THOMAS A. STANDISH

University of California at Irvine

DATA

STRUCTURE

TECHNIQUES

ADDISON-WESLEY
PUBLISHING COMPANY

Reading, Massachusetts
Menlo Park, California • London
Amsterdam • Don Mills, Ontario
Sydney

This book is in the
ADDISON-WESLEY SERIES IN COMPUTER SCIENCE

Consulting Editor
Michael A. Harrison

Library of Congress Cataloging in Publication Data

Standish, Thomas A.   1941–
  Data structure techniques.

  Includes bibliographical references.
  1. Data structures (Computer science) I. Title.
QA76.9.D35S73   001.6 ′42   78–67454
ISBN 0–201–07256–4

ISBN 0–201–07256–4
ABCDEFGH–MA–89876543210

To my wonderful father,

1907–1979

PREFACE

This book is a compendium of knowledge and programming techniques focusing on data structures and their associated underlying algorithms for storage allocation and management. It analyzes well-established methods for processing a variety of data structures including lists, trees, strings, arrays, stacks, files, tables, and multilinked structures.

Methods are explained for a variety of important processes such as hash coding, searching, compacting, garbage collecting, encrypting, conversion, compression, and many others.

One of the aims of the book is to provide an advanced level of expertise for professional programmers and computer scientists. The book introduces, surveys, and compares a broad variety of important material including many recent developments in the field, and provides an extensive bibliography of the data structure literature. Professionals should find it valuable for extending their knowledge of useful "tricks of the trade" and for finding relevant references to the literature, should they need to pursue certain advanced topics in depth.

Another aim of the book is to serve as a basis for courses on data structures. For this purpose, the book has been written to provide the opportunity to choose topics appropriate to courses at different levels and of different duration.

The book contains sufficient material for a one-year course at the first-year graduate or advanced undergraduate levels. For a one-semester course at this level, the instructor will want to select only essential topics. The following table gives one possibility that has been used successfully on three occasions in a graduate course offered by the Computer Science Department at Irvine:

Advanced course	
Chapter	List of sections
1	1.1, 1.2
2	2.1, 2.2, 2.5
3	3.1, 3.3, 3.4.1, 3.4.2, 3.5.1, 3.6.2, 3.7
4	4.1, 4.2, 4.3
5	5.1, 5.3.3, 5.4, 5.6, 5.7
6	6.1, 6.2, 6.3
7	7.1, 7.2.6, 7.3, 7.5.2
8	8.1, 8.5
9	9.1, 9.2, 9.3

The book has also been written so as to contain the proper introductory material to make it suitable for an introductory course on data structures at the undergraduate level. Sections intended for use in a first course on data structures have been marked so that advanced readers may skip them. A great deal of the material in the book is within the reach of those who have had modest experience in programming, which should, however, have included at least some exposure to machine-level concepts (such as bytes, addresses, binary representations of numbers, and the like).

A first course in data structures for undergraduates with this level of background, which has been taught successfully several times at Irvine, is composed from the following material:

Introductory course

Chapter	List of sections
1	1.1, 1.2, 1.3, 1.4
2	2.1, 2.2, 2.3, 2.4
3	3.1, 3.2, 3.3.1, 3.4.1, 3.4.2, 3.5, 3.6.1, 3.6.2, 3.7
4	4.1, 4.2.2, 4.3.1, 4.3.2, 4.3.3, 4.3.10, 4.4, 4.5
5	5.1, 5.2, 5.3, 5.4.1.1, 5.4.2, 5.5
6	6.1, 6.2.1, 6.3
7	7.1, 7.2, 7.4, 7.5.1
8	8.1, 8.2, 8.3.1, 8.4
9	9.1, 9.2, 9.3.1, 9.3.2, 9.3.3, 9.3.5, 9.3.6

With few exceptions, the book covers the material of ACM's Curriculum '68 Data Structures course (I1) in depth, and it covers much of the material in ACM Curriculum '78's courses CS-5, "Introduction to File Processing," and CS-7, "Data Structures and Analysis of Algorithms." It used to be normal practice to cover sorting in a course on data structures, and Curriculum '68, for instance, includes sorting as one of the topics recommended for such a course. However, since this book is not organized by algorithmic topic but instead by data structure topics, sorting is covered only modestly and in a manner different from the usual treatment.

In a book on algorithms, for example, one might find a chapter on sorting in which all the different methods are studied and compared. Such methods use a variety of data structures such as arrays, trees, stacks, and heaps. In a book on data structures, however, it seems to make more sense to use sorting methods as illustrations of the applications for these various data structures. Accordingly, the treatment is distributed in this book across the chapters that introduce data structures useful in sorting. Thus, Quicksort is discussed in the chapter on stacks and queues, Heapsort is discussed in the chapter on trees, and various other kinds of sorting techniques, such as selection sort, which use in-place rearrangements of linear arrays, are given as exercises at the end of the chapters on arrays and trees.

Algorithms and data structures go hand in hand. Neither can be studied fruitfully without knowledge of the other, and programs without data are just as uninteresting as data without programs. Accordingly, there is bound to be a close relation between many of the topics in a data structures course and companion topics in courses on analysis of algorithms. In a curriculum that offers courses both on data structures and on analysis of algorithms, the coordination between the two should be carefully studied and arranged. This book provides much more information on various low-level data representation techniques than many books on analysis of algorithms. At the same time, it does not strive to provide comparative algorithmic analysis for algorithmic topics such as searching and sorting. On the other hand, performance properties of data structures in these contexts are often cited, and in some cases proved. This should serve to whet the student's appetite for deeper study of analysis of algorithms. If the book succeeds in exciting the student's curiosity in this fashion, it should serve as excellent motivation for a later course in analysis of algorithms.

The following conventions are used throughout the book for numbering and referencing. Algorithms, exercises, figures, theorems, definitions, and tables are numbered sequentially in each chapter, as the examples in the following table show.

	Examples of numbering
Algorithm 6.11	is the eleventh algorithm in Chapter 6
Exercise 7.3	is the third exercise in Chapter 7
Figure 3.2	is the second figure in Chapter 3
Theorem 5.1	is the first theorem in Chapter 5
Definition 5.1	is the first definition in Chapter 5
Table 7.1	is the first Table in Chapter 7

The sections in each chapter are numbered using the Dewey Decimal system. Each section number begins with the number of the chapter in which it is found. For example, Section 4.3.9 refers to Subsection 9 of Section 3 of Chapter 4. Each odd-numbered page in the book has a section number and a section title printed at the top.

In each chapter the formulas to be referenced later are numbered sequentially using a parenthesized number in the righthand margin. For example, the second formula referenced in Chapter 4 is presented as follows:

$$C_N \approx \frac{1}{2}\left(1 + \frac{1}{1-\alpha}\right) \qquad \text{successful search.} \qquad (2)$$

Inside Chapter 4, we refer to this formula using the phrase "formula (2)," and outside Chapter 4, we refer to it using the phrase "formula (2) of Chapter 4."

References to articles, books, and reports are given by listing the last name(s) of the author(s) followed by the year of publication in square brackets. For instance, "Bell and Kaman [1970]" refers to an article entitled "The Linear Quotient Hash Code" published in the November 1970 issue of *Communications of the ACM*. The full reference is given in the list of references near the end of the book in the following form:

BELL, J. R. and KAMAN, C. H. [1970]. The Linear Quotient Hash Code, *CACM* **13:11** (November), 675–677.

This yields the further information that the article appears on pages 675 through 677, and that the November 1970 issue is issue 11 of volume 13 of the *Communications of the ACM* (abbreviated *CACM* in the reference). If an author published more than one referenced item in a given year, references are disambiguated by appending a letter of the alphabet to the year. For instance, Bays[1973a], Bays[1973b], and Bays[1973c] refer to three distinct publications in 1973 by Carter Bays.

ACKNOWLEDGMENTS

I am deeply indebted to many individuals who have kindly offered me their ideas and suggestions for improving earlier drafts of this book. Special thanks are due to the following people for their valued assistance: F. L. Bauer, Bob Boyer, Walt Burkhard, Sue and Steve Cirivello, Ron Colman, Paul Edelstein, Michael Harrison, Dan Hirschberg, Bob Jardine, Don Knuth, John Lowther, George Lueker, Dan Moore, J Strother Moore, Alan Perlis, Tom Szymanski, and Mark Tadman.

It was a great pleasure working with a number of highly gifted people at Addison-Wesley, each of whom contributed vitally to the editing and production of this book. Bill Gruener, the Computer Sciences editor, did a superb job of gathering helpful reviews and advising me how earlier drafts could be rewritten and improved. In my opinion, Bill is the most highly talented editor in the contemporary field of computer science, and I greatly appreciate his encouragement and support. One of the pleasant experiences I had in the production phase of this book was working with production editor Mary Cafarella, a professional craftsman of extraordinary perspicacity; we quickly developed a harmonious and cooperative working relationship. It makes an enormous difference to an author to have a production editor with whom he can work smoothly, and Mary was a teammate of the highest professional excellence. My thanks also go to Martha Morong, who assisted in copy-editing, to Gail Goodell, secretary to Bill Gruener, who helped coordinate communications and who was generally very helpful, to book designers Judy Fletcher and Herbert Caswell, to cover designer Ann Scrimgeour, to artists Joseph Vetere and ANCO/Boston for preparation of the figures, and to Mary Clare McEwing and Sharnel Murray for help with the promotion work. All of these individuals did splendid jobs.

I owe special thanks to many at the University of California at Irvine, who contributed their time and effort during the writing of this book. Jane Peirano, of the UC Irvine Library, kindly furnished me with a private study room in the Library adjacent to the computer science books and periodicals, to which I could retreat in complete privacy while I ploughed through the literature; this was an enormous help to me in completing this project. Mary Kay Clarke, Phyllis Siegel, Shirley Rasmussen, Sue Rose, and Susan Hyatt of the Irvine Computer Science Department helped enormously with copying, proofreading, mailing, and indexing. My father kindly assisted me in reading galley proofs. Tamara Taylor was a marvelous help in checking the page proofs.

Finally, I would like to thank the following graduate students who helped to certify the algorithms. I cannot declare with certainty no errors remain in the extensive collection of algorithms given in this book as we go to press for the first edition; however, I do know that the following individuals helped find and eliminate a great many errors in the algorithms in the first draft: Brien Amspoker, Sherry Cameron, Sue and Steve Cirivello, Narayan Char, Seth Cohen, John Conery, Evelyn Loo Corbitt, Bjorn Dahlberg, Lief Eriksen, Joe Giordano, Steven Hampson, Liang-Te Hu, Bob Jepson, Bob Jardine, Martin Katz, Greg Keilin, Hank Kleppinger, Jim Longers, Stephen McHenry, Tony Menges, Roger Mintzlaff, Jim Norris, Kim Poindexter, Bill Rockwell, John Tangney, Craig Taylor, Ashok Viswanathan, Mary Yaeger, and James Zmuda.

I am most of all indebted to my wife, Elke, for providing me the devotion and encouragement without which this book could not have been written.

Laguna Beach, California   T. A. S.
November, 1979

CONTENTS

1.1 INTRODUCTION AND MOTIVATION

The contemporary digital computer is an extraordinarily versatile problem-solving device. Its versatility derives, in part, from our ability to program it to represent and manipulate usefully a wide range of different kinds of information.

The basic information structures provided at the level of the naked machine are often simple, inelastic, and serially arranged. This underlying, general-purpose, information-bearing medium must be shaped into structures of higher orders that faithfully represent the information required to solve problems and that retain information essential to the stepwise progress of problem-solving computations.

A significant body of technique has arisen for composing machine-level information structures into versatile, higher-level data representations. Efficient algorithms are known for allocating storage, managing dynamic structural changes, searching for items with required properties, and a host of other useful tasks.

The development of systematic, basic understanding of these data representation techniques and of their associated processing algorithms lies at the core of computer science because it serves as a foundation for knowledge about what computers can do and the resources they require to attain given ends.

At the heart of our study of data structures lies the concept of a *data representation*. Informally, one constructs a data representation by organizing the data and processes of a given representational medium to satisfy required properties and behaviors of some specified system of objects and operations being represented. The key notion is one of *faithful imitation* of required behaviors. In certain simple cases, this notion can be captured formally, using the concept of a *model* of an axiomatic system in contemporary logic, wherein the axioms specify the behavioral requirements on objects and operations, and the model supplies the faithful imitation.

Often two distinct levels of language are associated with the representational process. One level describes the structures being modeled, and the second level describes the objects and operations in the underlying representational medium. In some systems, more than two levels of language are employed, with the intermediate layers serving both as representational media for higher layers and as specifications for underlying representations by lower layers.

Thus, data representations are often cascaded one or more times, at several levels of abstraction, spanning the gap from the machine domain to the problem domain. For example, in an airline reservation system, the entities at the problem-domain level might include schedules, flights, dates, and reservations. At an intermediate level in the system implementation, the entities might include files, tables, records, and strings. At the machine level, the entities might include bytes and linear sequences of machine words.

In this book we shall be concerned primarily with general-purpose, intermediate-level data structures (such as files, lists, arrays, and strings) and with their underlying data representations at the machine level. Experience has shown that these general-purpose, intermediate-level data structures have a high utility in applications programming. A given intermediate-level structure (such as a rectangular array or a table), however, often has a range of underlying representations, each with different space–time resource requirements.

A basic aim of this book is to develop understanding of the range of significant possible underlying representation techniques for each of the intermediate-level data structures studied, and to equip the reader with the means for choosing appropriately among them or designing new ones to suit new purposes.

1.2 HOW THE BOOK IS ORGANIZED

When the author began to write the first draft of this book, he settled on what he thought, at the time, was a perfectly sensible sequence for treating the topics in a data structures book. Since it seemed natural to progress from the less difficult to the more difficult in an orderly fashion, his idea was to arrange the chapters to treat data structures of increasing complexity, starting with the simplest first.

Strings, it was thought, should come first. These might be viewed as the simplest of data structures inasmuch as strings are just linear sequences of symbols. Stacks and queues are slightly more complex than strings since they have growth properties and can change size, so it was argued that stacks and queues should be treated next. Arrays might well be covered immediately thereafter. Arrays of several dimensions seem more complex than linear data structures. Yet since arrays usually don't change shape during use and since they have a uniform addressing structure, arrays seem less complex than trees. Trees, in turn, can contain substructures of arbitrary size, and can change shape in breadth and depth, so they seem more complex than arrays. Yet trees are less complex than lists and multilinked structures, since the latter can contain cycles and shared substructures, while trees cannot. Tables and files seem potentially most complex of all since they are sometimes similar to arrays of entries occasionally indexed by trees and occasionally containing entries tied together with multilinking techniques.

Thus, there seemed to be a reasonable argument for arranging the chapters around the following topics and in the following order: strings, stacks and queues, arrays, trees, lists, multilinked structures, tables, and files.

While the notion of progressing from simple to complex seemed sound at first, and while some data structures books indeed follow such a progression, the author discovered that the idea was fraught with unpleasant difficulties.

For example, while strings are superficially simple, their underlying representation techniques tend to employ data structures of greater complexity. Certain types of trees are used to obtain minimal-length encoding of strings, some string pattern-matching techniques use variations of hashing techniques, and some string representations involve linking together blocks of characters of varying sizes.

Similarly, while arrays are overtly simple, their underlying representations tend to involve techniques relying on notions of hash addressing, tree indexing, and multilinking.

Thus, the first draft of this book was plagued repeatedly by irritating situations in which concepts were used before being defined. These annoying forward references forced the author to abandon the early intention of ordering the chapters in a progression from the simple to the complex.

Fortunately, it does not hurt to move some of the chapters covering simple structures such as strings to a position near the end of the book. This is largely for pragmatic reasons, one of which is that strings are not used as efficient underlying representations for several of the more complex data structures such as multi-linked structures or indexed files.

The author undertook an analysis of the prerequisite relationships between the chapters. The results are presented in Fig. 1.1, in which a path from box X to box Y signifies that knowing about the topic in box Y is prerequisite to studying the topic in box X.

To the author's surprise, the graph in Fig. 1.1 is free of cycles, implying that there exists an ordering of the chapters that is free of mutually dependent systems of chapters each of which is prerequisite to each of the others. Comparing Fig. 1.1 and the table of contents, it is possible to see that the ordering of the chapters used in this volume presents each topic after its prerequisite topics have been covered.

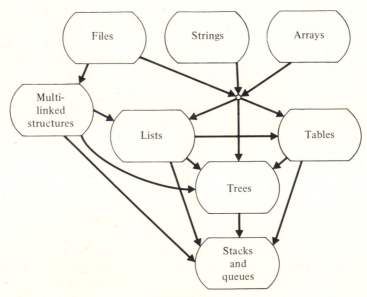

FIGURE 1.1

† 1.3 BASIC CONCEPTS AND NOTATION

1.3.1   Cells, fields, and pointers

Data representations often reside in underlying memory media that are composed of individually addressable units of storage. Often, too, the addresses of the addressable units consist of the integers lying in some designated range $(m \le i \le n)$. For instance, in a core memory consisting of 262,144 separate 36-bit words, the addresses of the words may consist of the integers in the range $(0 \le i \le 2^{18} - 1)$, and such addresses may be represented by 18-bit binary integers.

A *cell* is an addressable unit of storage. Frequently, cells are further divided into named fields. For example, Fig. 1.2 depicts a cell with address α having two fields named *Info* and *Link* respectively.

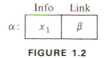

FIGURE 1.2

In this book, α and β are frequently used to signify the addresses of cells. The address of a cell is given to the left of the cell diagram and is followed by a colon. The names of fields of a cell are usually attached to the border of the cell diagram (usually on the top border, but sometimes on the sides or on the bottom as well). In Fig. 1.2, x_1 is the *contents* of the Info field and β is the *contents* of the Link field. In general, a *field* is a designated portion of a sequence of data, usually consisting of a subsequence of adjacent symbols. In this book, we assume that the fields of a cell are nonoverlapping. The fields of a cell are not assumed to correspond to addressable units of storage, and generally are not assumed to be individually addressable.

We shall always assume that distinct cells have distinct addresses. It is not necessarily the case that cells correspond exactly to the distinct addressable units of a given underlying memory medium. Sometimes cells may correspond to contiguous groups of underlying addressable units. For example, in a memory whose addressable units consist of 36-bit words, we can decree that the memory be divided into cells each consisting of two adjacent words. In this case, the address of each two-word cell is taken to be the address of its first (i.e., lowest addressed) word. By convention, the address of a multiword cell is the address of its first word. Thus, cells are a form of organization that we impose on an underlying memory medium, in which we partition the addressable units of the medium into pairwise disjoint, contiguous groups of addressable units and in which we take, for

---

† Advanced readers: Skip to Chapter 2.

cell addresses, the lowest of the addresses of the addressable units comprising each group. Occasionally we shall refer to a multiword cell as a *block*.

When a field F of a cell A contains the address of another cell B, we say that the F field of A contains a *pointer* to B (or, equivalently, that the F field of A *links* to B). Figure 1.3 depicts two cells each of which has a Link field containing a pointer to the other.

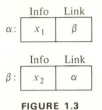

FIGURE 1.3

We often designate the occurrence of pointers by means of arrows. For example, Fig. 1.4 is intended to give exactly the same information as Fig. 1.3. The tail of each arrow (O——) resides in the field where the pointer address is stored, and the head of each arrow ($\rightarrow$) touches the diagram of the cell bearing the pointer address.

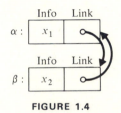

FIGURE 1.4

We frequently draw diagrams with linked cells in which several of the cells are not labeled with explicit addresses. Figure 1.5 illustrates such a diagram.

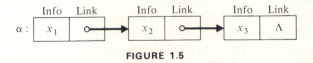

FIGURE 1.5

In Fig. 1.5, even though only the leftmost cell diagram is labeled with an explicit address, the other cells are assumed implicitly to possess distinct addresses independently of whether labels signifying such addresses have been included in the diagram. Thus the occurrences of the arrows in Fig. 1.5 each correspond to distinct pointer addresses. Figure 1.5 also illustrates a technique for linking cells together into a chain in which each cell, except the last, points to a successor in the chain. Such a configuration of linked cells is called a *linked list* of cells. Note that the Link field of the rightmost cell in Fig. 1.5 contains the symbol Λ. In this book, Λ designates a special *null pointer*, used to signify the termination of linked lists. We assume that Λ is an address distinct from the addresses of all cells.

1.3.2 Variables and assignments

In the text and in algorithms, we shall use *variables*, such as X or *Head*. Variables have *values* that are quantities of various sorts. Values are assigned to variables by performing *assignment statements*. For example, performing the assignment statement $X \leftarrow 3$ sets the value of the variable X to be the integer 3, and performing the assignment statement Head $\leftarrow \alpha$ sets the value of the variable Head to be the address α. The value of a variable at any moment is the value most recently assigned to it. An assignment statement such as Head $\leftarrow \alpha$ replaces the value last assigned to Head with the new value α, and Head has the value α until the moment that a value distinct from α is assigned by performing a new assignment statement. In diagrams, when a variable has the address of a cell as its value, we illustrate such a fact by a pointer from the variable to the cell its value addresses. For example, if we assume that a collection of cells is linked together as shown in Fig. 1.5 above, and we assume we have performed the assignment statement Head $\leftarrow \alpha$, we can depict the state of affairs that results by a diagram such as that in Fig. 1.6.

FIGURE 1.6

The notation Info(Head) designates the contents of the Info field of the cell whose address is the value of the variable Head. Thus, in Fig. 1.6, Info(Head) $= x_1$. Likewise, Link(Head) is the contents of the Link field of the leftmost cell in Fig. 1.6. Thus, Link(Head) is the address of the middle cell in Fig. 1.6, and Info(Link(Head)) $= x_2$. When we use an expression such as Info(Head) on the lefthand side of an assignment, as in Info(Head) $\leftarrow x_4$, we designate that the value in the Info field of the cell to which Head points is to be replaced by the new value x_4. Thus, for example, if we start with the diagram in Fig. 1.6 and perform the assignment Info(Head) $\leftarrow x_4$, we obtain a new diagram, given in Fig. 1.7, in

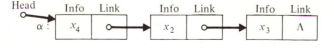

FIGURE 1.7

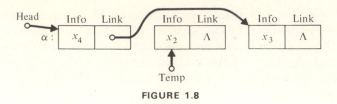

FIGURE 1.8

which the Info field of the leftmost cell has been changed to contain the new value x_4. Similarly, performing the three assignments

$$\text{Temp} \leftarrow \text{Link(Head)}, \qquad \text{Link(Head)} \leftarrow \text{Link(Link(Head))},$$

and

$$\text{Link(Temp)} \leftarrow \Lambda,$$

changes the diagram of Fig. 1.7 into the diagram given in Fig. 1.8.

1.3.3 Notation for algorithms

The notation used to present algorithms in this book is similar to that introduced in D. E. Knuth's series *The Art of Computer Programming* (see Knuth [1973a]) and widely used with minor variation in the literature on data structures. To illustrate the variant of this notation used in this book, we examine an example of a table look-up algorithm.

In data structure applications we often need first to record and later to retrieve information associated with given symbolic entities. For example, in compiling a FORTRAN program, we may need to set up a correspondence between FORTRAN identifiers and the storage locations corresponding to them in the compiled program. Compilers often use *symbol tables* for this purpose. Such a symbol table might record, for each distinct identifier I used in a program P, an address α in the compiled program. Given an occurrence of an identifier I, we might wish to search such a table to determine whether I is in the table or not and, if it is, what address α has been previously associated with it. One way of performing this task is simply to store a list of identifiers in the table and to search through the list each time. However, this could get to be very time-consuming if there are many identifiers. The task would be made easy if we could use the representation of the identifier I as a direct index into such a table. Unfortunately, since FORTRAN identifiers consist of from one to six letters or digits beginning with a letter, there are 1,617,038,306 possible distinct FORTRAN identifiers. Such a directly indexed table would obviously be too large to use in any practical compiler. Instead, we must turn to methods that store identifier–address pairs (I, α) in space suitable for handling at most several thousand distinct identifiers out of the more than a billion possibilities. Such techniques often store both a representation of each identifier I and its associated address α directly in the table entries. One technique for representing such a table relies on a method called *hash-addressing*. Though we shall illustrate this method on a small example, for reasons of brevity and clarity, the method has important practical applications in more realistic cases of large size. A range of such techniques is studied in greater depth in Chapter 4.

Our example concerns recording and then looking up the relative frequencies of occurrence of the seven letters used most frequently in English text. These seven most frequently used letters and their associated relative frequencies (derived from samples of actual English text) are given in Table 1.1.

TABLE 1.1

Letter	Frequency
E	1231
T	959
A	805
O	794
N	719
I	718
S	659

To simplify later exposition, we subscript each letter with an integer giving its position in the alphabet. Thus, for the letter E, we use E_5 since E is the fifth letter in the alphabet, and for A we use A_1 since A is the first letter in the alphabet. We use the term *keys* to refer to the entities of the form L_n, where L is a letter and n is its position in alphabetic order. For each letter L with frequency f given in Table 1.1, we construct a cell of the form

Key	Freq	Link
L_n	f	Λ

For example, the cell constructed for the letter N is

Key	Freq	Link
N_{14}	719	Λ

We then construct a table T with seven entries numbered 0 to 6, and we load the table entries to point to linked lists of cells, in the fashion indicated in Fig. 1.9.

We now define a hash-addressing function h, which maps keys onto indexes in Table T, by defining $h(L_n) = n \bmod 7$. Here, $n \bmod 7$ denotes the remainder of n after division by 7. For instance, $h(I_9) = 2$, since 2 is the remainder of 9 after division by 7, and $h(N_{14}) = 0$, since 0 is the remainder of 14 after division by 7.

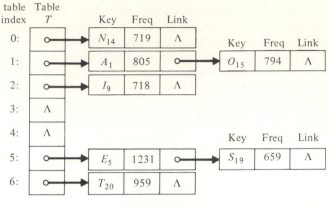

FIGURE 1.9

Since there are 26 possible keys of the form L_n and only seven table entries in Table T, we see that $h(L_n)$ cannot always send distinct keys onto distinct table indexes. If h maps two such keys L_n and $L'_{n'}$ onto the same table index, we say we have a *collision* at the common index $h(L_n) = h(L'_{n'})$. If we examine Fig. 1.9, we see that, for each i $(0 \le i \le 6)$, the linked list pointed to by the ith table entry contains keys that are mapped by h onto the index i. For example, since $h(A_1) = h(O_{15}) = 1$, the linked list starting at position 1 of Table T contains the keys A_1 and O_{15} in the Key fields of its linked cells. In fact, Fig. 1.9 can be constructed by inserting cells for each key L_n in order of decreasing frequency of L specified in Table 1.1. First, the cell $\boxed{\quad E_5 \quad | \quad 1231 \quad | \quad \Lambda \quad}$ is inserted into an initially empty table by computing $h(E_5) = 5$, and placing a link to this cell in the entry of Table T indexed by 5. Next, the cell $\boxed{\quad T_{20} \quad | \quad 959 \quad | \quad \Lambda \quad}$ is inserted by placing a pointer to it in the entry of T indexed by $h(T_{20}) = 6$. Continuing in this fashion, the last cell to be inserted is $\boxed{\quad S_{19} \quad | \quad 659 \quad | \quad \Lambda \quad}$. Since $h(S_{19}) = 5$, this cell is inserted at the end of the linked list pointed to by the address stored in the entry of T indexed by 5. To accomplish this, the quantity Λ in the Link field of the cell $\boxed{\quad E_5 \quad | \quad 1231 \quad | \quad \Lambda \quad}$ is replaced by a pointer to the cell $\boxed{\quad S_{19} \quad | \quad 659 \quad | \quad \Lambda \quad}$.

The following algorithm, used to illustrate the notation for algorithms in this book, searches the Table T for a cell containing a given key L_n. If a cell exists whose Key field contains L_n, the algorithm returns the address of the cell; otherwise the algorithm returns the null address Λ. The notation $T[i]$ stands for the value stored in the ith location in Table T.

Algorithm 1.1 *Searching a hash table T for a Key L_n.*

Let T be a table with seven entries numbered from 0 to 6. Let L_n be a key, where L is a letter of the alphabet, and n is the position of L in the alphabet. Define a hash function $h(L_n) = n \bmod 7$. Given L_n, the algorithm searches the linked list pointed to by the address stored in $T[h(L_n)]$ and returns the address of the cell whose Key field contains the key L_n. If no cell containing the key L_n appears on the linked list, the algorithm returns Λ.

1. [Initialize.] Set $C \leftarrow T[h(L_n)]$.
2. [End of list?] If $C = \Lambda$ (that is, if the linked list contains no more cells to examine), terminate the algorithm with C containing Λ.
3. [Key matches?] If $\text{Key}(C) = L_n$, the algorithm terminates with the result C. (C contains the address of the cell whose Key is L_n.)
4. [Continue search.] Set $C \leftarrow \text{Link}(C)$ and go back to step 2.

Each algorithm in this book is given a number and a title. The title immediately follows the algorithm number on the same line. Just below the number and title is a descriptive text, which describes properties of inputs and outputs and mentions relevant assumptions and facts. The body of the algorithm consists of a set of numbered steps. Normally, each step begins with a brief [bracketed] indication of its purpose. Thus, for example, at the beginning of step 2, we find "[End of list?]." This indicates that the purpose of step 2 is to *check to see* whether the linked list contains any more cells to examine and, if not, to take appropriate action. Comments (in parentheses) may appear in steps of an algorithm to help the reader understand the details. An example of a comment in Algorithm 1.1 is the remark "(C contains the address of the cell whose Key is L_n.)," which appears at the end of step 3.

To use Algorithm 1.1 to retrieve the frequency associated with a letter L, we execute the algorithm using key L_n and, after it terminates, if $C \neq \Lambda$, $\text{Freq}(C)$ gives the value of the frequency for L.

1.3.4 Mathematical notation

The mathematical notation used in this book has been selected from notation commonly used in the literature on data structures. This notation tends to differ only slightly from that in general use in the mathematical literature. For example, because base 2 logarithms occur so frequently in the data structure literature, it is convenient to introduce a special notation for them. We use $\lg x$ to stand for $\log_2 x$ in this book.

The following four notations are used with sufficient frequency in the remaining chapters that it profits us to define them in this chapter.

1. The *floor of x*, denoted $\lfloor x \rfloor$, stands for the greatest integer less than or equal to x (where x is any real number).
2. The *ceiling of x*, denoted $\lceil x \rceil$, stands for the smallest integer greater than or equal to x (where x is any real number).

3. If x and y are real numbers, we define $x \bmod y$ as follows:

$$x \bmod y = \begin{cases} x, & \text{if } y = 0, \\ x - y\lfloor x/y \rfloor, & \text{if } y \neq 0. \end{cases} \tag{1}$$

4. If x and y are bits (either 0 or 1), we define the *exclusive or* of x and y, denoted $x \oplus y$, by the equations:

$$\begin{array}{ll} 1 \oplus 0 = 1 & \qquad 1 \oplus 1 = 0 \\ 0 \oplus 1 = 1 & \qquad 0 \oplus 0 = 0 \end{array} \tag{2}$$

If x is a sequence of bits of the form $x = b_1 b_2 \cdots b_n$ and y is a sequence of bits of the form $y = c_1 c_2 \cdots c_n$, then $x \oplus y$ is defined to be the bit-wise *exclusive or* of the respective bits of x and y, by the equation:

$$x \oplus y = (b_1 \oplus c_1)(b_2 \oplus c_2) \cdots (b_n \oplus c_n). \tag{3}$$

Other notations are defined at the point of first use and references are supplied.

1.4 MATHEMATICAL BACKGROUND

A great deal of the material in this book is accessible to readers with modest mathematical backgrounds. For example, beginning college undergraduates who have mastered a first course in programming and who have had sufficient mathematical training to prepare for college should find that most of the ideas and explanations fall within their reach.

In this regard, for instance, it is assumed that all readers will know how to change the bases of logarithms, and facts such as

$$\log_b N = \frac{\log_c N}{\log_c b} \tag{4}$$

are usually invoked without specific mention.

On the other hand, many of the developments have been taken from the general research literature on data structures and involve a knowledge of more advanced concepts in mathematics and computer science. Some of these sections may fall beyond the reach of some readers. Mathematical facts in these sections are usually invoked with a reminder and a reference to the literature. An example of such a fact is the relation

$$H_n = \ln n + \gamma + O\left(\frac{1}{n}\right), \tag{5}$$

where H_n is the nth harmonic number

$$\left(H_n = 1 + \frac{1}{2} + \frac{1}{3} + \cdots + \frac{1}{n} \right)$$

and $\gamma = 0.57721566$ is Euler's constant (Knuth [1973a], pp. 73–78). Since the general research literature on data structures draws on quite a variety of mathematical knowledge, it is inevitable that this variety be reflected in any book that attempts reasonable coverage of the known results. However, the mathematical treatment herein deliberately avoids extremely advanced or intricate mathematics in an attempt to provide explanations comprehensible to a broad variety of advanced undergraduates, graduate students, and professional computer scientists.

One important system of description used throughout the book is the use of notation of the form $O(f(n))$ to describe the time or space requirements of running algorithms. If n is a parameter that characterizes the size of the input to a given algorithm, and if we say the algorithm runs to completion in $O(f(n))$ steps, we mean that the actual number of steps executed is no more than a constant times $f(n)$, for sufficiently large n. The following definition makes this concept precise.

Definition 1.1 We say that $g(n) = O(f(n))$ if there exist two constants K and n_0 such that $|g(n)| \leq K|f(n)|$ for all $n \geq n_0$.

For example, suppose Algorithm A arranges a sequence of n numbers into ascending order by exchanging pairs of numbers in some fashion, and suppose it can be shown that the exact number of steps Algorithm A executes is $g(n) = 3 + 6 + 9 + \cdots + 3n$ steps. Then it can be asserted that the algorithm runs in $O(n^2)$ steps by the following reasoning: First, $g(n)$ can be written in closed form since it is known that

$$\sum_{1 \leq i \leq n} 3i = \frac{3n(n+1)}{2}.$$

Thus, choosing $K = 3$, $n_0 = 1$, and $f(n) = n^2$, we can demonstrate that $|g(n)| \leq K|f(n)|$ for all $n \geq n_0$, provided we can demonstrate that the following inequality holds true:

$$\frac{3n(n+1)}{2} \leq 3n^2.$$

Multiplying both sides by $\frac{2}{3}$ and multiplying out the left side yields:

$$n^2 + n \leq 2n^2.$$

Subtracting n^2 from both sides gives:

$$n \leq n^2.$$

But the latter inequality holds for all $n \geq 1$.

Most of the algorithms studied in this book have running times that fall into one of the following classes:

constant	$O(1)$
log log	$O(\lg \lg n)$
logarithmic	$O(\lg n)$
linear	$O(n)$
$n \log n$	$O(n \lg n)$
quadratic	$O(n^2)$
cubic	$O(n^3)$
exponential	$O(2^n)$

It is important to gain an intuitive feeling for these classes in order to have a comparative framework in which to understand performance properties of algorithms. Table 1.2 lists some values of various functions for arguments that are powers of 2. Somehow, such tables never seem to dramatize sufficiently the performance differences between the functions $f(n)$. Plotting the functions on a graph is only slightly more informative and is still insufficiently memorable.

TABLE 1.2

	Values of $f(n)$ for:				
$f(n)$	$n = 2$	$n = 16$	$n = 256$	$n = 1024$	$n = 1048576$
$\lg \lg n$	0	2	3	3.32	4.32
$\lg n$	1	4	8	1.00×10^1	2.00×10^1
n	2	1.6×10^1	2.56×10^2	1.02×10^3	1.05×10^6
$n \lg n$	2	6.4×10^1	4.48×10^2	1.02×10^4	2.10×10^7
n^2	4	2.56×10^2	6.55×10^4	1.05×10^6	1.10×10^{12}
n^3	8	4.10×10^3	1.68×10^7	1.07×10^9	1.15×10^{18}
2^n	4	6.55×10^4	1.16×10^{77}	1.80×10^{308}	6.00×10^{315652}

Another way of looking at the matter, therefore, which is a bit more dramatic, is to ask an inverse question. Suppose we have a fast computer that can perform one step of a given computation C each microsecond. Suppose that n gives some fundamental measure of the size of the problem. For instance, n might be the number of nodes in a tree being searched, the number of records in a file being updated, or the number of nodes in a list structure being scanned and marked. Now assume that the computation C is being executed under control of an algorithm A, and that algorithm A takes exactly $f(n)$ steps, at one microsecond per step, to finish its task, where $f(n)$ is one of the functions given in Table 1.2. Now we can ask: How big can n be if we expect the computation C to terminate before a year (a week, a day) has expired?

The number of seconds in a year is $60 \times 60 \times 24 \times 365 = 31,536,000$, so the number of microseconds in a year is 3.15×10^{13}. Thus, the answer to our question is determined by finding the largest n such that $f(n) \leq 3.15 \times 10^{13}$. If $f(n) = 2^n$, then n can be at most 44 if C is to finish in less than a year. In other words, if Algorithm A takes exactly 2^n steps of a microsecond each, then the largest problem we can handle with a year's worth of computing effort is a problem of size $n = 44$. If $f(n) = 10^n$, matters are even worse—we can solve only a problem of size $n = 13$ in a year. If a year seems impossibly long to wait for our answer, or the solution seems infeasible because contemporary computers can't usually operate reliably for that long, we might see what size problem we could solve in an hour, a day, or a week. If $f(n) = 10^n$, we are still in deep trouble—the biggest n can be if the computation is to terminate in less than an hour is $n = 9$, and if we are allotted a week, the biggest n can be is 11. Thus, if the running time of our algorithm is characterized by an exponential function, we cannot expect to solve practical problems of very large size. Table 1.3 gives more results along these lines for functions $f(n)$ of linear or greater complexity.

TABLE 1.3
Size of Largest Problem that Algorithm A Can Solve if Solution Is to be Computed in Time T at 1 Microsecond/Step.

When number of steps is:	$T = 1$ min.	$T = 1$ hour	$T = 1$ day	$T = 1$ week	$T = 1$ year
n	6×10^7	3.6×10^9	8.64×10^{10}	6.04×10^{11}	3.15×10^{13}
n^2	7.75×10^3	6.0×10^4	2.94×10^5	7.77×10^5	5.61×10^6
n^3	3.91×10^2	1.53×10^3	4.42×10^3	8.45×10^3	3.16×10^4
2^n	25	31	36	39	44
10^n	7	9	10	11	13

Thus, we see that, given an hour, we can solve a problem of size 3.6 billion if Algorithm A takes n steps, but only size 60,000 if A takes n^2 steps, size 1,500 if A takes n^3 steps, and size 31 if A takes 2^n steps. These dramatic shifts in the sizes of problems we can handle as we ascend the scale of complexity are equally dramatically reversed as we descend the scale. Thus, if we can replace an algorithm A that takes n steps by an algorithm A' that takes only $\lg n$ steps of equal duration, or by an algorithm A'' that takes $\lg \lg n$ steps, then a problem that is solved by Algorithm A in one hour, would be solved by Algorithm A' in just 25.84 microseconds, and by Algorithm A'' in 4.7 microseconds!

On the other hand, we have to be quite careful in using these rough comparisons between functions in classes $O(\lg \lg n)$, $O(\lg n)$, and $O(n)$, because the step sizes for different algorithms often do not consume equal amounts of time, but instead they differ, sometimes by large multiples.

For example, if we use straightforward *sequential search* to try to find an item in an ordered list, we must inspect $(n + 1)/2$ (which is $O(n)$) items on the average (assuming each item searched for is equally likely to be chosen). If we use *binary search*, the number of comparisons needed to locate the item searched for is $O(\lg n)$; and if we use *interpolation search*, then, under proper conditions, we need make only $O(\lg \lg n)$ comparisons, on the average. (These search methods are studied in Chapter 4.) However, we cannot conclude too hastily that interpolation search is superior to the other methods. In fact, it is more costly to execute a step of a program for interpolation search than it is to execute the corresponding steps in binary search and sequential search.

Thus, one set of empirical data (Horowitz and Sahni [1976], p. 342) shows that interpolation search is faster for searching tables of upwards of 500 items, whereas binary search is fastest for searching tables of between 20 and 500 items, and sequential search is fastest for tables of up to 20 items. Another set of empirical data (Perl, Itai, and Avni [1978]) shows interpolation search faster only for tables of upwards of 5,000 items. (These boundaries are rough, of course, and depend on details of the implementations.) Nevertheless, the discussion should serve to explain why computer scientists are interested in finding algorithms that solve given types of problems with the lowest possible complexity class for time and space. Thus, in this book, the discussion and comparison of management algorithms for data structures, and of space consumed by data representations, often comments on the complexity class $O(f(n))$ characterizing the time and space resources required.

For example, in the discussion of computing optimal binary search trees in Chapter 3, if it is discovered that the best algorithm requires time $O(n^3)$ steps to find the optimal binary search tree for a tree with n nodes, then in an hour's worth of computing, we could expect to discover optimal trees for only a few hundred nodes. However, if we can discover how to find the optimum in time $O(n^2)$ steps, we can hope to find optimal trees containing on the order of 100,000 or so nodes. This is still not good enough to use for finding an optimum binary search tree for a file with, say, a million search keys, in a period of an hour or so. Rather, it might take a couple of months or so of continuous computing to find such a tree using an $O(n^2)$ algorithm.

These brief remarks will have served their purpose if they have helped the reader develop (or, more likely, confirm) his intuitions about the principal complexity classes that apply to algorithms in this book, and if, at the same time, he has been reminded of the possible abuse of this rough scale of measure.

EXERCISES

1. (Chapter ordering) Show that the order of presentation of chapters in this book is consistent with the prerequisite relationships depicted in Fig. 1.1.

2. (Finding last cell) Suppose the variable Head points to the first cell of a linked list composed of cells of the form

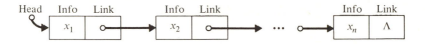

Write an algorithm to set the pointer Last to point to the last cell in the list pointed to by Head. [*Hint:* The last cell is the only cell whose Link field contains Λ.]

3. (List insertion) Given a linked list, such as that shown in Exercise 2, pointed to by a variable Head, and given a cell pointed to by New,

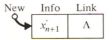

write an algorithm to change the last cell of the list pointed to by Head so that its Link field points to the cell pointed to by New. Thus, the algorithm is to insert a new cell at the end of a given linked list.

4. (Hash-table insertion) Let New be a variable that points to a cell containing a new letter key L_n and a new frequency f

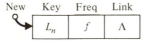

Given a hash-table in the form illustrated by Fig. 1.9, write an algorithm to insert the cell pointed to by New into Table T of Fig. 1.9 last on the linked list pointed to by table entry $T[h(L_n)]$. [*Hint:* Modify Algorithm 1.1, and use the solution to Exercise 3 to perform the list insertion.]

5. (Floor functions) Prove that $\lfloor x \rfloor + \lfloor y \rfloor \le \lfloor x + y \rfloor$ for any real numbers x and y.

6. (Fractional parts) The quantity $(x \bmod 1)$ is sometimes called the fractional part of the real number x. Prove that

$$x = \lfloor x \rfloor + (x \bmod 1).$$

7. (Logarithm base change) How can lg x be computed on a pocket calculator that computes only natural logarithms of the form ln x? [*Hint*: Apply base-change operation using formula (4).]

8. (Identities for exclusive-or) Prove that the exclusive-or operator obeys the following three identities:

$$(x \oplus y) \oplus x = y, \qquad (x \oplus y) = (y \oplus x).$$
$$(x \oplus y) \oplus y = x,$$

9. (O-notation) Prove that $f(n) = 1^2 + 2^2 + \cdots + n^2$ is $O(n^3)$.

10. (List reversal) Let the variable Head point to the first cell of a linked list, as in Exercise 2. Write an algorithm to reverse the links, as indicated in the following diagram:

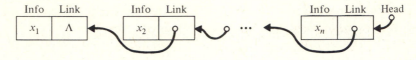

At termination of the algorithm, the variable Head should point to the former last cell.

CHAPTER

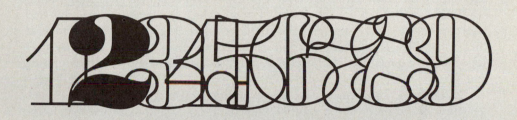

STACKS AND QUEUES

2.1 INTRODUCTION AND MOTIVATION

Stacks and queues have a wide number of applications in contemporary computer systems and are used frequently in the algorithms in this book. The purposes of this chapter are, first, to introduce a representation-free notation for stack and queue operations and, second, to study alternatives for stack and queue representations in an underlying memory medium. While the underlying representations using linking techniques are straightforward, the sequentially allocated representations have several subtle features. The use of stack notation is illustrated by an efficient algorithm to sort a sequence of distinct numbers into increasing order.

Stacks and *queues* are sequences of items, which are permitted to grow and contract only by following special disciplines for adding and removing items at their endpoints. In a *stack*, we add and remove items at only one end of a sequence. In a *queue*, we add items at one end and remove them from the opposite end.

As the name stack suggests, it is conventional to think of the items in a stack as being piled on top of one another, with the most recently inserted item at the top and the least recently inserted item at the bottom. Deleting the topmost item is often called *popping* the stack, and inserting a new item on top is often called *pushing* the item onto the stack. The visual image of pushing and popping items on the top of stacks is similar to the effect of adding and removing trays from a spring loaded pile in a cafeteria, in the sense that the whole pile shifts up and down as elements are deleted and added so that the level of the top of the stack does not change. This visual image is often used in automata theory where the top of a stack is visualized as sitting abreast of a read/write head that can push and pop stack elements. Thus, in automata theory, stacks are sometimes called *pushdown lists* (or *pushdown stacks*), connoting that the whole stack is "pushed down" under the displacement caused by adding new elements at its top.

However, in the sequentially allocated representations of stacks that we shall study, we shall find that the bottom of the stack sits in a fixed position, and that only the top of the stack is displaced under the addition of new elements. As the top of such a stack gets higher, it travels through memory and may bump into other previously allocated structures, necessitating a reorganization of memory if the stack is to be permitted further growth. We shall examine how this can be done both in this chapter, when we study the so-called *coexistence regimes* for several stacks, and later, in Chapter 5, when we study coexistence regimes for stacks and list structures.

Stacks have the property that the last item inserted is the first item that can be removed and, for this reason, they are sometimes called LIFO lists, after this "last-in, first-out" property. Thus, stacks implicitly provide a linear order for their items corresponding to the order of "*most recent* to *least recent* insertion." This property makes stacks natural to use for processing *nested structures of un-*

predictable depth, in which we wish to ensure that nested substructures get processed before the structure containing them. Suppose that we are processing the elements on a given level ℓ of a nested structure, and suppose further that we encounter a nested substructure S. At this point, we can interrupt the processing on level ℓ by placing information on top of a stack that later enables us to resume processing on level ℓ after the processing of substructure S has been completed. Thus, at any moment, the stack contains a sequence of *postponed obligations* whose completion in the order of removal from the stack is guaranteed to complete the processing of more deeply nested structures before the shallower structures that contain them.

Such nested structures occur frequently in applications and algorithms, and it is important to be able to recognize them in both their explicit and implicit forms. For example, the syntax of arithmetic expressions and blocks in programs, subroutine-calling sequences, and goal–subgoal structures exemplify nested structures in which, at any level, we may encounter a substructure having an arbitrary number of levels of similar substructures itself. Since trees form a natural representation for such nested structures, we devote considerable attention to them in Chapter 3. Not surprisingly, therefore, *stacks* play a key role in algorithms for tree processing, and we shall see later that several ingenious tree algorithms marry together the notions of stacks and trees by encoding into portions of a tree a stack of postponed obligations for further processing.

In this chapter, we establish the convention that items are added to the *rear* of *queues* and are deleted from the *front*. This is analogous to a waiting line in which people at the *front* of the line obtain service and depart and new arrivals join the *rear* of the line to await their turn for service. Queues thus have the property that the first item inserted is the first item that can be removed and, for this reason, they are sometimes called **FIFO** lists, after this "first-in, first-out" property. Queues implicitly provide a linear order for their items corresponding to their "*order of arrival.*" Thus, queues are used where we wish to process items under a "first-come, first-served" discipline.

It is common to use queues in operating systems where task queues are established, to regulate the order in which tasks receive processing and are allocated various system resources. Sometimes the order of items in such queues is rearranged to facilitate more efficient use of equipment, as in sorting queues of disk input–output requests to minimize mechanical delays; but in this chapter we shall use queues in the strict sense in which additions are made only at the rear and deletions only at the front, and in which the internal order is never perturbed.

If we represent a queue by allocating space for its items sequentially in memory, then additions make the rear expand and deletions make the front contract. So long as the queue is nonempty, it tends to travel rearward, eating up fresh space behind it and discarding used queue cells in front of it. Thus, if queues must coexist with each other or with other structures, it isn't long before the rear of some queue bumps up against some other neighboring structure.

Sometimes queues are guaranteed to be of bounded length. For example, in some operating systems, each job can be in only one of a number of possible "states." To each state, a queue is associated (such as the "I/O wait queue," the "high-priority run queue," and the "low-priority run queue"). In this case, no queue can be longer than the maximum number of jobs permitted by the operating system. More generally, in *closed queuing systems*, there are a number of *process servers*, each serving a queue of tasks awaiting service in order of arrival. When a server completes service on a task, the task is transmitted to the end of the queue for some new server. Arrival time and service time distributions affect the queue length at each server, but the total number of tasks in the system remains constant. Any queue representation that reserves enough space for all tasks to be in any single queue can function without need for reallocation of space for queues. However, in Section 2.5, a technique is presented whose performance suggests that initially allocating space for sequentially represented queues of only half the maximum length and reallocating space when needed can save half the total space without overly expensive penalties in reorganization costs. We also discuss queue representation techniques similar to those used for operating system buffers in which modular arithmetic is used to contain the motion of a queue representation in a bounded region of memory.

2.2 NOTATION

It is convenient to have a representation-independent notation for the actions of inserting and deleting items in stacks and queues. This notation can then be used later in the description of algorithms without implying a commitment to a particular representation of a stack or queue. Algorithms involving stacks and queues can then be implemented by choosing an appropriate stack or queue representation to suit the circumstances.

Let S be a stack and let X be a variable capable of containing an item of S as its value. We write $S \Leftarrow X$ to denote the action of pushing the contents of X on S. After we execute the operation $S \Leftarrow X$, the value of X becomes the new top item of S, the previous top item of S becomes the new second item of S, the previous second item of S becomes the new third item of S, and so on. On the other hand, writing $X \Leftarrow S$ denotes the action of assigning to X the value of the topmost item of S and then popping S by deleting its topmost item. The *empty stack* is denoted by Λ. In case S is empty to begin with, the effect of executing $X \Leftarrow S$ is to set the value of X to Λ and to leave the value of S unchanged.

If Q is a queue and X is a variable capable of containing a queue item as its value, writing $Q \Leftarrow X$ adds a new item to the rear of Q equal to the value of X, and writing $X \Leftarrow Q$ places the value of the item at the front of Q in X and removes the front item from Q, except that if Q is empty to begin with, X is set to the value Λ. The *empty queue* is also denoted by Λ.

For example, if Q is initially an empty queue, performing the operation $Q \Leftarrow 3$ places 3 in Q so that $Q = (3)$. If we next perform $Q \Leftarrow 17$, then Q is enlarged with the new rear element 17, so $Q = (3, 17)$. Again, performing $Q \Leftarrow 9$ changes Q to the form $Q = (3, 17, 9)$. Here, by convention, the front of the queue is taken to be the leftmost element of $(3, 17, 9)$ and the rear of the queue is taken to be the rightmost element. Thus, with $Q = (3, 17, 9)$, performing the operation $X \Leftarrow Q$ assigns X the value 3 and deletes 3 from the front of the queue, after which $Q = (17, 9)$.

We shall take some liberties with these notations, as the following example shows. Suppose S is a stack whose items are ordered pairs of integers. Performing $S \Leftarrow (3, 7)$ on an initially empty stack S sets S to have the value $S = ((3, 7))$, and subsequently performing $S \Leftarrow (2, 5)$ further changes S to be $S = ((2, 5), (3, 7))$. Here the topmost item in the stack is the leftmost item in $((2, 5), (3, 7))$. If now, we perform $X \Leftarrow S$, X is assigned the ordered pair $(2, 5)$ from the top of the stack, and the stack is popped so that $S = ((3, 7))$. We shall find it convenient to allow X to be an n-tuple of variables matching the structure of items that can be stored on S. For instance, if $S = ((3, 7))$, performing $(\ell, r) \Leftarrow S$ assigns 3 as the value of ℓ, assigns 7 as the value of r, and pops the integer pair $(3, 7)$ from S, leaving S empty. Such an operation may have no meaning when performed on an empty stack, so we can check first to see if S is nonempty by, for example, writing "*if* $S \neq \Lambda$, *then* $(\ell, r) \Leftarrow S$."

†2.3 QUICKSORT—A SORTING METHOD USING STACKS

The version of the Quicksort algorithm examined in this section rearranges a table of n *distinct* numbers into ascending order. An early version of the Quicksort algorithm was invented by C. A. R. Hoare when he was a British Council Visiting Student at Moscow State University in 1959–60. At the time, Russian scholars were attempting to use computers to provide mechanical translation from one natural language to another. The idea was to take a portion of the text to be translated, to sort the words in it into alphabetical order, and to use the sorted word list to look up word meanings in an alphabetized dictionary. The dictionary meanings were to provide further data for continuing the mechanical translation. In studying the sorting problem in this context, Hoare invented the initial version of Quicksort, which he published after subsequent refinement (see Hoare [1961] and Hoare [1962]).

The basic idea behind Quicksort is to break the problem of sorting a sequence of n numbers into two smaller sorting problems. These smaller sorting problems are then solved, and their solutions are combined to produce the solution to the larger problem. The subproblems are formulated by first picking one of the numbers, say X, and then rearranging numbers so that all numbers less than X lie to

---

† Advanced readers: Skip to Section 2.5.

the left of X, and all numbers greater than X lie to the right of X. If the subproblems of sorting the numbers to the left of X and sorting the numbers to the right of X are then solved, the entire sequence is sorted.

For example, picking $X = 41$ in the sequence

$$[41 \quad 62 \quad 13 \quad 84 \quad 35 \quad 96 \quad 57 \quad 28 \quad 79]$$

and partitioning the sequence into numbers $< X$, followed by X, followed by numbers $> X$, yields a sequence such as:

$$[28 \quad 35 \quad 13] \quad 41 \quad [84 \quad 96 \quad 57 \quad 62 \quad 79]$$

First subproblem   Second subproblem

in which there are two subproblems to be solved. Sorting the numbers in the subproblem [28 35 13] gives [13 28 35], and sorting the numbers in the subproblem [84 96 57 62 79] gives [57 62 79 84 96]. After the subproblems have been solved, the entire sequence is sorted:

$$[13 \quad 28 \quad 35 \quad 41 \quad 57 \quad 62 \quad 79 \quad 84 \quad 96].$$

One method that can be used to partition a sequence into subproblems is the following. We start with two pointers i and j, pointing to the leftmost and rightmost numbers in the sequence, respectively. In the following line, i points to 41 and j points to 79.

$$[41 \quad 62 \quad 13 \quad 84 \quad 35 \quad 96 \quad 57 \quad 28 \quad 79]$$
$$\;\;i \qquad\qquad\qquad\qquad\qquad\qquad\qquad\qquad j$$

First we move j to the left stopping at the rightmost number smaller than the number to which i points. Thus j is moved left until it comes to rest under 28 since 28 is smaller than 41.

$$[41 \quad 62 \quad 13 \quad 84 \quad 35 \quad 96 \quad 57 \quad 28 \quad 79]$$
$$\;\;i \qquad\qquad\qquad\qquad\qquad\qquad\qquad j$$

Then we exchange the numbers pointed to by i and j. This gives:

$$[28 \quad 62 \quad 13 \quad 84 \quad 35 \quad 96 \quad 57 \quad 41 \quad 79]$$
$$\;\;i \qquad\qquad\qquad\qquad\qquad\qquad\qquad j$$

Now we move i to the right until it comes to rest under a number that is greater than the number j points to. This yields:

$$[28 \quad 62 \quad 13 \quad 84 \quad 35 \quad 96 \quad 57 \quad 41 \quad 79]$$
$$\qquad\quad i \qquad\qquad\qquad\qquad\qquad\qquad j$$

Then we exchange the numbers pointed to by i and j a second time:

$$[28 \quad 41 \quad 13 \quad 84 \quad 35 \quad 96 \quad 57 \quad 62 \quad 79]$$
$$\qquad\quad i \qquad\qquad\qquad\qquad\qquad\qquad j$$

Attention then switches back to j. We move j leftward until it comes to rest under a number less than the one i points to,

$$[28 \quad 41 \quad 13 \quad 84 \quad 35 \quad 96 \quad 57 \quad 62 \quad 79]$$
$$\quad\;\; i \qquad\qquad\qquad\; j$$

and we exchange again:

$$[28 \quad 35 \quad 13 \quad 84 \quad 41 \quad 96 \quad 57 \quad 62 \quad 79]$$
$$\quad\;\; i \qquad\qquad\qquad\; j$$

Then attention shifts back to i as we move i rightward until it comes to rest under a number greater than that j points to,

$$[28 \quad 35 \quad 13 \quad 84 \quad 41 \quad 96 \quad 57 \quad 62 \quad 79]$$
$$\qquad\qquad\quad i \quad\; j$$

and we exchange a final time:

$$[28 \quad 35 \quad 13 \quad 41 \quad 84 \quad 96 \quad 57 \quad 62 \quad 79]$$
$$\qquad\qquad\quad i \quad\; j$$

The sequence is now partitioned into the numbers less than 41, followed by 41, followed by those greater than 41. Note that 41 was used in every comparison to create the partition in which 41 becomes the partition "boundary."

Algorithms 2.1 and 2.2 below implement Quicksort. Algorithm 2.2 partitions subsequences using the technique illustrated above of alternately decreasing j and exchanging, then increasing i and exchanging, until pointers i and j meet and the process terminates. Algorithm 2.1 calls Algorithm 2.2 to perform partitioning and to deliver back descriptions of subproblems to work on. Algorithm 2.1 acts as an "administrator," by deciding which of the subproblems to work on next and which to postpone until later. To postpone working on a subproblem, Algorithm 2.1 pushes the subproblem boundaries onto a stack. Thus, at any instant, the stack contains descriptions of all postponed subproblems awaiting later attention. After completion of a current problem, the stack is popped to obtain the boundaries of a new subproblem to work on. When the stack becomes empty, there are no more subproblems to solve, so the algorithm terminates. Algorithm 2.1 is written so it always chooses to postpone the larger of the two subproblems whose descriptions it receives from calling Algorithm 2.2. Using this trick, it can be shown that the depth of the stack is at most $\lceil \lg n \rceil$ stack entries (see Exercises 2.4 and 2.8).

Algorithm 2.1 *Quicksort*

Quicksort sorts a sequence of n distinct numbers in Table T into ascending order. The numbers in T are referred to as $T[1]$, $T[2]$, ..., $T[n]$. The algorithm uses an auxiliary stack S, which is initialized to the empty stack. Algorithm 2.2 is used as a subroutine to partition subsequences of the numbers in T into suitable subproblems. We assume n is at least two.

1. **[Initialize.]** Set $\ell \leftarrow 1$, $r \leftarrow n$, and $S \leftarrow \Lambda$. (ℓ is the leftmost index of the interval (ℓ, r) in Table T and r is the rightmost index.)

2. **[Partition interval.]** Call Algorithm 2.2 with input (ℓ, r) to partition interval (ℓ, r) of T into two intervals: an interval (ℓ_1, r_1) of numbers $< T[\ell]$ and an interval (ℓ_2, r_2) of numbers $> T[\ell]$. (Algorithm 2.2 uses a suitable pattern of exchanges to do this.)

3. **[Postpone larger subproblem.]** If $(r_1 - \ell_1) > (r_2 - \ell_2)$, then perform $S \Leftarrow (\ell_1, r_1)$, set $\ell \leftarrow \ell_2$, set $r \leftarrow r_2$, and go to step 4. Otherwise, perform $S \Leftarrow (\ell_2, r_2)$, set $\ell \leftarrow \ell_1$, set $r \leftarrow r_1$, and go to step 4. (This step stacks the larger interval on S and goes to step 4 to sort next the numbers in the smaller interval.)

4. **[Interval nontrivial?]** If $r > \ell$, then go to step 2. (Otherwise, $r \leq \ell$ so the interval (ℓ, r) contains at most one number and need not be sorted. Thus, the stack can next be examined at step 5 to see if there are any more postponed subproblems to consider.)

5. **[Done?]** If $S = \Lambda$, the algorithm terminates. Otherwise, perform $(\ell, r) \Leftarrow S$ and go back to step 4.

At step 4 of Algorithm 2.1, we examine the interval (ℓ, r) for a new subproblem. If the interval contains two or more numbers, we return to step 2 to partition it. However, if the interval contains just one number or is empty, we ignore it and proceed to examine the stack to see if any postponed subproblems remain to be considered. This ensures that the partitioning algorithm is never called unless its required input condition $\ell < r$ is met.

Algorithm 2.2 *Partition the interval (ℓ, r) in Table T.*

Using repeated exchanges, this algorithm partitions the distinct numbers in positions $T[\ell]$, $T[\ell + 1]$, ..., $T[r]$ into two subintervals: the interval (ℓ_1, r_1) containing numbers less than $T[\ell]$ and the interval (ℓ_2, r_2) containing numbers greater than $T[\ell]$. The output consists of the ordered pairs of indices (ℓ_1, r_1) and (ℓ_2, r_2) for these two intervals. At termination, the number originally in $T[\ell]$ lies between and separates the two subintervals. It is assumed initially that $\ell < r$.

1. **[Initialize.]** Set $i \leftarrow \ell$ and set $j \leftarrow r$.

2. **[Decrease j.]** If $T[j] > T[i]$, set $j \leftarrow j - 1$ and repeat this step. (This step finds the greatest j such that $T[j] \leq T[i]$.)

3. **[Exchange or done?]** If $j > i$, then $T[i] \leftrightarrow T[j]$ (that is, exchange $T[i]$ and $T[j]$) and go to step 4. Otherwise, set $(\ell_1, r_1) \leftarrow (\ell, i - 1)$, set $(\ell_2, r_2) \leftarrow (i + 1, r)$, and terminate the algorithm.

4. [Increase i.] If $T[i] < T[j]$, set $i \leftarrow i + 1$ and repeat this step. (This step finds the least i such that $T[i] \geq T[j]$.)

5. [Exchange or done?] If $j > i$ then $T[i] \leftrightarrow T[j]$ (that is, exchange $T[i]$ and $T[j]$) and go to step 2. Otherwise, set $(\ell_1, r_1) \leftarrow (\ell, j - 1)$, set $(\ell_2, r_2) \leftarrow (j + 1, r)$, and terminate the algorithm.

Figure 2.1 illustrates the successive subproblems considered by Algorithm 2.1 as it sorts. The subsequences enclosed in boldface square brackets [...] indicate the subproblems considered at each stage. The stack of intervals of postponed subproblems is also shown.

1	2	3	4	5	6	7	8	9	Stack
[41	62	13	84	35	96	57	28	79]	Λ
[28	35	13]	41	[84	96	57	62	79]	((5,9))
[13]	28	[35]	41	[84	96	57	62	79]	((3,3)(5,9))
13	28	[35]	41	[84	96	57	62	79]	((5,9))
13	28	35	41	[84	96	57	62	79]	Λ
13	28	35	41	[79	62	57]	84	[96]	((5,7))
13	28	35	41	[79	62	57]	84	96	Λ
13	28	35	41	[57	62]	79[	]84	96	((5,6))
13	28	35	41	[57	62]	79	84	96	Λ
13	28	35	41[	]57	[62]	79	84	96	((6,6))
13	28	35	41	57	[62]	79	84	96	Λ
13	28	35	41	57	62	79	84	96	Λ

FIGURE 2.1

Algorithm 2.2 fails to partition sequences of numbers that are not distinct. Exercise 2.5 challenges the reader to extend Algorithm 2.2 to cover this case. In addition, Algorithm 2.2 always uses the element $T[\ell]$ as a partition boundary. In Quicksort it is important to choose the partitioning element carefully. If the numbers in the input sequence are "almost sorted" already, $T[\ell]$ is a poor choice of a partition boundary. Exercise 2.6 shows how a better choice can be made.

It can be shown that Quicksort runs in $O(n \log n)$ steps on the average and in $O(n^2)$ steps in the worst case. R. Sedgewick [1977] has given an enlightened discussion and comparison of various versions of Quicksort, and his paper illustrates the intriguing mathematics that arises in the analysis of algorithms of this kind. While the analysis of versions of the Quicksort algorithm is beyond the scope of this book, the reader is invited to pursue this topic by independent reading or by taking a companion course in analysis of algorithms. For a practical study of how to implement the best variants of Quicksort on real computers, see Sedgewick [1978].

2.4 REPRESENTATIONS OF STACKS AND QUEUES

In this section we consider both linked and sequential allocation techniques for the underlying representations of stacks and queues. We treat the linked allocation techniques first, since these are the simpler of the two.

2.4.1 Linked representations

The items of a stack can be stored conveniently in cells of a linked list. Only a single pointer to the top of a stack S need be kept. Figure 2.2 illustrates this representation schematically.

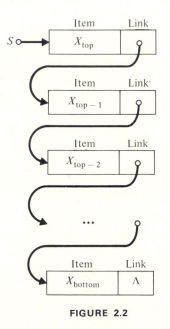

FIGURE 2.2

To provide a supply of empty cells to hold items of stacks and queues, it is convenient to divide a region of memory into cells containing *Item* and *Link* fields, and to link the empty cells into a linked list. This is called an *available space list* and we shall use a variable *Avail* in what follows to point to the first cell of such a list. Figure 2.3 illustrates an available space list.

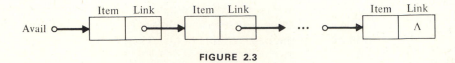

FIGURE 2.3

In this chapter, we shall assume Avail never points to the empty list Λ. If Avail should ever become empty, we can invoke one of the storage reclamation processes treated thoroughly in Chapter 5 to recover unused cells and to place them back on the Avail list. Here, to simplify the exposition, we shall assume an appropriate storage reclamation process is invoked behind the scenes when needed.

The operations of pushing and popping stack items can then be implemented as follows:

$$S \Leftarrow X \begin{cases} \text{Temp} \leftarrow \text{Avail}, \text{Avail} \leftarrow \text{Link(Avail)}, \\ \text{Item(Temp)} \leftarrow X, \text{Link(Temp)} \leftarrow S, \text{ and} \\ S \leftarrow \text{Temp}. \end{cases}$$

$$X \Leftarrow S \begin{cases} \text{If } S = \Lambda, \text{ then the stack is empty so set } X \leftarrow \Lambda. \\ \text{Otherwise, } X \leftarrow \text{Item}(S), \text{Temp} \leftarrow \text{Link}(S), \\ \text{Link}(S) \leftarrow \text{Avail}, \text{Avail} \leftarrow S, \text{ and } S \leftarrow \text{Temp}. \end{cases}$$

To use a linked list to represent a queue Q, it is profitable to keep pointers both to the front and to the rear of Q.

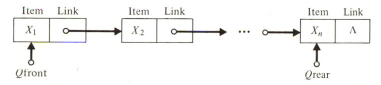

Then, to add an item X to the rear of Q, we do:

$$Q \Leftarrow X \begin{cases} \text{Temp} \leftarrow \text{Avail}, \text{Avail} \leftarrow \text{Link(Avail)}, \\ \text{Link}(Q\text{rear}) \leftarrow \text{Temp}, Q\text{rear} \leftarrow \text{Temp}, \\ \text{Item}(Q\text{rear}) \leftarrow X, \text{ and } \text{Link}(Q\text{rear}) \leftarrow \Lambda. \end{cases}$$

and to remove an item X from the front of Q, we do:

$$X \Leftarrow Q \begin{cases} \text{If } Q\text{front} = \Lambda \text{ then the queue is empty so set } X \leftarrow \Lambda. \\ \text{Otherwise, } X \leftarrow \text{Item}(Q\text{front}), \text{Temp} \leftarrow Q\text{front}, \\ Q\text{front} \leftarrow \text{Link}(Q\text{front}), \text{Link(Temp)} \leftarrow \text{Avail}, \text{ and } \text{Avail} \leftarrow \text{Temp}. \end{cases}$$

2.4.2 Sequentially allocated representations

Suppose that the representations of items to be stored in stacks or queues each occupy a fixed amount of storage c. The size of an item representation c may be either a fraction of a word (e.g., two bytes) or a multiple of a word length (e.g., three words). In order to simplify the exposition, however, we assume that each item representation occupies exactly one addressable unit of storage (e.g., one word). Adjustments to the algorithms in case $c \neq 1$ can be made rather easily if required.

2.4.2.1 *Managing a single stack in a fixed region.* If we are given a fixed region of addressable memory units, with addresses consisting of the integers in the range $L_0 < i \leq L_{max}$, we can allocate the representation of a stack S by anchoring the bottom of S at either end of the region and by allowing the top of S to grow towards the other end of the region. Without loss of generality, we could choose L_0 as the base address for items of S and we could maintain a pointer *Top* to point to the item currently on top of the stack. Initially, when the stack is empty, we set Top to point to the base address L_0. Then, to push an element X onto S, we do:

$$S \Leftarrow X \begin{cases} \text{Top} \leftarrow \text{Top} + 1. \text{ If now, Top} > L_{max}, \text{ then the stack} \\ \text{has overflowed the allocated region of memory.} \\ \text{Otherwise, store } X \text{ in the location given by Top.} \end{cases}$$

To pop an element off the stack S, we proceed as follows:

$$X \Leftarrow S \begin{cases} \text{If Top} = L_0, \text{ then the stack is empty, so set } X \leftarrow \Lambda. \\ \text{Otherwise, set } X \text{ to the value stored in the location} \\ \text{given by Top, and set Top} \leftarrow \text{Top} - 1. \end{cases}$$

When the stack overflows, either we must reallocate the memory to provide space for more stack items, or the computation must terminate. An alternative to passing back the value Λ when the stack becomes empty is to transfer control to a special algorithm to handle stack underflows, or to set an *underflow condition flag*, which will be interrogated by subsequent routines. The manner of communicating the stack's empty or overflowed condition is a matter that must be chosen to suit the implementation environment. In certain operating system environments, for instance, when two concurrent sequential processes pass data to each other using a stack or queue, it may be desirable to suspend a process that is attempting to remove an item from an empty stack or queue until another concurrent process inserts an item, at which point the suspended process can be resumed and can proceed normally. This situation occurs frequently, for example, when implementing input/output buffers in operating systems. Special control concepts are useful for coordinating the activities of producers and consumers of information stored in buffers. For an example of a buffer using a queue shared between concurrent producers and consumers, see Hoare [1974b].

To provide a simple uniform treatment in what follows, we shall communicate the empty stack and queue conditions by passing back the special value Λ. We shall further assume, in algorithms that use stacks, that overflow can never occur or, if it does, that memory is automatically reallocated behind the scenes to make more room for stack growth. Section 2.5 gives one technique for implementing such automatic reallocation policies.

2.4.2.2 *The coexistence of two stacks.* Two stacks can coexist conveniently in a fixed storage region by anchoring the base of one stack at the beginning of the region, anchoring the base of the other stack at the end of the region, and by arranging the tops of the stacks to grow toward each other.

In Fig. 2.4, Top_1 is incremented when new items are added, and Top_2 is decremented when new items are added. In this fashion, each stack can grow into the unused space in the middle, and neither stack overflows before all the space in the original fixed region has been consumed entirely.

FIGURE 2.4

2.4.2.3 *Representing queues using modular arithmetic.* Because sequentially al-located queues travel through memory when we add elements at the rear and delete elements from the front, it is convenient to confine their travel to a fixed region. Using modular arithmetic, we can cause a given interval of memory addresses to behave like a "circular track" in which, if a queue travels off one end, it "wraps around" and travels onto the opposite end. Letting N be the capacity of the interval, we can picture the cells as if they were arranged in a circular region, as depicted in Fig. 2.5. To implement a queue Q in such a circular region, we main-tain two pointers Qfront and Qrear, and we maintain a counter Qcount, which records the number of items currently in Q. Whereas Qfront contains the index of the item that can next be removed from Q, the variable Qrear points to the location where the next item to be inserted in Q will be stored. The queue insertion

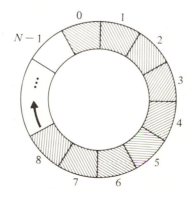

FIGURE 2.5

and deletion operations can now be represented as follows:

$$Q \Leftarrow X \begin{cases} \text{If } Q\text{count} = N, \text{ then the queue overflows. Otherwise,} \\ \text{store } X \text{ in the location } Q\text{rear, set } Q\text{rear} \leftarrow (Q\text{rear} + 1) \text{ mod } N, \\ \text{and set } Q\text{count} \leftarrow Q\text{count} + 1. \end{cases}$$

$$X \Leftarrow Q \begin{cases} \text{If } Q\text{count} = 0 \text{ then the queue underflows, so set } X \leftarrow \Lambda. \\ \text{Otherwise, set } X \text{ to the contents of the cell whose address is } Q\text{front,} \\ \text{set } Q\text{front} \leftarrow (Q\text{front} + 1) \text{ mod } N, \text{ and set } Q\text{count} \leftarrow Q\text{count} - 1. \end{cases}$$

The variables Qfront, Qrear, and Qcount contain redundant information, since the relationship

$$Q\text{rear} = (Q\text{front} + Q\text{count}) \text{ mod } N$$

is always true. It is therefore possible to eliminate one of the three variables by, for instance, altering the first definition above to eliminate Qrear, as follows:

$$Q \Leftarrow X \begin{cases} \text{If } Q\text{count} = N, \text{ then the queue overflows. Otherwise,} \\ \text{store } X \text{ in the location } (Q\text{front} + Q\text{count}) \text{ mod } N, \text{ and} \\ \text{set } Q\text{count} \leftarrow Q\text{count} + 1. \end{cases}$$

Similarly, if we retain Qrear and Qcount, Qfront can be eliminated from the second definition (see Exercise 2.10). It is also possible to give up one location in the region 0 to $N - 1$, and to dispense with Qcount, using certain conventions about whether Qrear = Qfront denotes the empty or the full queue (see Exercise 2.11).

2.5 GARWICK'S TECHNIQUE FOR MANAGING THREE OR MORE STACKS

Given a fixed storage region $L_0 < i \leq L_{\max}$, and three stacks S_1, S_2, and S_3, it is impossible to allocate contiguous sequential space for the three S_i in such a fashion that the bottoms of the stacks remain fixed and such that the top of any stack can grow sequentially until all the storage in the fixed region is exhausted. So long as we allocate at least one location for each stack, then no matter where we anchor the bottoms of the stacks and no matter in which directions we choose for the tops of the stacks to grow, there is always a way to add items to various of the S_i so that two of the three stacks will run out of room in which to grow, while the third still has room. Thus, unlike the case for two contiguous sequential stacks, in the case of three stacks, we cannot ensure that no stack will overflow before all available storage is consumed.

This leads us to the consideration of techniques for handling overflow in a single stack by moving the other stacks around so as to borrow part of the growing space from those that still have room and allocate it to those stacks that are cramped for space.

One rather elementary policy for providing space for a new element on an overflowed stack is to scan the stacks above the overflowed stack, searching for the nearest unit of free space and, if such a unit can be found, to shift all stacks between the top of the overflowed stack and the nearest unit of free space upwards one unit. If no free space can be found above, then an analogous search can be conducted below. If free space can be located below, a downshift of one unit will provide room for the overflowed element; and if no space can be located below, the entire region of storage has been exhausted and all stacks are full. While this policy is simple to implement, it can cause unnecessary repetitive unit shifts of many stacks in the case where consecutive additions to an overflowed stack are encountered. An alternative is to shift the stacks by several units in anticipation of possible bursts of local growth in the most active current stacks. This leads to the consideration of Garwick's technique.

Garwick's idea (see Garwick [1964]) for reallocating space for stacks upon overflow is to measure the growth in the respective stacks since the most recent reallocation, and to apportion space so that each stack receives some *fixed fraction* of the total remaining space plus additional space *proportional to its growth* since the last reallocation. This way, the stacks with the biggest recent appetites for space receive the most room in which to grow subsequently, yet every stack tends to get some room for growth. Garwick reports (*cf.* Garwick [1964], p. 140) that tests show that allocating between one and ten percent of the remaining space to each stack uniformly, and allocating the rest of the remaining space proportional to recent growth, appears to give good results. Knuth gives a variation of Garwick's technique using ten percent of the remaining space for uniform distribution, and 90 percent for distribution proportional to recent growth (*cf.* Knuth [1973a], p. 245, Algorithm G). Experiments with Knuth's variation reveal that it is advisable to add an additional capability to Garwick's technique to enable some of the remaining space to be distributed *proportional to stack size*, in addition to recent growth. The variation given in this book incorporates this feature. Circumstances in which it is appropriate to use it are considered in the next section.

In Algorithms 2.3 and 2.4 below, we assume that N ($N \geq 3$) stacks are allocated in a sequence of memory locations collectively called *Table*, where the addresses available lie in the range ($\text{Table}_{base} < i \leq \text{Table}_{max}$). The tops and base addresses of the respective stacks are kept in vectors *Top* and *Base*, such that the locations used by the ith stack ($1 \leq i \leq N$) are given by $\text{Base}[i] < j \leq \text{Top}[i]$. Whenever $\text{Base}[i] = \text{Top}[i]$, the ith stack is empty. All stacks grow in the direction of increasing i, and are nonoverlapping with their alternate bases and tops forming a nondecreasing sequence. The vectors *OldTop*, *NewBase*, and *Increase* hold quantities used during stack reallocation. By convention, $\text{Base}[N + 1] = \text{Table}_{max} - 1$ and $\text{Base}[1] = \text{Table}_{base}$. Figure 2.6 presents these facts pictorially.

We assume that Algorithm 2.3 is called when, for some k ($1 \leq k \leq N$), the kth stack has overflowed (i.e., performing $\text{Top}[k] \leftarrow \text{Top}[k] + 1$ makes $\text{Top}[k] >$

Base[$k + 1$]). The new element to be inserted on top of stack k is stored at location Top[k] only after Algorithms 2.3 and 2.4 have been performed and have shifted the respective stacks to make room (if possible).

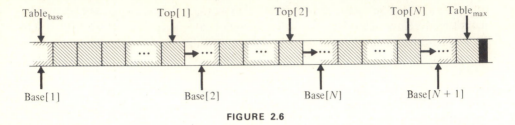

FIGURE 2.6

Algorithm 2.3 *Reallocate space for sequential stacks*

1. [Initialize.] Set TotalUsed $\leftarrow 0$ and SumOfIncreases $\leftarrow 0$. Then, for each i in the range ($1 \leq i \leq N$), do
   a) Set TotalUsed $\leftarrow$ TotalUsed + (Top[i] − Base[i])
   b) *if* Top[i] > OldTop[i], *then*
      > set Increase[i] $\leftarrow$ Top[i] − OldTop[i] and
      > set SumOfIncreases $\leftarrow$ SumOfIncreases + Increase[i]
      otherwise set Increase[i] $\leftarrow 0$.

   (The effect of this step is to set the value of TotalUsed to the sum of the sizes of the stacks, and to set SumOfIncreases to the sum of the increases in stack size since the most recent reallocation. In addition, for each stack $1 \leq i \leq N$, if stack i increased in size, Increase[i] contains the amount of the increase, whereas if stack i did not increase, Increase[i] = 0.)

2. [Table full?] Set Rem $\leftarrow$ (Table$_{max}$ − Table$_{base}$) − TotalUsed. If Rem < 0, then the table has no more room, and the algorithm cannot proceed. (Here Rem gives the amount of remaining empty space that can be reallocated.)

3. [Set policy.] $\rho \leftarrow 0.5$ (ρ is a fraction in the range $0 \leq \rho \leq 1$ used to help determine what portion of the 90% of the remaining space to allocate proportional to recent stack growth (ρ) versus what proportion to allocate proportional to stack size $(1 - \rho)$).

4. [Compute allocation factors.] $\alpha \leftarrow (.10 \times \text{Rem})/N$; $\beta \leftarrow (\rho \times .90 \times \text{Rem})/\text{SumOfIncreases}$; $\gamma \leftarrow ((1 - \rho) \times .90 \times \text{Rem})/\text{TotalUsed}$. (Here, α is set so that 10% of the remaining free space in the table will be distributed equally to each of the N stacks. Then 90% of the remaining space is split so that $\rho \times 90\%$ is allocated proportional to recent increases, using β, and so that $(1 - \rho) \times 90\%$ is allocated proportional to stack size, using γ.)

5. [Determine new base addresses.] Set NewBase[1] ← Base[1] and set $\sigma \leftarrow 0$. Then for $i \leftarrow 2, 3, \ldots, N$, do

   a) $\tau \leftarrow \sigma + \alpha + \beta \times$ Increase$[i - 1] + \gamma \times$ (Top$[i - 1] -$ Base$[i - 1])$
   b) NewBase$[i] \leftarrow$ NewBase$[i - 1] + ($Top$[i - 1] -$ Base$[i - 1]) + \lfloor \tau \rfloor - \lfloor \sigma \rfloor$
   c) $\sigma \leftarrow \tau$

6. [Move stacks.] Move the stacks to their proper new locations by performing Algorithm 2.4 below.

7. [Save tops.] For $1 \leq i \leq N$, do OldTop$[i] \leftarrow$ Top$[i]$ (so that stack growth between this reallocation and the next can be determined).

Algorithm 2.4 *Move stacks to new locations.*

1. [Initialize.] $i \leftarrow 2$ (We leave the first stack in place, and start considering shifts for stacks 2, 3, ..., N). NewBase$[N + 1] \leftarrow$ Base$[N + 1]$ (so that the "shift up" step below works properly). Top$[k] \leftarrow$ Top$[k] - 1$. (In Algorithm 2.3, we reallocated the stack boundaries assuming space for the overflowed element Top$[k]$ was present. However, when we move stacks, we assume Top$[k]$ is not yet inserted.)

2. [Terminate?] If $i > N$, then all stacks have been moved, so set Top$[k] \leftarrow$ Top$[k] + 1$ (to restore a space at the top of the kth stack to accommodate the overflowed element) and terminate.

3. [Shift down?] If NewBase$[i] <$ Base$[i]$, then the ith stack must be moved down by an amount $\delta = ($Base$[i] -$ NewBase$[i])$. We must perform this shift in increasing order of elements in stack i to avoid clobbering part of the stack. Thus, for $h \leftarrow$ Base$[i] + 1$, Base$[i] + 2, \ldots,$ Top$[i]$, we set Table$[h - \delta] \leftarrow$ Table$[h]$. Then, we readjust the Base and Top of stack i by setting Base$[i] \leftarrow$ NewBase$[i]$ and Top$[i] \leftarrow$ Top$[i] - \delta$. Now we consider the next stack in sequence by setting $i \leftarrow i + 1$ and returning to step 2.

4. [Shift up?] If NewBase$[i] >$ Base$[i]$, then the ith stack must be shifted up. But to avoid possible overwriting of stacks above it, we must first move all upward-bound stacks between stack i and the first stack above i that need not be moved up (if any). Hence, we first find the smallest j in the range $i < j \leq N + 1$ such that NewBase$[j] \leq$ Base$[j]$ (note that the initialization in step 1 guarantees the existence of such a j). Now, we shift stacks upward in decreasing order on the interval of upward-moving stacks. For $t \leftarrow j - 1$, $j - 2, \ldots, i$, do

   a) $\delta \leftarrow$ NewBase$[t] -$ Base$[t]$
   b) for $h \leftarrow$ Top$[t]$, Top$[t] - 1, \ldots,$ Base$[t] + 1$, set Table$[h + \delta] \leftarrow$ Table$[h]$
   c) set Base$[t] \leftarrow$ NewBase$[t]$ and Top$[t] \leftarrow$ Top$[t] + \delta$.

Finally, set $i \leftarrow j$ and return to step 2.

5. [No change?] (Take care of case where NewBase[i] = Base[i])
Set $i \leftarrow i + 1$ and go back to step 2.

2.5.1 Degradation of performance in
Garwick allocation as memory becomes saturated

Empirical explorations of the behavior of Algorithm 2.3 suggest that the cost of
reallocating stacks is often relatively inexpensive when at least a quarter of the
total available space is unused. However, as the memory approaches full saturation, the stacks vibrate back and forth in a frenzied fashion, as the algorithm
makes minor, often ineffective, readjustments in the last few driblets of free space it
allocates. For instance, in one sample of runs investigated, the algorithm performed 92% of its space reorganizations when the last 5% of the free space was
being allocated. As the graphs in Figs. 2.7 and 2.8 indicate, the final paroxysms of
the algorithm before space is exhausted tend to incur very high reallocation costs.

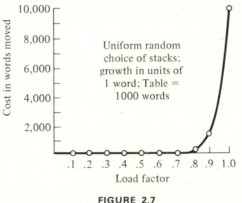

FIGURE 2.7

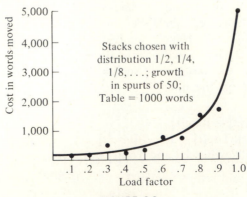

FIGURE 2.8

2.5.2 Choosing a reallocation policy

The variable ρ in step 3 of Algorithm 2.3 can be set to a value between 0 and 1 to determine what fraction of 90% of the unused space to allocate proportional to recent stack growth and what fraction to allocate proportional to stack size. How shall a value for ρ be chosen? Experiments with the behavior of Algorithm 2.3 show that there are some circumstances in which (by setting $\rho = 1$) allocation proportional to recent growth alone outperforms allocation proportional to stack size while, in other circumstances (by setting $\rho = 0$), allocation proportional to stack size outperforms allocation proportional to recent growth, and in yet other circumstances (by setting $\rho = 0.5$) a mixed strategy outperforms the two extremes.

While program behavior is highly variable in general, there exist circumstances under which it can be measured and found to behave according to certain principles that make it sensible to apply certain sampling and estimation disciplines. Two such principles that apply frequently to program behavior are the principles of *locality* and *recency*. Two instances of the principle of locality are that in many programs, over 90% of the instructions executed lie in 10% of the code and that, often in file processing, 20% of the records are accessed 80% of the time. Two instances of the principle of recency are that over half the references in large LISP programs are references to one of the ten most recently referenced cells (Clark [1979]) and that, in a virtual-memory operating system, pages referenced most recently tend, in the near future, to be referenced again and that, all other things being equal, swapping out the least recently referenced pages tends to minimize page faulting. Thus, at first sight, for a choice of a fixed, general table reallocation policy, Garwick's technique of reallocating free space proportional to recent growth agrees well with these two frequently encountered principles of program behavior.

However, closer inspection of the actual running behavior of Garwick's policy reveals circumstances in which it does a poor job of reapportioning unused space. These circumstances occur when recent growth samples are so small as to be a bad measure of even recent short-term trends, and they cause inappropriately skewed space reapportionments that invite a cascade of further badly skewed reapportionments based on a succession of small, inadequate samples of recent growth. Given program execution behavior in which the principles of locality and recency are determined by measurement to hold, samples of recent growth must be adequately reflective of actual short-term trends if they are to be of use in predicting the short-term future. As the simulations discussed below show, better predictions can sometimes be achieved by using stack size as a factor in calculating space reallocations, because stack size partly reflects cumulative recent growth over time independent of the interval since the last reallocation, and because, therefore, its use avoids the distortions implicit in small, inadequate samples of recent growth.

On the other hand, stack size is of very little predictive value when the stacks are of nearly equal size and when growth tends to occur in randomly chosen

stacks in sizable, consecutive spurts. It is here that recent growth measurements
alone provide the best predictions.

These ideas are illustrated in some results of simulation experiments performed on Algorithm 2.3, using repeatable sequences of random numbers. A table
of 1000 memory locations was preallocated into ten regions of 100 locations each
to provide room for ten stacks. In one sequence of experiments, stacks were
chosen at random with uniform probability. In a second sequence, stacks were
selected with a skew distribution with probabilities proportional to the numbers $\frac{1}{2}$,
$\frac{1}{4}, \frac{1}{8}, \ldots, (\frac{1}{2})^{10}$. Growth in the selected stacks was chosen to occur either a single
word at a time, or in consecutive spurts of 20 or 50 words, before a new stack was
selected. The allocation policy factor ρ was set to 1, 0.5, and 0 for each possible
combination of distribution (uniform or $\frac{1}{2}^n$) and growth spurt size (1, 20, or 50).
Then the number of memory reorganizations as well as their costs (measured in
total number of words moved) were accumulated for various intervals of memory
saturation, as words were added repeatedly to the initially empty stacks until all
free space was consumed and the entire table overflowed. Table 2.1 compares the
results (each averaged over 10 runs) by giving, for each combination of experimental conditions, the cumulative cost of reorganization up to 70% full, the cumulative cost up to 100% full, and the average total number of reorganizations.

TABLE 2.1

		Uniform random choice of stacks			Stacks chosen with frequency $\propto 1/2^n$		
Growth	$\rho = 1$	0.0	19571.9	22.3	272.3	9888.5	11.0
in	$\rho = 0.5$	0.0	10364.6	11.8	272.3	7432.3	8.5
units	$\rho = 0$	0.0	8847.1	10.1	272.3	7228.9	8.3
Growth	$\rho = 1$	2526.5	18075.7	24.4	3152.6	16350.5	23.3
in spurts	$\rho = 0.5$	1889.2	15840.0	20.7	1534.0	11103.2	14.7
of 20	$\rho = 0$	1634.6	26250.0	32.5	1152.5	16150.2	19.7
Growth	$\rho = 1$	2856.1	12435.2	17.8	1837.4	9884.6	13.3
in spurts	$\rho = 0.5$	2945.7	14264.8	19.7	1351.3	9934.6	12.7
of 50	$\rho = 0$	4688.8	33036.2	43.0	2049.6	24139.8	28.4
	ρ	a	b	c	a	b	c

a = total work < 70% saturation in words moved.
b = total work up to full saturation in words moved.
c = total number of reorganizations of memory.

As the results show, at over 70% saturation stack size is a better predictor
than recent growth when stacks grow only a word at a time, regardless of whether
the stacks grow uniformly or have growth that is highly skewed. At below 70%

saturation, the choice of policy makes no difference. Close inspection of the running behavior at high saturation (upwards of 95%) shows that the recent-growth policy uses poor sampling.

If stacks grow in spurts of 20 consecutive words, then, regardless of the distribution used for stack choices, a setting of $\rho = 0.5$ (a "half-and-half" policy) gives the best behavior at between 70% and 100% saturation, whereas stack size alone ($\rho = 0$) is the best predictor at less than 70% saturation. On the other hand, if stacks grow in spurts of 50 consecutive words, and stacks are chosen at random with each stack equally likely to be chosen, then recent growth ($\rho = 1$) is the best predictor (stack size having little predictive value since, on the average, the stacks are the same size). The use of recent growth alone ($\rho = 1$) is seldom the best policy.

2.5.3 Other applications and observations

Historically, Garwick devised his method in order to deal with sequential tables in a compiler (Garwick [1964]). He observed that, if each of a set of tables used during compilation has a fixed size, then one gets a series of independent restrictions on the compiler, each restriction corresponding to the maximum size of a table (e.g., no more than 1000 identifiers allowed, no more than 10 array subscripts, expression nesting no more than 64 levels deep, strings no more than 500 characters, etc.). Garwick noted that this situation could be avoided only if sequential tables could be made dynamically variable in size. Thus, while Algorithm 2.3 is written to reallocate space for stacks, nothing in it depends on how the space between Base[i] and Top[i] is used ($1 \le i \le N$). Hence, it can be used to reallocate space for queues, or for sequential tables of any sort (with appropriate precaution taken to shove the queues and tables as far left as possible beforehand).

Knuth observes that, since the first stack is never moved by the algorithm, the programmer can arrange to place the largest stack first, if he knows which it is in advance. Also, space can be initially allocated proportional to expected stack size although, even if space is initially divided equally, the algorithm will quickly readjust allocations to the proper proportions during the early phases of its operation. Finally, Knuth shows a method for having the arrays OldTop, NewBase, and Increase share space in Algorithm 2.3 (*cf.* Knuth [1973a], p. 246).

EXERCISES

1. (Queue reversal) Let Q be a nonempty queue and let S be an empty stack. Using only the temporary variable X, the four operations

$$X \Leftarrow S, \qquad S \Leftarrow X, \qquad X \Leftarrow Q, \qquad Q \Leftarrow X,$$

and the two tests

$$S = \Lambda \qquad \text{and} \qquad Q = \Lambda,$$

write an algorithm to reverse the order of the elements in Q.

2. (Linked queue reversal) Let Q be a representation of a queue using a linked list, as shown in the uncaptioned diagram in Section 2.4.1. Let Qfront and Qrear point to the front and rear cells of Q, respectively. Write an algorithm to reverse the direction of the links in Q and to swap the pointers Qfront and Qrear. Compare the efficiency of your solutions to Exercises 1 and 2.

3. Will Quicksort work if stack S is replaced by a queue Q?

4. In Algorithm 2.1, show that the depth of the stack S is at most $\lceil \lg n \rceil$ entries.

[*Note.* Exercises 5 and 6 extend and improve the partition Algorithm 2.2.]

5. (Generalization) Extend Algorithm 2.2 so that it works on sequences of numbers that are not necessarily distinct.

6. (Improved partitioning) Note that Algorithm 2.2 always uses $T[\ell]$ (that is, the leftmost number in the interval (ℓ, r)) on which to partition.
   a) Rewrite Algorithm 2.2 to save $T[\ell]$ in a variable X for use in comparison with the $T[i]$ in the range $\ell + 1 \le i \le r$.
   b) Rewrite Algorithm 2.2 to choose X equal to the median of the numbers $T[\ell]$, $T[\lfloor(\ell + r)/2\rfloor]$, and $T[r]$ and to partition on X.

7. (Worst case for Quicksort) Given Algorithms 2.1 and 2.2 as written in the text.
   a) What sequence of 15 distinct integers $(1 \le i \le 15)$ takes the most time to sort?
   b) What sequence of 15 distinct integers $(1 \le i \le 15)$ causes the stack S to reach its deepest possible limit on problems of length 15?

8. Without the trick of postponing the largest subproblem on the stack, how deep can the Quicksort stack grow in the worst case?

9. (Hoare) Show that Quicksort can be modified to find the kth smallest of a given sequence of n numbers (and that this modified algorithm does less work to achieve its goal than Quicksort does).

10. (Removal of Qfront) Using the representation for circular queues given in Subsection 2.4.2.3, show how the value of the variable Qfront can be expressed as a function of the values of Qcount and Qrear, and show how to implement the operation $X \Leftarrow Q$ without reference to Qfront.

11. (Knuth) Show that by giving up a queue item location (so that, for N item locations, the queue is said to be full when $N - 1$ items have been entered in the queue) it is possible to implement the operations $X \Leftarrow Q$ and $Q \Leftarrow X$

knowing only the values of Qfront, Qrear, and N. [*Hint*. Establish conventions for setting up Qfront and Qrear so that, when we attempt $Q \Leftarrow X$, we do Qrear $\leftarrow (Q$rear $+ 1)$ mod N and, if now Qfront $= Q$rear, the queue has overflowed, and when we attempt $X \Leftarrow Q$, if Qfront $= Q$rear, the queue has underflowed.]

12. Can circular queues be implemented using modular arithmetic, values for Qfront and Qrear, and a single Boolean variable to indicate whether the queue is empty or nonempty, without giving up any locations, as in Exercise 11?

CHAPTER

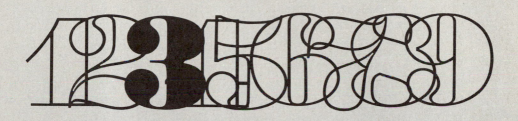

TREES

3.1 INTRODUCTION AND MOTIVATION

Trees are a species of nonlinear structure of considerable importance in computer science, partly because they provide natural representations for many sorts of nested data that occur in computer applications, and partly because they are useful in solving a wide variety of algorithmic problems.

Trees are used in each of the remaining chapters of this book. The chapter on tables studies how trees can be used to organize *symbol tables* in assemblers and compilers, and how *decision trees* can be constructed to represent *decision tables*. The traversal algorithms for trees studied in this chapter form the backbone of the algorithms in the chapters on lists and multilinked structures that perform printing, marking, copying, and equality testing. In addition, trees provide a basis for fast dynamic storage allocation of blocks of storage of variable size. In the chapter on strings, trees provide the basis for minimal-length encodings of characters using the so-called *Huffman code* technique. The chapter on arrays describes how to provide fast array element access using pointer trees. Finally, in the chapter on files, trees provide valuable indexing structures for large collections of records. This chapter lays the groundwork for all of these techniques.

Trees have many rich and varied applications in the solution of algorithmic problems. Trees are used as intermediary structures in certain methods for sorting, searching, and the determination of equivalence relations. Trees are used to implement *priority queues* having a "largest-in, first-out" behavior, in which the value of each item establishes its priority for leaving the queue. Tree-structured search spaces are used in game playing, theorem proving, and problem solving. *Parse trees* are sometimes used in compilers to represent the phrase structure of sentences in context-free languages.

Tree representations inside the computer are subjected to operations such as traversal, searching, copying, and compacting. Elements of trees and subtrees of trees are inserted, deleted, and replaced. The representation techniques used for trees yield behaviors that are well adapted to some of these operations, and not others, and that exhibit various costs in space and time. For instance, one distinction is whether a tree representation is *static* or *dynamic*. Static trees remain fixed in shape during an application, whereas dynamic trees change shape under various shape-changing operations such as element insertion, element deletion, and total tree restructuring. An objective for this chapter is to understand the range of techniques available for these purposes, and to study and compare their performance properties and advantages.

In preparation for this, we first define several varieties of trees in a representation-independent manner, and we study their quantitative properties briefly. Three particular varieties of highest importance are *binary trees*, *oriented trees*, and *ordered trees*. We introduce these notions by first talking about *free trees* (which are unoriented and unordered), and then by introducing the concepts of orientation and order.

Following the introduction of these representation-independent definitions of trees, we study several concrete representation techniques. Principally, we examine techniques for representing trees by linking and threading and for representing trees sequentially in storage.

For several reasons, we study traversal algorithms for these representations in some depth. First, tree-traversal algorithms form the basis for many later algorithms dealing with more complex structures. Often an algorithm for manipulating a complex structure consists of a tree-traversal technique extended in ingenious ways. In the chapters on lists and multilinked structures, for instance, we shall see that algorithms for copying, compacting, and garbage collection often fit this theme. It is important to study tree-traversal ideas in their simplest dress before progressing to these more advanced topics. A second reason for studying traversal algorithms is that different representations require different traversal techniques, some of which are nontrivial. Traversal algorithms are the carriers of a number of quite beautiful tricks and themes, and their careful study can equip the programmer with a stock of ideas and methods applicable in a range of other situations. A third reason for studying traversal algorithms is that they provide a microcosmic example of a progression of research contributions, which illustrate successful steps by computer scientists in their quest to discover the least resources (in time and memory) with which an important algorithmic task can be performed. Perhaps the reader will share the author's sense of excitement and pleasure when he reads about these developments.

In the final section of the chapter, we study several additional tree structures and their applications. The concept of a *heap* is introduced and applied to a sorting technique, Heapsort, and to the implementation of priority queues. Minimum spanning trees and trees used for efficient union of disjoint sets are then studied. Finally, a study of trees used in searching is undertaken, which treats both static and dynamic cases. In this connection, we study both *optimum static binary search trees* and *Tries*, and also dynamically balanced trees, such as *AVL trees*, *height-balanced k-trees*, *2–3 trees*, and *B-trees*.

†3.2 DEFINITIONS AND BASIC CONCEPTS

Since trees are a special sort of *graph*, we begin by considering a bit of graph theory. A graph consists of a collection of *vertices V*, and a collection of *edges E*, where each edge in *E* is a line joining a pair of vertices in *V*. In this chapter, we restrict attention to graphs for which each edge joins two distinct vertices and no two distinct vertices are joined by more than one edge (though in the next two chapters, we relax this restriction, and consider graphs with *self-references* $\bigcirc$, and *multiply-connected* vertices $\Longleftrightarrow$).

---

† *Advanced readers:* Read only Definitions 3.1 through 3.6 and skip to Section 3.3.

Two distinct vertices are *adjacent* if they are joined by an edge. A sequence of edges $e_1, e_2, \ldots, e_n$ forms a *path* of length n if each edge e_k shares one vertex in common with the preceding edge e_{k-1}, and the other vertex in common with the succeeding edge e_{k+1}. A path is *simple* if all the vertices used in it are distinct, save possibly for the first and last, which are permitted to be identical. A path can also be specified by giving a sequence of vertices $v_0, v_1, \ldots, v_n$ such that v_{k-1} is adjacent to v_k for $1 \le k \le n$; and in this case, we say the path connects v_0 and v_n. A *cycle* is a path of length three or more that connects a vertex v_0 to itself. A *simple cycle* is a cycle whose path is simple.

A graph is *connected* if there is at least one path from any vertex to any other. If a graph is not connected, we can separate it into *connected components* formed from single isolated vertices (connected to nothing else) or from maximal subsets of vertices that are connected to each other.

A *free tree* is defined to be a finite, connected graph with no simple cycles. It is interesting that there are six equivalent restrictions on finite graphs that can be used to define free trees. Before studying these, we must first examine the relationship between the number of vertices, edges, components, and cycles in a graph.

Suppose we take a graph $G = (V, E)$, where V is a vertex set and E is an edge set. Consider building up G by starting with all the vertices and no edges, and then by adding the edges in E one at a time. Each time we add an edge in E to the subgraph of G built up at any point, one of two things can happen: (1) we can form a bridge that joins two separate connected components into one new single connected component while not adding any new simple cycles, or (2) we can add an edge to a pair of previously nonadjacent distinct vertices within a connected component, forming more cycles but not changing the number of distinct connected components. Thus, adding an edge either decreases the number of components, or increases the number of simple cycles, but not both at once. In particular, following Berge ([1958], p. 27), if we define the *cyclomatic number* $v(G)$ by the relation $v(G) = e - v + c$, where e is the number of edges, v is the number of vertices, and c is the number of connected components, then adding an edge either decreases c by one and leaves $v(G)$ constant, or leaves c constant and increases $v(G)$ by one. In particular, G contains no simple cycles, iff $v(G) = 0$, and G possesses a unique simple cycle iff $v(G) = 1$. (Here, *iff* is an abbreviation for "if and only if".) We are now prepared to prove a theorem used several places in what follows.

Theorem 3.1 (Berge [1958]) Let G be a graph with $v > 1$ vertices. Any one of the following six equivalent properties characterizes a free tree:

1. G is connected and has no simple cycles.
2. G has no simple cycles and has $v - 1$ edges.
3. G is connected and has $v - 1$ edges.

4. G has no simple cycles, and if an edge is added which joins two nonadjacent vertices, exactly one simple cycle is formed.

5. G is connected, but if an edge is deleted, G becomes disconnected.

6. Every pair of vertices is connected by exactly one path.

Proof We proceed to show

$$(1) \Rightarrow (2) \Rightarrow (3) \Rightarrow (4) \Rightarrow (5) \Rightarrow (6) \Rightarrow (1).$$

$(1) \Rightarrow (2)$: Letting c be the number of disjoint connected components of G, and e be the number of edges of G, we have $c = 1$ since G is connected, and $v(G) = 0$ since G has no simple cycles. Now, since $v(G) = e - v + c$, we find that $e = v - 1$.

$(2) \Rightarrow (3)$: If $v(G) = 0$ and $e = v - 1$, then $c = v(G) - e + v = 1$, so G must be connected.

$(3) \Rightarrow (4)$: If $c = 1$ and $e = v - 1$, then $v(G) = e - v + c = 0$, so G has no simple cycles. However, if we add an edge connecting two nonadjacent vertices, $v(G)$ is incremented to 1, so G must contain exactly one simple cycle.

$(4) \Rightarrow (5)$: If vertices v_0 and v_1 of G belong to separate connected components of G, then adding the edge that joins them adds no new simple cycles, contradicting (4), so G must be connected and $c = 1$. If G is acyclic, $v(G) = 0$, this together with $c = 1$ means $e = v - 1$, so deleting an edge implies that $c = v(G) - e + v = 2$. Hence, there are two components, so G becomes disconnected.

$(5) \Rightarrow (6)$: Since G is connected, any two vertices are joined by at least one path. Suppose there were two vertices v_0 and v_1 joined by two distinct paths. Then removing an edge that belongs only to the first path does not disconnect the graph, since a connection equivalent to the deleted edge is still established through v_0 and v_1 using the second path.

$(6) \Rightarrow (1)$: Suppose G contains a simple cycle. Then G has two vertices on this simple cycle that are connected by two distinct paths.   ∎

Figure 3.1 gives an example of a free tree (a) and of graphs (b) and (c) that are not free trees. The edges in these graphs are assumed to be unoriented; that is, no direction is prescribed for travel along the edges. If we prescribe a direction of travel along each edge of a graph, we produce a *directed graph* (sometimes called a *digraph* or an *oriented graph*). This is conventionally done by letting the edge set E of the graph $G = (V, E)$ be a subset of the set of ordered pairs of vertices of G; that is, $E \subset V \times V$. Each edge $e \in E$ then has the form (v, v'), and we say v is the *origin* of e, v' is the *terminus* of e, and that the direction of travel along e is from v to v'.

An *oriented tree* is a free tree in which some particular vertex r has been designated as the *root*, and in which orientations have been assigned to the edges in such a fashion that, for any vertex v distinct from the root, the orientations travel in the direction from r toward v along the unique path that connects them. It is easy to see that once a vertex has been chosen as the root, then the orientations along the paths away from the root can be uniquely determined. Thus, to any free tree on n vertices, there correspond n distinct oriented trees on the same set of vertices, each with a distinct root.

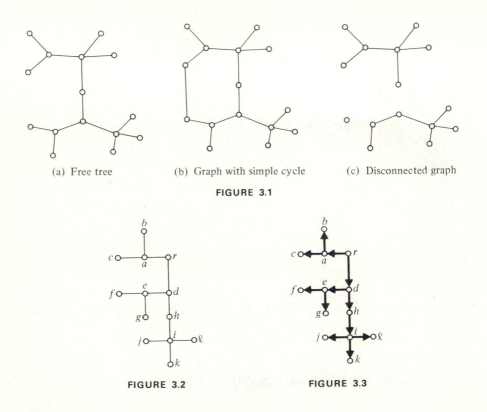

(a) Free tree　　　　(b) Graph with simple cycle　　　(c) Disconnected graph

FIGURE 3.1

FIGURE 3.2　　　　　　　　　　FIGURE 3.3

Suppose we take a free tree such as that shown in Fig. 3.2, and that we select vertex r as the root. The orientations assigned to the edges are then determined as shown in Fig. 3.3. Now, suppose we take this tree, grab it by the root r, and hold r up, while allowing the remaining nodes to dangle below. We might picture the result of this operation as shown in Fig. 3.4.

Once this is done, we can speak of the *level* of a vertex in an oriented tree, and of family relationships between the vertices. The level of a vertex v in an oriented tree is just 1 plus the length of the path between the root and v (*special case*: the root is at level 1). Shifting to a consideration of family relationships, let v be a vertex other than the root r in an oriented tree, and let $v_0, v_1, v_2, \ldots, v_n$ be the path from r to v, where $v_0 = r$, and $v_n = v$. Then, v_{n-1} is called the *parent* of v, and

$v_0 = r, v_1, \ldots, v_{n-1}$, are called *ancestors* of v. Correspondingly, if v is the parent of a node v_{n+1}, then v_{n+1} is a *child* of v, and if v is an ancestor of some node v_k at some level $k > n$ in the tree, then v_k is a *descendant* of v. If two or more vertices have the same parent, they are siblings to each other. Thus, in Fig. 3.4, vertices b and c are siblings with the common parent vertex a.

FIGURE 3.4

In addition to family relationships, terminology related to oriented trees includes terms such as leaves, subtrees, and branches. A *leaf* of an oriented tree is a vertex with no descendants. Sometimes we will call leaves *terminal nodes*, while nonleaves will be called *internal nodes*. The *subtree* of a given tree *rooted at* a vertex v consists of the subgraph of the whole tree formed by taking v and its descendants together with the paths in the whole tree originating at v. For example, the subtree of the tree in Fig. 3.4 rooted at vertex h is shown in Fig. 3.5.

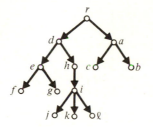

FIGURE 3.5

In an oriented tree, the left-to-right order of the children of a given parent is immaterial. Thus, the oriented tree pictured in Fig. 3.6 is to be considered identical to the oriented tree in Fig. 3.4, even though the order of several groups of siblings has been permuted.

FIGURE 3.6

By contrast, in an *ordered oriented tree* (or *oriented tree*, for short), the order of the children of each parent node is specified, and is important. While it is easy to give a definition for an oriented tree that is stated in terms of general constraints on a directed graph, it turns out to be convenient to give a recursive definition for ordered trees. Putting the definitions for *free trees, oriented trees,* and *ordered trees* together, we have:

Definition 3.1 A *free tree* is a connected graph with no simple cycles.

Definition 3.2 An *oriented tree* is a directed graph having a designated vertex r, called the *root*, and having exactly one oriented path between the root and any vertex v distinct from the root, in which r is the origin of the path and v is the terminus.

Definition 3.3 An *ordered tree* T is a finite set of one or more vertices such that there is one designated vertex r called the root of T, and such that the remaining vertices (in $T - \{r\}$) are partitioned into $n \geq 0$ mutually exclusive subsets $T_1, T_2, \ldots, T_n$, each of which is, in turn, an *ordered tree*. The $T_i \, (1 \leq i \leq n)$ are said to be *subtrees* of T, and T_i is said to be to the *left* of T_j if $i < j$.

By convention, in this book, we place the root of an ordered tree at the top of a drawing of it, the subtrees are arranged in left-to-right order below the root and edges are drawn from the root to each subtree. It is then permissible (and, indeed, often useful) to mix metaphors liberally, when talking about ordered trees. The metaphors can come from spatial relations (up, down, right, left), family relationships (parent, sibling, descendant), or botanical trees (roots, leaves, branches, twigs). Thus, we might find a sentence such as: "Starting at the root, keep descending downward and to the left visiting leftmost descendants in sequence until a leaf is encountered." In this sentence we have succeeded in mixing all three classes of metaphors. In fact, the idea contained in this sentence is a key part of a traversal algorithm for ordered trees. Several theories of intelligent problem-solving behavior emphasize the role of representation shifts as an aid to problem solving. Metaphor mixing appears to be a way of bringing several systems of representation to bear on a problem simultaneously, and it seems sound to encourage its use in intuitive stages of problem solving and for informal explanation. For example, in comments in algorithms we frequently use such metaphorical remarks to help make the meaning of low-level details intuitively clear.

Starting with Definition 3.3, by directing edges from the root of an ordered tree to the roots of its respective ordered subtrees (if any), we obtain recursively the directed graph of an oriented tree. Free trees, oriented trees, and ordered trees are related by the fact that each is more constrained than its predecessor. In particular, by ignoring the ordering constraints among subtrees of an ordered tree, we obtain an oriented tree, and by ignoring the identity of the root and the directions on the edges in an oriented tree, we obtain a free tree.

A *binary tree* is another sort of tree with important applications in computer science. It is different from free, oriented, and ordered trees, and should not be thought of as a natural extension or restriction of any of these former three kinds of trees. A binary tree is defined recursively as follows:

Definition 3.4 A *binary tree* is a finite set of vertices that either is *empty*, or consists of a vertex called the *root* together with two binary subtrees, which are disjoint from each other and from the root, and are called the *left* and *right* subtrees.

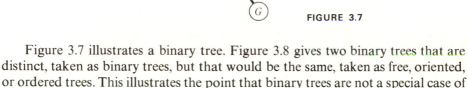

FIGURE 3.7

Figure 3.7 illustrates a binary tree. Figure 3.8 gives two binary trees that are distinct, taken as binary trees, but that would be the same, taken as free, oriented, or ordered trees. This illustrates the point that binary trees are not a special case of these other sorts of trees.

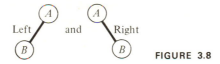

FIGURE 3.8

Definition 3.5 A *full binary tree* is a binary tree in which each node either is a leaf or has exactly two nonempty descendants.

Thus, in a full binary tree each node has either two children or no children. The binary tree of Fig. 3.7 is not full because some vertices have both empty and nonempty subtrees. Figure 3.9 illustrates a full binary tree.

Definition 3.6 A *complete binary tree* is a binary tree with leaves on at most two adjacent levels $\ell - 1$ and ℓ in which the leaves at the bottommost level ℓ lie in the leftmost positions of ℓ.

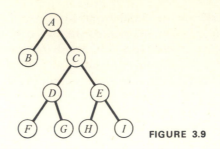

FIGURE 3.9

Figures 3.10 and 3.11 illustrate complete binary trees. Complete binary trees are used both explicitly and implicitly in many of the algorithms and quantitative analyses that follow. Complete binary trees can be thought of as completely balanced binary trees in which some number of rightmost leaves at the lowest level may have been deleted.

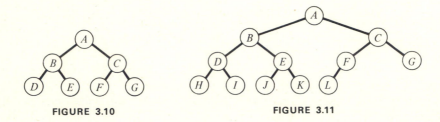

FIGURE 3.10   FIGURE 3.11

A *forest* is a possibly disconnected graph, each of whose connected components is a tree. Thus, a forest is a collection of zero or more trees. The trees in a forest can be made into a single tree by adding a new vertex (which serves as a new root in the case of ordered or oriented trees), and by joining the new vertex to the roots of the trees in the forest (or to any vertex in each tree in a forest of free trees). If the trees are ordered, then the collection of trees in the forest must also be ordered (forming what is then called an *ordered forest*) if this construction is to have meaning.

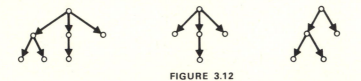

FIGURE 3.12

There is an important construction relating binary trees to ordered forests. Take an ordered forest such as that shown in Fig. 3.12. Remove the edges from each parent to each of its children except the leftmost, and install edges from each child to its right sibling. Then link the roots of the trees in the original forest so that each root is connected by an installed edge to its right sibling root. The result is a binary tree, as illustrated in Fig. 3.13. This construction establishes a 1–1 correspondence between ordered forests and binary trees and is used, among other things, to help derive quantitative facts about trees permitting us to reason about compressed tree representations taking the least possible amount of space. Here, the newly established rightward horizontal edges denote the right subtree relationship, while the retained vertical edges give the left subtree relationship in the newly constructed binary tree.

FIGURE 3.13

3.3 TWO QUANTITATIVE FACTS ABOUT BINARY TREES

In this section we develop two quantitative facts about binary trees. The first relates the number of leaves to the number of internal nodes in full binary trees, and is used in Chapter 5 to study the efficiency of certain list-processing algorithms. The second determines the number of distinct binary trees that can be constructed from n vertices, and is used in the study of minimal space representations of ordered trees in Section 3.5.

3.3.1 The relation between leaves and internal nodes in full binary trees

In a full binary tree, each vertex is either an internal node with two nonempty left and right subtrees, or a leaf (having no descendants). In such a tree, we can show that the number of leaves always exceeds the number of internal nodes by one.†

Following our convention of putting the root of a tree at the top of a tree diagram and the subtrees (if any) on the levels beneath it, we can think of each edge in a tree as having an *edge top*, touching the parent, and an *edge bottom*, touching the child, of the parent–child pair that the edge connects. In a tree with k edges, there are k such edge tops and k such edge bottoms, since each edge contributes exactly one top and one bottom. Hence,

$$\# \text{ edge tops} = k = \# \text{ edge bottoms}$$

(where the symbol # is read as "the number of").

---

† I am grateful to Tom Szymanski for suggesting I should use a proof based on the equality of in-degrees and out-degrees in place of the clumsy induction proof I gave in an earlier draft.

In a full binary tree of n nodes and k edges, the number of edge bottoms is exactly the number of nodes minus one, since each node except the root lies at the bottom of exactly one edge. Hence,

$$\# \text{ edge bottoms} = n - 1.$$

Also, in a full binary tree each internal node is at the top of exactly two edges, so

$$2 \times (\# \text{ internal nodes}) = \# \text{ edge tops}.$$

We note further that the number of nodes n is the sum of the number of leaves and the number of internal nodes:

$$n = (\# \text{ leaves}) + (\# \text{ internal nodes}).$$

Putting these facts together, we get:

$$2 \times (\# \text{ internal nodes}) = \# \text{ edge tops} = \# \text{ edge bottoms}$$

$$= n - 1$$

$$= (\# \text{ leaves}) + (\# \text{ internal nodes}) - 1.$$

Solving for the number of leaves in terms of the number of internal nodes gives:

$$\# \text{ leaves} = (\# \text{ internal nodes}) + 1. \tag{1}$$

This relationship is used in numerous places throughout the text.

3.3.2 The number of binary trees with n nodes

The objective of this section is to determine for a given n the number b_n of binary trees with distinct shapes that can be formed each containing n nodes. Figure 3.14 illustrates the different binary tree shapes obtainable for each of the n from 1 to 4. If $n = 1$, $b_n = 1$. If $n > 1$, we can pick one of the n nodes as the root of the tree, and we can partition the remaining $n - 1$ nodes into left and right subtrees. Let j be the number of nodes assigned to form the left subtree $(0 \leq j \leq n - 1)$. Then $n - 1 - j$ nodes remain to form the right subtree. In this instance, $b_j b_{n-1-j}$ gives the total number of binary trees that can be formed with j nodes in the left subtree, but to get all possible binary trees on n nodes, we must sum up product terms of this form over all possible values j of the number of nodes in the left subtree. This gives us the relation

$$b_n = b_0 b_{n-1} + b_1 b_{n-2} + \cdots + b_{n-1} b_0. \tag{2}$$

We now solve this recurrence relation using a generating function† of the form

---

† For a good introduction to generating functions and their uses, see Knuth [1973a].

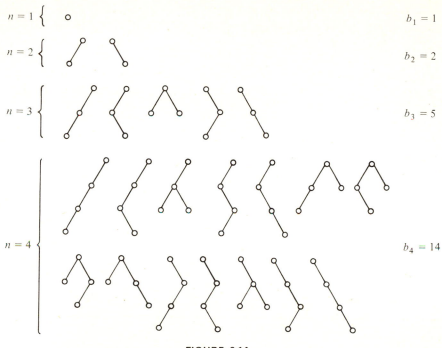

$$n = 1 \left\{ \quad \circ \right. \qquad\qquad b_1 = 1$$

$$n = 2 \left\{ \right. \qquad\qquad b_2 = 2$$

$$n = 3 \left\{ \right. \qquad\qquad b_3 = 5$$

$$n = 4 \left\{ \right. \qquad\qquad b_4 = 14$$

FIGURE 3.14

$$G(x) = b_0 + b_1 x + b_2 x^2 + \cdots$$

When we multiply $G(x)$ by itself, we get

$$G(x)G(x) = (b_0 + b_1 x + b_2 x^2 + \cdots)(b_0 + b_1 x + b_2 x^2 + \cdots)$$
$$= (b_0 b_0) + (b_0 b_1 + b_1 b_0)x + (b_0 b_2 + b_1 b_1 + b_2 b_0)x^2 + \cdots$$
$$= \sum_{n \geq 0} \left(\sum_{0 \leq j \leq n} b_j b_{n-j} \right) x^n.$$

Thus, we observe that the coefficient of x^n in this expansion of $G(x)^2$ is exactly the formula for b_{n+1} (or, equivalently, that b_n is the coefficient for x^{n-1}). Hence, if we multiply $G(x)^2$ by x, we can get the coefficients of x^n to match those of $G(x)$, except for the first term, since then $xG(x)^2 = b_1 x + b_2 x^2 + b_3 x^3 + \cdots$. Indeed, we can make $xG(x)^2$ match the expansion of $G(x)$ exactly, by adding a term of the form b_0 to $xG(x)^2$. But since $b_0 = 1$, this implies

$$1 + xG(x)^2 = G(x).$$

The latter equation is quadratic in $G(x)$, and yields two solutions, one of which is

$$G(x) = \frac{1 - \sqrt{1 - 4x}}{2x} = \frac{1}{2x}(1 - \sqrt{1 - 4x}). \tag{3}$$

Using a Taylor series expansion of $(1 + z)^r$, we get a binomial generating function

$$(1 + z)^r = 1 + rz + \frac{r(r-1)}{1 \cdot 2}z^2 + \frac{r(r-1)(r-2)}{1 \cdot 2 \cdot 3}z^3 + \cdots. \tag{4}$$

The coefficients of powers of z in this generating function can be written more succinctly using the following generalized definition of binomial coefficients, where r is any real number and k is an integer:

$$\binom{r}{k} = \frac{r(r-1)(r-2)\cdots(r-k+1)}{1 \cdot 2 \cdot 3 \cdots k} \qquad \text{for } k > 0;$$

$$\binom{r}{0} = 1, \quad \text{and} \quad \binom{r}{k} = 0 \qquad \text{for } k < 0. \tag{5}$$

Thus, the binomial generating function (4) can be rewritten as

$$(1 + z)^r = \sum_{k \geq 0} \binom{r}{k} z^k. \tag{6}$$

Since $\sqrt{1 - 4x} = (1 + (-4x))^{1/2}$, we can replace $\sqrt{1 - 4x}$ in (3) with an appropriately substituted version of (6) to get

$$G(x) = \frac{1}{2x}\left(1 - \sum_{k \geq 0} \binom{1/2}{k}(-4x)^k\right).$$

Using a change of dummy variable in which k is replaced by $n + 1$, and then simplifying, gives

$$G(x) = \frac{1}{2x}\left(1 - \sum_{n+1 \geq 0} \binom{1/2}{n+1}(-4x)^{n+1}\right)$$

$$= \frac{1}{2x} + \sum_{n+1 \geq 0} \binom{1/2}{n+1}(-1)^n 2^{2n+1} x^n$$

$$= \sum_{n \geq 0} \binom{1/2}{n+1}(-1)^n 2^{2n+1} x^n. \tag{7}$$

But the latter yields coefficients of x^n which match b_n in the original definition of $G(x)$. Hence,

$$b_n = \binom{1/2}{n+1}(-1)^n 2^{2n+1}. \tag{8}$$

The latter form of b_n is unpleasantly messy so it is worthwhile attempting to tidy it up a bit. This can be done as follows. We first expand $\binom{1/2}{n+1}$ using definition (5):

$$\binom{1/2}{n+1} = \frac{\frac{1}{2}\left(\frac{1}{2}-1\right)\left(\frac{1}{2}-2\right)\cdots\left(\frac{1}{2}-n\right)}{1\cdot 2\cdot 3\cdots(n+1)}$$

$$= \frac{\frac{1}{2}\left(-\frac{1}{2}\right)\left(-\frac{3}{2}\right)\cdots\left(\frac{-2n+1}{2}\right)}{1\cdot 2\cdot 3\cdots(n+1)}$$

$$= \frac{(-1)^n}{2^{n+1}}\cdot\frac{1\cdot 3\cdot 5\cdots(2n-1)}{1\cdot 2\cdot 3\cdot 4\cdots(n+1)}.$$

We observe that the numerator of the latter expression contains a product of odd numbers of the form $1\cdot 3\cdot 5\cdots(2n-1)$. Such a product can be expressed by taking the product of all the numbers from 1 to $2n$ and striking out the even numbers

$$1\cdot 3\cdot 5\cdots(2n-1) = \frac{1\cdot 2\cdot 3\cdot 4\cdot 5\cdots(2n-1)(2n)}{2\cdot 4\cdots(2n)} = \frac{(2n)!}{2^n\cdot n!}.$$

This permits us to rewrite

$$\binom{1/2}{n+1} = \frac{(-1)^n}{2^{n+1}}\cdot\frac{1}{(n+1)!}\cdot\frac{(2n)!}{2^n\cdot n!} = \frac{(-1)^n}{2^{2n+1}}\cdot\frac{1}{(n+1)}\binom{2n}{n}.$$

Substitution of the latter result back into (8) yields, after cancellation, the following final form

$$b_n = \frac{1}{n+1}\binom{2n}{n}. \tag{9}$$

Using Stirling's approximation (see Exercises 3.4 and 3.6), we can show that the latter is $4^n/n\sqrt{\pi n} + O(4^n n^{-5/2})$.

A corollary of importance to our later discussion is the following:

$$b_{n-1} = \text{the number of distinct ordered trees on } n \text{ vertices.} \tag{10}$$

If we take an ordered tree on n vertices and remove its root, together with the edges connecting the root to the subtrees of the root (if any), we obtain an ordered forest on $n-1$ vertices. The construction of Figs. 3.12 and 3.13 then shows a way of establishing a 1–1 correspondence between such ordered forests and appropriately constructed binary trees, and the result in (10) follows.

3.4 LINKED TREE REPRESENTATIONS

In this section, we study linking and threading techniques for binary trees, and the use of linked blocks of nonuniform length to represent ordered trees. The threading of a linked representation encodes certain relationships derived from the order in which nodes are encountered during particular tree traversals. Three such traversal orders of special significance are defined in this section.

3.4.1 Linked binary trees

An often used representation for binary trees is the *linked representation*. Figure 3.16 illustrates the linked binary-tree representation of the binary tree shown in Fig. 3.15. Each cell in the linked representation of Fig. 3.16 is of the form

LLINK INFO RLINK

L	X	R

where the LLINK and RLINK fields contain pointers L and R to the cells corresponding to the left and right descendants of X in the tree of Fig. 3.15. The pointer fields are set to Λ if the corresponding descendants are empty.

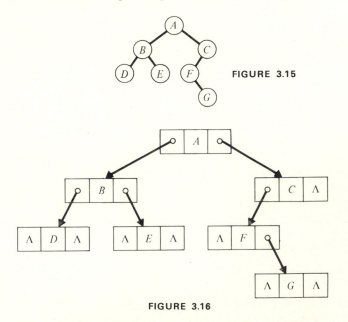

FIGURE 3.15

FIGURE 3.16

In the linked representation of binary trees, such as that shown in Fig. 3.16, the number of Λ's always exceeds the number of cells by one, independent of the shape or size of the tree. To see why this is so, observe that the tree of Fig. 3.16 can be converted to a diagram of a full binary tree by replacing each occurrence of Λ by a pointer to an empty leaf node ($\frac{\text{\textbullet}}{\square}$), and that formula (1) of Section 3.3.1 can then be applied, to conclude that the number of such leaves is one greater than the number of cells. Thus, because more than half of the links in the linked binary tree representation are Λ, more than half of the link space is "wasted." This fact raises the question of whether more efficient representations might exist.

One technique is to supply separate encodings for leaf nodes. These nodes need not contain pointer fields and, for example, can be stored in a region of the address space separate from that used to store internal nodes of the tree. An address range check can then be used to detect the fact that such leaf nodes have no left and right pointer fields. This representation tends to be most useful for full binary trees, such as those used to represent binary arithmetic expressions, as illustrated in Fig. 3.17.

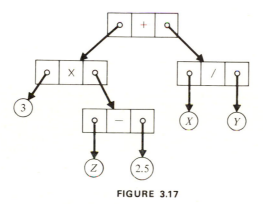

FIGURE 3.17

The circular nodes of Fig. 3.17 can be stored, say, in an address range $[\alpha_1, \beta_1]$, and the rectangular nodes can be stored, say, in a disjoint address range $[\alpha_2, \beta_2]$. Then, given the address of a node, one can tell immediately whether it has non-empty left and right subtrees or not.

Another use for the Λ fields in Fig. 3.16 is to hold links called "threads" that aid in the traversal of the nodes of the tree in particular useful orders. The following section defines three such useful orders, and in the section after that, threading techniques are introduced and studied.

3.4.2 Traversal orders for binary trees

A *traversal* of a tree is a process that enumerates each of the nodes in the tree exactly once. When a node is encountered in the order of enumeration specified by a particular traversal process, we shall say that we *visit* the given node. Traversals are used as the basis for algorithms that perform such actions as printing, marking, or copying nodes in a tree. Thus, when we *visit* a node during a traversal, we intend that there be an opportunity to take particular special actions such as printing, marking, or copying the node.

Table 3.1 gives recursive definitions of three traversal orders in which binary trees may be traversed. For example, the various orders of traversal applied to the binary tree of Fig. 3.18 yield:

Preorder	*A*	*B*	*D*	*E*	*G*	*C*	*F*
Symmetric order:	*D*	*B*	*G*	*E*	*A*	*C*	*F*
Postorder:	*D*	*G*	*E*	*B*	*F*	*C*	*A*

TABLE 3.1

Preorder	Symmetric order	Postorder
Visit root	Traverse left subtree	Traverse left subtree
Traverse left subtree	in symmetric order	in postorder
in preorder	Visit root	Traverse right subtree
Traverse right subtree	Traverse right subtree	in postorder
in preorder	in symmetric order	Visit root

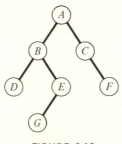

FIGURE 3.18

3.4.3 Threaded trees

Suppose we wish to print the infix representation of the algebraic expression represented in the tree of Fig. 3.17. By enumerating the contents of the nodes of Fig. 3.17 in symmetric order, as defined in the previous section, we observe that subexpressions appear in infix order. (See Exercise 3.9 for a more complete version of this process, which inserts parentheses where required by the relative precedence of the arithmetic operators.) In general, to aid in such symmetric traversals, we can replace the Λ fields of a tree such as that of Fig. 3.19 with special links, called *threads*, which point to the successors and predecessors of a given node in symmetric order. This yields a tree such as that given in Fig. 3.20, in which

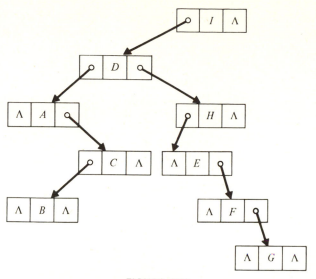

FIGURE 3.19

the dashed upward-pointing links point to the symmetric-order successors and predecessors.

Algorithm 3.1 finds the symmetric successor of a node in a threaded binary tree linked according to the method shown in Fig. 3.20.

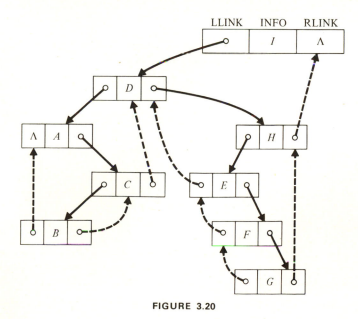

FIGURE 3.20

Algorithm 3.1 *Finding the symmetric successor of a node N in a symmetrically threaded binary tree.*

Let N contain the address of a node in a symmetrically threaded binary tree whose successor we wish to find. At termination, N contains the address of the desired successor.

1. [Move right once and test.] Set $N \leftarrow \text{RLINK}(N)$. If N is a thread or $N = \Lambda$, then terminate the algorithm.

2. [Move downward to left as far as possible.] If $\text{LLINK}(N)$ is not a thread then set $N \leftarrow \text{LLINK}(N)$ and repeat this step. Otherwise, terminate the algorithm.

In Algorithm 3.1, we assume that there is a way to tell whether a link is a thread (such as those indicated by dashed lines in Fig. 3.20) or is not a thread (such as those indicated by solid lines in Fig. 3.20). A pair of tag bits can be added to each node to record this fact for the left and right link fields. Alternatively, if the addresses of descendants of a node are always higher than the address of the node itself, threads can be detected as addresses that point to lower locations in memory.

An algorithm to find the symmetric predecessor of a given node can be obtained from Algorithm 3.1 by exchanging the words LLINK and RLINK, and by exchanging the words "left" and "right" in the comments.

To traverse the nodes of a symmetrically threaded tree in symmetric order, one first finds the initial node in symmetric order, and then enumerates successors with Algorithm 3.1 until reaching the node Λ.

Algorithm 3.2 *Traversal of nodes in symmetric order in a symmetrically threaded binary tree.*

Let R be the address of the root of the symmetrically threaded binary tree.

1. [Initialize.] Set $N \leftarrow R$.

2. [Find first node to visit.] If $\text{LLINK}(N) \neq \Lambda$, then set $N \leftarrow \text{LLINK}(N)$ and repeat this step. Otherwise, proceed to step 3.

3. [Visit.] Visit node N.

4. [Find successor.] Replace N by the symmetric successor of N using Algorithm 3.1. If, now, $N = \Lambda$, then terminate the algorithm. Otherwise, go to step 3.

Algorithm 3.2 can be shown to run in linear time as follows: If the threaded tree T contains n nodes, then the $2n$ link fields in its nodes contain:

a) 2Λ's (found in the nodes having no symmetric predecessor and no symmetric successor).

b) $n - 1$ downward pointing links (since each of the n nodes except the root is pointed to by exactly one downward pointing link distinct from the others), and

c) $n - 1$ threads (an application of formula (1) in Section 3.3.1 shows there must be $n + 1$ thread fields, two of which are occupied by Λ's, so there must be $n - 1$ nonnull threads).

Working in conjunction, Algorithms 3.1 and 3.2 visit the nodes of T by travelling along the downward links and right successor threads of T until reaching a Λ link, in such a fashion that each distinct link or thread is traversed exactly once. As a consequence, the cumulative number of times that steps which traverse links or threads can execute in Algorithms 3.1 and 3.2 is bounded above by the following:

$$\text{\# Downward links} + \text{\# Right threads} + \Lambda \le (n - 1) + (n - 1) + 1 = 2n - 1.$$

If we decide to use threaded trees to represent algebraic formulas in an algebraic-formula manipulation system, we must program operations on threaded trees that mirror algebraic operations. For example, to implement substitution, we need to be able to replace a leaf of a tree with a new subtree. Having determined, say, that a leaf is the right child of a given node N, the following algorithm inserts a new subtree in place of this leaf as the right subtree of N.

Algorithm 3.3 *Inserting a symmetrically threaded tree T_1 as the right subtree of a given node N in another symmetrically threaded tree T_2.*†

1. [Initialize.] Let R point to the root of T_1.
2. [Locate pointer to successor of N in T_2.] $S \leftarrow N$. **repeat** $S \leftarrow \text{RLINK}(S)$ **until** either S is a thread or $S = \Lambda$.
3. [Adjust RLINK of N to point to root of T_1.] $\text{RLINK}(N) \leftarrow R$.
4. [Find place in T_1 to insert pointer to right successor.] $Q \leftarrow R$. **while** $\text{RLINK}(Q)$ is not a thread and $\text{RLINK}(Q) \ne \Lambda$ **do** $Q \leftarrow \text{RLINK}(Q)$.
5. [Insert right successor pointer into T_1.] $\text{RLINK}(Q) \leftarrow S$.
6. [Find place in T_1 to insert pointer to left successor.] $Q \leftarrow R$. **while** $\text{LLINK}(Q)$ is not a thread and $\text{LLINK}(Q) \ne \Lambda$ **do** $Q \leftarrow \text{LLINK}(Q)$.
7. [Insert left successor pointer into T_1.] $\text{LLINK}(Q) \leftarrow N$.

Subtree insertion algorithms such as this can be made less time-consuming if it is not necessary to search for the respective places in T_1 in which to plant

---

† In this algorithm, the notation "**repeat** S **until** B" has the same effect as a part of a step such as: "(a) Do S. If B is *false*, repeat part (a) of this step." Also, the notation "**while** B, **do** S" has the same effect as a part of a step such as: "(a) If B is *true*, then do S and repeat part (a) of this step."

pointers to the left and right symmetric successors in T_2. As shown in Fig. 3.21, a special header element can be employed for this purpose containing pointers to the leftmost and rightmost nodes of T_1 in symmetric order, as well as containing a pointer to the root of T_1.

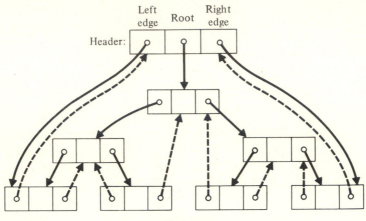

FIGURE 3.21

Using a symmetrically threaded tree to keep items in an updatable, alphabetized index involves inserting and deleting nodes, while maintaining proper threading. The threads help to print the index in alphabetical order without unbounded auxiliary memory (such as a stack), and they permit location of alphabetic successors and predecessors, given only the address of a node as initial information.

Since only the right threads in a threaded tree are used for alphabetical index printing, the left threads may be replaced by Λ. Under these circumstances, a *right-threaded tree* (with left threads omitted) may suffice as a representation.

Exercises 3.10 to 3.14 explore some algorithmic problems in threaded trees. Threaded trees (in the form of right-threaded trees) were introduced by Perlis and Thornton [1960] and refined by Knuth [1973a], who discusses symmetric threading. Anatol Holt's thesis (Holt [1963]) independently introduces threading in both directions. Perlis and Thornton's paper gives numerous examples of formula manipulation using right-threaded trees.

3.4.4 Linked blocks of nonuniform length

Consider an ordered tree, such as that given in the left part of Fig. 3.22, in which different internal nodes have differing numbers of children. Suppose we want to represent such a tree by a linked representation, in which each cell contains links to its children in order. We might accomplish this by using cells with a size field, an information field, and a variable number of link fields, such as shown in the right part of Fig. 3.22. There, cells corresponding to leaf nodes contain no link fields, only size and information fields. Also, a cell corresponding to an internal node contains size and information fields and an ordered sequence of link fields pointing to the children in order.

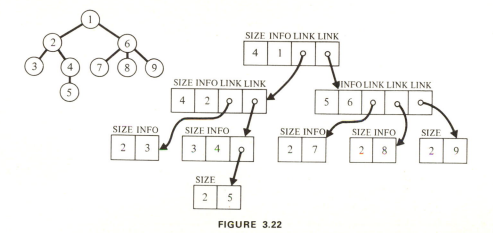

FIGURE 3.22

The cells in this representation are frequently represented by linked blocks of contiguous storage. Since the blocks are usually of nonuniform length, memory-management techniques are required for allocating nonuniform blocks within a larger region of contiguous storage. These techniques are studied in Chapter 6. Normally, some additional fields are added to such cells, giving additional data required by the tree-processing and memory-allocation algorithms.

3.5 REPRESENTATIONS IN CONTIGUOUS STORAGE

Representations for nodes of trees can be arranged sequentially in a contiguous region of linear storage in various ways. Often the addresses in which such nodes reside bear interesting relationships to one another which mirror relationships in the original tree. Thus, given α, the address of residence of a particular tree node in a sequential representation, it may be possible to calculate the address of the parent, ith child, or right sibling of the node stored at α as simple functions of α. A number of algorithms using this sort of address arithmetic implicitly use tree-structured data representations, even though the data are stored sequentially and the tree-processing operations are encoded arithmetically. In such cases, it becomes important to recognize explicitly what is happening, particularly when circumstances might favor a change of representation to an explicit tree structure in order to promote efficiency.

3.5.1 Contiguous representation of complete binary trees

If we number the nodes in a complete binary tree first by levels (with all nodes at level k being numbered before any at level $k + 1$), and then left to right within each level, we obtain an ordering such as that illustrated in Fig. 3.23.

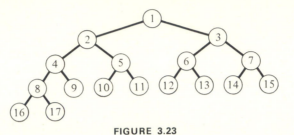

FIGURE 3.23

Letting N be the total number of nodes in such a tree, and letting n be the number of any node in this tree, we see that the node number of certain relatives in the tree can be calculated by the following rules:

Parent $(n) = \lfloor n/2 \rfloor$ (provided $n > 1$, since root has no parent)

Left child $(n) = 2n$ (provided $2n \leq N$; otherwise left child doesn't exist)

Right child $(n) = 2n + 1$ (provided $2n + 1 \leq N$; otherwise right child doesn't exist)

Right sibling $(n) =$ (**if** n is even and $n < N$ **then** $n + 1$ **else** right sibling doesn't exist)

Left sibling $(n) =$ (**if** n is odd and $n \neq 1$ **then** $n - 1$ **else** left sibling doesn't exist) (11)

Hence, by placing representations for the N nodes of a complete binary tree in the contiguous sequence

we can use the simple arithmetic relationships (11) to process the nodes as if they were explicitly represented as a binary tree.

An important natural generalization of this numbering system for complete binary trees is that for complete k-ary trees. In a complete k-ary tree, each node has exactly k descendants except for those on the bottommost two levels, and each level except the last is completely filled with nonempty nodes. On the last level, some number of rightmost leaves are permitted to be empty. Figure 3.24 illustrates a complete quaternary tree.

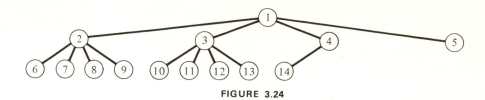

FIGURE 3.24

Since the number of nodes on the successive levels of a complete k-ary tree follows a geometric progression $1, k, k^2, k^3, \ldots$, the relations shown in (12) can be used to compute parents, children, and siblings, with the proviso that, for a node to exist, its node number must lie in the range 1 to N, where N is the total number of nodes in the tree.

$$\text{Parent } (n) = \left\lfloor \frac{n + k - 2}{k} \right\rfloor$$

ith child of $(n) = k(n - 1) + i + 1$ (for $1 \le i \le k$)

Right sibling $(n) = (\textbf{if } ((n - 1) \bmod k) \ne 0 \textbf{ then } n + 1 \textbf{ else}$
right sibling doesn't exist)

Left sibling $(n) = (\textbf{if } ((n + k - 2) \bmod k) \ne 0 \textbf{ then } n - 1 \textbf{ else}$
left sibling doesn't exist)

(12)

3.5.2 Sequential enumerations

Let us now turn our attention to sequential representations of ordered trees of arbitrary shape. These need not be complete, and different nodes may have different numbers of children. These sequential representations are useful when we need a compact technique (yielding efficient use of storage) and when the trees remain of fixed size and shape during the running of algorithms that use them, or are subject to infrequent shape-changing operations such as deletions and insertions. Indeed, any systematic policy for enumerating the nodes of an ordered tree yields a sequential representation. So, if we have an application that demands extensive repetitive enumeration of the nodes of a tree in some particular order, it may make sense to use a sequential representation that encodes that order. In the following sections, the Preorder and Postorder traversals of ordered trees are analogous to those for binary trees. However, the Symmetric Ordering for binary trees has no direct analogue in ordered trees. Instead the concept of Level Order is studied in ordered trees.

3.5.2.1 *Preorder.* In a preorder enumeration, we first enumerate the root of a tree and then we perform a preorder enumeration of each of the subtrees of the root in left to right order. For example, given the ordered tree of Fig. 3.25, the preorder enumeration is ①, ②, ..., ⑨.

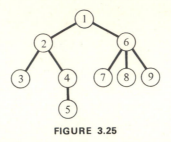

FIGURE 3.25

In former times, the order of inheritance prescribed by the English law of primogeniture, which specified the eldest living son as heir of his father's estate, illustrates a preorder enumeration of the ordered tree of living male members of an English family, where sons of each father are ordered by date of birth.

In order to encode the information necessary to reconstruct an ordered tree for a preorder enumeration of its nodes, we can use parentheses and commas. Here, we follow the designation of a node with a parenthesized list of expressions for its subtrees (if any). The expressions for the subtrees are separated by commas. Thus, the preorder enumeration of Fig. 3.25 can be rendered as (1(2(3, 4(5)), 6(7, 8, 9))). In addition to this simple technique, there are other ways of adding information to the preorder sequence that enable recovery of the original ordered tree. These are worth studying since they can provide a basis for compact tree representations with efficient storage utilization.

One such method involves the use of two bits per node, as follows. Consider the nodes of a tree T in preorder: $n_1, n_2, \ldots, n_k$. If node n_i *has no left descendant* in T, mark it as $n_{i)}$, and if node n_i *has a right sibling* in T, mark it as $n_i^($. [*Note:* Since these conditions are not mutually exclusive, it is possible to have a node n_i marked $n_i^($ to signify that it has a right sibling, but has no left descendant.] For example, the tree in Fig. 3.25 would lead to a marked preorder node sequence such as that shown in Fig. 3.26.

FIGURE 3.26

From this information it is easy to reconstruct a linked binary tree corresponding to T (using the correspondence of Figs. 3.12 and 3.13). In particular, we proceed as follows. Consider the marked nodes $n_1, n_2, \ldots, n_k$ in sequence. If n_i is not marked as $n_{i)}$, then it has a left descendant and in preorder, since left descendants of nodes are considered before right siblings, n_{i+1} is its left descendant. Therefore, draw a left descendant link from n_i to n_{i+1}. However, if n_i is marked as $n_{i)}$, then n_{i+1} is not the left descendant of n_i, but is the right sibling of some previously enumerated node. In fact, n_{i+1} must be the right sibling of the most recent node in the sequence marked as having a right sibling (as a consequence of the preorder procedure). Thus, we can draw a right sibling link from the node n_j to n_{i+1}, provided j is the largest integer $\leq i$ for which node n_j is marked as $n_j^($. After drawing the right sibling link, we delete the right sibling mark on n_j.

In an algorithm to process the preorder node sequence, we can stack nodes marked $n_j^($ on a stack, and upon encountering a node $n_{i)}$, we can link the node on top of the stack to node n_{i+1}, and pop it off the stack.

The following algorithm accomplishes this representation conversion process.

Algorithm 3.4 *Conversion of marked preorder node sequence for an ordered tree into the linked binary representation.*

Let $n_1, n_2, \ldots, n_k$ be a sequence of marked nodes each of the form

| L | INFO | R |

, where INFO holds information associated with the node, where $L = $ ')' if the node has no left descendants and is blank otherwise, and where $R = $ '(' if the node has a right sibling and is blank otherwise. We are to construct a linked binary representation using nodes of the form

| LLINK | INFO | RLINK |

, where, again, INFO holds information associated with the node, and LLINK and RLINK hold pointers to the left and right binary subtrees respectively (or point to Λ, if the corresponding subtree is empty). S is a pushdown stack.

1. [Initialize.] Create a sequence of empty linked binary nodes $b_1, b_2, \ldots, b_k$ in 1–1 correspondence with the sequence of marked nodes $n_1, n_2, \ldots, n_k$, having $\text{LLINK}(b_i) = \text{RLINK}(b_i) = \Lambda$ for $(1 \leq i \leq k)$, and set $\text{INFO}(b_i) \leftarrow \text{INFO}(n_i)$ for $(1 \leq i \leq k)$. Let S be an empty stack.

2. [Link together.] **for** $i \leftarrow 1$ **step** 1 **until** $k - 1$ **do**
   a) **if** $R(n_i) = $ '(' **then** $S \Leftarrow b_i$.
   b) **if** $L(n_i) = $ ')' **then** $[t \Leftarrow S$ **and** $\text{RLINK}(t) \leftarrow b_{i+1}]$ **else** $\text{LLINK}(b_i) \leftarrow b_{i+1}$.

Executing this algorithm on the marked node sequence of Fig. 3.26 yields the linked binary tree shown in Fig. 3.27. This figure can be redrawn with left links

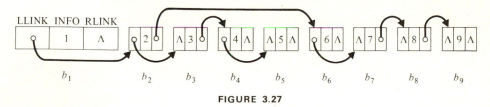

FIGURE 3.27

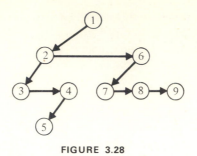

FIGURE 3.28

pointing downward and to the left, and right links pointing horizontally to the right, as in Fig. 3.28.

This is easily seen to be the binary tree representation of Fig. 3.25. Indeed, the tree of Fig. 3.25 can be recovered from it by first drawing parent–child links between any two nodes X and Y such that Y is a sibling of the leftmost child of X, and then by dropping the rightward horizontal links. This is just the inverse of the construction shown in Figs. 3.12 and 3.13 (see Exercise 3.8).

Thus, we have seen that by adding two bits per node to the preorder sequential enumeration of the nodes of an ordered tree, we can adequately represent and recover the shape of the original tree. Is this the best we can do as far as minimizing the storage required to store the tree is concerned? An equivalent question is whether or not we can encode the shape of the tree in less than $2n$ bits for an ordered tree of n nodes. We have seen, in (10) above, that there are b_{n-1} distinct ordered trees on n vertices. If b_{n-1} can be encoded in less than $2n$ bits, then we can represent the original tree by supplying a "shape number" followed by the sequence of values to be stored at the nodes (enumerated in preorder, say); and such a representation will consume less space than that discussed above, which uses two bits per node. In fact, it is easy to show that $b_{n+1} < 4b_n$ (starting with formula (9) (see Exercise 3.5)); and this, together with the fact that $b_1 < 4$, implies that $b_n < 4^n$ for all $n \geq 1$. Hence, b_{n-1} can be encoded in binary in at most $2n - 2$ bits.

Asymptotically, the number of bits required for b_n is approximately $2n - (\frac{3}{2}) \lg n$ (as can be derived from the fact that b_n is $O(4^n/n^{3/2})$). Thus, the use of the "shape number" encoding does not produce dramatic savings in space over the two-bit-per-node representation. (See Exercises 3.3 and 3.6 for more refined results.) Rather remarkably, it has been discovered that it is possible to convert a shape number k $(1 \leq k \leq b_n)$ to the kth binary tree on n vertices in linear time (Knott [1977]).

In the special case of a full binary tree, it is possible to recover the structural information about the tree from a preorder enumeration of the nodes, together with *one* information bit per node. The single bit tells whether the node to which it is attached is a leaf or an internal node. For example, let a node be marked with a bit that is set to 0 if it is a leaf, and to 1 if it is an internal node. Then the sequence

$$A^1 \ B^1 \ C^1 \ D^0 \ E^0 \ F^0 \ G^1 \ H^0 \ I^0$$

represents the full binary tree shown in Fig. 3.29.

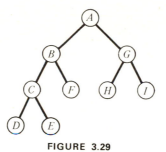

FIGURE 3.29

Exercise 3.15 explores the procedure for converting the one-bit preorder sequential enumeration into the corresponding full linked binary tree.

The following two methods of adding tree-structure information to the preorder sequential enumeration of the nodes in a tree might be called *arithmetic tree representations*, since they use arithmetic facts, stored in a vector parallel to the vector of nodes, to encode the tree structure. The *preorder sequence with degrees* gives the number of children of each node (sometimes called the degree of the node) above the information stored in the node. For example, the tree of Fig. 3.25 would be represented in this fashion as indicated in Fig. 3.30.

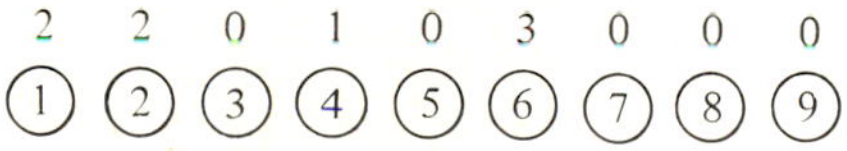

2   2   0   1   0   3   0   0   0

(1) (2) (3) (4) (5) (6) (7) (8) (9)

FIGURE 3.30

The *preorder sequence with weights* is a similar representation, in which the information stored above each node in the preorder sequence signifies the *weight* of the subtree of which the node is a root. The weight of a subtree is defined to be the number of nodes in a subtree excluding the root. Thus, the tree of Fig. 3.25 would be represented in preorder sequence with weights as shown in Fig. 3.31. These arithmetic representations are often convenient to use in programming languages that supply arithmetic and character arrays as the principal composite data structures.

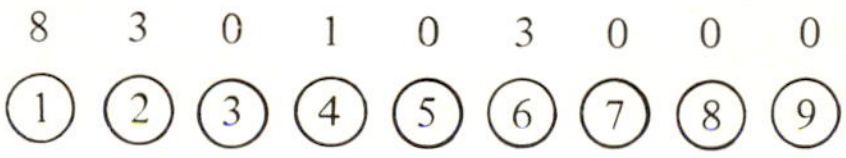

8   3   0   1   0   3   0   0   0

(1) (2) (3) (4) (5) (6) (7) (8) (9)

FIGURE 3.31

In the preorder sequence with weights, the extent of the subtree of which node
i is a root can be immediately determined, since the weight $w(i)$ of node i is the
number of nodes to the immediate right of node i in the preorder sequence that
constitute the subtree rooted at node i. For example, in Fig. 3.31 the subtree
rooted at node ② consists of node ② together with the three nodes to the
immediate right of node ②, since the weight of node ② is 3. Thus, it is easy to
find a subtree, or to replace a subtree with another subtree of the same weight. On
the other hand, deleting a subtree or replacing a subtree with another subtree of
different weight requires modifying the weights of every node in the whole tree on
the path from the root of the whole tree to the root of the subtree being modified.

By comparison, in the preorder sequence with degrees, replacing a subtree
with another of the same or different weight can be done locally with no need for
alteration of degrees elsewhere in the representation. However, finding the extent
of a subtree rooted at a given node requires computation.

Perlis has developed methods for manipulating trees represented in preorder
sequence with weights using concise expressions in the programming language
APL (see Perlis [1972], pp. 272–282).

Exercises 3.19 to 3.20 explore efficient conversions between the various preorder representations in this section.

3.5.2.2 *Postorder.* A *postorder* enumeration of the nodes of an ordered tree is
performed as follows:

1. Traverse in postorder the subtrees of the root from left to right.

2. Visit the root.

This definition is recursive. The postorder sequential enumeration of the tree
of Fig. 3.25 is shown in Fig. 3.32. Tree structure information may be added to such
a node sequence to enable recovery of the tree structure in several ways similar to
that explored in the previous section for preorder sequential enumerations. For
example, the postorder sequence augmented either by degrees or by weights is
sufficient.

FIGURE 3.32

A postorder enumeration of an operator–operand tree for an arithmetic expression yields a *postfix* representation. For example, the expression $(1/n) \times
\log (n + 1) - 3 \times n$ has the operator–operand tree given in Fig. 3.33 and has the
corresponding postfix representation given in Fig. 3.34. Postfix representations of
expressions are popular in programming language interpreters, since a simple
pushdown stack evaluator can be used for expression evaluation.

The theme of such a postfix-representation evaluator is as follows. We consider the items in the postfix representation in sequence from left to right. When we encounter a constant or a variable, we push its value onto a stack S. When we encounter a binary operator β, we pop the two topmost values from the stack, $S[\text{top}]$ and $S[\text{top} - 1]$, and we push the value of the expression $S[\text{top} - 1]\beta S[\text{top}]$ back onto the stack. When we encounter a unary operator α, we pop $S[\text{top}]$ from the stack and push the value of the expression $(\alpha S[\text{top}])$ back on the stack. (Exercise 3.26 asks the reader to develop an algorithm setting forth the precise details.)

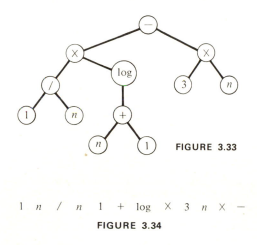

FIGURE 3.33

$$1 \quad n \quad / \quad n \quad 1 \quad + \quad \log \quad \times \quad 3 \quad n \quad \times \quad -$$

FIGURE 3.34

3.5.2.3 *Level order*. A *level-order* sequential enumeration of the nodes of an ordered tree consists of a list of the nodes in order of increasing levels, given left-to-right within each level. For example, the level-order enumeration of the nodes in the tree in Fig. 3.25 is:

$$① ② ⑥ ③ ④ ⑦ ⑧ ⑨ ⑤$$

By adding degrees or weights to the level-order enumeration, the tree structure can be encoded. For example, the above sequence with degrees added becomes:

2	2	3	0	1	0	0	0	0	Degrees
①	②	⑥	③	④	⑦	⑧	⑨	⑤	Nodes

Exercise 3.21 explores reconstruction of the original tree of Fig. 3.25 from this latter information.

3.6 BINARY TREE TRAVERSAL ALGORITHMS

In this section, we study techniques for traversing nodes in binary trees in various orders. One of the themes underlying the algorithms presented is that of attempting to discover the least resources (in time and memory) with which we can perform the traversal task. In all cases, the algorithms run in linear time (i.e., time proportional to the number of nodes in the binary tree), so the challenge is to minimize the auxiliary memory the algorithms must use. We start by examining traversal techniques using pushdown stacks as auxiliary memory.

The use of stack traversal techniques requires that we set aside an area of memory to contain the largest stack we contemplate using for any potential traversal. At worst, such a stack can contain the same number of entries as there are nodes in the binary tree being traversed. Thus, to avoid abandoning a computation because of violation of an implementation limit during program execution, it is tempting for programmers to allocate large stack spaces. If more than one tree is being stack-traversed on an interleaved basis, more than one stack will be required, leading potentially to the problems of managing several stacks simultaneously studied in Chapter 2.

The disadvantages of stack traversals can be overcome when we discover how to eliminate such pushdown stacks, using link inversions and marking bits within the binary tree itself. The link-inversion traversal has the disadvantage that it temporarily disrupts the topology of the binary tree, so that only one process can traverse the tree at a given time. In fact, it is possible to represent a binary tree in read-only memory in such a way that several processes can traverse the tree simultaneously, each in a different stage of traversal independent of the others. This read-only traversal technique works in linear time and bounded workspace but requires tag bits on the nodes.

Even tag bits on the nodes can be eliminated. There exists a linear time traversal technique using no stacks and no tag bits. Of course, the threaded traversal we have already seen requires neither stacks nor tag bits, but the space required to store threads at the leaves of the tree may be substantial. An important question, then, is to determine whether the space reserved for threads in leaf nodes can be eliminated in the stackless traversals with no tag bits, if the latter are to be considered as improvements with respect to space, over threaded traversal.

It is important to study properties of various stackless traversal techniques for binary trees for two reasons (among others). First, marking algorithms for garbage collection in list structures (to be studied in Chapter 5) are based on the ideas presented in binary tree traversals. Second, several of the main ideas involved can be generalized to stackless traversals of more complicated multilinked structures studied in Chapter 6. The idea of traversal itself lies at the core of many algorithms for such tasks as copying, printing, garbage collection, and equality testing. Therefore it is useful to study the main ideas of traversal first in their simplest form before advancing to more complicated themes in which the idea of traversal plays a supporting role.

3.6.1 Stack traversals

The idea behind stack traversals is to save on a pushdown stack a set of postponed obligations for nodes or subtrees to be traversed later. Algorithm 3.5 performs a preorder traversal of a binary tree T, where T is assumed to be represented using the linked representation exemplified in Fig. 3.16.

Algorithm 3.5 *Preorder stack traversal of binary tree.*

1. [Initialize.] Let S be an empty stack. Let PRES contain a pointer to the root of the binary tree T.
2. [Is tree empty?] If PRES $= \Lambda$, then go to step 5.
3. [Preorder visit.] Visit the node pointed to by PRES.
4. [Postpone right and descend left.] (First, save the address of the right subtree on the stack to postpone its traversal until the left subtree has been processed.) Set $S \Leftarrow$ RLINK(PRES). (Then proceed to process left subtree.) Set PRES $\leftarrow$ LLINK(PRES) and go to step 2.
5. [Done?] If the stack S is empty, then terminate the algorithm (since no more postponed work remains). Otherwise, set PRES $\Leftarrow S$ and go to step 2.

Exercises 3.24 to 3.25 explore other sorts of traversals using stacks and queues.

3.6.2 Link inversion traversals

In a link-inversion traversal, as we descend into a binary tree, we replace normally downward pointing pointers in the link fields of nodes with upward pointers, which point to immediate ancestors. On the way up again, we restore pointer fields to their original condition containing downward pointers. Thus, as the algorithm traces out a path down into the lower parts of the tree, it leaves a "reverse" path to use to climb back out again. In Algorithm 3.6 below, we assume that each node N, in a linked representation such as that of Fig. 3.16, contains an additional TAG field such that initially TAG$(N) = 0$. The TAG field is set to 1 when the RLINK field is set to point upwards to its parent. It is reset to 0 when the RLINK field is reset to point downward to its original right child node. The following algorithm can be used to perform link inversion traversals in preorder, symmetric order, or postorder; and it works for binary trees with shared subtrees (i.e., subtrees pointed to by more than one ancestral node in the whole tree). [*Note.* In such a tree no node may be an ancestor of itself.]

Algorithm 3.6 *Link inversion traversal of binary tree.*

1. [Initialize.] Set PRES to point to the root of the tree, and set PREV ← Λ.
2. [Preorder visit.] Visit node PRES if traversing in preorder.
3. [Descend left.] Set NEXT ← LLINK(PRES). If NEXT ≠ Λ, then set LLINK(PRES) ← PREV, PREV ← PRES, PRES ← NEXT, and go to step 2.
4. [Symmetric order visit.] Visit node PRES if traversing in symmetric order.
5. [Descend right.] Set NEXT ← RLINK(PRES). If NEXT ≠ Λ, then set TAG(PRES) ← 1, RLINK(PRES) ← PREV, PREV ← PRES, PRES ← NEXT, and go to step 2.
6. [Postorder visit.] Visit node PRES if traversing in postorder.
7. [Go up.] If PREV = Λ, then the algorithm terminates. Otherwise, if TAG(PREV) = 0, then set NEXT ← LLINK(PREV), LLINK(PREV) ← PRES, PRES ← PREV, PREV ← NEXT, and go to step 4. Otherwise, set NEXT ← RLINK(PREV), TAG(PREV) ← 0, RLINK(PREV) ← PRES, PRES ← PREV, PREV ← NEXT, and go to step 6.

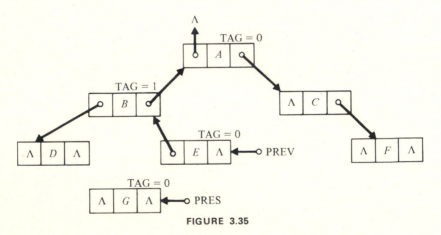

FIGURE 3.35

Figure 3.35 shows the status of link inversions after Algorithm 3.6 has executed step 3, and the variable PRES points to node *G* of the tree of Fig. 3.18. Note that the node with TAG = 1 contains an RLINK that points to its original parent; that nodes with TAG = 0 either are in the original condition or contain LLINKS that point to their original parent; and that there is a chain of upward-pointing links from the node referenced by PREV through the original root to the (mythical) parent Λ of the entire tree. At termination, Algorithm 3.6 restores all pointers to their original condition.

The TAG fields in Algorithm 3.6 are used when ascending the tree to determine whether ascent comes from a left subtree or a right subtree. The question arises as to whether this tag field can be eliminated so as to give a traversal technique requiring neither stacks nor tag bits. J. M. Robson has answered this question affirmatively, using an ingenious technique shown in the next section.

3.6.3 Robson traversal

J. M. Robson (see Robson [1973]) has given a link inversion traversal algorithm for binary trees in which the function of the tag bits in Algorithm 3.6 is replaced by a stack of pointers threaded through unused fields of certain leaves in the tree. This stack is built using the leftmost leaves of subtrees in the whole tree that have already been traversed. The LLINK fields of these leaves are used to chain the stack elements together, while the RLINK fields point to interior nodes in the tree having nonempty left subtrees already traversed, and nonempty right subtrees in the process of being traversed. During ascent, when a node N with two nonempty subtrees is discovered, if the top of the stack points to N, then ascent is from the right; otherwise it is from the left. Hence, the threaded stack provides the same information as the TAG bits in Algorithm 3.6.

In the following algorithm, the variable TOP, when nonempty, holds the contents of the top of the stack, and points to the most recently encountered node whose nonnull left subtree is already traversed, but whose nonnull right subtree is not yet completely traversed. The variable STACK, when nonempty, points to a leaf of the tree that holds references to the second-to-the-top stack element and to the remainder of the stack.

Algorithm 3.7 *Robson traversal of binary tree.*

1. [Initialize.] Set PRES ← t and PREV ← t (where t is the address of the root of the tree) and set TOP ← Λ and STACK ← Λ.

2. [Leaf?] (Steps 2 through 4 descend repeatedly to find the leftmost leaf of the subtree rooted at PRES, making necessary visits and planting upward-pointing links on the way down. When the leftmost leaf is discovered, control passes to step 5.) If LLINK(PRES) = Λ and RLINK(PRES) = Λ, then PREVISIT(PRES), SYMVISIT(PRES), POSTVISIT(PRES) and set AVAIL ← PRES (to make the leaf available for use as the next stack element, if required). Go to step 5.

3. [Descend left.] (If left subtree is nonempty, descend left and plant upward link in LLINK field.) If LLINK(PRES) ≠ Λ, then PREVISIT(PRES), NEXT ← LLINK(PRES), LLINK(PRES) ← PREV, PREV ← PRES, PRES ← NEXT, and go back to step 2.

4. [Descend right.] (If the left subtree is empty, descend to right and plant upward link in RLINK field.) PREVISIT(PRES), SYMVISIT(PRES), NEXT ← RLINK(PRES), RLINK(PRES) ← PREV, PREV ← PRES, PRES ← NEXT, and go back to step 2.

5. [Done?] If PRES = t, the algorithm terminates.

6. [Ascend from left.] (Provided the parent PREV to which ascent is being made has an empty right subtree, there can be no doubt ascent is from the left. Original left downward pointer is restored.) If RLINK(PREV) = Λ, then SYMVISIT(PREV), POSTVISIT(PREV), NEXT ← LLINK(PREV), LLINK(PREV) ← PRES, PRES ← PREV, PREV ← NEXT, and go to step 5.

7. [Ascend from right.] (Provided the parent PREV to which ascent is being made has an empty left subtree, there can be no doubt that ascent is from the right. Original right downward pointer is restored.) If LLINK(PREV) = Λ, then POSTVISIT(PREV), NEXT ← RLINK(PREV), RLINK(PREV) ← PRES, PRES ← PREV, PREV ← NEXT, and go to step 5.

8. [Ascending from right or left?] (If the top of the stack TOP points to the parent PREV to which ascent is being made, then ascent is from the right. Otherwise it is from the left.) If PREV = TOP, then go to step 10. (Otherwise, continue with step 9.)

9. [Left subtree finished.] (When traversal of the nonempty left subtree of the node PREV is completed, a pointer to PREV is pushed onto the stack, and processing of the right subtree commences.) SYMVISIT(PREV), LLINK(AVAIL) ← STACK, RLINK(AVAIL) ← TOP, STACK ← AVAIL, TOP ← PREV, NEXT ← RLINK(PREV), RLINK(PREV) ← PRES, PRES ← NEXT, and go to step 2.

10. [Right subtree finished.] (When traversal of the nonempty right subtree of the node PREV is finished, the stack is popped and ascent continues.)

POSTVISIT(PREV), NEXT ← STACK, TOP ← RLINK(STACK), STACK ← LLINK(STACK), LLINK(NEXT) ← RLINK(NEXT) ← Λ, NEXT ← LLINK(PREV), LLINK(PREV) ← RLINK(PREV), RLINK(PREV) ← PRES, PRES ← PREV, PREV ← NEXT, and go to step 5.

Figure 3.36 shows a tree about to be traversed by Algorithm 3.7 after initialization in step 1. Figure 3.37 shows the status of the pointers in the tree of Fig. 3.36 when descent has reached the rightmost leaf of the tree (after step 2 of Algorithm 3.7 has been executed). The top of the stack points to node E using the pointer in the variable TOP. This is the most recently encountered node whose nonnull left subtree has been traversed and whose nonnull right subtree is being traversed. The variable STACK points to the stack of nodes F, D, and B whose LLINK fields chain the stack elements together (shown by upward-pointing wavy lines), and whose RLINK fields point to nodes with left subtrees traversed and right subtrees not yet completed (shown by dashed lines).

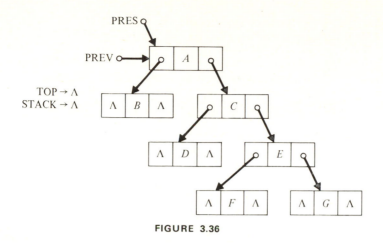

FIGURE 3.36

Comparing Robson traversal to threaded traversal, if we assume that the threads used in Algorithm 3.2 are distinguished from normal tree links by the use of tag bits, then threaded traversal takes more space than Robson traversal. However, though Robson traversal uses no tag bits while it is in progress, it modifies the tree being scanned with link inversions and an *in situ* stack. This is not true for threaded traversal, so threaded trees could be placed in read-only memory and could be traversed by more than one process concurrently, each in a different stage of traversal. Also, in threaded trees, the address of any node is

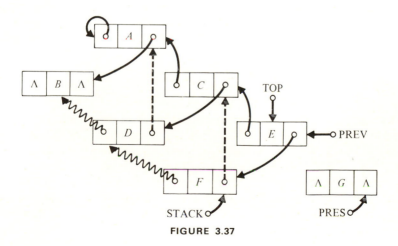

FIGURE 3.37

sufficient starting information with which to access any other node, while in Robson traversal, only the address of the root will suffice.

3.6.4 Lindstrom scanning

If we are willing to give up traversal of nodes in a particular order (such as preorder, postorder, or symmetric order) in a binary tree and if, instead, we are willing to settle for scanning the nodes in some order that is unpredictable and possibly repetitive, it is possible to improve upon the space requirements of threaded traversal and Robson traversal.† In particular, Lindstrom [1972] has given a technique for binary tree *scanning* using neither stacks nor tag bits. For instance, such scanning techniques can be used to mark the nodes of a structure in use during list garbage collection (studied in Chapter 5), where, unlike the requirements for printing an alphabetical index, the order and multiplicity in which we visit nodes is unimportant.

In the case of Lindstrom scanning, we assume that the leaf nodes of a binary tree (i.e., those with empty left and right subtrees) are *atomic* and are represented in memory without fields to contain LLINK and RLINK addresses. The predicate ATOM(X) is true if X is an atom and false if X is not an atom. Nonatoms are assumed to have LLINK and RLINK fields pointing to their respective left and right subtrees.

In the absence of leaf nodes with LLINK and RLINK fields, neither threaded traversal nor Robson traversal can work, since they each use the LLINK and RLINK fields of leaf nodes to contain threads and stacks respectively.

The idea behind Lindstrom scanning can be readily grasped by representing a binary tree as a system of roads built from "three-way intersections" and "dead

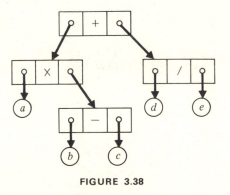

FIGURE 3.38

---

† Actually, Lindstrom scanning is repetitive only as far as internal nodes are concerned. The leaves are scanned only once each and in order.

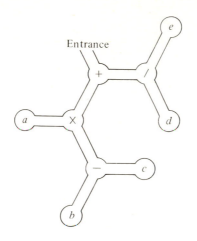

FIGURE 3.39

ends." For example, the binary tree of Fig. 3.38 corresponds to the roadway in Fig. 3.39.

To visit all places along the roadway of Fig. 3.39, one could use two simple rules: (a) when traveling through an intersection, *turn right*, and (b) when at a dead end, *turn around*. Another way of thinking about this is to imagine the line in Fig. 3.39 as a wall of a building. To visit all rooms of the building, one can place one's hand on the right inside wall at the entrance and move forwards, always keeping the right hand on the wall. This process implies that each intersection is crossed three times, and each dead end is encountered exactly once. In Lindstrom scanning, the act of "traveling through an intersection and turning right" corresponds to a cyclical permutation of three pointers at a nonatomic node. The act of turning around at a dead end corresponds to swapping pointers to a present and a previous node. The cyclical permutation during a "right turn at an intersection" is performed three times, and restores pointers to their original configuration.

The following version of Lindstrom scanning scans the nonatomic nodes in a binary tree represented as in Fig. 3.38, where circular nodes represent atoms (which must be assumed nonnull if this version of the algorithm is to work).

Algorithm 3.8 *Lindstrom scanning of a binary tree.*

1. [Initialize.] Set PREV ← Λ and PRES to a pointer t to the root of the tree.

2. [Visit node and turn right.] Set NEXT ← LLINK(PRES), LLINK(PRES) ← RLINK(PRES), RLINK(PRES) ← PREV. Scan the node PRES. Set PREV ← PRES and PRES ← NEXT.

3. [Done?] If PRES = Λ, then halt. If ATOM(PRES), then swap PRES and PREV. Go back to step 2.

Algorithm 3.8 works for trees with shared subtrees, which are scanned with appropriate multiplicity. (We say t is a *shared subtree* of tree t' if two or more pointers to the root of t are contained in cells of t' at levels of t' higher than that at which the root of t appears.)

3.6.5 Siklóssy traversal

Siklóssy [1972] has given a method for traversing binary trees in read-only memory. Each internal node has two link fields LLINK and RLINK, and each has a TAG field. These fields are preset in read-only memory as follows: The TAG field of node N is set to + if N is a left child of its parent, and is set to − if N is a right child of its parent. By convention, the tag of the root is set to − (as if the root were imagined to be a right child of its empty parent Λ). Let N be an internal node, for which the address of its parent is P, the address of its left child is L, and the address of its right child is R. Then the LLINK field of N is set to contain $P \oplus L$ and the RLINK field of N is set to contain $P \oplus R$. (See Fig. 3.40.)

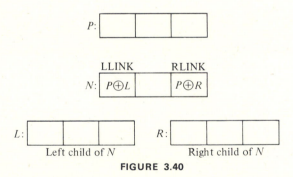

FIGURE 3.40

For the purpose of calculating $P \oplus L$ or $P \oplus R$: (a) if the left (or right) subtree is empty, then L (or R) is taken to be the address Λ, and (b) for the root of the tree, P is taken to be the address Λ. For example, the binary tree of Fig. 3.18 would be represented in read-only memory suitable for Siklóssy traversal as shown in Fig. 3.41.

The Greek letters in Fig. 3.41 represent addresses of nodes. Given a representation such as that of Fig. 3.41, Siklóssy traversal proceeds as follows:

Algorithm 3.9 *Siklóssy traversal of a binary tree.*

1. [Initialize.] Set PRES to the address of the root of the tree and set PREV ← Λ. If PRES = Λ, then (the tree is empty, so) terminate the algorithm.

2. [Preorder visit.] If traversing in preorder, VISIT(PRES).

3. [Go left.] Set NEXT ← LLINK(PRES) ⊕ PREV. If NEXT ≠ Λ, set PREV ← PRES, PRES ← NEXT, and go to step 2.

4. [Symmetric order visit.] If traversing in symmetric order, VISIT(PRES).

5. [Go right.] Set NEXT ← RLINK(PRES) ⊕ PREV. If NEXT ≠ Λ, set PREV ← PRES, PRES ← NEXT, and go to step 2.

6. [Postorder visit.] If traversing in postorder. VISIT(PRES).

7. [Go up.] If PREV = Λ, then terminate the algorithm. Otherwise, if TAG(PRES) = +, set NEXT ← LLINK(PREV) ⊕ PRES, PRES ← PREV, PREV ← NEXT, and go to step 4. Otherwise, NEXT ← RLINK(PREV) ⊕ PRES, PRES ← PREV, PREV ← NEXT, and go to step 6.

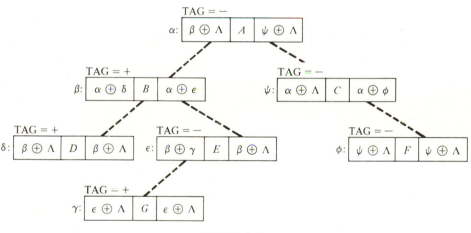

FIGURE 3.41

The key to understanding how this algorithm works is contained in the identities for the exclusive-or operation developed in Exercise 1.8. These identities, applied to the addresses of cells in Fig. 3.40, are $(P \oplus L) \oplus P = L$, $(P \oplus L) \oplus L = P$, $(P \oplus R) \oplus R = P$, and $(P \oplus R) \oplus P = R$. Thus, for instance, given the addresses P and N, the value of the expression LLINK$(N) \oplus P$ gives the address L and enables the traversal to advance downward and to the left to cell L. Similarly, given N and L, the value of the expression LLINK$(N) \oplus L$ is P, whence RLINK$(N) \oplus P = R$, enabling the traversal process to come up from the left and to go down to the right. Finally, to come up from the right, given N and R, the value of the expression RLINK$(N) \oplus R$ gives the address of the parent P of N.

3.7 ADDITIONAL TREE STRUCTURES AND THEIR APPLICATIONS

There are a number of interesting variants of tree data structures used in algorithms and applications. These exhibit important properties, and often enable
algorithms to be devised having surprisingly efficient execution times. These are
such tree structures as *heaps, spanning trees, binary search trees, 2–3 trees, B-trees,*
and *Tries.* This section investigates various of these types of trees and develops
their properties.

3.7.1 Heaps, heapsort, and priority queues

The word *heap* is used in two senses in this book (and in the literature). One use
applies to complete binary trees whose nodes contain "search keys," which are
arranged in descending order along every path from the root to a leaf. The other
use applies to a zone of memory in which multilinked nodes of variable size are
allocated (see Baecker [1970]). We shall study techniques for managing this latter
sort of heap in Chapter 6. In this section, we shall study the former sort of heap.

Let $K_1, K_2, \ldots, K_n$ be chosen from a set of *keys* on which a *total order* has
been defined. (Recall that in a *total order,* two laws hold: (a) the law of *trichotomy,*
namely, for any two keys K_i and K_j, exactly one of the relations $K_i < K_j$, $K_i = K_j$,
or $K_i > K_j$ holds, and (b) the law of *transitivity,* namely, if $K_i < K_j$ and $K_j < K_\ell$,
then $K_i < K_\ell$.) Further, let the keys K_i be assigned to the nodes of a complete
binary tree in level order. Figure 3.42 illustrates this assignment for $n = 9$.

FIGURE 3.42

We define such a binary tree to be a *heap* provided the key K_i at each node in
the tree is greater than or equal to the keys K_{2i} and K_{2i+1} of its children nodes.
We say that the keys $K_1, K_2, \ldots, K_n$ satisfy the *heap property* provided $K_{\lfloor j/2 \rfloor} \geq K_j$
for every j satisfying the relation $1 \leq \lfloor j/2 \rfloor < j \leq n$.

Note that every subtree of a heap is a heap, and (by transitivity) that the key at
the root of a heap is the largest key in the heap.

Suppose now that we have a complete binary tree whose nodes contain keys
not satisfying the heap property. How can we exchange keys between parent–child
pairs in the tree so that a heap can be established? Consider a system of promo-

tions in a hierarchy, in which, if the value of a key K_j at a node is greater than the value of the key $K_{\lfloor j/2 \rfloor}$ at its parent node, we exchange K_j and $K_{\lfloor j/2 \rfloor}$. (This process resembles the mad rush characterized by the Peter Principle, in which each person in a hierarchical organization tends to be promoted until he reaches his level of incompetence—at which point he is said to have achieved *final placement*.) Repeatedly performing such promotions until no more can be performed will convert the hierarchy into a heap. For example, starting with the tree of Fig. 3.43, we could perform the following promotions (let $a \leftrightarrow b$ stand for exchanging a and b):

$$3 \leftrightarrow 2, \quad 3 \leftrightarrow 1, \quad 2 \leftrightarrow 1, \quad 4 \leftrightarrow 2, \quad 4 \leftrightarrow 3, \quad 6 \leftrightarrow 5, \quad 6 \leftrightarrow 4, \quad 4 \leftrightarrow 5, \quad 7 \leftrightarrow 5, \quad 6 \leftrightarrow 7.$$

The tree resulting from these ten promotions is given in Fig. 3.44.

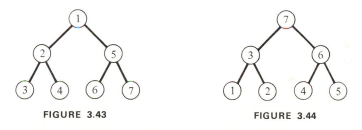

FIGURE 3.43   FIGURE 3.44

It turns out that using ten promotions to establish this heap is rather wasteful. For instance, only four promotions,

$$7 \leftrightarrow 5, \quad 4 \leftrightarrow 2, \quad 7 \leftrightarrow 1, \quad 6 \leftrightarrow 1,$$

are needed to establish the heap in Fig. 3.45, starting from the tree of Fig. 3.43.

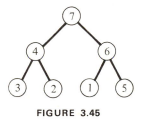

FIGURE 3.45

Given n keys, it is interesting to inquire whether we can arrange them into a heap in at most $O(n)$ exchanges. (The reader might find pleasure in attempting to solve this problem before reading on.)

A bottom-up process can be used to solve this problem. Let's suppose that we are given a binary tree T of the form

where K is the key in the root of the tree, and K_L and K_R are the keys in the respective roots of the left and right subtrees T_L and T_R. Suppose, further, that the left and right subtrees have already been arranged into heaps. Then the only way in which the whole tree T could fail to be a heap is if K is less than K_L or less than K_R. If this is the case, we can exchange K with the *larger* of K_L and K_R. Without loss of generality, suppose $K_R \geq K_L$. Then we exchange K and K_R, giving a new tree

Since T_L is already a heap, and since $K_R \geq K_L$, the only way in which this new tree could fail to be a heap is that key K could be less than the keys of one or both of its new children in tree T_R. These new children are already roots of respective heaps since they are roots of subtrees of the original tree T_R (assumed to be a heap at the outset). Hence, the altered subtree T_R with new root K is a tree which, like the original tree, departs from the heap property only at its root if at all. The key at the root of T_R can be exchanged repeatedly with the larger of the keys of its children until, after some amount of downward travel, it comes to rest at a node where it is not less than the keys of its children. At this point, the entire original tree is a heap.

This process, originally called the *sift-up* procedure by Floyd (see Floyd [1964]), is given more precisely by the following algorithm.

Algorithm 3.10 *Sift up.*

Let T point to the root of a nonempty binary tree with key K at its root, and let T_L and T_R be subtrees that are heaps. The key K is repeatedly exchanged with the larger of the keys of the children of the node where it currently resides until T is made into a heap. For convenience, if a subtree is the empty tree Λ, we assume that the key of its root is a quantity $-\infty$ less than every key K_i.

1. [Initialize.] Set $N \leftarrow T$. (N is the current node containing key K).
2. [Extract keys and subtrees.] $K \leftarrow$ key of N. $T_L \leftarrow$ left subtree of N. $T_R \leftarrow$ right subtree of N. $K_L \leftarrow$ key of T_L. $K_R \leftarrow$ key of T_R.
3. [Terminate?] If $K \geq K_L$ and $K \geq K_R$, the algorithm terminates.
4. [Exchange with bigger child.] If $K_L > K_R$, then exchange the keys of N and T_L, set $N \leftarrow T_L$, and go to step 2. Otherwise, exchange the keys of N and T_R, set $N \leftarrow T_R$, and go to step 2.

Given a complete binary tree T, not initially a heap, we can convert T into a heap by repeatedly applying the sift-up procedure, first to its smallest subtrees, and then later to subtrees whose left and right subtrees have already been made into heaps. Any order of application of sift-up to the nodes of T which processes the subtrees of each node before it processes the node itself will suffice to create a heap out of the whole tree.

(For the sake of specificity, and as a preparation for our later treatment of the Heapsort algorithm, we can assume that we apply sift-up to the nodes in the reverse of level order—i.e., from bottom to top and right to left within each level.)

The running time for sift-up is proportional to the number of times it exchanges keys in step 4. Let us now show that the number of key exchanges required in applying sift-up to all n nodes of a complete binary tree is at most $O(n)$.

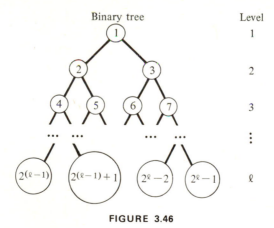

FIGURE 3.46

Suppose we have a tree of ℓ levels as in Fig. 3.46. A key K in a node at level i could be exchanged with children along any downward path at most $(\ell - i)$ times before coming to rest—since, in the worst case, it would come to rest in a leaf at the bottommost level ℓ. Since there are 2^{i-1} nodes on level i of the tree, each of whose keys could be exchanged at most $(\ell - i)$ times, the total number of exchanges required in applying sift-up to all nodes in the tree could not exceed E, where

$$E = \sum_{1 \leq i \leq \ell} 2^{i-1}(\ell - i).$$

By exchanging $(\ell - i)$ and i, the sum for E becomes

$$E = \sum_{1 \leq \ell - i \leq \ell} 2^{(\ell - i) - 1}(i) = \sum_{0 \leq i \leq \ell - 1} i2^{(\ell - 1) - i}.$$

Here $2^{\ell - 1}$ can be removed as a factor, and the term for $i = 0$ can be dropped, giving

$$E = 2^{\ell - 1} \sum_{1 \leq i \leq \ell - 1} \frac{i}{2^i}.$$

But since it can be shown that $\sum (i/2^i) < 2$ (see Exercise 3.34 for outline of intermediate steps) we get

$$E = 2^{\ell - 1} \sum_{1 \leq i \leq \ell - 1} \frac{i}{2^i} < 2^{\ell - 1} \cdot 2 = 2^\ell.$$

So E is bounded above by 2^ℓ, where ℓ was the number of levels in the original tree. If n is any number of nodes sufficient for at least one node to reside on level ℓ, then n lies in the range $2^{\ell - 1} \leq n \leq 2^\ell - 1$. Hence, $2^\ell \leq 2n$. Putting these results together, we see that the total number of exchanges required in applying sift-up to all nodes of the tree is at most E, which is, in turn, bounded above by 2^ℓ, which is at most $2n$. Therefore, the number of exchanges required to make an n-node complete tree into a heap is $O(n)$.

A heap is used as the basic data structure of the Heapsort algorithm. (See Floyd [1964] and Williams [1964.) The basic ideas behind this sorting algorithm are as follows:

1. Take the n keys to be sorted $K_1, K_2, \ldots, K_n$ and consider them to be arranged in a complete binary tree.

2. Convert this tree into a heap by applying sift-up to the nodes in reverse level order. (This takes time $O(n)$.)

3. Repeatedly do the following steps (a, b, and c) until the heap is empty:
   a) Remove the key at the root of the heap (which is the largest in the heap) and place it on an output queue.
   b) Detach from the heap the rightmost leaf node at the bottommost level, extract its key K, and replace the key at the root of the heap with K.
   c) Finally, apply sift-up to the root to convert the tree to a heap once again.

Original tree T

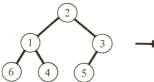

T converted to a heap by the exchanges 5⟷3, 6⟷1, 6⟷2, 4⟷2

Key at root placed on output queue.
Rightmost leaf at bottom level detached,
and its key placed at root.

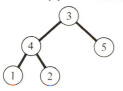

Output queue

Tree converted back into heap by
applying sift-up to root (3 ⟷ 5 exchanged).

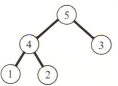

Key at root placed on output queue.
Rightmost leaf at bottom level detached, and
its key placed at root.

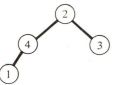

Output queue

⑤ , ⑥

Tree converted back into heap (by 2 ⟷ 4).

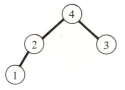

FIGURE 3.47

(*Continued on next page*)

Key at root placed on output queue.
Rightmost leaf at bottom level detached,
and its key placed at root.

                                          Output queue

Tree converted back into heap (by 1 ⟷ 3).

Root key queued, last leaf detached, etc.

                                          Output queue

Tree heapified (by 1 ⟷ 2).

Root key queued, last leaf detached, etc.

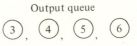   Output queue

Tree heapified.

Root key queued, tree empty.   Output queue
Heapsort terminates.

FIGURE 3.47 (concluded)

Figure 3.47 shows the progression of events in Heapsort, starting with a complete binary tree of six keys 2, 1, 3, 6, 4, 5, distributed over the nodes of the tree in level order. Removing the key at the root of a heap, queuing it, and replacing it with the key of the detached leaf occurring last in level order are operations that take constant time. Applying sift-up to the root of a tree may cause at most $\lfloor \lg n \rfloor$ exchanges in the worst case, in which the key at the root is moved down to a lowest position in a complete binary tree of n nodes. Hence, the cumulative total cost of applying sift-up operations to the roots of the trees being reheapified in the latter stages of the algorithm is $O(n \log n)$.† Since the original tree is converted to a heap initially in time $O(n)$, the dominant cost in the algorithm is $O(n \log n)$.

Heapsort has the advantage of being an $O(n \log n)$ sorting algorithm whose worst case performance is fairly close to its *average* performance (see Knuth [1973b], pp. 154–157]).

If we use the contiguous representation of complete binary trees (see Eq. (11) in Section 3.5.1), both the tree and the queue in the Heapsort algorithm can be represented sequentially and made to lie adjacent to one another in a single linear sequence. This gives rise to an *in situ* variant of the Heapsort algorithm of unusual elegance, put forth by Floyd (see Floyd [1964]). This is rendered as Algorithm 3.11 below.

Two fine points of Algorithm 3.11 are worth noting. First, during conversion of the initial tree to a heap, at least half the nodes need not be considered. The nodes numbered $\lfloor n/2 \rfloor + 1, \lfloor n/2 \rfloor + 2, \ldots, n$ have no children (as a consequence of Eq. (11)) and thus cannot exchange keys with lower nodes in the tree. Hence it suffices to apply sift-up only to nodes $\lfloor n/2 \rfloor, \lfloor n/2 \rfloor - 1, \ldots, 1$ in reverse level order, to heapify the tree. Second, instead of repeatedly exchanging pairs of keys in sift-up, the root key can be held in a temporary variable *Temp* while being compared to various "upward-sifting" keys; and finally it can be placed in the hole left by the upward migration of the keys bigger than it.

Algorithm 3.11 *Heapsort.*

Let M be a sequence initially containing keys $K_1, K_2, \ldots, K_n$ in locations $M[1], M[2], \ldots, M[n]$. The algorithm performs an *in situ* sort of the keys in bounded workspace and $O(n \log n)$ time. The algorithm uses the subroutine Siftup(i, n) given below.

1. [Convert M almost to a heap.] *For* $i \leftarrow \lfloor n/2 \rfloor$ *step* -1 *until* 2 *do* Sift-up(i, n). (After this step, the subtree containing the root may not have the heap property, but all other subtrees do).

2. [Iterate.] (Repeatedly apply Sift-up to root, exchange root and last leaf, and consider last leaf to be deleted from tree and joined to output queue, until M is sorted.) *For* $i \leftarrow n$ *step* -1 *until* 2 *do* steps (a) and (b):
   a) Sift-up$(1, i)$.
   b) Exchange $M[1]$ and $M[i]$.

Subroutine 3.11 Sift-up(i, n).

Let i be a pointer to the root and let n point to the last leaf in level order.

1. [Initialize.] Set Temp $\leftarrow M[i]$.

---

† More precisely, $\sum_{1 \le k \le n} \lfloor \lg k \rfloor = (n + 1)q - 2^{q+1} + 2$, where $q = \lfloor \lg (n + 1) \rfloor$ (see Knuth [1973a], p. 400).

2. [Set j to point to left child of i.] $j \leftarrow 2i$.

3. [Move promotees up.] *If* $j \leq n$ (that is, if left child of node i exists in tree), *then*
   a) *If* $j < n$ (that is, if right child of node i also exists in tree), *then* (set j to point to larger child by doing) *if* $M[j + 1] > M[j]$, $j \leftarrow j + 1$.
   b) *If* $M[j] >$ Temp (that is, if larger child is bigger than the root key), *then* set $M[i] \leftarrow M[j]$, $i \leftarrow j$, and go back to step 2.

4. [Final placement of root.] $M[i] \leftarrow$ Temp.

Applications of heaps—priority queues. In a number of applications, we have a set of items on which we perform only two operations: (1) add an item to the current set, and (2) extract the item from the set having maximum (minimum) value. For example, in discrete-event simulation systems, we wish to simulate events in the temporal order in which they occur. The simulator may schedule future events by adding events to the current set, and it must be able to extract the next (i.e., minimum time) event, in order to know which future event to simulate next. Often the operations *add* and *extract* come in pairs or, over the course of an algorithm, occur in equal numbers. Similar requirements for a *largest-in, first-out* set representation are found in algorithms for such tasks as: (a) operating-system task scheduling, (b) solving sparse linear systems using matrix row elimination, and (c) iteration in numerical schemes based on the idea of repeated selection of an item with smallest test criterion.

Let us call a set with a largest-in, first-out behavior a *priority queue* (since the value of each item establishes its priority for leaving the queue). It is obvious that there are a number of different representations for priority queues. We could keep all n items in the queue in a sorted list—in which case, extraction takes constant time but addition takes time $O(n)$; or we could leave the items in random order in a sequential list—in which case addition takes constant time, but extraction takes time $O(n)$. An advantage of the heap representation is that addition and extraction each take $O(\log n)$ time. This becomes very advantageous for large n. As Gonnet [1976] points out, for a heap containing 1000 items, the average number of comparisons needed to do an insertion followed by an extraction is 12. Priority queues can also be represented as height-balanced trees (see next section) and as the so-called *leftist* trees of Crane [1972] (see Knuth [1973b], pp. 150ff for discussion and see Section 3.8 for references to further representations).

3.7.2 Minimum spanning trees

Suppose we have a network of n nodes connected by edges having distance measures attached. Supposing the network is connected, in the sense that from any node there is at least one path to any other node; we may wish to find the least costly way to connect all nodes in the network together, using edges in the network. For example, let $n_1, n_2, \ldots, n_k$ be nodes consisting of terminals on a circuit board, and suppose we wish to solder wires between the terminals to connect them together so they will all have the same voltage. We might want to know what is the way to solder pairs of terminals together (n_i, n_j) so that the least amount of wire is used to connect all k terminals together. Here, the edges between terminals (n_i, n_j) represent physical distance on the circuit board. Clearly, we never need to connect the terminals together in any fashion that contains a cycle since, in any cycle, we can remove one wire and the remaining terminals are still electrically connected at less expense. Also, we need to ensure that any two terminals are connected by at least one path, to solve the problem. These two conditions—cycle-free and connected—imply (by Theorem 3.1) that the solution to the problem will be a *free tree* containing all the nodes in the network.

Let us call a free tree that connects all n nodes in a network N, a *spanning tree* for N. A *minimum spanning tree* for N is a spanning tree for N of least cost, where the cost of a tree is the sum of the distances of its edges. Minimum spanning trees are not necessarily unique. There exist connected graphs with distance-bearing edges having more than one spanning tree of minimum cost.

There is a remarkably simple process† for computing a minimum spanning tree. To start with, we pick any node n in the network. Then among all the edges that connect n to other nodes, we pick some edge e of shortest distance, connecting n to some node n', and we add e and n' to the partial spanning tree being constructed. Then, at each stage, we choose a new edge e of shortest distance connecting some node n already selected to some node n' not yet selected, and we add e and n' to the partial spanning tree being constructed. We repeat this process until no more nodes can be added. A minimum-cost spanning tree results.

For example, consider the cities on the map given in Fig. 3.48. Suppose that the South Numpshire Telephone Company installs a multidrop line (a common telephone circuit) to all the offices of a customer's firm in each of the cities in Fig. 3.48, and that it charges for the multidrop line on the basis of the minimum-cost spanning tree for the map in Fig. 3.48, in which the distances between cities are marked on the edges connecting them.

To find the minimum-cost spanning tree, we proceed as follows:

1. Pick some city to start with, say, Kincaid.

2. Now the shortest edge connecting Kincaid to some other city is the edge of distance 10 connecting Kincaid to Blentham, so we mark Kincaid, Blentham, and the edge connecting them as selected.

3. Now the shortest edge connecting either Kincaid or Blentham to some other city is the edge of length 12 connecting Kincaid to Durfee, so we mark as selected both Durfee and the edge connecting Kincaid and Durfee.

---

† Sometimes called Prim's Algorithm.

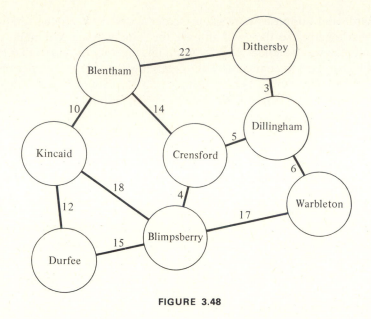

FIGURE 3.48

4. Next, the shortest edge connecting Durfee, Kincaid, or Blentham to some city not marked as selected is the edge from Blentham to Crensford, so we mark as selected both Crensford and the edge connecting it to Blentham.

5. Continuing in this fashion, we add the edges from Crensford to Blimpsberry and Dillingham, and finally the edges from Dillingham to Dithersby and Warbleton.

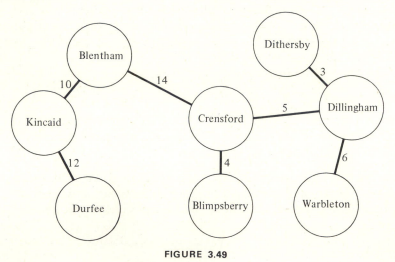

FIGURE 3.49

The resulting spanning tree is shown in Fig. 3.49 and is of cost 54. The reader can verify that starting with any city on the map and adding cities not yet selected via the shortest-distance edges to cities already selected will result in finding a minimum spanning tree.

To prove that the process P outlined above, in fact, succeeds in finding a minimal spanning tree, we proceed as follows. Let the process P of starting at an arbitrary node v_1 and repeatedly adding the shortest edge that connects some new node not previously selected to some node previously selected define an ordering on the nodes according to the order in which they are added: $v_1, v_2, \ldots, v_n$. Let edge e_i be defined as the edge connecting (v_i, v_{i+1}) in this process. Suppose now that there is some connected graph $G = (V, E)$, where V is a set of n vertices, and some assignment of costs to its edges $c(e)$ for e in E, such that process P fails to find a minimum-cost spanning tree. If $v_1, v_2, \ldots, v_n$ is the ordering in which P adds vertices v_i, then let e_j $(1 \leq j < n)$ be the lowest-numbered edge added by P such that the vertices $(v_1, \ldots, v_{j+1})$ and edges $(e_1, \ldots, e_j)$ chosen so far cannot be extended to a minimum-cost spanning tree for G. Thus, $V_1 = (v_1, \ldots, v_j)$ and $(e_1, \ldots, e_{j-1})$ can be extended to a minimum-cost spanning tree, say T.

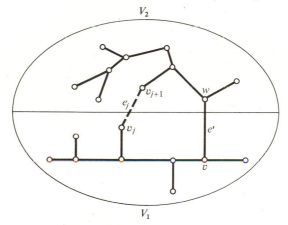

Let $V_2 = (v_{j+1}, \ldots, v_n)$. Then there exists a path p in T connecting vertex v_j to vertex v_{j+1} (since a spanning tree connects any two distinct vertices). For some edge $e' = (v, w)$ in this path p, we have $v \in V_1$ and $w \in V_2$, since path p starts at vertex $v_j \in V_1$ and ends at vertex $v_{j+1} \in V_2$. Suppose now that the cost of edge e' is greater than the cost of edge e_j, $c(e') > c(e_j)$. Then, in spanning tree T, suppose we add edge e_j (which connects vertices v_j and v_{j+1} and forms exactly one cycle, by Theorem 3.1), and suppose further that we then delete edge e' (this disconnects the cycle just formed, but leaves a free tree, which connects V, by Theorem 3.1). Let this new tree be called T'. Then T' is a spanning tree of cost less than the cost of spanning tree T, contradicting the minimality of T. Hence, edge e' could not have been of greater cost than edge e_j (so we have established $c(e_j) \geq c(e')$). But process

P chose edge e_j to be a least-cost edge connecting vertices in V_1 to vertices in V_2, so we must have had $c(e_j) \leq c(e')$, and this, together with the fact that $c(e_j) \geq c(e')$ implies that $c(e_j) = c(e')$. Thus, spanning tree T' is of the same minimal cost as spanning tree T. But T' contains the edge e_j, assumed to be the lowest-numbered edge preventing the subgraph $(V_1, \{e_1, \ldots, e_{j-1}\})$ from being extended to a minimum-cost spanning tree. Because the assumption that there exists such an e_j leads to a contradiction, no such e_j can exist. This proves that process P always finds a minimum-cost spanning tree.

This spanning-tree construction process is interesting because, among other things, it is an example in which a sequence of locally opportunistic choices succeeds in finding a global optimum. Such algorithms are called *greedy algorithms*.

But aside from spanning trees being important tree data structures in themselves (which will find application in Chapters 5 and 6), our main interest in minimal-spanning-tree construction is motivated by the fact that the construction algorithm itself can use interesting tree data structures.

The use of heaps might come in handy if, at each stage, we have a heap that contains all edges connecting a vertex in V_1 (the vertices selected so far) to the vertices in V_2 (the vertices remaining to be chosen), with the heap ordered on edge length. Then it is a simple matter to choose the edge e_j of least cost connecting a vertex in V_1 to one in V_2. After making this choice, we must set $V_1 \leftarrow V_1 \cup \{v_{j+1}\}$ and $V_2 \leftarrow V_2 - \{v_{j+1}\}$, and update the heap to contain only edges from the new V_1 to the new V_2. (This involves deleting edges originating in the old V_1 and terminating on v_{j+1} while adding edges originating at v_{j+1} and terminating in the new V_2.) Since only the edges touching v_{j+1} are involved at each stage, and since these edges can be kept on an edge list attached to v_{j+1}, the algorithm need consider each edge in the original graph $G = (V, E)$ only once, and for each edge its processing cost for heap insertion and deletion is at most $2 \log |E|$, making the entire cost of the algorithm $O(|E| \log |E|)$.

Actually, though, there is a more efficient way to build the minimum-cost spanning tree using yet another form of treelike data structures to keep track of unions of subsets of a partition on the vertices. This is a variation of Kruskal's algorithm, as given by Aho, Hopcroft, and Ullman [1974], and is presented as Algorithm 3.12 below.

Algorithm 3.12 actually constructs a spanning forest at intermediate stages of the construction of the minimal spanning tree. A spanning forest is a set of disjoint free trees that cover all the vertices in G. Arguments similar to the one given above prove that the choice of the least-cost edge at each stage correctly constructs the minimal spanning tree at termination.

Algorithm 3.12 *Kruskal's minimum-spanning-tree algorithm.*

Let $G = (V, E)$ be a connected, undirected graph, with a cost function $c(e)$ defined on edges in E. Let Part be a partition on the vertex set V into a collection S_1, S_2, ..., S_k of disjoint, nonempty subsets of vertices. The partition Part is manipulated by operations in the algorithm and keeps getting coarser and coarser until it finally equals V.

1. [Initialize.] (Initialize the partition Part by putting each vertex in V into a separate subset of the partition.) *For each vertex $v \in V$ do* add $\{v\}$ to Part. Also, let T (the spanning tree constructed so far) be initialized to the empty set, $T \leftarrow \varnothing$. Now construct a priority queue Q from all edges $e \in E$ with least cost $c(e)$ having highest priority.

2. [Choose next edge.] If $|\text{Part}| = 1$, the algorithm terminates. Otherwise, remove from Q an edge (v, w) of lowest cost. If now, v and w are in different subsets S_i and S_j of the partition, then merge S_i and S_j into a single subset in Part, and add (v, w) to T.

3. [Return for more.] Go back to step 2.

We see that the idea behind this algorithm is to enumerate the edges of E in order of increasing cost. As each edge (v, w) is considered in sequence, if v and w are already in the same subset of the partition Part on the vertices, the edge is ignored, but if v and w are in distinct subsets of the partition, we merge the two subsets, and add the edge (v, w) to the final spanning tree T. At any given stage in the algorithm, Part contains disjoint subsets of vertices, and each subset corresponds to a spanning tree of the spanning forest for the whole graph.

While we already know how to represent the priority queue Q in Algorithm 3.12 efficiently, how can we efficiently represent the union of disjoint sets required to manipulate the vertex partition? One interesting way to do this is given in the following section.

3.7.2.1 *Efficient union of disjoint sets.* We illustrate the union problem with a set of thirteen elements numbered 1 through 13. Suppose we partition this set into pairwise disjoint, nonempty subsets S_i as follows:

$$S_1 = \{1, 5, 7, 8, 10\},$$

$$S_2 = \{2, 11, 12, 13\},$$

$$S_3 = \{3, 4, 9\},$$

$$S_4 = \{6\}.$$

We represent each set by a tree

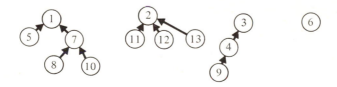

in which each node represents an element of that set. Each node points to its parent, and the root points to 0. To determine whether two elements v and w belong to the same or different sets, we follow the pointers upwards from the respective nodes ⓥ and ⓦ until reaching the roots of their respective trees Root(v) and Root(w). If now, Root(v) = Root(w), then v and w are in the same subset of the partition. Otherwise, they are in disjoint subsets.

To construct the union $S_i \cup S_j$ of two subsets, all we have to do is set the root of one to point to the root of the other (instead of to 0). But which one shall we choose to make into a subtree of the other? It might be best to avoid depth and encourage breadth, in order to minimize the time it takes to find Root(x) from node x. One thing we could try is a *weighting rule* of the form: If $|S_i| > |S_j|$, then make Root(S_i) the parent of Root(S_j); otherwise make Root(S_j) the parent of Root(S_i).

It can be shown that starting with subsets containing single nodes, if we repeatedly perform the union operation $S_i \cup S_j$ using the weighting rule, then a tree of n nodes has maximum level $\lfloor \lg n \rfloor + 1$.

In an application such as Kruskal's algorithm, where we alternately perform unions $S_i \cup S_j$ and find roots Root(v) and Root(w), a further improvement can be made. The idea is to apply a *path compression* transformation when we perform Root(x) in which, after locating Root(x) by traversing an upward path p from x to Root(x), we make a second pass and traverse p again, setting the parent of every node on path p except the root to Root(x). This path compression idea is made more precise as follows:

Subroutine Root(x).

1. [Initialize.] Set Root ← x.
2. [Locate root.] **While** Parent of (Root) > 0 **do** Root ← Parent of (Root).
3. [Compress path.] **While** $x \neq$ Root **do** steps (a), (b), and (c):
    a) Set temp ← Parent of (x)
    b) Set Parent of (x) ← Root
    c) Set x ← temp.

Now it takes a little longer to find Root(x) (because of the time for compression), but after executing Root(x), the tree containing x is made shallower, on the average.

A rather remarkable result, due to Tarjan, can be proved about the total time taken by interspersed sequences of Root(x) and union instructions of the form $S_i \cup S_j$. It can be shown that, while it takes more time to process k of these instructions than time proportional to k, nevertheless, if there are more Root(x) instructions in the sequence than unions, then the total time required is not more than proportional to the number of Root(x) instructions times a very slowly growing function, which, although not quite constant, hardly grows at all. This slowly growing function is obtained by taking a sort of inverse of a very rapidly growing function, Ackermann's function.

As a consequence of these developments, if we use these fast root-finding and set-union techniques to implement the operations in step 2 of Kruskal's algorithm (Algorithm 3.12), and we use heaps to implement the priority queue Q in Algorithm 3.12, we can analyze the overall running time as follows. Initialization requires building the heap Q from $|E|$ edges, which takes time $O(|E|)$, and constructing the initial partition, which takes $O(|V|)$. Then, in step 2, we remove the edge of lowest cost from Q, which takes $O(\log |E|)$, we do $2|E|$ root-finding operations (two for each edge (v, w) in E), and we do $|T| - 1$ set-union operations. Following Aho, Hopcroft, and Ullman ([1974], pp. 129ff), it can be shown that the interspersed sequence of root and union operations takes $O(|E|G(|E|))$, where $G(n)$ is an almost-not-growing function such that $G(n) \leq 5$ for all $n \leq 2^{65536}$ (that is, for all "practical" values of n). Step 2 of Algorithm 3.12 may terminate before all $|E|$ edges are examined; so, supposing that $d \leq |E|$ such edges are examined up to termination, the time to process the edges is $O(d \log |E|)$, and the total running time of the algorithm is at most $O(|E| \log |E|)$.

3.7.3 Binary search trees

Suppose we are given n distinct keys $K_1, K_2, \ldots, K_n$, in ascending order, and suppose we are given a binary tree T of n nodes. Define N_i to be the ith node visited if we traverse T in symmetric order. Then, if we store key K_i in node N_i, the resulting tree has the following property:

Binary search tree property. At each node N_i having key K_i, all keys in nodes in the left subtree of node N_i are less than K_i, and all keys K in the right subtree of node N_i are greater than K_i.

A binary tree with this property is called a *binary search tree.* Given a key K, the process of searching for K in such a tree T is straightforward. If K matches the key in the root of T, the search terminates successfully. Otherwise, if K is less than the key at the root of T, search continues in the left subtree of T; whereas if K is greater than the key in the root of T, search continues in the right subtree of T. Figure 3.50 illustrates a binary search tree containing the names of the eleven brightest stars in the sky. These stars, in order of apparent magnitude, are listed in Fig. 3.51.

To search for the star Rigel in the binary search tree of Fig. 3.50 we begin by comparing Rigel to the star Sirius whose name is stored at the root of the tree. Since Rigel comes before Sirius in alphabetic order, we continue the search in the left subtree of the node containing Sirius. Now the name Rigel is compared to Canopus, and it is discovered that Rigel comes after Canopus in alphabetical order, so the search continues in the right subtree of the node containing Canopus. Rigel is then compared to Capella and found to be greater, so the search continues in the right subtree of the node for Capella. It is then discovered that Rigel matches the name in the root of the right subtree of Capella, so the search terminates successfully.

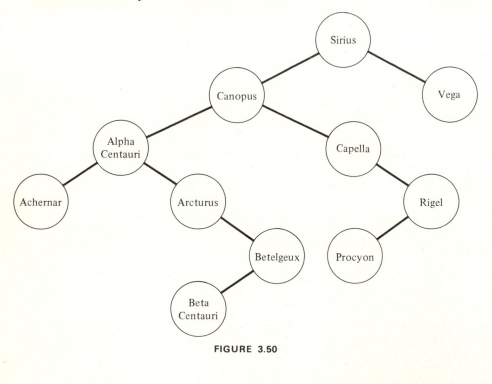

FIGURE 3.50

1.   Sirius
2.   Canopus
3.   Alpha Centauri
4.   Arcturus
5.   Vega
6.   Capella
7.   Rigel
8.   Procyon
9.   Achernar
10. Betelgeux
11. Beta Centauri

FIGURE 3.51

If we search for the star Antares in the tree of Fig. 3.50, we conclude that Antares is not present, since the search path traced out by the decisions Antares < Sirius, Antares < Canopus, Antares > Alpha Centauri, and Antares < Arcturus leads us to the empty left subtree of Arcturus. If we insert a new node for Antares as the left subtree of Arcturus, we obtain a new binary search tree of twelve nodes. In fact, the binary search tree of Fig. 3.50 was built up in this fashion by repeated insertion of the stars in Fig. 3.51, considered in order of apparent magnitude. Thus, Sirius was considered first and placed at the root of the tree. Canopus was considered second and inserted as the left subtree of Sirius, Alpha Centauri was considered next and inserted as the left subtree of Canopus, followed by Arcturus inserted as the right subtree of Alpha Centauri, and Vega inserted as the right subtree of Sirius, and so on.

How efficient is the search process in a binary search tree? Suppose that we consider a sequence of searches for names of stars in Fig. 3.50, in which the names of stars are chosen equally often. The work needed to find a given star could be measured by noting the number of comparisons needed to locate it in the binary search tree. For the name K, this is just the level of K in the tree, namely, $1 +$ the length of the path from the root to the node containing key K. Let us define *internal path length* of a binary tree as the sum of the lengths of the paths from the root to each of the nodes. For the tree of Fig. 3.50, for instance, the internal path length is

$$28 = (0 + 1 + 1 + 2 + 2 + 3 + 3 + 3 + 4 + 4 + 5).$$

If search for each of the keys K in a binary search tree of n nodes is equally likely and if I is the internal path length of the tree, then the number of comparisons required by an average search is $(I + n)/n$. Thus, the average number of comparisons in a search of the tree of Fig. 3.50 is $(28 + 11)/11 = 3.55$.

For unsuccessful searches, it turns out to be convenient to examine properties of *extended binary trees*, in which the empty subtrees are indicated by small square boxes ☐. Figure 3.52 shows an extended binary search tree corresponding to the search tree of Fig. 3.50.

We can now define the *external path length* of a binary tree to be the sum of the lengths of the paths from the root to each of the square boxes in the extended binary tree having boxes as leaves and circular internal nodes. The external path length of the tree of Fig. 3.52 is

$$50 = (4 + 4 + 4 + 6 + 6 + 5 + 3 + 5 + 5 + 4 + 2 + 2).$$

If a binary tree has n nodes and has external path length E, then an average unsuccessful search (with each of the $n + 1$ boxes† an equally likely target) re-

---

† Recall from Eq. (1) of Section 3.3.1 that there are $n + 1$ leaves in a full binary tree with n internal nodes.

quires $E/(n + 1)$ comparisons. Hence, an average unsuccessful search of the tree in Fig. 3.52 requires $50/12 = 4.17$ comparisons.

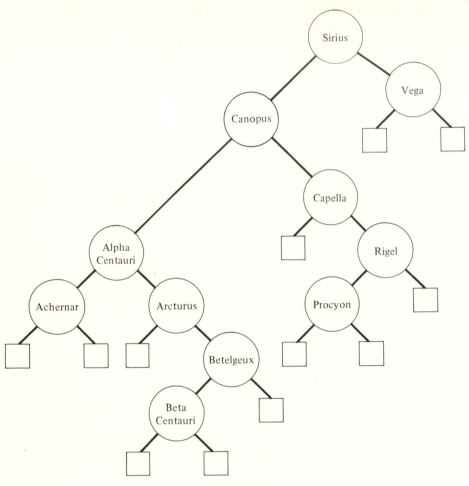

FIGURE 3.52

It turns out that the external and internal path lengths of a binary tree are related in an interesting and useful way. In particular, in a tree with n internal (circular) nodes and $n + 1$ external (square) nodes, we have

$$E = I + 2n. \qquad (13)$$

To prove this, consider replacing an external node ☐ at distance k from the root by an internal node with two new external nodes as children . Then I is increased by k, and E is decreased by k but increased by $2(k + 1)$. Then after the replacement, we have

$$(E - k + 2(k + 1)) - (I + k) = E - I + 2.$$

But if $E = I + 2n$ held true before the replacement, then the value of $E - I$ was $2n$, so

$$(E - I) + 2 = 2n + 2 = 2(n + 1).$$

Since there are $n + 1$ internal nodes in the tree after the replacement, (13) holds for a tree of $(n + 1)$ internal nodes if it held previously for a tree of n internal nodes. Note also that (13) holds true for the tree $\triangle$. Now, since any extended binary tree can be built up via a sequence of replacements of the sort mentioned, starting with the tree $\triangle$, (13) holds for all extended binary trees.

Now we can ask what are the shapes of binary trees having minimum and maximum average search times, assuming the search keys are chosen with equal likelihood. The answers can be obtained by finding the shapes that minimize (or maximize) either the internal or external path length (since these latter differ by a constant).

It can be shown that the shape a tree must take to minimize the internal path length is one in which all leaves occur on at most two adjacent levels (see Knuth [1973a], p. 400). Thus, complete trees minimize average search times for equally likely keys. It can also be seen that the degenerate trees with linear structure (having exactly one internal node on each level) maximize the internal path length. Trees such as those in Fig. 3.53 are examples of such degenerate cases.

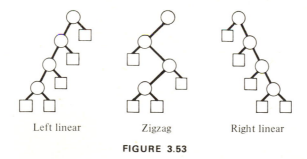

Left linear   Zigzag   Right linear

FIGURE 3.53

In a minimal search tree, with leaves on at most two adjacent levels, the internal path length takes the form

$$0 + 1 + 1 + 2 + 2 + 2 + 2 + 3 + \cdots,$$

since one node is at the root, two nodes are at depth 1, four nodes are at depth 2, and so on. As shown in Knuth ([1973a], p. 400), this sum takes the form $\sum_{1 \le i \le n} \lfloor \lg i \rfloor$. From the equation in Exercise 3.35 this sum can be seen to be essentially $n \lg n$. Hence, an average successful search requires about $\lg n + 1$ comparisons, in the best case.

In the worst case, the internal path length takes the form

$$0 + 1 + 2 + \cdots + (n - 1) = \frac{(n - 1)n}{2},$$

so an average search takes $(I + n)/n$ or $(n - 1)/2 + 1 = (n + 1)/2$ comparisons.

Now suppose that we build up binary search trees by the insertion method used to create Fig. 3.50 from the keys in Fig. 3.51. We might consider taking n keys $K_1, K_2, \ldots, K_n$ and building up search trees considering each possible permutation of the n keys as equally likely. What would it cost to perform an average search in the average such tree? Rather remarkably, it can be shown that only about $1.386 \lg n$ comparisons are required. In other words, the average tree is only about 38.6 percent worse than the best possible tree, in the number of comparisons required for average search. This means that if keys are inserted in a tree in random order, well-balanced trees are rather common, and degenerate trees rare. Knuth ([1973b], p. 427) presents a beautiful proof of this fact, as follows: Assuming each of the $n!$ orderings of n keys to be equally likely as a sequence of insertions for building up search trees, let C_n be the average number of comparisons for a successful search, and let C'_n be the average number of comparisons for an unsuccessful search. Since the number of comparisons needed to find a key is just one more than the number required when that key was inserted, we have $C_n = (\sum_{0 \le i \le n-1} (C'_i + 1))/n$, so

$$C_n = 1 + \frac{C'_0 + C'_1 + \cdots + C'_{n-1}}{n}. \tag{14}$$

However, the relation $E = I + 2n$ between external and internal path length, together with $C_n = (I + n)/n$ and $C'_n = E/(n + 1)$, implies

$$C_n = \left(1 + \frac{1}{n}\right) C'_n - 1. \tag{15}$$

Combining (14) and (15), we get a recurrence relation

$$(n + 1)C'_n = 2n + C'_0 + C'_1 + \cdots + C'_{n-1}, \tag{16}$$

which can be solved as follows. First, write out (16) with n replaced by $(n - 1)$, getting

$$nC'_{n-1} = 2(n - 1) + C'_0 + C'_1 + \cdots + C'_{n-2}.$$

Then subtract this from (16) to get

$$(n + 1)C'_n - nC'_{n-1} = 2 + C'_{n-1},$$

whence

$$C'_n = C'_{n-1} + \frac{2}{n+1}.$$ (17)

Now, since $C'_1 = 1$, we can expand (17), getting

$$C'_n = 1 + \frac{2}{3} + \frac{2}{4} + \cdots + \frac{2}{n+1}.$$ (18)

But (18) is very close to twice H_{n+1}. In fact, we see that

$$C'_n = 2H_{n+1} - 2.$$ (19)

We can combine (19) with (15) and simplify, to get

$$C_n = 2\left(1 + \frac{1}{n}\right) H_n - 3.$$ (20)

Now, recalling (from Chapter 1, Eq. (5)) that $H_n = \ln n + \gamma + O(1/n)$, we see that $C_n \approx 2 \ln n \approx 1.386 \lg n$.

Now we know what to expect in the worst case, the best case, and the average case, for binary tree searching, with equally likely keys. The case where the keys are not equally likely is considered in the following section.

3.7.3.1 *Static binary search trees.* In some applications, a binary search tree can be set up in advance, and can be repeatedly searched during the course of the application with no worry that the tree will change shape through insertions of new nodes or through deletions. Such a binary search tree is called a *static* tree, whereas a tree that changes shape during the application, through insertions and deletions, is called a *dynamic* binary search tree. An example of a static binary search tree is one used to provide a searching index for the operation codes of an assembler. Since the op-codes remain fixed through all assemblies, the binary search tree is static.

We have already seen that if searching for each of the operation codes is equally likely, then a complete binary tree minimizes the average search time. But how can we minimize search time if the search keys are used with some nonuniform distribution? Given a distribution of frequencies of use for the keys, can we find an *optimum binary search tree*—one that minimizes expected search times?

This problem has been formulated and solved by Knuth (see Knuth [1971b]) in the following way. Suppose we are given a set of n search keys $K_1, K_2, \ldots, K_n$ in ascending order, and suppose further that the probability of using key K_i in a successful search is α_i, while the probability of using some key K between K_i and K_{i+1} in an unsuccessful search is β_i. (Here, there are two special end cases: β_0 is the probability that $K < K_1$ is used, and β_n is the probability that $K > K_n$ is used.)

All of these probabilities add up to 1, so that

$$1 = \beta_0 + \alpha_1 + \beta_1 + \alpha_2 + \beta_2 + \cdots + \alpha_n + \beta_n.$$

In a binary search tree of n nodes, we know that the keys K_i are assigned to the internal nodes in symmetric order, and if we extend such a tree to contain external nodes numbered ⓪ to Ⓝ in left-to-right order, then α_i is the probability of reaching internal node Ⓚ, and β_i is the probability of reaching Ⓘ. For a tree with $n = 4$, Fig. 3.54 illustrates how probabilities α_i and β_i are associated with internal and external nodes.

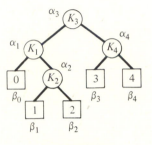

FIGURE 3.54

Now we can define a weighted cost function that measures the expected number of comparisons needed for an average search, as follows:

$$\text{Average cost} = \sum_{1 \leq i \leq n} \alpha_i (\text{level of } Ⓚ) + \sum_{0 \leq i \leq n} \beta_i ((\text{level of } Ⓘ) - 1).$$

We define the optimum binary search tree as one that minimizes this average cost function among all possible binary search trees of n nodes with keys K_i. We can see that, if T is an optimum binary search tree on n keys, then any subtree of T must be an optimal subtree over the keys it contains. Otherwise, we could replace the nonoptimal subtree with an optimal one, leading to an improvement in the average cost of the whole tree.

This consideration leads to a bottom-up algorithm for computing the optimal solution. We compute larger and larger optimal subtrees, and we save the solutions. At each stage, we use optimal subtrees of smaller size to find the optimal trees of a given size, for sizes $1, 2, 3, \ldots, n$, considered in sequence. This process can be formulated precisely, and can be shown to take $O(n^3)$ time, and $O(n^2)$ cells of memory. However, Knuth [1971b] found an improvement that reduces the overall time to $O(n^2)$. This is achieved by noting that it is not necessary to try all the trees of a given size to find the optimum; rather, the optimum will be found in a certain subset with weights lying in a certain range that isn't "too far out of balance." Details are given in Knuth [1971b] and in Knuth ([1973b], p. 436).

In the case that all $\alpha_i = 0$ (that is, we have only unsuccessful searches), Hu and Tucker [1971] show how to compute the optimum tree in time $O(n \log n)$ and space $O(n)$.

Since Knuth's method uses time proportional to n^2, it isn't practical to find optimal subtrees for very large n. For example, it would be impossible to use the algorithm to compute the optimum binary tree to use for searching a file with, say, a million keys, if we expect to use a reasonable amount of computing time finding the optimal solution. However, as we shall see in later chapters, we wouldn't want to use binary tree techniques for searching large files anyway.

Nonetheless, the difficulty of computing the optimum has led to a search for heuristic methods for inserting nodes to attempt rapid construction of binary trees that have near-optimal search times, assuming unequal frequencies for the search keys. This can result in trees that are within two to three percent of the optimum, in terms of average search times. These approaches are reported on in Knuth [1973b], Nievergelt [1974], and Bruno and Coffman [1971]. (See also Sheil [1978] for an interesting approach to this problem.)

3.7.3.2 *Dynamic binary search trees.* Suppose now that a binary search tree is being used under conditions involving insertions and deletions of keys, as well as searches. Over time, the shape of the tree might change. Suppose we assume that each key K in the tree is equally likely to be used in a search. We know that the average search time can be minimized by keeping the tree completely balanced (so its leaves appear on at most two adjacent levels). Perhaps after each insertion or deletion, we could make some local changes to keep the tree completely balanced. Unfortunately, this idea doesn't work very well. For instance, if we insert a node ① into the tree in Fig. 3.55(a), and then attempt to rebalance it completely, we obtain the tree of Fig. 3.55(b), in which every node of the former tree has been moved. This shows that the attempt to rebalance completely after each insertion cannot be managed locally, but may instead lead to global changes of sweeping proportions.

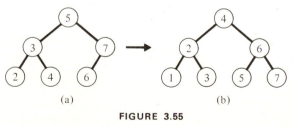

(a)   (b)

FIGURE 3.55

Martin and Ness [1972] have devised an algorithm for rebalancing the linked representation of binary search trees that works in linear time using two push-down stacks, and that rebalances a binary tree in place. However, using this algorithm after every insertion and deletion is very time-consuming, since it involves looking at every node in the tree. Perhaps we could content ourselves with rebalancing only every so often, such as when some performance measure degrades below some limit. We know that random insertions seldom tend to produce degenerate expensive cases and, after rebalancing, it may take, on the average, a considerable number of insertions and deletions before performance can be expected to degrade very far.

Another idea for maintaining good search times in dynamic binary search trees is to give up the idea of maintaining complete balance, and to compromise by keeping the tree "almost balanced." This way, it may be possible to achieve good search times, while not paying very much during insertion and deletion to maintain the almost-balanced condition. This idea lies behind a range of techniques such as *weight-balanced*, *height-balanced*, and *bounded-balance* binary trees. We will consider only the height-balanced trees in this section. The interested reader can consult Nievergelt [1974] for a survey and references to the other techniques.

Height-balanced trees. We define the *height* of a binary tree to be the length of the longest path from the root to some leaf. A binary search tree T is said to be a *height-balanced k-tree*, or *HB[k]-tree*, for short, if T and each of its subtrees have the $HB[k]$ property. A tree has the $HB[k]$ property if the respective heights of the left and right subtrees of the root differ by at most k. An $HB[1]$ tree is called an *AVL tree*, after the two Russian mathematicians Adel'son-Vel'skii and Landis, who first defined them. We will use AVL trees in our examples, but the results can be generalized from $HB[1]$ to $HB[k]$.

Figure 3.56 illustrates an AVL tree, whereas Fig. 3.57 illustrates a tree that is not an AVL tree because the right subtree of the root fails to have the $HB[1]$ property.

FIGURE 3.56   FIGURE 3.57

Now let us consider how many comparisons it takes to perform binary search in an AVL tree. The minimum number of comparisons in an extended binary tree of n internal nodes occurs in a tree balanced so that all leaves (i.e., external nodes) appear on at most two levels, as we have seen before. An extended binary tree of height h has at most 2^h external nodes (in the case that all external nodes appear at the same bottommost level in a complete tree). Therefore, the number of internal nodes n is bounded above by $n \le 2^h - 1$ (since the number of internal nodes is one less than the number of leaves or, alternatively, since the number of internal nodes is a sum of the form $1 + 2 + 4 + \cdots + 2^{h-1}$, which is a geometric series with sum $2^h - 1$). Because $n \le 2^h - 1$ implies that $h \ge \lceil \lg (n + 1) \rceil$, we know that the height h (and therefore the maximum number of comparisons in a search of a completely balanced extended tree) is bounded below by $\lceil \lg (n + 1) \rceil$. But what about the worst case? How deep, at its very deepest, can an $HB[1]$ tree get? To answer this question, we can take n internal nodes and attempt to arrange them to produce the AVL tree of greatest depth. The idea is, say, systematically to favor the right subtree by using the least possible number of nodes to create the left subtree of height h, and the least possible number to produce a right subtree of height $h + 1$. Since the $HB[1]$ property must hold for all subtrees of an AVL tree, similar conditions must hold recursively for the left and right subtrees. Figure 3.58 illustrates a sequence of such right-leaning AVL trees of deepest extent for n internal nodes.

  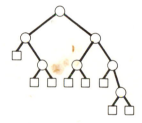

FIGURE 3.58

TABLE 3.2

Height	Number of nodes in left subtree	Number of nodes in right subtree	Number of nodes in whole tree
0	0	0	1
1	0	1	2
2	1	2	4
3	2	4	7
4	4	7	12

If we now make a table of the number of internal nodes in the left and right subtrees of the trees in Fig. 3.58, we get the results in Table 3.2. It is easy to see that there is a recurrence relation that characterizes the numbers in each of the columns of this table, namely:

$$G_h = 1 + G_{h-1} + G_{h-2},\tag{21}$$

where, say, $G_0 = 0$ and $G_1 = 1$. It is also easy to see why this must be so—each tree of height h is formed by taking a tree of height $h - 1$ on its right (containing G_{h-1} nodes), a tree of height $h - 2$ on its left (containing G_{h-2} nodes), and a new root (containing 1 node).

The recurrence (21) seems to be a close relative of the recurrence relation for the Fibonacci sequence $F_n = F_{n-1} + F_{n-2}$. In fact, comparing the Fibonacci sequence

$$0, 1, 1, 2, 3, 5, 8, 13$$

to the numbers in the columns of Table 3.2 suggests that G_h is just one less than some corresponding Fibonacci number, $G_h = F_{h+2} - 1$. In fact, this can be proved easily by induction. For this reason, the trees of Fig. 3.58 are called *Fibonacci trees*. Since these Fibonacci trees have the fewest nodes among all possible AVL trees of height h, we know that the number of internal nodes in any AVL tree of height h obeys the relation $n \geq G_h$; so

$$n \geq F_{h+2} - 1.\tag{22}$$

But the kth Fibonacci number F_k is bounded below by a power of the inverse of the *golden ratio* $\phi = (1 + \sqrt{5})/2$. For example, we know that $F_k \geq \phi^{k-2}$ (Knuth [1973a], p. 18, Ex. 4) and, more precisely, $F_k > \phi^k/\sqrt{5} - 1$ (Knuth [1973a], p. 82). Hence, we can conclude

$$n > \phi^{h+2}/\sqrt{5} - 2.$$

From this,

$$\log_\phi (n + 2) > \log_\phi (\phi^{h+2}/\sqrt{5}) = (h + 2) - \log_\phi \sqrt{5}.$$

So $h < \log_\phi (n + 2) + \log_\phi \sqrt{5} - 2$. Now, using the fact that $\phi = 1.618034$ and applying a logarithm base conversion $\log_\phi x = (\lg x/\lg \phi)$, we get:

$$h < 1.4404 \lg (n + 2) - 0.328.\tag{23}$$

Thus, an AVL tree can have search processes that never involve more than 45 percent more comparisons than the optimum number.

Empirical tests by Knuth (see Knuth [1973b], p. 460) support the conjecture that the average search in AVL trees takes about $\lg n + c$ comparisons for some small constant c ($c = 0.25$ for large n).

Putting these results together, we have Table 3.3 for AVL trees. Thus, if we agree to give up complete balance in favor of being almost balanced, we find that AVL trees must pay 45 percent more comparisons in the worst case, and hardly anything in the average case. But now, by paying this price, can we make the cost of insertion much cheaper than insertion followed by complete rebalancing?

TABLE 3.3

Comparisons used in a search	Completely balanced tree of n nodes	AVL tree of n nodes
Worst possible number	$\lg (n + 1)$	$1.44 \lg (n + 2)$
Average number	$\lg (n + 1) - 2$	$\lg n + 0.25$†

† Based on empirical studies.

When we insert a new node into an AVL tree, some external node is replaced by a new internal node, and the height of one of the subtrees of the immediate parent of the new node is increased by one. This may or may not increase the heights of the subtrees of the grandparents and ancestors of the newly inserted node (back along the trace path of the insertion from the root down to the point of insertion), depending on whether or not, for a given ancestor on the trace path, the $HB[1]$ property is lost as a result of the insertion. In Fibonacci trees, for instance, such as those given in Fig. 3.58, insertion of a new rightmost node increases the height of the right subtree of every ancestor on the trace path by one, whereas insertion of a new leftmost node changes at most only the height of the left subtree of its immediate parent.

When insertion of a new node thus causes an AVL tree to lose the $HB[1]$ property at one or more nodes, the $HB[1]$ property can be restored by applying exactly one of the four *rotations* in Fig. 3.59.

To see how these rotations can be used to maintain the $HB[1]$ property, consider the following example. Suppose we insert the keys consisting of the names of the brightest stars in the order given in Fig. 3.51 into a binary search tree, and that we apply rotations as required to maintain the AVL property at all times. The first node is Sirius.

We can add the next node, Canopus, without destroying the AVL property:

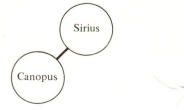

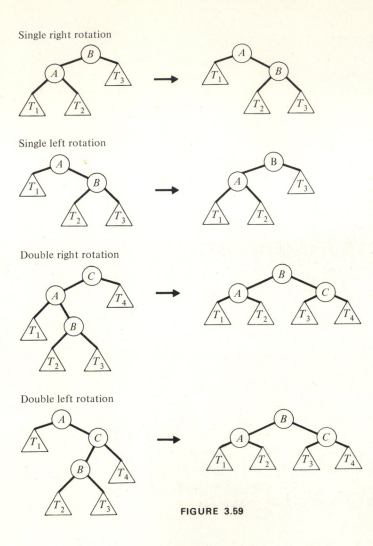

Single right rotation

Single left rotation

Double right rotation

Double left rotation

FIGURE 3.59

But adding the next node, Alpha Centauri, creates an imbalanced tree:

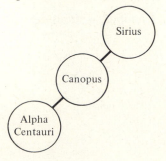

This imbalance must be removed by applying a single right rotation to yield:

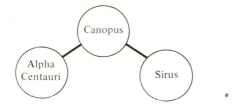

Now the next four stars in sequence: Arcturus, Vega, Capella, and Rigel, can be inserted without requiring any rotations to yield:

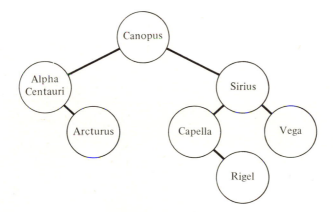

However, when we try to add Procyon, the subtree rooted at Capella becomes imbalanced and requires a double left rotation to restore the AVL property.

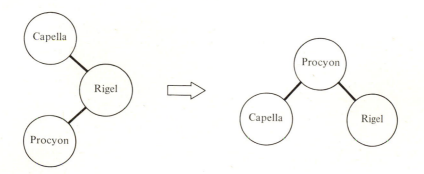

The next two stars, Achernar and Betelgeux, can be added without requiring rotations, to yield:

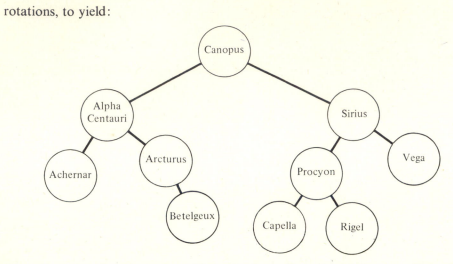

Now, however, the attempt to add the final star, Beta Centauri, causes formation of an imbalanced subtree,

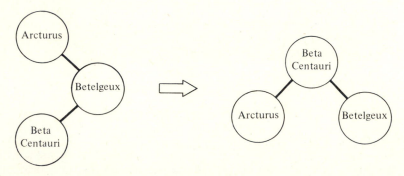

whose imbalance must be removed by application of another double rotation. The final AVL tree is shown in Fig. 3.60.

Assuming that search keys are equally likely, the average successful search in this tree requires

$$\text{Average} = \frac{11 + (0 + 1 + 1 + 2 + 2 + 2 + 2 + 3 + 3 + 3 + 3)}{11}$$

$$= \frac{11 + 22}{11} = 3.0 \text{ comparisons.}$$

This is an improvement over the random-insertion tree of Fig. 3.50 (for the same insertion order, but with no rebalancing), since the average number of comparisons required to search the tree of Fig. 3.50 is 3.55.

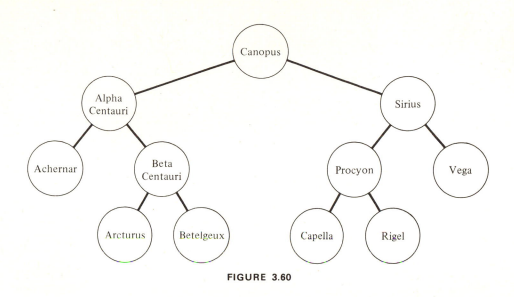

FIGURE 3.60

There is a close analogy of single and double rotations to applications of the associative law to algebraic formulas, if we represent algebraic formulas as binary trees such as that of Fig. 3.33. In particular, writing the trees of Figure 3.59 as parenthesized infix formula transformations gives:

Single right rotation

$$((T_1 \, \textcircled{A} \, T_2) \, \textcircled{B} \, T_3) \Rightarrow (T_1 \, \textcircled{A} \, (T_2 \, \textcircled{B} \, T_3))$$

Single left rotation

$$(T_1 \, \textcircled{A} \, (T_2 \, \textcircled{B} \, T_3)) \Rightarrow ((T_1 \, \textcircled{A} \, T_2) \, \textcircled{B} \, T_3)$$

Double right rotation

$$((T_1 \, \textcircled{A} \, (T_2 \, \textcircled{B} \, T_3)) \, \textcircled{C} \, T_4) \Rightarrow ((T_1 \, \textcircled{A} \, T_2) \, \textcircled{B} \, (T_3 \, \textcircled{C} \, T_4))$$

Double left rotation

$$(T_1 \, \textcircled{A} \, ((T_2 \, \textcircled{B} \, T_3) \, \textcircled{C} \, T_4)) \Rightarrow ((T_1 \, \textcircled{A} \, T_2) \, \textcircled{B} \, (T_3 \, \textcircled{C} \, T_4))$$

Since the parenthesized forms of the rotations are obtained by traversing the trees in Fig. 3.59 in symmetric order, we can see by inspection that none of the rotations changes the symmetric order of the keys in a binary search tree. The double left (and right) rotation(s) are called *double* because they can each be obtained by making a single right (left) rotation followed by a single left (right) rotation. For example, if

$$(T_1 \, ⒜ \, (T_2 \, ⒝ \, T_3))$$

is first rotated left to obtain

$$((T_1 \, ⒜ \, T_2) \, ⒝ \, T_3),$$

and then

$$(((T_1 \, ⒜ \, T_2) \, ⒝ \, T_3) \, ⒞ \, T_4)$$

is rotated right to make ⒝ the root, we obtain the double right rotation above. However, it is unnecessary to implement double rotations by two successive calls on single-rotation subroutines. Any of the four kinds of rotations can be obtained by permuting the contents of pointer fields in a small local portion of the overall tree. (Specifically, single rotations can be performed with five assignments, and double rotations with seven assignments.)

By adding two bits to each internal node of a binary search tree, we can keep track of whether the left and right subtrees are of equal height, or whether one is higher than the other. Let the symbols $\oslash$, $\ominus$, and $\oslash$ denote the situations where the subtrees of a node make the node *left heavy*, *balanced*, or *right heavy*, respectively. Then we can discover the conditions when certain of the above rotations must be applied. For instance, suppose that trees T_1, T_2, and T_3 each have height h. Suppose that a new node is inserted that makes tree T_1 into a new AVL subtree T_1' with height $h + 1$. If the balance factors before changing T_1 into T_1' are indicated by

$$((T_1 \, \ominus \, T_2) \, \oslash \, T_3),$$

then after changing T_1 into T_1', the tree loses its $HB[1]$ property at the root. However, the $HB[1]$ property can be restored by using a single right rotation to produce the new tree

$$(T_1' \, \ominus \, (T_2 \, \ominus \, T_3)).$$

Note now that if $\text{height}(T_i) = h$ (for $i = 1, 2, 3$) and $\text{height}(T_1') = h + 1$, then the heights of

$$((T_1 \, \ominus \, T_2) \, \oslash \, T_3) \quad \text{and} \quad (T_1' \, \ominus \, (T_2 \, \ominus \, T_3))$$

are both $h + 2$, so no balance factors need be changed in the entire tree above the subtree where the rotation was applied, and the single rotation is sufficient to restore the AVL condition for the entire tree. In the case of double rotations, similar considerations apply. For instance, if T_1 and T_4 have height h, T_2 and T_3 have height $h - 1$, and trees T_i (for $i = 1, 2, 3, 4$) are arranged into a larger tree of the form

$$(T_1 \, \oslash \, ((T_2 \, \ominus \, T_3) \, \ominus \, T_4)),$$

then any insertion that unbalances the tree by increasing the height of either T_2 or T_3 by one (creating, say, T'_2 or T'_3 in the process) can have the imbalance removed by applying a double left rotation to create a tree of the form

$$((T_1 \ominus T'_2) \ominus (T'_3 \ominus T_4)).$$

If the height of

$$(T_1 \oslash ((T_2 \ominus T_3) \ominus T_4)$$

before insertion was $h + 2$, then after insertion of the new item to create T'_2 or T'_3, followed by double rotation to restore the AVL property, the subtree

$$((T_1 \ominus T'_2) \ominus (T'_3 \ominus T_4))$$

also has height $h + 2$, and therefore none of the nodes above this subtree needs to have its balance factor changed, and one double rotation suffices to restore the $HB[1]$ property everywhere in the tree.

From these considerations, it is possible to write an algorithm that searches for a node N in an AVL tree T having a search key K, and if the search is unsuccessful, inserts a new node $\widehat{K}$, adjusts balance factors, and applies a rotation to remove imbalances if necessary. At first sight, such an algorithm might be thought to require a stack to retain a record of the nodes on the trace path from the root to the point of insertion, so that balance factors may later be adjusted, but Knuth has shown (cf. Knuth [1973b], pp. 455–457, Algorithm A) that such a stack is unnecessary.

While it is true that insertions require at most one rotation, deletions of nodes may require lg n rotations. (To see this, consider deleting the leftmost node of a Fibonacci tree, such as those given in Fig. 3.58.)

An empirical study of the performance of height-balanced trees by Karlton, Fuller, Scroggs, and Kaehler [1976] has shown that for sufficiently large trees, the execution times of all procedures for maintaining $HB[1]$ trees are *independent* of the size of the trees! In particular, an average of 0.465 restructures are required per insertion, with an average of 2.78 nodes revisited to restore the $HB[1]$ property. An average of 0.214 restructures are required per deletion, with an average of 1.91 nodes revisited to restore the $HB[1]$ property. As a further breakdown, a random insertion into an AVL tree required no rebalancing 53.5 percent of the time, a single left or right rotation 23.3 percent of the time, and a double left or right rotation 23.2 percent of the time. The cost of maintaining $HB[k]$ trees dropped sharply as allowable imbalance (k) was increased.

A subsequent empirical study by Baer and Schwab [1977] compared the performance of (a) $HB[k]$ trees for various k, (b) weight-balanced and bounded-balance trees, and (c) application of total restructuring disciplines. If insertion and subsequent searches are the only operations of interest, then pure AVL (that is, $HB[1]$) trees were found to have the best performance. Further, they showed conditions in which increasing k in $HB[k]$ trees was unprofitable, since the relaxation of the balancing criterion caused an increase in average path length not compensated for by the decrease in the number of balancing operations.

Knuth [1973b] shows how to use AVL trees to provide a representation for linear lists in such a way that the times required to insert an item, delete an item, find the kth item given k, and find an item with a given key K, are all $O(\log n)$. The idea is to put the items into an AVL tree in order of their keys K, but to add to each node a new field giving one plus the number of nodes in its left subtree. Thus, one can perform rapid insertion (overcoming the difficulty of sequential allocation) and rapid random access (overcoming the difficulty of linked allocation).

3.7.4 *B*-trees and 2–3 trees

We have seen that under optimal conditions when search keys are equally likely, complete binary search trees require lg $n + 1$ comparisons in the worst (deepest) searches. By increasing the branching factor m of a tree, and using a multiway search tree, instead of a binary tree, this worst case (and, indeed the average cases, too) can be improved to on the order of $\log_m n$ comparisons. In other words, the branching factor m in the multiway tree becomes the base of the logarithm that gives the tree depth in the case of complete balancing. For example, if $m = 256$, then $\log_{256} 16777216 = 3$, whereas $\log_2 16777216 = 24$. Suppose we are constructing a completely balanced m-ary tree on 16777215 keys. We can do this in general by placing $m - 1$ of the keys in the root node, placing m nodes each containing $m - 1$ keys on the first level, placing m^2 nodes each containing $m - 1$ keys on the second level, and, in general, placing m^k nodes each containing $m - 1$ keys on the kth level. Then, for $m = 256$, a complete search tree has just three levels containing 255, 65280, and 16711680 keys, respectively, whereas for $m = 2$, the binary case, we need 24 levels containing 1, 2, 4, ..., 2^{23} keys, respectively.

If we are constructing tree-structured indexes for use with large files (containing, say, 16777215 records), and if we are storing nodes of the tree-structured index on an external rotating memory device such as a disk or drum,† then the number of levels in the tree index may relate to the number of disk or drum accesses we have to perform to search the tree. Since such accesses tend to be relatively expensive compared to operations in primary memory, it is advantageous to attempt to minimize their number. Obviously, then, increasing the branching factor of a tree can cut down dramatically on the number of tree levels that must be examined in searching an index for such a large file. Thus, if we have static indexes, a completely balanced m-ary tree such as that shown in Fig. 3.61 may be ideal.

---

† See Chapter 9, Section 9.2.2 for a detailed explanation of properties.

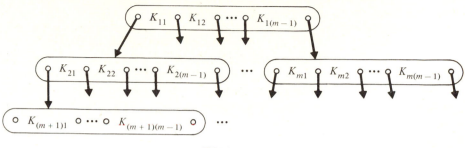

FIGURE 3.61

Here we assume that the $(m-1)$ keys $K_{j1} K_{j2} \cdots K_{j(m-1)}$ in node j are given in ascending order. To search for a given key K, if we find K as one of the keys in the root, the search terminates. Otherwise, we *locate* a pair of adjacent keys K' and K'' such that $K' < K < K''$, and we follow the pointer between K' ⅃ K'' to the root of a subtree where search continues. Visiting all keys in the tree in alphabetical order causes us to scan the nodes of the tree in a pattern that is a generalization of symmetric traversal for binary trees. We call this *generalized symmetric order.*

However, what happens if, instead of having static trees, we have dynamic trees that are expected to change shape under insertions and deletions? We must reject the idea of performing a complete rebalancing of the tree after each insertion because of cost. But can we arrange for some way to maintain a multiway tree so that insertions and deletions can be cheaply performed, that still guarantees $\log_m n$ search times? The notion of *B*-trees provides an affirmative answer to this question. However, unlike the case of $HB[k]$ trees, where we allowed the heights of the subtrees to get out of balance by no more than k, instead, in the case of B-trees, we maintain trees of uniform depth, and permit ourselves the luxury of varying the number of keys contained in the nodes. This notion of nodes with a variable number of keys provides us the elasticity we need to perform cheap insertions and deletions.

This motivates the following definition for *B*-trees (a notion due to Bayer and McCreight [1972]):

Definition 3.7 A *B-tree* of order m is a tree with the following properties:

a) The root has at least two children unless it is a leaf.

b) No node in the tree has more than m children.

c) Every node except for the root and the leaves has at least $\lceil m/2 \rceil$ children.

d) All leaves appear on the same level and contain no information.

e) An internal node with k children contains exactly $k-1$ keys.

The special case where $m = 3$ is of special interest.

Definition 3.8 A *2–3 tree* is a *B*-tree of order 3.

We will use 2–3 trees as examples in the following discussion. Reflecting briefly on the definitions, we see that every internal node in a 2–3 tree must have either two or three children, and each such internal node must contain either one or two keys. Finally, all leaves appear on one level. Figure 3.62 exemplifies a 2–3 tree with letters of the alphabet used as keys.

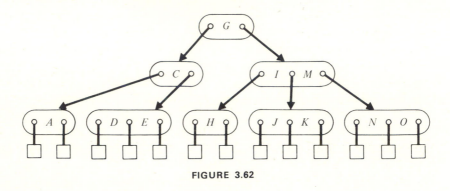

FIGURE 3.62

To search for the key *J*, for instance, we start at the root and note that $J > G$, so we follow the pointer to the right subtree of the root. Since now, $I < J < M$, we follow the middle pointer between *I* and *M* to the node containing keys *J* and *K* and, in this node, the search terminates successfully.

What can we say about search times in *B*-trees of order *m*? In the worst case, the deepest *B*-tree on *n* keys will be constructed by taking the minimum number of children allowed for each node, by Definition 3.7. Thus, the root will have two children, and each node on the levels below the root will have $\lceil m/2 \rceil$ children. So the number of nodes on levels 1, 2, 3, ... follows the geometric progression 2, $2\lceil m/2 \rceil$, $2\lceil m/2 \rceil^2$, ... If the tree has *k* levels and all the leaves appear on level *k*, then the number of leaves is a term in this progression of the form $2\lceil m/2 \rceil^{k-1}$. But the number of leaves is just one more than the number of keys,† and since there are *n* keys, there are $n + 1$ leaves. Therefore, we get, for the deepest tree,

$$n + 1 \geq 2\lceil m/2 \rceil^{k-1}.$$

Solving for *k* yields

$$k \leq 1 + \log_{\lceil m/2 \rceil}\left(\frac{n+1}{2}\right).$$

---

† To see this, enumerate the leaves and keys of Fig. 3.62 in generalized symmetric order, and note that the leaves and keys alternate, and leaves are at both ends of the sequence.

Since we need to access at most k levels in the worst case, we see that the number of levels is quite modest. For instance k is at most 3 if $n = 1{,}999{,}998$ and $m = 199$.

Now let's look at the process of inserting new keys. Sometimes we can find room for a new key in a given node. For example, in Fig. 3.62, to insert the key B, we just change the node containing A to a node containing $(\circ A \circ B \circ)$. On the other hand, if we try to insert a key into a node that is full (that is, has $m - 1$ keys in it already in a B-tree of order m), we can "split the node into two nodes and pass the middle key up to the parent," which may cause a cascade of further splits leading possibly to splitting the root, adding a new root, and deepening the B-tree by one more level. To see how this works, consider first the 2–3 tree of Fig. 3.62. Let's insert the key L. The attempt to add L to the node $(\circ J \circ K \circ)$ where it belongs in symmetric order would create a node $(\circ J \circ K \circ L \circ)$ with four children and three keys, in violation of the 2–3-tree constraints. Hence, we split $(\circ J \circ K \circ L \circ)$ into two new nodes $(\circ J \circ)$ and $(\circ L \circ)$, and we pass the middle key K up to the parent node $(\circ I \circ M \circ)$. The attempt to add K to $(\circ I \circ M \circ)$ leads to a sequence $(\circ I \circ K \circ M \circ)$ which is too long, so we again split it into two nodes $(\circ I \circ)$ and $(\circ M \circ)$, and we pass the middle key K up to the root. Now there is room for K in the root, which changes from $(\circ G \circ)$ to $(\circ G \circ K \circ)$. The new tree is illustrated in Fig. 3.63.

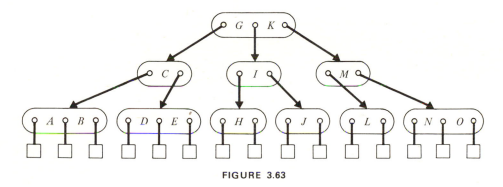

FIGURE 3.63

If we were to attempt to add keys P, Q, and R to the tree of Fig. 3.63, the root of the tree $(\circ G \circ K \circ)$ would split when O was passed up from below, and we would pass K up to form a new root with two children. This would deepen the B-tree by one level. (To generalize to B-trees of order m—if we attempt to add a key K to a node with $m - 1$ keys in it, we place K into the sequence of keys in order, getting an ascending sequence of m keys, and these are split into two nodes with keys $(\circ K_1 \circ \cdots \circ K_{\lceil m/2 \rceil - 1} \circ)$ and $(\circ K_{\lceil m/2 \rceil + 1} \circ \cdots \circ K_m \circ)$, while the middle key $K_{\lceil m/2 \rceil}$ is passed up.)

Now let us ask how much splitting can go on, on the average? When we add a new key at level k, as many as k nodes can be split as the split progresses up to the root. But it turns out that this is very rare. If we construct a tree from scratch, the total number of splits is one less than the total number of nodes in the tree (since each new split adds exactly one node). Let there be n keys and p nodes. Then there are at least $1 + (\lceil m/2 \rceil - 1)(p - 1)$ keys contained in the p nodes, so

$$1 + (\lceil m/2 \rceil - 1)(p - 1) \leq n,$$

and therefore (simplifying to isolate p):

$$p \leq \frac{n - 1}{\lceil m/2 \rceil - 1} + 1.$$

Now it follows that we need only split nodes, on the average, less than once every $\lceil m/2 \rceil - 1$ insertions. Put differently, the average is less than $1/(\lceil m/2 \rceil - 1)$ splits per insertion!

In particular, for 2–3 trees, we get worst-case search times of $1 + \lg((n + 1)/2)$ comparisons, and an average of less than one split per insertion.

In Chapter 9 on files, we will discover that *B*-trees are appropriate for maintaining dynamic tree indexes to files. A number of subtle variations and improvements to the use of *B*-tree indexes are considered in Knuth [1973b, pp. 476–479] and by Bayer and McCreight [1972].

Aho, Hopcroft, and Ullman [1974] have used 2–3 trees extensively in the design and analysis of efficient algorithms; and recently optimal 2–3 trees have been studied by Miller, *et al.* [1977].

3.7.5 Tries

Tries are a species of search tree originally introduced by Fredkin [1960]. While the word *trie* comes from the word re*trie*val, it has become fashionable in certain circles recently to pronounce the word *trie* as "try" (rhyming with "pie"), in order to distinguish it, when spoken, from the word "tree."

If we take the names of the stars in Fig. 3.51, and consider the way they are spelled from sequences of letters, we can develop a discrimination process in which branches diverge at places where the names are spelled differently. For instance, grouping together all star names spelled with the same initial letter into separate trees in the following forest, we get Fig. 3.64.

Here, to look up the entry for a particular star Xyzw ... we find the tree whose root is X and follow the yzw ... path from X until, after sufficient alphabetic discrimination, we arrive at the full name for the star. In the cases of Procyon, Rigel, Sirius, and Vega, the first letter alone is sufficient to distinguish the star from all others. However, in the case of Canopus and Capella, since both stars begin with the letters "Ca", we have to wait until seeing the third letter "n" or "p" to distinguish them from all others. Similarly, for the stars beginning with "A", the second letter distinguishes them from all others, and for the "B" stars, the fourth letter discriminates. Assuming choices of star names to be equally likely, the average number of letters we must inspect to distinguish the average star name completely is

$$\frac{2+2+2+4+4+3+3+1+1+1+1}{11} = \frac{24}{11} = 2.18.$$

This is a smaller average number of comparisons than that needed for the optimal binary search tree (which required 3.0, on the average). Tries can be represented by a set of nodes that are vectors of pointers long enough to contain one pointer for every character in the alphabet. Then Trie searching consists of using the character code X_i for the ith character of a word to select the X_ith pointer in the vector for the node; and this process is repeated until sufficient characters have been examined to distinguish the word from all others in the Trie. Other representations are possible using binary representations for the nodes (see, for instance, Knuth [1973b, pp. 481–499], Maly [1976], and Severance [1974]).

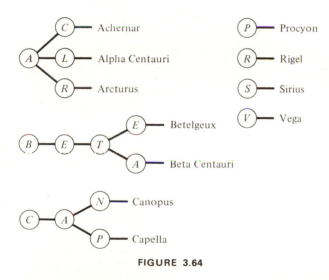

FIGURE 3.64

Search times are surprisingly good in Tries. The number of characters examined during a random average search is approximately $\log_m N$, for nodes with m links and N random keys stored in the Trie.

Here, random keys are keys chosen, say, with representations in a base m number system to be evenly distributed in the interval $[0, 1]$. Tries are insensitive to the order of insertion of the keys, but they are sensitive to bunching in the spelling of prefixes of the keys.

3.8 BIBLIOGRAPHIC NOTES

KNOTT [1977] gives a numbering system for binary trees, and ROTEM and VARAL [1978] give a correspondence between binary tree shapes and the stack-sortable permutations. Ranking, listing, and generation techniques for k-ary trees are studied in TROJANOWSKI [1978] and RUSKEY [1978]. The properties of ternary search trees are studied in SZWARCFITER and WILSON [1978].

VUILLEMIN [1978] defines binomial trees and studies the use of labeled binomial-tree forests to represent priority queues. GONNET [1976] comments on the use of heaps to represent event-driven simulation mechanisms, and an alternative structure for simulation event sets is introduced and compared to heaps in FRANTA and MALY [1977, 1978]. CRANE [1972] studies the use of balanced binary trees to represent priority queues and linear lists.

KRUSKAL [1956] gives an early version of the minimum-spanning-tree algorithm.

FOSTER [1975] studies AVL trees, and FOSTER [1973] generalizes AVL trees to $HB[k]$ trees. Two empirical studies of the behavior of height-balanced binary trees are KARLTON, FULLER, SCROGGS, and KAEHLER [1976], and BAER and SCHWAB [1977]. NIEVERGELT [1974] is a readable introduction to the subject of binary search trees. Binary trees of *bounded balance* are defined and studied in NIEVERGELT and REINGOLD [1973]; and BAER and SCHWAB [1977] define and compare $HB[k]$, bounded-balance, and weight-balanced binary search trees. Given unequal access frequencies for the keys, BRUNO and COFFMAN [1971] study heuristics for constructing nearly optimal trees. HIBBARD [1962], in an early and significant study of binary trees, was the first to prove that the total expected path length of randomly constructed binary trees was $2 \ln 2\, n \lg n + O(n)$ (where random construction meant that each permutation of the keys was equally likely to be used in tree construction). HIBBARD [1962] also proved that, in a certain sense, random deletions do not alter the statistical properties of trees that have been randomly constructed. KNUTH [1973b] gives further developments along these lines.

Since height-balanced trees normally require two bits per node to encode whether the subtree rooted at a node is left-heavy, balanced, or right-heavy, a number of studies are aimed at reducing the storage requirements to one bit per node. HIRSCHBERG [1976] studies techniques for restricting height-balanced trees to be one-sided (say, either balanced or right-heavy), requiring just one bit per node to signify the balance status. HIRSCHBERG [1976] gives an insertion algorithm for such one-sided trees, and KOSARAJU [1978], OTTMANN and WOOD [1978], and ZWEBEN and MCDONALD [1978] give deletion algorithms. BROWN [1978] gives a clever method for representing AVL trees with one bit per node that is not restricted to one-sided trees, by using the two bits in the two children of each node with two nonempty children to encode the balance factor.

OTTMANN, SIX, and WOOD [1978] provide $O(\log n)$ insertion and deletion algorithms for one-sided brother trees. In a *right-brother tree*, for example, all leaves have equal depth and each node with only one son has a right brother with exactly two sons. LUCCIO and PAGLI [1978] define *power trees*, a class of binary trees in which balance is maintained only for nodes belonging to certain paths. When compared to AVL trees, the power trees reduce the average number of restructurings required after insertion.

SHEIL [1978] defines and studies *split trees*. A split tree is a binary search tree each node of which contains two keys—a *node* value that is the maximally frequent key in the subtree rooted at the node, and a *split* value that partitions the remaining keys with respect to their lexical ordering between the left and right subtrees of the node. Median split trees use lexical medians as split values so that the search tree is perfectly balanced. Median split trees can be built in time $O(n \log n)$ as opposed to time $O(n^2)$ for optimal binary search trees. Thus, they are good both for large key sets that remain fixed for the duration of an application and also for key sets with highly skewed search frequencies.

BAYER and MCCREIGHT [1972] study B-tree properties, define a new class of trees called B^*-trees with nodes ranging from two-thirds full to completely full, and give B-tree maintenance algorithms. MCCREIGHT [1977] studies pagination of B^*-trees with variable-length records. BAYER [1972a] introduces a binary variant of B-trees and gives maintenance processes. BAYER and METZGER [1976] study the use of B-trees in enciphering environments for encrypted files.

ROSENBERG and SNYDER [1978] characterize 2-3 trees that are minimal in the expected number of comparisons per access for a given number of keys. Optimal 2-3 trees are studied by MILLER, PIPPENGER, ROSENBERG, and SNYDER [1977]. YAO [1978] provides an analysis of the average storage utilization of 2-3 trees. KRIEGEL, VAISHNAVI, and WOOD [1978] provide an $O(\log n)$ insertion algorithm for a class of trees called 2-3 *brother trees*, and they show that 2-3 brother trees have better storage utilization than 2-3 trees.

SUSSENGUTH [1963] derives an optimal branching factor for tree-structured indexes.

COMER and SETHI [1977] prove that determining minimal size Tries for certain variants is an NP-complete problem, and they consider other questions in the complexity of Trie index construction.

KARP, MILLER, and ROSENBERG [1972] study questions of rapidly identifying tree-structured patterns within larger trees.

EXERCISES

1. (Representations) For each of the following, which kind of tree provides the most natural representation, a binary tree, an oriented tree, or an ordered tree?
   a) An elimination tree for a tennis tournament.
   b) A parse tree of a program.
   c) A hierarchical organization chart of a firm.
   d) A pedigree for a dog.
   e) Nested sets.
   f) Arithmetic expressions.

2. (Parenthesizing arithmetic expressions) Derive a formula that gives the total number of distinct ways of parenthesizing the expression $a_0 + a_1 + \cdots + a_n$, where each parenthesis pair surrounds a pair of subexpressions connected by one plus sign.

3. (Binary encoding of b_n) Obtain an estimate of the number of bits required to encode b_n as a binary integer starting with formula (9) and using $\lg x =$

ln x/ln 2 and

$$\ln n! = \left(n + \frac{1}{2}\right) \ln n - n + \ln\sqrt{2\pi} + \frac{1}{12n} - \frac{1}{360n^3} + O\left(\frac{1}{n^5}\right)$$

(Knuth [1973a], p. 111).

4. (Stirling's approximation) From the expression for ln $n!$ in Exercise 3, derive Stirling's approximation:

$$n! = \sqrt{2\pi n}\left(\frac{n}{e}\right)^n\left(1 + \frac{1}{12n} + O\left(\frac{1}{n^2}\right)\right)$$

5. (Upper bound for b_n) Using formula (9) for b_n, show that

$$b_{n+1} = 4b_n - \left(\frac{6}{n+2}\right)b_n$$

and thus that $b_{n+1} < 4b_n$. Then prove that $b_n \le 4^{n-1}$.

6. (Estimating b_n) Use Stirling's approximation (in Exercise 4) to show the result cited in the text that

$$b_n \approx \frac{4^n}{n\sqrt{\pi n}} + O(4^n n^{-5/2}).$$

7. (Knott [1977]) Discover a linear-time algorithm for converting distinct shape numbers in the range 1 to b_n into corresponding distinct binary trees on n vertices.

8. (Forests from trees) Give an algorithm to convert a binary tree into an ordered forest according to the correspondence shown in Figs. 3.12 and 3.13.

9. (Printing arithmetic expressions) Write an algorithm to print infix expressions from binary trees representing arithmetic expressions (such as that shown in Fig. 3.17). Your algorithm should insert parentheses only when required by the relative precedence of infix operators. For example, an expression for a sum or difference should be parenthesized if it is an operand of a division or multiplication, but an expression for a product that is an operand of a sum should not be parenthesized. Thus, your algorithm should print $3 \times (Z - 2.5) + X/Y$ to correspond to the tree of Fig. 3.17.

10. (Left subtree insertion) Write an algorithm to insert a symmetrically threaded subtree T_1 as the left subtree of a node N in a given symmetrically threaded subtree T_2.

11. (Knuth) Write an algorithm to insert a single node N as the right (left) descendant of a node P in a symmetrically threaded tree.

12. (Deletion in threaded trees) Write an algorithm to delete the right (left) descendant node P of a given node N in a symmetrically threaded tree.

13. (Threading) Write an algorithm to insert symmetric threads in an initially unthreaded linked binary tree.

14. (Utility of threads) Are symmetric threads useful for stackless preorder (postorder) traversal of the nodes in a symmetrically threaded binary tree?

15. (Construction of full binary trees) Give an algorithm for converting the preorder enumeration of the nodes of a full binary tree into the linked representation for the binary tree, where each node X in the enumeration has a bit set to 1 if X is an internal node and set to 0 if X is a leaf.

16. (Perlis [1972]) Let a tree be represented as a sequence of nodes V together with a sequence of weights W (as in Fig. 3.31). Write algorithms to:
a) Find the path from the root of the tree to a particular node n.
b) Find the subtree rooted at n.
c) Delete the subtree rooted at n.

17. (Trees with weights) Let V_1, W_1 and V_2, W_2 be pairs of sequences giving the nodes and weights for two trees T_1 and T_2. Write algorithms to:
a) Insert tree T_2 as the last child of node n in tree T_1.
b) Replace the subtree of T_1 rooted at node n by subtree T_2.

18. (Trees with degrees) Repeat Exercises 16 and 17 using sequences of degrees instead of sequences of weights (as shown in Fig. 3.30).

19. (Conversion of weights to degrees) Give an algorithm for efficiently converting a tree represented as a preorder sequence with weights to one represented as a preorder sequence with degrees. (For example, convert the representation of Fig. 3.31 to that of Fig. 3.30.)

20. (Conversion of degrees to weights) Give an algorithm for converting efficiently from a preorder sequence with degrees to a preorder sequence with weights.

21. (Tree construction) Give an algorithm to construct an ordered tree from the level-order enumeration of its nodes with degrees.

22. (Representation for full binary trees) Give a method of adding two bits per node to a postorder enumeration of the leaves of a full binary tree that enables conversion to the linked binary-tree representation in linear time and bounded workspace.

23. (Symmetric-order stack traversal) Give an algorithm that traverses the nodes of a linked binary tree in symmetric order using a stack.

24. (Postorder stack traversal) Give a stack-traversal algorithm which traverses the nodes of a binary tree in postorder.

25. (Level order traversal) Give an algorithm that traverses the nodes of a linked binary tree in level order. [*Hint:* Use a queue instead of a stack to hold pointers to subtrees awaiting subsequent traversal.]

26. (Stack evaluator) Write an interpreter to evaluate postfix arithmetic expressions (such as that shown in Fig. 3.34).

27. (Siklóssy) Modify Algorithm 3.6 so that it uses TAG fields on nodes that are set in advance of the running of the algorithm and left fixed, such that $TAG(N) = +$ if N is the left child of its parent, and $TAG(N) = -$ if N is the right child of its parent.

28. (Tagless Siklóssy traversal?) Is it possible to eliminate the TAGs on cells in Algorithm 3.9 if we assume that cell addresses in a binary tree are ordered in some suitable fashion? [*Hint.* Suppose that, as we traverse the cells in symmetric order in the binary tree, the addresses of the cells form a strictly increasing sequence.]

29. (Termination of Algorithm 3.9) Would Algorithm 3.9 work properly if the TAG of the root of the binary tree had been set to $+$ in Fig. 3.41?

30. (Read-only traversal) As given in Fig. 3.41, the leaves in the representation used in Siklóssy traversal take as much space as the leaves in the representation in Fig. 3.20 used for threaded traversal. Is there a variant of Siklóssy traversal that uses leaves that are atomic or Λ, with no LLINK or RLINK fields, which can save space in read-only memory compared to that required for threaded traversal?

31. (Start up information in Siklóssy traversal) The address of any single node anywhere in a threaded binary tree is sufficient information to initiate traversal. How many addresses are required in Siklóssy traversal to initiate traversal starting anywhere in the tree, and what relationship must these addresses bear to one another?

32. (Burkhard [1975b]) Devise a stackless, link-inversion traversal, using no tag bits, for linked binary trees with an address ordering on its nodes as follows: For all nodes N in the binary tree T, assume $LLINK(N) < N$ and $RLINK(N) < N$, and let Λ be the address of a special cell such that $N < \Lambda$ for all N in T and such that $LLINK(\Lambda) < \Lambda$ and $RLINK(\Lambda) < \Lambda$. [*Hint.* Use a normal link-inversion traversal such as that given in Algorithm 3.6, but upon ascent from a subtree to a parent node P, if the right link of P points down (to a higher address than that of P), the right subtree has not yet been processed, whereas if the right link of P points upward (to a lower address than that of P), the right subtree has been traversed and ascent can continue.]

33. (Burstall and Darlington) Let A and B be two binary trees with respective frontiers $f(A)$ and $f(B)$. [The frontier of a binary tree consists of the sequence of leaves in left to right order.] Write an efficient algorithm to determine whether $f(A) = f(B)$.

34. $(\sum i/2^i < 2)$ Verify $\sum_{1 \leq i \leq n} i/2^i < 2$ by justifying the steps in the following derivation:

$$\sum_{1 \leq i \leq n} \frac{i}{2^i} = \sum_{1 \leq i \leq n} \sum_{1 \leq j \leq i} \frac{1}{2^i} = \sum_{1 \leq j \leq n} \sum_{j \leq i \leq n} \frac{1}{2^i} = \sum_{1 \leq j \leq n} \left(\frac{1}{2^{j-1}} - \frac{1}{2^n} \right)$$

$$= \left(2 - \frac{1}{2^{n-1}} \right) - \frac{n}{2^n}$$

$$= 2 - \frac{n+2}{2^n} < 2.$$

35. $(\sum \lfloor \lg i \rfloor)$ Show that $\sum_{1 \leq i \leq n} \lfloor \lg i \rfloor = (n+1)q - 2^{q+1} + 2$, where

$$q = \lfloor \lg (n+1) \rfloor.$$

36. (Deletion in AVL trees) Write an algorithm to delete a node N in an AVL tree.

37. (Deletion in B-trees) Write an algorithm to delete a key K in a B-tree of order m.

38. (AVL tree representation of sequences) Show how to use an AVL tree to represent a finite sequence of keys $K_1, K_2, \ldots, K_n$ so that accessing the ith element as well as accessing an element with a random key K are both operations implementable in $O(\log n)$ time.

39. (Tree insertion sort) Write an algorithm to sort n distinct $K_1, K_2, \ldots, K_n$ by inserting them into a binary-search tree and then using the symmetric-order enumeration of the tree to read out the result in sorted order. Analyze the running time of your algorithm.

40. (Martin and Ness [1972]) Develop an algorithm to relink the linked representation of a binary tree so that it is balanced (i.e., all leaves on at most two levels). The algorithm should use linear time and two pushdown stacks and should manipulate the linked-tree representation in place.

41. (Full k-ary trees) Define a full k-ary tree to be an oriented tree in which each node has either k children or no children. Generalize the proof of Section 3.3.1 to show that in such a full k-ary tree

$$\# \text{ Leaves} = (k-1) \times (\# \text{ internal nodes}) + 1.$$

CHAPTER

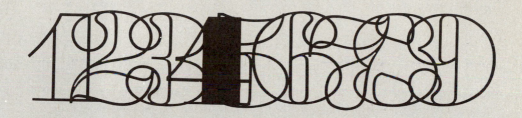

TABLES

4.1 INTRODUCTION AND MOTIVATION

It is often said that *tables* and *files* are aggregates of individual components called *records*. The records are, in turn, often viewed as collections of information associated with distinct named entities. Frequently, distinct records in a *table* or *file* contain distinct *keys*, and each record stores information associated with its key. Sometimes the key is the name of the entity to which a record pertains. Other times, a key is chosen so as to identify a particular record uniquely in a table or file.

Suppose $K_1, K_2, \ldots, K_n$ are distinct keys, and that we have a collection T of records of the form

$$(K_1, I_1), (K_2, I_2), \ldots, (K_n, I_n),$$

in which I_j is some information associated with K_j for $1 \leq j \leq n$. Given a particular key K, the process of *table look-up* or *file searching* consists of a systematic method for locating the record (K_j, I_j) in T such that $K = K_j$, in which case the search is said to be *successful*, or for determining that there is no record in T whose key matches K, in which case the search is said to be *unsuccessful*.

There are many ways that we might choose to represent information in T so that operations such as searching, updating, inserting, deleting, and enumerating can be done efficiently and conveniently.

The distinction between a *table* and a *file* is often one of informal usage, and usually centers around two attributes—size and lifetime. Thus, if size alone were important, a file could be a large table, and a table could be a small file. Sometimes, though, a file refers to a collection of information that is stored on tapes, disks, or other long-term external memory media, regardless of its internal format. In time-sharing systems, for instance, a user's files refer to the information saved in long-term memory between active sessions; and these may consist of files of program text, compiled relocatable machine code, formatted data, cross-reference listings, and so forth.

By contrast, tables are often created in internal memory with lifetimes confined to the execution of a particular program. For instance, symbol tables in assemblers and compilers store associations between identifiers and program data created during the course of a particular assembly or compilation. If the information in the symbol table is not needed later for debugging, loading, or listing, the table may vanish at the conclusion of the compilation or assembly. As another example, one may create a temporary table of values of a function during the execution of an algorithm, and this table may vanish when the end result is computed and the values in the table are no longer needed.

Thus, the word *table* is sometimes associated with short lived entities created in internal memory during program execution, whereas the word *file* is associated with longer-lived entities stored on external memory. The quality of persistence through time independently from program execution thus sometimes distinguishes files from tables.

But these distinctions are not hard and fast, and are subject to many exceptions. In actual pattern of usage, tables of values of functions and decision tables may be considered and treated more as files than as tables, and the files containing indexes to other files may be considered and treated more as tables than as files.

Thus, there seems to be no way to define tables and files with precision that covers and characterizes all the various contemporary uses of these words. Therefore, the division of subject matter between this chapter on *tables* and Chapter 9 on *files* should not be regarded as rigid. Roughly speaking, though, we will treat organization techniques for large collections of information in external memory in Chapter 9 on files. For the present, it suffices to think of a *table* as a set of pairs of the form $(x, F(x))$ for some function F and some finite domain.

In this chapter, we study binary search, hash tables, and symbol tables, all of which can be used in internal memory and are useful in table processing. However, as we shall see, some of the techniques (such as *hashing*) apply also to large files and to large-scale information retrieval applications (where they are sometimes known by different names, such as *scatter storage* or *associative memory* techniques).

In the following section, we study techniques for searching tables stored contiguously in memory. These are sequential collections of records of the form (K_j, I_j) for $1 \leq j \leq n$. In this context, we explore *sequential search*. Then, on the assumption that the table is *ordered*—i.e., that the records are arranged so that $K_j < K_{j+1}$ $(1 \leq j \leq n - 1)$—we study *binary search* and *Fibonaccian search*.

Second we study hashing techniques such as open addressing, use of buckets, and chaining. Phenomena such as primary and secondary clustering, and search time as a function of table saturation are described. Various policies for collision resolution are investigated. Also presented are Knuth and Amble's techniques for ordered hashing, and Bays' algorithm for reallocating a hash table *in situ* to make it larger or smaller.

Decision tables are covered in the next section. An introduction and overview is given, together with pointers to the literature. The so-called rule-mask techniques are given for decision-table interpretation, and the problem of translating decision tables into computer programs is examined.

Finally, techniques for organizing symbol tables are discussed, drawing comparisons between binary search, hashing, and binary tree techniques discussed in the previous chapter on trees.

4.2 SEARCHING SEQUENTIAL TABLES

Let T be a *table* consisting of a finite collection of ordered pairs

$$(K_1, I_1), (K_2, I_2), \ldots, (K_n, I_n)$$

and let K be a search key. Suppose that we represent table T by storing the pairs (K_j, I_j) sequentially in memory. For instance, we might use an n by 2 rectangular table T such that $T[j, 1] = K_j$ and $T[j, 2] = I_j$ for $1 \le j \le n$, or we may use two "parallel" sequential tables each of length n, say Tkey and Tinfo, such that Tkey$[j] = K_j$ and Tinfo$[j] = I_j$. Let us use the notation Key($T[j]$) to denote the key K_j stored in the jth entry of the sequential representation of T, no matter which sequential representation technique is chosen.

Simple *sequential search* of Table T for a record containing the *search key K* can be performed by the following (poorly written) program:

1. [Initialize.] Set $i \leftarrow 1$.
2. [Unsuccessful?] If $i = n + 1$, then the algorithm terminates unsuccessfully.
3. [Successful?] If Key($T[i]$) $= K$, then the algorithm terminates successfully.
4. [Continue searching.] Set $i \leftarrow i + 1$ and go back to step 2.

Actually, this algorithm can be improved upon in important ways. Note that the main loop of the algorithm is given in steps 2, 3, and 4. As a small initial improvement, we can replace the test $i = n + 1$ in step 2 with the test $i > n$, which saves one addition each trip around the loop. Another modest improvement results on some computers from changing the loop to count down from n to 1 instead of counting up from 1 to n. This way, the test for exhaustion of the search in step 2 can be changed to the test $i = 0$, which is cheaper on some computers than the test $i > n$, since one less memory reference is involved. By far the biggest improvement, however, results from extending the table to contain a new 0th element. This element is initialized to contain the search key K. Then it is possible to eliminate the exhaustion test from the inner loop entirely, as follows:

Algorithm 4.1 *Searching a sequential table.*

1. [Initialize.] Set Key($T[0]$) $\leftarrow K$ and set $i \leftarrow n$.
2. [Done?] If Key($T[i]$) $= K$, then go to step 3. Otherwise, decrease i by 1 and repeat this step.
3. [Termination.] If $i = 0$, the search terminates unsuccessfully. Otherwise, the search terminates successfully with the ith entry containing the search key K.

Algorithm 4.1 will run upwards of 20 percent faster than the first version given in steps 1 through 4 above on many machines (Knuth [1977], p. 64). This algorithm solves the search problem for on the order of 25 or fewer records efficiently compared to other methods we shall presently investigate (such as binary search or hash addressing).

4.2.1 Most frequent to least frequent order

Sequential search has some interesting properties if we are permitted the luxury of arranging the records in the order of most frequently searched to least frequently searched. The expected number of comparisons required to locate a record with key K under sequential search is given by

$$\overline{C}_n = 1p_1 + 2p_2 + \cdots + n \cdot p_n,$$

where p_i is the probability that the ith record searched contains the search key, and where $p_1 + p_2 + \cdots + p_n = 1$.

Under different probability distributions the quantity $\overline{C}_n$ assumes several interesting values. Suppose $p_i = 1/2^i$ for $1 \le i \le n - 1$ and (to make the sum of the p_i equal to unity), suppose $p_n = 1/2^{n-1}$. In this case, the ith record is accessed twice as often as the $(i + 1)$st.

From the observation that $\overline{C}_n = (1/2)\overline{C}_{n-1} + 1$, it follows that $\overline{C}_n = 2 - (1/2^{n-1})$; that is, the average search involves looking at less than two of the records for such a skew distribution.

If each record is equally likely to be accessed during search, we have $p_i = 1/n$ for $1 \le i \le n$, and $\overline{C}_n = (n + 1)/2$. That is, about half the records are searched on the average, each time a search is conducted.

A family of distributions that often describes naturally occurring frequencies is the family of *Zipf distributions*. Let $H_n^{(s)}$ be the nth harmonic number of order s defined by

$$H_n^{(s)} = \frac{1}{1^s} + \frac{1}{2^s} + \cdots + \frac{1}{n^s}.$$

Then, letting $c = 1/H_n^{(1+\theta)}$, we define the *Zipf distribution of order* θ by

$$p_1 = \frac{c}{1^{1+\theta}}, \quad p_2 = \frac{c}{2^{1+\theta}}, \quad \ldots, \quad p_n = \frac{c}{n^{1+\theta}}.$$

If $\theta = 0$, we obtain the law that Zipf observed for words in natural language, namely that the nth most frequently occurring word in natural language text occurs with a frequency proportional to $1/n$ (Zipf [1949]). Subsequently, Schwartz studied word frequencies (Schwartz [1963]), and found a more appropriate fit for word frequencies if θ has a small positive value. Zipf also found that cities ranked in order of decreasing population obeyed the distribution for $\theta = 0$, and that for $\theta = -\frac{1}{2}$, the distribution of personal income is obtained. Knuth ([1973b], p. 398) observes that, with $\theta = -\log 0.80/\log 0.20$, the Zipf distribution approximates the 80—20 rule observed in commercial file-processing applications, in which 80 percent of the transactions deal with the most active 20 percent of the records in a file, and within the most active 20 percent, the same ratio applies.

For the Zipf distribution of order θ, we find that

$$\overline{C}_n = \frac{H_n^{(\theta)}}{H_n^{(1+\theta)}},$$

whence, in the special case that $\theta = 0$, we get $\overline{C}_n = n/H_n$. For example, for the 80–20 rule, $\overline{C}_n \cong 0.122n$ (Knuth [1973b], p. 398).

4.2.2 Ordered table search

Consider a telephone book. Given a name, it is easy to look up the corresponding phone number. But given a phone number, it is hard to look up the corresponding name(s). In the latter case, nothing short of exhaustive search can be guaranteed to work. However, if the names in a phone book were not given in alphabetical order, the search for a particular name would be as hard as the search for a particular phone number. Thus, for people, the efficiency of search in phone books, library card catalogues, and the index to this book, is critically dependent on the entries being given in order.

Conceptually, the reason is straightforward. If we compare a search key K with a key K_i in a table with records arranged in order by key (*viz.*, $K_j \leq K_{j+1}$ for $1 \leq j \leq n - 1$), and we find that K is less than K_i, then K is also less than all keys K_j with $j > i$. So we can eliminate further search among all keys K_j with $j \geq i$. Thus, the result of a single comparison may eliminate the necessity of search in a large subset of the records. By contrast, in an unordered table, the result of a single comparison of K with a nonmatching key K_i can eliminate only K_i from consideration.

By taking advantage of the potential for elimination of searching certain subsets in an ordered table, we obtain various efficient search strategies.

Let T be a table of n ordered records (K_1, I_1), (K_2, I_2), ..., (K_n, I_n) ordered on the values of K_i such that $K_1 < K_2 < \cdots < K_n$. Suppose we want to search for a record in T containing the search key K. We might consider splitting our table in half by locating the record (approximately) in the middle of the table $(K_{\lfloor n/2 \rfloor}, I_{\lfloor n/2 \rfloor})$, extracting its key $K_{\lfloor n/2 \rfloor}$, and comparing it to K. If we have a stroke of good fortune, and find that $K = K_{\lfloor n/2 \rfloor}$, we have found what we're looking for and the search terminates successfully. On the other hand, if $K < K_{\lfloor n/2 \rfloor}$, then we do not have to search the upper half of the table, and if $K > K_{\lfloor n/2 \rfloor}$ then we do not have to search the lower half of the table. So, in any case, either we are lucky and the search terminates with just one comparison, or we are fortunate and can continue the remainder of the search on a table half as big as the original. In the worst case, at each step, we can discard half the remaining records to be searched, and so by repeated halving of the size of the problem, we can soon narrow the search to at most a single record. Thus, we can either find the record containing key K, or we can conclude that no such record is in the table. This process is called *binary search* (or sometimes *logarithmic search*, since the maximum number of times we need to halve the table is the base two logarithm of the number of table entries n).

Actually, the informal description of binary search given here sounds easy to implement, but it glosses over some important details. It is actually known to be tricky to program all the details correctly. For instance, Knuth ([1977], p. 65) reports that when students are asked to program binary search for the first time,

80 percent get the program wrong (even if they have had over a year of programming experience). In the face of this challenge, the reader who has never programmed a binary search before may take pleasure in working out the details before reading the algorithm given below.

It is not our only choice to divide the table in half at each stage of an ordered search procedure. We may instead choose to divide the table, say, into portions such as $\frac{1}{5}$ and $\frac{4}{5}$, or in a ratio of x to $1 - x$ for any x in the range $0 < x < 1$, or in proportions governed, say, by the Fibonacci numbers 1, 1, 2, 3, 5, 8, 13, …

Another idea is the concept of *interpolation search*. When we search a phone book, if looking for a name beginning with, say, the letter C, we tend to choose a starting point that is near the front of the phone book. However, if looking for a name beginning with the letter V, we tend to choose a starting point near the end. Generalizing, if we believe the keys are more or less uniformly distributed over the alphabet, we might define a distance measure $|x - y|$ between two keys x and y in alphabetical order; and if looking for key K between keys K_ℓ and K_u, we might choose a division point between K_ℓ and K_u that divides the segment of keys between K_ℓ and K_u into parts proportional to $|K - K_\ell|$ and $|K_u - K|$. In fact, A. C. Yao and F. F. Yao have shown that if the keys are independent and randomly distributed numbers, interpolation search requires an average of ($\log_2 \log_2 n$ plus a small constant) key comparisons to locate a record containing the search key (Yao and Yao [1976]). However, a possible snag in this idea is that the expense of computing the interpolated search points may not be repaid by increased search efficiency when compared, say, to pure binary search for modestly sized tables in internal memory (see Perl, Itai, and Avni [1978]). On the other hand, for external memory containing large files, where the access time for a record exceeds by far the computation time for an interpolated search point, the idea may have merit. Yet, as we shall see, this is just the size of file for which hash addressing techniques may be competitive.

The following algorithm gives the method for *binary search*.

Algorithm 4.2 *Binary search in an ordered table.*

Let T be a table with n entries. Assume that

$$\text{Key}(T[1]) < \text{Key}(T[2]) < \cdots < \text{Key}(T[n]).$$

The variables ℓ and r hold the *left* and *right* boundaries of the search at each point. Thus, at any given moment, the position i of the key K we are searching for, such that $K = \text{Key}(T[i])$, must lie strictly between ℓ and r; that is, $\ell < i < $ r.

1. [Initialize.] Set $\ell \leftarrow 0$ and r $\leftarrow n + 1$.
2. [Compute midpoint.] Set $i \leftarrow \lfloor (\ell + \text{r})/2 \rfloor$.

3. [Unsuccessful?] If $i = \ell$ (the key is not in the table), output $i = 0$, and terminate the algorithm unsuccessfully.

4. [Compare.] (We know $\ell < i < r$ at this point). In the following cases, take the following actions.

Case	$\Rightarrow$	Action

a) $K < \mathrm{Key}(T[i]) \Rightarrow$ Set $r \leftarrow i$ and go to step 2.
b) $K = \mathrm{Key}(T[i]) \Rightarrow$ Output i and terminate algorithm successfully
c) $K > \mathrm{Key}[T(i)] \Rightarrow$ Set $\ell \leftarrow i$ and go to step 2.

On some small computers, instructions may be lacking to compute the midpoint in step 2 efficiently. Under these circumstances, a multiplicative version of binary search may prove fruitful. In order for this multiplicative version to work, the records must be ordered in a special fashion. In particular, for n keys, let B be a complete binary tree of n nodes. For example, if we have $n = 13$ keys, we choose B as the complete binary tree on 13 nodes. Then, letting $N_1, N_2, N_3, \ldots$ be the sequence of nodes of B enumerated in symmetric order, and letting $K_1, K_2, \ldots, K_n$ be the sequence of keys in ascending order, we place K_i in N_i for each i ($1 \le i \le n$). Figure 4.1 shows an example of how key K_i is inserted in node N_i for each i ($1 \le i \le n$).

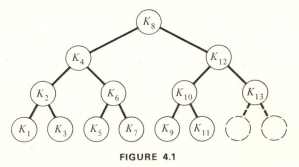

FIGURE 4.1

Next, we enumerate the keys in the nodes of tree B in level order. Let T be a table of n records whose keys are given in the same order as that obtained by the level order of the keys in B. For example, for the 13 keys in Fig. 4.1, we would get the following table T:

	1	2	3	4	5	6	7	8	9	10	11	12	13
T:	K_8	K_4	K_{12}	K_2	K_6	K_{10}	K_{13}	K_1	K_3	K_5	K_7	K_9	K_{11}

Then, the following algorithm can be used to search for a search key K.

Algorithm 4.3 *Multiplicative binary search.*

Let T be a table with n keys K_i ordered as prescribed above, and let i be an index into the table. Let K be a search key.

1. [Initialize.] Set $i \leftarrow 1$.

2. [Failure?] If $i > n$, the algorithm terminates unsuccessfully.

3. [Compare.] If $K = \text{Key}(T[i])$, then the algorithm terminates successfully. Otherwise, set $i \leftarrow 2i$ or $2i + 1$ according as $K < \text{Key}(T[i])$ or $K > \text{Key}(T[i])$, respectively, and go back to step 2.

For example, to search for $K = K_{10}$ in the table T, Algorithm 4.3 starts by examining $T[1]$, since $i = 1$. The key stored in $T[1]$ is K_8. Since the search key K_{10} is greater than K_8, the value of i is replaced by $2i + 1$, so i becomes 3. Now, $K_{10} < \text{Key}(T[3]) = K_{12}$ so the value of i is replaced by $2i$. At this point, the algorithm finds that $K_{10} = \text{Key}(T[6]) = K_{10}$, so the algorithm terminates successfully. If we are lacking efficient multiplication on a particular machine, the multiplication $2i$ in Algorithm 4.3 can be replaced by $(i + i)$.

Another method of search similar to binary search that uses only addition and subtraction is that called *Fibonaccian search*. This method relies on properties of the Fibonacci numbers:

$$F_0 = 0, \quad F_1 = 1, \quad \text{and} \quad F_n = F_{n-1} + F_{n-2} \quad \text{for} \quad n \geq 2.$$

In particular, suppose we have a table T containing $F_n - 1$ elements for some Fibonacci number F_n. Then we split the table into three parts as follows:

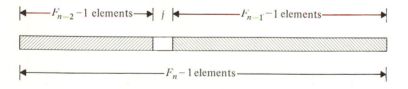

The left part contains one fewer than F_{n-2} elements. The right part contains one fewer than F_{n-1} elements, and the jth element divides the table into such left, right, and middle parts. Adding up the sizes of the three parts, we see that

$$(F_{n-2} - 1) + 1 + (F_{n-1} - 1) = (F_{n-2} + F_{n-1}) - 1 = F_n - 1 \text{ elements.}$$

How shall we select j, then, to divide the table in this fashion? If the elements are numbered from 1 to $F_n - 1$, it suffices to set $j = F_{n-2}$. To use this as a basis for a search technique, we proceed as follows: First check to see if the search key K matches the key in position $T[F_{n-2}]$. If so, the search terminates successfully. If not, then if $K < \text{Key}(T[F_{n-2}])$, search the left portion of the table, while if

$K > \text{Key}(T[F_{n-2}])$, search the right portion of the table. The search of the left and right portions proceeds by the same principle of decomposition applied iteratively. The following algorithm implements this idea. The first step is modified to allow the algorithm to apply to a table T of any size $n > 1$, rather than just to tables of size $F_n - 1$.

Algorithm 4.4 *Fibonaccian search.*

Let T be a table of n records arranged in ascending order of their keys $K_1 < K_2 < \cdots < K_n$. Let K be a search key. Let F_k be the largest Fibonacci number such that $F_k \leq n$. In the following steps, $f1$ and $f2$ are two consecutive Fibonacci numbers, and i is an index into the table.†

1. [Initialize.]   Set $i \leftarrow (n+1) - F_{k-1}$, $f2 \leftarrow F_{k-2}$,   and $f1 \leftarrow F_{k-3}$.   If $K < \text{Key}(T[i])$, then $i \leftarrow f2$ (shift search range to lowest end of table if K lies below initial probe).

2. [Branch.]
   a) If $K > \text{Key}(T[i])$, then go to step 3.
   b) If $K = \text{Key}(T[i])$, then the algorithm terminates successfully.
   c) If $K < \text{Key}(T[i])$, then go to step 4.

3. [Search upper part.] If $f1 = 0$, the algorithm terminates unsuccessfully. Otherwise, set $i \leftarrow i + f1$ and $(f1, f2) \leftarrow (f2 - f1, f1)$, and go back to step 2.

4. [Search lower part.] If $f2 = 1$, then the algorithm terminates unsuccessfully. Otherwise, set $i \leftarrow i - f1, f2 \leftarrow f2 - f1, f1 \leftarrow f1 - f2$, and go back to step 2.

In this algorithm, when probing at location i in the table, the range of further search always extends $(f2 - 1)$ elements below the ith position and $(f1 + f2 - 1)$ positions above the ith position. If $f1 = F_k$ and $f2 = F_{k+1}$ for two consecutive Fibonacci numbers F_k and F_{k+1}, then the transformation $(f1, f2) \leftarrow (f2 - f1, f1)$ in step 3 changes the values of $f1$ and $f2$ to $f1 = F_{k-1}$ and $f2 = F_k$. Similarly, the transformation $f2 \leftarrow f2 - f1, f1 \leftarrow f1 - f2$ changes the values of $f1$ and $f2$ to $f1 = F_{k-2}$ and $f2 = F_{k-1}$. Pictorially, if $f1$ and $f2$ are two adjacent pointers into the Fibonacci sequence:

$$0 \quad 1 \quad 1 \quad 2 \quad 3 \quad 5 \quad 8 \quad 13 \quad 21 \quad \cdots$$
$$\uparrow \quad \uparrow$$

then $(f1, f2) \leftarrow (f2 - f1, f1)$ shifts the pair of pointers one place to the left:

$$0 \quad 1 \quad 1 \quad 2 \quad 3 \quad 5 \quad 8 \quad 13 \quad 21$$
$$\uparrow \quad \uparrow$$

---

† In this algorithm the notation $(x, y) \leftarrow (e_1, e_2)$ signifies a "parallel assignment" in which the values of the expressions e_1 and e_2 are first computed and are then assigned simultaneously to be the respective values of x and y.

whereas $f2 \leftarrow f2 - f1, f1 \leftarrow f1 - f2$ shifts the pointers two places left:

$$0 \quad 1 \quad 1 \quad 2 \quad 3 \quad 5 \quad 8 \quad 13 \quad 21$$
$$\uparrow \quad \uparrow$$

These shifts in the values of $f1$ and $f2$ are exactly what is required to deal iteratively with the upper and lower portions of the search range in case $K > \text{Key}(T[i])$ or $K < \text{Key}(T[i])$, respectively.

It can be shown that the binary search technique of Algorithm 4.2 minimizes the average number of comparisons required to perform search among all comparison-based methods, assuming the search for each of the keys is equally likely. This is obtained by showing that binary search can be modeled by search in a complete binary search tree, and that the internal path length of such a tree is minimized when all the leaves occur on at most two adjacent levels. Accordingly, Fibonaccian search does not use as few comparisons as binary search, on the average, assuming search for each key to be equally likely, since the binary search tree corresponding to Fibonaccian search does not have its leaves on at most two adjacent levels. For instance, the binary search tree corresponding to Fibonaccian search of the lowest 12 elements in a table of $n > 12$ elements is given in Fig. 4.2. In this tree, the key at the root is the key first examined, and the keys of the left and right sons of the root are those examined next if the search key is respectively less than and greater than the key at the root. It can be shown, by techniques similar to that used to prove that AVL trees have log n search times (*cf.* Section 3.7.3.2) that the worst-case search time in Fibonaccian search is $O(\log n)$.

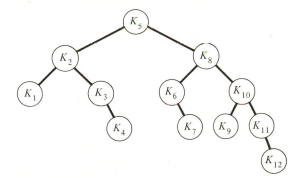

FIGURE 4.2   *A right heavy Fibonacci tree.*

4.3 HASH TABLES

In the search methods examined so far in this chapter, we have searched for a given key K by rummaging around amongst the table entries according to some systematic policy, such as eliminating half the remaining elements each time we do a comparison, or running through the elements in order.

It would be nice if we could calculate quickly the address where key K is stored directly as a function of K itself. This way we would not have to examine irrelevant entries, but instead could locate K without trial and error. In fact, the character tables we shall study in Chapter 7 and the array representations we shall study in Chapter 8 can both be viewed as tables of this sort—we go directly from the character C or the n-tuple of indices $(i_1, i_2, \ldots, i_n)$ to the corresponding table location by a 1–1, onto indexing function.

However, suppose the number N of possible keys that could be stored is much larger than the number of table entries M. For instance, we may have a symbol table capable of holding $M = 997$ of the $N = 1,617,038,306$ possible FORTRAN identifiers. In this case, any function $h(K)$ that maps FORTRAN identifiers onto the table locations $0, 1, \ldots, 996$ cannot be 1–1, so some subset of two or more identifiers must map onto the same location. If we have two keys, K_1 and K_2, and an address β in a table such that $h(K_1) = \beta = h(K_2)$, we say K_1 and K_2 have a *collision* at β under the mapping h.

Suppose we could devise an efficient way to deal with collisions so that, any time we map a key K into a location $h(K)$ where collisions occur, we could find quickly the record containing K amongst all records with keys K' that also mapped to location $h(K) = h(K')$. Our search procedure for finding the record containing key K in the table would then involve two steps: (a) compute the table location $h(K)$; (b) starting at address $h(K)$, locate the record containing key K using (if necessary) some sort of *collision-resolution policy*.

In order for such a method to work acceptably, we need to solve two problems: (a) find a function $h(K)$, called a *hash function*, which produces a low number of collisions given a distribution of possible input keys K and a target address space $0, 1, \ldots, M - 1$ for the table; and (b) devise a *collision-resolution policy* for finding a record containing a given key K amongst those whose keys collide at the same location.

If we know nothing about the distributional properties of the keys that will be used, we might attempt to find a hash function that gives a uniform random distribution of values $h(K)$ assuming that distinct keys K are chosen with equal likelihood. On the other hand, if we know something about the distribution of the keys (such as the fact that arithmetic progressions are likely, as in sequences of identifiers used in programming, such as X1, X2, X3 or PLOTA, PLOTB, PLOTC), then we might attempt to devise *distribution-dependent hash functions* that assign separate hash locations to groups of related keys.

Even if we have uniform random hash functions, the probability of collisions is high for all but fairly sparsely occupied tables. For instance, the von Mises birthday paradox (Feller [1957], p. 31) states that among 23 or more people in a room, there is a greater than even chance that two or more will have a common birthday, and if there are 88 or more people in the room, there is a better than even chance of finding three people with the same birthday. Similarly, a hash table with 365 locations containing 88 or more keys whose hash addresses were calculated as if they had been chosen uniformly and randomly, would have a greater than even chance of having a collision of three or more keys at some address. Thus, even under apparently favorable circumstances, we must expect collisions.

Three *collision-resolution policies* that have received attention in the literature are (1) *chaining*, (2) the use of *buckets*, and (3) *open addressing*.

4.3.1 Chaining

One way of resolving collisions is to maintain M linked lists, one for each possible address in the hash table. A key K hashes to an address $\beta = h(K)$ in the table. At address β, we find the head of a list containing all records having keys that have hashed to β. This list is then searched for a record containing key K. (Here the word *chain* is a synonym for a linked list.)

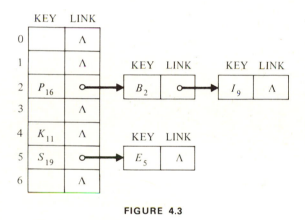

FIGURE 4.3

Figure 4.3 (constructed to be similar to but slightly different from Fig. 1.9 in Chapter 1) illustrates a hash table with collision resolution by chaining. The table has seven entries numbered 0 through 6. The keys to be hashed are each of the form L_n, where n is a number giving the position of letter L in the alphabet. For example, Z_{26} and B_2 are keys, since Z is the 26th letter in the alphabet and B is the second letter in alphabet. Given a key L_n, we define the hash function h by $h(L_n) = n \bmod 7$. Thus,

$$h(P_{16}) = 16 \bmod 7 = 2.$$

We also see, for example, that $h(P_{16}) = h(I_9) = h(B_2) = 2$, since

$$16 \bmod 7 = 9 \bmod 7 = 2 \bmod 7 = 2.$$

The table in Fig. 4.3 shows the result of inserting, in order, the keys $K_{11}, P_{16}, B_2,$

S_{19}, E_5, and I_9 into an initially empty table. Keys that collide at address β are stored on the same chain whose head starts at address β. In Fig. 4.3 we have shown only keys stored on these chains instead of the records containing the keys.

If the keys in each chain are kept, say, in ascending order, then a search for keys that are *not* in the table goes faster. If N keys are stored in chains in a table with M entries, the average number of keys in a list is N/M. Thus, the average list length is quite short, even if it is highly probable that collisions will occur. Thus, this form of hashing decreases the average amount of work involved in list searching by a factor of M.

4.3.2 The use of buckets

Suppose we divide a table into M groups of records, with each group containing exactly b records. Each group of b records is called a *bucket*. The hash function $h(K)$ computes a bucket number from the key K, and the record containing K is stored in the bucket whose bucket number is $h(K)$. If a particular bucket verflows, an overflow policy is invoked.

As we shall see in greater detail in Chapter 9 on files, hashing methods are not only good for tables stored in internal memory; they are also helpful for searching files of records stored on secondary memory devices such as disks and drums. When retrieving records from, say, a disk, whole groups of records can frequently be brought into primary memory at a time (for instance, by reading an entire track on a particular cylinder of the disk). Since it is relatively costly in time to move read/write arms on disks and to wait for rotational delays, it often pays to take care in computing a hash function (by perhaps more expensive means) since the extra cost of hash computation is often repaid by reducing costly mechanical repositioning and rotational delay. Also, once the transfer of a track of records is initiated from disk or drum into primary memory, the remainder of the transfer does not take much time. After reading a whole track into main memory, a binary search, for example, can be used to locate a particular record of interest. This is much faster than conducting the search by bringing in a record at a time by repeated disk or drum accesses (each one with possible rotational delays). Thus, bucketing techniques go hand in hand with hash techniques applied to files stored on external memory.

If a bucket overflows, a chaining technique can be used to link to an "overflow" bucket. This link can be planted at the end of the overflowed bucket. It is convenient to keep overflow buckets on the same cylinder of a rotating memory device, to avoid having to reposition cylinder read/write heads. Since comparatively few overflows occur with a proper choice of bucket size, all overflowed records from all overflowed buckets on a cylinder can be placed together in a common overflow bucket. Knuth ([1973b], p. 535) has analyzed this method, and has found the average number of accesses required as a function of the percentage of occupancy to be quite good. For instance, less than three accesses are required for all bucket sizes tried from $b = 1$ to $b = 50$, even at 95% of full table saturation. For a bucket size $b = 50$ at 95% saturation, only 1.2 accesses were required on the average for a successful search.

We shall investigate the cylindrical surface index techniques to support such hash methods with bucketing more carefully in Chapter 9 on files.

4.3.3 Open addressing

Suppose we have a key K such that $h(K)$ is already occupied by another record R' with a key K' distinct from key K. To resolve such a collision in open addressing, we search for an empty table entry at an address other than $h(K)$. Let $\beta_0 = h(K)$ and let $\beta_0, \beta_1, \ldots, \beta_{M-1}$ be a permutation of the table addresses called a *probe sequence*. We might choose to inspect the table entries in the order given by the probe sequence until finding a record containing key K (in which case the search is *successful*) or until finding an empty record or concluding that the table is full (in which case the search is *unsuccessful*). If we adopt the convention that a *full table* is one with exactly one empty entry and $M - 1$ nonempty entries, we can avoid having to make a test for table exhaustion, since each probe sequence will eventually locate an empty entry. This open addressing policy is summarized in the following algorithm.

Algorithm 4.5 *Hash table search by open addressing.*

Let T be a table with M entries $T[0], T[1], \ldots, T[M - 1]$. For convenience, we assume that all keys inserted in T have strictly positive numerical values, whereas a key in each empty entry is 0. We let K be the search key. At least one entry must be empty.

1. [First hash.] Set $i \leftarrow h(K)$.
2. [Successful?] If $K = \text{Key}(T[i])$, then the algorithm terminates successfully.
3. [Unsuccessful?] If $\text{Key}(T[i]) = 0$, then the algorithm terminates unsuccessfully.
4. [Compute next probe.] $i \leftarrow i - p(K)$. If now $i < 0$, set $i \leftarrow i + M$. Go back to step 2.

In order for this algorithm to work properly, we must assume that $p(K)$ is defined so as to generate a permutation of the table addresses for use in probing; that is, we must assume that the addresses $(h(K) - i \cdot p(K)) \bmod M$ form a permutation of $0, 1, \ldots, M - 1$ for $0 \le i \le M - 1$, so that the probe sequence will exhaustively search all addresses in the table in some order.

The simplest way to choose the probe sequence function is to define $p(K) = 1$ for all keys K. This is called *linear probing* since the probe sequence for any key K

is always of the form

$$h(K), \quad h(K) - 1, \quad h(K) - 2, \quad \ldots, \quad 1, \quad 0, \quad M - 1, \quad M - 2, \quad \ldots, \quad h(K) + 1.$$

That is, we first inspect the entry at address $h(K)$ to see if it contains K, and if not we search in decreasing order of table addresses until we run down to the lowest address 0. At this point we "wrap around" and continue to search downward from the highest address $M - 1$.

Linear probing gives rise to a phenomenon called *primary clustering*. For example, Fig. 4.4 shows a table after inserting in order the keys $M_{13}, G_7, Q_{17}, Y_{25}, R_{18}$ with the hash function $h(K_n) = (n \bmod 11)$, where insertion of key K_n consists of placing K_n into the first empty location in the probe sequence $h(K_n), h(K_n) - 1, \ldots$ In Fig. 4.4, two clusters have formed. All keys that collide at address β will extend the cluster containing β. Worse yet, adjacent clusters tend to join up to form composite clusters as the number of table entries grows. For example, adding keys Z_{26} and F_6 to the table in Fig. 4.4 generates the table in Fig. 4.5. Here, when Z_{26} is added, the two clusters occupying locations 2–3 and 5–6–7 are joined, and when F_6 is added, it is inserted at the low-address end of the one big cluster in the table.

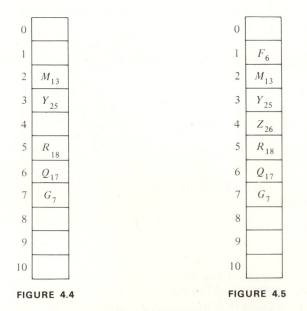

FIGURE 4.4   FIGURE 4.5

Returning to Fig. 4.4, we see that if a new key K is inserted with a hash address $h(K)$ randomly chosen in the range 0 to 10, then location 4 has a 4/11 chance of being filled with key K, whereas locations 0, 8, 9, and 10 each have a 1/11 chance of being filled. The most important reason for the growth of primary clusters is that the bigger clusters are bigger targets. Thus, big clusters grow faster than small clusters, a situation that is unstable. This phenomenon increases retrieval and insertion times dramatically as the table approaches full saturation.

If we define the *load factor* α of a table to be the ratio of the number of occupied entries N in the table to the total number of entries M in the table,

$$\alpha = \frac{N}{M} \quad \text{(load factor)}, \tag{1}$$

then it can be shown (for large N and reasonably small α, say $\alpha \leq 0.7$) that the average number of probe addresses examined, C_N, for a successful search in open addressing with linear probing is approximately

$$C_N \approx \frac{1}{2}\left(1 + \frac{1}{1-\alpha}\right) \quad \text{(successful search)}, \tag{2}$$

and that, for an unsuccessful search (or for an insertion), the average number of probes is approximately

$$C'_N \approx \frac{1}{2}\left(1 + \left(\frac{1}{1-\alpha}\right)^2\right) \quad \text{(unsuccessful search)}. \tag{3}$$

(See Knuth [1973b], pp. 529ff. These derivations are among the prettiest in computer science, in the author's opinion). This implies that the performance of linear probing deteriorates rapidly as the table approaches full saturation (i.e., as N approaches M).

Might there be a way to break apart the primary clusters that damage the performance of linear probing? The search for good answers to this question led to a number of ideas for calculating exhaustive probe sequences. Two such ideas are given in the next two sections.

4.3.3.1 *Pseudo random probing.* Following Morris [1968], use a probe sequence of the form

$$h(K) + 0, \quad h(K) + r_1, \quad h(K) + r_2, \quad \ldots, \quad h(K) + r_{M-1},$$

reduced modulo the table size, where the numbers $0, r_1, r_2, \ldots, r_{M-1}$ are a permutation of the numbers $0, 1, \ldots, M-1$. The numbers r_i can be generated by a cheap random number generator (see Morris [1968]). Alternatively, for example, setting $p(K) = c$ for all K, where c is an integer relatively prime to the table size M in Algorithm 4.5, generates a pseudo random probe sequence.

4.3.3.2 *Quadratic residue search.* Following Radke [1970], use a probe sequence of the form

$$h(K), \quad h(K) + i^2, \quad h(K) - i^2, \quad \ldots$$

all reduced modulo the table size, for values of i increasing in the interval $1 \leq i \leq (M - 1)/2$. With M chosen to be a prime number of the form $4j + 3$ for some integer j, it can be guaranteed that the probe sequence is a permutation of the table address space (see Radke). This overcomes a difficulty of earlier quadratic search techniques, which trace out only half the addresses in the table in their probe sequences (e.g., see Maurer [1968]).

A problem with these methods is that two keys K and K' which collide trace out the same probe sequence. This leads to a phenomenon called *secondary clustering*.

Following Amble and Knuth [1974], we define any technique for which $p(K)$ in step 4 of Algorithm 4.5 is of the form $p(K) = f(h(K))$ as *open addressing with secondary clustering*.

Analysis of open addressing with secondary clustering yields the following approximations for the average number of probes in successful and unsuccessful searches (see Knuth [1973b], pp. 522–523, and Bell [1970], p. 109):

$$C_N \approx 1 - \ln (1 - \alpha) - \frac{\alpha}{2} \qquad \text{(successful search)}, \qquad (4)$$

$$C_N' \approx \frac{1}{(1 - \alpha)} - \alpha - \ln (1 - \alpha) \quad \text{(unsuccessful search)}. \qquad (5)$$

An idea even better than those of Sections 4.3.3.1 and 4.3.3.2 is the following one, which eliminates the effects of both primary and secondary clustering.

4.3.3.3 *Double Hashing.* Following de Balbine ([1968], pp. 149–150) and Bell and Kaman [1970], use a probe sequence of the form $h(K) - i \cdot h_2(K)$ reduced modulo the table size for $0 \leq i \leq M - 1$, where $h_2(K)$ is a second hash function that gives for key K an integer relatively prime to the table size M. The difference between this method and pseudo random probing is that, in double hashing, different keys K and K' produce possibly different probe sequences even though they collide at the same table address, whereas in pseudo random probing and quadratic residue search, two keys that collide at the same address lead to the same probe sequence.

It has been found empirically that double hashing eliminates secondary clustering. Also, empirical studies show that the average number of probes agrees with formulas derived for "uniform probing" (see Knuth [1973b], pp. 527–528), in which we assume that keys go into random locations in the table independently of one another (so that there is no primary or secondary clustering):

$$C_N \approx \frac{1}{\alpha} \ln \frac{1}{(1-\alpha)} \quad \text{(successful search)}, \tag{6}$$

$$C_N' \approx \frac{1}{(1-\alpha)} \qquad \text{(unsuccessful search)}. \tag{7}$$

Recently, L. Guibas [1977] has shown that formulas (6) and (7) describe the average number of probes theoretically for $\alpha < 0.31$, but the proof for higher load factors has been difficult to achieve. (However, see Guibas [1978].)

Bell and Kaman [1970] discovered double hashing independently of de Balbine [1968] and called it the *linear quotient hash code*. This discovery was in sequel to Bell's discovery (see Bell [1970]) that the quadratic residue search could be modified to eliminate secondary clustering by letting the probe sequence be of the form

$$h(K) + a \times i + h_2(K) \times i^2,$$

where $h_2(K)$ supplied different coefficients for distinct keys colliding at $h(K)$. It was a short step from this observation to the idea that the quadratic steps in the probe sequence were not as important as the idea that colliding keys should lead to distinct probe sequences after the first collision, and that using a double hash could accomplish this.

Returning to Algorithm 4.5, how should we choose $p(K)$ in step 4 so as to guarantee double hashing? One convenient way is as follows: Let the table size M be a prime number, and choose $p(K)$ as any value in the range $1 \le p(K) \le M - 1$. Another possibility is to choose M as a power of 2, such as 2^k, and to choose $p(K)$ as an odd value between 1 and $2^k - 1$. All that is required is that $p(K)$ be *relatively prime* to M. In Bell and Kaman's variation [1970], the table size M is chosen to be a prime number. Then, letting Q and R be the quotient and remainder of dividing the key K by the table size M, Bell and Kaman set $h(K) = R$ and

$$p(K) = (if\ Q = 0\ then\ 1\ else\ Q).$$

Of these variations of open addressing, the *double hashing* methods are superior because they incur no penalties for primary or secondary clustering. However, there are further improvements that can be achieved under favorable circumstances.

4.3.4 Ordered hashing

By using an ordering on the keys K of a hash table search algorithm, Amble and Knuth [1974] obtain a new algorithm almost identical to the old.

Algorithm 4.6 *Ordered hash table search by open addressing.*

Let T be a table with M entries $T[0]$, $T[1]$, ..., $T[M-1]$ and let K be a search key. We assume that empty entries have keys $K = 0$, and that nonempty entries have keys whose values are positive integers. At least one entry must be empty $(\text{Key}(T[j]) = 0$ for some $j)$.

1. [First hash.] Set $i \leftarrow h(K)$.
2. [Successful?] If $K = \text{Key}(T[i])$, then the algorithm terminates successfully.
3. [Unsuccessful?] If $\text{Key}(T[i]) < K$, then the algorithm terminates unsuccessfully.
4. [Compute next probe.] Set $i \leftarrow i - p(K)$. If now $i < 0$, set $i \leftarrow i + M$. Go back to step 2.

Note that the only difference between this algorithm and Algorithm 4.5 is that the test in step 3 of Algorithm 4.5 has been changed from $\text{Key}(T[i]) = 0$ to $\text{Key}(T[i]) < K$ to produce Algorithm 4.6.

However, we cannot use Algorithm 4.6 unless the hash table T has been filled (or otherwise rearranged) in a suitable way. Suppose that we have inserted keys into table T in decreasing order. That is, starting with an empty table, we first insert the largest key, then the second largest, and so on, until finally we last insert the smallest key. Now suppose we are searching for a search key K. Let this key generate the probe sequence β_0, β_1, ..., β_{M-1} (where $\beta_i = (h(K) - i \times p(K))$ mod M, and $p(K)$ is guaranteed to be relatively prime to M.) Now the interesting thing is that if K is in the table, the keys we examine at locations $T[\beta_0]$, $T[\beta_1]$, ..., $T[\beta_i]$ (where β_i is the location containing key K) must all occur in decreasing order. This is because, when key K was inserted in the table, all keys inserted before it were greater than K. Hence, when K came to be inserted, the probe sequence β_0, β_1, ... was followed, hitting a succession of occupied locations until finally at β_i, an empty location was found in which key K was inserted. All the occupied locations contained keys greater than K since all keys in the table were greater than K when K was inserted. From this we see that if we are searching for K by examining successive locations in the probe sequence β_0, β_1, ..., and if we come across a location β_j containing a key $K_j < K$, then key K could not possibly be in the table T (since we have just shown that all predecessors of the location of key K in the probe sequence β_0, β_1, ... contain keys greater than K). Hence, we can conclude that the search is unsuccessful whenever we find the condition $\text{Key}(T[i]) < K$ to be true. This is the reason why step 3 of Algorithm 4.6 works.

Now it is unreasonable to assume that we can ensure that the keys in a dynamically changing hash table can be loaded in decreasing order (although for a preloaded static table, this is not too much to swallow). Fortunately, there is a method for inserting keys into an ordered hash table in any order, that is guaranteed to produce the same results as inserting keys in strictly decreasing order. This process is given as follows:

Algorithm 4.7 *Key insertion in an ordered hash table.*

Assume that key K is not in table T, so that $\text{Key}(T[i]) \neq K$ for $0 \leq i \leq M - 1$. Also, assume that T is ordered and contains at most $N \leq M - 2$ keys. After insertion of K in T, T will be ordered, and at least one empty entry will remain in T.

1. [First hash.] Set $i \leftarrow h(K)$.
2. [Termination?] If $\text{Key}(T[i]) = 0$, set $\text{Key}(T[i]) \leftarrow K$ and terminate.
3. [Exchange?] If $\text{Key}(T[i]) < K$, exchange the values of K and $\text{Key}(T[i])$.
4. [Probe further.] Set $i \leftarrow i - p(K)$. If now $i < 0$, set $i \leftarrow i + M$. Go back to step 2.

Roughly speaking, this algorithm works as follows. We start examining locations in T according to the probe sequence corresponding to K. We continue following this probe sequence for K so long as K is less than the key at each place visited. If we are lucky, we find an empty entry, place K in it, and terminate. However, if, in following K's probe sequence, we examine a location with a key K' smaller than K, we swap K and K', and we proceed along the probe sequence for K' trying to find an empty entry in which to place K'. In turn, K' may be exchanged for a lesser key K'' before an empty entry is located, in which case the probe sequence for K'' is followed, and so on. This process more or less resembles a game of "musical chairs," in which an unseated child is trying to find an empty chair to sit in while the rest of the children are already seated. The unseated child examines chairs in some order (his personal probe sequence, let us say) until locating an empty chair to sit in, or until finding a smaller child. If he finds a smaller child he bullies him into releasing his seat, and sets the smaller child roaming on his own (probably different) personal probe sequence looking for an empty seat or a smaller child to bully into an exchange.

To show that Algorithm 4.7 leaves table T ordered after insertion, we reason as follows. When table T is ordered, then for every key K in it, we have the (invariant) property that every key K' found in table locations given by the probe sequence leading up to the location β_j where K is stored must be bigger than K. In symbols, if $\text{Key}(T[\beta_j]) = K$, then $\text{Key}\,(T[(h(K) - i \times p(K)) \bmod M]) > K$ for $0 \leq i < j$. Since Algorithm 4.7 never decreases the value of a key stored in any table position, it maintains the invariant property.

It is a rather remarkable fact that no matter the order in which we insert keys into T using Algorithm 4.7, the final arrangement of keys in T is unique, and is identical to that obtained by inserting the keys in decreasing order.

Theorem 4.1 (Amble and Knuth [1974]). A set of N keys $K_1, K_2, \ldots, K_N$ can be arranged in an ordered hash table $T[0], T[1], \ldots, T[M-1]$ of $M > N$ entries in exactly one way such that Algorithm 4.6 is valid.

Proof At least one arrangement is possible, since we can insert keys in strictly decreasing order. Suppose there are two or more distinct arrangements of keys in T that are each valid. Let K_j be the largest key that appears in different locations in at least two different arrangements. Then, all keys larger than K_j occupy fixed positions in all possible arrangements. Now examine the probe sequence for K_j and consider the sequence of table locations indexed by this probe sequence. The table locations of keys larger than K_j occur earlier in the probe sequence than K_j's address, and the locations of keys smaller than K_j occur later in the probe sequence. Thus, K_j must sit in the first location in its probe sequence after locations occupied by the fixed larger keys in each valid arrangement. This contradicts the assumption that K_j can appear in two different locations. ∎

Now we would like to know the average behavior of these ordered hashing methods, assuming that the hash addresses of the keys are independent and randomly distributed on the interval 0 to $M-1$, and assuming that each of the N keys in the table is equally likely to be used in a search.

We see that the number of probes C_N required to locate a key K with Algorithm 4.5 is identical to the number required to insert it in the first place (exactly the same probe sequence being followed in both cases). Thus, if C'_{k-1} is the average number of probes needed to insert the kth item, we have

$$C_N = \frac{C'_0 + C'_1 + \cdots + C'_{N-1}}{N}. \tag{8}$$

Turning now to the performance of Algorithm 4.6, since the position of any particular set of keys in an ordered table is unique by Theorem 4.1, we can assume they have been inserted in decreasing order. Under these circumstances consider the key arrangement that results from inserting the keys with Algorithm 4.5 (wherein, to insert a key K, we place K in the location i with which Algorithm 4.5 terminates after unsuccessful search in step 3). This key arrangement is exactly that required by Algorithm 4.6. Then, the average number of probes D_N needed by Algorithm 4.6 to find a key in the table is

$$D_N = \frac{C'_0 + C'_1 + \cdots + C'_{N-1}}{N} = C_N, \tag{9}$$

since the average number of probes needed for Algorithm 4.6 to find the kth largest item is C'_{k-1}. Hence, with respect to successful searching, Algorithms 4.5 and 4.6 use the same number of probes.

For unsuccessful searching, however, Algorithm 4.6 does considerably better than Algorithm 4.5. In unsuccessful searching, the number of probes D'_N required by Algorithm 4.6 is the same as the number required by Algorithm 4.5 to perform a successful search if, after inserting in decreasing order the keys $K_1, K_2, \ldots, K_N$, the search key K had been inserted. In other words,

$$D'_N = D_{N+1} = C_{N+1}. \tag{10}$$

Remarkably, the average number of probes needed by the order-preserving insertion algorithm, Algorithm 4.7, is the same as that required using insertion by Algorithm 4.5. However, even though the average is the same, the probability distribution differs, and certain (rare) insertions may take up to $O(N^2)$ iterations (see Amble and Knuth [1974], p. 137).

4.3.5 Using pass bits

At the expense of more memory, the open addressing techniques of Algorithm 4.5 and 4.6 can be extended to make unsuccessful searching still faster. Suppose we extend the table T by adding a bit B_i to each table entry $(0 \leq i \leq M - 1)$. Initially suppose that these bits are all set to 0. Now suppose that, each time we execute step 3 of Algorithm 4.7, we set $B_i \leftarrow 1$ during the key-insertion process. This implies that, whenever a key K comes to rest in position $T[j]$ in the table, all the locations in its probe sequence $\beta_0, \beta_1, \ldots, \beta_{j-1}$ that were *passed over* (i.e., inspected and found to be nonempty) during the insertion process have their pass bits set to 1. Then, if the ordered search algorithm, Algorithm 4.6, ever gets to step 3 and finds that the pass bit in $T[i]$ is 0, the search must be unsuccessful because this location could never have been passed over during an insertion of the key being searched for, and hence the key being searched for was never inserted in the first place.

The pass bit method is especially attractive in the case of ordered hash table search because the extra bit can be appended as the leftmost (most significant) bit of each key in the table, making it possible to perform the extra testing at almost no extra cost. Algorithm 4.6 can be rewritten in this fashion as follows (Amble and Knuth [1974], p. 137):

Algorithm 4.8 *Pass bit search in an ordered hash table.*

Assume that the pass bits in the table entries have been set as prescribed above.

1. [First hash.] Set $i \leftarrow h(K)$.
2. [First termination test.] If $(B_i, \text{Key}(T[i])) < (1, K)$, then if $K = \text{Key}(T[i])$ the algorithm terminates successfully, whereas if $K \neq \text{Key}(T[i])$, then it terminates unsuccessfully.

TABLE 4.1

Average Number of Probes Required for Search as a Function of Load Factor α = N/M (from Amble and Knuth [1974]. p. 137. Theoretical Data, two decimal places. Empirical Data, one decimal place.)

Method	Successful search							Unsuccessful search						
Saturation = 100α = % full	25	50	75	80	85	90	95	25	50	75	80	85	90	95
Unordered search (Alg. 4.5)														
Linear probing	1.17	1.50	2.50	3.00	3.83	5.50	10.50	1.39	2.50	8.50	13.00	22.72	50.50	200.50
Secondary clustering	1.16	1.44	2.01	2.21	2.47	2.85	3.52	1.37	2.19	4.64	5.81	7.71	11.40	22.04
Double hashing	1.15	1.39	1.85	2.01	2.23	2.56	3.15	1.33	2.00	4.00	5.00	6.67	10.00	20.00
Ordered search (Alg. 4.6)														
Linear probing	1.17	1.50	2.51	3.00	3.83	5.50	10.50	1.17	1.50	2.50	3.00	3.83	5.50	10.50
Secondary clustering	1.16	1.44	2.01	2.21	2.47	2.85	3.52	1.16	1.44	2.01	2.21	2.47	2.85	3.52
Double hashing	1.15	1.39	1.85	2.01	2.23	2.56	3.15	1.15	1.39	1.85	2.01	2.23	2.56	3.15
Pass bit search (Alg. 4.8)														
Linear probing	1.17	1.50	2.51	3.00	3.83	5.50	10.50	1.0	1.2	2.0	2.4	3.6	5.4	10.3
Double hashing	1.15	1.39	1.85	2.01	2.23	2.56	3.15	1.0	1.1	1.3	1.4	1.6	1.7	2.2

3. [Second termination test.] If $(B_i, \text{Key}(T[i])) = (1, K)$, the algorithm terminates successfully.

4. [Next probe.] Set $i \leftarrow i - p(K)$. If now $i < 0$, set $i \leftarrow i + M$. Go back to step 2.

The average number of probes for an unsuccessful search with the pass bit method has been found difficult to analyze. However, empirical results reveal that the idea can be worthwhile. (See Table 4.1.)

Putting all the results on open addressing methods together we obtain Table 4.2, showing theoretical and empirical results.

TABLE 4.2

Theoretical Approximate Values for Successful and Unsuccessful Average Search Times for Unordered and Ordered Hash Tables.

Increment method	C_N, D_N, and D'_{N-1}	C'_N
Linear probing	$\frac{1}{2}(1 + (1-\alpha)^{-1})$	$\frac{1}{2}(1 + (1-\alpha)^{-2})$
Secondary clustering	$1 - \ln(1-\alpha) - \alpha/2$	$(1-\alpha)^{-1} - \ln(1-\alpha) - \alpha$
Double hashing	$-\alpha^{-1}\ln(1-\alpha)$	$(1-\alpha)^{-1}$

$(C_N, C'_N) = $ (Successful, Unsuccessful) unordered search times.
$(D_N, D'_N) = $ (Successful, Unsuccessful) ordered search times.
$\alpha = N/M = $ load factor of the table.

4.3.6 Binary tree hashing

While the ordered search and pass bit techniques reduce the unsuccessful search times in hashing quite significantly, they do not improve the successful search times. In some applications, however, successful searches are much more numerous than insertions and unsuccessful searches. Under these circumstances, if one is willing to do more work when inserting an item, by moving keys around in the hash table, it is possible to reduce average search times.

A situation in which this sort of consideration might prove favorable is that of designing a symbol table for a compiler. For instance, Bell and Kaman ([1970], p. 676) report using a hash table in compiling a COBOL program in which 735 keys were used and which the hash routine was entered 10,988 times. In other words, there were $(10988 - 735)/735 \approx 13.95$ searches, on the average, for each insertion.

One method of relocating keys at insertion time to reduce average retrieval times is *binary tree hashing* (Gonnet and Munro [1977]). Suppose K is a key to be inserted in a hash table where retrieval is to be organized, say, using double hashing with open addressing, as in Algorithm 4.5. The main observation on which binary tree hashing is founded is that, if K hashes to a location occupied by another key K', then we have two choices: (a) leave K' in place and examine the next location on the probe sequence for K to see if there is a free location in which to place K, or (b) replace K' with K and examine the next location on the probe sequence for K' to see if there is a free location in which to place K'. If only one of K and K' hashes next to an empty location, it is placed there, while the other is allowed to occupy the original point of collision. If both "secondary" locations for K and K' are occupied, however, we extend the consideration another "level," where there are four "tertiary" locations to consider (in general), corresponding to the new locations to which K and K' hash after collision at their secondary locations, and to the locations to which the occupants of these secondary locations hash. In general, we perform a level-order search of the "binary tree" generated by the locations encountered by rehashed keys until an empty location is found. Gonnet and Munro note that an elegant implementation of this level-order search can be implemented using the contiguous representation of complete binary trees (see formulas (11), Chapter 3) in which the children of node i are at $2i$ and $2i + 1$. Then the binary representation of the node in the complete binary tree of the first empty location indicates the way in which the keys in the hash table are to be relocated.

Gonnet and Munro report that this reordering scheme leads to an average of roughly 2.13 probes for retrieval from a full table and to an apparent worst case of $O(\log n)$ probes.

TABLE 4.3
Number of Probes for
Successful Search C_N versus 100α.

Percent full = 100α	80%	90%	95%
Binary tree hashing	1.58	1.75	1.88
Brent's method	1.60	1.80	1.97
Alg. 4.5, double hashing	2.01	2.56	3.15

Brent [1973], in an earlier development, had investigated a reordering scheme also based on the idea of rearranging the keys encountered on probe sequences generated by the attempt to insert a given key K so as to shorten the search paths for keys. Brent's analysis showed that the time for unsuccessful searches does not differ from that for open addressing with double hashing. Empirical data that compare successful search times for Algorithm 4.5, for binary tree hashing, and for Brent's method are shown in Table 4.3

4.3.7 Optimal preloading

In some applications, such as a hash table of opcodes for an assembler, the keys can be inserted all at once when the table is being set up, before any searches are performed. Subsequently, the table stays fixed since no insertions are performed. Under these circumstances it is profitable to preload the table in some order of insertion of keys that minimizes expected average search times with respect to some anticipated set of frequencies of access for the keys. Poonan [1976] found a method for computing the optimal placement of keys in time $O(N^3)$ to minimize average search times by noting that the optimal-placement problem is a variant of the assignment problem in operations research. Some empirical data (see Poonan) show successful search times on the order of 1.4 probes for $\alpha = 0.50$, 1.5 probes for $\alpha = 0.80$, 1.6 probes for $\alpha = 0.90$, and 1.7 probes for $\alpha = 0.95$. This is slightly better than the results for binary tree hashing, but the $O(N^3)$ time restricts the application of the method to smaller-size problems than those that binary tree hashing can handle. For further information on optimal key placement see Rivest [1978a], and for an approach that comes close to the optimal packing but uses only $O(n)$ packing costs, see Lyon [1978, 1979].

4.3.8 Deletions

Deleting items from hash tables set up using chaining is straightforward. But for the open addressing techniques, we cannot simply remove an item from a table, since it may be on the probe sequence used to locate some other item, and replacing it with an empty item would have the effect of removing the other item as well from view to algorithms such as Algorithms 4.5 and 4.6. Under the circumstances, one possible method is to mark an item as deleted, but to leave it in the table. Then, when searching for a key K, we should treat the deleted items as if they were present while, when inserting an item, we can use the first empty *or deleted* entry we locate in the probe sequence explored. The trouble with this policy is that entries never become empty once they are first occupied, so the table clogs up and performance degrades. In the unordered open-addressing techniques, eventually unsuccessful searches may each take M probes if all empty entries have been consumed after a long sequence of insertions and deletions. The situation can be improved, however, by periodically rehashing the table *in situ* (i.e., with the table kept in place) under the agreement that *deleted entries are not rehashed*.

4.3.9 Rehashing *in situ*

When a hash table becomes full, room for additional entries can be created by allocating space for a larger hash table. Entries in the original table can be removed, one by one, and inserted into the new table, using a new hashing function appropriate to its larger size. This process is called *rehashing*.

Even when a hash table has not overflowed, rehashing to a larger table may be beneficial, if, for example, it lowers average search times. Rehashing can also be used to compress a hash table by discarding a fraction of the empty entries while retaining the nonempty ones. In this case, the new table is chosen to be smaller than the original, but still sufficiently large to contain all the original entries to be saved.

So long as the original table and the new table are allocated in disjoint regions of memory, rehashing is straightforward. One need merely enumerate the elements of the old table serially, and insert each nonempty (and nondeleted) entry so enumerated into the new table, using a hash-insertion algorithm for the new table. However, if it is desired to expand (or contract) a given table on the spot, say by adding (or removing) space at one end of the table, then the rehashed entries may be inserted in the same table space where unrehashed entries lie, and collisions may occur between them. Thus, rehashing a table in place presents problems different from those met in rehashing into a disjoint table.

The *in situ* rehashing algorithm given below as Algorithm 4.9 is a variant of the one given by Bays [1973a], adapted to the use of open addressing with double hashing.

Algorithm 4.9 *In Situ rehashing of a hash table.*

Let T be a hash table with $0, 1, \ldots, M_1 - 1$ entries and $N < M_1$ occupied entries. We extend (or retract) the table by adding (or subtracting) entries at the top so that its new address space is $0, 1, \ldots, M_2 - 1$, where, again, $N < M_2$. We have $h(K)$ and $p(K)$ as two new hash functions, where $h(K)$ maps key K onto 0 through $M_2 - 1$ and $p(K)$ is relatively prime to M_2.

1. [Initialize.] Set $i \leftarrow 0$, and set X to contain an empty table entry.

2. [Rehashable?] If $T[i]$ is marked neither *empty* nor already *rehashed*, then exchange $X \leftrightarrow T[i]$ and go to step 4. Otherwise, continue linear enumeration at step 3.

3. [Advance to next.] Set $i \leftarrow i + 1$. If $i = M_1$, then the algorithm terminates. Otherwise, go back to step 2.

4. [Compute hash constants.] Set $K \leftarrow \text{Key}(X)$, $a \leftarrow h(K)$, and $c \leftarrow p(K)$.

5. [Find unrehashed location.] If $T[a]$ is marked already *rehashed*, then repeatedly compute new probe addresses $a \leftarrow (a - c) \bmod M_2$ until finding an address a such that $T[a]$ is not marked *rehashed*.

6. [Insert in Table.] Exchange $T[a] \leftrightarrow X$. Mark $T[a]$ as *rehashed*. (The entry originally in $T[a]$ has been saved as the value of X and becomes the displaced entry.)

7. [Process displaced entry?] If the displaced entry X is marked *empty*, then go

back to step 3 to resume linear enumeration of T. Otherwise, go back to step 4 to rehash it and place it in the table in turn.

The algorithm assumes that it is possible to distinguish between *empty* and *nonempty* table entries, and that entries can be marked *rehashed* or *not-rehashed*. Initially, it is assumed that all entries are marked *not-rehashed*.

Informally, the *in situ* rehashing algorithm works as follows. We conduct an ascending linear sweep of the table addresses from 0 to $M_1 - 1$, examining each entry as we go. When we find an entry X that has not been rehashed, we extract its key and compute hash constants $a = h(K)$ and $c = p(K)$ with which to compute the probe sequence for K. This probe sequence is $\beta_0, \beta_1, \ldots, \beta_{M_2-1}$, where $\beta_i = (a - i \times c) \bmod M_2$. We locate the first address, say β_j, in this probe sequence not containing a rehashed entry. This is the location where the rehashed entry X is to be relocated; but if it contains an unrehashed entry, the unrehashed entry must be relocated to make room for X. The unrehashed entries that are displaced by the insertion of rehashed entries are themselves immediately rehashed, perhaps causing a cascade of subsequent similar displacements. Eventually, any such cascade of displacements must die out, at which point the original linear sweep is resumed in search of more unrehashed entries to process. The algorithm terminates when the linear sweep exhausts the limits of the old table.

Using a variation of the algorithm, we can rehash a table into itself *in place* to remove deleted entries. The deleted entries (say, marked for deletion, as discussed above), are replaced with true empty entries when they are examined in step 2.

The *in situ* algorithm takes roughly the same amount of time as the conventional algorithm to rehash an old table into a disjoint new table, since the *in situ* and disjoint versions each require a linear sweep of the address range for the old table, plus similar cumulative times to insert rehashed items into the address range for the new table. The two versions differ mainly in the order in which they rehash nonempty entries.

Hopgood [1968] studies two questions related to rehashing: (a) determining the load factor α at which it is profitable to rehash, given that the cost of rehashing can be repaid by making k cheaper accesses in the rehashed table, and (b) the related question of how big the new table should be.

4.3.10 Hashing functions

Underlying the discussion on hashing so far has been an assumption that we could find suitable hashing functions $h(K)$ mapping the domain of keys K into the range of addresses 0, 1, ..., $M - 1$ in a hash table. How shall we choose such hashing functions?

We present here only two of the many techniques known for selecting hashing functions. One method uses division and the other uses multiplication. An exten-

sive survey of hashing functions is given by Knott [1975], and valuable information is given in the treatment of this topic by Knuth [1973b].

4.3.10.1 *The division method.* In the division method, we simply let $h(K)$ be
the remainder of K after division by the table size M:

$$h(K) = K \bmod M. \tag{11}$$

However, we must choose M carefully. For example, if M is a power of the radix of
the computer, such as $M = 2^r$, then $h(K)$ would simply consist of the r least
significant bits of K. Thus, the distributional features of the r last bits of the keys K
would determine the distribution of the values $h(K)$. Choosing M as a prime
number is a step in the right direction; but further precautions are necessary. For
example, suppose we are working on a computer with a 24-bit word length, and
we choose keys composed of three 8-bit characters of the form $C_1 C_2 C_3$ (chosen,
say, from the EBCDIC character set, which might not be uncommon for IBM
equipment). Suppose we choose a table size $M = 65537$, which, it so happens, is of
the form $2^{16} + 1$, a number verified by Fermat to be prime. Thus, to compute the
hash function $h(C_1 C_2 C_3)$, we use the formula $(C_1 C_2 C_3) \bmod (2^{16} + 1)$. If we
express $C_1 C_2 C_3$ as a radix-256 number, we get

$$h(C_1 C_2 C_3) = (C_1 \times 256^2 + C_2 \times 256 + C_3) \bmod (256^2 + 1);$$

and if, now, $256 C_2 + C_3 > C_1$, the quotient of $C_1 C_2 C_3$ divided by $2^{16} + 1$ will be
simply C_1, and the remainder will be of the form

$$(C_1 \times 256^2 + C_2 \times 256 + C_3) - C_1 \times (256^2 + 1) = (C_2 \times 256 + C_3) - C_1.$$

Thus, expressed as a base-256 number, the value of $h(C_1 C_2 C_3)$ is
$(C_2 C_3 - C_1)_{256}$. This shows that the values of $h(K)$ tend to be simple superposi-
tions of the characters in the key K, an unfortunate outcome.

Generalizing, we should avoid choosing the table size M as a prime of the
form $r^k \pm a$, where r is the radix of the character set (such as $r = 64$ for ASCII,
$r = 256$ for EBCDIC, or $r = 100$ for some binary-coded decimal machines), and
where k and a are small integers. If this choice is avoided, experience shows that
the division method produces satisfactory results in many cases. For example,
studies by Lum, Yuen, and Dodd [1971], Lum [1973], and Buchholz [1963] indicate that using the division method with a prime divisor or a divisor relatively
prime to the table size yielded the best average performance among the methods
investigated. The study of Lum, Yuen, and Dodd [1971], for instance, compared
the performance of eight types of hashing functions (including the *division method*,
digit analysis, mid-square hashing, folding, algebraic coding, and others) on eight
sets of keys (some numeric, some alphabetic, and some alphanumeric) of varying
key length (from 5 to 12 symbols), with the size of the sets of keys varying from 500
to 33575 and drawn in seven out of the eight cases from actual files used in practice

(such as product codes, personnel locations, customer codes, applicants, and the like). They conclude that the division method outperforms even theoretical randomization when collisions are resolved by chaining.

4.3.10.2 *The multiplicative method.* Suppose we start with the *golden ratio*

$$\phi^{-1} = \frac{\sqrt{5} - 1}{2} = 0.61803399,$$

and suppose we examine its multiples $i\phi^{-1}$ for $1 \le i \le 20$, the fractional parts of those multiples, and the floor of 10 times the fractional parts of the multiples. This gives Table 4.4 (where $\{x\}$ denotes $x - \lfloor x \rfloor$).

TABLE 4.4

i	Multiple $i\phi^{-1}$	Fractional part $\{i\phi^{-1}\}$	Floor of 10 × fractional part $\lfloor 10 \times \{i\phi^{-1}\} \rfloor$
1	0.618034	.618034	6
2	1.236068	.236068	2
3	1.854102	.854102	8
4	2.472136	.472136	4
5	3.090170	.090170	0
6	3.708204	.708204	7
7	4.326238	.326238	3
8	4.944272	.944272	9
9	5.562306	.562306	5
10	6.180340	.180340	1
11	6.798374	.798374	7
12	7.416408	.416408	4
13	8.034442	.034442	0
14	8.652476	.652476	6
15	9.270510	.270510	2
16	9.888544	.888544	8
17	10.506578	.506578	5
18	11.124612	.124612	1
19	11.742646	.742646	7
20	12.360680	.360680	3

Note that the first ten values of $\lfloor 10 \times \{i\phi^{-1}\} \rfloor$ are a permutation of the numbers 0, 1, ..., 9. Thus, if we are dealing with a table of size $M = 10$ entries, we might be able to use as hash addresses multiples of the golden ratio with the integer part thrown away, scaled to the table size, and then rounded appropriately. When we examine the fractional parts of the multiples of the golden ratio $\{i\phi^{-1}\}$ and look closely at how these fractional parts fall into the interval $[0, 1)$, we find a remarkable phenomenon—each newly added point falls into one of the largest remaining intervals and divides it into the golden ratio! Note in Table 4.5 the progression of interval splitting as we add points to the interval $[0, 1)$ taken from column 3 of Table 4.4.

TABLE 4.5

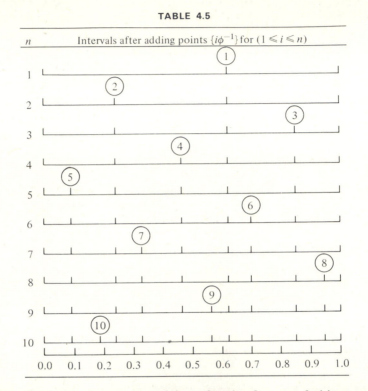

n	Intervals after adding points $\{i\phi^{-1}\}$ for $(1 \leqslant i \leqslant n)$

In fact, the intervals are created in a first-in, first-out fashion, so that the interval split by the next point added is the oldest of the largest intervals remaining (as can be verified by examining Table 4.4). This phenomenon generalizes: If θ is an irrational number, the fractional parts of n multiples of θ, of the form

$$\{\theta\}, \{2\theta\}, \ldots, \{n\theta\},$$

when placed in the interval $[0, 1)$, will divide the interval into $n + 1$ line segments of at most three lengths, and the next point $\{(n + 1)\theta\}$ always falls into the oldest of the largest existing segments. (See Knuth [1973b], p. 511 for further discussion.) It turns out that choosing the numbers $\theta = \phi^{-1}$ and $\theta = 1 - \phi^{-1}$ leads to the most uniformly distributed interval-splitting points among all possible values of θ between 0 and 1.

Suppose now that we use the key K as a multiplier for θ, compute the fractional part of $K\theta$, scale by the table size $M \times \{K\theta\}$, and choose as a hash address the greatest integer less than or equal to $M \times \{K\theta\}$. This computes a hash address in the proper range 0 to $M - 1$. Hence, we can use as a hashing function something of the form $h(K) = \lfloor M\{K\theta\} \rfloor$. Actually, though, we want $h(K)$ to have two properties: (1) $h(K)$ should be fast to compute, and (2) $h(K)$ should minimize collisions. We can compute the multiplicative version of $h(K)$ faster, if we think of integers in the computer as being fixed-point fractions with the radix point to the left of the word. This way, we might be able to find an integer A such that $\theta \approx A/w$, where w is the word size of the computer. Now, suppose further that we choose a table size that is a power of 2, say $M = 2^m$. Then the following steps enable rapid calculation of $h(K)$ multiplicatively:

1. $X \leftarrow A \times K$

2. $X \leftarrow X \bmod w$

3. $X \leftarrow$ the leftmost m bits of the value of X

Following Knuth ([1973b], p. 509), the general formula for $h(K)$ is

$$h(K) = \left\lfloor M\left(\left(\frac{A}{w} K\right) \bmod 1\right) \right\rfloor, \tag{12}$$

where A is relatively prime to w. Further considerations (Knuth [1973b], p. 512) indicate that taking $\theta = 0.6125423371$ gives even better dispersion of certain groups of related keys than $\theta \approx \phi^{-1}$.

4.3.11 Choosing a hashing technique

We have seen that the choice of a hashing technique involves two decisions: (1) choosing a hashing function $h(K)$ that is cheap to compute and minimizes collisions, and (2) choosing a collision-resolution policy.

With regard to collision-resolution policies, we have seen that there are some rather remarkable techniques that cost very few probes even at near saturation of the table, and that we can choose methods (such as binary tree hashing) to minimize probes for successful search if unsuccessful searches and insertions are expected to be rare, or methods (such as ordered hash table search with double hashing and pass bits) to minimize insertion times and unsuccessful searches, if the latter are expected frequently.

However, minimizing the number of probes does not tell the whole story. This is particularly the case for the use of hashing techniques for files stored on external memory devices—a topic explored in Chapter 9 on files. Actually, hashing with separate chains kept in order of the keys can be shown to yield the least number of probes of any of the techniques examined for both successful and unsuccessful searches (see Knuth [1973b], p. 518, and p. 546, Exercises 34–35, where it can be shown that it costs an average of $1 + \alpha/2$ probes for a successful search and less than $1 + \alpha/4$ probes for an unsuccessful search). Practical considerations sometimes intrude with the pure application of these methods. For instance, consider the case of using hash symbol tables for compilers handling variable-length identifiers. In some implementations a level of indirection is employed. That is, the hash table itself consists of n pointers, which point to the actual keys used. But if variable-length identifiers are stored in the symbol table directly in packed form, double hashing is rendered inoperable by the nonuniform size of the table entries. However, chaining the entries in place in the table can be made to work. On the other hand, chaining requires space for keeping links, and this space might by released to provide for more entries if an open-addressing technique were selected. The open-addressing technique might then operate at lower load factors and, using tight inner loops, it might prove superior to chaining methods at such lower load factors.

4.4 DECISION TABLES

Decision tables are a tabular system of notation that have acquired popularity in areas such as business data processing and systems analysis. Decision tables display various combinations of conditions that, when satisfied, imply that certain associated prescribed actions are to be taken. In situations where hundreds of possible combinations of conditions arise and where numerous possible subsets of prescribed actions may be invoked, decision tables help cope with complexity. For example, they provide a framework for systematically checking such matters as:

a) *consistency* (whether there exist two or more sets of conditions that can be satisfied simultaneously, yet which imply different actions);

b) *completeness* (whether every possible legitimate combination of conditions has been covered); and

c) *redundancy* (whether a set of conditions implying a set of actions is given more than once).

In some instances, these properties can be checked mechanically. Furthermore, decision tables can be translated into computer programs that are optimized for space or time.

Advocates of decision tables maintain that, in addition to promoting reliability and efficiency, the use of decision tables helps programmers and analysts to deal systematically with inherent complexity, to communicate better with each other, and to clarify the logic of complex designs.

The literature on decision tables is voluminous. For instance, one survey by King [1967] lists 29 papers, the survey article by Pooch [1974] lists 108 papers and the bibliography of Metzner and Barnes [1977] lists 191 references. In fact, one author of a letter to the *ACM Forum* mentions he has looked at over 180 works on decision tables, 80 percent of which are devoted to decision-table conversion

(Chvalovsky [1976]). Four books on the subject are Montalbano [1974], London [1972], Metzner and Barnes [1977], and Pollock, Hicks, and Harrison [1971]. Our purpose here is to introduce the subject and to indicate some of the interesting problems.

Suppose an auto insurance company has the following decision rules for deciding which male customers it will insure and whether they are to pay just the basic premium or the basic premium plus a surcharge for higher risk.

1. A customer pays only the basic premium if he has had less than two accidents in the past three years and is either over 25 years of age or is married.

2. A customer is uninsurable if he has had two or more accidents in the last three years and is 25 or under.

3. A customer pays the basic premium plus a high risk surcharge of 50 percent extra if he has had two or more accidents in the last three years and is older than 25, or if he is single and 25 or under but has not had two or more accidents in the last three years.

	1	2	3	4	5
1. Married?	–	N	–	N	Y
2. Age is 25 or less?	Y	Y	N	N	–
3. Two or more accidents in last three years?	Y	N	Y	N	N
4. Uninsurable. Deny application.	X				
5. Pay basic premium.		X	X	X	X
6. Pay risk surcharge.		X	X		

FIGURE 4.6

These rules can be represented in a decision table such as that given in Fig. 4.6. This decision table is divided into four quadrants by the horizontal and vertical double lines. The list of questions in the upper left quadrant is called the *condition stub*, and the list of actions in the lower left quadrant is called the *action stub*. The entries in the upper right quadrant are called *condition entries*. These are of the form Y (for yes), N (for no), and – (for don't care which). The entries in the lower righthand quadrant are called *action entries* and are either blank (meaning "Don't take the action") or X (to indicate that the action is to be taken).

The columns numbered 1 through 5 are called *rules*. The rule in column 2, for instance, is read "If (not married) and (age is 25 or less) and (not had two or more accidents in last three years), then (pay basic premium) and (pay risk surcharge)." The rule in column 3 is read "(No matter whether married or not), if (not 25 or less) and (has had two or more accidents in last three years), then (pay basic premium) and (pay risk surcharge)."

A decision table, some of whose entries are dashes "–" (or *don't-care* entries), can be expanded to a table containing no don't-care entries. To do this, two copies of a column containing a dash, say, in row *i*, are made. In one of the copies, the dash in row *i* is replaced by *Y*, and in the other copy, the dash in row *i* is replaced by *N*. This eliminates one dash, and creates two rules where one had been before. The process is repeated until all dashes have been eliminated. For example, rule 5 of Fig. 4.6 has condition entries

$$\begin{matrix} Y \\ - \\ N \end{matrix}.$$

These are expanded to

$$\begin{matrix} Y \\ Y \\ N \end{matrix} \quad \text{and} \quad \begin{matrix} Y \\ N \\ N \end{matrix}.$$

The fully expanded version of the table of Fig. 4.6 is given as Fig. 4.7.

	1	2	3	4	5	6	7	8
Married?	Y	N	N	Y	N	N	Y	Y
Age ⩽ 25?	Y	Y	Y	N	N	N	Y	N
Accidents ⩾2?	Y	Y	N	Y	Y	N	N	N
Uninsurable.	X	X						
Pay premium.			X	X	X	X	X	X
Pay surcharge.			X	X	X			

FIGURE 4.7

The decision table of Fig. 4.6 is not the only one whose fully expanded form is Fig. 4.7. The table in Fig. 4.8 also expands to Fig. 4.7. This illustrates the point that sets of rules with identical action parts may be simplified in various alternative ways to obtain condensed tables. The method that produces the greatest number of don't-care entries, starting with the fully expanded table, produces the greatest condensation.

	1	2	3	4	5
Married?	–	N	–	–	Y
Age ≤25?	Y	Y	N	N	Y
Accidents ≥2?	Y	N	Y	N	N
Uninsurable.	X				
Pay premium.		X	X	X	X
Pay surcharge.		X	X		

FIGURE 4.8

The problem of condensing decision tables in this fashion is similar to a problem that occurs in the design of switching circuits, in which one tries to find the smallest number of circuit elements that realize a given Boolean function. In an expanded decision table, a subset of rules each having the same subset of actions A corresponds to a Boolean function in disjunctive normal form. For example, in Fig. 4.7, consider rules 6, 7, and 8, implying the common action "Pay basic premium." If we represent the conditions in the condition stub by the propositonal variables C_1, C_2, and C_3, then the Boolean function $f(C_1, C_2, C_3)$ corresponding to rules 6, 7, and 8 is

$$f(C_1, C_2, C_3) = \overline{C_1} \cdot \overline{C_2} \cdot \overline{C_3} \vee C_1 \cdot C_2 \cdot \overline{C_3} \vee C_1 \cdot \overline{C_2} \cdot \overline{C_3}.$$

(Here, $\vee$ means logical disjunction, $\cdot$ means logical conjunction, and $\overline{C_i}$ is the logical negation of C_i.) Schwayder [1975] has shown how to apply both Karnaugh maps and Quine–McCluskey techniques for Boolean function simplification to the solution of the rule minimization problem for decision tables. Informal logical simplification, using rules such as *ground resolution* ($A \cdot \overline{B} \vee A \cdot B \Rightarrow A$) and *subsumption* ($A \vee A \cdot B \Rightarrow A$) can be used to simplify small examples of such disjunctive normal forms by hand. However, if the goal of the optimization process is to minimize expected processing time, some procedures accomplish this at the expense of increasing rather than decreasing the number of rules (Reinwald and Soland [1966]).

In a fully expanded decision table, it is easy to define the concepts of *completeness, consistency* and *redundancy*. Let T be a fully expanded table with n conditions. Then two rules of T are said to be *inconsistent* if they have identical condition entries but nonidentical action entries. A table with no pair of inconsistent rules is said to be *consistent*. Two rules are *redundant* if they are identical, and a table with a pair of redundant rules is said to be *redundant*. The table T is *complete* if it consists of 2^n rules, no two of which are either inconsistent or redundant.

	1	2	3
C_1	–	Y	Y
C_2	N	N	–
C_3	–	–	Y
A_1	X	X	
A_2			X

FIGURE 4.9

Let a rule whose condition part consists only of "Y" and "N" entries be called a *simple* rule, and let a rule whose condition part consists of "Y", "N", and "–" entries be called a *composite* rule. A composite rule R_1 is said to *overlap* with another rule R_2 if R_1 and R_2 can be expanded into respective sets S_1 and S_2 of rules such that some rule in S_1 has a condition part identical to the condition part of some rule in S_2. For example, in Fig. 4.9, Rules 1 and 2 overlap because rule 1 can be expanded to the two rules

	1a	1b
C_1	Y	N
C_2	N	N
C_3	–	–
A_1	X	X
A_2		

the first of which is identical to rule 2. In this case, the overlap is said to be redundant. Rules 2 and 3 also overlap in Fig. 4.9 because one expansion of rule 2, namely

	2a
C_1	Y
C_2	N
C_3	Y
A_1	X
A_2	

has a condition part identical to one of the expansions of rule 3, namely

3b

C_1	Y
C_2	N
C_3	Y
A_1	
A_2	X

In this case, the overlap is said to be inconsistent because identical condition parts in the overlapping expansions correspond to different actions A_1 and A_2 respectively.

	1	2	3	4
C_1: Age $\leqslant 25$?	Y	N	Y	N
C_2: Age $= 25$?	N	Y	N	N
C_3: Age > 50?	N	N	Y	Y

FIGURE 4.10

Another sort of inconsistency is that called *intra-rule* inconsistency. Heretofore, we have tacitly assumed that the conditions in the condition stub have been logically independent. This need not be the case, however, in some applications. For instance, consider the conditions shown in Fig. 4.10. It is impossible for one person to have an age x satisfying the conditions of columns 2 or 3 of Fig. 4.10, since whenever $C_2 = Y$, C_1 is forced to be Y, and C_3 is forced to be N. Also, if $C_3 = Y$, C_1 and C_2 are forced to be N. Let us call the combinations in columns 2 and 3 *forbidden combinations*. Some authors (e.g., King [1969], Pooch [1974], Verhelst [1972], and Pollock, Hicks, and Harrison [1972]) use special symbols to indicate whether condition entries are forced to take on given values resulting from dependency on the outcomes of other condition tests. Intra-rule inconsistency occurs if mutually inconsistent responses are given as condition entries in a rule in violation of the logical dependency of the conditions. King [1968] observes that it is often unrealistic to assume that the conditions in decision tables are mutually independent in practice.

A decision table is said to be *ambiguous* if there is a logically permissible datum that satisfies the condition entries of two rules having different action sets. If we are dealing with logically independent conditons, then a decision table is ambiguous iff it has a pair of inconsistent rules. However, when the conditions are logically dependent, the following interaction may occur between overlapping inconsistent rules and dependent conditions. Let R_1 and R_2 be the condition parts of two composite rules with different action sets, whose expansions $E(R_1)$ and $E(R_2)$ into simple rules have overlapping condition parts $E(R_1) \cap E(R_2)$. Suppose that each of the condition combinations in $E(R_1) \cap E(R_2)$ is a *forbidden combination*—i.e., that, due to the logical dependencies of the conditions, none of the condition combinations in $E(R_1) \cap E(R_2)$ can ever arise for any possible datum tested against the conditions. Then the decision table has only an *apparent ambiguity*, not a real one.

	1	2	3
Age < 18?	Y	–	N
Age > 65?	–	Y	N
A_1	X		
A_2		X	
A_3			X

FIGURE 4.11

For example, consider the decision table of Fig. 4.11. The overlap between the condition parts of rules 1 and 2 occurs for expanded rules

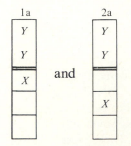

having inconsistent actions A_1 and A_2, respectively. But ^Y_Y is a forbidden combination of conditions, since there exists no age x such that $x < 18$ and $x > 65$. Hence, the ambiguity is apparent rather than real.

Considering forbidden combinations leads to refinements of the definitions of completeness, consistency, and redundancy given earlier. The idea of completeness was to ensure that decision tables "cover all possible combinations of conditions." The basis of the earlier definition of completeness was that, if a decision table has n logically independent conditions, it has 2^n possible combinations of n logically independent truth values. If, now, the conditions are dependent in such a fashion as to exclude k forbidden combinations, the table could be said to be *complete* if its expansion covers all $2^n - k$ combinations none of which is forbidden. Similarly, a fully expanded table is *redundant* (*inconsistent*) if it contains a pair of rules R_1 and R_2 with the same (different) action sets, and having identical condition parts that are not forbidden combinations. An unexpanded table is *complete* (*redundant, inconsistent*) iff the corresponding fully expanded table is *complete* (*redundant, inconsistent*). In these terms, a table is *ambiguous* just when it is inconsistent.

The discussion of decision table ambiguity in the literature has given rise to an extended debate. While it is clearly easy to check mechanically for consistency and redundancy in the case of logically independent conditions, the relations between conditions may be complicated in actual practice and not subject to programmed investigation (King [1968]). This has led some authors to advocate dialogs between decision-table processors and the analyst constructing the table (King [1968]). Other authors have advocated systems of run-time diagnostics (Muthukrishnan and Rajaraman [1970]) for pinpointing ambiguities. Still others have advocated compile-time analysis (Pollock [1971]). For further developments in the debate, see King and Johnson [1973].

The decision tables discussed so far (with condition entries Y, N, or $-$, and action entries X or blank) are called *limited-entry decision tables*. A generalization of this notion is the *extended-entry decision table*, in which the condition and action entries can be chosen from subsets of integers. An example of an extended-entry decision table is given in Fig. 4.12 (adapted from Schumacher and Sevcik [1976]).

	1	2	3	4	5	ELSE	Meaning of codes
Meal service.	1	2	3	4	3		1 best, 2 good, 3 poor, 4 foul
Want to come back.	1	–	–	3	1		1 yes, 2 maybe, 3 no
Pennies in pocket.	1	–	2	1	1		1 yes, 2 no
Investments doing well.	1	2	2	–	1		1 well, 2 poorly
Tip amount indicated.	1	2	3	3	2	2	$1 = 15\%, 2 = 10\%, 3 = 0\%$
Get rid of pennies.	1	2	2	1	1	2	1 yes, 2 no

FIGURE 4.12 *Decision table for tipping in a restaurant.*

Figure 4.12 contains a column labeled ELSE, which has a set of actions. This column is called the ELSE rule, and its action part is executed in case the combination of conditions being tested matches none of the conditions of the other rules. Extended-entry decision tables can be translated to limited-entry decision tables by a technique of Press (Press [1965]). Thus, perhaps because no generality is lost, much of the theory of translation of decision tables to computer programs has concerned limited-entry decision tables. However, because efficiency may be lost, some recent explorations have concerned direct translation of extended-entry tables.

4.4.1 Conversion to computer programs

Once a decision table has been developed by a problem analyst or programmer, it is convenient to be able to convert it mechanically into an efficient running program. Two broad categories of methods have received the bulk of attention in the literature, *rule-mask techniques* and *decision-tree techniques*.

In the *rule-mask techniques*, binary images of the condition entries are prepared. In some treatments, such as that of Kirk [1965], one of these binary images is a *masking matrix M* prepared from the matrix of condition entries in the table by replacing dashes "–" with the bit 0, and replacing both Y and N with the bit 1. Another matrix R is defined from the matrix of condition entries by replacing Y by 1 and other entries by 0. Given a datum d to be tested, a vector V of responses to the conditions applied to d is prepared in which 1 stands for a "yes" answer, and 0 stands for a "no" answer. A rule j of the decision table applies to the response vector V provided

$$V \wedge M[j] = R[j],$$

where $M[j]$ and $R[j]$ are the jth columns of M and R, respectively. (For variations on this idea, see Kirk [1965], King [1966], and Muthukrishnan and Rajaraman [1970]).

An interesting variation is that given by Barnard [1969] (which is closely related to a technique in Muthukrishnan and Rajaraman [1970]).

4.4.1.1 *Barnard's technique.* The technique is illustrated by Figs. 4.13, 4.14, and 4.15. The *true matrix T* in Fig. 4.14 is derived from the condition entries of Fig. 4.13 by replacing "Y" and "–" by 1, and replacing "N" by 0. The *false matrix F* in Fig. 4.15 is obtained by coding 1 in all positions of Fig. 4.13 containing "N" or "–" and 0 in all positions containing "Y".

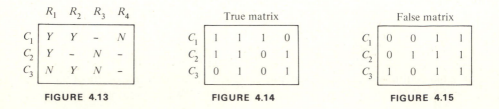

	R_1	R_2	R_3	R_4
C_1	Y	Y	–	N
C_2	Y	–	N	–
C_3	N	Y	N	–

FIGURE 4.13

True matrix

C_1	1	1	1	0
C_2	1	1	0	1
C_3	0	1	0	1

FIGURE 4.14

False matrix

C_1	0	0	1	1
C_2	0	1	1	1
C_3	1	0	1	1

FIGURE 4.15

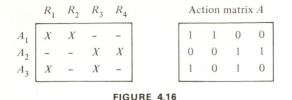

FIGURE 4.16

Let there be m rules $R[1], R[2], \ldots, R[m]$ and n conditions $C[1], C[2], \ldots, C[n]$. Let W be a *cumulative rule vector* of length m bits, which contains 1 in all positions initially. Each condition is tested in sequence, and if the outcome is true, the corresponding row of the true matrix T is *and*ed with the cumulative rule vector, while if the outcome is false, the corresponding row of the false matrix F is *and*ed with the cumulative rule vector. When all conditions have been tested, the cumulative rule vector has 1's in positions corresponding to satisfied rules, and 0's elsewhere. If the action entries are coded as a matrix, as in Fig. 4.16, the cumulative rule vector W (after condition testing) can be *and*ed with each row of the action matrix in sequence. If the result of *and*ing W with row $A[i]$ of the action matrix is a nonzero vector, the corresponding action A_i is executed. Otherwise, the action A_i is not executed, and the next row of the action matrix is considered in sequence. Barnard's technique is given as Algorithm 4.10.

Algorithm 4.10 *Barnard's rule mask interpretation procedure.*

Let T, F, and A be matrices coded as specified above, and let there be n conditions, m rules, and k actions.

1. [Initialization.] Set $W \leftarrow$ a row vector of m 1's. (W is the cumulative rule vector).
2. [Test conditions.] For $i \leftarrow 1, 2, \ldots, n$, do the following. If condition C_i is true for the test datum d, then $W \leftarrow W \wedge T[i]$. Otherwise, set $W \leftarrow W \wedge F[i]$.
3. [Take actions.] For $i \leftarrow 1, 2, \ldots, k$, if $W \wedge A[i] \neq 0$, then perform action A_i.

Rule-mask techniques have high storage-utilization efficiency (2 bits per table entry) and can take advantage of hardware capabilities for word-at-a-time execution of logical operations.

4.4.1.2 *Decision-tree techniques.* *Decision-tree* techniques result from conversion of the condition entries in a decision table into binary decision trees, in which condition tests are placed at each internal node of the tree and in which the outcomes of the tests determine which subtree to use for subsequent testing. The leaves of the trees select rules.

A common framework for many approaches is to decompose the original problem recursively into two subproblems of smaller size, as follows. Let C be an n-row table of condition entries ($n > 1$). Select a condition for some i ($1 \leq i \leq n$). Make two smaller tables C_Y and C_N from C by deleting the ith row of C and retaining in C_Y those columns j such that

$$C[i, j] = \text{``}Y\text{''} \quad \text{or} \quad C[i, j] = \text{``}{-}\text{''},$$

while retaining in C_N those columns j such that

$$C[i, j] = \text{``}N\text{''} \quad \text{or} \quad C[i, j] = \text{``}{-}\text{''}.$$

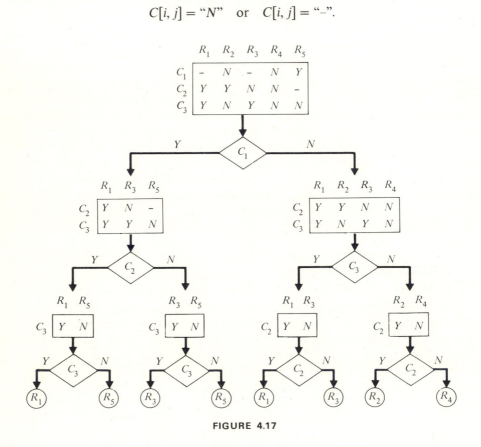

FIGURE 4.17

Create decision subtrees recursively for C_Y and C_N and make them the "Y" and "N" children of the root node. Finally, place the condition test C_i in the root node. When C_Y or C_N has just one row, a final decision can be made, and rules can be selected for the leaves of the tree. Figure 4.17 illustrates this process. We start at the top with the condition entries taken from Fig. 4.6. Choosing the conditions to test in different orders leads to different decision trees. For instance, choosing to test the conditions in the order C_3, C_2, then C_1 leads to the decision tree of Fig. 4.18. In this decision tree, some paths do not require testing all conditions to determine a unique outcome.

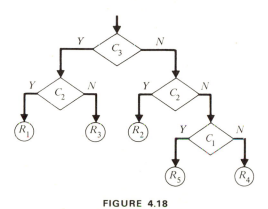

FIGURE 4.18

If we are given a set of execution costs c_i $(1 \leq i \leq n)$ for testing the conditions C_i, and a set of frequencies f_j $(1 \leq j \leq m)$ that characterize how often the various rules R_j $(1 \leq j \leq m)$ will be executed, we can try to find an *optimal decision tree*—one whose expected cost is minimal for the given cost and frequency data.

There are a number of approaches to this problem in the literature. It is easy to see that the search space for solutions is large and grows rapidly with the number of conditions. Let $f(n)$ be the number of complete decision trees on n conditions (those in which each path from the root to a leaf tests n distinct conditions). We have only one decision tree on one condition, so $f(1) = 1$. But for n conditions, there are n ways of choosing the condition to test at the root, and both subtrees can be chosen independently from amongst the $f(n-1)$ subtrees on $n - 1$ conditions. This gives rise to the following recurrence relations:

$$f(1) = 1,$$

$$f(n) = n \cdot f(n-1)^2,$$

which is solved by

$$f(n) = \prod_{1 \leq i \leq n} i^{(2^{n-i})}.$$

This grows quite rapidly. For instance,

n	$f(n)$
1	1
2	2
3	12
4	576
5	1.66×10^6
10	5.84×10^{224}
12	1.68×10^{902}

(see Schumacher and Sevcik [1976]).

Reinwald and Soland [1966] have solved the problem of finding the decision tree with minimum execution time using branch-and-bound techniques in this search space. Schumacher and Sevcik [1976] observe that the Reinwald and Soland algorithm is effective for $n \leq 6$. It takes several seconds for $n = 5$, several hours for $n = 6$, and is estimated to take years or centuries for $n > 6$ (Schumacher and Sevcik [1976], p. 349). Schumacher and Sevcik [1976] and Bayes [1973] adopt a bottom-up approach in which they calculate and save the optimal decision trees of size k for $k = 1, 2, \ldots, n$. This way the optimal tree of size $k + 1$ can utilize the optima for sizes k and less. An important saving is introduced in this fashion, since, in contrast to the recursive decomposition methods, the same subproblem is never considered twice. Schumacher and Sevcik found it feasible to compute optimal decision trees for $n \leq 12$ (using 4×10^6 32-bit words of storage when $n = 12$). Storage requirements grow proportional to 3^n with use of their technique.

Since Hyafil and Rivest [1976] have shown that constructing optimal binary decision trees is *NP*-complete, it is not surprising that the above-mentioned algorithms take exponential time. Thus there is motivation for finding efficient heuristics for constructing near-optimal decision trees. For decision tables there are heuristics that approach the optimum trees reasonably well. For instance, Schumacher and Sevcik [1976] report that the heuristic of Ganpathy and Rajaraman [1973] came within two percent of optimal for $n = 8$. Schwayder [1974] argues, on information theoretic grounds, that the curve along which the optimum decision tree is located is relatively flat in the region of the optimum, so that heuristic techniques have a good chance of finding near-optimal solutions. Heuristic techniques have also been investigated by Verhelst [1972] (see comments by King and Johnson [1974]) and Schwayder [1974]. A fast heuristic for selecting which of the remaining conditions to test in the recursive decomposition method is studied in Pollock [1965].

4.5 SYMBOL TABLES

Symbol tables are used in assemblers, compilers, loaders, and lexical analyzers to store associations between *names* and *values*. Names are items such as identifiers, opcodes, and keywords. Values may be items such as relative addresses, block nesting levels, identifier type indicators, and pointers. For example, in a simple compiler, a symbol table might consist of a collection of records of the form:

IDENTIFIER VALUE TYPE

I	v	t

Suppose that the type of an identifier I can be one of the following codes from 0 through 4:

Type	Meaning
0	A keyword such as *if, then, begin, end, for*, or *goto*
1	An undefined label
2	A defined label
3	An integer-valued variable
4	A floating-point valued variable

The contents of the VALUE field in a record depend on the TYPE. For example, for an identifier of types 3 or 4, the VALUE field in the record containing I might contain the run-time address of the storage location to be used for storing values of the variable named I. For an identifier of type 2, the VALUE field might contain the address of the machine-code instruction to jump to corresponding to the label I on some statement in the program.

In general, a *symbol table* can be thought of as a set of n-tuples of the form $(I, v_1, v_2, \ldots, v_{n-1})$, where I is a *name*, and where v_i $(1 \leq i \leq n - 1)$ are values of attributes of the name, such that distinct tuples have distinct names. The names can then be used as keys to access the tuples containing them.

How shall we organize a representation for a symbol table? The answer to this question depends heavily on the intended operations to be performed on the symbol table when it is used. For example, some symbol tables (such as a table of opcodes for an assembler) may be *static*, in the sense that they are only used to look up values associated with their names, and are never subjected to insertion or deletion operations during use. On the other hand, some tables may be *dynamic*, in the sense that new records are inserted and deleted during use (as happens, for instance, in symbol tables for handling definitions of identifiers in block-structured programming languages such as ALGOL 60). In yet other cases, we may perform searches, updates, and insertions, but never deletions; and further, the insertions may happen only immediately after unsuccessful searches (in which, if we don't find a name already in the table, we immediately insert it). Occasionally, we may wish to enumerate the names in the table in alphabetical order (say, to print the contents of the table as an index of some sort). Thus, for a particular symbol table of interest, some subset of the following operations may apply:

Symbol Table Operations

1. *retrieve* the values of some attributes of a given name I
2. *update* the values of some attributes of a given name I
3. *insert* a new record consisting of a name and attribute values
4. *delete* a record having a given name I
5. *enumerate* the records in the table in alphabetical order of names

We could organize the representation for the symbol table in at least the following four possible ways:

1. *Ordered sequence:* Place the records in sequential order according to the alphabetical order of their names.
2. *Balanced binary tree:* Create an AVL search tree from the names and place the records at the nodes (or pointers to the portions of records containing values of attributes at the nodes).
3. *Linked list:* Link the records together into a one-way linked list in the order of their names.
4. *Hash table:* Store the records in a hash table with hashing performed on their names.

The choice of which of these four methods to use should be based on an examination of the costs of performing the required operations. Accordingly, we should prepare a table giving the average cost of the above operations for each of the four methods. This is given as Table 4.6.

Some explanation is in order for the figures in this table. If we store the records in a sequentially allocated linear region in order of their names, then *binary search* (Algorithm 4.2) or *Fibonaccian search* (Algorithm 4.4) can be used, to give $O(\log n)$ times for random access; but for insertion (deletion), on the average, half the records must be moved down (up) to make (close) a gap for the record inserted (deleted), leading to $O(n)$ processing costs. In a linked list, once the place for an insertion (deletion) has been located, the insertion (deletion) can be performed at constant cost; but random access in a linked list involves inspecting half the records on the average, an $O(n)$ cost. Using AVL trees or 2–3 trees leads to $O(\log n)$ search times and, in AVL trees, to constant insertion times, once the price for access to the insertion/deletion point has been paid. Also, $O(n)$ enumeration of the records in alphabetical order is possible using symmetric tree traversal (Algorithm 3.7). Hash tables have the fastest random-access, insertion, and deletion times, but they suffer two potential disadvantages. First, to list the records in alphabetical order, the records must first be sorted, at cost $O(n \log n)$. Second, as noted before in this chapter, some hashing techniques (not including chaining) do not have convenient deletion policies; and the tables can become clogged with records marked for deletion, but still physically present to facilitate search for other records.

TABLE 4.6
Expected Processing Times
for Operations on Symbol Tables.

	Random-access retrieval/updating	Insertion/ deletion†	Sequential enumeration
Ordered sequence	$O(\log n)$	$O(n)$	$O(n)$
Balanced binary tree	$O(\log n)$	constant	$O(n)$
Linked list	$O(n)$	constant	$O(n)$
Hash table	constant	constant	$O(n \log n)$

† The times in column 2 assume search for the record to be inserted/deleted has taken place.

One can note from a study of Table 4.6 that, while binary search trees are not the best performers in every column, they are also "uniformly not the worst." That is, in any column of Table 4.6, some technique other than balanced search trees performs worse. Thus, balanced search trees can be warmly recommended if all the operations in the heading of Table 4.6 are involved. On the other hand, for dynamic tables with no deletions and no enumerations, hashing techniques seem best (provided there is no real-time requirement, since, with the exception of binary tree hashing, the worst-case access times for hash tables involve looking at all the table entries).

In some applications of symbol tables, such as those for handling identifiers in block-structured languages, it is convenient to combine the advantages of *stacks* and *hash tables*, creating a *hybrid* representation. For instance, in ALGOL 60, a given identifier can be used at more than one block level for two or more different purposes, as in the program:

$$\textbf{begin integer } x, i;$$
$$\vdots$$
$$\textbf{begin real } x, y;$$
$$\vdots$$
$$\textbf{end};$$
$$\textbf{end};$$

Here, the scope of use of the variable x as an integer extends over the outer block, excluding the inner block, and the scope of the use of x as a real variable is confined to the inner block. In a symbol table, to handle this scope-occlusion policy, two symbol-table records must be associated with the same name x. This situation violates the previous assumptions of our analysis, in which distinct records were required to possess distinct names used as search keys.

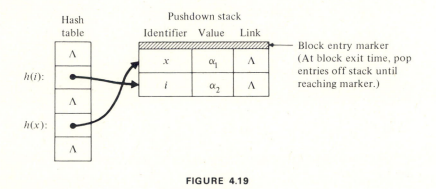

FIGURE 4.19

One solution to this problem is to use a hash table with collision resolution by chaining, and to allocate the records in each chain on a pushdown stack. Figure 4.19 shows the status of the hash table and the stack after the outer block above has been entered, but before the inner block has been entered. Figure 4.20 shows the status of the hash table and stack after both the outer and inner blocks have been entered. When the inner block is exited, the records on top of the pushdown stack are popped one by one until all records associated with the most recent block entry have been removed from the stack. (A marker can be entered on the stack at block entry time, and records can be popped until reaching the shallowest marker, in order to implement this policy.) Each time a record with identifier I is popped, the chain pointer associated with the hash address $h(I)$ in the hash table is reset to point to the successor of record(I) in its chain, instead of to record(I). After exit from the inner block, the hash table and stack are restored to the configuration given in Fig. 4.19. Thus, the operation for entering a record

$$\boxed{I \mid \alpha_i \mid \beta_i}$$

into the symbol table becomes:

Enter record:

1. Push $\boxed{I \mid \alpha_i \mid \beta}$ on the stack. Let θ be the address of the new stack top.

2. Set the link field of θ to point to $T[h(I)]$ and set $T[h(I)] \leftarrow \theta$, where T is the hash table.

Then, to pop a record from the stack:

Pop a record

1. Let I be the identifier in the identifier field on top of the stack, and let θ be the pointer in the link field of the record on top of the stack. Set $T[h(I)] \leftarrow \theta$.

2. Pop the topmost record off the stack.

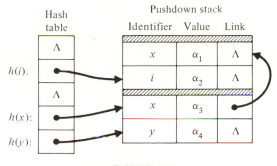

FIGURE 4.20

4.6 BIBLIOGRAPHIC NOTES

Fibonaccian searching was introduced by FERGUSON [1960]. Its efficiency was studied by OVERHOLT [1973] and KNUTH ([1973b], p. 421, Exercise 18). Interpolation searching is studied in YAO and YAO [1976], PERL and REINGOLD [1977], and PERL, ITAI, and AVNI [1978]. PERL and REINGOLD [1977] give a simple analysis showing that interpolation search has log log n behavior, based on a quadratic application of binary search.

Jump searching is studied in SCHNEIDERMAN [1978]. In tables of entries arranged in increasing order of their search keys, jump searching jumps over portions of the ordered table until the search is localized to a small block, after which sequential search or smaller jumps are performed to locate the target key. SCHNEIDERMAN [1978] shows the optimal jump size to be $\sqrt{N}$ for a table of N records. Self-organizing search deals with heuristic policies for placing more frequently accessed keys toward the beginning of a sequence to be searched in sequential order. RIVEST [1976] studies such self-organizing search policies.

TENNENBAUM [1978] presents data on simulations of self-organizing search policies. ALLEN and MUNRO [1978] consider heuristics for maintaining a binary search tree in near optimal form, assuming keys are searched for with independent, fixed, but unknown frequencies.

Surveys of hash table methods are given in MORRIS [1968], MAURER and LEWIS [1975], and KNUTH [1973b]. An extensive survey of hashing functions is provided in KNOTT [1975]. SORENSON, TREMBLAY, and DEUTSCH [1978] define and give examples of distribution-dependent hashing functions and present empirical test data.

Further developments in the chaining technique for handling collision resolution include the method of *coalesced chaining* discussed in KNUTH ([1973b], p. 514) and originally given in WILLIAMS [1959]. HALATSIS and PHILOKYPROU [1978] introduce *pseudochaining* as a collision-resolution method halfway between pure chaining and open addressing. Link fields are present in each cell and the first overflow item is chained. The performance of pseudochaining is between that of direct chaining and the best known open-addressing method.

Perfect hashing functions providing a single probe retrieval method for static sets are discussed in SPRUGNOLI [1977] and in ANDERSON and ANDERSON [1979].

A progression of developments on the topic of quadratic residue search is MAURER [1968], DAY [1970], BELL [1970], RADKE [1970], LAMPORT [1970], HOPGOOD and DAVENPORT [1972], ECKER [1974], BURKHARD [1975a], and BATAGELJ [1975].

DUMEY [1956] contains the first mention of hashing in the open literature. PETERSON [1957] is an early work on hashing that introduced open addressing and provided an influential analysis of uniform hashing. KRAL [1971] studies properties of hashing with linear probing. ULLMAN [1972] proves that there exist nonrandom hashing functions that perform better than uniform hashing, but that it is impossible to sustain uniform improvement at all load factors over uniform hashing. ATAI, KOMLÓS, and SZEMERÉDI [1978] prove that, in a certain sense, there is no fast single hashing algorithm. GUIBAS [1978] studies the phenomenon of k-ary clustering in hashing techniques. Clustering is a pile-up phenomenon that occurs because many keys may probe the same table locations in the same order. A hashing technique exhibits k-ary clustering if the search for a key begins with k independent random probes and subsequent probes are completely determined by the location of the k initial probes. GUIBAS [1978] shows that for $k > 1$, average performance is asymptotically equivalent to the performance of uniform probing.

Optimal placement of keys in a hash table under the assumption of known access frequencies is studied in POONAN [1976] and RIVEST [1978a]. The optimal placement solution takes $O(n^3)$ steps and thus is impractical for fixed tables of very large size. LYON [1978, 1979] studies recursive entry displacement policies, cutoffs for unsuccessful searches, and auxiliary cost functions that yield new techniques for improved open addressing that resemble exact-solution optimal packings, but that impose only $O(n)$ packing costs. Displacements are depth-limited approximations to the optimal solutions. Such techniques are good for large fixed tables (such as dictionaries).

FAGIN, NIEVERGELT, PIPPENGER, and STRONG [1978] introduce *extendible hashing*, an access technique guaranteed to use no more than two page faults to locate a record having a given search key K. Extendible hashing uses Tries that are well balanced and it provides an attractive alternative to balanced-tree methods. LARSON [1978] introduces *dynamic hashing*, a file-organization technique that permits space to be increased and decreased without reorganizing the file. The expected storage utilization is sixty-nine percent at all times. An index is maintained based on a forest of binary trees and there are no overflow records.

FISHER [1966] cites some experience on the effectiveness of using decision tables in a software application. MAES [1978] argues that classical decision-table format is not well suited to represent flow-chart-like programs, and that there may be limitations to decision-table methodology. Ambiguity in decision tables is discussed in KING [1968], KING [1969], KING and JOHNSON [1973], POLLACK [1971], and MUTHUKRISHNAN [1971]. Detection of logic errors in decision tables is studied in IBRAMSHA and RAJARAMAN [1978].

MUTHUKRISHNAN and RAJARAMAN [1970] give a technique similar to BARNARD's (presented in Subsection 4.4.1.1), which yields a rule-mask technique for extended-entry tables. LEW [1978] gives a dynamic programming algorithm for converting extended-entry decision tables to optimal decision trees.

Two surveys on decision tables are presented in POOCH [1974] and KING [1967]. Four books on decision tables are MONTALBANO [1974], LONDON [1972], POLLACK, HICKS, and HARRISON [1971], and METZNER and BARNES [1977].

Two surveys that examine identifier searching techniques applicable to symbol tables are PRICE [1971] and SEVERENCE [1974]. Some statistics for FORTRAN identifiers used in hashing are given in LURIE and VANDONI [1973].

EXERCISES

1. (Self-organizing search) As happens in several situations in practice, suppose the keys K_1, K_2, ..., K_n are accessed in an uneven fashion, with some keys accessed much more frequently than others. Consider keeping the keys in a sequence, recording the frequency of access for each key, and searching the sequence in straight ascending linear order. Investigate policies for reordering the location of keys and their associated frequencies to place more frequently accessed keys toward the beginning of the sequence. For example, suppose that, whenever a key has been located, we move it to the beginning of the sequence. Under various assumptions about the distribution of frequencies of access to the keys, how do your policies behave? (Rivest [1976]).

2. (Merge search, Price [1971]) Let T be a table containing R records, sorted on the value of keys K, and let F be a sequence of keys K sorted in the same order as the keys in T. Each record R in T is of the form [Key: K, Info: I] where I is a number. Write a program to compute the average of the Info fields associated with the keys in F.

3. (Multiplicative binary search setup) Devise an efficient linear-time method for rearranging the records in a table T from an initially ascending order of their keys $K_1 < K_2 < \cdots < K_n$ into the order required for multiplicative binary search (as given in Algorithm 4.3).

4. (Interpolation search) Write an algorithm to perform interpolation search on

records with keys chosen as independent and uniformly distributed random numbers in the range $[0, 1]$.

5. (Probe sequences) Prove that if m and n are relatively prime integers, the sequence of m numbers of the form $(i \times n) \bmod m$ for $1 \le i \le m$ forms a permutation of the numbers $0, 1, \ldots, m - 1$.

6. (Amble and Knuth) Show how to generalize the ordered hashing method of Algorithm 4.6 to apply to external searching where each of the M table positions is a *bucket* containing b or fewer keys.

7. (Choosing hashing functions). Mr. Alf Witt selects as a hashing function $h(K) = K \bmod M$. For a value of his table size, Witt chooses $M = 1024$ since it is easy to use 10-bit addresses for his application. Prove that Witt's function maps even keys onto even hash locations and odd keys onto odd hash locations. Show that Witt's function consists of extracting the last 10 bits of a key. Is this a good hash function?

8. (Knuth [1973b], p. 540) Values for a function $F(x)$ are to be stored in a table. We wish to interpolate the value for $F(x)$ between two stored values $F(x_1)$ and $F(x_2)$. What search method would you select for storing values in the table?

9. (Searching for an interval of keys) You want to locate all items in a table between two keys K and K'. Which search method would you use?

10. (Improving open addressing algorithms) Modify Algorithms 4.5 and 4.6 so that they compute $p(K)$ only once for each key K searched for.

11. (Decision tables) Let $C_1, C_2, \ldots, C_n$ be n logically independent conditions in a decision table. Let A be a set of actions. Let F be an arbitrary expression in the propositional calculus with $C_1, C_2, \ldots, C_n$ as propositional variables. Prove that it is possible to construct a decision table in which actions A are taken iff F is satisfied. [*Hint*: Expand F to disjunctive normal form.]

12. (Decision-table expansion) Suppose rule R_j $(1 \le j \le m)$ of a limited-entry decision table T contains n_j dashes "–" $(n_j \ge 0)$. Prove that, when the composite rules of T are completely expanded to simple rules, the expanded table contains $\sum_{1 \le j \le m} 2^{n_j}$ rules iff no rules of T overlap.

13. (Decision-table design) If your country has an income tax for which you must file an income-tax return, translate the policy for answering the question "Who must file?" into a decision table.

14. (Kirk) Let T be an extended-entry decision table. Develop an algorithm for converting T into a limited-entry decision table. Analyze the increase in the number of table entries as a result of the conversion process.

15. (Symbol-table management) What happens if, in Figs. 4.19 and 4.20, $h(x) = h(i) = h(y)$? Does the chaining method of collision resolution work properly with pushing and popping the stack in this instance?

CHAPTER

LISTS

5.1 INTRODUCTION AND MOTIVATION

Lists are useful because they organize computer memory into an elastic commodity that can be allocated on demand in various amounts and shapes during the running of a program. Lists can be lengthened by the insertion of new elements or by adjoining a new list to a given list. Also, one list can be embedded inside another list. Embedding can be performed repeatedly producing structures of unrestricted depth. Thus, lists can grow both in length and in depth by nesting. Lists can also shrink. Elements or embedded lists can be deleted and lists can be broken into constituent parts.

Thus, lists have interesting growth, combining, and decay laws that permit them to change size and shape dynamically under programmed control. By contrast, certain other methods of storage allocation must preallocate storage in a fixed size and shape before a program is run; and during program execution, size and shape either cannot vary or are costly to vary. This happens, for instance, with the allocation of tables, arrays, and record structures in some programming languages. Often, in order to use these structures advantageously one must be able to predict demand for storage before a program is run so that one can preallocate a sufficient amount of space.

With lists, one need not preallocate the size or shape of storage structures in advance. Being elastic, lists can grow during program execution to handle unpredictable amounts of information of unpredictable shapes. This property makes lists ideal for applications whose natural information requirements grow and shrink unpredictably, and whose parts change shape and combine with each other in ways that cannot be easily forecast.

For example, in symbolic formula manipulation, subexpressions may be nested within expressions to an unpredictable depth, and the number of terms of a formula may grow without limit. Therefore, lists are natural to use. Again, in process scheduling for clock-driven simulation, an unpredictable number of processes may be created, and these must be scheduled for execution. Lists may be useful to keep track of the status of these processes. Sometimes lists are useful in partnership with structures of fixed size and shape. Overflow in a table of fixed size can be absorbed by lists, since lists can grow to meet unforeseen demand for table space. Lists may also be useful in devising efficient algorithms in which they can be used to keep track of internal information at intermediate stages in the execution. For example, the "chaining algorithms" used in one-pass assemblers and compilers sometimes use lists to resolve undefined forward references to labels. For reasons such as these, lists and list structures are an important topic in the study of data structures.

One of the goals of this book is to study, classify, and compare the known significant techniques for representing each of the major types of intermediate data structures that are the focal points of the respective chapters. As might be expected, there are a number of different possible underlying representations for lists, each with particular advantages and disadvantages. Three broad classes of such underlying representations are *sequentially allocated lists*, *linked lists*, and *associative lists*. In Section 5.3, we study these three classes but we devote the most attention to exploring representations for linked lists, because they are the richest in terms of variety and possess a number of special cases such as one-way linked lists, symmetrically linked lists, threaded lists, circular lists, and orthogonal lists.

A second goal for this chapter is to examine the best known techniques for major linked-list management tasks. These methods are rich in interesting ideas for manipulating generalized linked representations; and considerable attention has been devoted to them in the data structure literature. Our goal is to understand and compare the significant results in the literature on list management algorithms.

To support linked-list representations, memory is organized into cells and unused cells are linked together into a list of available (or unallocated) cells. As demands for storage arise, cells are removed from the list of available space and are added to structures in use. It is also possible for various list cells to become disconnected from the set currently in use by a program, and such cells may be reclaimed and used again. This leads to the study of storage reclamation policies.

Some such reclamation policies, such as the "reference count" techniques, reclaim unused cells at the instant they become inaccessible to the main program. Other techniques, such as the so-called "garbage collection" techniques, are usually invoked when the list of available cells becomes exhausted. Such techniques normally operate by tracing and marking all cells currently accessible from (and therefore in use by) the program, following which there is a "gathering" phase consisting of a linear sweep of memory, in which all unused cells are linked together and all marked cells are unmarked. The available space list is then reconstituted.

Other important storage management algorithms that come into play during list processing are algorithms for such tasks as:

1. *compacting*—i.e., moving all list cells currently in use into a single contiguous region of memory, leaving another adjacent contiguous region for the unused cells;

2. *copying*—in which a copy of a list (together with all sublists) is created in another region of memory, leaving the original list unaltered;

3. *moving*—in which a list is moved to a new region of memory and the old copy can be destroyed; and

4. *traversal*—in which the nodes of a list are visited in some particular order of interest (such as during printing or marking).

The complexity of algorithms for tracing, marking, copying, compacting, and moving is dependent on the complexity of the connectivity of the underlying list structure representations on which they operate. The algorithms in this chapter are sensitive to three classes of representations of lists of increasing complexity: *pure lists*, *reentrant lists*, and *cyclic lists*. Each of these classes is properly contained in the next:

$$\text{Pure lists} \subset \text{Reentrant lists} \subset \text{Cyclic lists.}$$

Hence, algorithms that operate on cyclic lists are valid for reentrant and pure lists, and algorithms working on reentrant lists also work for pure lists, but not necessarily vice versa.

An important aspect of the study of algorithms for managing linked lists is to find algorithms for each of these three complexity classes that work with the least amount of resources. Interesting developments have been revealed in the literature on such algorithms recently. For example, it has been discovered possible to copy cyclic lists in linear time (i.e., in an amount of time linearly proportional to the number of lists cells being copied), using *bounded workspace* (i.e., using a fixed amount of storage for the operation of the algorithm independent of the size of the list structure being copied).

Sometimes list processing occurs in environments requiring special considerations. For example, in a paging environment (or in a virtual memory system), care must be taken to ensure that lists do not become fragmented and spread sparsely over a large number of distinct pages, causing excessive page swapping. In Section 5.4.4, techniques for controlling lists in a paging environment are examined. In other cases, lists must live side by side with other forms of storage allocation, such as that for stacks, tables, and arrays. It is important to study coexistence regimes for several classes of storage allocation in this context. For example, to make more room for a stack, a linked list area can be garbage-collected and compacted in the region farthest from the growth end of the stack. Section 5.5 presents a technique for accomplishing this.

5.2 DEFINITIONS AND BASIC CONCEPTS †

A *list* is a finite, ordered sequence of items $(x_1, x_2, \ldots, x_n)$ where $n \geq 0$. The list ( ) of no items occurs as a special case where $n = 0$, and is called the *empty list*. The empty list is denoted by the symbol Λ. The items x_i $(1 \leq i \leq n)$ in a list can be arbitrary in nature. In particular, it is possible for a given list to be an item in another list. For example, let L be the list $(x_1, x_2, (y_1, y_2, y_3), x_4)$. Then, the third item of L is the list (y_1, y_2, y_3). In this case, we say (y_1, y_2, y_3) is a *sublist* of L. If a

---

† Advanced readers: Skip to Subsection 5.3.3.1.

list L has one or more sublists, we say that L is a *list structure*. If a list has no sublists, we will call it either a *linear list* or a *chain*.

A list such as $(x_1, x_2, (y_1, y_2, y_3), x_4)$ can be mapped into an ordered tree such as

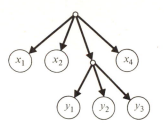

in which the list and each of its sublists are made to correspond to distinct internal nodes whose children are the ordered trees corresponding to the items they contain. If the edges of such an ordered tree are redirected to form directed graphs containing cycles or multiple distinct paths between nodes, more complicated topological organizations result. The action of redirecting edges corresponds to certain pointer-manipulation operations that can be performed on linked and associative list representations; and the classes of directed graphs that portray the resulting connectivity patterns can be used to provide the classification of lists into *pure lists*, *reentrant lists*, and *cyclic lists* mentioned earlier as being important to the discussion of list processing algorithms. These three classes are as follows:

Pure lists: A pure list is a list structure whose graph corresponds to a rooted, ordered tree in which there is exactly one path between any two distinct nodes; for example,

(1)

Reentrant lists: A reentrant list is a list structure whose graph corresponds to a rooted, connected, ordered, acyclic, directed graph. These have the property that their graphs may contain nodes accessible by two or more distinct paths from the root, but having the property that all paths from the root are of finite length. A node is said to be *shared* if it is the terminus of two or more directed edges. Shared nodes in the graph correspond to shared sublists or shared items of the original

list; for example,

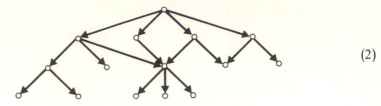

(2)

Cyclic lists: A cyclic list is a list structure whose graph corresponds to a rooted, directed, ordered graph, possibly containing cycles. Cycles in the graph correspond to situations in which the list or its sublists "contain themselves" (and for this reason, cyclic lists are sometimes called *recursive lists*); for example,

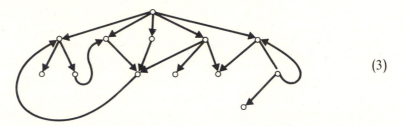

(3)

The use of parenthesized linear notation for list structures can specify only pure lists, since shared sublists or recursive sublists cannot be indicated. Thus, some sort of additional notation is required to denote reentrancies and cycles. One way to do this involves the use of "labels" and "references." In linear form, one instance of a shared or recursively used substructure is labeled, and references to the label are planted elsewhere. We do not pursue this notational development further, however. (The interested reader is referred to Knuth [1973a], p. 407, and to Elgot and Snyder [1977].)

Thus, our notational policy is identical to that used in several list processing languages in which the syntactic expressions denoting lists in programs of the language can designate only pure lists. Reentrant and cyclic list structures can then be created from pure lists by application of pointer-manipulation operations to the underlying list representations in such a way as to create the topological properties described in (1), (2), and (3).

In the algorithms that follow, we shall find it necessary to distinguish between an element of a list being another list and not being another list. In most situations we shall use a class of undefined items called *atoms* to refer to entities that are not lists; and the predicate "X is an Atom" evaluates to *true* or *false*, depending on whether X is not a list or is a list, respectively. In several list processing languages, atoms correspond to quantities such as numbers and symbol strings, which are stored as items in lists. While our figures will show examples of atoms of these sorts, the algorithms will rely on the more abstract notion that an *atom* is any object that is not a list.

In most branches of science, the adjective *atomic* is intended to describe indecomposable objects. However, with regard to data structures (see Standish [1978]), the notion of what is and what is not atomic is not absolute, but instead is relative to the set of decomposition operators used in a given system.

5.3 LIST REPRESENTATION TECHNIQUES

In this section we examine three classes of underlying representations for lists: (1) sequentially allocated lists, (2) linked lists, and (3) associative lists.

5.3.1 Sequentially allocated lists

Let $L = (x_1, x_2, \ldots, x_n)$ be a linear list with elements x_i $(1 \leq i \leq n)$, where each element requires one word to be represented in memory. In sequential allocation the representations of the items x_i are stored consecutively in memory beginning at address α, as exemplified in Fig. 5.1.

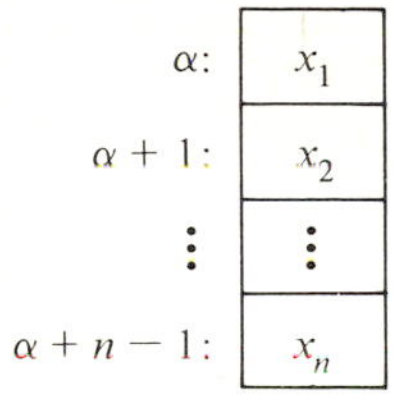

FIGURE 5.1

In general, we can store x_i in location $\alpha + i - 1$ $(1 \leq i \leq n)$. As immediate generalizations, the items x_i might each take k words, and we could store L either in ascending or in descending order of addresses, so that item x_i would be stored in the k words beginning at address $\alpha + k(i - 1)$ for ascending storage order and $\alpha - k(i - 1)$ for descending storage order.

If the items x_i have nonuniform sizes, we may store them contiguously, as long as we provide some means for recognizing the boundaries between adjacent elements. For example, we could mark the first word of each item specially, or we could store the number of words per item in a special field in each item. However, such storage policies entail loss of ability to perform direct arithmetic indexing of list elements.

If we consider list structures with nested sublists of various depths, sequential allocation demands that we nest sublists linearly within lists, distinguishing the boundaries of sublists in some fashion. The printed, linear representation of pure lists in this book is an example of linear allocation in which sublists are separated by matching parenthesis pairs and elements are delimited by commas.

Sequential representations of lists save space (i.e., make efficient use of storage) at the expense of element access time and increased cost of growth and decay operations. Further, as we have seen in Chapter 2, managing the growth of three or more sequentially allocated lists at or near the saturation of the available memory is quite costly.

5.3.2 Linked allocation for lists

Linked allocation of list structures provides a natural way of allocating storage for cyclic and reentrant lists, and provides allocation for pure lists that conveniently accommodates growth and decay properties, as well as certain natural traversals of the elements. The cost of such representations is borne in increased expense for access to arbitrary elements and in a reduction in storage utilization efficiency because of the extra space required to hold links.

5.3.2.1 *One-way linked allocation.* Let $L = (x_1, x_2, \ldots, x_n)$ be a list. Let α_i ($1 \leq i \leq n$) be a set of distinct addresses of memory cells. In this chapter, we consider only cells of uniform size. In the next chapter, on multilinked structures, cells can be allocated in varying sizes. The *link* fields of a particular cell are assumed to be fields that hold addresses (or relative addresses) of other cells. Thus, relationships such as contiguity of elements in a list, or sublists of a list, can be represented by explicit links stored in particular fields of cells. This permits contiguous or nested list elements to be represented in nonadjacent cells in memory.

Since the possibilities for such representation schemes are numerous, we proceed, by example, to give various illustrations, in the hope that the reader will be able easily to generalize to a set of linked representation "themes" of general utility that can be adapted to the peculiarities of the many machine environments and many representation requirements encountered in practice.

We have already examined the linked list representation for *linear lists* in Chapter 1. These form the basis for direct generalization to linked representations for list structures. In Chapter 1, we showed that we could allocate cells to represent the linear list $L = (x_1, x_2, \ldots, x_n)$ as shown in Fig. 5.2.

In Fig. 5.2, each cell has two fields, an INFO field containing an item x_i in L and a LINK field containing an address of another cell. The LINK field of the last cell α_n contains the quantity Λ, which denotes the address of the empty list.

To represent the more general case of list structures, as opposed to linear lists, we must enlarge upon the idea illustrated in Fig. 5.2. For example, suppose we are fortunate enough to have representations of atoms and pointers that take identical amounts of space. Then, to represent list structures with items that are either sublists or atoms x_i, we can store either an atom x_i or the address of a sublist in

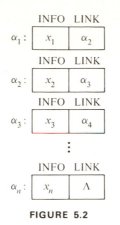

FIGURE 5.2

the INFO field of a given cell. However, we now need a systematic way to tell whether the INFO field contains the address of a sublist or contains an atom directly. For example, in Fig. 5.3 a TAG field containing $+$ is used to indicate that the contents of the INFO field is an atom x_i, and a TAG field containing $-$ is used to indicate that the INFO field contains the address of a sublist of the list. Figure 5.3 shows how the pure list structure $(x_1, x_2, (y_1, y_2, y_3), x_4)$ is represented using these conventions.

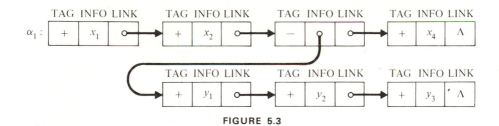

FIGURE 5.3

In some representations, there may not be enough space in the INFO field to hold representations of atoms, but there may be enough space in a single word to hold either (a) an atom and a tag bit, or (b) two addresses and a tag bit. In such a circumstance, the allocation regime of Fig. 5.4 can be used.

If a word cannot contain two full machine addresses plus a tag bit, then it may be possible to use relative addresses instead of absolute addresses. A relative address may be given relative to the base address of the region of memory used for linked allocation, or relative to the address α_i of the cell containing the link. This scheme saves space at the expense of the time required to locate a successor or sublist address relative to the address of a given cell. In Fig. 5.4 a clear TAG field

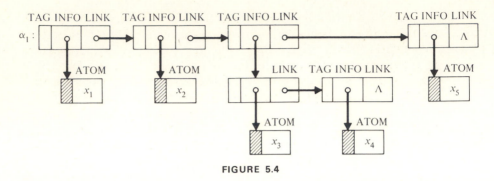

FIGURE 5.4

indicates that the remainder of the word holds an INFO field and a LINK field, each containing (possibly relative) addresses, and a cross-hatched TAG field indicates that the rest of the word contains the representation of an atom x_i.

In many cases, all bits in a cell are required to contain efficient machine representations of such atoms as integers, double-precision floating-point numbers, and so forth; and there is no space left over for a tag bit. Under these circumstances, cells containing atoms x_i and cells containing pairs of machine addresses can be placed in distinct regions of memory, and an *address range discrimination* can be used to detect whether a given link points to an atom x_i or to a cell containing a pair of machine addresses. Figure 5.5 illustrates this allocation scheme.

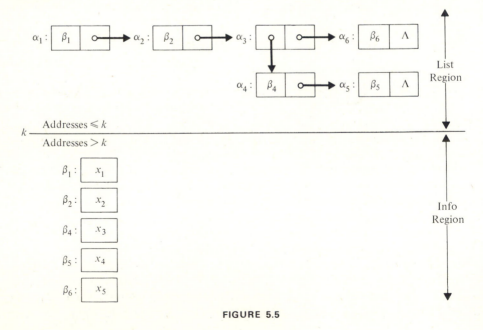

FIGURE 5.5

Again, if a single word cannot contain two full machine addresses in Fig. 5.5 it may be possible to fit two relative addresses in a word instead. The representation scheme exemplified in Fig. 5.5 requires separate management of atom-spaces and linked-pair spaces, and so it complicates the management algorithms for lists.

As a final example, in the case where a machine word can hold either an atom x_i or an address pair, but cannot hold a TAG bit in addition, one can allocate a *bit map* with a 1–1 correspondence between words in the linked-list space and bits in the bit map. Then, a bit in the bit map can be turned "on" to indicate that the corresponding word contains an atom x_i, and it can be left "off" to indicate that the corresponding word contains a machine-address pair.

From these five examples, it should be evident that a wide range of techniques is available for the representation of one-way linked lists, and that a technique can usually be chosen that fits the requirements of the underlying machine and those of the implementation efficiencies desired.

One-way, linked-list spaces can always represent cyclic and reentrant lists if they can represent pure lists. This is accomplished by using multiple occurrences of particular cell or atom addresses in the same list structure, as illustrated in Fig. 5.6.

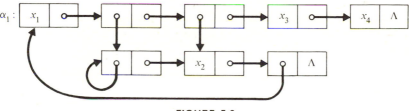

FIGURE 5.6

In a paging environment, it is often advantageous to allocate space for atoms on separate pages, as the atoms are sometimes required only during special operations such as printing or equality testing. This implies that the pages containing atoms need be called into fast memory only during the execution of operations requiring use of the contents of individual atom addresses.

5.3.2.2 *Symmetrically linked allocation.* Consider the diagram of Fig. 5.7. In this diagram, each cell contains links to its left and right neighbors (except for the first cell, which has no left neighbor, and the last cell, which has no right neigh-

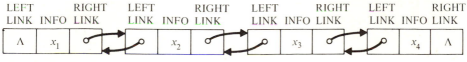

FIGURE 5.7

bor). Each cell has an INFO field, which contains an item x_i, and has two address fields LEFT LINK and RIGHT LINK. Such a structure is called a *symmetrically linked list*.

It is easy to traverse a symmetric list in either direction (forwards or backwards), starting from the address of any cell. By contrast, given the address of an arbitrary cell on a one-way linked list, traversal is possible only in the forward direction. Similarly, if α is the address of an arbitrary cell on a symmetric list S, one can delete cell α of S, or one can insert a new cell before or after cell α of S. For example, if C contains the address of cell α on S, the steps shown in Fig. 5.8 delete cell C from S.

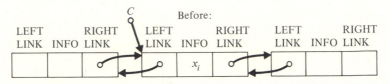

To delete a cell C from a symmetric list S:

1. If Left Link $(C) \neq \Lambda$ then Right Link (Left Link (C)) ← Right Link (C).
2. If Right Link $(C) \neq \Lambda$ then Left Link (Right Link (C)) ← Left Link (C).
3. (Optional Clean Up) Left Link (C) ← Right Link (C) ← Λ.

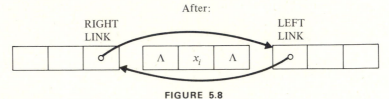

FIGURE 5.8

Again, by contrast, if α is the address of an arbitrary cell on a one-way linked list L, it is not always possible to delete cell α from L, nor is it possible to insert a new cell before cell α. [*Note.* In the case of one-way linked representations of pure linked lists, a copying trick can be used to perform deletion. To delete the cell at address α, if cell α links to cell β, we copy the contents of β into α. Unfortunately, this trick doesn't work for the last cell on a list.]

As shown above, one must pay extra space for the extra flexibility of symmetric lists, since each cell of a symmetric list has two address fields instead of one. However, there are two similar techniques that can be used to store symmetric lists using only one address field per cell.

In Fig. 5.9, the link field of each cell contains the quantity $L \oplus R$, where L is the address of the left neighbor's cell, R is the address of the right neighbor's cell, and $\oplus$ is the exclusive-or operator of logic defined in Section 1.3.4. Starting with the addresses of any two adjacent cells in a symmetric list set up according to the

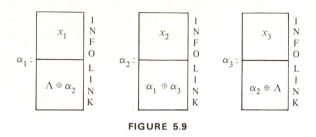

FIGURE 5.9

method of Fig. 5.9, it is possible to traverse in either the left or the right direction. The key properties of the exclusive-or operation used to accomplish this are given in the equations

$$(L \oplus R) \oplus R = L \quad \text{and} \quad (L \oplus R) \oplus L = R$$

(see Exercise 8 in Chapter 1). Now, in Fig. 5.9, by starting at the lefthand address α_1, and also using the starting address Λ, one traverses to the right by extracting $\Lambda \oplus \alpha_2$ from the LINK field of cell α_1 and calculating $(\Lambda \oplus \alpha_2) \oplus \Lambda$, which has the value α_2. At cell α_2, one extracts $\alpha_1 \oplus \alpha_3$ from the LINK field, and, having saved α_1 from the previous step, one calculates $(\alpha_1 \oplus \alpha_3) \oplus \alpha_1$, which yields α_3. At cell α_3, the evaluation of $(\alpha_2 \oplus \Lambda) \oplus \alpha_2$ yields Λ, which signals the end of the traversal to the right. Symmetrically, one can start at the righthand end and can use the address α_3 and the address Λ to start traversing to the left.

In general, given any two consecutive addresses on such a symmetric list, not only can one scan either left or right; one can insert and delete cells in the neighborhood.

A second method for symmetric linking using one address field per cell arises from giving a second interpretation to the operation $L \oplus R$ in Fig. 5.9. If we redefine $L \oplus R$ by the equation

$$L \oplus R = (L + R) \bmod M,$$

where M is a number larger than all cell addresses, we then have the relations:

$$L = ((L \oplus R) - R) \bmod M,$$

and　　　　　　　　　　　　　　　　　　　　　　　　　　　　　　　　　　　　(4)

$$R = ((L \oplus R) - L) \bmod M.$$

(See Exercise 5.1 for the justification.)

Using either the exclusive-or interpretation or the modular arithmetic interpretation of $X \oplus Y$, we can write a traversal algorithm that traverses symmetric lists with $X \oplus Y$ links, starting with any two consecutive addresses.

Algorithm 5.1 *Symmetric traversal in direction of A to B.*

In step 3 of this algorithm, the operation $X \circleddash Y$ is to be interpreted as

$$X \oplus Y \qquad \text{or} \qquad (X - Y) \bmod M,$$

depending on whether the links have been stored using the exclusive-or interpretation or the modular arithmetic interpretation, respectively. A and B are
addresses of two consecutive cells on the list.

1. [Done?] If $B = \Lambda$, then terminate the algorithm.

2. [Visit.] Visit B.

3. [Advance.] Set Successor $\leftarrow$ LINK$(B) \circleddash A$, set $A \leftarrow B$, set $B \leftarrow$ Successor, and
   go back to step 1.

Thus, calling Algorithm 5.1 with $A = \Lambda$ and $B = \alpha_1$ traverses the cells of Fig.
5.9 from left to right, whereas calling Algorithm 5.1 with $A = \Lambda$ and $B = \alpha_3$
traverses the cells of the same list from right to left.

While the exclusive-or and modular arithmetic representations save one
address per cell over symmetric linking, they always require two consecutive
addresses to "prime their pumps" and to get started, whereas ordinary two-way
symmetric linking requires only one address.

To make list structures composed from symmetrically linked cells, it is
sometimes convenient to use special header cells that point to the left and right
ends of symmetrically linked chains (as done in Weizenbaum [1963], for example).
An example of a symmetric list structure using header cells is given in Fig. 5.10.

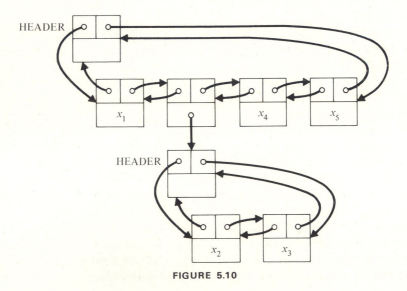

FIGURE 5.10

Each header cell links to the leftmost and rightmost cells of a symmetrically linked chain, and the leftmost and rightmost cells of the chain each link back to the header cell. A list item that points to a sublist, points to the header for the sublist. The information field of a list header can frequently be used to contain storage management information. For example, as we will see later in more detail, one policy for storage reclamation of symmetric lists is to keep a "reference count" in the header cell for each list. Such a reference count is an integer equal to the total number of external references to the header. Each time a new reference to a symmetric list S is created, the reference count of S is increased by one; and each time a reference is destroyed, the reference count is decreased by one. Whenever the reference count reaches zero, there are no external references, so the cells on the symmetric list can be returned to the available space list. It is easy to return all the cells since the header points to the left and right end of its subordinate chain and allows the chain to be spliced into the available space list conveniently.

5.3.2.3 *Circular lists.* Circular lists are formed by linking the last cell of a chain to the head of the chain, as illustrated in Fig. 5.11. Circular lists have the property that all elements can be accessed starting from any cell on the list.

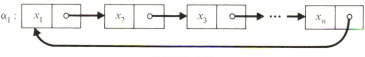

FIGURE 5.11

An example of circular lists occurs in Roberts' CORAL language (see Roberts [1965]), used in the context of computer graphics programs. A picture element might consist of a set of points joined by lines, with the lines in a given plane defining "faces" of polyhedra. For example, the triangle of Fig. 5.12 might be defined by the three points p_1, p_2, and p_3 joined by lines ℓ_1, ℓ_2, and ℓ_3, which in turn bound the triangle T_1.

It is convenient in this context to define a data representation for the triangle T_1 by a system of circular lists, in which each point is connected to the lines touching it, each line is connected to its endpoints and to the polygons of which it is an edge, and each polygon is connected to the lines forming it. Figure 5.13 gives a schematic representation of how data blocks for points, lines, and polygons can be tied together by rings.

As illustrated in Fig. 5.13, the elements that tie the blocks together into rings each contain two pointers. One of the pointers links the ring elements together in the forward direction. The other departs slightly from the conventional symmetrically linking back-pointer. In a CORAL ring, the even-numbered back pointers

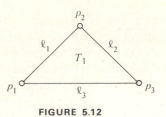

FIGURE 5.12

point to the special ring-header element, and the odd-numbered back-pointers point back two elements in the ring. This enables fast access of the header element from any ring position, as well as traversal in the backwards direction. Also illustrated in Fig. 5.13 is an example of a data block. A data block has enough ring elements to allow the block to be a member of several rings, and to contain locally, data (such as point coordinate data, or symbolic identification data) that pertain to its particular block type.

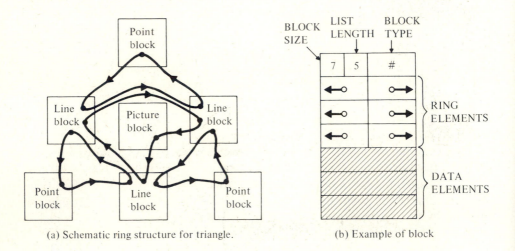

(a) Schematic ring structure for triangle.

(b) Example of block

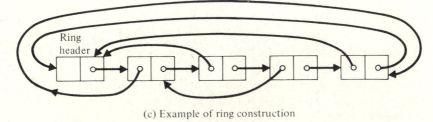

(c) Example of ring construction

FIGURE 5.13

(Other examples of the use of rings for associative data structures can be found in Gray [1967], Williams [1973], and Lang and Gray [1968ab].)

In a three-dimensional CORAL representation, each point is defined by its position coordinates and is on a ring that threads through each line segment of which it is an endpoint; each line segment has subordinate rings leading to its left and right endpoints and lies on a ring threaded through every polygon of which it is an edge; and each polygon has subordinate rings leading to each of its edges, and lies on a ring threaded through each polyhedron of which it is a face.

Using this representation it becomes easy to move pictures and parts of pictures by transforming the coordinates of the relevant points (which define the lines that define the edges that define the polygons that define the polyhedra). If a point p is moved from location (x, y) to $(x + a, y + b)$, then all lines of which p is an endpoint are automatically adjusted, since p is on a ring through all such lines touching it; and automatically this applies to all polygons of which the lines are edges and all polyhedra of which the polygons are faces. Thus, units of a picture of any dimension (points, lines, faces, polyhedra) can be conveniently transformed, since each such unit is connected ultimately to the points that define it, and to the higher-dimensional units of which it forms a part of a boundary.

5.3.2.4 *Threaded lists.* Threaded lists are pure lists in which additional linkage structures called "threads" have been added to provide for traversals in special orders. Since we have covered threading techniques in Chapter 3 on trees, we will cover only one brief example in this section to illustrate the flavor of the method. Generally speaking, threading permits bounded-workspace, read-only traversals along the direction provided by the threads. This implies that we can use both stackless traversal, and read-only traversal in bounded workspace by one or more processes simultaneously, with each in a possibly different stage of traversal. Also, given the address of any cell in a threaded list, it is possible to find any successor along the thread. However, threading increases the time for insertion and deletion of cells and costs extra tag bits per cell.

Consider the pure list $(+, (\times, a, (-, b, c)), (\times, d, e))$. Using one-way linked allocation, we can represent this list as shown in Fig. 5.14.

By adding a Tag field to each cell, and agreeing that a Tag $= -$ for a "normal" link, and a Tag $= +$ for a "thread" link, we can replace all occurrences of Λ in Fig. 5.14 with "up" links pointing to cells from which it is possible to continue a left-to-right traversal of atoms in the list. This is depicted in Fig. 5.15.

The "thread" links in Fig. 5.15 are indicated by dashed lines $(----)$. To traverse the atoms of Figs. 5.14 and 5.15 in "left-to-right" order, we must traverse all left descendants of any cell before any right siblings. The traversal of the list in Fig. 5.14 can be accomplished using a pushdown stack, as illustrated in the following algorithm.

LEFT RIGHT

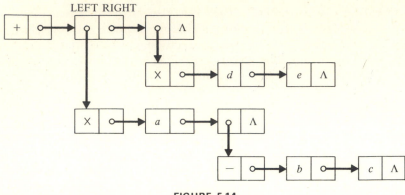

FIGURE 5.14

Algorithm 5.2 *Traverse X using a pushdown stack A.*
Let A be a stack of pointers initialized to Λ and let X initially hold the address of the root of the list.

1. [Initialize.] Set $A \leftarrow \Lambda$.

2. [New cell—start on left half.] *If* Left(X) is an atom, *then* (visit the atom); Process (Left(X)) and go to step 3. Otherwise (to go down) $A \Leftarrow X$, $X \leftarrow$ Left(X), and go to step 2.

3. [Left side done—process right side.] If Right$(X) \neq \Lambda$, *then* $X \leftarrow$ Right(X), go to step 2. Otherwise (pop the stack) $X \Leftarrow A$. If now $X = \Lambda$, then terminate the algorithm. Otherwise, go to step 3.

The corresponding stackless algorithm to traverse the threaded list of Fig. 5.15 is as follows:

TAG   RIGHT
LEFT

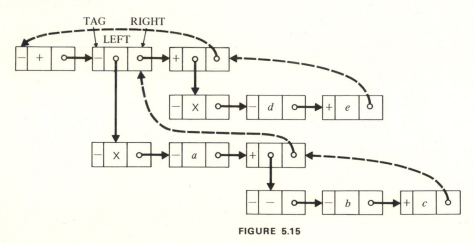

FIGURE 5.15

Algorithm 5.3 *Traverse X using threads in bounded workspace.*

X points initially to the root of the list. $\text{Tag}(X) = +$ means $\text{Right}(X)$ is a thread or "up" link.

1. [Initialize.] Set Original Root $\leftarrow X$.
2. [New Cell—start with left side.] If $\text{Left}(X)$ is an atom, then (visit the atom); $\text{Process}(\text{Left}(X))$ and go to step 3. Otherwise, (go down by setting) $X \leftarrow \text{Left}(X)$ and repeat this step.
3. [Left side done—now do right side.] If $\text{Tag}(X) = -$, then set $X \leftarrow \text{Right}(X)$ and go to step 2. Otherwise (to go up), set $X \leftarrow \text{Right}(X)$. If now, $X = $ Original Root, then terminate the algorithm. Otherwise, go to step 3.

These two algorithms execute the same number of steps for lists of the same number of cells. To see this, we argue as follows.

For each of the above traversal algorithms, the total number of steps executed, Total, is the sum of three contributions:

$$\text{Total} = \begin{cases} 1 \text{ (for step 1)} + \\ (\text{Cumulative number of times step 2 is executed}) + \\ (\text{Cumulative number of times step 3 is executed}). \end{cases}$$

Each time step 2 is executed, either we visit an atom or we descend a left link; so the cumulative number of times step 2 is executed is:

$$\# \text{atoms} + \# \text{left links} \quad (\text{pointing to sublists, not atoms}).$$

Likewise, each time step 3 is executed, we either traverse a right link, or we go up to a higher node (by popping the stack or following a thread in the respective cases of Algorithm 5.2 and Algorithm 5.3), or we terminate execution; so the cumulative number of times step 3 is executed is:

$$\# \text{right links} + \# \Lambda\text{s} \quad (\text{for Algorithm 5.2})$$

or

$$\# \text{right links} + \# \text{threads} \quad (\text{for Algorithm 5.3}).$$

Thus, adding up all these contributions, we get

$$\text{Total} = 1 + (\# \text{atoms} + \# \text{left links}) + \left(\# \text{right links} + \begin{Bmatrix} \# \Lambda\text{s} \\ \text{or} \\ \# \text{threads} \end{Bmatrix} \right) \quad (5)$$

which simplifies, in turn, to

$$\text{Total} = 1 + 2 \times (\# \text{cells}),$$

since each cell in the list structure contributes exactly two of the quantities counted in the second and third terms of (5). Thus, both algorithms execute in an identical number of steps.

Bounded-workspace algorithms such as Algorithm 5.3 may often turn out to be superior to stack algorithms. If stacks are implemented sequentially, they usually have bounds that impose an arbitrary limit on list depth before stack overflow occurs. This can either cost extra stack space initially, which is seldom used, or it can imply that the stack overflow policy must provide for moving and enlarging a stack. Complex applications requiring simultaneous traversals of more than one list at a time may then require the management of several stacks simultaneously; this can imply time-consuming stack shuffling. If stacks are implemented as lists, the time for pushing and popping usually exceeds the time for following "up-threads" in a threaded list. Bounded-workspace, read-only traversal algorithms alleviate these problems.

The disadvantages of threading are that insertion and deletion are more costly and more space is needed if tag bits are required. In some representations, list cells can be allocated in increasing order of left-to-right traversal. In this case, "up-links" can be distinguished from other links because they point "backwards" in memory. That is, if $\text{Right}(x) < x$, then $\text{Right}(x)$ is an "up-link." If this is the case, there is no extra space required for tag bits; but normally this situation does not hold. To insert a new cell Y after a cell X in a threaded list such as that given in Fig. 5.15, if $\text{Tag}(X) = +$, then four steps are required:

$$\text{Tag}(X) \leftarrow -, \quad \text{Tag}(Y) \leftarrow +, \quad \text{Right}(Y) \leftarrow \text{Right}(X), \quad \text{and} \quad \text{Right}(X) \leftarrow Y.$$

By contrast, in a pure list, insertion of Y after X takes just two steps:

$$\text{Right}(Y) \leftarrow \text{Right}(X), \quad \text{and} \quad \text{Right}(X) \leftarrow Y.$$

One tricky situation occurs if one tries to delete the root of a threaded list such as that given in Fig. 5.15; namely, the thread that terminates on the root must be adjusted by searching down to the end of the chain of right links at the top level, and changing the thread to point to the new root. This problem can be avoided by starting each threaded list with a special "header cell" whose left link points to the original root, and whose right link is an "up-link" to itself. Figure 5.15 would then be rendered as shown in Fig. 5.16.

The use of such a header introduces one kind of consistency at the destruction of other kinds.

5.3.2.5 *Orthogonal lists*. If we arrange for list cells to link symmetrically both left and right to horizontal neighbors, and also to link upwards and downwards to vertical neighbors, we obtain a two-dimensional *orthogonal list*. Figure 5.17 illustrates such a list.

HEADER:

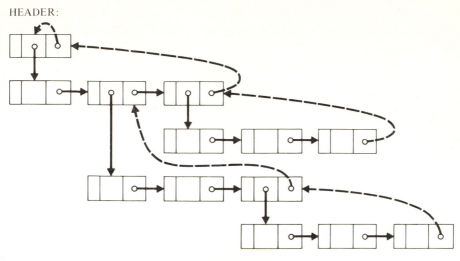

FIGURE 5.16

Higher-dimensional orthogonal lists can be obtained by adding more perpendicular dimensions to the two shown in Fig. 5.17, and by establishing symmetric links to new list cells in the new dimensions. In Chapter 8 on arrays, we will study how to use orthogonal lists such as that of Fig. 5.17 to provide storage-efficient

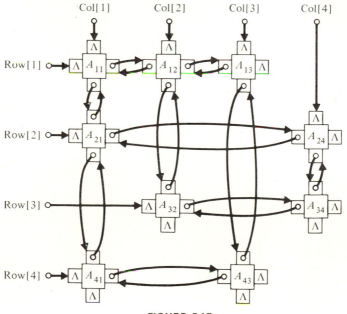

FIGURE 5.17

representations for sparse matrices. The notion of orthogonal lists can be made more general by requiring that each cell be on k different lists simultaneously, regardless of the representation technique selected for the lists.

5.3.2.6 *List headers.* We call attention, briefly, to a device of which we have so far seen three instances in this chapter—the *list header*. Representations with special header cells occur frequently enough in applications and in the published literature that they deserve mention as a representation technique. Some uses for headers are:

1. To provide a stopping place on circular lists, or to define a unique starting place.
2. To hold both ends of a symmetric list (for fast garbage return, insertion, etc., or to hold a reference count as in Weizenbaum [1963]).
3. To form a root of a threaded tree, or a threaded pure list with properties consistent with other cells that are roots of sublists.
4. To hold an extra "utility" field (or fields) for each sublist of a list that can be used to aid management algorithms such as copying, traversal, equality testing, or storage reclamation—especially in the case of cyclic lists.
5. To permit ease of deletion of the first cell on a sublist when that sublist is multiply referenced (in a cyclic or reentrant list) without having to search for and update all references to the head of the sublist.

5.3.3 List representations in associative memory

An *associative memory*, sometimes called a *content-addressed memory*, permits accessing of data through a partial specification of its content. Rather than relying on explicit addresses to gain access to its cells, a reference to an associative cell is given by specifying a portion of what a cell contains. All cells containing a given item are "referenced" and, in contrast to addressable memory, either none or more than one of the cells may be referenced by a given content specification.

For example, suppose we use an ideal associative memory to represent the contents of a telephone book. Suppose, further, that the cells in the memory are organized to contain the following information:

Last name	First name and initials	Street address and city abbreviation	Telephone number

For instance, one entry might be:

| JONES | WILLIAM, F. | 381 MAPLE ST. CAMB. | 482–1076 |

In such an ideal associative memory, it would be equally easy to find all entries (a) having name fields containing "JONES, WILLIAM, F.", (b) having a street address "381 MAPLE ST. CAMB.", (c) having a phone number "482–1076", (d) having just the last name "JONES", or (e) having a first name and middle initial "WILLIAM, F.". In ordinary phone books, looking up a phone number, given a name, is easier than looking up the name corresponding to a given phone number (because, as we saw in the previous chapter, the alphabetical properties of the listing of names can be utilized to avoid exhaustive search). In Chapter 9 on files, we shall examine techniques for indexing records on values found in several fields that help approximate the properties of ideal associative memories. For the present, it suffices to imagine that the ideal associative memory is available.

A normal addressable memory can be obtained as a special case of an associative memory when we consider cells of the form

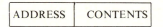

provided we can create distinct addresses and assign them to distinct cells.

From this observation, it follows that one way of representing pure lists in an associative memory is to create and assign distinct addresses to nodes and to use the associative representation above. For instance, suppose the list $(A_1, (A_2, A_3), A_4)$ is represented first in linked form as in Fig. 5.18, where the symbols λ_i $(1 \leq i \leq 5)$ represent distinct cell addresses. Figure 5.18 can, in turn, be transformed into a

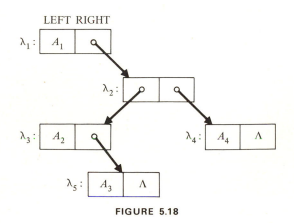

FIGURE 5.18

ADDRESS	LEFT	RIGHT
λ_1	A_1	λ_2
λ_2	λ_3	λ_4
λ_3	A_2	λ_5
λ_4	A_4	Λ
λ_5	A_3	Λ

FIGURE 5.19

set of triples in an associative memory as shown in Fig. 5.19. This yields Wilkes' method for representing lists in associative memory (Wilkes [1972]). Wilkes points out that the triples in the representation in Fig. 5.19 can be represented as rows of a normal three-column table and can be moved about (by interchange of rows in the table) without disturbing the linking topology of the list and without requiring update. Further, he observes that the links to cells are essentially symmetric.

Wilkes [1972] argues that the use of these properties can help a user keep his program data compact in memory, leading to lowered processing costs and to better response time in multiprogrammed systems, particularly in a paging environment. Even though, in the absence of hardware support, the use of associative links involves searching memory, Wilkes states that, for structures of modest size for which care is taken to exploit and preserve natural ordering, searching need not be a very time-consuming operation.

Feldman and Rovner [1969], in their ALGOL-based associative language LEAP, use triples of the form:

denoted $A \cdot O \equiv V$, as a basis for associative list processing.

One of the ways that associative triples can be represented in memory is by use of hash codes. An early version of an associative language by Feldman and Rovner (see Feldman [1965]) represented $A \cdot O \equiv V$ triples in the following cell format:

A	t	O	V
LINK		USE	

Here, the fields A, t, O, and V stand for attribute, tag, object, and value, respectively. The A, O, and V values are small integers standing for the identifiers used to name the attributes, objects, and values.

The address fields LINK and USE chain together all cells having certain properties. In particular, the LINK fields link together all triples that hash to a particular hash address (using hash-collision resolution by chaining, as discussed in Chapter 4). The USE field links together all cells having a particular value V. The heads of the USE lists are kept in a table indexed on values V. To compute the hash address for a triple, a hash function of the form $h(A, O)$ is used, so that the hash address is determined by the pair consisting of the Attribute and the Object. It is possible that there exist distinct attribute–object pairs (A', O') and (A, O) such that $h(A, O) = h(A', O')$. All such (A, O) pairs hashing to the same location reside on the same linked list, linked through the LINK fields. The USE lists (akin to inverted file indexing techniques, which will be studied in Chapter 9) make it possible to answer inverse questions. For example, to answer an attribute-retrieval question such as what is COLOR(ROSE) or SON(JOHN), one computes the hash addresses h(COLOR, ROSE) and h(SON, JOHN) and searches the respective chains for cells containing the proper (A, O) pairs. The appropriate values are stored in the V-fields of these cells. On the other hand, to answer a question such as "Find all objects having the COLOR PINK", the USE list for $V = $ PINK is searched for cells having $A = $ COLOR.

5.3.3.1 *Hash linking.* An intriguing notion, due to D. G. Bobrow (see Bobrow [1975]) is the idea of *hash linking*. As pointed out above, a normal coordinate-addressed memory is a special case of a content-addressed memory whose cells are of the form:

such that there is exactly one cell having a given address for each address in some range (such as $(0 \leq i \leq 2^m - 1)$). If we relax this restriction a bit and allow more than one cell with a given address, then it is possible to think of associating more than one CONTENTS field with a given address. In particular, we can use the normal memory address, say α, to access the normal contents CONTENTS_1 of address α; and we can use an auxiliary hash table to store additional contents associated with α by, say, storing $(\alpha, \text{CONTENTS}_2)$ in a hash table at some address related to the hash address $h(\alpha)$. Bobrow calls this technique *hash linking* because one hashes on the address α to discover the link to the additional cell containing the additional contents associated with α, instead of using the normal linking method of planting a link to an overflow cell within the cell addressed by α itself.

Some examples of uses for this technique are as follows.

1. *Table compression:* Suppose we have a computer with 18-bit words. Suppose, further, that we want to keep the current balance of bank accounts in a compressed table, where 98 percent of the customers have current balances less than $2,621.43 (note that $2^{18} = 262,144$). Then, if customer k has a balance less than $2,621.43, we can store the current balance as an 18-bit integer in cell k of the compressed table; but if customer k has a balance of $2^{18} - 1$ cents or more, we place the quantity $2^{18} - 1$ in cell k of the table, and hash on the address k. Then we store k and the customer's balance in an overflow hash table using address $h(k)$ for some hash-addressing function h. The entries in the overflow table are big enough to contain larger balances for the two percent of the customers who need them.

2. *Traversing list structures:* Suppose we are attempting to traverse cyclic list structures, and there is insufficient room to put a tag bit in the list cells to prevent endless revisiting of cells already visited. Suppose, further, that allocating a bit-map is too costly because it takes M/w bits, where w is the word size and M is the number of words in the memory zone under consideration. Another alternative is to use hash linking. As we traverse a cyclic structure, we hash on the addresses α of cells visited, and deposit the addresses α so visited in a hash table at the appropriate place determined by $h(\alpha)$. Then we can determine whether a cell has been visited before during traversal by determining whether its address is in the hash table. If the structures to be visited take up only a small portion of the total space M, then the use of such a hash table can be economical of storage compared to a bit map.

3. *Pointer compression:* Suppose we are dealing with list structures stored in a paging environment for a virtual-memory system. Let the virtual addresses be chosen in the range (0 through $2^B - 1$) and let the page addresses be chosen in the range (0 through $2^p - 1$). For example, we may have 1024 word pages ($p = 10$) in a virtual address space of size 1048576 ($B = 20$). To combat the phenomenon of page thrashing and to keep working set sizes small, we may have attempted to copy list structures onto pages after the fashion of, say, Fenichel and Yochelson [1969], wherein we endeavor to put cells in the same connected component of a list structure on the same page, insofar as possible, and thereby to minimize references from one page to another. One way of representing pointers in this scheme is to use 10-bit pointers for on-page links, and 20-bit pointers for off-page links. However, we could allocate 10-bit fields for all pointers; and for off-page links, we could store a link of 0, and hash-link on the address α of the cell containing the pointer 0 to find a hash table entry of the form (α, β) containing the true link β. This hash table could be stored on the page containing α, or in a global hash table.

5.4 STORAGE RECLAMATION

In this and the following sections, we shall study the best-known techniques for managing regions of list cells of uniform size, so as to provide the basic raw material out of which linked list representations can be fashioned and so as to rearrange allocated linked list structures for purposes of dynamic efficiency. In the next chapter on multilinked structures, we study management techniques for regions of cells of nonuniform size.

Attention to details of explicit storage allocation and deallocation distracts a programmer from solving the problem at hand. Thus, although some of the early list processing languages such as IPL-V (Newell and Tonge [1960]) placed responsibility on the programmer for returning list cells no longer in use to the pool of free storage, many contemporary list processing systems have adopted the philosophy of easing this burden by providing automatic storage allocation and reclamation. Thus, an important contemporary topic in the understanding of underlying representations for lists is that of automatic storage allocation and reclamation.

As we have seen in Section 5.3.2, linked lists have numerous possible underlying representations. For the purpose of exploring and comparing the themes of various list management algorithms we are about to study, it is important to establish a single such linked representation as a framework for explanation and comparison. Once understood, the algorithms we present can then easily be modified to suit the details of other linked-representation conventions as required.

A good choice for a linked list representation is that used by the programming language LISP (McCarthy [1960]), since much of the literature giving significant list algorithms assumes the basic features of LISP representations and uses its terminology and notation. If the reader has not already been introduced to this notation, his exposure to the few features of it utilized in the present chapter will help to make accessible to him further developments in the research literature cited.

Thus, we shall assume that list cells are divided into two distinct varieties, atomic cells used to contain data such as integers, and nonatomic cells used to contain pairs of pointers. All linked list representations will be assumed to be fashioned from these two sorts of cells.

We shall follow the LISP convention of naming the left and right pointer fields of nonatomic cells the *car* and *cdr* fields respectively. This tradition appears to have come from an early IBM machine (the 7090) on which early versions of LISP were programmed, on which *car* was short for "contents of the *a*ddress *r*egister" and *cdr* was short for "contents of the *d*ecrement *r*egister".

We shall assume, for the following algorithms, that we are dealing with cyclic list structures, the most general of the three classes discussed earlier. Figure 5.20 illustrates such a list structure.

The first technique for storage reclamation we shall study is a "garbage collection" method based on *marking* and *gathering*. If at some point in the execution of a program, the list of available free cells *Avail* becomes exhausted, the garbage collection process is invoked. In the *marking phase* all cells accessible to the program are marked as being *in use*. In the *gathering phase*, a linear sweep over the

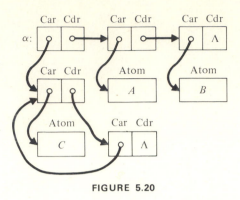

FIGURE 5.20

memory is conducted, and all cells not marked as *in use* are linked together into a free list, which becomes the new value of Avail. (Additionally, the *in use* marks of all cells are reset to *not in use* to prepare for future garbage collection.)

The second approach to storage reclamation we shall study is called *incremental garbage collection*. In the reference-counter methods for incremental garbage collection, a field is kept in each cell which contains an integer called the *reference count*. The reference count in a given cell equals the total number of pointers that reference the cell. When a new pointer is created that links to a cell whose address is α, the reference-count field in cell α is incremented by one, and when a link to α is destroyed, the reference count in cell α is decremented by one. If the reference count ever reaches 0, there are no external references to cell α, so cell α can be put back on the available space list. This technique is called incremental because a cell is returned to free storage the instant it is no longer referenced, causing storage reclamation to occur incrementally, instead of all at once (as in the marking and gathering method).

Another variation of incremental garbage collection is parallel collection. We assume there are two machines sharing the same list-structured memory. One machine is totally devoted to garbage collection and goes about marking and gathering garbage all the time. The other machine utilizes free cells from the Avail list, and changes pointers in cells accessible to its controlling program. It is a challenging matter to devise a method whereby the two computers can cooperate without locking each other out over 50 percent of the time (making it better to use a single computer that interleaves its garbage collection and list manipulation activities).

5.4.1 Marking algorithms

In this section, we study *marking algorithms* for cyclic list structures. As we shall see, the developments in this area are not entirely satisfactory. Ideally, we should like to be able to mark N cells in accessible list structures in rapid linear time $O(N)$

and with no more memory than a marking bit on each cell and a fixed number of variables private to the marking algorithm (this being called *bounded workspace*). Unfortunately, this desirable goal has not been reached at the date this book is written. (It may well be that someone can prove that such a goal is unattainable, but such "impossibility proofs" have been hard to come by.)

The reason it is important to attempt to find marking algorithms that work with *bounded workspace* is that marking is invoked at the very moment of free-storage exhaustion—the exact instant when there is no space available for holding stacks or other storage structures whose size grows unboundedly. Thus, traversal techniques using stacks and tag bits for marking are undesirable. As a starting point, and as a basis for comparison, we begin by giving a marking algorithm based on the use of pointer stacks and tag bits.

A technique that eliminates the stacks but fails to eliminate a set of *tag* bits (independent of the marking bits required to denote that nodes are *in use*) is the Schorr–Waite–Deutsch technique, which relies on link inversion. This technique is a slight generalization of the link-inversion traversal for binary trees given in Algorithm 3.6. Because the list structures involved may contain cycles and reen-trancies (as opposed to binary trees, which are analogous to pure lists), the link-inversion technique must be applied to a spanning tree of the structure. It requires a tag bit, in addition to the marking bit, because, on ascent from the traversal of subtrees of the spanning tree, it is necessary to know whether the ascent is from the right or the left. Allocation of this extra tag bit may require a bit map if no room can be found in the cells themselves (Schorr and Waite [1967]).

A technique that uses only a stack of bits for workspace external to the list structure being marked is due to Wegbreit [1972]. This technique is a considerable improvement over the Schorr–Waite–Deutsch method with regard to space, even though the space it uses is still unbounded.

A linear-time, bounded-workspace algorithm that uses no tag bits was dis-covered by Fisher [1974], provided that the list structure is acyclic and that it can be assumed that the addresses of the nodes are arranged in a certain order. Unfortunately, this assumption does not often hold for circumstances en-countered in actual practice.

Finally, Lindstrom [1974] discovered a bounded-workspace algorithm for marking cyclic structures which uses no auxiliary tag bits and does not depend on an address order-preserving environment. Unfortunately, its running time is $O(n \log n)$. Thus, nobody has yet devised the ideal $O(n)$, bounded-workspace marking algorithm that uses no tag bits.

We will now study this progression of results.

5.4.1.1 *Marking with pointer stacks.* Let each cell C of the list structure to be marked contain a mark bit $MARK(C)$ initially set to "−" to denote *not in use* and let each nonatomic cell C have, in addition to its mark bit, two link fields designated car(C) and cdr(C), respectively. We further assume that, given the address of a cell C, the predicate Atom(C) returns *true* if C is the address of an atom, and returns *false* otherwise.

The idea behind the algorithm is to perform a preorder traversal of a spanning tree of the cyclic list structure being marked. To accomplish this, whenever an unmarked nonatomic node is encountered, first its cdr link and then its car link are stacked on a stack containing postponed obligations to traverse substructures not yet examined. Since the car link is stacked after the cdr link, the substructure the car link points to will be traversed before the substructure to which the cdr link points. Any links to cells already marked (i.e., with MARK(C) = "+") need not be traversed.

Algorithm 5.4   *Marking cyclic list structures with a pointer stack*

Let S be a stack, and let C be a variable containing the address of a node. The algorithm marks node C and all nodes accessible from C via any chain of pointers in the *car* and *cdr* fields of nonatomic cells accessible from C. Λ is assumed to be an Atom such that MARK(Λ) = "+".

1. [Initialize.] Let S be an empty stack.
2. [Mark.] Set MARK(C) ← "+".
3. [Process links.] If C is not an Atom (i.e., if Atom(C) = *false*), then $S \Leftarrow$ cdr(C) and $S \Leftarrow$ car(C).
4. [Done?] If stack S is empty, then the algorithm terminates.
5. [Process next node.] $C \Leftarrow S$. If MARK(C) = "−" then go to step 2. Otherwise, go to step 4.

Algorithm 5.4 is organized so that it tends to produce shallow stacks in real applications. Data collected by Clark and Green [1977] demonstrate that, on the average, in list structures used in practice, nonatomic car fields occurred $\frac{1}{3}$ of the time, while nonatomic cdr fields occurred $\frac{3}{4}$ of the time. Thus a preorder traversal will restrict the depth of the stack to be proportional to the longest car path in the preorder spanning tree of the list structure. Under the circumstances, the longest car path is likely to be shorter than the longest cdr path.

5.4.1.2 *Marking with link-inversion and tag bits.* The link-inversion traversal algorithm for binary trees given in Chapter 3 (Algorithm 3.6) used special tag bits in nodes to signify whether, upon ascent, a node was being revisited from the left or from the right. If ascent was from the left, descent and traversal of the right subtree was next attempted. If ascent was from the right, further ascent to ancestral nodes was attempted. In the generalization of Algorithm 3.6 presented below, the tag bits in nodes are used for the same purpose. In addition, since cyclic lists are admissible for marking, separate mark bits are maintained in nodes. Initially, all TAG and MARK fields of all nodes are assumed to contain "–". Infinite looping is avoided by not traversing any node already marked "+".

Algorithm 5.5 *Schorr–Waite–Deutsch marking of cyclic list structures.*

Let PRES contain the address of the start node. The algorithm sets the MARK bits in the start node and all nodes accessible from it to "+". Assume Λ is the address of an Atom having a MARK field set to "+". During the course of the algorithm, occasionally the MARK field of Λ is redundantly set to "+" by actions that mark atoms.

1. [Initialize and check for Atom.] Set PREV ← Λ. If PRES is an Atom, then set MARK(PRES) ← "+" and terminate the algorithm.

2. [Mark node.] Set MARK(PRES) ← "+".

3. [Is *car* marked or Atomic?] If MARK(car(PRES)) = "+", go to step 5. Otherwise, if car(PRES) is an Atom, then set MARK(car(PRES)) ← "+" and go to step 5.

4. [Follow *car* path and invert links.] Set NEXT ← car(PRES), car(PRES) ← PREV, PREV ← PRES, PRES ← NEXT, and go back to step 2.

5. [Is *cdr* marked or Atomic?] If MARK(cdr(PRES)) = "+", go to step 7. Otherwise, if cdr(PRES) is an Atom, then set MARK(cdr(PRES)) ← "+" and go to step 7.

6. [Follow *cdr* path and invert links.] Set TAG(PRES) ← "+", NEXT ← cdr(PRES), cdr(PRES) ← PREV, PREV ← PRES, PRES ← NEXT, and go back to step 2.

7. [Ascend.] If PREV = Λ, then the algorithm terminates. Otherwise, if TAG(PREV) = "+", then set TAG(PREV) ← "–", NEXT ← cdr(PREV), cdr(PREV) ← PRES, PRES ← PREV, PREV ← NEXT, and go to step 7 (for further ascent). Otherwise, set NEXT ← car(PREV), car(PREV) ← PRES, PRES ← PREV, PREV ← NEXT, and go to step 5.

5.4.1.3 *Wegbreit marking with a bit stack.* If it is not possible to allocate tag bits in addition to mark bits in nodes of a list structure, recourse must be made to other ideas in order to get the Schorr–Waite–Deutsch method to work. One alternative is to allocate a bit map with bits in 1–1 correspondence with nodes of the list space. But if the word length of the computer is w bits, and there are M list cells that are either free or reserved, using a bit map to hold tag bits will occupy M/w words, perhaps an unacceptable price to pay. Another possibility is to use hash linking, and to hash link cells whose TAG bit is set to "+" into an auxiliary table. With this method, however, the number of hash entries in the table can be as great as the longest cdr chain in a list structure spanning tree.

What appears to be the most space-efficient, linear-time technique is based on the idea of using a bit stack to contain one bit for each node having two non-atomic fields on the path from the present point of traversal back to the root (called the trace path). This idea is due to Wegbreit (see Wegbreit [1972]).

Wegbreit's algorithm uses link inversion similar to the Schorr–Waite–Deutsch method. However, instead of using TAG bits in every node, a stack of flag bits is used. A stack is used because the trace path grows and shrinks in last-in, first-out order. Also, nodes with one or more atomic fields require no trace bits in the stack since, when revisiting a node with one atomic field and one nonatomic field, it is known that the traced field must be the nonatomic one. Hence, only those nodes on the trace path having two nonatomic fields require a flag bit in the stack.

Algorithm 5.6 *Wegbreit marking with a bit stack.*

Let PRES point to the start node, and let S be a bit stack. Assume that MARKED(X) is a predicate with a side effect that marks the node X and returns *true* iff the node was previously marked.

1. [Initialize.] Set PREV $\leftarrow \Lambda$ and $S \leftarrow \Lambda$.

2. [Process new node.] If (PRES is an Atom) or (MARKED(PRES)) or (both car(PRES) and cdr(PRES) are Atoms), then go to step 4.

3. [Process car.] If car(PRES) is an Atom, set NEXT $\leftarrow$ cdr(PRES), cdr(PRES) $\leftarrow$ PREV, PREV $\leftarrow$ PRES, PRES $\leftarrow$ NEXT, and go to step 2. Otherwise, set NEXT $\leftarrow$ car(PRES), car(PRES) $\leftarrow$ PREV, PREV $\leftarrow$ PRES, and if now, cdr(PRES) is not an Atom, stack $S \Leftarrow 1$, set PRES $\leftarrow$ NEXT, and go to step 2.

4. [Backup.] If PREV $= \Lambda$, then the algorithm terminates. Otherwise, if cdr(PREV) is an Atom, set NEXT $\leftarrow$ car(PREV), car(PREV) $\leftarrow$ PRES, PRES $\leftarrow$ PREV, PREV $\leftarrow$ NEXT, and go to step 4. Otherwise, if car(PREV) is an Atom, then go to step 6 (to ascend).

5. [Pop stack.] Set FLAG $\Leftarrow S$. If FLAG $= 1$, then $S \Leftarrow 0$, set NEXT $\leftarrow$ cdr(PREV), cdr(PREV) $\leftarrow$ car(PREV), car(PREV) $\leftarrow$ PRES, PRES $\leftarrow$ NEXT, and go to step 2.

6. [Ascend.] Set NEXT $\leftarrow$ cdr(PREV), cdr(PREV) $\leftarrow$ PRES, PRES $\leftarrow$ PREV, PREV $\leftarrow$ NEXT, and go to step 4.

The list structure that produces the worst-case space requirements for this algorithm is a single chain in which each node has a nonatomic *car* and *cdr* pointing to some successor in the chain. The chain uses all nodes in the system and the bit stack can be of depth N. Most cases of practical use will not approach this pathological case. However, the system must reserve in advance some fixed amount of space for the bit stack; and there is always a chance that this implementation limit could be transgressed. Notwithstanding this risk, the Wegbreit technique is the best linear algorithm with regard to space efficiency now known. However, if we are willing to loosen our marking time requirement from $O(N)$ to $O(N \log N)$, we can avail ourselves of Lindstrom's technique, which uses no tag bits at all.

5.4.1.4 *Lindstrom marking without stacks or tag bits.* We assume that all mark bits are set to 0 initially. During the course of Lindstrom's algorithm, the mark bit of each cell on the trace path is 0 if return will be from the right and its left descendant is nonatomic. All other cells on the trace path, as well as completely processed cells, have mark bits set to 1. When a zero-marked cell is accessed from above, the trace path is searched to see if the trace path contains it. If it is on the trace path, further tracing is avoided. If it is not on the trace path, normal descent is initiated.

Algorithm 5.7 *Lindstrom marking without stacks or tag bits.*

In the following, we use two macro instructions defined as follows. Let *move right* stand for the sequence of instructions: "Set $V \leftarrow cdr(S)$, $cdr(S) \leftarrow car(S)$, $car(S) \leftarrow P$, $P \leftarrow S$, and $S \leftarrow V$." Let *move left* stand for the sequence of instructions: "Set $V \leftarrow car(S)$, $car(S) \leftarrow cdr(S)$, $cdr(S) \leftarrow P$, $P \leftarrow S$, and $S \leftarrow V$." Initially, all cells have mark bits set to 0. We assume that S points to the start node of the structure to be marked.

1. [Initialize.] If S is an Atom, then set $MARK(S) \leftarrow 1$ and terminate the algorithm. Otherwise, set $P \leftarrow \Lambda$. If now, $car(S)$ is an Atom, go to step 3.
2. [Descend from S.] Set $MARK(S) \leftarrow 1 - MARK(S)$, move left, and go to step 4.
3. [Descend to right.] Set $MARK(S) \leftarrow 1$, and if $cdr(S)$ is an Atom, go to step 8. Otherwise, move right.
4. [Is S new?] If $MARK(S) = 1$, then go to step 8. Otherwise, if $car(S)$ is an Atom, go to step 3. Otherwise, if $cdr(S)$ is an Atom, go to step 2. Otherwise, set $Q \leftarrow P$.
5. [Search for S.] In the following cases, take the following actions:
           Case $\Rightarrow$ Action
   a) $Q = \Lambda \Rightarrow$ if $car(S)$ is an Atom, go to step 3. Otherwise, go to step 2.
   b) $Q \neq \Lambda \Rightarrow$ if $MARK(Q) = 0$, go to step 6. If $cdr(Q)$ is an Atom, go to step 7. Otherwise, set $Q \leftarrow cdr(Q)$ and repeat this step.
6. [Found S?] If $Q = S$, go to step 8.
7. [Search up to left.] Set $Q \leftarrow car(Q)$ and go to step 5.
8. [Skip S.] (Exchange the values of S and P) $S \leftrightarrow P$.

9. [Move up from P.] If $S = \Lambda$, then the algorithm terminates. Otherwise, if MARK$(S) = 0$, set MARK$(S) \leftarrow 1$, and go to step 11.

10. [Up from right or left?] If cdr(S) is not an Atom, go to step 12.

11. [Up from right.] Move left and go to step 9.

12. [Process right descendant?] If car(S) is not an Atom, go to step 2. Otherwise, move right and go to step 9.

5.4.2 Collection

The marking algorithms of the previous section can be used to mark all cells accessible to the program. All inaccessible cells will then remain unmarked, and a linear sweep of the memory can be used to link all such unmarked cells together.

A word of caution is in order, however, before proceeding to a version of the collection algorithm. The use of marking algorithms must be carefully arranged to be *completely thorough*. Not only must one mark all list structures accessible from such usual places as program variables with pointer values or pointers on the execution stack (if there is one); one must also protect from erasure data structures being constructed but only partially completed. The garbage collection process is triggered by running out of available free cells. This happens when a request is made for a free cell during a construction process. Therefore, when garbage collection occurs, it is frequently the case that a partially constructed list structure is in the list cell space, perhaps referred to only by pointers in machine accumulators (not by pointers in program variables and execution-time structures), and perhaps malformed in the sense that, since it is only a partially complete construction, the pointers and tags do not obey the constraints of finished, well-formed list structures.

Two dangers arise from this state of affairs: (1) If we forget to mark partially completed structures accessible from machine accumulators, the cells in the partially completed structure are erased and returned to the free storage list. (2) A malformed structure may derail the proper operation of the marking algorithm.

Unfortunately, experience shows that failure to observe these precautions leads to some of the most vexing errors in list structure programming. Of the two dangers above, the first is the more serious. The reason bugs arising from the first are hard to detect is that they occur only intermittently and the symptoms are not obviously related to the source of the error, making diagnosis difficult. The intermittent nature of the errors is due to the fact that only if the garbage collector is invoked during an inadequately protected construction (a chance occurrence) will the partially completed structure be partly erased. Even so, the partly erased structure may lie unperturbed for quite a while before it is accessed, altered, or used in further construction, if it is even noticed at all. At the point that unexpected erroneous behavior is detected, frequently all one knows is that a given structure is malformed but one may not know the source of malformation. A general hint that is usually significant, however, is when pointers in normal structures point to cells in the available space list. This is usually a signal that partial erasure of a construction has accidentally occurred when garbage collection was invoked in the middle of the construction episode.

Let us assume now that all accessible cells have been properly marked such that $MARK(C) = $ "$+$", and inaccessible cells are marked "$-$". We assume that cells are distributed in a zone of memory from address M_1 up to M_2 (that is, $M_1 \leq a < M_2$) and that they use c words per cell. The following algorithm links unmarked cells in ascending order of cell addresses and reconstitutes the available space list, Avail.

Algorithm 5.8 *Collection of unmarked cells.*

1. [Initialize.] Avail $\leftarrow \Lambda$.
2. [Conduct linear sweep.] For $A = M_2 - c$, $M_2 - 2c$, $M_2 - 3c$, ..., $M_1 + c$, M_1 do step (a):
   a) If $MARK(A) = $ "$-$", set $cdr(A) \leftarrow$ Avail, and Avail $\leftarrow A$. Otherwise, set $MARK(A) \leftarrow$ "$-$".

Note that the linear sweep of the cells is conducted in descending order so that the cells on Avail will lie in ascending order (a property we shall make use of in Section 5.5 below). Note also that the algorithm resets all mark bits to "$-$".

It is convenient to add an additional step to Algorithm 6.8 to count the number of cells being reclaimed and appended to the Avail list. This cumulative total is useful for such processes as compacting the memory and deciding on garbage collection policies, as we will see later. Thus, we assume in what follows that the number of cells N on Avail is readily available.

5.4.3 Incremental garbage collection

Three methods for incremental garbage collection are: (1) the *reference count* technique, (2) *interleaved collection*, in which a single processor devotes its activities alternately to normal list processing and garbage collection, and (3) *parallel collection*, in which a normal list processing computer and a devoted garbage collection computer share the same list processing memory.

Incremental garbage collection techniques find application in real-time systems where response-time requirements forbid pausing to collect garbage by marking-and-gathering methods. A perhaps apocryphal instance of this relates to a robot project once undertaken at M.I.T. An attempt was made to program a hand–eye system to catch a pingpong ball thrown in its reach. The experimenter wound up for the pitch and tossed the ball at the robot. The robot instantly tracked the trajectory of the ball with its TV camera eye, and computed where to stretch out its arm to catch the ball. As it came near to issuing instructions to its arm to catch the ball, however, it paused to garbage-collect its 256K list memory. This process took 2.31 seconds at roughly 9 microseconds per cell. Result—the pingpong ball whistled by the frozen robot, and clacked along the floor behind it. (A sequel to this apocryphal story is that, after fixing the garbage collection problem, the investigators discovered that the robot systematically missed its catches in a certain quadrant. Further diagnosis led to the discovery that it had a sick sine routine. Apparently the commercial sine-routine package, lifted from a popular compiler, was systematically wrong for certain ranges of its argument values—a fact that users of the commercial package had never noticed over many years of use.)

5.4.3.1 *Reference counter methods*. Suppose we allocate a field in each list cell capable of containing an integer. Let us call this field the *reference count* field of a cell C, designated, say, as REF(C), and let us agree to maintain an integer in REF(C) equal to the number of times C is pointed to by link fields in other allocated cells. In our diagrams, this simply means that REF(C) contains the number of arrows pointing at cell C.

When a new pointer to cell C is created and stored in a link field of some cell, we increment the reference count of C by one: REF(C) $\leftarrow$ REF(C) + 1; and when a pointer to C is destroyed, we decrement the reference count of C by one: REF(C) $\leftarrow$ REF(C) − 1. Now, whenever the reference count of a cell drops to 0, there are no external references to it, so it has become available and can be adjoined to the available space list.

Weizenbaum [1963] developed an intriguing variation on the policy for returning newly freed cells to the Avail list. Normally, the policy for freeing a cell C whose reference count has just dropped to 0 is first to append C to the Avail list and then to process the pointers contained in C, say by overwriting them with Λ, and dropping the reference counts of cells they reference. In turn, this may lead to a cascade of further cells becoming free (as happens to all nodes in a tree in some order when the root is discovered to be free, for instance.) Weizenbaum's policy differs from this, however. A newly freed cell is placed on the end of the Avail list, but its internal pointers are not immediately processed. This end cell is considered for use when it advances to the front of the Avail list, by virtue of the cells in front of it having been used up. Only at this moment are the pointers internal to the cell processed (by decrementing the reference counts of their referents). This delayed action of reference-count processing is quite efficient in running time, and it provides a smoother incremental collection policy—one not so vulnerable to significant real-time delays caused by cascades of cell releases implicit in the former policy.

Two classical complaints levied against reference-count techniques are:

1. The extra reference-count field may take up too much space and thereby decrease storage utilization efficiency; or, perhaps worse, if we are too stingy in the allocation of reference-count fields of suitable size, it may become possible for the reference-count field to overflow, torpedoing the validity of the reclamation policy.

2. If cyclic structures are permitted, it becomes possible for islands of inaccessible garbage to exist, all cells of which have nonzero reference counts, because the cells on a cycle mutually support each other's nonzero reference counts. Figure 5.21 illustrates such an island of inaccessible yet unfreed garbage.

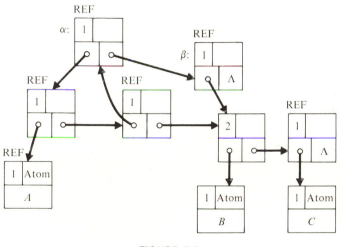

FIGURE 5.21

Generalizing, it can be seen that any list structure containing a cycle can never be liberated by normal reference-count decrementing, and that all pure lists or reentrant lists to which a cell on such a cycle points are also never liberated. On the other hand, pure lists or reentrant lists are capable of being liberated once their roots are liberated. Some authors therefore restrict use of reference-count techniques to acyclic list structures. Other authors (for example, Weizenbaum [1969]) advocate use of a hybrid policy involving reference counts for normal use and marking for collection of cyclic structures.

It is a common opinion (found in print in many places, such as Schorr and Waite [1967]) that it is impossible to collect islands of inaccessible garbage containing cyclic structures. But let's reflect on this problem for a moment—is it really impossible?

Let C be an inaccessible connected component of a list structure graph each of whose constituent cells has a nonzero reference count. Suppose we start at some cell S in C and traverse the cells in C accessible from S, and that while traversing we maintain two cumulative sums, R, the sum of the reference counts in the fields of cells traversed, and P, the sum of the number of pointers contained in the cells traversed. At the end of the traversal, if $P = R$, then the entire connected component C can be liberated. Liberation is possible because all references to cells in C are accounted for by pointers in C, and hence no external references can exist. For example, in Fig. 5.21, if we sum the number of arrows in the diagram we find 10 arrows, and if we sum the numbers in the reference-count fields, we also get a sum of 10. Hence, the entire connected structure in Fig. 5.21 has no external references and is collectable in its entirety. On the other hand, if the result of a traversal yields a sum of pointers $P < R$, then there are fewer pointers internal to the connected component C than there are references to cells. Hence, some of the cells must be referenced by external pointers not accounted for by the P pointers in the diagram. Note that, if tracing of the diagram in Fig. 5.21 is begun at the cell marked α, then all cells are accessed and $P = R = 10$. However, if tracing is begun at the cell marked β, then $P = 4$ and $R = 6$, so the connected component accessible from β is not collectable even though it is a part of a larger island of collectable garbage. Thus, our method succeeds in finding an island of collectable garbage only if we are fortunate enough to choose a start cell S from which all other cells in the connected component are collectable.

Unfortunately, there exist some uncollectable structures C, not externally referenced, that do not have single start nodes from which all the others are accessible. A pathological example of this is given in Fig. 5.22. Here, we assume that the memory has $2N + 1$ list cells. We join all cells into a single inaccessible

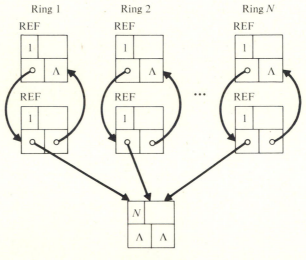

FIGURE 5.22

structure formed from N rings of two cells each, such that each of the N rings points once at the single remaining cell, which is referenced N times.

Now, no matter where we start tracing, we never find $P = R$. Thus, we conclude that we must be able to select multiple starting points from which to trace the structure and compute the cumulative sums P and R. The structure in Fig. 5.22 forces us to choose N starting points, one on each ring. It is clear that analogous structures with $k \leq N$ independent starting points could be built from k rings and one cell referenced k times, once from each ring. Thus, we might be forced to try all possible combinations of starting points $\binom{M}{k}$ in the memory, for each k ($1 \leq k < M/2$). But $\sum_k \binom{M}{k}$ is $O(2^M)$ combinations, and for each combination tried, we may have to trace out at least some fraction of the memory. Hence, the whole process may at worst be $O(M \cdot 2^M)$.

This analysis shows that, while the idea of collecting islands of inaccessible garbage may not be *impossible*, it certainly is *unthinkable*. Clearly, a marking and gathering policy, independent of the reference-count techniques, is a better route to travel, when considering how to gather cells that the reference-count method fails to release.

Perhaps the marking and gathering process could be invoked for occasional "spring housecleaning" if the sum of the number of cells on the available space list and the number of cells in use should be substantially less than the number of cells in the memory, indicating the presence of substantial amounts of uncollectable free islands.

A reference count scheme that works well in the context of a hierarchy of memory devices has recently been studied by Deutsch and Bobrow [1976]. In this paper, it is pointed out that the disadvantage of mark-and-sweep techniques is that the time required to collect unused space is proportional to the amount of space in use, since that all must be traced, and additionally, in an extended hierarchy of memories, that marking may entail tracing of structures spread over pages of secondary storage, an inherently slow process. By contrast, the reference counter methods are what Deutsch and Bobrow call *transaction-oriented*; that is, the overhead required for reclamation (involving incrementing and decrementing reference counts) is proportional to the number of transactions that affect the accessibility of the data. Here, only operations that change pointers can affect accessibility.

Deutsch and Bobrow argue that pointer-change operations, such as updating pointer fields in data blocks or records, and changing pointer values of reference variables are usually distributed uniformly in a computation, making the overhead for storage maintenance roughly proportional to the total computational effort. Since this is not true for marking-and-gathering-based garbage collection, in which the overhead in the marking phase is proportional to the amount of data in the system, reference counts seem to be suggested as a basis for incremental reclamation schemes.

A problem still remains with the two sources of potential inefficiency: (1) that every allocated datum must contain space for a reference count, leading to potentially significant space overhead, and (2) that every transaction affecting the accessibility of a datum must alter the reference count, leading to intolerable overhead for operations such as altering the reference count of referents on every assignment.

These two sources of inefficiency are overcome in the Deutsch and Bobrow scheme by the following device. A *transaction file* is built up consisting of three sorts of transactions: allocation of a new cell from free space, creation of a pointer to a cell, and destruction of a pointer to a cell. At suitable intervals, the transactions accumulated serially during the course of a computation are examined and used to adjust a table of reference counts kept separate from the cells with which they are in 1–1 correspondence.

We now take note of empirical data on LISP use given by Clark and Green [1977] in order to provide a sensible basis for developing a method for storage of the reference-count table. For LISP data, Clark and Green found that, most of the time, when a cell is created, another cell is created very soon thereafter that references it, and that (less frequently) a created cell is abandoned with no reference remaining anywhere. The abandoned cells are often holders of temporary values used in computations, such as real numbers or strings. More startling, perhaps, is the fact that only two to ten percent of the cells are ever referenced by more than one cell.

Thus, since the vast majority of data have a reference count of 1, we can use the hash linking technique of Bobrow [1975] discussed earlier (in Section 5.3.3.1) to maintain hash links only to those cells with reference counts that are not 1. Cell addresses are used as keys for two such hash link tables. The first table is called the *multireference table*, or MRT, and it holds cell addresses with reference counts of two or greater. Another separate table, called the *zero count table*, or ZCT, is used to hold addresses of cells whose reference count from other list cells is zero, but which are nonetheless referenced by program variables or execution stack positions. (Such latter references are to be considered separately from references generated in cell space.)

Here now is how the three classes of transactions are handled. For an *allocation transaction*: An entry is made in the ZCT except when the allocation transaction is followed by a create-pointer transaction (a common case, in which the pair of transactions cancel and can thus be ignored). For a *create-pointer transaction*: If the datum referenced is in the ZCT, it is deleted since its reference count has been incremented to 1. If the datum is in the MRT, its reference count is incremented. Otherwise, if the datum is not in the MRT, it is entered with a reference count of 2. For a *destroy-pointer transaction*: If the referenced datum is in the MRT, it is deleted if its reference count is 2. Otherwise, its reference count is decremented by one. On the other hand, if the referenced datum is not in the MRT, it is entered in the ZCT.

Once the transactions have been processed and the tables have been updated to be correct, the free cells are those referenced in the ZCT that are not pointed to by program variables or the program execution stack entries.

When a datum is reclaimed, the pointers it contains may be destroyed, leading to more pointer-destruction transactions that can be saved for later processing. However, there is a good chance that sizable structures will be freed all at once; and, since the hash tables must be in core during the reclamation process, it may be preferable to process all transactions generated during the reclamation process immediately as they arise.

During the accumulation of transactions for storage on an external sequential medium, an in-core buffer can be used. This in-core buffer can be organized as a table hashed on the addresses involved in the transactions. Thus, allocate–create transaction pairs that occur closely in time and that cancel, can be omitted from the readout of the buffer to secondary storage, for further economy.

Finally, Deutsch and Bobrow argue that the mark-and-sweep garbage collector (that can be run in conjunction with a reference count scheme at infrequent intervals to reclaim inaccessible cyclic structures) should also serve the function of compacting and reorganizing list structures to minimize paging. This topic is pursued further in Section 5.4.4.

The reference-count technique was introduced in early papers by Gelernter, Hansen, and Gerberich [1960], and by Collins [1960]. The inadequacy of the method in relation to cyclic structures was mentioned in McBeth [1963]. Further developments in reference count ideas were given in Weizenbaum [1963] and Weizenbaum [1969].

5.4.3.2 *Minsky's algorithm for interleaved collection.* Knuth [1973a] (p. 422, Exercise 12, and p. 594, answer 12) attributes to M. Minsky an interleaved, garbage collection process in which, when the available space list Avail contains less than N nodes, a coroutine is initiated that shares computer time with the main program, and performs the following garbage collection processes:

a) Marks all nodes on the Avail list.

b) Marks other nodes accessible to the program.

c) Links unmarked nodes together to form a new Avail list to use when the current Avail list becomes exhausted.

d) Resets the mark bits in all nodes.

Now, one must find a way to compute N, the number of nodes on Avail, used to trigger the garbage collecting coroutine, and one must additionally select a ratio of time-sharing that guarantees that steps (a), (b), (c), and (d) can be completed before the N cells on Avail are used up, while still guaranteeing that the main program continues to run.

5.4.3.3 *Parallel garbage collection.* Parallel garbage-collection algorithms govern the operation of two computers that share a common list memory. One computer executes the main program and the other collects garbage and restores it to the available space list.

Parallel garbage collection algorithms are difficult to devise because of potential conflict between the list processing computer, which we shall call the *mutator*, and the garbage collecting computer, which we shall call the *collector*. For instance, if both the mutator and collector are attempting to perform an operation on a given cell at address α, one may overwrite and thereby erase the work done by the other if care is not taken to synchronize their respective actions. Naively, suppose that the mutator wishes to change the car field of α and that the collector wishes to set a mark field of α to the mark $+$. Suppose further that the mutator and the collector each read the contents of α in some order, and that the mutator changes the car field while the collector changes the mark field, each in its own respective internal registers. Now, if the mutator writes back into α first and the collector writes back into α second, the overwriting by the collector undoes the car change performed by the mutator whereas, if the collector writes back into α first and the mutator writes back into α second, the overwriting by the mutator undoes the mark change performed by the collector. If the goal of the collector was first to mark all accessible cells and then to collect them to reconstitute the available space list, the latter circumstance may cause an accessible cell to be linked improperly onto the available space list during the collection phase. In the former circumstance, the collector clobbers a car pointer that the mutator has just set, and this may wreck the connectivity of the structure the mutator was trying to establish.

In Steele's solution to the parallel garbage collection problem (see Steele [1975], and also the corrigendum in *CACM* 19:6 (June), p. 354), each processor can be thought of as having a global "seize register," which contains a pointer to the cell α to which the processor desires exclusive access. If the other processor tries to seize α before the first processor releases α, then the other processor will loop (or hang) until it can seize it. Thus, each processor can complete a read–modify–write cycle on a cell α as an indivisible unit in a fashion guaranteed free from interference by the other processor. For marking, Steele's collector algorithm uses a stack traversal similar to that in Algorithm 5.4, which assumes the existence of a separate stack outside the list cell space to hold pointers to accessible cells awaiting marking. Steele [1975] notes that the use of a Schorr–Waite–Deutsch link-inversion traversal for marking (as in Algorithm 5.5) by the collector would disrupt the topology of the accessible cell structure for the mutator, and is therefore inappropriate.

Algorithm 5.9 below, for parallel collection, is a variant of one given by Gries [1977b], which Gries ascribes to Dijkstra. Gries [1977b] has proved his version of this algorithm to be correct, and has noted that the proofs of correctness of parallel algorithms of this sort are challenging because of the potential interaction between the parallel processors (see also the letter by Gries [1977a] and the reply by Wadler in *CACM* 20:2 (February 1977), p. 120). Wadler [1976] provides a valuable analysis of the efficiency of this class of algorithms and, among other things, demonstrates that if a real-time garbage collector is being used at its maximum capacity, real-time garbage collection requires only twice as much processing power as regular garbage collection. Further, Wadler shows that supplementing a list processor with a second processor devoted to garbage collection leads to an increase in execution speed.

In order for Algorithm 5.9 to work properly, we establish the following conventions. We assume that a region of memory with addresses α in the range $0 < \alpha \le M$ holds list cells of the form

with one such cell at each address α. The address of the special cell Λ is taken to be 0. The Λ cell has color, car, and cdr fields the same as all others that can be assigned and accessed. The program variable *Root* holds a fixed address β in the cell memory, which is assumed to contain the root cell of the cyclic list structure containing all cells accessible to the mutator. The mutator can access any cell reachable from the root via some sequence of car and cdr pointers. The available space list Avail is a one-way linked list of free cells that can be detached one by one by the mutator and linked into the set of cells accessible from the root cell. The program variable Avail holds the address of a fixed address θ in memory containing a list cell whose cdr field points to the first free cell on the Avail list, if there is one. The program variable *EndAvail* holds the address of the last cell on the Avail list, as shown in Fig. 5.23.

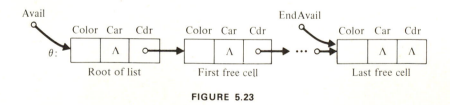

FIGURE 5.23

Note that the cell at address θ is *not* a free cell, but is used only to hold a pointer to a linked list of free cells in its cdr field. If the cdr field of θ contains Λ, the Avail list is empty.

The color field of each cell contains one of three colors: *black*, *gray*, and *white*, coded in two bits as 11, 01, and 00, respectively. The following actions for coloring nodes are taken to be *indivisible*:

whiten(α):   color(α) $\leftarrow$ white
blacken(α):   color(α) $\leftarrow$ black
darken(α):   *if* color(α) = white *then* color(α) $\leftarrow$ gray

In order for the last of these three operations to be *indivisible*, one must assume that the underlying computer has something like an "or-to-memory" operation, in which one can *or* the pattern 01 directly into color(α). Implementing the darken(α) operation by the sequence

$$\text{temp} \leftarrow \text{color}(\alpha) \ or \ 01; \quad \text{color}(\alpha) \leftarrow \text{temp}$$

would violate the indivisibility requirement on a computer with a memory reference as its only indivisible action. Other than the three indivisible actions above, only the memory reference is considered indivisible in Algorithm 5.9.

The mutator will be assumed to perform an unending sequence of any of the following operations in any order and at any speed independent of the actions of the collector.

Mutator operations

Let α and β be addresses of cells reachable from Root such that $\alpha \neq \Lambda$ and $\beta \neq \Lambda$. The mutator can perform any of the following:

1. [Nullify car.] Set car(α) $\leftarrow \Lambda$.
2. [Nullify cdr.] Set cdr(α) $\leftarrow \Lambda$.
3. [Link car.] Set car(α) $\leftarrow \beta$ and darken(β).
4. [Link cdr.] Set cdr(α) $\leftarrow \beta$ and darken(β).
5. [Link car to new cell.] Set NewCell $\leftarrow$ cdr(Avail), car(α) $\leftarrow$ NewCell, darken(NewCell), **wait until** NewCell $\neq$ EndAvail, cdr(Avail) $\leftarrow$ cdr(NewCell), darken(cdr(NewCell)), and cdr(NewCell) $\leftarrow \Lambda$.
6. [Link cdr to new cell.] Set NewCell $\leftarrow$ cdr(Avail), cdr(α) $\leftarrow$ NewCell, darken(NewCell), **wait until** NewCell $\neq$ EndAvail, cdr(Avail) $\leftarrow$ cdr(NewCell), darken(cdr(NewCell)), and cdr(NewCell) $\leftarrow \Lambda$.

The operation **wait until** NewCell $\neq$ EndAvail causes the mutator to wait until the Avail list contains at least one free cell before proceeding, and can be implemented by an action such as "L: *if* NewCell = EndAvail, *then go to L*".

The collector is assumed to be operating in parallel with the mutator and follows the instructions given in the nonterminating Algorithm 5.9.

Algorithm 5.9 *Parallel collection.*

1. [Initialize.] Set $i \leftarrow 0$, darken(Root), darken(Avail), and darken(Λ).

2. [Blacken.] (This step blackens gray nodes and those reachable from gray nodes.) If $i \le M$ and color(i) $\ne$ gray, then set $i \leftarrow i + 1$ and repeat this step. Otherwise, if $i \le M$ and color(i) = gray, then darken(car(i)), darken(cdr(i)), blacken(i), set $i \leftarrow 0$, and repeat this step.

3. [Collect.] (This step links the white nodes onto Avail and whitens the black nodes in preparation for another cycle.) *for* $i \leftarrow 0, 1, \ldots, M$ *do* steps (a) and (b):
   a) *if* color(i) = white, *then* (link i to Avail by setting) car(i) $\leftarrow \Lambda$, cdr(i) $\leftarrow \Lambda$, cdr(EndAvail) $\leftarrow i$, and EndAvail $\leftarrow i$.
   b) *if* color(i) = black, *then* whiten(i).

4. [Repeat.] Go back to step 1 (to repeat the collection cycle over again).

If we assume initially that all cells in the memory ($0 \le \alpha \le M$) are white, then the mutator and the collector cooperate to make reachable cells first gray and later black. The collector starts by graying the roots. Then it scans memory in an ascending linear sweep in which, if it finds a gray cell α, it grays the children of α, blackens α, and begins another sweep (starting at 0 again) in an attempt to find another gray cell to blacken. If it completes a sweep without finding any more gray cells to blacken, it progresses to the final phase in which it links all white cells onto Avail and whitens the black cells in preparation for another cycle.

Suppose that the mutator takes a cell β and grays it (by using mutator operations 5 or 6) and then overwrites a link to β to make β unreachable. After this, the mutator cannot reference β until it has been linked back into the Avail list. But during marking, the collector blackens β once it is gray and fails to link it onto Avail since it is not white. What prevents β from being permanently lost to the system is that, on the next cycle, the collector whitens β since it was black and then links it back onto Avail. Thus, we may have to wait for two cycles of the collector to retrieve certain unreachable cells, but eventually they will be recovered.

The reason for using the color gray in addition to the colors black and white can be seen from considering the cell configurations in Fig. 5.24, in which "b" stands for black, "w" for white, and "C" for the name of the color field.

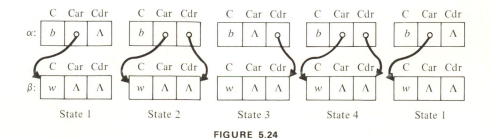

FIGURE 5.24

Suppose the mutator endlessly transforms the cell α in Fig. 5.24 by starting with the configuration in state 1, setting $\text{cdr}(\alpha) \leftarrow \beta$ to get state 2, setting $\text{car}(\alpha) \leftarrow \Lambda$ to get state 3, setting $\text{car}(\alpha) \leftarrow \beta$ to get state 4, and setting $\text{cdr}(\alpha) \leftarrow \Lambda$ to get state 1 again. Then β is always reachable from α in Fig. 5.24 no matter what state the cells are in. Suppose that β starts out with the color white and that the collector is supposed to blacken β eventually because it is attached to α, which is already black. However, the collector might never notice that β is attached to α since it might inspect the car pointer of α in state 3 when it is Λ and might later inspect the cdr pointer of α in state 1 when it is Λ, thus never noticing that β is attached to α. Thus, the mutator must cooperate in some fashion, which it does by graying any white node that it makes reachable by pointing to it.

The marking step of Algorithm 5.9 is written so as to be appropriate for proving that the algorithm works, even though it is unacceptably inefficient (see Wadler [1976] for analysis). Gries ([1977b] p. 925) notes that it is possible to substitute more efficient traversal processes to blacken the reachable cells provided they make a final pass through all the cells without finding gray ones. (This is pursued in the exercises.)

Baker [1977] gives another approach to parallel garbage collection in which he divides the list cell space into two semi-spaces. During execution of a user program, all list cells in use are located in one of the two semi-spaces. During garbage collection, all accessible cells are traced and *moved* to the other semi-space and the "from" semi-space contains only garbage. Then the "to" and "from" semi-spaces are reversed, and the cycle repeats. This technique follows an early method given by Fenichel and Yochelson [1969] and later refined by Cheney [1970]. One might initially think that this technique would be too inefficient in its use of space, since only half the total memory can be used; but Baker [1977] shows that this assumption is premature if one uses cdr-direction linearization (as discussed next in Section 5.4.4) to compact the list storage.

5.4.4 Garbage collection in multi-level storage environments

The garbage collection techniques studied in Sections 5.4.1 through 5.4.3 are oriented primarily toward use in rapid-access primary memory. Often, though, list processing programs are of such large size that they cannot be conveniently accommodated entirely in primary memory and, for reasons of cost, portions of the programs and data are then stored on secondary memory, such as drums or disks. If a reference is made to a portion of the program or data not in primary memory, the relevant external portion of the program or data is retrieved from secondary memory, transferred to primary memory, and execution continues.

As we shall see in greater detail in Chapter 9, the average time to retrieve a word from a rotating memory device such as a drum might be on the order of 10 to 50 milliseconds (half the rotation time). On the other hand, word-transfer rates from a drum are much faster, say, on the order of 2 to 10 microseconds/word in current technology. To use a drum as if it were a core memory by reading single words as required might increase the data-reference times by a factor in the range of 10,000 to 40,000. On the other hand, the cost of accessing an additional 250 to 500 words of contiguous data from a drum is hardly more than that for accessing a single word. This implies that we might consider dividing drum memory into units called *pages*, and bringing an entire page into core from a drum whenever a single word from a page is required. If then, we could find some technique for increasing the likelihood that subsequent references would occur on the same page (or on pages currently in core), the number of slow, external, secondary-memory accesses might be drastically reduced—perhaps bringing list processing techniques for large program and data spaces further toward the realm of the practical.

Thus, we find a significant body of literature devoted to the problem of concentrating nearby references to list cells on the smallest number of pages via techniques of compacting, copying, and reorganizing. One important time to consider such techniques is *garbage collection time.*

Straightforward use of the garbage collection techniques discussed earlier in a two-level memory tends to lead, after a while, to a diffusion of small, active sections of virtual pages amongst a large mass of mostly inactive pages, resulting in too many references to secondary storage and, ultimately, to unacceptable degradation of performance. Remedial techniques are required to oppose this tendency and to structure lists in virtual memory so as to reduce the exchange rate of primary and secondary storage during execution of a job. Finding the appropriate occupancy disciplines for pages in virtual memory has been an important way to attempt achievement of this goal.

One technique is that of Fenichel and Yochelson [1969]. Fenichel and Yochelson assumed lists to be written in an effectively unbounded virtual memory space. They divided this virtual memory space into two *semi-spaces*, one of which is designated as *current*. When garbage collection is invoked, the active lists in the current semi-space are moved into a compact, contiguous region of the second space, using a recursive list-moving algorithm. The second space is then designated as *current*. Clark and Green [1977] used an algorithm closely resembling that of Fenichel and Yochelson, in which each list is traced recursively; following the *cdr* links before the *car* links, to produce *cdr-direction linearization*. As new cells are encountered during this trace, they are marked and assigned to sequential locations in a second linearized address space. In Clark and Green's experiments, a striking result was that after cdr-direction linearization, over 98 percent of each program's list cdrs pointed to the next cell in memory. Also, with 512-word pages, the percentage of list cell pointers pointing off a given page varied from 2.7 to 8.4 following cdr-direction linearization. The use of linearization can also permit the use of compact pointer encodings to increase the number of on-page pointers and the number of list cells that can fit on a page. One such technique is called *cdr-coding*, in which a bit per cell is used to indicate whether or not the cdr-successor of a cell appears immediately after in sequential order, or whether an actual pointer occurs next to link to the cdr cell. Other studies of list-linearization and compaction appear in Minsky [1963], Cheney [1970], and Hansen [1969].

In addition to applying list reorganization and compaction disciplines at garbage collection time, it is possible to try to apply sensible disciplines at list *construction time*. In LISP, the function cons[x; y] can be used to detach a cell from the available space list, and to plant references to x and y in the respective car and cdr fields. Bobrow and Murphy [1967] (see also Bobrow and Murphy [1968] for experimental data) study a policy for attempting to allocate new list cells nearby to recently allocated cells. In particular, instead of keeping one large list of available space, they allocate an available space list on each page of memory. This way, new cells can be allocated on the same pages as the pointers referring to them, if possible; and references tend, then, to be confined to the same page. Garbage collection is also attempted on a page-by-page basis to maintain this discipline.

An example of this sort of policy, taken from Clark and Green [1977], but essentially a minor modification of the policy given in Bobrow and Murphy ([1967], p. 158), is as follows. Let cons[x; y] denote the action of fetching an available cell C and planting links to x and y in its respective car and cdr fields. Then, cons[x; y] is placed:

1. on the page with y if y is a list and there is room; otherwise,
2. on the page with x if x is a list and there is room; otherwise,
3. on the same page as the most recent cons, if there is room; otherwise,
4. on any page with at least 16 free cells.

Unfortunately, the data of Clark and Green [1977] suggest that this clever cons policy contributes little, whereas linearization of lists contributes greatly to performance improvements. In addition, linearization permits space compression through cdr-coding and the use of on-page pointers with small relative offsets.

Additional studies of list memory and garbage collection policy in two-level hierarchies are found in Cohen [1967], Rochfeld [1971], Baecker [1972], and Deutsch and Bobrow [1976]. In particular, Deutsch and Bobrow examine the concept of *incremental linearization*, accompanying the use of incremental reference-count-based garbage collection. Deutsch [1973] studies the issue of compact representation of LISP programs, and Hansen [1967] studies list compaction techniques.

5.5 COMPACTING AND COEXISTENCE REGIMES

As noted in the previous section, compacting can be accomplished by copying or moving lists from one space into a disjoint space. These techniques are useful in connection with list management in multilevel storage environments. The distinction between *list moving* and *list copying* in this connection is that, after a list is copied, the original is left unperturbed, but when a list is moved, the original may be destroyed. We study list moving and copying algorithms in Sections 5.6 and 5.7. In this section we study the problem of compacting a zone of list memory *in situ* without reliance on the availability of separate zones of disjoint contiguous memory in which to place copies or to move lists.

The *in situ* compacting process is useful, among other purposes, for providing for the coexistence of list memory with other sorts of memory, such as stacks. For example, in some programming languages with a strictly subroutine-oriented control structure, space for working storage for subroutines, blocks, and expression evaluation is stacked on an execution stack in last-in-first-out order. If such a language simultaneously permits the use of list structures allocated from a zone of garbage collected list cells, it may be desirable to arrange matters so as to be able to accommodate overflows in the initial allocation of either the execution stack or the list space. Suppose that the execution stack and list space are located next to one another, as depicted in Fig. 5.25 with the growth end of the execution stack aimed at the bottom end of the list memory zone. If the list memory zone now becomes full, it is an easy matter to chew off an adjacent contiguous area below the list zone in the area of potential growth of the stack, and to link it together into fresh free cells for the available space list. This extends the list zone. But what about the other case? Suppose the stack grows until it runs out of space by bumping up against the bottom of the list zone. Suppose, further, that the length of the Avail list in the list zone is substantial. How can we reorganize the list zone to place the in-use cells at the top of memory in a contiguous region so that the bottom will consist entirely of free cells, some of which can be released to provide for additional growth of the stack? The *in situ* list-compacting algorithm (Algorithm 5.10) given below accomplishes exactly this and enables implementation of a cooperation policy between a list zone and a stack, called a *coexistence regime*.

Assume now that the available space list, Avail, has been linked in ascending order of memory addresses in a list zone with addresses α in the range

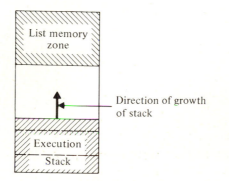

FIGURE 5.25

$M_1 \leq \alpha \leq M_2$, in which there is one list cell at each separate address α. Assume further that there are N cells on Avail, and that cells C in use are marked such that $\text{MARK}(C) = \text{"+"}$ while cells C on the Avail list are marked such that $\text{MARK}(C) = \text{"−"}$. (A slight modification of Algorithm 5.8 is required to leave the in-use cells marked "+" and to count the number of cells on Avail.)

The idea behind the *in situ* compacting algorithm presented below is as follows. We draw a line in the list zone so that N cells are below the line and the rest are above the line. The objective of the algorithm is to move all free cells down below the line, and to move occupied cells below the line into available free cells above the line. To make cells below the line free, we move their contents into an Avail cell above the line. Since Avail is ordered in the direction of increasing memory addresses, detaching successive cells from Avail ensures that the cells used are above the line. However, a problem remains. References from certain cells may point to old locations below the line, instead of to the new locations above the line, where the old contents have been moved. This requires that we update the links of any cells pointing to addresses below the line. To do this we use an *address-forwarding technique*. When the contents of a cell α below the line are moved to a new location β above the line, we place the address β in the cdr field of cell α, and we call β the *forwarding address*. Then we scan cells above the line for occurrences of links α pointing below the line, and we replace each such α with its forwarding address β stored in cdr(α). The whole process operates in three phases:

1. Move occupied cells below the line to new addresses β above the line, and leave the forwarding addresses in the old locations;

2. Scan the cells above the line for links pointing below the line and update them using forwarding addresses; and

3. Link up the available space below the line into a reconstituted available space list.

Algorithm 5.10 gives the details.

Algorithm 5.10 *In situ compacting of a list zone.*

Throughout the algorithm, A and C are addresses of cells. There are N cells on Avail, which are linked in order of increasing memory addresses in the zone $M_1 \leq \alpha \leq M_2$. Cells in use are marked "+" while those on Avail are marked "−".

1. [Initialize.] (Draw the line.) LINE $\leftarrow M_2 - N + 1$.

2. [Relocate reserved cells.] For $A \leftarrow$ LINE, LINE $+ 1, \ldots, M_2$, do step (a):
   a) If $\text{MARK}(A) = \text{"+"}$, then $C \Leftarrow$ Avail and move the contents of the cell with address A into the cell with address C. Then (to save the forwarding address) set cdr$(A) \leftarrow C$.

3. [Update links.] For $A \leftarrow M_1, M_1 + 1, \ldots,$ LINE $- 1$ do step (a):
   a) If A is not an Atom, then if the link in car(A) $\geq$ LINE, replace car(A) with cdr(car(A)), and also, if the pointer in cdr(A) $\geq$ LINE, replace cdr(A) with cdr(cdr(A)).

4. [Relink Avail.] (This step is optional and relinks Avail again in ascending order of addresses in the free zone.) Set Avail $\leftarrow \Lambda$. For $A \leftarrow M_2, M_2 - 1,$ $M_2 - 2, \ldots,$ LINE, set cdr(A) $\leftarrow$ Avail and set Avail $\leftarrow A$.

Figure 5.26 shows the Avail list and the line before the compacting process is begun. Figure 5.27 shows the status of the compacting process after step 2 of Algorithm 5.10, with forwarding addresses posted in relocated cells.

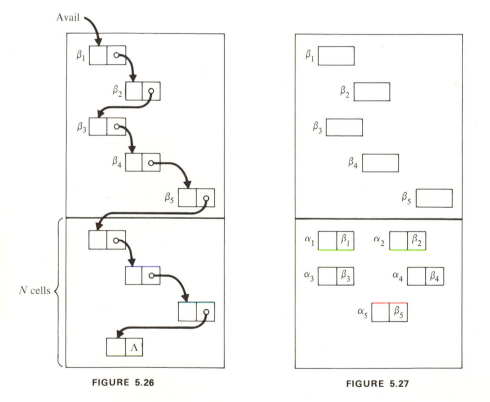

FIGURE 5.26   FIGURE 5.27

5.6 COPYING CYCLIC LISTS IN BOUNDED WORKSPACE

In Section 5.4.1 we saw that minimal-resource marking algorithms required, in addition to their mark bits, either additional tag bits and $O(N)$ time, or $O(N \log N)$ time and no tag bits, in order to operate successfully. If we now wish to copy a possibly cyclic list, what are the least resources required to accomplish the task? Can we possibly copy lists in linear time without tag bits or other unbounded auxiliary memory, aside from the space required for the list and its copy? If we could solve this problem, we would have a *bounded-workspace, linear-time* copying algorithm. Even though a copying algorithm requires that we leave the original list unchanged and that we produce a graph-isomorphic copy with link fields analogous to those in the original, there is a ray of hope that we can copy in bounded workspace and $O(N)$ time, since space allocated to hold the copy can be used as an unbounded memory to store intermediate stages of the construction (unlike the case for marking, where no unbounded intermediate space excluding marks would be available in the tag-free case). A rather remarkable progression of increasingly better results has been achieved over the past few years in the attack on this problem.

In Lindstrom [1974] copying algorithms were given for copying an arbitrary (possibly cyclic) list of N cells in time $O(N^2)$ with no mark bits, and in time $O(N \log N)$ if a mark bit is available in each cell. Subsequently, Fisher [1975] developed a linear-time algorithm (using three passes over the structure being copied) that required no mark bits but assumed the copy was placed into a block of sequential locations. Clark [1975] improved on this by devising a copying process that took slightly more than two passes under the same assumptions as Fisher; and Clark was able to demonstrate an improvement in running time of between 1.26 to 2 times faster than Fisher's algorithm, with a speedup of about 1.62 for list structures encountered in practice. The culmination of these developments is an algorithm discovered by Robson [1977], which uses bounded workspace (i.e., a fixed number of program variables independent of the size of the list) and linear time to copy an arbitrary list, and which does not rely on any assumptions about address ordering or contiguity. The Robson algorithm, presented as Algorithm 5.11 below, traverses the same spanning tree of a structure twice, with the first traversal being from left to right, and the second traversal being from right to left.

Algorithm 5.11 *Robson's linear, bounded-workspace copying algorithm.*

This algorithm uses four special cell addresses m_0, m_1, m_2, and m_3 as marks, planted in the cdr fields of cells. The addresses m_i are assumed to be set aside from normal use, and are assumed to be in sequential order. Thus, $m_i + j = m_{i+j}$, so that the process "increase the mark in cdr(f) by 1" sends marks m_0 and m_1 into marks m_2 and m_3 respectively. A cell is said to be unmarked if the value of its mark $> m_3$. Also, marks m_1 and m_3 are said to be "odd". The variables have mnemonic significance, as follows: gf = grandfather, f = father, *newf* = new node corresponding to f, s = son, and $s1$ and $s2$ = sons in old and new structures. Since atoms are not copied, but instead only the references to atoms are copied, the algorithm assumes that all atoms are the same as Λ and that Λ is not marked. Let Marks = $\{m_0, m_1, m_2, m_3\}$ be the set of marks.

1. [Initialize.] Set $gf \leftarrow \Lambda$ and $f \leftarrow n$ (where n is the address of the start node for the list to be copied). Set direction $\leftarrow$ down.

2. [Phase 1 done?] If $f = \Lambda$, go to step 8. Otherwise, if direction $\neq$ down, go to step 5. Otherwise (get a new cell) $newf \Leftarrow$ Avail, and copy the contents of f into $newf$. Then mark f by setting $\text{cdr}(f) \leftarrow m_0$, and set $\text{car}(f) \leftarrow newf$.

3. [Trace further or start up from bottom.] If $\text{car}(newf) = \Lambda$ or $\text{car}(newf) \in$ Marks, set $s \leftarrow \text{car}(newf)$, $\text{car}(newf) \leftarrow gf$, and direction $\leftarrow$ up. Otherwise, increase the mark in $\text{cdr}(f)$ by 2, set $s \leftarrow \text{car}(newf)$, $\text{car}(newf) \leftarrow gf$, $gf \leftarrow f$, and $f \leftarrow s$.

4. [Return to process next node.] Go back to step 2.

5. [Ascending from right?] Set $newf \leftarrow \text{car}(f)$. If now, the mark in $\text{cdr}(f)$ is odd (we have returned from the right branch of the spanning tree), set $gf \leftarrow \text{cdr}(newf)$, $\text{cdr}(newf) \leftarrow s$, $s \leftarrow f$, $f \leftarrow gf$, and go back to step 2.

6. [Ascending from left.] Set $gf \leftarrow \text{car}(newf)$, $\text{car}(newf) \leftarrow s$. If now $\text{cdr}(newf) = \Lambda$ or $\text{cdr}(\text{cdr}(newf)) \in$ Marks, set $s \leftarrow f$ and $f \leftarrow gf$. Otherwise, (we need to follow the right branch, so) increase the mark in $\text{cdr}(f)$ by 1, set $s \leftarrow \text{cdr}(newf)$, $\text{cdr}(newf) \leftarrow gf$, $gf \leftarrow f$, $f \leftarrow s$, and direction $\leftarrow$ down.

7. [Return to process next node.] Go back to step 2.

8. [Prepare for phase 2.] Set $gf \leftarrow \Lambda$, $f \leftarrow n$, and direction $\leftarrow$ down.

9. [Done?] If $f = \Lambda$, the algorithm terminates.

10. [Going down?] Set $newf \leftarrow \text{car}(f)$. If direction $\neq$ down, go to step 13.

11. [Descend to right.] If the mark in $\text{cdr}(f)$ is odd (then need to follow right branch, so) set $s \leftarrow \text{cdr}(newf)$, $\text{cdr}(newf) \leftarrow gf$, $gf \leftarrow f$, $f \leftarrow s$, and go to step 9.

12. [Descend left.] Set $s1 \leftarrow \text{cdr}(newf)$. Now set $s2$ to Λ if $s1 = \Lambda$ or to $\text{car}(s1)$ if $s1 \neq \Lambda$. Finally, set $\text{cdr}(newf) \leftarrow gf$, direction $\leftarrow$ up, and return to step 9.

13. [Father marked?] If $\text{cdr}(f) \in$ Marks, go to step 17. Otherwise, set mark $\leftarrow$ $\text{cdr}(f)$ (the field used for the mark is about to be overwritten), $s \leftarrow \text{car}(newf)$, $\text{car}(newf) \leftarrow \text{cdr}(newf)$, $\text{cdr}(newf) \leftarrow s2$, $\text{cdr}(f) \leftarrow s1$.

14. [Follow left branch.] If mark $\geq m_2$ (need to follow left branch) then set $gf \leftarrow f$, $f \leftarrow s$, direction $\leftarrow$ down, and return to step 9.

15. [Follow right branch.] Set $gf \leftarrow \text{car}(newf)$. If now, $s = \Lambda$, then set $\text{car}(f) \leftarrow \text{car}(newf) \leftarrow \Lambda$. Otherwise, set $\text{car}(newf) \leftarrow \text{car}(s)$ and $\text{car}(f) \leftarrow s$ (the order of these two is critical since f and s may be the same node).

16. [Ascend.] Now set $s \leftarrow s1 \leftarrow f$, $s2 \leftarrow newf$, $f \leftarrow gf$, and return to step 9.

17. [Ascend.] Set $gf \leftarrow \text{car}(newf)$, $\text{car}(f) \leftarrow s1$, $\text{car}(newf) \leftarrow s2$, $s1 \leftarrow f$, $s2 \leftarrow newf$, $f \leftarrow gf$, and return to step 9.

As can be seen, this process uses the standard link-inversion technique to avoid use of an explicit stack. To understand the spanning tree that the algorithm traverses (first in phase 1 in preorder and then in phase 2 in reverse preorder), we can distinguish between two types of pointers: *spanning-tree pointers* and *back pointers*. Spanning-tree pointers are links in the car or cdr fields of cells that are encountered during the preorder traversal in phase 1, and which, during the order implicit in this traversal, point from a given cell to an unmarked child. All other pointers are back pointers, and these may include pointers from a node to itself, its descendants, its ancestors, or its cousins. During the first phase, the nodes are marked in preorder to prevent infinite looping or rescanning of shared subtrees. The marking process begins at the instant a node is first encountered and copied. Thus, when node

is first encountered, a fresh cell is allocated for the copy, the contents of the old cell are copied into the new cell, the car field of the old cell is made to point to the new cell, and the cdr field of the old cell is made to hold a mark m_0, as follows:

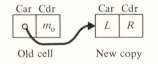

Here, we let L and R be the addresses of the children of the old cell. Now suppose that circumstances imply that we should scan down to the left from the old cell. Let F be the father of the old cell. We then store the inverted link to the father in the copy as follows:

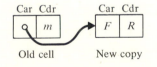

Similarly, when we have finished processing the left subtree of the old cell in the spanning tree and we need to process its right *spanning subtree*, we restore the L field, plant the inverted link to the father F in the cdr field of the new copy, and descend to the right. The configuration now appears as follows:

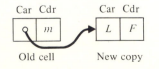

Finally, after preorder traversal of the right spanning subtree, we ascend back

from the right and encounter the node. The nature of the mark now tells us that
we are ascending from the right, so we restore the original pointers L and R in the
car and cdr fields of the new copy, and follow the inverted link F back up to the
father, for further ascent. At the end of phase 1, then, each cell of the old structure
points to its corresponding cell in the copy in the following configuration:

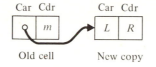

The corresponding copy at the end of phase 1 has exactly the contents of the old
cell before the copying process began.

Actually, the marks in the old cell are set up by phase 1 to contain additional
useful information. A choice of four marks m_0, m_1, m_2, and m_3 is available, and
phase 1 overwrites the initial mark m_0 with some of the others to indicate whether
the L and R pointers are spanning-tree pointers or backward pointers. Phase 2
uses this information on the second scan in reverse preorder.

Phase 2 now begins, and the encodings of the marks, being in the cells pointing to the copies rather than in the copies, enable phase 2 to remove the marks as
it uses them in reverse symmetric order, even while the pointers from old to new
nodes are removed in reverse preorder. The four stages that phase 2 creates as it
processes a given node are indicated in Fig. 5.28.

Here L' and R' are the addresses of the cells in the new copy that correspond
to the cells with addresses L and R in the old list structure, respectively.

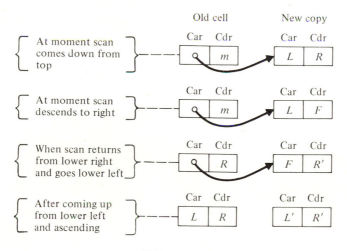

FIGURE 5.28

5.7 MOVING CYCLIC LISTS IN BOUNDED WORKSPACE

Moving a list differs from copying it, in that the original list can be destroyed by a list-moving algorithm, whereas it must be preserved by a list-copying algorithm.

Moving algorithms have been studied in previous sections in connection with garbage collection and compacting. The list-moving algorithms of Minsky [1963] and Fenichel and Yochelson [1969] both require stacks. Cheney's algorithm (Cheney [1970]) was the first to utilize only constant workspace and to take linear time. It was oriented toward compacted lists in cdr-coded form. Cheney's method does not require much modification to apply to the ordinary LISP format, however. Reingold [1973] gave an algorithm that applied the link-inversion technique to avoid reliance on an explicit stack.

Both Reingold's and Cheney's algorithms utilize at least two visits to each cell. Clark [1976] improved on these processes by arranging for a moving process in which only cells with both pointers pointing to lists need be visited more than once. This improves on the previous versions in light of empirical data (see Clark and Green [1977]) showing that only about $\frac{1}{3}$ of the cars and $\frac{3}{4}$ of the cdrs in real lists point to other lists. Assuming cars and cdrs to be independent as to their data types (pointing to lists or not), this means that only about $\frac{1}{4}$ of the cells would be revisited in Clark's moving algorithm. Clark's algorithm is given below.

Algorithm 5.12 *Clark's list-moving algorithm.*

The algorithm works in two parts. Steps 1 through 6 copy the top level of a list. Steps 7 through 9 find the most recently visited sublist. The algorithm moves the list pointed to by h from its old region to a new region. At termination, h points to the new list, and Avail to the next free cell in the new area. Note that it is necessary to be able to distinguish cells in the new area to which the list is being moved from old cells in the structure via the predicate "x is new?"

1. [Initialize.] Set $x \leftarrow h$, $n \Leftarrow$ Avail, $h \leftarrow n$, and $k \leftarrow \Lambda$.

2. [Save car and cdr.] $a \leftarrow$ car(x) and $d \leftarrow$ cdr(x).

3. [Store forwarding address.] car(x) $\leftarrow n$.

4. [Is car a list?] If a is a list, then set cdr(x) $\leftarrow k$ and $k \leftarrow x$. (k points to the most recently visited cell whose car is a list.)

5. [Copy old car.] Set car(n) $\leftarrow a$. (If a is an Atom, car(Avail) has its final value now.)

6. [Compute and write new cdr.] If d is an Atom, then cdr(n) $\leftarrow d$, $n \Leftarrow$ Avail, and go to step 7. If car(d) is new, then set cdr(n) $\leftarrow$ car(d), $n \Leftarrow$ Avail, and go to 7. Otherwise, d must be an unvisited list, so set cdr(n) $\Leftarrow$ Avail, $n \leftarrow$ cdr(n), $x \leftarrow d$, and return to step 2. (In all cases, cdr(n) gets its final value in this step. If d is an Atom or an already visited list, cdr-direction tracing stops and we go to

steps 7 through 9 to find the most recently seen sublist. Otherwise, we continue cdr-following and return to step 2.)

7. [Done?] If $k = \Lambda$, the algorithm terminates with h pointing to the new list, and n to the first cell on Avail.

8. [Remove first element of k-list.] Set $x \leftarrow \text{car}(\text{car}(k))$, $t \leftarrow k$, and $k \leftarrow \text{cdr}(k)$.

9. [Compute and write new car.] If $\text{car}(x)$ is new, then set $\text{car}(\text{car}(t)) \leftarrow \text{car}(x)$ and return to step 7. Otherwise, set $\text{car}(\text{car}(t)) \leftarrow n$ and go to step 2. (Car of the copy of the cell just removed from k gets its final value in this step.)

If it is not possible to implement the predicate "x is new?", then Reingold's algorithm (see Reingold [1973]) may be used instead, with guarantees that the list can be moved in linear time, constant workspace, and no additional bits per node for marking or other assumptions about the nature of the area to which the list will be moved. Reingold's algorithm relies on the Schorr–Waite–Deutsch link-inversion technique.

5.8 OPTIMAL STORAGE FOR GARBAGE COLLECTION

If we are using a marking-and-gathering garbage collector, as opposed to an incremental garbage collector, the performance degrades rapidly as the available space in the list zone approaches zero. Suppose, for the sake of argument, that a list processing computation is operating in equilibrium at some given load factor α (where $0 \leq \alpha \leq 1$). The load factor α is defined as the ratio of the list cells in use (i.e., accessible to the program) to the total list cells in the list zone. When the computation is in equilibrium, then the rate at which new cells are utilized from the available free-space list is equal to the rate at which garbage is created. Suppose, for instance, that a list computation is in equilibrium at a load factor of $\alpha = 0.95$, meaning that 95 percent of the cells in the list zone are in use, and that the remaining five percent are either on the available-space list or constitute cells inaccessible to the program (and thus are garbage). When the Avail list is exhausted, a garbage collection is performed, returning this five percent of the list cells to the Avail list. But in order to gather this five percent, the 95 percent of the cells in use have to be traced and marked. At $\alpha = 0.99$, we have to trace and mark 99 percent of the cells to gather 1 percent of the cells that are free. If the small percentage of cells gathered at high load factors are quickly exhausted, another garbage collection will soon be triggered. Thus, it is possible that when list use approaches full saturation, the processor will devote nearly all of its time to repeated garbage collections of small yield. This behavior is, indeed, observed in practice.

A question now arises of whether, if possible, it might be better to request more core storage (if such an option is available) when the load factor α exceeds a certain fraction, than to incur the potential waste of time implied by operating the garbage collection policy at high load factors, and if so, how such a fraction should be chosen. To sharpen the question, we can assume that we are in an environment (such as a commercial time-sharing environment) in which charges are based on the number of kilo-core seconds (a time-memory product) used by a computation. We might then inquire whether we could minimize the number of kilo-core seconds used by a garbage collecting computation. If we request too much core and operate at low load factors, we garbage collect only rarely but the space in use is large. If we operate at high load factors, the space is minimized, but garbage collection uses up a large amount of time.

This problem has been examined by Hoare [1974a]. Hoare's method for optimizing the storage size is as follows. Define:

S = Total size of list zone in words;

N = Total number of list cells (at one per word) collected during all runs of a garbage collector over the entire computation;

K = Average number of list cells in use (i.e., accessible to the main program) after a garbage collection;

T = Time spent by the program on useful computation exclusive of garbage collection.

For computations of long duration, S is small in comparison with N, and so we may regard S and N as independent. We may then conclude that

$S - K$ = Average number of words collected on each garbage collection;

$N/(S - K)$ = Number of collections invoked during the course of the entire computation.

We now formulate the cost, in time, spent during each garbage collection as $aK + b(S - K)$ where a is the average time taken to mark and unmark each word in use and b is the average time taken to unmark and gather each free word. (Here, b is usually smaller than a.) Then the total time spent garbage collecting is the number of collections times the cost per collection:

$$\frac{N}{S - K}(aK + b(S - K)) = N(aK/(S - K) + b).$$

Now, let $g = T/N$ be defined as the useful computing time per word collected. Then the total cost of the program (in, say kilo-core seconds) is proportional to the product of the total time spent times the space used. The total time spent has two contributions, the time T exclusive of garbage collections and the garbage collection time $N[(aK/(S - K)) + b]$. The sum of these two is multiplied by the space in use, S, to get

$$\text{COST} = S\left[T + N\left(\left(\frac{aK}{S-K}\right) + b\right)\right] = \frac{S}{S-K}\, aKN + (b + g)SN.$$

This expression is minimized by setting

$$S = K(1 + r)$$

where $r = \sqrt{a/(b+g)}$ and the associated minimum cost is $(\sqrt{a} + \sqrt{b+g})^2 KN$.

The constants a and b are obtained from program measurement, and the constant g can be estimated by dividing the running time used by the program since the last garbage collection by the number of words collected. This provides a dynamic estimating policy for deciding the amount of storage to request from (or release to) the operating system for use up to the next garbage collection.

Hoare [1974a] found that the COST curve was shallow around the minimum cost value, so that crude estimates of g will be adequate to give good performance. A particularly simple strategy is to check to see whether S/K (the overallocation factor) lies between 1.2 and 1.7 after garbage collection and, if not, to request or release storage to bring $S/K = 1.5$. (Put differently, if, after collection, Avail contains less than 20 percent of the total list space or more than 70 percent, it should be adjusted to contain 50 percent.) Hoare's curves show serious performance penalties for Avail less than 20 percent (Hoare [1974a], p. 166).

The conclusions of Hoare's analysis can be applied to the segregated storage techniques of the next chapter, where blocks of different sizes are kept in different zones of uniform-size blocks, each zone being separately garbage collected. The Hoare analysis gives a technique for deciding when to expand or contract these various zones.

Campbell [1974] offers additional analysis of the optimization process, and comments on Hoare's analysis under circumstances when space and time are not of equal significance, and when S and N are not independent.

5.9 BIBLIOGRAPHIC NOTES

Early development of list processing ideas is found in NEWELL, SHAW, and SIMON [1956], NEWELL, and SHAW [1957], BLAAUW [1959], and CARR [1959].

Two early list processing languages of considerable influence are IPL-V (see NEWELL [1964], and NEWELL and TONGE [1960]) and LISP (see MCCARTHY [1960] and MCCARTHY, ABRAHAMS, EDWARDS, HART, and LEVIN [1962]).

Symmetric lists are studied in WEIZENBAUM [1963] and WEIZENBAUM [1969]. Threaded lists are studied in PERLIS and THORNTON [1960], and in KNUTH [1968]. Ring-structured lists are studied in ROBERTS [1965], WILLIAMS [1973], GRAY [1967], LANG and GRAY [1968a, b], FELDMAN [1965], and FELDMAN and ROVNER [1969].

The reference-count methods have been studied in GELERNTER, HANSEN, and GERBER-ICH [1960], COLLINS [1960], WEIZENBAUM [1963], WEIZENBAUM [1969], MCBETH [1963], and DEUTSCH and BOBROW [1976]. Recently, BARTH [1977] has studied compile-time-based incremental collection based on the Deutsch and Bobrow method and on data-flow analysis.

Multiword list elements are treated in the next chapter, and are studied in ROSS [1961], ROSS [1967], WEIZENBAUM [1962], COMFORT [1964], and D'IMPERIO [1969].

ROHL and CORDINGLY [1970] examine list processing facilities in the context of Atlas Autocode. WILKES [1965] develops ideas about why lists are useful. A book on list processing has been written by FOSTER [1967]. ELGOT and SNYDER [1977] have given careful attention to the problem of defining lists rigorously.

DIJKSTRA, LAMPORT, MARTIN, SCHOLTEN, and STEFFENS [1978] give a parallel garbage collection technique exhibiting very little mutual interference with weak exclusion and synchronization constraints. KUNG and SONG [1977] also report on an efficient parallel garbage collection system and provide a correctness proof.

CLARK and GREEN [1978] study measurements of shared cells in LISP—those pointed to by more than one pointer—and find that, in practice, shared cells are quite rare. CLARK [1979] presents an empirical study of how three large LISP programs use their list structures during execution which discovers that over half of all references were references to one of the ten most recently referenced cells.

HANSEN [1978] studies a predecessor algorithm for ordered lists.

EXERCISES

1. (Symmetric link representation) Verify the relations (4) to show that

$$L = ((L \oplus R) - R) \bmod M \qquad \text{and} \qquad R = ((L \oplus R) - L) \bmod M,$$

where $L \oplus R = (L + R) \bmod M$, and $L, R < M$. [*Hint.* The following facts may be useful:

$$x \bmod y = x - y\lfloor x/y \rfloor,$$

$$\lfloor a - b \rfloor = \lfloor a \rfloor - \lfloor b \rfloor \quad \text{if } b \text{ is an integer},$$

and

$$\lfloor \lfloor b \rfloor \rfloor = \lfloor b \rfloor.]$$

2. (Relations on pure lists) In analyzing algorithms that run on the linked representation of pure lists, the following relations are sometimes helpful:
   a) $1 + \#\text{cells} = \#\text{atoms} + \#\Lambda\text{s}$
   b) $\#\text{links (to nonatoms and non-}\Lambda\text{s)} = \#\text{cells} - 1$
   c) $\#\text{left-links (to sublists, not to atoms)} = \#\text{cells} - \#\text{atoms}$
   d) $\#\text{right-links} = \#\text{cells} - \#\Lambda\text{s}$
   e) $\#\Lambda\text{s} = \#\text{left-links (to sublists, not atoms)} + 1$

   Prove each of these relations. [*Hints:* (a) In a full binary tree the number of leaves is the number of internal nodes plus 1; (b) each cell except the root has one pointer coming into it; (c) the number of left fields equals the number of cells; (d) the number of right fields equals the number of cells, and (e) each left-link initiates a chain of right-linked cells ending in Λ with 1 added for the right-linked chain starting at the root.]

3. (List structure reversal) Given the linked representation of a pure list such as

$$(x_1, (y_1, y_2, (z_1, z_2), y_4), (w_1, w_2), x_4),$$

write an *in situ* reversal algorithm to reverse the sublists at all levels including the topmost level, resulting in a linked representation corresponding to

$$(x_4, (w_2, w_1), (y_4, (z_2, z_1), y_2, y_1), x_1).$$

4. (Reversal analysis) Using the relations in Exercise 2, analyze the running time of your algorithm for Exercise 3.

5. (Deletion) Write an algorithm to delete the nth cell of a linked linear list.

6. (Concatenation) Write an algorithm to concatenate the linked linear lists

$$(x_1, x_2, \ldots, x_n)$$

and

$$(y_1, y_2, \ldots, y_m)$$

to form the linked linear list

$$(x_1, x_2, \ldots, x_n, y_1, y_2, \ldots, y_m).$$

7. (Merging) Write an algorithm to merge the two linked lists

$$(x_1, x_2, \ldots, x_n)$$

and

$$(y_1, y_2, \ldots, y_n)$$

to form

$$(x_1, y_1, x_2, y_2, \ldots, x_n, y_n).$$

8. (Membership test) Write an algorithm to test whether an item x is stored in the Info field of a symmetrically linked list $(y_1, y_2, \ldots, y_n)$ stored using the representation of Fig. 5.7.

9. (Sublist test) Let L_1 and L_2 be two one-way linked representations of list structures. Write an algorithm to test whether L_2 properly contains a sublist identical to L_1.

10. (Insertion trick) Given the one-way linked representation of a list $L = (x_1, x_2, \ldots, x_n)$, given a cell containing an Info field y pointed to by C (using the representation shown in Fig. 5.2), and given the address α of just one cell on L,

show how to insert cell C before cell α on L. [*Hint:* Set up a pointer field in C in the proper way and swap contents of C and α.]

11. (Parallel garbage collection) Write an improved version of Algorithm 5.9 by substituting a more efficient marking process.

12. (Parallel garbage collection) Extend Algorithm 5.9 to handle contents of car and cdr fields that point to atoms in addition to pointing only to list cells or to Λ.

13. (V. Stenning) Write a mutator–collector parallel garbage collection system using just two colors: black and white.

14. (Compacting) Reimplement Algorithm 5.10 to use two pointers that start at the respective ends of the zone and move toward each other, so that when they collide or pass each other the relocation phase of Algorithm 5.10 terminates. Can the variable LINE then be eliminated?

15. (Reingold [1973]) Develop a linear-time, bounded-workspace algorithm for moving a list using no stacks or tag bits, and making no assumptions about address ordering or segregation of the new area to which the list is to be moved from the old area.

16. (Open problem) Is it possible to write a bounded-workspace, linear-time algorithm for marking cyclic list structures having one mark bit per cell, or, if it is impossible, can the impossibility be proved?

CHAPTER

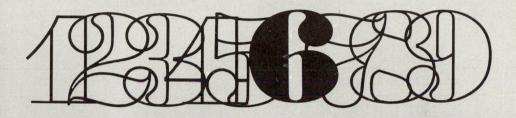

MULTILINKED STRUCTURES

6.1 INTRODUCTION AND MOTIVATION

In the previous chapter on list structures, we examined linking techniques that permitted us to organize memory as a flexible commodity that could be allocated in varying sizes and shapes dynamically during the running of a program. However, we tacitly assumed that the cells we linked together had uniform size and information-bearing capacity. As a consequence, to accommodate varying amounts of information, the excess information incapable of being stored in a particular cell was stored in additional cells, and links were planted to these additional cells to tie the cells together. Thus, while the method of linking uniform-size cells together allowed us to accommodate varying amounts of information, this accommodation was purchased at the expense of certain forms of efficiency loss. For instance, access to the nth cell of a linked list required following $n - 1$ links, making list search and update inefficient compared to arithmetic indexing, or to binary search, as in the ordered tables treated in Chapter 4. In addition, cells of fixed size have bounded capacity for containing pointers, so nodes of multiway trees with variable numbers of pointers to children nodes could not be conveniently represented.

In the study of the so-called multilinked structures, we allocate nodes consisting of different numbers of contiguous words of storage. Thus, different nodes can have different sizes. This permits us, for example, to allocate a node large enough to contain all the pointers to children nodes of a node in a multiway tree, or to contain a local sequential list of information allocated contiguously. Storage utilization efficiency is thereby increased (by elimination of the links that tie together a number of fixed-size cells to hold the information that can now be allocated in one multiword node). Search time in local lists stored in the nodes can also be decreased for certain kinds of operations (by, for instance, using binary search on ordered, sequentially allocated sequences of elements).

We can link together nodes of differing size into topological structures such as trees, rings, and directed graphs. We shall use such multilinking techniques elsewhere in this book when we study multilinked storage representations for arrays (Chapter 8), inverted files using multilinked techniques (Chapter 9), and multiway tree indexes for files (Chapter 9).

The management of storage for allocating nodes of varying size poses for us some new problems not encountered in the allocation of nodes of fixed size. These underlying storage-management techniques require careful study. One of the purposes of this chapter is to examine and compare a range of techniques for this purpose that have been investigated in the literature.

The management algorithms for the large connected topological organizations of nodes that are linked together in multilinked structures also require consideration. These algorithms are more complicated than their simpler relatives for the more specialized structures such as trees and simple linked lists. Algorithms for such tasks as traversal (used in, say, printing and marking for garbage collection), copying, moving, compacting, and equality testing, all become more challenging when nodes of varying size and internal composition are permitted and when the linking topologies include the full generality of connected directed graphs with cycles. A number of algorithms based on the notion of a *utility cell* are examined for performing these tasks on multilinked structures.

6.2 DYNAMIC STORAGE ALLOCATION TECHNIQUES

Dynamic storage allocation techniques are methods for managing contiguous linear regions of memory in such a fashion that requests for blocks of n contiguous words can be granted for variable n, and such that blocks released from active use can be reclaimed and reallocated on further demand.

Two notable applications for such dynamic storage allocation methods are: (1) allocating space for nodes of varying size for the construction of multilinked data structures in programming languages and systems programs, and (2) allocating space for running programs and data in the main memory of a computer under control of a multiprogrammed operating system. The typical request sizes for blocks of storage for running programs in an operating system may run into the thousands of words, whereas the typical requests for blocks of storage for nodes in multilinked data structures may be just a few words. Thus, dynamic storage allocation methods must deal with a range of applications exhibiting a large variance in the distribution of block sizes, block lifetimes (the durations that reserved blocks are in use), and interarrival times for block allocation requests. Methods that work well under some sets of circumstances perform poorly in others. Some methods give fast allocation at the expense of poor storage-utilization efficiency. Others give good storage-utilization efficiency at the expense of slower allocation times.

One category of methods is the set of *sequential-fit methods* such as *first fit*, *best fit*, *optimal fit*, and *worst fit*. In these methods, as in the others, storage blocks are divided into two classes: *free* and *reserved*. In the sequential-fit methods, the free blocks are linked into a sequential list. When a request for a block of storage of size n words is serviced, a search is made along this linked list until a block of appropriate size is found. This block is then detached from the list, and becomes a reserved block.

Another category of methods are the so-called *buddy-system methods*. Memory is broken down into blocks of prescribed sizes such as blocks whose sizes are powers of 2 $(1, 2, 4, 8, \ldots, 2^n, \ldots)$ or blocks whose sizes are numbers in the Fibonacci sequence starting at 3 $(3, 5, 8, 13, 21, \ldots, F_n, \ldots)$. Blocks with sizes in these sequences can be subdivided into smaller blocks whose sizes are also numbers in the sequence. Free blocks of the various sizes are placed on lists of blocks of the same size. To service a request for a block of size n, a block of size $k \geq n$ is located on one of the lists, and if possible, the unused portion of size $k - n$ is subdivided into smaller blocks, which are placed on the lists of appropriate size to minimize the waste when a block of request size n is stored in a reserved block of size k, for some k in the sequence of permissible block sizes.

A third category of methods are the so-called *segregated-storage methods*. These methods have a number of variations. One variation is to divide the entire memory into a number of smaller units called *pages*, and to allocate blocks of uniform size to each page. Different pages can have different uniform-size blocks, however. An index is then maintained to the various pages, and available-space lists of blocks of uniform size are maintained on each page. Another method is to keep a number of lists each of which links blocks of the same size (or range of sizes) together. A table or a tree-structured index is kept leading to the heads of lists each containing free blocks of the same size (or range of sizes). Yet another method is to maintain a tree-structured index to blocks of various sizes, and to use one of the tree-balancing techniques of Chapter 3 to guarantee $O(\log n)$ search times. Finally, some techniques involve a hierarchy of these methods.

Operation of any of these methods for a period of time may lead to the phenomenon of *storage fragmentation*. When a request for a block of size n cannot be satisfied exactly because no block of size n is currently free, and a block of size $k > n$ is selected to satisfy the request, the various methods follow different procedures for dispensing with the excess storage of size $k - n$. In the sequential-fit methods, a new free block of size $k - n$ is created and placed back on the free storage list. In the buddy-system methods, a block of size n may be stored in the block of smallest permissible block size $k \geq n$, so that $k - n$ of the words in the block of size k are unused. After a while, in the absence of any policy for forming larger free blocks from adjacent free smaller ones, storage blocks may become divided into smaller and smaller fragments. In the case of the sequential-fit methods, the fragments appear on the free list and the phenomenon is called *external fragmentation*. In the buddy-system methods, by contrast, some of the unused storage dwells inside the reserved blocks, and this is called *internal fragmentation*. Thus, the buddy-system methods are subject to both internal and external fragmentation, while the sequential-fit methods and segregated-storage methods are often subject to external fragmentation alone.

If fragmentation persists for some period of time and the free storage blocks become more and more finely divided, there may come a time when a request for a block of size n is encountered that cannot be satisfied, because no block of size $k \geq n$ is free. Under these circumstances, the allocation method *fails*, and resort must be made to a failure policy of some sort, such as

1. moving reserved blocks to create larger regions of free space (including, at the extreme, compacting all reserved blocks into one end of the region of memory being allocated, and freeing up one large contiguous block of free storage at the other end),

2. aborting the computation,

3. queuing the request on a wait queue to wait for a subsequent moment when a free block large enough to accommodate the request has been released, or

4. allocating more memory for use in satisfying block-reservation requests.

External fragmentation may be combated by attempting to *coalesce* adjacent free blocks into free blocks of larger size. One time to do this is when blocks are being liberated (i.e., made free after being in use for some period of time). It is possible to devise methods that allow inspection of adjacent neighbors (or buddies) of a block being liberated, to see if they are already free and, if so, to join them together into larger free blocks. These policies for coalescing are important because they allow the allocation method to operate in an equilibrium wherein the fragmentation resulting from splitting blocks to satisfy allocation requests is counteracted by coalescing liberated blocks to join other free blocks.

In the following algorithms, we assume no simple temporal relationship between the times of requests for block reservation and liberation. For example, if the times of reservation and liberation follow a simple temporal relation—the most recently reserved block is always the first to be liberated—then the stack techniques of Chapter 2 suffice to handle the dynamic storage allocation problem for variable-size nodes, and the involved techniques of this section are unnecessary.

6.2.1 Sequential fit methods

Let us suppose that the free blocks B_1, B_2, ..., B_n of storage in a region R of sequential memory are linked together with symmetric links into a ring, using their block addresses. (By definition, the address α of a block B is the address of the first word of B. B always consists of a sequence of contiguous words w_i $(1 \leq i \leq k)$. In symbols, then, $\alpha = \min \{\alpha_i | \alpha_i$ is the address of word w_i for $1 \leq i \leq k\}$.) Figure 6.1 illustrates such a ring of symmetrically linked free blocks.

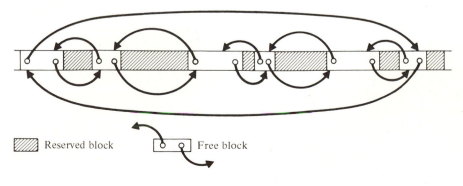

FIGURE 6.1

Figure 6.1 shows the symmetric linking of free blocks into a ring in order of ascending block addresses. In general, this need not be the case. The ring can contain free blocks in any order.

In our subsequent discussion of coalescing policies, we will need to make the following additional assumptions about the internal structure of each block B:

1. The first and last words of B have *boundary tags* that are one-bit quantities. The boundary tags of each free block are set to $+$, and the boundary tags of each reserved block are set to $-$. We denote the boundary tag field of a word stored at address α by TAG(α).

2. The first word of each block B has a size field containing an integer k, where k is the length of B in words. This is denoted SIZE(B).

3. Each free block B has left and right link fields containing the addresses of free blocks to the left and right on the symmetrically linked ring of free blocks. These fields are denoted LLINK(B) and RLINK(B), respectively.

4. The last word of each free block B has a SIZE field whose contents are identical to the SIZE field in the first word.

In short, reserved blocks have tag fields on their first and last words set to $-$ (to indicate they are in use), and they have a size field SIZE in their first word. Free blocks have tag fields set to $+$ in their first and last words, as well as size fields in their first and last words. Also, free blocks link left and right to their left and right neighbors (in ring order, not in address order). Figure 6.2 illustrates the formats of free and reserved blocks.

In the *sequential-fit methods*, a request for reservation of a block of size n is handled by scanning to the right along the ring of free blocks until finding a block of size $k \geq n + 2$ (according to one of the sequential-fit policies). If an exact fit is found (that is, if $k = n + 2$), then the block is detached from the ring of free blocks and its tags are set $-$ to mark it as reserved. If $k \gg n + 2$, the block is split into

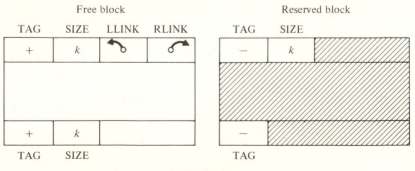

FIGURE 6.2

two smaller blocks, one of size $n + 2$, which is marked as reserved and satisfies the request, and one of size $k - (n + 2)$, which is formatted as a free block and is joined to the ring of free blocks. When a block B is liberated, an attempt is made to coalesce it with its near neighbors (in address order, not in ring order) to form a larger free block, if possible; and then the resulting possibly enlarged free block is placed on the free block ring. Algorithms 6.1 and 6.2 give the procedures for reservation and liberation.

Algorithm 6.1 *Block reservation using the sequential-fit method.*

Assume that P is a pointer to one of the free blocks on the ring of free blocks. Let n be the size of the request for a block of storage. At successful termination, B points to the block reserved.

1. [Find block.] According to the sequential-fit policy being used (first-fit, best-fit, optimal-fit, or worst fit), successively examine blocks on the ring of free blocks, until finding one of size k satisfying the policy. If no such block exists, the algorithm terminates unsuccessfully. At the conclusion of this step, P points to the block selected.

2. [Exact fit?] If $\text{SIZE}(P) = n + 2$ (we have an exact fit). Set $\text{TAG}(P) \leftarrow -$ and $\text{TAG}(P + \text{SIZE}(P) - 1) \leftarrow -$ (to mark the block reserved). $B \leftarrow P$. Then (to detach the block from the free ring) if $P = \text{RLINK}(P)$, (the block pointed to by P is the only one on the ring) so set $P \leftarrow \Lambda$ (to signify that the ring is empty). Otherwise, $\text{LLINK}(\text{RLINK}(P)) \leftarrow \text{LLINK}(P)$ and $P \leftarrow \text{RLINK}(\text{LLINK}(P)) \leftarrow \text{RLINK}(P)$. The algorithm now terminates successfully.

3. [Make new free block.] Otherwise, if $\text{SIZE}(P) \geq n + 5$ (there is enough excess of $\text{SIZE}(P)$ over the request size $n + 2$ to make a new free block), set $Q \leftarrow P + (n + 2)$, $\text{SIZE}(Q) \leftarrow \text{SIZE}(P + \text{SIZE}(P) - 1) \leftarrow \text{SIZE}(P) - (n + 2)$, $\text{TAG}(Q) \leftarrow \text{TAG}(P + \text{SIZE}(P) - 1) \leftarrow +$, and if now $P = \text{RLINK}(P)$, set $\text{LLINK}(Q) \leftarrow \text{RLINK}(Q) \leftarrow Q$; otherwise set $\text{LLINK}(Q) \leftarrow \text{LLINK}(P)$ and $\text{RLINK}(Q) \leftarrow \text{RLINK}(P)$ (all of which set up the new free block Q and link it into the free ring). Now, $\text{TAG}(P) \leftarrow \text{TAG}(P + (n + 1)) \leftarrow -$ and $\text{SIZE}(P) \leftarrow n + 2$ sets up the fields of the block satisfying the reservation request. Finally $B \leftarrow P$ and $P \leftarrow \text{RLINK}(Q)$ sets up the pointers for successful exit, and the algorithm terminates successfully.

4. [Excess too small?] If now $n + 2 < \text{SIZE}(P) < n + 5$, block P is large enough to satisfy the request, but too small to allow its excess after the request is satisfied to be made into a new free block. In this case, we can allocate the block as if it had been an exact fit, using the operations in step 2; but we might first want to record the actual number n of elements in use by placing n in a new field $\text{USED}(P) \leftarrow n$. In this case, internal fragmentation exists.

Algorithm 6.2 *Liberation with coalescing in sequential-fit method.*

Let B point to the block to be liberated, and let P point to some block on the ring of free blocks. If $P = \Lambda$, the ring is empty. The algorithm places B back on the ring in ring-sequential order after first trying to coalesce it with free neighbors in address order.

1. [Ring empty?] If $P = \Lambda$, the free ring is empty, so set $P \leftarrow B$, $\text{LLINK}(B) \leftarrow \text{RLINK}(B) \leftarrow B$, $\text{TAG}(B) \leftarrow \text{TAG}(B + \text{SIZE}(B) - 1) \leftarrow +$, and $\text{SIZE}(B + \text{SIZE}(B) - 1) \leftarrow \text{SIZE}(B)$, and exit.

2. [Left neighbor free?] If $\text{TAG}(B - 1) = +$, then (the left neighbor is a free block on the free block ring suitable for coalescing) set $Q \leftarrow B - \text{SIZE}(B - 1)$, $\text{SIZE}(Q) \leftarrow \text{SIZE}(B + \text{SIZE}(B) - 1) \leftarrow \text{SIZE}(Q) + \text{SIZE}(B)$. If now, $Q = \text{RLINK}(Q)$, then (Q was the only free block on the ring) exit. Otherwise, remove Q from the ring and continue) $B \leftarrow Q$, $\text{LLINK}(\text{RLINK}(B)) \leftarrow \text{LLINK}(B)$, and $\text{RLINK}(\text{LLINK}(B)) \leftarrow \text{RLINK}(B)$.

3. [Right neighbor free?] If $\text{TAG}(B + \text{SIZE}(B)) = +$, then (the right neighbor is free and can be coalesced), $Q \leftarrow B + \text{SIZE}(B)$, $\text{SIZE}(B) \leftarrow \text{SIZE}(Q + \text{SIZE}(Q) - 1) \leftarrow \text{SIZE}(B) + \text{SIZE}(Q)$, $\text{LLINK}(B) \leftarrow \text{LLINK}(Q)$, and $\text{RLINK}(B) \leftarrow \text{RLINK}(Q)$. If now $B = \text{LLINK}(B)$, then (B was the only remaining block on the free ring, so) set $P \leftarrow B$, and exit. Otherwise, proceed to step 4.

4. [Join B to free ring] (This joining is performed to the left of the node pointed to by P), $\text{RLINK}(\text{LLINK}(P)) \leftarrow B$, $\text{LLINK}(B) \leftarrow \text{LLINK}(P)$, $\text{RLINK}(B) \leftarrow P$, and $\text{LLINK}(P) \leftarrow B$.

Let us now examine several alternative sequential-fit policies. In each of these policies, assume that P initially points to a block on the free ring. (If $P = \Lambda$, the ring is empty, and each of the following policies fails immediately. Hence, we assume that $P \neq \Lambda$). Also, in some of the policies, we travel around the entire ring, and if we come back to the starting point, not having found a suitable block, the policy fails. For this reason, assume that we initially perform the assignment $P_0 \leftarrow P$, to save the starting address P_0 for ring traversal for use in a ring-search termination test.

6.2.1.1 *First fit.* In the *first-fit* policy, we search the free ring starting at P_0 until locating the first block P with a size $\text{SIZE}(P) \geq n + 2$ big enough to accommodate the block request size n. To convert Algorithm 6.1 into a *first-fit* algorithm, we replace step 1 with the following:

1. [First-fit policy.] If $P = \Lambda$ (the free ring is empty, and) the algorithm terminates unsuccessfully. Otherwise, set $P_0 \leftarrow P$, and perform steps (a) and (b) repeatedly.
   a) If $\text{SIZE}(P) \geq n + 2$, the algorithm continues at step 2.

  b) Otherwise, set $P \leftarrow \text{RLINK}(P)$. If now $P = P_0$, the algorithm terminates unsuccessfully (since the entire ring has been traversed without locating a suitable block).

    6.2.1.2 *Best fit.* In the *best-fit* policy, we examine blocks along the ring in right neighbor sequence until finding an exact fit or until, having examined the entire ring, we find a block of smallest size on the ring such that $\text{SIZE}(P) \geq n + 2$. To convert Algorithm 6.1 to a *best-fit* algorithm, we replace step 1 with the following:

1. [Best-fit policy.] If $P = \Lambda$, (the free ring is empty, and) the algorithm terminates unsuccessfully. Otherwise, set $P_0 \leftarrow P$, $Q \leftarrow \Lambda$, and $S \leftarrow \infty$ (where S is the best size, so far), and perform steps (a), (b), and (c) repeatedly.
  a) If $\text{SIZE}(P) = n + 2$ (we have an exact fit), continue at step 2.
  b) If $\text{SIZE}(P) > n + 2$, then, if $\text{SIZE}(P) < S$, set $Q \leftarrow P$ and $S \leftarrow \text{SIZE}(P)$.
  c) Set $P \leftarrow \text{RLINK}(P)$. If now $P = P_0$, then (we have completed a trip around the ring, and we must fail or pick the best so far, hence) if $Q = \Lambda$ (no block was large enough to satisfy the request, and) the algorithm terminates unsuccessfully. Otherwise (Q points to the block of smallest size greater than $n + 2$, so), set $P \leftarrow Q$ and continue at step 2.

    6.2.1.3 *Optimal fit.* *Optimal fit* is a technique due to J. A. Campbell [1971] who found circumstances under which it performed better than first fit. The idea is to scan the ring of free blocks for a while, building up a sample of the free blocks that would satisfy the request, and then to choose the first block past the end of the sample better than the best block in the sample. This involves more work than first fit and chooses a tighter-fitting free block than first fit, although the result may not be as tight a fit as best fit.

    We might make an analogy with a touring cyclist who can choose one of N known hotels at which to stop for the night. He is assisted by a very strong tail wind and cannot turn back once he has visited a particular hotel and has gone on toward the next. What should be his optimal strategy for selecting a hotel? The solution (see Campbell [1971]) is to calculate a sample size $s(N)$ governed by inequality (1) below, and to pick the first hotel better than the best among the first $s(N) - 1$ hotels examined in the sample:

$$\frac{1}{s(N)} + \frac{1}{s(N) + 1} + \cdots + \frac{1}{N - 1} \leq 1 < \frac{1}{s(N) - 1} + \frac{1}{s(N)} + \cdots + \frac{1}{N - 1}. \quad (1)$$

For large N, (1) may be approximated by $N/e < s(N) < N/e + (2 - e^{-1})$ subject to an error of at most 1 in $s(N)$. Hence, for large N, a good approximation for $s(N)$ is $\lceil N/e \rceil$. If we try out the algorithm a number of times, say K times, the fraction of times out of K that it picks the best hotel (i.e., its probability of success) is given by:

$$p(N) = \frac{s(N) - 1}{N} \sum_{s(N) \leq i \leq N} \frac{1}{i - 1} = \frac{s(N) - 1}{N} (H_{N-1} - H_{s(N)-2}).$$

For instance, if $N = 1097$ ($\approx e^7$), then $N/e = 403$ ($\approx e^6$), and $p(N) \approx 0.366$ ($\approx (402/1097) \times (7 - 6)$). In other words, if we sample approximately 38 percent of the blocks on the free ring, and pick the best block after completing the sample, we get the optimum block (that would have been chosen by best fit) about 37 percent of the time. We see that optimal fit gives us a policy that is intermediate between first fit and best fit, in that it looks at more blocks than first fit and less than best fit, but selects a fit closer to the request size than first fit, but not as close (on the average) as best fit.

Of course, we need a failure policy to go along with optimal fit should we find no free block after examining the sample that is better than the best block in the sample. Campbell's routine simply keeps track of the best block examined so far; and therefore, if, at the end of the free ring, no block better than the best in the sample is discovered, it reverts to best fit. Campbell's data showed that this reversion to best fit occurred roughly once in four times, so the average probability of success over many requests was not much smaller than $3/4e \approx 0.276$—still a considerable improvement over the first-fit strategy.

In an application with simplification of expressions in a physics calculation, Campbell showed that optimal fit outperformed first fit with regard to the external fragmentation of blocks on the free ring, with first fit leading to an excess of small fragments that usually forced termination of the simplification computation considerably before optimal fit, due to failure to satisfy a request for a free block.

6.2.1.4 *Worst fit.* Another strategy for choosing a free block is to choose the largest block on the free list, on the grounds that, after it is split, it has the largest remainder of any of the blocks, and so will lead after a time to the least amount of small external fragments on the free ring. This policy is called *worst fit*.

6.2.1.5 *Variations in ring ordering.* We have kept free blocks on the free ring in random order in Algorithms 6.1 and 6.2. Two other possibilities are: (1) keep blocks on the free ring in address order, and (2) keep blocks on the free ring in order of increasing block size. These two methods have the following two respective difficulties:

1. When returning a liberated block to the free ring, which has not coalesced with near neighbors, one must search the free ring for the proper place in which to insert the newly liberated block; and

2. When searching for a block with a large request size n, one must search past all blocks of size smaller than n before reaching blocks big enough to satisfy the request.

Note that Algorithms 6.1 and 6.2 make use of the notion of a *roving pointer P*. The pointer P is stepped around the ring systematically by following RLINKs in the successive blocks. At the end of satisfying one request, P is stepped to the right of the block B that is detached to satisfy the request. Search for a block to satisfy the next request picks up at the place following that where the most recent request was satisfied. Thus the pointer P keeps circulating to the right around the ring. This means that fragments deposited behind it from previous splits have had the longest time to coalesce by the time it reaches them again. Knuth ([1973a], p. 449, and p. 452, Ex. 6) found that the notion of a roving pointer made it necessary to inspect only 2.8 blocks in a first-fit search (using block request sizes chosen uniformly between 100 and 2000, and block lifetimes chosen uniformly between 1 and 1000). By contrast, when the roving pointer was not used but instead search was always begun at one point (the beginning of a free list), small fragments tended to accumulate near the front of the list, and (using the same distribution of request sizes and lifetimes) about 125 blocks had to be examined on the free list on the average (which was about half of the list), and 20 percent of the time, 200 or more iterations were necessary.

Unfortunately, the sequential-fit methods have proved difficult to analyze mathematically, and recourse to simulation experiments has been necessary in order to characterize their behaviors. We will study later how the sequential-fit methods compare to the buddy-system and segregated-storage methods with regard to various sets of experimental performance data.

First Midterm

6.2.2 Buddy-system methods

Following Knowlton [1965] and Knuth ([1973a], pp. 442–445), suppose we have available a region of 2^m storage locations (for some m) to use for allocating blocks of variable size, and suppose we decide to break the memory into blocks of sizes 1, 2, 4, ..., 2^k, ... Then, when presented with a request for a block of size n, we find the smallest k such that $2^k \geq n$, and see if there is a block of size 2^k available. If there is, we allocate it (and we allow some waste if there are $2^k - n$ cells left unused in the block of size 2^k). If there isn't, we see if there are any larger blocks of size 2^{k+1}, 2^{k+2}, ..., 2^m available that we could split up into smaller blocks, producing one of size 2^k to use to satisfy our request, and some split ones of various sizes to place in the pool of free blocks for later use.

When we liberate a block B and attempt to return it to the free storage pool, we first attempt to coalesce it. In the coalescing process, we check the *buddy* of block B to see if it is also free, and we combine buddies of size 2^k and 2^k to form a larger free block of size 2^{k+1}. This larger coalesced block may reside next to a *buddy* of size 2^{k+1} of its own which is also free, and which can be coalesced into a new free block of size 2^{k+2}. This coalescing process proceeds until some free block is obtained whose buddy is reserved (or until the whole memory of size 2^m is one large free block).

The buddy B' of a block B of size 2^k resides at an address β' which is closely related to the address β of block B. To understand the exact relationship, we first examine the binary addresses of blocks of sizes 1, 2, 4, 8, ..., 2^{m-1} in a region of memory with addresses from 0 through $2^m - 1$. For, example, picking $m = 4$, we get the results shown in Table 6.1.

TABLE 6.1

Addresses of blocks of Size 1	Addresses of blocks of Size 2	Addresses of blocks of Size 4	Addresses of blocks of Size 8
0000	0000	0000	0000
0001	0010	0100	1000
0010	0100	1000	
0011	0110	1100	
0100	1000		
0101	1010		
0110	1100		
0111	1110		
1000			
1001			
1010			
1011			
1100			
1101			
1110			
1111			

We observe that the block addresses for blocks of size 2^k are binary numbers such that the last k bits are 0, and such that the $(k + 1)$st bit from the last alternates in the sequence 0, 1, 0, 1, ... For example, for blocks of size $4 = 2^2$ the last two bits of the block addresses are 00, and the third bit from the last alternates in the sequence 0, 1, 0, 1.

Let us define as (binary) *buddies* of size 2^k, any two adjacent blocks of size 2^k, of which one has an address ending in

$$\overbrace{10\ldots\ldots0}^{k \text{ zeros}}$$

and the other has an address ending in

$$\overbrace{0\ldots\ldots0.}^{k+1 \text{ zeros}}$$

For example, if we split a block of size 16 whose address is of the form $bb\ldots b0000$, into two buddies of size 8, the addresses of the buddies of size 8 are $bb\ldots b1000$ and $bb\ldots b0000$. Hence, given the address $bb\ldots b000$ of a block of size 8, to find the address of its binary buddy, we complement the fourth bit from the last. In general, given the address of a block of size 2^k, to find the address of its binary buddy, we complement the $(k+1)$st bit from the last. (The binary buddy can be readily computed by using an exclusive-or with a word whose $(k+1)$st bit is 1 and all of whose other bits are 0.) Note that, when a block is split, the two sub-blocks formed will be buddies and they can recombine with each other but not with any other block.

The idea behind coalescing, then, is to look at the buddy B' of a block B being liberated, and if B' is free, to make a new block of size twice B. This process is iterated until no more free buddies of the same size as the current one can be coalesced.

The method of allocating blocks of size 2^k $(0 \le k \le m)$ in a binary-buddy system differs from that used in the sequential-fit methods, and herein lies the power of the buddy systems. We maintain separate symmetrically linked rings of each size block that is free, for sizes 1, 2, 4, ..., 2^m. Let AVAIL[k] point to a block of size 2^k on the ring of symmetrically linked free blocks of size 2^k (for $0 \le k \le m$). If there are no free blocks of size 2^k, then AVAIL[k] = Λ. Then, to satisfy a request for a block of size n, we find the smallest-size block on one of the avail lists whose size is greater than or equal to n, split it if necessary to obtain a block of size $2^{\lceil \lg n \rceil}$ (tossing the unused split pieces onto the appropriate free rings), and we allocate the block of size $2^{\lceil \lg n \rceil}$. Algorithms 6.3 and 6.4 illustrate block reservation and liberation in such a binary-buddy system under the assumed formats of blocks given in Fig. 6.3.

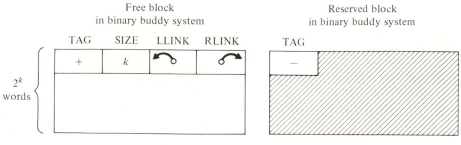

Free block
in binary buddy system

Reserved block
in binary buddy system

FIGURE 6.3

Note that the TAG field is the only field common to both free and reserved blocks, and that it contains + for free blocks and − for reserved blocks. The SIZE field contains the exponent k to which 2 is to be raised to yield the length of the block in words 2^k (hence, $k = $ lg(size in words)). Also, left and right links are provided in each free block to link free blocks symmetrically into a ring.

Algorithm 6.3 *Reserving a block in the binary buddy system.*

This algorithm attempts to reserve a block B of at least n words in an address zone whose addresses range from 0 to $2^m - 1$. The array of pointers AVAIL[k] ($0 \leq k \leq m$) point either to the empty ring Λ, or to a symmetrically linked ring of free blocks of size 2^k.

1. [Find size.] Let $s = \lceil \lg n \rceil$, and let k be the smallest integer in the range $s \leq k \leq m$ such that AVAIL[k] $\neq \Lambda$. If no such k exists, the algorithm terminates unsuccessfully.

2. [Detach block from ring.] Set $B \leftarrow$ AVAIL[k] and TAG(B) $\leftarrow -$. If LLINK(B) = RLINK(B), then (B was the only block on the ring, so) set AVAIL[k] $\leftarrow \Lambda$ and go to step 3. Otherwise, (to remove B from the ring and advance the pointer AVAIL[k]) set LLINK(RLINK(AVAIL[k])) $\leftarrow$ LLINK(AVAIL[k]) and

$$\text{AVAIL}[k] \leftarrow \text{RLINK}(\text{LLINK}(\text{AVAIL}[k])) \leftarrow \text{RLINK}(\text{AVAIL}[k]).$$

3. [Split block if too big.] If $k = s$, block B is of the proper size and the algorithm terminates successfully. Otherwise, (split B into two smaller blocks B and $B2$, and place $B2$ on the ring of its size) set $k \leftarrow k - 1$ and set $B2 \leftarrow B + 2^k$ ($B2$ is the address of the buddy of B). Now, set TAG($B2$) $\leftarrow +$, SIZE($B2$) $\leftarrow k$, and LLINK($B2$) $\leftarrow$ RLINK($B2$) $\leftarrow$ AVAIL[k] $\leftarrow B2$. (Note that AVAIL[k] was previously empty and now contains a ring with one block, $B2$, on it.) Now, repeat this step.

Algorithm 6.4 *Liberation of a block in the binary buddy system.*

This algorithm liberates block B in a binary buddy system and attempts to coalesce B with its liberated buddy as many times as possible before inserting the resulting block of largest possible coalesced size containing B on the list of appropriate size.

1. [Find buddy address.] Set $k \leftarrow$ SIZE(B), and set $B2 \leftarrow$ the address of B with bit $k + 1$ complemented. ($B2$ is now the address of the buddy of B of size 2^k).

2. [Is buddy unavailable?] If TAG($B2$) $= -$ or $k = m$ or (TAG($B2$) $= +$ and SIZE($B2$) $\neq k$), then (buddy is unavailable, so B can be joined to ring AVAIL[k]) by proceeding as follows. If AVAIL[k] $= \Lambda$, then (ring was empty, so) AVAIL[k] $\leftarrow$ LLINK(B) $\leftarrow$ RLINK(B) $\leftarrow B$. Otherwise, LLINK(B) $\leftarrow$

LLINK(AVAIL[k]), LLINK(AVAIL[k]) ← B, RLINK(LLINK(B)) ← B, and RLINK(B) ← AVAIL[k]. The algorithm now terminates.

3. [Coalesce with buddy.] (Remove $B2$ from its ring.) If $B2 = $ RLINK($B2$) then ($B2$ was the only block on its ring, so) set AVAIL[k] ← Λ. Otherwise, set LLINK(RLINK($B2$)) ← LLINK($B2$) and RLINK(LLINK($B2$)) ← RLINK($B2$), and if AVAIL[k] = $B2$, then set AVAIL[k] ← RLINK($B2$). (Now, coalesce buddies.) Set B ← min(B, $B2$), TAG(B) ← +, and k ← SIZE(B) ← $k + 1$. (Now calculate the new buddy of B). Set $B2$ ← (the address of B with bit $k + 1$ complemented), and return to step 2.

Some data by Weinstock [1976] shows that the buddy-system reservation scheme is quite efficient for a distribution of block sizes used by the BLISS/11 compiler. For the binary-buddy system of Algorithms 6.3 and 6.4, an average of only one ring had to be checked per operation for a sequence of block reservations and liberations. Unfortunately, the binary-buddy system was the worst of all methods compared with regard to efficiency of memory utilization. For six of Weinstock's data distributions, the unused memory due to internal fragmentation ranged between 25 and 41 percent of the memory. Thus, while the binary-buddy system spent the least amount of time in reservation and liberation, it had the worst storage-utilization efficiency. Knuth [1973a] (pp. 448–449) simulated the binary buddy system and found that it was seldom necessary to split or coalesce blocks. Further, although the buddy system sometimes allows two adjacent blocks of the same size to be available but uncoalescible (because they are not buddies), both Knuth [1973a] and the mathematical analysis of Purdom and Stigler [1970] found this seldom to be a problem. Theoretically, if we pick random block sizes uniformly and independently between 1 and N, the binary-buddy system forces us to round each request of size n up to $2^{\lceil \lg n \rceil}$, so the waste due to internal fragmentation can be studied by studying the ratio of a_n/b_n, where a_n is the sum of the first n terms of

$$1 + 2 + 3 + \cdots + n$$

and b_n is the sum of the first n terms of

$$1 + 2 + 4 + 4 + 8 + 8 + 8 + 8 + 16 + 16 + \cdots$$

Knuth ([1973a], p. 453, Exercise 21, and p. 600, Answer 21). This ratio lies in the range $\frac{2}{3} \leq a_n/b_n \leq \frac{3}{4}$, so the internal fragments occupy between 25 and 33.3 percent of the total block space reserved. (See also Russell [1977] for an interesting general study of internal fragmentation.) This waste due to internal fragmentation has a more significant debilitating impact on performance than that due to external fragmentation (Randell [1969], Purdom and Stigler [1970], and Randell and Kuehner [1968]). Hence, methods that reduce the internal fragmentation phenomenon of the binary-buddy system are important to pursue. This led to investigations into the *Fibonacci buddy system* (by Hirschberg [1973b]), a *weighted buddy system* (by Shen and Peterson [1974]), and a *generalized Fibonacci buddy system* (by Hinds [1975]). Hirschberg's simulation data revealed an internal fragmentation that used up 27.6 percent of the allocated space in the binary buddy method, whereas Fibonacci buddy allocation (based on blocks chosen from sizes in the Fibonacci sequence) reduced the internal fragmentation to 20 percent. The weighted-buddy system permits blocks of sizes 2^k and $3 \cdot 2^k$ (making the allowable sizes members of the sequence 1, 2, 3, 4, 6, 8, 12, ...). Shen and Peterson's data, comparing the performance of binary-buddy and weighted-buddy systems under two distributions of block sizes, one uniform and one exponential, give the results (Shen and Peterson [1974], p. 560) shown in Table 6.2.

TABLE 6.2

Type of fragmentation	Uniform distribution		Exponential distribution	
	Binary buddy	Weighted buddy	Binary buddy	Weighted buddy
Internal	26%	12%	28%	14%
External	1%	22%	1%	8%
Total	27%	34%	29%	22%

Thus, the results show that while the weighted-buddy system purchases a reduction in internal fragmentation at the cost of increased external fragmentation, it reduces the overall fragmentation, under favorable circumstances. Hinds' generalized Fibonacci method notes that the recurrence

$$\text{Size}_n = \text{Size}_{n-1} + \text{Size}_{n-k}$$

(originally observed by Hirschberg [1973b]) can be specialized to obtain the binary and Fibonacci buddy block sizes:

For binary-buddy block sizes:

$$\text{Size}_n = \text{Size}_{n-1} + \text{Size}_{n-1}, \quad \text{Size}_0 = 1.$$

For Hirschberg's Fibonacci-buddy block sizes:

$$\text{Size}_n = \text{Size}_{n-1} + \text{Size}_{n-2}, \quad \text{Size}_0 = 3, \quad \text{Size}_1 = 5.$$

In general, though, other choices of k and Size_i $(0 \le i \le k - 1)$ yield the basis for a buddy system. For instance, $k = 3$, and $\text{Size}_0 = 1$, $\text{Size}_1 = 1$, and $\text{Size}_2 = 2$, yield the sequence of block sizes

$$1, \quad 1, \quad 2, \quad 3, \quad 4, \quad 6, \quad 9, \quad 13, \ldots$$

6.2.3 Segregated-storage methods

The dynamic storage allocation methods discussed so far intermingle blocks of various sizes in one common allocation zone. Another strategem is to divide the entire region to be allocated into a number of smaller zones, each with its own storage-allocation policy. Some of the zones can be devoted to reserving and liberating blocks of one uniform fixed size (using the simpler techniques of Chapter 5). Others can still be devoted to handling requests of variable size. Using zones of uniform size blocks can alleviate the problem of unusable sizes that uncontrolled intermingling of storage sizes often creates. However, this is paid for by unused space in some of the zones. The AED Free-storage Package (Ross [1967]) is an example of this philosphy. Some programming language implementations make use of a similar strategy of allocating memory in pages devoted to blocks of fixed uniform size. We call this sort of strategem a *partitioned storage method*.

Another sort of segregated storage method is to maintain separate lists of blocks of uniform size (or, more generally, ranges of sizes). All the blocks of various sizes reside in a common allocation zone, however. For example, in the method of Purdom, Stigler, and Cheam [1971], k lists of free blocks are kept. A size partition is chosen of the form $(a_0, a_1, \ldots, a_k)$, which is a strictly increasing sequence of sizes such that $a_0 = 0$ and a_k is the total amount of space to be allocated. Then, the ith list contains all free blocks with sizes s in the range $a_{i-1} < s \leq a_i$. One possibility, for instance, is to let $a_1 = 1$ and $a_{i+1} = 2 \cdot a_i$. This yields the size partition

$$(0, 1, 2, 4, \ldots, 2^i, \ldots),$$

so the ith list consists of all free blocks with sizes s lying in the range $2^{i-2} < s \leq 2^{i-1}$. When a block of size n is requested, the first block from list i is taken, where i is chosen so that $a_{i-1} < n \leq a_i$. If list i is empty, list $i + 1$ is used. If list $i + 1$ is also empty, list $i + 2$ is used, and so on. If all lists from i to k are empty, the allocation fails. Once a block of sufficient size is located, n cells are used to meet the request, and the remainder is put on the appropriate available list (except that, when only a small number of cells remain, it may be better to give all the cells in the block to the requester). As usual, when a block of storage is released it is coalesced with its neighbors, if possible, and placed on the list of appropriate size.

Instead of accessing the k lists with a vector of pointers AVAIL[i], we could instead index them using a balanced binary tree (or other sort of balanced search tree such as a 2-3 tree, or a B-tree, using the methods of Chapter 3). This would guarantee $O(\log k)$ search times to find a relevant list.

6.2.3.1 *Tree-indexed segregated storage.* Let us agree to partition all free blocks into a number of equivalence classes. Each equivalence class consists of all free blocks of the same size. We further agree to keep the blocks of each fixed size k

on a symmetrically linked ring. Thus, for each possible size s, the free blocks of that size are either the empty ring Λ, or a nonempty, symmetrically linked ring with one or more blocks on it each of size s. For each nonempty ring, we pick a block on it, and designate this block as the representative of the ring. We then organize the representatives for each of the nonempty rings into a balanced search tree (such as an AVL tree), using the block size as the search key. For example, using an AVL tree index, if, at a particular moment there exist k nonempty rings with k distinct sizes of blocks, then organizing the representatives of the rings into an AVL tree guarantees search times of at worst $1.44 \log_2 k$ comparisons of the request size to the sizes of nodes in the tree to find the best fit (or to determine that the request cannot be satisfied). When a block is liberated, it can be coalesced with near neighbors (if possible), joined to the ring of blocks of its size (if one exists), or made into a new ring, which is then added to the tree index. Coalescing may entail deletion of blocks from rings, which may in turn cause some rings to vanish, and therefore cause nodes to be deleted from the tree index.

While the $O(\log k)$ search times will not do as well as, say, first-fit sequential search (under some circumstances such as those explored by Knuth [1973a], p. 449, in which an average of 2.8 inspections of available blocks were required to satisfy a request), there are other circumstances in which $O(\log k)$ search times will beat sequential list searching by a considerable margin (as in best-fit searching for large blocks on lists containing many small blocks).

6.2.3.2 *Fast-fit segregated storage.* As we shall see later, Weinstock's data (Weinstock [1976]) indicate that best-fit sequential methods yield the best storage utilization, while buddy systems give the fastest satisfaction of requests. Therefore, it would be best if we could combine the advantages of best-fit allocation with the use of separate lists to service allocation requests, if at all possible.

In the Weinstock data (Weinstock [1976]), the distribution of block sizes used by the BLISS/11 compiler were concentrated among blocks of sizes 1 through 15 over 90 percent of the time. Therefore, Wulf, Weinstock, and Johnsson designed a storage-allocation method called *QuickFit*, which used a hierarchy of search methods, the first of which was to maintain 15 exact lists with blocks of uniform sizes 1 through 15 stored on the 15 respective lists. If a request fell in the range 1 to 15, it was handled by first consulting its appropriate exact list to find a block of exactly the right size. If that failed, a large block was split (if large enough) in order to satisfy the request; and if, in turn, that failed, a larger exact list was searched. Finally, if all of these failed, a first fit was performed on all blocks larger than the range of the exact lists. (Various other hierarchies of policies were used for requests falling initially outside the range of the exact lists (Weinstock [1976]). The end result of measuring the QuickFit policy, was that QuickFit allocated blocks as fast as the fastest methods—the buddy-system methods—using an average of between one and two inspections of blocks. However, with regard to storage utilization efficiency, the data show it did not perform as well as best-fit.

The following *Fast-Fit* method has been arranged to use a vector of exact lists to give the speed advantages of the buddy systems and QuickFit systems for the bulk of requests typical of the compiler data, but also to produce a best fit, using search in a balanced tree index for requests outside the range of the exact lists, if necessary. Thus, the method combines the advantages of best-fit and exact-list searches, while guaranteeing search times at worst $O(\log k)$, where k is the number of distinct block sizes among free blocks.

Figure 6.4 shows an example of a *Fast-Fit* index with five exact lists and one balanced tree index. The free blocks stored in the index of Fig. 6.4 are blocks of sizes

1, 1, 1, 1, 2, 2, 2, 4, 4, 4, 4, 4, 5, 5, 8, 9, 9, 10, 10, 10, 27, 27, 77, 77,   and   102.

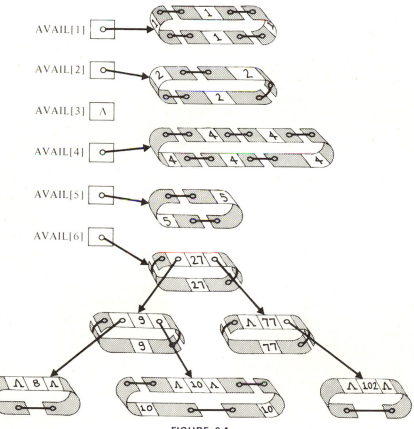

FIGURE 6.4

The blocks of sizes 1 through 5 are placed on exact lists. For instance, the first exact list is pointed to by a pointer in AVAIL[1], and consists of four free blocks, each of size 1, symmetrically linked into a ring. The second exact list consists of three free blocks of size 2, symmetrically linked into a ring and pointed to by a pointer in AVAIL[2]. The third exact list is empty since there are no free blocks of size 3, so AVAIL[3] contains the pointer Λ, which stands for a pointer to an empty ring. AVAIL[4] and AVAIL[5] point to exact lists containing free blocks of sizes 4 and 5, respectively.

In Fig. 6.4, all free blocks of size 6 or greater are too big to fit on the exact lists of sizes 1 through 5. We again link free blocks of identical size into symmetrically linked rings. Then, for each ring, we pick a representative block on the ring, and we link the ring representatives into a balanced search tree. For the sake of specificity, an AVL tree has been used in Fig. 6.4, and the root of this AVL tree is pointed to by a pointer in AVAIL[6].

Now, to service a request to reserve a block of size n, we do the following. If $n \leq 5$ and the exact list L pointed to by AVAIL[n] is nonempty, we detach a free block of size n from L. If the exact list pointed to by AVAIL[n] is empty, however, we search for a pointer AVAIL[j] to a nonempty structure with free blocks of the next biggest size $s > n$. If no nonempty structure with free blocks bigger than n exists, the allocation fails. Otherwise, we seize a free block of next biggest size s, divide it into blocks of size n and $(s - n)$, and place the remainder of size $(s - n)$ back into the Fast-Fit index. If we are searching for a block of size $n \geq 6$, we use n as a search key to search the AVL tree pointed to by AVAIL[6] in Fig. 6.4, and we locate a ring of blocks whose size is the smallest $s \geq n$ (if such a ring exists), detach a block from the ring and, if necessary, split it and file the remainder back in the index. To liberate a block, we coalesce it with neighbors, if possible, and file it on an exact list or on one of the rings in the tree index.

In general, we define a *Fast-Fit Index of order k* as follows. Let there be k *exact lists* $(1 \leq i \leq k)$, where list i is either the empty ring Λ or contains all free blocks of size i symmetrically linked into a ring. AVAIL[i] is set to point to some block on list i if list i is nonempty. Otherwise AVAIL[i] = Λ. If there are no free blocks of size $s \geq k + 1$, we define AVAIL[$k + 1$] = Λ. Otherwise, we set AVAIL[$k + 1$] to point to the root of an AVL tree T formed from a set of nonempty rings R_1, $R_2, \ldots, R_m$, each of which contains free blocks of uniform size given by SIZE(R_i). The search key for insertion of rings R_i into the tree index T is the size field of any of the blocks on the ring. We know that

$$\text{SIZE}(R_i) \geq k + 1 \quad \text{for all } R_i \ (1 \leq i \leq m).$$

To allocate a block of size n in a Fast-Fit index of order k we do the following:

1. Find the smallest j in the range $1 \leq j \leq k + 1$ such that AVAIL[j] $\neq \Lambda$, and either $j \geq n$ or $j = k + 1$. If no such j exists, the allocation is said to *fail*.

2. If now $j = n$ and $j \leq k$, the request can be satisfied exactly and we detach a block from the jth list to do so.

3. If however, $j > n$ and $j \leq k$, we must split a block of smallest size greater than n into one of size n and a remainder of size $(j - n)$ to be placed back on the list AVAIL$[j - n]$.

4. If $j = k + 1$, we must search the tree index T using search key n to find the ring containing free blocks of smallest size $s \geq n$. If no such ring exists, the allocation is said to *fail*. If $s = n$, we detach a block of size n and readjust the ring and T as required. If $s > n$, we split the block of size s into blocks of size n and $(s - n)$ and place the remainder of size $(s - n)$ on the appropriate exact list or ring of T making adjustments as required.

Whenever we insert a block into the tree index or into an exact list, we first attempt to coalesce it with its neighbors, if possible, to form a block of larger size. (Also, we keep blocks on rings in first-in, first-out order.)

6.2.4 Comparison of the methods

Weinstock [1976] and Nielsen [1977] have performed the most extensive set of comparative performance experiments on dynamic memory allocation to date. Weinstock found it useful to establish a descriptive framework for classifying dynamic memory allocation algorithms in terms of a six-tuple of parameters (S, F, E, R, C, M), where

    S is a searching criterion,
    F is the order in which the list of free blocks is maintained,
    E is a procedure for handling the excess when a block is split,
    R is a rule for rounding up the request size n to a nearest block size,
    C is a coalescing policy, and
    M is a compacting policy.

Examples of searching criteria are: Best Fit (B), First Fit (F), Next Fit (N)—First Fit with a roving pointer in which the next search begins where the previous one left off—Worst Fit (W), and Buddy-system Fit $(\bar{B})$. Examples of the order in which the list of free blocks can be maintained are: order on physical location of blocks in ascending order (L), order on ascending size of blocks (S), last-in, first-out order (I), and random order (R). Examples of procedures for handling the excess after block splitting are: return the excess to a free class (R); if the excess is smaller than a system parameter k, keep it with the allocated block; otherwise return it to the free list (R_k); and Buddy-system return (B). Examples of rounding rules are: do not perform rounding but allocate exactly what was asked for (Λ), round up to the nearest power of two (B), and round up to the nearest Fibonacci number (F). Examples of coalescing rules are: do not coalesce (Λ), coalesce blocks if they are physically adjacent (L), and coalesce only if adjacent free blocks are buddies (B).

Finally, examples of compacting rules are: do not compact (Λ), and perform total compacting (C).† Since coalescing can be performed either at the time a block is liberated or at the time it is requested, the coalescing policy can be rendered more accurately as a pair such as (free, L) or (reserve, L) to stand for coalescing physically adjacent free blocks at liberation time and reservation time, respectively.

Thus, using a Weinstock six-tuple, we can compactly describe various allocation methods. For instance, in a First-Fit method without a roving pointer, we might have the description

$$(F, L, R, \Lambda, (\text{free}, L), \Lambda),$$

meaning that the First-Fit search method (F) is used on a free list kept in location order (L), with the excess after a split returned to the free list (R). Further, while no rounding is done (Λ), coalescing is performed on adjacent free blocks at liberation time (free, L), and no compacting is performed (Λ).

As another example, Knowlton's binary-buddy method (Knowlton [1965]) can be described by the six-tuple

$$(\bar{B}, I, B, B, (\text{free}, B), \Lambda),$$

meaning that the Buddy System Fit ($\bar{B}$) is used for searching, the free list is maintained in LIFO order (I), excesses after block splitting are handled by the Buddy System policy (B), the rounding is performed to the nearest power of two (B), coalescing is done at block liberation time on adjacent free buddies (B), and no compacting is performed (Λ).

Perhaps the reader feels that this system of description is overly detailed but, as Weinstock points out, many of the algorithms in the literature, for which performance data or analyses are offered, are not described in sufficient detail to ascertain certain of their implementation details (ordering of free list, policy for handling excess after split, when coalescing is performed or whether it is performed at all, whether a roving pointer is used or whether search begins at the head of the free list each time a request is handled, etc.). Unfortunately, performance is often sensitive to such implementation details. Therefore, if these details are missing from a paper giving performance data and analysis, it is hard to know exactly which variant of the method is being analysed and compared.

Weinstock's data compare eleven variations of the dynamic storage allocation methods discussed, including variations of First-Fit, Best-Fit, Next-Fit, and Buddy-System methods. Also, a Quick-Fit method, used in the BLISS/11 compiler, consisting of a segregated storage method combined with a first-fit method, is compared.

Six different distributions were used in Weinstock's experiments, including size distributions that were Poisson distributed, exponentially distributed, uni-

---

† The notion of compacting is defined and studied in Section 6.3.2.

Block size in words	Percent of total	Request frequency	Cumulative percent
2	4	XXXXXXXXXXX	4
3	44	XXXXXXXXXXXXXXXXXXXXXXXXXXXXXXX . . . XXX	49
4	3	XXXXXXXX	52
5	3	XXXXXXXX	55
6	9	XXXXXXXXXXXXXXXXXXXXXXX	64
7	9	XXXXXXXXXXXXXXXXXXXXXXX	73
8	2	XXXXX	74
9	4	XXXXXXXXX	78
10	14	XXXXXXXXXXXXXXXXXXXXXXXXXXXXXXXXXXXXX	92
11	4	XXXXXXXXXXX	96
12	2	XXXXX	98
13	0	XX	98
14	1	XX	99
15	0	X	99
16	0	X	99
17	0	X	99
22	0	XX	99
65	1	XX	100

FIGURE 6.5

formly distributed, and distributed over two values, as well as two naturally occurring distributions drawn from the BLISS/11 compiler and from a University of Virginia study of B5500 system data (see Batson, Ju, and Wood [1970]). Figure 6.5 gives the distribution of allocated block sizes from the BLISS/11 data (Weinstock [1976], p. 33). The Batson, Ju, and Wood data measured segment sizes in the B5500 operating system (which utilizes variable size segments), and found that about 60 percent of the segments used contained less than 40 words apiece under routine operating conditions. Table 6.3 presents a subset of Weinstock's timing data for a subset of the methods compared. The methods compared are:

1. *Best-Loc:* Best-Fit with free list in location order.

$$(B, L, R, \Lambda, (\text{free}, L), \Lambda)$$

2. *First-Loc:* First-Fit with free list in location order.

$$(F, L, R, \Lambda, (\text{free}, L), \Lambda)$$

3. *Next-Loc:* First-Fit with roving pointer, and location order.

$$(N, L, R, \Lambda, (\text{free}, L), \Lambda)$$

4. *Buddy:* Binary Buddy method with liberation time coalescing

$$(\bar{B}, I, B, B, (\text{free}, B), \Lambda)$$

5. *Quick-Fit:* With segregated exact lists and hierarchy of fitting policies. Request-time coalescing.

TABLE 6.3

Method	Distributions					
	Bliss/11	Two-valued	Univ. of Va.	Expo-nential	Uniform	Poisson
Best-Loc	2.70, 18	3.83, 32	3.01, 22	2.52, 18	2.29, 15	2.84, 21
First-Loc	2.68, 23	4.06, 42	2.85, 26	3.11, 30	2.27, 21	3.46, 33
Next-Loc	3.82, 28	4.04, 30	3.13, 24	3.87, 29	3.43, 26	3.86, 30
Buddy	0.78, 1	0.84, 2	0.79, 2	0.79, 2	0.76, 1	0.73, 1
Quick-Fit	0.59, 1	0.54, 1	0.71, 1	0.61, 1	0.63, 1	0.62, 1

The figures given in Table 6.3 are of the form ($m.mm$, n) where $m.mm$ gives the time in milliseconds to perform an average reservation or liberation of a block, and n is the number of blocks examined to satisfy a reservation request.

It can be seen from these data that, under the distribution conditions tested, the maintenance of segregated-storage lists as in the Buddy System and Quick Fit, clearly reduces search times for blocks to satisfy requests by factors of between 4 and 8 in raw time consumed, and by factors of 9 to 40 in the number of blocks searched, in comparison to the sequential-fit methods. As mentioned before, however, Knuth ([1973a], p. 449) found distribution conditions in which Next-Loc takes only 2.8 block comparisons on the average to satisfy a request, rendering it competitive if the circumstances are right.

With regard to storage-utilization efficiency, Weinstock [1976] found the five methods compared in Table 6.3 to be ranked in order of decreasing partial order of superiority as shown in Fig. 6.6.

An example of a space-time trade-off diagram for the Poisson distribution data is given in Fig. 6.7. Also shown in Fig. 6.7 are some results of simulations by Tadman [1978] which calibrated and compared *Fast-Fit* to the methods in-

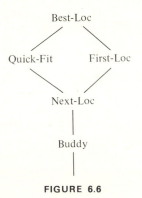

FIGURE 6.6

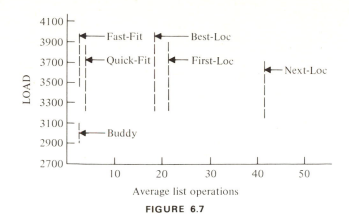

FIGURE 6.7

vestigated by Weinstock. The Fast-Fit method used has a Weinstock description of (Fast, I, R, Λ, (Free, L), Λ).

On the vertical axis in Fig. 6.7, the Load is the total number of words in the reserved blocks in memory. The vertical line for each method ranges from the load at which the probability of an allocation failure becomes nonzero (*viz.*, 0.001) on the low end upwards to the load at which the probability of an allocation failure is 1. For the Poisson distribution used in Fig. 6.7, we see that Fast-Fit and Best-Loc achieve the best performance of any of the methods, in allowing us to operate at the highest load without significant probability of allocation failure. Thus, if we intend to run at high loads without failure for such Poisson data, Fast-Fit and Best-Loc are the best methods. However, if we can run at low loads and allocation time is at a premium, Fast-Fit, Quick-Fit and the Buddy method give the greatest speed. Tadman's data (see Tadman [1978]) show the average number of list operations for Fast-Fit to be one less than that for Quick-Fit, over a number of the Weinstock test distributions (so Fast-Fit is slightly faster than Quick-Fit, much faster than Best-Fit, and can operate successfully at the high load factors previously associated only with Best-Fit).

A number of studies compare the performance of Best-Fit to First-Fit. Collins [1961] discovered circumstances under which Best-Fit outperformed First-Fit, whereas in Knuth's simulations [1973a], First-Fit always outperformed Best-Fit. Most recently, a comparison between First-Fit and Best-Fit was conducted by Shore [1975]. Shore found the time–memory product efficiencies of First-Fit and Best-Fit to be within 1 to 3 percent of each other. Shore also found that the performance of both methods could depend heavily on the first moment and the second-central moment of the request distribution, and that there is strong evidence that the relative performance of the two strategies depends on the frequency of requests that are large compared to the average request. When this frequency is high, First-Fit outperforms Best-Fit, by preferentially allocating toward one end of memory and encouraging large blocks to grow toward the other end. (Note here that Shore's First-Fit has a Weinstock description of

$$(F, L, R, \Lambda, (\text{free}, L), \Lambda),$$

whereas Knuth's best performance First-Fit method was a Next-Fit with roving pointer, described by

$$(N, R, R, \Lambda, (\text{free}, L), \Lambda).)$$

Segregated storage, First-Fit, and the Buddy system were compared by Purdom, Stigler, and Cheam [1971], using a simulation with requests arriving as a Poisson process with rate λ, block sizes distributed geometrically with mean c, and exponential block lifetimes. They claim such a distribution is similar in shape to many distributions measured on actual systems, such as those measured by Batson, Ju, and Wood [1970]; and that, under these conditions, the following results are obtained. First, with regard to storage utilization efficiency, segregated storage and First-Fit exhibit almost identical performance, with segregated storage slightly more efficient. The Buddy system rejects up to about 15% more requests under heavily loaded conditions, however. Second, with regard to running time, measured in mean number of searches per request, the Buddy system ran faster than First-Fit (except for some runs with light loading or large mean block size), with the Buddy system being much faster than First-Fit for the important cases of heavy loading with many small blocks. Segregated storage with the ranges for the segregated lists divided by the numbers $a_i = 2^{i-1}$ ran nearly as fast as the Buddy system (except for runs with light loading). Table 6.4 gives some of the results with table entries of the form $(xx, n.nn)$, where xx is the percentage of requests accepted, and $n.nn$ is the mean number of searches required to accept or reject requests.

There are some circumstances in which First-Fit allocation will fail while Best-Fit will succeed, and vice versa. For example, suppose we are given requests for blocks of sizes 6 and 8 in a memory whose list of free blocks contains a block of size 10 followed by a block of size 7. Figure 6.8 shows that First-Fit fails while Best-Fit succeeds. However, with requests for blocks of sizes 5, 5, and 6, First-Fit succeeds, while Best-Fit fails.

Actually, the phenomenon exhibited by Fig. 6.8 is much deeper than it might first appear. Robson [1971] shows that, if blocks are never allowed to move, there will always be some sequence of requests the total of whose sizes is less than the total of the sizes of the free block list, but which cannot be satisfied under a fixed choice of allocation policy. Unfortunately, for example, no matter what allocation method is used, overflow with blocks restricted to sizes 1 and 2 might occur when memory is only $\frac{2}{3}$ full.

Under equilibrium conditions, Knuth and Gelenbe have derived some interesting rules. For instance, suppose we use a Best-Fit strategy, and suppose there

TABLE 6.4

**Data for Segregated Storage,
First-Fit Method, and Buddy System.**

Mean rate of requests, λ	Mean size of blocks requested (c)†			
	2	4	11	45
3			99, 2.95 99, 1.30 96, 1.92	66, 1.99 66, 1.70 60, 1.90
14		100, 1.91 100, 1.50 99, 1.35	79, 2.05 79, 3.23 72, 1.89	
50	99, 1.49 98, 2.39 96, 1.28	74, 2.43 76, 5.82 72, 2.14		

† Total memory size 128 cells.

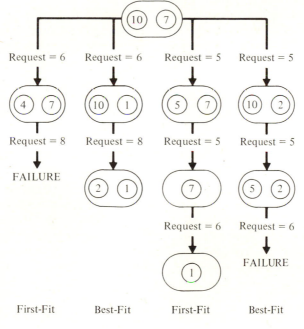

FIGURE 6.8

are N reserved blocks and M free blocks at a moment of equilibrium. Then, if $(1 - p)$ is the probability that a request of size n is satisfied exactly (i.e., there is no excess), the *fifty-percent rule* of Knuth ([1973a], p. 445) states that $M = \frac{1}{2}pN$. In particular, if the block sizes are infrequently equal to one another, and any excess is split off (so the probability of an exact fit $(1 - p) \approx 0$), then the number of free blocks, M, is about half the number of reserved ones, N.

Gelenbe's *two-thirds rule* provides a relationship between the average size f of free blocks on the free list, and the average size r of reserved blocks, under equilibrium conditions. With N and M roughly constant under equilibrium, Gelenbe [1971] defines the ratio between the total amount of reserved space and the total space (reserved and free) as the fraction ρ:

$$\rho = \frac{rN}{fM + rN}.$$

When the probability $(1 - p)$ of an exact fit is near 0, Gelenbe finds that $\rho = \frac{2}{3}$. In general, at equilibrium, $\rho = (1 + p/2)^{-1}$.

Weinstock's data ([1976], p. 32) point to the conclusion that the sizes of the exact lists in the segregated-storage methods mirror the actual distribution of reserved blocks, assuming independently distributed block sizes, lifetimes, and request arrival rates. At equilibrium, the number of free blocks on a given exact list will be proportional to the number of blocks of that size that are reserved (roughly). This helps explain why the segregated-storage methods with exact lists so frequently satisfy small requests in an average of only one search.

Additional references on these topics are Cranston and Thomas [1975], Bays [1977], Peterson and Norman [1977], Shore [1977], and Nielsen [1977].

6.3 MANAGEMENT ALGORITHMS FOR MULTILINKED STRUCTURES

As we mentioned in the introduction to this chapter, multilinked structures often consist of a collection of cells of various sizes linked together by pointers into what amounts to a connected directed graph, possibly containing cycles. One of the earliest expositions of this point of view as a basis for synthesizing data representations was given by Ross [1961]. Ross called multilinked cells *plexes*. "The components of an element may be of any form. They may be one-bit quantities, machine addresses, machine instructions, symbolic information, or numerical data in any appropriate number form. In particular (and this is the means whereby the system includes all other known symbol manipulation schemes), a component of an element may be a 'link' or reference to another element." (Ross [1961], p. 147).

To allocate the space for variable-size cells, one of the dynamic memory allocation techniques of Section 6.2 can be used. However, in connection with a chosen allocation technique, other categories of operations on multilinked structures are frequently necessary.

For example, if an allocation request to a dynamic memory allocation algorithm should fail, one possible remedy is to *compact* the reserved cells—moving them into one end of memory so that they are adjacent and contiguous, and so that the other end of memory is a single large free block. *Compacting* is also of use in coexistence regimes, wherein, say, a stack and a heap (i.e., a region of variable-size cells) live next to one another. Should the stack overflow, the heap can be compacted with the reserved cells placed in the end of memory farthest from the growth end of the stack (which, in turn, grows toward the heap). If a free area is liberated by this means, the stack can be allocated extra space in what formerly was the heap, the heap space can be reduced, and the execution of the algorithm can continue.

Traversal of multilinked structures is another important process. This is used in such applications as printing and garbage collection, and as an underlying basis for other algorithms (as we shall see). It is important to be able to traverse a multilinked structure with minimal auxiliary space at traversal time. In thinking about traversal, it is convenient to think of a multilinked structure as a directed graph in which cells correspond to nodes of the graph and in which links correspond to directed edges. In what follows, we will use the words *node* and *cell* interchangeably, and the words *link* and *edge* interchangeably, on the understanding that we are thinking of a multilinked structure as a directed graph.

Other algorithms of importance include those for *copying, moving,* and *equality testing.* When we copy a multilinked structure consisting of nodes arranged by their links into a connected, possibly cyclic, directed graph, we wish to create a disjoint set of multilinked nodes that are graph-isomorphic to the original structure, and that contain identical, nonlink information fields in corresponding nodes. *Moving* a multilinked structure consists of displacing some or all of its constituent nodes to new memory locations and of updating the links to point to the new, as opposed to the former, node locations. *Equality testing* of two multilinked structures consists of checking to see whether there exists a graph isomorphism between their node–link topologies and, if so, whether corresponding nodes under this graph isomorphism contain identical information in nonlink fields.

Many of these algorithms can be rendered straighforward if we assume the existence of a *utility cell*† in each node of a multilinked structure. A *utility cell* is a field large enough to contain a pointer to another cell, if necessary, or, alternatively, large enough to contain an integer at least as large as the number of pointers the cell contains.

---

† Actually, a *utility cell* should be called a *utility field*, since it is a *field* of a cell, for consistency with our terminology. For historical reasons, however, we shall permit this abuse of terminology.

We give outlines for algorithms for *traversing, compacting, copying, moving,* and *equality testing* in this chapter, based on the assumption of utility cells in each node. These are called *utility-cell algorithms.* Actually, we give just the themes behind these algorithms, distilling the abstract features of them for the reader. The actual details of application in particular applications can easily be worked out.

6.3.1 Traversal

Traversal consists of visiting each node in a multilinked structure. Traversal can be used for printing, marking during garbage collection, and many other purposes.

One method of traversal is to use an auxiliary stack and an *already visited* bit in each node. The main idea is to enumerate the nodes of the spanning tree of the structure (which possibly contains cycles, but is a connected, directed graph). To enumerate the nodes of a spanning tree, we begin at the starting node of the structure by setting its *already visited* bit to *true* (assuming that all bits are initially set to *false*). If the starting node contains n pointers to other nodes, we treat it as the root of a multiway tree (the spanning tree), which we proceed to visit in preorder.

If a link points to a node whose already visited bit is set to *true*, then it has already been enumerated in the preorder traversal of the spanning tree. However, if the already visited bit is set to *false*, it has not yet been enumerated in preorder, and we must visit it.

For any node N with n pointers, suppose we have already visited the first $(i - 1)$ nodes pointed to by the first $(i - 1)$ pointers, that we are currently about to visit the node pointed to by the ith pointer, and that the nodes referred to by pointers $i + 1$ to n have not yet been visited. Then we push on a stack the number $(i + 1)$ together with the address α of node N. Then we proceed to visit the node pointed to by the ith pointer in node N, together with all of its descendants in the spanning tree. This may cause further items to be pushed onto the stack. When we have finished this subtree of the spanning tree, we will find the address α and the number $(i + 1)$ on top of the stack. We then pop the number $(i + 1)$ and the address α from the stack and, if, now, $i + 1$ is larger than the number of pointers n in node N, we have finished visiting all descendants of N, and the new top of the stack can be considered, in turn. However, if $i + 1$ does not exceed n, we push α and $(i + 2)$ on the stack, and we proceed to visit the subtree rooted at the address given by the $(i + 1)$st pointer of N. This process is only a slight generalization of Algorithm 3.5, and so the details are left to the reader as an exercise (see Exercise 6.2).

The disadvantage of a preorder stack traversal, of course, is that it requires a stack of maximum depth equal to the maximum depth of the preorder spanning tree for the multilinked structure. This may at worst be proportional to the number of nodes in the structure. It may well be that, at the time we wish to traverse such a structure, we have the least amount of free memory available (as in garbage collection applications, where we call the garbage collector when the storage allocator fails to allocate space for a requested node).

6.3.1.1 *Schorr–Waite–Deutsch traversal.* A more space-efficient method is to use a link-inversion, preorder traversal of the spanning tree analogous to Algorithm 3.6 (for link-inversion traversal of a binary tree). This process is called the *Schorr–Waite–Deutsch traversal* (see Schorr and Waite [1967]). As before, we assume the use of an *already visited* bit in each node to prevent further traversal of nodes encountered by following two or more identical pointers generated in the structure. Upon descent into the spanning tree, we reverse pointers to point upward, and upon ascent we restore them to their original condition. The utility cell in each node is set to contain the number i of the pointer currently inverted to point to the node's spanning tree ancestor. This is analogous to the two-valued TAG bit in Algorithm 3.6. The details are a straightforward generalization of Algorithm 3.6, and are left to the reader (Exercise 6.3).

Assuming the use of the utility cell to contain the number of the currently inverted pointer in an n-pointer cell, the link-inversion, preorder-traversal algorithm requires only a constant number of cells of memory. Here, it must be further assumed that the number of pointers in (and, in general, the format of) each node can be determined from inspection of the node (say, by looking at its node type, or by accessing a special field) if nodes in the structure can have nonuniform numbers of pointers.

(See also Knuth [1973a], p. 421, Ex. 8, and p. 593, Ans. 8, for variations on the Schorr–Waite–Deutsch algorithm.)

6.3.1.2 *Thorelli traversal.* Let us assume that the structure we wish to traverse is a directed graph, in which, while we do not specify a representation for the nodes, we assume that nodes are assigned distinct addresses and that each node has the property that, given its address α, we can determine the list of addresses $(\beta_1, \beta_2, \ldots, \beta_n)$ of its immediate successors. This is called the *successor list* of α.

We shall further assume that $P0$ contains the address α of a starting node in the graph, and that our objective is to visit and mark all nodes in the graph that can be reached by a path starting at $P0$. We mark a node by setting its TAG field to $+$. Initially, we assume all tag fields of all nodes have been set to $-$. For example, in Fig. 6.9, the cross-hatched nodes are those visited and marked if we start traversal at $P0$. The others are neither visited nor marked.

We must, of course, prevent the traversal algorithm from chasing endlessly around cycles in such a graph. Algorithm 6.5 is an abstract traversal algorithm

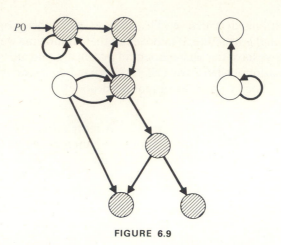

FIGURE 6.9

based on tree traversal methods given in Nilsson [1971] and Thorelli [1972]. As we shall see, it can be specialized to traverse the spanning tree of a graph in preorder or level order.

Algorithm 6.5 *Abstract Nilsson–Thorelli traversal.*

Let AUX be an auxiliary list of addresses of nodes waiting to be traversed, and let $\text{TAG}(N) = +$ if node N has been visited, whereas, if node N has not been visited, assume $\text{TAG}(N) = -$.

1. [Initialize.] Set $\text{AUX} \leftarrow \Lambda$ and $P \leftarrow P0$ (where $P0$ contains the address of the starting node).

2. [Visit and mark.] Visit node P, and set $\text{TAG}(P) \leftarrow +$.

3. [Process successors.] Insert the addresses of the successors of P on the list AUX.

4. [Done?] If $\text{AUX} = \Lambda$, then the algorithm terminates.

5. [Process next.] Extract one element P from AUX. If $\text{TAG}(P) = -$, then go to step 2. Otherwise, go to step 4.

If we choose to insert the successors of node P at the front of the AUX list, and also to extract elements to process next from the front of AUX, then AUX behaves like a pushdown stack, and the algorithm performs a preorder traversal of the spanning tree of the component of the graph accessible from $P0$. However, if we choose to treat AUX as a queue, by inserting successors of P at one end, say the *rear*, and choosing nodes to process next from the other end, say the *front*, then the spanning tree of the component of the graph accessible from $P0$ is traversed in *level order* (see Thorelli [1972], and Nilsson [1971]).

One rather interesting way of traversing the nodes N of a graph each of which contains a *utility cell* field UC(N), is to thread the AUX queue through the utility cell fields. This way, the nodes of a graph accessible from $P0$ are threaded together in level order of the spanning tree via a chain through addresses

$$P0, \text{UC}(P0), \text{UC}(\text{UC}(P0)), \ldots, \text{UC}^k(P0).$$

This chain, called the *Thorelli chain*, is useful for other utility-cell management algorithms, as we shall see.

In the utility-cell algorithms in the following sections, we shall assume the following further representational details for the storage of information in the nodes. Each node is of the form shown in Fig. 6.10.

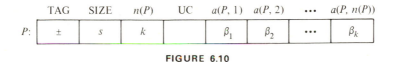

FIGURE 6.10

Thus, if the address of the node is the value of variable P, TAG(P) is a bit set to $+$ for marked nodes and $-$ for unmarked nodes. Initially all nodes are assumed unmarked and have TAGs set to $-$. The quantity SIZE(P) gives the size in words of the contiguous storage block reserved for node P. The quantity $n(P)$ gives the number of information fields (containing pointers to other nodes or nonpointer data) stored in node P. The field UC(P) is a utility cell belonging to node P, and has sufficient capacity to hold a pointer. The fields $a(P, 1)$, $a(P, 2)$, ..., $a(P, n(P))$ each contain either pointers or nonpointer data. The expression $(a(P, k)$ is a pointer) evaluates to *true* or *false* depending on whether $a(P, k)$ contains a pointer or not (for any k between 1 and $n(P)$).

Under these assumptions about representation, the following algorithm traverses the nodes of a graph accessible from initial node $P0$, and links the nodes together into a Thorelli chain.

Algorithm 6.6 *Thorelli traversal of a multilinked structure.*

We assume the existence of an auxiliary cell $Q0$ having a utility cell field UC($Q0$). The pointers FRONT and REAR point to separate ends of a queue of nodes to be processed, the queue being threaded through the utility cells of the nodes.

1. [Initialize.] Set FRONT $\leftarrow$ UC($Q0$) $\leftarrow$ $P0$, set REAR $\leftarrow$ the address of cell $Q0$ and set TAG($P0$) $\leftarrow$ $+$.

2. [Done?] If FRONT = REAR, then set UC(REAR) $\leftarrow \Lambda$ and terminate the algorithm.

3. [Process next node.] Set REAR ← UC(REAR) and for $i = 1, 2, \ldots, n$(REAR) do the following steps:
   a) $X \leftarrow a$(REAR, i)
   b) If (X is a pointer) and (TAG(X) = −), then set TAG(X) ← +, set UC(FRONT) ← X, and set FRONT ← X.
4. [Return for more.] Go back to step 2.

6.3.2 Compacting

Suppose now that nodes such that TAG(N) = − are reserved and nodes such that TAG(N) = + are free. Suppose we wish to move all reserved nodes into one end of memory so they sit adjacent to one another in a contiguous sequence, while all free space is concentrated at the other end of memory. If we do this, we must also update the pointer fields in the reserved nodes so that they point to the new addresses to which their referents have been moved, instead of the former addresses at which they used to reside. Otherwise, the linking topology of the pointer fields would not be left invariant.

Such a process is called *compacting*. Some authors advance the opinion that compacting algorithms are too expensive to include in storage allocation packages. One often heard argument is that, when a memory allocation algorithm fails to grant a request, the algorithm is nearly out of space and, if memory were compacted and the request granted, then, in many cases, the memory would soon overflow anyway. On the other hand, as Haddon and Waite [1967] put it, "compaction is used only when the program would otherwise fail, and in such circumstances no expedient is too expensive." Haddon and Waite give the following (pathological) example, to emphasize this point. Suppose 20,000 words of memory are allocated to contain one- and two-word elements, and suppose odd-numbered words are occupied by one-word elements. Then one cannot allocate a two-word element, even though half of the memory is free, in the absence of compacting. Perhaps a reconciliation of these opposite viewpoints can be achieved by observing that, if an allocation attempt fails, then, if the memory is nearly fully reserved, it is preferable to try to obtain more memory before compacting (if such an alternative is available). With this precaution, we proceed to study a utility-cell algorithm for compacting. Other approaches to compacting are given by Haddon and Waite (who use an address correspondence table), Cheney [1970] (which has been studied in Chapter 5), Wegbreit [1972a], Fitch and Norman [1978] (which improves on the Haddon–Waite method), and Morris [1978] (see Exercise 6.5).

Algorithm 6.7 below uses the utility cells in each reserved block that needs to be moved to contain the forwarding address where it will reside in the future. It is a three-pass procedure consisting of three linear sweeps. During the first pass, the forwarding addresses are computed from a running total of space needed by the

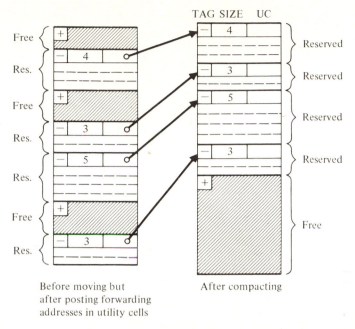

TAG SIZE   UC

Before moving but
after posting forwarding
addresses in utility cells

After compacting

FIGURE 6.11

reserved blocks, and these addresses are posted to the utility cells of each reserved block. During the second pass, the pointer fields in reserved blocks are updated to point to the future addresses of their referents. Finally, during a third pass, the reserved blocks are moved to their new addresses in the compacted end of memory. Figure 6.11 illustrates the noncompacted and compacted stages of the Algorithm.

Algorithm 6.7 *Compacting multilinked nodes.*

We assume that the nodes are allocated in a region of memory $M_1 \le \alpha \le M_2$.

1. [Initialize.] Set $P \leftarrow M_1$ and $S \leftarrow M_1$ (S contains a running total of the sizes of the reserved blocks).

2. [Store forwarding addresses.] If $\text{TAG}(P) = -$, then set $\text{UC}(P) \leftarrow S$, and set $S \leftarrow S + \text{SIZE}(P)$.

3. [Advance to next.] Now set $P \leftarrow P + \text{SIZE}(P)$ (to advance to next block). If now, $P \le M_2$, then return to step 2. Otherwise, set $P \leftarrow M_1$ and continue at step 4.

4. [Update pointers.] If $\text{TAG}(P) = -$, then for $i = 1, 2, \ldots, n(P)$ do the following step:
   a) If $a(P, i)$ is a pointer, then set $a(P, i) \leftarrow \text{UC}(a(P, i))$.

5. [Advance to next.] Set $P \leftarrow P + \text{SIZE}(P)$. If now, $P \leq M_2$, then return to step 4. Otherwise, set $P \leftarrow M_1$ and continue at step 6.

6. [Move reserved blocks.] If $\text{TAG}(P) = -$, then move the words from P through $P + \text{SIZE}(P) - 1$ to the new locations $\text{UC}(P)$ through $\text{UC}(P) + \text{SIZE}(P) - 1$.

7. [Advance to next.] Set $P \leftarrow P + \text{SIZE}(P)$. If $P \leq M_2$, return to step 6. Otherwise, continue at step 8.

8. [Set up free block.] If $S \leq M_2$, then (create a free block at the M_2 end of memory). Set $\text{TAG}(S) \leftarrow +$, $\text{SIZE}(S) \leftarrow (M_2 + 1 - S)$. Now the algorithm terminates.

6.3.3 Copying

Sometimes we need to copy a directed graph consisting of node $P0$ and all nodes accessible from it via any path of pointers. A special case of compacting consists of copying all structures in use into a fresh region of contiguous memory. This can be especially valuable in paging environments where such copying tends to place the nodes of a connected component (in level order) on the same page.

Algorithm 6.8 below is a utility-cell method for copying. To create the copy of a multilinked directed graph, we must create a linking topology that is graph-isomorphic to the graph of the original structure, using a disjoint set of newly allocated nodes. To do this, we first create the Thorelli chain for the structure accessible from start node $P0$, using Algorithm 6.6. Then we traverse the Thorelli chain, and insert, after every node N on the chain, a blank freshly allocated node of size identical to the size of N. Thus, odd positions in the chain are nodes of the structure to be copied, even nodes are new blank nodes of proper size, and all nodes are linked together into a common chain via pointers in their utility cells. We then pass down the chain and set up a graph-isomorphic linking topology in the new cells, while also copying nonpointer fields directly. Figure 6.12 illustrates the stages of this process.

Algorithm 6.8 *Copying a multilinked structure.*

This copies the connected component of nodes accessible from starting address $P0$ and leaves the address of the starting node of the copy in the variable COPY at termination.

1. [Construct chain.] Using Algorithm 6.6, construct the Thorelli chain for the structure with starting address $P0$. Then set $P \leftarrow P0$.

2. [Allocate storage for copy.] While $P \neq \Lambda$ do steps (a), (b), and (c):
   a) Allocate a block of storage of size $\text{SIZE}(P)$ words and store its address in Q.
   b) Set $\text{TAG}(Q) \leftarrow -$, $\text{SIZE}(Q) \leftarrow \text{SIZE}(P)$, and $n(Q) \leftarrow n(P)$.

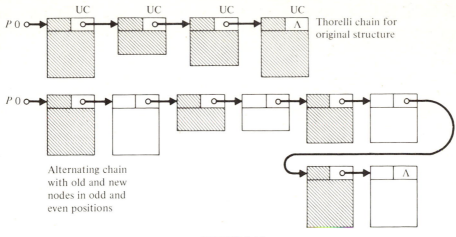

Thorelli chain for original structure

Alternating chain with old and new nodes in odd and even positions

FIGURE 6.12

   c) Then set TEMP ← UC(P), UC(P) ← Q, UC(Q) ← P ← TEMP (to insert the copy block on the chain and to advance the pointer P to the next node on the original chain.)

3. [Reinitialize.] Set P ← P0 (for another pass down the chain.)

4. [Set up fields in copy nodes.] If P = Λ, then set COPY ← UC(P0) and terminate the algorithm. Otherwise, set Q ← UC(P) and, for i = 1, 2, ..., n(P) do steps (a) and (b):
   a) If (a(P, i) is a pointer), then set a(Q, i) ← UC(a(P, i)).
   b) Otherwise, set a(Q, i) ← a(P, i).

5. [Advance to next.] Set P ← UC(Q) and go back to step 4.

6.3.4 Equality testing

In some applications, such as programming languages, we wish to test two structures for exact equality. If the structures are represented in the underlying storage with multilinked nodes of variable size, we face the problem, not only of ascertaining whether corresponding nonpointer fields contain identical information, but also of checking whether corresponding pointer fields contain pointers that correspond.

   Algorithm 6.9 below is a utility-cell algorithm for checking the equality of two structures formed from multilinked nodes. The sets of nodes for the two structures are assumed disjoint in memory. If the starting addresses for the nodes are given as values of the variables R and Q, we first construct the respective Thorelli chains for these structures using Algorithm 6.6. Then the two chains are merged so that odd nodes are from the R chain and even nodes are from the Q chain. All nodes on the merged chain are linked, as usual, through the utility-cell fields. It is then an easy matter to check for the correspondence between pointers of the two corresponding sets of nodes accessible from R and Q.

Algorithm 6.9 *Equality-testing of two multilinked structures.*

In the following, if the algorithm terminates unsuccessfully, the two structures accessible from R and Q are not equal, whereas successful termination implies equality.

1. [Construct chains.] Construct the Thorelli chains for the structures accessible from starting addresses R and Q using Algorithm 6.6.
2. [Merge chains.] $P \leftarrow R$. Now, while $R \neq \Lambda$ do the following:
   a) If $Q = \Lambda$, then the algorithm terminates unsuccessfully.
   b) Otherwise, TEMP $\leftarrow$ UC(R), UC(R) $\leftarrow Q$, $R \leftarrow$ TEMP, TEMP $\leftarrow$ UC(Q), UC(Q) $\leftarrow R$, and $Q \leftarrow$ TEMP.
3. [Chain lengths unequal?] If now $Q \neq \Lambda$, then the algorithm terminates unsuccessfully.
4. [Done?] If $P = \Lambda$, then the algorithm terminates successfully.
5. [Get next pair of nodes.] $R \leftarrow P$, $Q \leftarrow$ UC(R), $P \leftarrow$ UC(Q).
6. [Check for isomorphism.] If $n(R) \neq n(Q)$, then the algorithm terminates unsuccessfully. Otherwise, for $i = 1, 2, \ldots, n(R)$ do steps (a), (b), and (c):
   a) If ($a(R, i)$ and $a(Q, i)$ are both pointers) then if UC($a(R, i)$) $\neq a(Q, i)$, then the algorithm terminates unsuccessfully.
   b) If $a(R, i)$ and $a(Q, i)$ are not pointers, then, if $a(R, i) \neq a(Q, i)$, then the algorithm terminates unsuccessfully.
   c) If one of $a(R, i)$ and $a(Q, i)$ is a pointer and the other is not, then the algorithm terminates unsuccessfully.
7. [Continue processing.] Go back to step 4.

6.4 BIBLIOGRAPHIC NOTES

Isoda, Goto, and Kimura [1971] study a bit-table technique for allocating storage dynamically in blocks of size 2^n.

Robson [1971] and Robson [1974] are two papers studying the amount of storage needed in dynamic storage allocation methods. In Robson [1971] it is proved that the minimal amount of storage needed for any strategy is bounded below by a function that rises logarithmically with the size of blocks used. In Robson [1974] the amount of storage needed to operate without risk of allocation failure is considered. Upper and lower bounds stronger than those given in Robson [1971] are given. Garey, Graham, and Ullman [1972] study the worst cases for dynamic memory allocation algorithms.

Another early paper mentioning multiword items, in addition to Ross [1961] cited earlier, is Comfort [1964].

An interesting general discussion concerning multilinked structures and dynamic memory allocation is WODON [1969].

A challenging problem, in general, is to discover an arrangement whereby a set of fields of fixed length, but of varying sizes may be packed into contiguous words in a block of storage so as to minimize the total block length required. It is understood that the fields may not cross word boundaries, and that waste may occur in a word the sum of whose field lengths is less than the word length. This problem is equivalent to the *bin-packing* problem, and has been shown to be *NP*-complete so that, at the moment, only exponential algorithms are known for finding the optimum. However, it has been discovered that if we are willing to settle for slightly less than the optimum arrangement, polynomial-time algorithms exist that are considerably faster. (See JOHNSON [1974].)

Recently, ROBSON [1977] has discovered an improved algorithm for copying cyclic structures that operates in bounded workspace.

EXERCISES

1. (Hirschberg [1973b]) Using Hirschberg's generalized Fibonacci recurrence relation,

$$Size_n = Size_{n-1} + Size_{n-k},$$

   and given an integer m, show that it is possible to choose k and initial values for $Size_i$ $(0 \leq i \leq k - 1)$ so that $Size_n$ generates all block sizes $1, 2, \ldots, m$.

2. (Stack traversal) Devise an algorithm to perform a preorder traversal of the spanning tree of a multilinked structure using an auxiliary pushdown stack.

3. (Schorr–Waite–Deutsch) Devise a link-inversion traversal algorithm for traversing a multilinked structure that uses only utility cells to contain an integer that specifies which pointer is currently inverted in each node under partial completion of traversal of its descendants in the preorder spanning tree, but that uses bounded workspace otherwise.

4. (Fast-Fit AVL tree search) Let T be an AVL tree and let K be a search key. Devise an algorithm to search T to find the node of T containing the least key K' such that $K \leq K'$, if such a node exists.

5. (Morris [1978]) Devise an improved compacting algorithm that works in time proportional to the size of the storage area, that uses one bit for each pointer, and that reversibly encodes all pointers pointing to a given location as a chain emanating from the pointed to location through the pointing locations and terminating with the pointed to location's transplanted address.

6. (T. Dear) Devise a Worst-Fit policy for step 1 of Algorithm 6.1. Are there distributions of request sizes for which this policy does not perform well, and if so, what are they?

7. (Fitch and Norman [1978]) Using the idea of building a relocation map give a variation of the Haddon and Waite compacting algorithm that needs only

bounded workspace and that has running time proportional to the size of the heap.

8. (S. Reiss) Devise an algorithm for insertion of a free block of size n into a Fast-Fit free storage index consisting of five exact lists and one AVL-tree index.

9. (Equality testing) Devise an equality testing algorithm for testing the equality of two multilinked structures R and S, where the nodes of R and S need not be disjoint, but rather can be shared in some instances.

10. (Tree-indexed segregated storage) Are there distributions of request sizes for which the tree-indexed segregated storage techniques of Subsection 6.2.3.1 outperforms any of the sequential-fit policies?

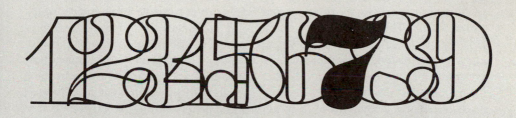

7.1 INTRODUCTION AND MOTIVATION

Strings are finite sequences of symbols. It is important to study techniques for representing and manipulating strings because of their widespread use.

A moment's glance at some of these uses reveals quite a diversity. First of all, strings are the basic medium in which programs are written and transmitted to the computer for subsequent linguistic analysis and execution. Strings can be composed into text which, in turn, is the medium manipulated by text editors and document-preparation systems. Strings are the principal medium of exchange in input/output transactions between a central processor and peripherals such as card readers, terminals, and printers. They are used in fields of records within files to store alphanumeric information, and within tables to name items and represent stored values. They are used in programming languages for names of identifiers, labels, and procedures, and are often a species of data that can be stored, printed, and, in some instances, manipulated. In assembly-language implementations they are used in symbol tables and in macro expansions. They are converted to and from internal forms for numbers, lists, arrays, and other data that can be expressed as linear strings in the text of programs. Some programming languages, such as COMIT and SNOBOL, are oriented toward string processing and provide ease of expression of string-processing programs. The study of the lexical and syntactical analyses of structures expressed initially in string form is an important part of the theory and construction of compilers and assemblers. Theoretically, strings can be used as a general-purpose computational medium since any computable function can be expressed as a string-manipulation process using, for example, Markov algorithms.

Within the computer, many different representations of strings are used in these many different contexts. Some are ideal for fast manipulation but are wasteful of space. Others use space efficiently but require more time to manipulate.

It is important to be able to select a string representation for a given intended application which has appropriate properties in the tradeoff between efficiency in time, utilization of space, and ease of programming and debugging. This chapter explores a number of possible representation choices and presents algorithms for just a few of the many string-manipulation tasks.

†7.2 REPRESENTATIONS OF STRINGS IN CONTIGUOUS STORAGE

We first consider methods for representing the successive characters of a string in contiguous memory in the same order that they occur in the string. That is, we consider *order-preserving*, *contiguous* representations of strings.

---

† Advanced readers: Skip to Section 7.3.1.

7.2.1 Fixed-length character codes

Given a set of N distinct characters, a popular method of providing binary character codes is to use bit strings of length $k = \lceil \lg N \rceil$ (that is, k is the least integer such that $N \leq 2^k$) and to assign distinct bit strings to distinct characters. Thus, all characters are represented by binary codes of the same length, and this length is the minimum uniform length that can provide a distinct code for each distinct character.

Some examples of codes based on this principle are ASCII (the American Standard Code for Information Interchange), EBCDIC (the Extended Binary-Coded Decimal Interchange Code), Hollerith, BCD (or Binary Coded Decimal), SIXBIT, and various codes for punched paper tape.

ASCII is an eight-bit code of which one bit is a parity bit, leaving seven bits for the character code. If the number of bits in the character code is odd, the parity bit is set to 1; otherwise the parity bit is set to 0. Hence, ASCII codes can represent $2^7 = 128$ distinct characters. When used in computer storage, the parity bit is sometimes omitted, so that ASCII characters can be treated as seven bits long. BCD is a code six bits long used for magnetic tapes, and EBCDIC (extended BCD) is an eight-bit code used in some IBM series machines. Hollerith is a code for punched cards and specifies the correspondence between a character and the punched-hole pattern in a column of a card.

7.2.2 Packed strings

Given a designated character code and assuming a word oriented machine, the packed representation of a string S consists in placing the successive character codes for characters of S in successive words, with as many character codes per word as possible. For example, in Fig. 7.1, the successive characters of the string "PACKEDSTRING" are shown packed six to a word in two consecutive words. Sometimes the character codes fit evenly in a word, as in packing the eight-bit EBCDIC codes into 32-bit, or 16-bit words. Sometimes, the character codes do not fit evenly, as in packing seven-bit ASCII codes into a 36-bit word. In this case, the left-over bits can be placed at the right- or lefthand boundary of the word and can occasionally be used for some separate useful purpose, such as marking bits for use in garbage collection.

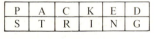

FIGURE 7.1

7.2.3 Unpacked strings

The unpacked representation for a string S consists of storing successive character codes for successive characters of S one to a word in contiguous words. To

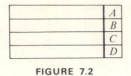

FIGURE 7.2

promote efficiency, whenever the integer values of the codes are to be used in indexing operations, the character codes are stored in the low-order bits of the word. Figure 7.2 gives an example of the unpacked representation for the string "ABCD".

The unpacked representation of strings is ideal for situations where speed is of the essence and low storage utilization is tolerable, since the unpacked representation wastes considerable space, although it requires no shifting, masking, or conversion for use in fast indexing and replacement operations.

7.2.4 Radix-*N* representations

Given N characters in an alphabet from which strings are to be composed, it is sometimes useful to view strings as base-N numbers, with each letter of the alphabet standing for a different base-N digit. One then computes the binary representation of the base-N number corresponding to the string, and stores this binary number.

An example where this technique pays off is in storing FORTRAN identifiers in a 32-bit-word machine. Each FORTRAN identifier can consist of from one to six letters and digits beginning with a letter. If an ASCII or EBCDIC character code is used, the packed representation yields a storage utilization factor of at most four characters per 32-bit word. However, assuming an alphabet of 26 letters, 10 digits, and 1 blank, for a total of 37 possible characters, one can convert each identifier to a corresponding base-37 number. Given that there are less than 37^6 possible identifiers, it turns out to be possible to represent each one with a distinct binary number of 32 bits, since $37^6 < 2^{32}$. Hence, one can store FORTRAN identifiers one to a word, using radix-37 representation. Similarly, using radix 37, one could represent three-character strings, one to a word, on a 16-bit machine (since $37^3 < 2^{16}$).

In general, strings of length k over an N-character alphabet will fit in a word of b-bits, using the radix-N representation, if $\lceil k \lg N \rceil \le b$.

7.2.5 Karlgren's representation

On some occasions, one wants to use n-bit character codes of uniform size to represent all characters of an alphabet of more than 2^n symbols. For example, one might want to pack six characters per word on a 36-bit machine using six-bit codes to represent symbols in an alphabet of size 100. Karlgren's idea is to use some of the n-bit codes as "shift" or "shift-lock" symbols (see Karlgren [1963]). Then each of the remaining n-bit codes can represent distinct "uppercase" and "lowercase" symbols, depending on the case currently established. The appearance of a case symbol establishes a case for a specified scope. The use of the "shift-lock" symbol establishes "uppercase" mode until uppercase mode is revoked by the appearance of a "shift-release" code (or "lowercase" code). The use of a "shift" code specifies that the immediately following code is to be interpreted in "uppercase" no matter what current case has been established.

For example, let A be an alphabet consisting of lowercase letters, digits, and a blank. To represent uppercase alphabetic characters, one might designate "/" as a "shift" code, # as a "shift-lock" code, and = as a "shift-release" code. By convention, any lowercase letter preceded by / stands for the corresponding uppercase letter, all letters bounded by # and = are designated as uppercase letters, and all letters bounded by = and # are taken to be lowercase letters except those immediately preceded by /. Thus, for example, the string "/the #ibm c=orporation" represents the string "The IBM Corporation". Karlgren points out that more than two cases might be convenient. For example, a four-case system might consist of lower gothic, upper gothic, lower italic, and upper italic. In this case, in addition to characters designating shifts into upper- and lowercase, separate shift characters would be used to designate shifts into gothic and italic, respectively. With the addition of one more device, the characters used to designate shifts to and from various cases can serve dual purposes. If not preceded by the special character ¢, a shift character designates a shift of case. However, if preceded by the character ¢, a shift character stands for itself (*viz.*, it designates a symbol to be printed rather than a change of mode of interpretation of succeeding characters). For example, the string "/numerator¢/#d=enominator" represents the string "Numerator/Denominator". Karlgren's techniques are commonly used in contemporary text editors wherein one wants to compose text in an extended character set using a terminal with a restricted character set (for example, composing text to be printed in upper- and lowercase on a terminal offering only uppercase characters, or composing text to be printed in a variety of different type fonts and sizes from a terminal offering only one type font and size).

One might inquire under what conditions Karlgren's representation produces a net saving of space over standard techniques since, in many cases, two character codes of size k bits are used to represent the equivalent of one code of size $(k + 1)$ bits using standard uniform-length coding. Karlgren's analysis makes use of conditional probabilities. Suppose one divides an alphabet into two cases: u, for "upper", and ℓ, for "lower". Suppose, then, that one agrees to use a case-shift code only at boundaries where case shifts occur. Also, suppose that the basic code is k

bits long, and that we are given the following conditional probabilities:

$P_{u|\ell}$ = probability a lowercase letter follows an uppercase letter,

$P_{\ell|u}$ = probability an uppercase letter follows a lowercase letter,

$P_{u|u}$ = probability an uppercase letter follows an uppercase letter,

$P_{\ell|\ell}$ = probability a lowercase letter follows a lowercase letter.

Then, it costs $2 \times k$ bits to represent each letter whose case differs from its predecessor's case, and k bits to represent each letter whose case is the same as that of its predecessor. Hence, we can write an expression for the average number of bits k' per character:

$$k' = (P_{u|\ell} + P_{\ell|u}) \times 2 \times k + (P_{u|u} + P_{\ell|\ell}) \times k$$
$$= (2 \times P_{\neq} + P_{=}) \times k = (P_{\neq} + 1) \times k,$$

where

$$P_{\neq} = P_{u|\ell} + P_{\ell|u}, \qquad P_{=} = P_{u|u} + P_{\ell|\ell}, \qquad \text{and} \qquad P_{\neq} + P_{=} = 1.$$

Now suppose the size of alphabet A is n symbols ($n = |A|$). Using the standard coding technique (of Section 7.2.1), we require $S_1 = \lceil \lg n \rceil$ bits. Using Karlgren's representation, we require $S_2 = \lceil \lg ((n/2) + 2) \rceil$ bits. Thus, if $P_{\neq}$ is the probability that a symbol belongs to a case different from the preceding symbol, then Karlgren's representation is an improvement only if

$$(1 + P_{\neq}) \times S_2 < S_1.$$

In particular, this happens whenever $P_{\neq} < [(S_1/S_2) - 1]$. For example, supposing the alphabet A consists of 100 symbols, we would have

$$S_1 = \lceil \lg 100 \rceil = 7 \qquad \text{and} \qquad S_2 = \lceil \lg (\tfrac{100}{2} + 2) \rceil = 6,$$

so that Karlgren's representation would pay off whenever $P_{\neq} < \tfrac{1}{6}$.

Generalizing from two cases to c mutually exclusive cases (wherein the current case is specified by the most recently encountered of c distinct case codes), let

$$S_c = \left\lceil \lg \left(\frac{n}{c} + c \right) \right\rceil.$$

Then, c cases are more economical than c' cases provided

$$(1 + P_c) \times S_c < (1 + P_{c'}) \times S_{c'},$$

where P_c and $P_{c'}$ are the respective probabilities that case shifts occur between adjacent symbols.

A further generalization is required in order to handle the situation encountered in practical applications such as computer typesetting systems. Here,

TABLE 7.1

Source of sample	Total nonshift characters in sample	Number of different fonts	Number of different sizes	Font changes	Size changes	Case changes
Orwell's *1984* (p. 45, Harcourt-Brace edition)	1741	2	2	2	3	88
Shakespeare's *Hamlet*, Act I, Scene V	637	4	2	32	2	50
Chaucer's *Canterbury Tales*, "The Miller's Tale"	1398	3	4	6	3	100
Knuth, *The Art of Computer Programming*, Volume 1, p. 445 (first edition)	1954	5	2	62	34	104

one typically has a number of different type *fonts* (such as gothic, italic, boldface, special symbols), each of which can be printed in several *sizes* (such as 5-point, 7-point, 14-point), and each of which has a set of uppercase symbols and lower-case symbols. Hence, a triple of the form ⟨font, size, case⟩ is required in order to specify the interpretation of character codes. The three components of this triple can be varied independently. One can change from upper- to lowercase without changing the font or the size; one can change the font while leaving the size and case invariant; or one can change the size while leaving the font and case the same. Hence, the appearance of a case-shift code signals a change in one of the three components of the triple. To change two or more components, two or more consecutive shift codes are required. At most three consecutive shift codes are required to change from any arbitrary value of the triple to any other.

It is instructive to look at some numbers derived from samples of actual print, and to investigate the savings in storage that can result from using Karlgren's representation. Some findings are presented in Tables 7.1 and 7.2.

TABLE 7.2

Source of of sample	Number of single-shift codes	Number of occurrences of two consecutive shifts	Number of occurrences of three consecutive shifts	Probability of a case shift	Percent case shifts
Orwell	85	4	0	5.1	5.1
Shakespeare	82	1	0	13.0	11.7
Chaucer	97	3	0	7.3	7.2
Knuth	57	31	27	5.9	9.3

Four samples of text were investigated: a novel, a play, a poem, and a technical exposition. The largest percentage of font shifts occurred in the play (38% of all shift codes were font shifts). The largest percentage of size changes occurred in the technical exposition (17% of all shift codes were size changes). In all but the technical exposition, more than 95% of the shifts between successive characters of the text required only one shift code, and less than 5% required two or more consecutive shifts. By contrast, in the technical exposition, 50.4% of all shifts required two or more consecutive shift codes. Thus, there can be more than a factor-of-10 difference between technical exposition and running linguistic text, in the requirement to use two or more consecutive codes to signal a required shift.

Let's make the trial assumption that a font of a given size consists of 128 characters (64 uppercase and 64 lowercase). Then, using fixed-length character codes, we can compute the number of bits required to encode characters for each of the four samples of text. (See Table 7.3.)

TABLE 7.3

Source	Number of fonts	Number of distinct characters = x	Bits required for fixed-length code = $\lceil \lg x \rceil$
Orwell	2	$2 \times 128 = 256$	8
Shakespeare	4	$4 \times 128 = 512$	9
Chaucer	3	$3 \times 128 = 384$	9
Knuth	5	$5 \times 128 = 640$	10

Using a Karlgren representation with a six-bit code augmented by a set of shift codes, the savings in storage compared to the packed representation using fixed-length codes are as shown in Table 7.4. The savings appear to be most worthwhile when many type fonts are required, even if the percentage of shift codes approaches 10% and even if more than 50% of the shifts consist of two or more consecutive shift codes.

TABLE 7.4

	Bits required for packed representation with fixed-length codes	Bits required for Karlgren representation	Bits saved	Percent storage saved
Orwell	$8 \times 1741 = 13928$	$6 \times 1834 = 11004$	2924	21%
Shakespeare	$9 \times 637 = 5733$	$6 \times 721 = 4326$	1407	24.5%
Chaucer	$9 \times 1398 = 12582$	$6 \times 1507 = 9042$	3540	28.1%
Knuth	$10 \times 1954 = 19540$	$6 \times 2154 = 12924$	6616	33.9%

7.2.6 Huffman codes

Another idea for storing strings compactly is to measure the frequency of occurrence of various characters in a sample text, and to assign short codes to the most frequent symbols and longer codes to less frequent symbols in such a fashion as to minimize the total space required. This is the idea behind Huffman's code.

To see how this can be done, consider the following small example. Suppose that a text is composed of the letters S, I, P, O, and T, and suppose that the number of occurrences of these letters in the text is as given in Table 7.5.

We start with the frequencies (10, 29, 4, 9, 5) and rearrange them as (4, 5, 10, 29, 9) so that the first two frequencies (4 and 5) are the two smallest

TABLE 7.5

Letter	Frequency in sample
S	10
I	29
P	4
O	9
T	5

values. Then, we construct a binary tree from the two smallest values:

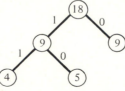

(1)

in which 4 and 5 are the values placed at the leaves, and in which the root contains the sum of the values at the leaves (4 + 5). We label the left branch "1" and we label the right branch "0". Returning to the sequence (4, 5, 10, 29, 9), we replace the first two terms (4 and 5) with their sum (9), and we rearrange the resulting sequence again so that the smallest values appear in the first two positions. This yields (9, 9, 10, 29). We again create a binary tree from the two smallest values:

(2)

with the root containing the sum of the values at the leaves. Then we substitute the tree (1) into the tree (2) to get the composed tree:

(3)

Continuing in this fashion, we return to the sequence (9, 9, 29, 10), replace the first two terms with their sum, and rearrange the sequence so that the two new smallest values appear first and second, getting (10, 18, 29). We again build a tree:

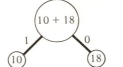

(4)

with the two smallest values at the leaves and their sum at the root, and we again compose tree (4) with tree (3) so as to substitute the root of (3) for a leaf of (4) that it matches, getting the composed tree:

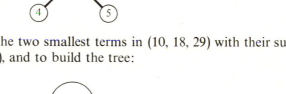

(5)

The final step is to replace the two smallest terms in (10, 18, 29) with their sum, getting the sequence (28, 29), and to build the tree:

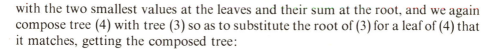

(6)

which can be composed with (5) by substituting the root of (5) for a leaf of (6) that it matches, getting the final composed tree:

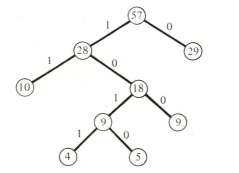

(7)

We now convert this final composed tree into a *Huffman coding tree* by making a one-for-one replacement of the frequencies at the leaves of (7) with letters having those frequencies specified in Table 7.5. This gives, for the final tree, Fig. 7.3.

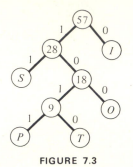

FIGURE 7.3

The coding tree in Fig. 7.3 is used to encode and decode strings in the alphabet $A = (S, I, P, O, T)$. The code assigned each letter is found by following the path from the root of the coding tree to the leaf containing the given letter and by reading the 0,1 labels along the path in succession. This results in the assignment of codes given in Table 7.6. Note that the most frequent letters have the shortest codes assigned and that the least frequent letters have the longest codes assigned.

TABLE 7.6

Letter	Code assigned	Frequency
S	1 1	10
I	0	29
P	1 0 1 1	4
O	1 0 0	9
T	1 0 1 0	5

To encode a string, we replace each letter with its corresponding code, using the correspondence in Table 7.6. Examples are:

String	Encoded string
S I P	1 1 0 1 0 1 1
T O P S	1 0 1 0 1 0 0 1 0 1 1 1 1
I T S	0 1 0 1 0 1 1

To decode an encoded string S, we use the successive bits of S to find a path through the coding tree of Fig. 7.3, starting at the root. A 1 means "turn right" and a 0 means "turn left." Each time we reach a leaf, we emit the letter the leaf contains, and we return to the root of the coding tree to start a fresh path using the next bit of the encoded string in sequence. For example, the encoded string

$$1 \ 1 \ 1 \ 0 \ 1 \ 1 \ 1 \ 0 \ 0 \ 1 \ 0 \ 1 \ 0 \ 1 \ 1$$

decodes as "SPOTS" because the initial 1 1 leads to an S, the adjacent 1 0 1 1 leads to a P, the succeeding 1 0 0 yields O, the next 1 0 1 0 yields T, and the final 1 1 yields S.

The following algorithm constructs Huffman coding trees for a set of $n \geq 2$ frequencies $(f_1, f_2, \ldots, f_n)$.

Algorithm 7.1 *Construction of Huffman coding tree on* $(f_1, f_2, \ldots, f_n)$.
1. [Base case.] If $n = 2$, then terminate, with the result

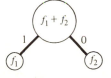

2. [Recursion step.] If $n > 2$, then rearrange $(f_1, f_2, \ldots, f_n)$ so that f_1 and f_2 are the two smallest values. Let T_1 be the Huffman coding tree that results from calling the algorithm recursively on $(f_1 + f_2, f_3, \ldots, f_n)$, and let T_2 be the Huffman coding tree that results from calling the algorithm recursively on (f_1, f_2). Terminate the algorithm with the tree that results from substituting T_2 for some leaf of T_1 having the value $f_1 + f_2$.

Note that Algorithm 7.1 does not necessarily produce a unique result corresponding to a given set of input frequencies $(f_1, f_2, \ldots, f_n)$, since step 1 does not specify an ordering on (f_1, f_2) and since step 2 permits substitution of T_2 for any of the leaves in T_1 with value $f_1 + f_2$ in case there are two or more leaves with the value $f_1 + f_2$. For example, the two Huffman coding trees in Fig. 7.4 could result from calling Algorithm 7.1 on the set of frequencies (2, 3, 4, 5).

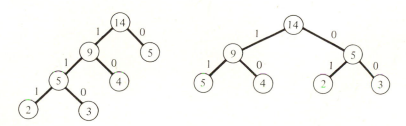

FIGURE 7.4

As we shall show in a moment, both trees in Fig. 7.4 provide minimal-length encodings under the assumed set of frequencies. However, the right tree in Fig. 7.4 is better balanced than the left tree in Fig. 7.4. In fact, Schwartz [1964] shows how to construct a Huffman coding tree that is as well balanced as possible among all possible Huffman coding trees that fit a given set of input frequencies $(f_1, f_2, \ldots, f_n)$, in the sense that it has the smallest depth among all the possible valid solution trees.

To complete our discussion of Huffman codes, we would like to show that Huffman codes minimize the length of encoded messages with character frequencies matching those used in the construction of the coding tree. The relevant measure to minimize is called the *weighted path length* of the coding tree. This is a sum of the form $\sum_{1 \le i \le n} f_i \ell_i$, where f_i is the frequency of the ith letter and ℓ_i is the length of the path (in number of edges) from the root of the coding tree to the leaf containing the ith letter. For example, the weighted path length of the coding tree in Fig. 7.3 is

$$10 \cdot 2 + 4 \cdot 4 + 5 \cdot 4 + 9 \cdot 3 + 29 \cdot 1 = 112.$$

The reason why the weighted path length is the relevant measure to minimize is that it is the sum of the frequencies times the length of the encoding which, when divided by the sum of the frequencies, yields the average length per character (in bits).

Theorem 7.1 A Huffman coding tree for the frequencies $(f_1, f_2, \ldots, f_n)$ has minimum weighted path length $\sum_{1 \le i \le n} f_i \ell_i$ amongst all full binary trees with leaves $(f_1, f_2, \ldots, f_n)$.

Proof. We proceed by induction on n. For $n = 2$, the weighted path length of any full binary tree with leaves f_1 and f_2 is $f_1 + f_2$. Now let $n \ge 3$. Rearrange the frequencies f_i so that $f_1 \le f_2 \le \cdots \le f_n$. Since there are only a finite number of full binary trees with leaves $f_1, f_2, \ldots, f_n$ there must exist one, say T, with minimum weighted path length. Let N be an internal node of T at greatest distance from the root of T amongst all internal nodes of T. If f_1 and f_2 are not the frequencies contained in the leaves that are the children of N, then we can exchange the frequencies of the children of N, say f_i and f_j, with f_1 and f_2 without increasing the weighted path length of T. (Since $f_i \ge f_1$, exchanging $f_1 \leftrightarrow f_i$ could at worst decrease the weighted path length by moving f_i closer to the root and f_1 farther from the root. But since T is already minimal, its weighted path length cannot be made smaller. A similar argument holds regarding the possible exchange $f_2 \leftrightarrow f_j$.) Thus, we know that there is a tree of minimal weighted path length having a subtree of the form

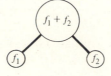

The induction will be complete if we can show that this tree is minimal if and only if the tree that results from dropping the leaves f_1 and f_2 is also minimal over the frequencies $(f_1 + f_2, \ldots, f_n)$. To establish the latter fact, we note that, in Huffman coding trees such as those of Fig. 7.4, the number contained in any internal node N is the sum of the numbers in the leaves of the subtree rooted at N. Therefore, the number in each leaf L is a summand of every number in each internal node on the path from the root to L. Consequently, the weighted path length of a Huffman coding tree can be obtained by adding the values of all of its internal nodes. (For example, the sum of the internal-node values of the tree in Fig. 7.3 is $9 + 18 + 28 + 57 = 112$.) Hence, using summations of the values of internal nodes, if W is the weighted path length of a tree T with subtree

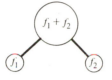

and W' is the weighted path length of the tree T' that results from dropping leaves f_1 and f_2 from T, then $W = W' + (f_1 + f_2)$, since

$$\left(f_1 + f_2\right)$$

is an internal node of T but not of T'. From this, we can see that T has minimum weighted path length if and only if T' does also, since their weighted path lengths differ by the constant $f_1 + f_2$. Thus, the existence of a tree of weighted path length smaller than either would lead, by direct construction, to the existence of a tree of weighted path length smaller than the other.   ∎

It is worth noting that the use of Huffman codes depends on having error-free storage and transmission media. If a bit in a Huffman encoding is dropped or spuriously changed, the entire decoding process can be thrown off. (Interestingly, however, simulation experiments reveal that Huffman coding trees have "self-correcting" properties such that erroneous decoding caused by a changed bit tends to die out after a short while, and normal correct decoding resumes (see Exercise 7.2).)

It is possible to design codes that contain enough information to detect and correct for some specified level of errors. If $A = a_1 a_2 \cdots a_n$ and $B = b_1 b_2 \cdots b_n$ are two sequences of n bits, we define the *Hamming distance* between A and B to be the number of places in which the bits in A and B differ. For instance, if $A = 01101$ and $B = 11001$, the Hamming distance between A and B is 2, because the first and third bits of A and B differ while the others are identical. Suppose we devise a set of n-bit encodings for the letters of the alphabet, and suppose the Hamming distance between the encodings for any pair of letters is 3 or more. Now suppose we send or store code C for a letter L in an unreliable medium, and suppose a bit in C is changed to its complement, yielding the damaged code C'. Then the Hamming distance between C and C' is 1, but the Hamming distance between C' and the code for any letter different from L will be 2 or more, since C differed from all codes for letters other than L by at least three to begin with. We might infer that C' is an erroneous version of C, and correct it back to C, since C' is closer to C than to any other code, using Hamming distance as a measure. The paper by Hamming [1950] stimulated much work in this direction. Information on error-detecting and -correcting codes can be found in Berztiss [1975], Birkhoff and Bartee [1970], Stone [1973], and Peterson and Weldon [1961].

7.2.7 Composing Huffman codes with Karlgren's representation

To help save space in string representations, one can first find a Karlgren representation using shift codes. Then one can conduct a frequency analysis of the text, and Huffman-encode the Karlgren codes.

The Karlgren representation works by exploiting the conditional probabilities of one subset in a partition following characters in another disjoint subset of the partition. The Huffman code works by exploiting the unconditional probabilities of occurrences of characters, with less probable characters assigned to longer codes. Using composition, the advantages of both systems can be used at once.

7.2.8 Encoding blanks and compressing decks

In some forms of text, strings of contiguous blanks occur frequently. An example is a card deck for a FORTRAN program. Many FORTRAN statements are short in length (Knuth [1971a]) and, when they are punched on cards, most of a card can frequently be left blank. Important savings in internal computer representations can be achieved by the simple device of encoding such strings of blanks specially. For example, one could replace a string of K blanks whenever $K \geq 3$, by the special escape character \$ followed by two digits $d_1 d_2$ representing the value of K.

Another example of repetitive character suppression is the *Crunch* representation, originally invented by D. J. Farber at Bell Laboratories. In the Crunch representation, the successive characters of a card are divided up into fields, such that each field ends with a contiguous string of blanks. The fields are then represented with the blanks removed and the nonblanks present, as follows: Let b stand for a blank, and suppose a character string is given as:

$$X\ 1\ b = Y + b\ b\ b\ 2\ 5\ b\ b\ b\ b.$$

This is divided into fields as follows:

$X\ 1\ b$	$= Y + b\ b\ b$	$2\ 5\ b\ b\ b\ b$
Field 1	Field 2	Field 3

such that each field is a string whose tail is a substring of one or more blanks and whose head is a substring of zero or more contiguous nonblanks. The fields are then encoded in the form

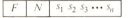

where F is the field length, N is the number of nonblank characters to follow, and $s_1 s_2 \cdots s_n$ are the nonblanks in the field. Thus, the example above would be encoded as follows:

where § is an end-of-line character.

Farber reports that a 7- or 8-to-1 savings in space resulted from the Crunch representation of FORTRAN decks. Half of the space is saved by converting from the "row binary" card representation to "column binary". The row binary representation of cards on the IBM 704–709 series machines consisted in taking two 36-bit words to encode each of the twelve rows of a Hollerith card. Only the first 72 columns of an 80-column card could be represented this way, so, by convention, the last eight columns were not represented. Thus, it took 24 words to encode a card. But since Hollerith has only 64 characters, it is possible to encode the symbol in each card column in 6-bits, yielding 6 characters per 36-bit word, or 12 words per card, in "column binary". An additional factor of 3.5 to 4 results from blank suppression in typical FORTRAN decks.

The Crunch representation was later used as the basis for IBM's *Prest* decks.

A more elaborate encoding for card decks came from the Share 709 Operating System's technique, called *Squoze* decks. This technique afforded approximately a 10:1 savings, according to Boehm and Steel [1959]. A Squoze deck represents 709 assembly code in a form that resembles the first pass of a conventional assembler. Symbols of up to six characters are stored in radix-50 representation in an ordered symbol table, and require only 34 of the 36 bits in a 36-bit word. Operation codes require either six bits or ten bits, as follows: (1) the 32 most frequently used instructions are encoded in five bits; (2) all others are encoded in nine bits; and (3) a distinguishing bit is added to tell which instruction category the code belongs to. The mean number of bits per op-code achieved was $7\frac{1}{2}$ bits. A Squoze deck consists of preface and introductory descriptions regarding layout and loading information, a dictionary of symbols and their associated formats, and a text consisting of 709 instruction descriptions. Some have maintained that the radix-50 encoding of identifiers was a bad choice of a great deal of conversion time for a two-bit saving, and that it could have been ignored.

These early case histories should demonstrate that a few commonsense compression techniques can buy very significant savings in space in practical circumstances.

7.3 STRING CONVERSIONS

Strings are often converted to and from other internal representations. There are several noteworthy string-conversion processes worth discussing. Among these are encrypting, fast code conversions, and a few subtleties of floating-point number conversions. Whenever we print an internal data representation on an external printed medium, we must perform a conversion into string form. However, printing will not be discussed here, since most techniques are relatively straightforward. Again, syntax analysis is a form of string conversion, as are assembly and compilation, in a very general sense. These topics will not be discussed here either since they are more properly covered in a treatment of parsing, translation, and compiling (see, for example, Gries [1971], and Aho and Ullman [1972], [1973]).

7.3.1 Encrypting

With the age of electronic mail and electronic funds transfer possibly about to dawn on us, it is important for computer scientists to provide publicly available technologies to ensure the privacy of electronic mail, the confidentiality of information stored in computer data banks, and some means for transmitting signed electronic transactions that prevents fraudulent manipulation.

Encrypting is a technique used to render the contents of messages and documents illegible to unintended readers. The basic notion of encrypting is to apply an invertible† transformation to text, rendering it into encrypted form called a *cryptogram* for storage or transmission, and later to apply the inverse transformation to the cryptogram to recover the original text, called *plaintext*, for subsequent use.

Encrypting transformations can be built up using one or both of the following two ideas: (a) *transposition* of the order of units of the text, and (b) *substitution* of units of text for corresponding units using an external correspondence table or function. The kind of transposition or substitution to be applied to units of the text is often controlled by a so-called *key*. Apart from periodically repeating keys, there are keys derived from the message, and nonrepeating keys, in usage.

In applying these two basic ideas, it is important to remove statistical properties of the text that could serve as a clue to cryptanalysts. For example, suppose a text is encrypted using Julius Caesar's method, in which each letter is replaced with one three places down in the alphabet (so A becomes D, B becomes E, etc.). Such a *monoalphabetic* substitution, as it is called, does not alter the frequencies of distinct letters. Thus, if you happen to know that the plaintext was in English, and that, in English, the most frequently used letter is E, then you might make the

---

† F. L. Bauer has pointed out to the author that, more generally, a one-to-many mapping that is uniquely invertible (called a *homophone*) can be used.

guess that the most frequently used letter in the cryptogram is a substitute for E. Pairs of letters, called *digrams*, have distinct frequencies as well. In English, for instance, TH is the most commonly occurring letter pair. On the assumption of a set of guesses made at a given stage, certain puzzles suggest themselves. For instance, on the assumption of substituting E for the most frequent letter, could E?E? stand for EVEN, EYED, or EVER? Could E?E?? stand for EXERT, EVENT, or ELECT? Thus, monoalphabetic substitution does not disguise letters sufficiently to form the basis for a secure encrypting method. Polyalphabetic substitution, if used with a periodic key, is also unsafe, as was shown by Kasiski [1863] and Kerckhoffs [1883] in the 19th century.

The principle of rearranging the order of letters in a text also is susceptible to attack. For instance, suppose a block of n-bits is permuted by a device such as that shown in Fig. 7.5, called a permutation box (or P-box, for short). One might, at first, think that, for respectable n, such a P-box would provide too large a set of possible permutations of its input to cryptanalyze easily, since for an n-bit input, $n!$ permutations are possible. Yet, by feeding a P-box inputs with single ones and the rest zeros and seeing where the ones come out (as shown in Fig. 7.5), we find that only $n - 1$ experiments are required to learn the internal permutation in any of the $n!$ possible distinct P-boxes. This process is called "*tickling* the P-box with ones."

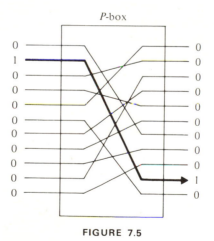

FIGURE 7.5

Of the two principles mentioned earlier, we have seen that *substitution* alone and *rearrangement* alone, if improperly used, can be susceptible to effective attack. Some combinations of them, e.g., polyalphabetic substitution with periodic key, followed by transposition, are much harder to break, but are also more complicated and thus more susceptible to manual, clerical errors. The use of a non-periodic key, however, in connection with a relatively simple polyalphabetic substitution, offers an interesting method (named after the sixteenth-century Frenchman Viginère), which is unbreakable if properly used, as shown by Shannon [1949]. Suppose we have a nonperiodic key consisting of an endless sequence of random digits, one portion of which reads 0910897625. Let us suppose the sender and receiver each have identical copies of the random-digit sequence, and that the sender wishes to send the receiver the message APRIL. The sender encrypts the message APRIL first by replacing each letter with a two-digit encoding representing the position of each letter in the alphabet. (Thus A becomes 01, B becomes 02, ..., and Z becomes 26). According to this, APRIL is 01 16 18 09 12. Now the numerical form of APRIL is placed beneath the portion of the random-digit sequence, as in Fig. 7.6, and digit pairs of the numerical form of APRIL are added modulo 100 to succcessive digit pairs of the random digit sequence.

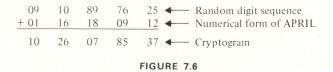

```
    09   10   89   76   25  ◄──── Random digit sequence
 +  01   16   18   09   12  ◄──── Numerical form of APRIL

    10   26   07   85   37  ◄──── Cryptogram
```

FIGURE 7.6

The resulting cryptogram is sent to the receiver, who proceeds to write it down above the identical portion of the random digit sequence used to encode the original. He then subtracts the successive pairs of digits in the random-sequence modulo 100 from the pairs of digits in the cryptogram, as indicated in Fig. 7.7.

```
    10   26   07   85   37  ◄──── Cryptogram
 −  09   10   89   76   25  ◄──── Random digit sequence

    01   16   18   09   12  ◄──── Numerical form of APRIL
```

FIGURE 7.7

It is essential to the method that, once a sequence of random digits has been used, it be discarded and never used again. Early in the 1920's the German Foreign Office embodied this concept into the "one-time pad." Two identical sheets of random digits are typed, one for the sender and one for the receiver. A number of such sheets are then bound into two identical pads. When a cipher clerk uses a sheet to encrypt a message, he tears off the sheet and throws it away. The receiver does likewise after using his corresponding sheet to decode the message. Even if a cryptanalyst gets to examine a cryptogram–plaintext pair and can thus recover a portion of the random-digit sequence used to encrypt the plaintext, this does him no good, since it cannot be used to discover any other portion of the random sequence. In essence, each different digit pair of the random sequence determines a different independent alphabetic substitution to be applied to the plaintext letter to which it corresponds, and thus the random sequence destroys statistical properties of the plaintext, rendering fruitless an attack based on frequency principles.

A more contemporary form of the one-time pad concept can be achieved using random-bit sequences, generated, say, with radioactive sources. Let A and B be two tapes filled with different random-bit sequences in this fashion. Let A' and B' be copies of tapes A and B. Suppose we send tapes A' and B' by separate courier from a sending station S to a receiving station R. Figure 7.8 shows how we can send messages from S to R.

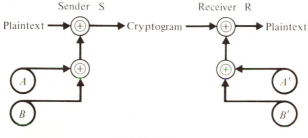

FIGURE 7.8

To see how the scheme depicted in Fig. 7.8 works, we recall the identity (*cf.* Exercise 1.8) characterizing the exclusive-or operator:

$$(x \oplus y) \oplus y = x.$$

If we let x be the binary representation of the plaintext and y be a random-bit sequence, we see that we can encrypt and send x as the cryptogram $(x \oplus y)$; and that, if the receiving station has a copy of y, it can recover the plaintext by computing

$$(x \oplus y) \oplus y.$$

In Fig. 7.8, the bit sequence y is obtained by computing the exclusive-or of the random-bit sequences on respective tapes A and B, for the sender, and respective copies A' and B' for the receiver. The use of two tapes enhances the security of the method since, if one of the two couriers is compromised into surrendering a copy of his tape, the single copy is still insufficient for decryption.

Since sending tapes and one-time pads is cumbersome and since, if more than one sender and one receiver are involved, problems of synchronizing the use of separate portions of the one-time pad become difficult, there is motivation for developing cipher machines that generate pseudo-random-bit sequences internally in response to given "keys". The internally generated bit sequences can then be exclusive-or'ed with the plaintext or cryptogram to encrypt or decrypt.

This theme can have highly sophisticated variations, the idea being to use a formula for generating the pseudo-random sequence sufficiently strong that, even given a cryptogram and its plaintext, a cryptanalytic procedure could not be devised to reconstruct and use the formula without spending centuries on the next generation of computers.

An example of a weak variation on this theme is the following. Let $p = p_1 p_2 \cdots p_m$ be a binary representation of a plaintext broken into m blocks of n bits per block, and let $k = k_1 k_2 \cdots k_m$ be a bit sequence composed of m blocks of n bits per block. Let the cryptogram c corresponding to plaintext p be defined as

$$c = (p \oplus k) = (p_1 \oplus k_1)(p_2 \oplus k_2) \cdots (p_m \oplus k_m).$$

If the n-bit blocks k_i of k are related to each other by the recurrence relation $k_i = V(k_{i-1})$, where k_1 is given as a "key" or "seed", we call c a *Vernam cipher of p with respect to key k_1*. An example of a recurrence relation $k_i = V(k_{i-1})$ is that given by a linear congruential random-number generator such as

$$k_i = (3141592631 \times k_{i-1} + 14522135347) \bmod 2^{35}. \tag{8}$$

If the user of a Vernam cipher supplies an integer key K and a plaintext p, then K can be used to generate a seed k_1 for a random-number generator such as (8); and (8) can be used repeatedly to generate $k_2, k_3, \ldots, k_m$ with which to encrypt p. (In general, linear congruential random-number generators are of the form

$$x_{i+1} = (a \cdot x_i + c) \bmod m,$$

where a is a multiplier, c is an increment, m is a modulus, and $x_0 = N$ is a starting value. An enlightened discussion is found in Knuth ([1969], pp. 9–24) where a number of important precautions are explored.) Exercise 7.4 explores the cryptanalysis of Vernam ciphers resting on publicly known random-number generators such as (8), under the usual assumption of a cryptogram–plaintext pair.

Returning now to the two earlier themes of transposition and substitution, we have seen how both transposition and substitution, considered alone, are subject to cryptanalytic attacks. Perhaps there is a way, however, to combine these two methods into a single method that is less vulnerable. This is the idea behind the so-called *block-substitution* methods. In a block-substitution method, we take an n-bit key k, we take a binary encoding of the plaintext $p = p_1 p_2 \cdots p_m$ broken into m blocks of n bits each, and we produce a cryptogram c from p by applying a block substitution $B(p_i, k)$ to each of the p_i ($1 \le i \le m$), getting

$$c = B(p_1, k)B(p_2, k) \cdots B(p_m, k).$$

The question arises of how we might select the properties of k and $B(p_i, k)$ so as to render this method resistant to attack. Figure 7.9 illustrates a substitution table for three-bit quantities called a substitution box (or S-box, for short).

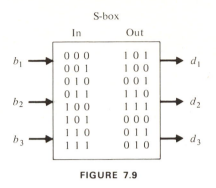

FIGURE 7.9

When a three-bit sequence $b_1 b_2 b_3$ is input to the S-box in Fig. 7.9, the row matching $b_1 b_2 b_3$ in the left column is determined, and the corresponding three-bit sequence $d_1 d_2 d_3$ in the right column of the same row is output on the output lines of the S-box. Thus, for instance, if 0 1 0 is input, 0 0 1 is the output. Returning to the P-box of Fig. 7.5, we can cascade layers of P-boxes and S-boxes to construct what Feistal [1973] calls a *product–cipher system*. Figure 7.10 illustrates this concept and shows what happens if a "tickle" bit is submitted to the leftmost input lines.

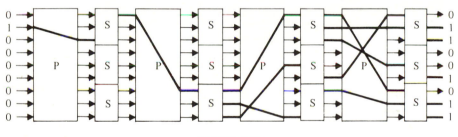

FIGURE 7.10

If the P-boxes are chosen to "diffuse" the results output by a layer of S-boxes, and the S-boxes are chosen to "confuse" the number of zeros and ones they transform, cryptographic strength can result; and the effect of several cascaded layers of P and S boxes can make every bit of the output depend on each bit of the input in a complicated way.

As a further refinement, we may wish to make the operation of a product–cipher system dependent on the value of an input key k. To do this, we can replace each S-box in Fig. 7.10 with two alternative S-boxes, and we can let the 0 or 1 value of a corresponding bit in key k determine which of the two alternatives is to be used in a given block transformation. Figure 7.11 illustrates this principle.

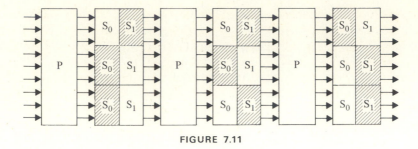

FIGURE 7.11

Figure 7.11 shows the alternatives for the two S-boxes that would be selected using a nine-bit key

$$k = 1\ 0\ 0\ 1\ 0\ 1\ 0\ 1\ 1$$

to select $S_1 S_0 S_0$ in the first S-layer, $S_1 S_0 S_1$ in the second S-layer, and $S_0 S_1 S_1$ in the third S-layer. (In Fig. 7.11 the selected alternatives S_i are cross-hatched, while the unselected S_i are clear.)

In IBM's Lucifer system (Smith [1971] and Feistal [1973]), which is a product–cipher system constructed along the lines of Fig. 7.11, each S-box has four-bit inputs, each P-box permutes 128 inputs, and the key is 128 bits. Needless to say, the P-box and S-box transformations must be chosen carefully to make it difficult to trace a given input–output pair back and to reconstruct the S and P transformations. Since an S-box, being perfectly general, can be set up to behave exactly like a P-box, in the worst case the whole system could behave just like a cascade of pure P-boxes and could be exposed by tickling. To avoid this possibility, the S and P boxes must be set up with transformations considered strong on an analytic basis (e.g., see Kam and Davida [1978]).

The recent National Bureau of Standards (NBS) Data Encryption Standard (DES) is a product–cipher system similar to the IBM Lucifer system; but it encrypts blocks of 64 bits each, subject to a key k of 56 bits. This Data Encryption Standard is being considered by NBS as a standard for use in enabling individuals and organizations to encrypt, and thus to protect, confidential data during storage and transmission. However, the DES has been attacked (e.g., see Diffie and Hellman [1976a] and [1977], and see also Bari Kolata [1977a]) on two grounds:

a) the 56-bit key may not be wide enough to prevent a successful cryptanalytic attack using fast parallel multichip computers of a coming generation; and

b) no public analysis of the S-boxes in the system has been offered to provide evidence of cryptographic strength. (See bibliographic notes in Section 7.6 for further references and developments.)

Public-key cryptosystems. Cryptosystems that depend upon the use of a common key K by both the sender and receiver to encrypt and decrypt messages are subject to the problem of keeping the key K secure. When a single key K is distributed among a community of users who share the use of the key, the problems of maintaining the secrecy of the key multiply (see Ehrsam, *et al.* [1978] and Matyas and Meyer [1978]). Also, there is a need for some system of "signing" encrypted messages, such as might be useful for signing "electronic checks" in an electronic funds transfer system, to identify provably that the sender alone signed a particular transaction and that no one else could have forged the signature. This is especially challenging when electronic "cut-and-paste" techniques could append a prestored signature to a plaintext message before or after encryption.

An elegant proposal for a system that does not depend on shared keys and that permits a signature technique has been advanced recently by Diffie and Hellman [1976b]. In a public-key cryptosystem, each user has two keys—a public key and a private key. Let the public key of a person in Atlanta be A and let his private key be a, and let the public key of a person in Buffalo be B and let his private key be b. We can think of the public keys as being published, say, in a telephone directory, and we can think of the private keys as being contained inside the hardware of a well-protected encrypting typewriter owned by each participant in the scheme. Such a typewriter might be constructed to erase its private key if tampered with.

Let us say the person in Atlanta wants to send the person in Buffalo a message M. To do this, the person in Atlanta encrypts message M using Buffalo's public key. Let $E(B, M)$ be this encrypted message. For any pair (p, P) of private and public keys, the encrypting function E has the two properties:

1. $E(p, E(P, M)) = M$, and
2. $E(P, E(p, M)) = M$.

Thus, everyone can see the coded message $E(B, M)$, but only Buffalo can read it by using his private key, since $E(b, E(B, M)) = M$.

Now suppose Atlanta wants to sign a purchase order in a way that Buffalo will know it could have come only from Atlanta. To do this, Atlanta first encrypts with his private key, getting $E(a, M)$, and then encrypts this with Buffalo's public key getting $E(B, E(a, M))$. When Buffalo receives this cryptogram, he first decrypts with his private key getting

$$E(b, E(B, E(a, M))) = E(a, M),$$

and then he decrypts again, using Atlanta's public key,

$$E(A, E(a, M)) = M.$$

Only Atlanta could have encrypted M with his private key, so a forger could not possibly have sent the signed message M.

Recently, Rivest, Shamir, and Adleman [1978] have proposed an implementation of this public-key cryptosystem concept relying on the difficulty of factoring large integers. Their proposal uses the encrypting function

$$E(k, M) = M^k \bmod n;$$

that is, if M is an integer representation of the message, one raises M to the kth power, where k is the key, and then takes the remainder after division by a suitably chosen integer n. The method for selecting the public and private keys and for choosing the divisor is as follows:

We first determine two large "random" primes p and q (using a technique explained in a moment). We multiply these together to get n:

$$n = p \times q.$$

It is intended to make n public but, due to the difficulty of factoring large n, p and q will be effectively hidden. This fact will also hide the relation between the public and private keys. Next, we choose a large, random integer d (to be used as the private decrypting key) having the property that d is relatively prime to $(p - 1) \times (q - 1)$. Finally, we choose e (the public encrypting key) to be the "multiplicative inverse" of d modulo $(p - 1) \times (q - 1)$, by finding an e that satisfies the relation

$$e \times d \equiv 1 \text{ modulo } (p - 1) \times (q - 1). \tag{9}$$

Relation (9) signifies that the difference $(e \times d - 1)$ must be an integer multiple of $(p - 1) \times (q - 1)$.

Now the integer pair (e, n) is made public. A message M to be encrypted must be encoded as an integer between 0 and $n - 1$. If the encoding of M is too large to fit in the range 0 to $n - 1$, it is broken into smaller blocks each of which is encrypted separately. Assuming $0 \leq M \leq n - 1$, we can then apply the encrypting transformation

$$E(e, M) = M^e \bmod n.$$

To decrypt, the privately kept pair (d, n) is used. Thus, $E(d, M) = M^d \bmod n$ decrypts M. The following algorithm can be used to implement $E(k, M)$ and requires at most 2 lg k multiplications and 2 lg k divisions.

Algorithm 7.2 *Exponentiation by repeated squaring and multiplication.*

Let M be a message in the range $0 \leq M \leq n - 1$, and let (k, n) be a pair of integers. The output C is the encrypted form of M using $E(k, M) = M^k \bmod n$. Let $k_r k_{r-1} \cdots k_1 k_0$ be the binary representation of the key k.

1. [Initialize.] Set $C \leftarrow 1$.
2. [Square and multiply.] For $i \leftarrow r, r - 1, \ldots, 0$ do (a) and (b).
   a) Set $C \leftarrow (C^2) \bmod n$.
   b) If $k_i = 1$, then set $C \leftarrow (C \times M) \bmod n$.

A procedure two times better than this is given in Knuth [1969] where the problem of exponentiation is studied in greater detail. Since encrypting and decrypting are identical, the operation given by Algorithm 7.2 could be implemented on a few special-purpose integrated circuit chips. Even using a high-speed general-purpose computer is not prohibitively expensive. Rivest, Shamir, and Adleman [1978] claim that a 200-digit message M can be encrypted in a few seconds.

Demonstrating correctness. To demonstrate that the encrypting function $E(k, M)$ works properly, we must show that the following two identities hold:

$$E(e, E(d, M)) = M,$$
$$E(d, E(e, M)) = M. \tag{10}$$

To do this, we use the Euler totient function $\phi(n)$, which gives the number of positive integers less than n that are relatively prime to n. For prime numbers p, we always have $\phi(p) = p - 1$. Now, defining the congruence relation $a \equiv b(\text{modulo } n)$ to mean the same as $((a - b) \bmod n) = 0$, we can state a theorem of Fermat and Euler: If M is an integer that is relatively prime to n, then

$$M^{\phi(n)} \equiv 1(\text{modulo } n). \tag{11}$$

Since we have chosen n as the product of two primes $n = p \times q$, we can manipulate the totient function $\phi(n)$ as follows.

$$\phi(n) = \phi(p \times q) = \phi(p) \times \phi(q) = (p - 1) \times (q - 1) = n - (p + q) + 1.$$

Now, since we chose d to be relatively prime to $(p - 1) \times (q - 1)$, it has a multiplicative inverse e in the ring of integers modulo $\phi(n)$,

$$e \times d \equiv 1(\text{modulo } \phi(n)). \tag{12}$$

Since we can manipulate positive exponents in congruence relations according to the usual laws

$$x^a \times x^b \equiv x^{a+b}(\text{modulo } n) \qquad \text{and} \qquad (x^a)^b \equiv x^{a \times b}(\text{modulo } n)$$

(*cf.* Knuth [1973a], p. 39), we can rewrite (10) above as:

$$E(e, E(d, M)) \equiv E(d, M)^e \equiv (M^d)^e \equiv M^{e \times d}(\text{modulo } n),$$
$$E(d, E(e, M)) \equiv E(e, M)^d \equiv (M^e)^d \equiv M^{e \times d}(\text{modulo } n).$$

Now, if we can prove that $M^{e \times d} \equiv M(\text{modulo } n)$, we will have proved that the encrypting and decrypting procedures have the right inverse properties. Restating (12), we know that $(e \times d - 1)$ must be an integer multiple of $\phi(n)$ for some integer k. That is, $(e \times d - 1) = k \times \phi(n)$ for some integer k. Thus, $e \times d = k \times \phi(n) + 1$.

This implies that:

$$M^{e \times d} \equiv M^{k \times \phi(n) + 1}(\text{modulo } n).\qquad(13)$$

From (11), if p does not divide a message M, then

$$M^{p-1} \equiv 1(\text{modulo } p);$$

and since $(p - 1)$ divides $\phi(n)$, we get:

$$M^{k \times \phi(n) + 1} \equiv M^{k \times (p-1) \times (q-1)} M^1 \equiv (M^{p-1})^{k \times (q-1)} M \equiv M(\text{modulo } p).$$

When p divides M, we have $M \equiv 0(\text{modulo } p)$, so no matter whether p does or does not divide M, we have established that $M^{e \times d} \equiv M(\text{modulo } p)$. A similar argument for q shows that $M^{e \times d} \equiv M(\text{modulo } q)$. Now we can apply the law that, whenever r and s are relatively prime,

$$x \equiv y(\text{modulo } r) \qquad \text{and} \qquad x \equiv y(\text{modulo } s)$$

imply that

$$x \equiv y(\text{modulo } rs)$$

(Knuth [1973a], p. 39) to see that $M^{e \times d} \equiv M(\text{modulo } p \times q)$ or, in other words, $M^{e \times d} \equiv M(\text{modulo } n)$, which is what we wanted to demonstrate.

Finding large primes and computing e and d. We must now turn to the topic of finding primes p and q such that if $n = p \times q$ is made public, it is not computationally feasible to factor n.

According to the best algorithm known to Rivest, Shamir, and Adleman [1978] for factoring n, Table 7.7 gives the number of operations required and the time required (at one microsecond per operation) to factor n versus the number of digits n contains.

Rivest, Shamir, and Adleman [1978] recommend using 100-digit primes p and q, so that n will have 200 decimal digits. To find a large 100-digit prime, a

TABLE 7.7†

Digits	Number of operations	Time
50	1.4×10^{10}	3.9 hours
75	9.0×10^{12}	104 days
100	2.3×10^{15}	74 years
200	1.2×10^{23}	3.8×10^9 years
300	1.5×10^{29}	4.9×10^{15} years
500	1.3×10^{39}	4.2×10^{25} years

† From Rivest, Shamir, and Adleman [1978].

probabilistic method can be used that determines whether a number is prime or composite to within a vanishingly small probability of incorrectness. Using Fermat's theorem, $a^{(p-1)} \equiv 1(\text{modulo } p)$ whenever p is prime and a is a positive number less than p (which is a special case of formula (11) above), we can test a number n to see whether it is prime or composite (i.e., a product of two or more primes). To do this, select a number a at random, raise it to the power $(n-1)$ and divide by n. If the remainder is not 1, n cannot be prime. By testing n with a properly arranged sample of values of a in this fashion, n can be determined prime within a certain probability of correctness. Rivest, Shamir, and Adleman recommend use of a primality test of Solovay and Strassen, which works as follows. Let gcd (a, b) stand for the "greatest common divisor" of a and b, and let $J(a, b)$ be a Jacobi symbol defined by:

$J(a, b) =$ **if** $a = 1$ **then** 1 **else**

if a is even **then** $J(a/2, b) \times (-1)^{(b^2-1)/8}$

else $J((b \bmod a), a) \times (-1)^{(a-1) \times (b-1)/4}$

where b is odd, and $a \leq b$.

Now let b be a large odd number that we wish to test for primality, and let a be chosen randomly from the numbers $(1, \ldots, b-1)$. We test whether

$$\text{gcd } (a, b) = 1 \qquad \text{and} \qquad J(a, b) \equiv a^{(b-1)/2}(\text{modulo } b). \tag{14}$$

If b is prime, then (14) will always be true; but if b is composite (14) is false with probability at least $\frac{1}{2}$. Therefore, if (14) is found to be true for 100 randomly chosen values of a, the chance that b is not prime is one out of 2^{100}.

Now to choose d, which must be relatively prime to $\phi(n)$, we could pick some prime greater than max (p, q). Here, d should be chosen from a large set of possibilities so that a cryptanalyst can't find it by direct search. The Gauss prime number theorem, which characterizes the "density" of primes we can expect to find in a given interval of integers, can be applied to estimate the difficulty of locating primes if we test successive odd large numbers. For instance, in trying to find p and q as 100-digit primes, about $(\ln 10^{100})/2 = 115$ numbers will be tested before a prime is found. This tells us that finding probabilistic primes p, q, and d should not take much computing effort. Rivest, Shamir, and Adleman [1978] attest that a high-speed computer can determine in several seconds whether a 100-digit number is prime, and can also find the first prime bigger than a given number in a few minutes.

Finally, to compute e such that $e \times d = 1(\text{modulo } \phi(n))$, given that d and $\phi(n)$ are relatively prime, we can use the Euclidean Algorithm to find integers e and k such that

$$e \times d + k \times \phi(n) = 1$$

(see Exercise 15 of Section 4.5.2 of Knuth [1969], p. 315). Then $(e \times d - 1)$ is a multiple of $\phi(n)$, as required.

Examples of the use of this public-key cryptosystem are given in Rivest, Shamir, and Adleman [1978] and in Gardner [1977]. In particular, Gardner challenges the reader to decrypt an encrypted text for a prize of $100.

One interesting possible line of attack on the Rivest, Shamir, and Adleman technique is to attempt repeatedly to apply the encrypting function in the forward direction. It is possible that, after some number of forward applications of the publicly known encrypting function, the original message could be recovered even when the decryption key is unknown. Simmons and Norris [1977], Rivest [1978b], and Herlestam [1978] comment on this idea.

The security of the Rivest, Shamir, and Adleman technique relies on the computational difficulty of factoring large integers. However, at the moment, nobody has proved that factoring large integers is computationally difficult. In fact, it is still possible that somebody will figure out a method for factoring large integers that is computationally efficient. On the other hand, this problem has been worked on by famous mathematicians for over three hundred years and no one has invented an algorithm that will factor 200-digit numbers in a reasonable amount of time (see Knuth [1969], Section 4.5.4, for a discussion of some of these factoring algorithms). Thus the history of the problem constitutes partial "certification" of the potential cryptographic strength of the method. Actually, to prove the method secure, one would like to have two strong results of the following form: (a) factoring large integers is provably difficult, and (b) any general way of breaking the method yields an efficient way to factor large integers. This would help establish the security of the method more firmly. Rivest, Shamir, and Adleman [1978] challenge the reader to examine closely the difficulty of factoring large numbers, and urge the exploration of other implementations of public-key cryptosystems based on provably difficult problems, in case the security of their implementation someday turns out to be inadequate.

7.3.2 Fast code conversions

Because the binary codes for fixed-length character encodings often occupy all binary numbers in the range $0 \leq b \leq 2^n - 1$, it is frequently possible to use them for indices to access items in a table. If T is a conversion table whose ith entry is a converted code for the character code i, then the conversion of the string S is:

$$S = c_1 c_2 \cdots c_n \Rightarrow S' = T[c_1]T[c_2] \cdots T[c_n].$$

Thus, a string in unpacked form can be converted rapidly using a process such as

for $i \leftarrow 1$ **step** 1 **until** Length(S) **do** $S[i] \leftarrow T[S[i]]$.

Converting packed representations takes longer, since words containing packed characters must be decomposed and their converted characters recomposed. Normally this is easy on machines offering byte-manipulation instructions or byte addressing.

Karlgren observes that conversion from codes with two case-shift signals to and from codes of fixed length can be done easily without the need for conversion tables (see [Karlgren 1963]). To convert a k-bit code with two case-shift signals to a $(k + 1)$-bit code, add an additional "channel" to the k-bit code to be used as a "carrier" of the case-shift information. Every time a shift code is encountered, the signal on its corresponding carrier channel is reassigned. To go the other way, every time the code on a carrier channel inverts, one outputs the corresponding case-shift signal; otherwise the carrier bit is stripped from the $(k + 1)$-bit code to produce the corresponding k-bit code.

7.3.3 Matula's test for number conversion

Most radix conversions are straightforward, but there is one situation that should be noted which can lead to considerable vexation if ignored.

Ideally, we would like to be able to take any possible decimal floating-point number N, of, say, K significant digits, translate it, say, into an underlying binary floating-point representation of P bits, using careful rounding, and then later, using careful rounding again, translate the binary representation back to decimal, recovering N. One might at first think that this would be possible whenever there are enough bits in the floating-point representation to "hold" all 10^K numbers possible in the decimal floating-point representation; i.e., that it would be possible whenever $10^K \leq 2^P$, as is the case for integer representations. But Matula and Goldberg have shown that this is not so (see Goldberg [1967] and Matula [1968a, 1968b]). In fact, all possible N can be recovered after two ideal conversion and rounding transformations if and only if $10^K \leq 2^{P-1}$.

To see what this means in practice, consider a 36-bit machine with a single precision floating-point representation having a 27-bit mantissa. Is it possible to convert decimal floating-point numbers of eight significant digits into and out of 27-bit binary mantissa form, and always to recover the identical input back again? According to Matula's test this is possible if $10^8 \leq 2^{27-1}$. But 2^{26} is, in fact, less than 10^8 even though $10^8 < 2^{27}$, leaving an inviting trap for the unsuspecting programmer. (In law, such a situation is termed an *attractive nuisance*.)

To gain a bit of insight into why this phenomenon exists, let us look at two examples given by Goldberg [1967]. When we attempt to represent the twenty decimal numbers 8.0, 8.1, ..., 9.8, 9.9 in binary using seven bits, we find that the integer part requires four bits and three bits XXX are left for the binary fraction part:

$$1\ 0\ 0\ 0\ .\ X\ X\ X$$

$$1\ 0\ 0\ 0\ .\ X\ X\ X$$

$$\vdots$$

$$1\ 0\ 0\ 1\ .\ X\ X\ X$$

$$1\ 0\ 0\ 1\ .\ X\ X\ X$$

No matter how the fraction bits XXX are computed, there are at most 16 distinct numbers in this representation, which implies that we can recover at most 16 of the original 20 decimal numbers. Shifting to a floating-point representation does not change matters, since the above binary numbers become $.1000XXX \times 2^4$ and $.1001XXX \times 2^4$. Therefore, 7 bits are not enough for two-digit accuracy (even though $10^2 < 2^7$). Hence, it is impossible to write string-conversion routines that map the 20 numbers from decimal-digit string form into seven-bit binary floating-point form and back again without loss of decimal precision.

Similarly, suppose we try to represent the 10,000,000 decimal numbers

$$9000000.0, \quad 9000000.1, \quad \ldots, \quad 9999999.8, \quad 9999999.9$$

by 27 bits. Since $2^{23} = 8388608$, we need 24 bits to represent the integer parts of these numbers. With three bits left over for the binary fraction part, there can be only 8,000,000 of the 10,000,000 original numbers represented distinctly; and the situation still holds if we move the binary point to obtain 27-bit binary mantissas in binary floating-point form. Hence, 27 bits are not enough for eight-digit accuracy.

7.4 REPRESENTATIONS FOR VARIABLE-LENGTH STRINGS

In some applications, it is necessary to process strings whose length cannot be predicted in advance of the running of an algorithm. This situation may arise, for example, in programs that compute new strings as a function of other data, as in the operations of string concatenation or macroexpansion in assemblers. It may also arise in text-processing systems or information-retrieval applications where the size of data to be read in is not foreknown. In the text of FORTRAN or ALGOL programs, the size of strings can be determined at compile time and remains constant during program execution, so that strings can be stored in a table whose size remains invariant during program execution. By contrast, in applications where string size can vary dynamically during program execution and cannot be predicted in advance, the underlying string representation must support strings of varying size, and must manage the variations that are encountered during program execution.

A basic idea for representing strings of varying size is to use linked blocks containing characters. A pointer can specify the location of the block containing the next character (or group of contiguous characters) in a string, allowing the characters to be stored in noncontiguous blocks of memory. Compared to the contiguous packed representation of strings, the use of pointers reduces memory utilization and destroys arithmetic indexing of the characters relative to a base address, but makes considerably easier various operations that change string length, such as insertion, deletion, or substitution of substrings. In this context, we must study the tradeoff between space, time, and ease of programming.

7.4.1   Representations using linked blocks of uniform size

An obvious linked representation for strings is to use chains composed of pairs of the form (Character, Pointer). The string $S = C_1 C_2 \cdots C_n$ would then be stored as shown in Fig. 7.12. Unused pairs can be chained together to form an available space list. Insertions and deletions are easy to program. The drawback lies in the poor storage utilization of this technique. For example, assuming a machine with 32-bit words, 24-bit addresses, and 8-bit characters, the storage utilization (namely, the fraction of memory used for storing characters) is only 25 percent.

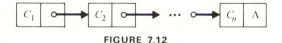

FIGURE 7.12

To increase the storage utilization at the expense of a bit more programming, we can use fixed-size blocks of n words each, with each block containing a substring of k contiguously packed characters and a pointer to a successor block, as shown in Fig. 7.13.

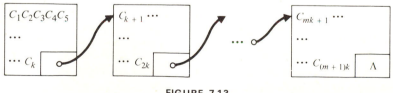

FIGURE 7.13

If there is more space in a block than is needed to store the characters at the end of a given string, the remainder of the block is conventionally filled with special "void" characters. While management of storage is easy using a linked list of n-word blocks for available space, insertions and deletions between arbitrary characters in a string can lead to storage waste or can cause time-consuming repacking of successive blocks. For example, taking our machine with 32-bit words, 8-bit characters packed four to a word, and using 24-bit pointers, suppose we consider blocks of three words each. A string such as "MARY'S GARDEN" would be represented:

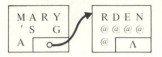

where "@" represents the void character. If now one wants to insert the string "ROSE" after the word "MARY'S", we can either (1) split the block for "MARY'S GA" into two blocks, and insert the block for "ROSE" in between, getting:

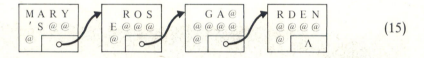   (15)

or (2) we can repack the resulting string "MARY'S ROSE GARDEN" into successive blocks, getting:

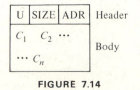   (16)

Here, method 1 saves time and programming effort at the cost of space (half the characters in (15) above were void), and method 2 saves space at the cost of time and programming effort.

As the size of the blocks in the fixed block-size method increases, waste due to incompletely filled blocks increases. As the size of the blocks decreases, percentage of waste due to pointers increases. These disadvantages lead to the consideration of methods using variable-size blocks.

7.4.2 Berztiss' representation

Each block in Berztiss' representation is composed of a *header* and a *body* (see Berztiss [1965]). The *header* has a use bit U, a size SIZE, and an address ADR. The *body* is a set of contiguous words containing packed characters $C_1 C_2 \cdots C_n$. (See Fig. 7.14.)

U	SIZE	ADR	Header
C_1 C_2 $\cdots$			Body
$\cdots C_n$			

FIGURE 7.14

The use bit has the value 0 if the block is in use and the value 1 if the block is available. If the size specifies the number of characters in the body, there is no need to use "void" characters to fill the unused remainder of the last word of the body, and the size of the whole block is then $\lceil SIZE/p \rceil + 1$, assuming a one-word header and characters packed p to a word in the body. By convention, the address of a block is the address of its first word.

The available blocks (those with $U = 1$) are chained together into an available space list Avail, and pointers are maintained to the first and last blocks on Avail, stored as values of the variables First and Last, respectively.

To store a string $S = C_1 C_2 \cdots C_n$, the first block B on Avail is obtained. If the characters of S fit evenly in the body of B, no further storage from Avail need be requested. If the characters of S fit into the body of B and leave a k-word remainder unused, this k-word remainder is given a new header, and is inserted as the new first block on Avail. If the storage capacity of the body of B is insufficient to contain the characters of S, successive blocks from Avail are obtained and filled with the successive characters of S in sequence. The general form of the result is a chain of blocks of variable size filled with the characters of S in order. The address α of the first block in such a chain is, by convention, the address of the string S in string storage. Berztiss assumes that this address α is stored in some location ℓ, external to the string storage region, and he forms a *ring* for each string by inserting the string address α in location ℓ, and by inserting ℓ in the ADR field of the last block on the chain. (See Fig. 7.15.) The use bits of the blocks in a *ring* representing a string are each set to 0.

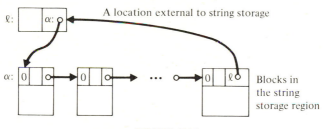

FIGURE 7.15

At the outset, the bounds on the region of string storage are obtained, and string storage is made into a single large available block that is placed on Avail. Successive block requests are allocated from Avail initially by splitting the single large block into smaller blocks of required size. When a block B is released, as in replacement of one substring by another, it is appended to the end of Avail. Eventually, Avail becomes a linked list of blocks of varying size.

After a program has run for a while, storage may become highly fragmented, with a significant fraction of storage used up as block headers. If this occurs, a string-compacting algorithm is needed that performs a "spring housecleaning" by rearranging strings represented as rings of blocks into single contiguously packed blocks, and which coalesces Avail into a single block. This algorithm is costly in time and should be used sparingly. It depends on having a nonempty Avail list to use as temporary storage for characters whose position in memory is being exchanged.

It works roughly as follows: At the start, to free up a region of contiguous space starting at one end of memory, blocks belonging to strings in use have their contents transferred to space on Avail, and the addresses of their predecessors are updated by travelling around the ring for the string to which they belong. (Travelling around these rings is costly in time. This cost can be eliminated at the expense of space by the usual device of linking the rings symmetrically. We are studying Berztiss' representation, however, for its economy of storage utilization.) The starting address of a string to be compacted is then located; and successive characters are removed from the successive blocks on its ring and packed contiguously into the linear region of memory previously made available. Once the body of such a block has been copied, the block itself is appended to Avail. This process continues until the last string has been compacted, at which time the blocks on the Avail list are all at the other end of memory in a contiguous region. This contiguous region can be reorganized as a single block, which becomes the new Avail list. The algorithm gets messy when it has to handle an Avail list that is of very small capacity and is highly fragmented, since its capacity to act as a buffer for displaced strings is small, and it is possible that only part of a string can be compacted before Avail requires more storage. The basic cycle is to free up as much new contiguous storage as possible using up Avail, transfer as much as possible of some string currently being compacted into the free contiguous region, and convert the released blocks (or parts thereof) that have just been compacted into a new Avail list.

7.4.3 Madnick's comparison

Madnick ran experiments on an IBM system/360 comparing six different string representations (Madnick [1967]). The six representations are given in Fig. 7.16.

The six methods are described as follows (quoted from Madnick [1967], p. 421):

Method 1 (*Double-word blocks*). The string is represented internally by linked two-word blocks. The first word contains a character; the second contains a pointer to the next character.

Method 2 (*Single-word blocks*). This method strongly resembles the double-word block technique but, rather than using two words, the 8-bit character and 24-bit pointer are packed into a single 32-bit word.

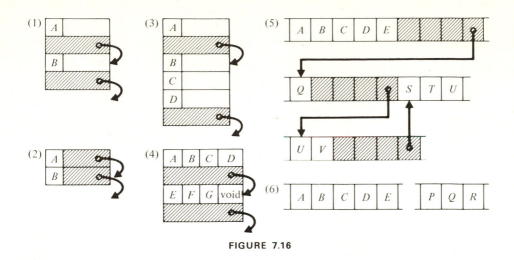

FIGURE 7.16

Method 3 (Variable-length blocks). The characters are stored one to a word consecutively in memory. Whenever the sequence is to be broken, a pointer indicates the location of the next block of characters. Characters and pointer can be identified by information stored in the unused portion of the 32-bit word.

Method 4 (Packed double-word blocks). The characters are stored in fixed-length packed blocks (4 per word, 8 per double word, etc.), followed by a pointer to the next block. ... A special character called the "void" character fills the empty spaces in data blocks that are only partially filled.

Method 5 (Linear linked strings). Characters are stored sequentially in memory, byte by byte. Whenever the sequence is to be broken, a special character is used to denote a pointer. In other words, the pointer is made 32 bits long where the leading 8 bits identify it as a pointer.

Method 6 (Linear string). Strings are maintained linearly throughout memory without any pointers.

Table 7.8 gives the results of Madnick's experiments comparing data-structure characteristics for the six methods.

Madnick used method 2 for an underlying string representation for a SNOBOL-compatible string-processing package on the IBM 360 model 40. He compared it with a SNOBOL implementation on the IBM 7094, which used a linear string technique (method 6). While acknowledging the difficulty of comparisons across machines and implementations, he observed that method 2 was about 2.5 times faster than method 6 in this application.

TABLE 7.8

Method	Packing density	Ease of scan	Ease of insert/delete	Speed of insert/delete	Localization of string for paging
1. Double word	12.5%	Easy	Easy	Fast	Poor
2. Single word	25%	Easy	Easy	Fast	Poor
3. Variable length	12.5–25%	Moderate	Moderate	Moderate	Fair
4. Packed double	12.5–50%	Moderate	Difficult	Slow	Fair
5. Linked linear	25–100%	Moderate	Difficult	Very slow	Good
6. Linear	100%	Easy	Moderate	Very slow	Excellent

7.4.4 Examples of string representations used in real systems

It is helpful to glance briefly at some string representations used in practice with success in several systems, *viz.*: (Teco, Apl, Macro-10, and Snobol from Harrison [1973]).

1. *A text editor.* Teco is a text editor written for the PDP-10. It edits one or more pages of text stored in a buffer in core memory. Substrings of text can be inserted, deleted, and replaced; one can search for occurrences of given substrings; and blocks of text can be moved. Teco's internal representation is a packed, linear string in contiguous memory. If characters are deleted or inserted, the entire text to the right of the point of insertion or deletion is shifted in the proper direction the required number of character positions to accommodate the change. The code that shifts the characters is executed in the PDP-10's fast accumulators.

2. Apl. In one implementation of Apl (on an IBM 360 model 50), strings are stored in blocks of variable size. Each block has a header with information declaring the string to be an array of linear dimension, of length ℓ, with characters for elements, and giving garbage-collection bits, and a backpointer to the location from which the string is externally referenced. The characters of the string are packed in contiguous linear form in the body of the block and are individually addressable and modifiable in the Apl language. Each time a new string is created, a new block of contiguous storage of appropriate size is allocated.

3. *A macro assembler.* In the Macro-10 assembler for the PDP-10, strings are stored in linked four-word blocks.

4. Snobol. A contiguous, linear packed sequence of characters is used in some Snobol implementations. Substrings of the packed sequence are indicated by pointer pairs that point to the beginning and end of each substring. This works

because in SNOBOL an existing string is never changed but can have new strings
formed from its substrings (see Harrison [1973], Madnick [1967], and Farber,
Griswold, and Polonsky [1964]).

7.5 EXAMPLES OF OPERATIONS ON STRINGS

In this section, we examine two string-manipulation and testing problems with
important applications—macroexpansion and string pattern matching.

7.5.1 Macroexpansion

In most assemblers and in some compilers, the user is permitted to *define* and *call*
macros. An example of a macro definition is:

$$\textit{macro}\ \ \textbf{F}(x1,\ x2,\ x3)$$
$$[\textbf{Fetch}\ x1$$
$$\textbf{Add}\quad x2$$
$$\textbf{Store}\ x3]$$

where **F** is called the *macro name*, $x1$, $x2$, and $x3$ are called *formal parameters*, and

$$[\textbf{Fetch}\ x1$$
$$\textbf{Add}\quad x2$$
$$\textbf{Store}\ x3]$$

is called the *macro body*. A macro call specifies a set of strings that are to be
substituted for formal parameters in a macro body. For example, $F(A, B, C)$ is a
macro call. Here A, B, and C are called *actual parameters*. When the actual
parameters A, B, and C are substituted for occurrences of the respective formal
parameters $x1$, $x2$, and $x3$ in the body of F, we get the "expanded" body:

$$[\textbf{Fetch}\ A$$
$$\textbf{Add}\quad B$$
$$\textbf{Store}\ C]$$

The *value* of the macro call $F(A, B, C)$ is the expanded body without the square
brackets [and].

Macro calls can be nested, as in the expression $G(A, H(B, C), D)$. In this case,
there is a choice in the order of macroexpansion between "inside-out" expansion
and "outside-in" expansion. In "inside-out" expansion, the innermost macro calls
in the actual parameter list (i.e., those at the deepest level of nesting) are expanded
first, and their values are used as actual parameters for macro calls containing
them. In "outside-in" expansion, the unexpanded inner calls are first substituted in
the body of the outermost call, and this substituted body is evaluated to expand
any macro calls it contains. (It should be mentioned that the two evaluation
orders can yield different results although this fact is not demonstrated here.)

$$macro \ \ G(x, y, z)$$
$$[\,z(x, y)\,]$$

$$macro \ \ D(u, v)$$
$$[\,Fetch \ u$$
$$v \qquad]$$

$$macro \ \ H(s, t)$$
$$[\,Xor \ \ s(t)\,]$$

FIGURE 7.17

For example, supposing we had defined three macros as shown in Fig. 7.17. Then the call $G(A, H(B, C), D)$, if expanded outside-in, would produce first

$$D(A, H(B, C)),$$

then

Fetch A
$H(B, C)$

and finally

Fetch A
Xor $B(C)$.

Expansion in inside-out order would produce first

$$G(A, \textbf{Xor} \ B(C), D),$$

then

$$D(A, \textbf{Xor} \ B(C))$$

and finally

Fetch A
Xor $B(C)$.

With respect to internal representations useful for macroexpansion, the supporting underlying representation is often selected to be able to handle strings of varying size, such as arise in the process of macroexpansion. The macro definitions can be preprocessed, producing an internal form convenient for fast expansion. As an example of the preprocessing involved, we might choose, as an underlying representation, Madnick's method 5—linear linked strings, in which characters are stored sequentially, except for the occurrences of pointers that are preceded by special characters identifying them as such. The body of the macro definition is scanned to find occurrences of the formal parameters, and a vector V is set up having one entry for each of the respective formal parameters. Each entry in V is a chain of occurrences of formal parameters in the body of the macro. For example, reconsider the macro definition given above:

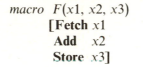

Suppose that the initial linear linked string for the macro body of F is given as shown in Fig. 7.18, where the symbol @ indicates that the next three bytes in sequence specify a pointer giving the continuation of the string, the symbol # is a character for upspacing a line and returning the carriage to the left margin, and the symbol & specifies the end of the string.

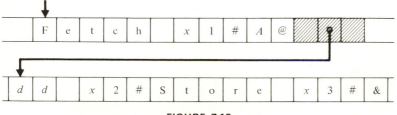

FIGURE 7.18

After preprocessing, the internal representation of the macro definition might appear as shown in Fig. 7.19.

We might imagine that the macro name F is stored in a (possibly hash coded) symbol table, wherein the entries contain information associated with F, such as the fact that F is a macro, in which case a pointer is given to its "formal parameter vector" V. V has a length field, giving the number of formal parameters, and for each formal parameter x_i it specifies the chain of occurrences of x_i in the text of the body of F. The vector V also contains a pointer to the preprocessed body. In the string for the preprocessed body, the occurrence of the symbol $ signals a pointer on one of the chains of occurrences of formal parameters.

Now suppose we are given a macro call, such as $F(A, B, C)$. A vector of pointers to actual parameter strings is constructed from this call (see Fig. 7.20), where each string ends in a null pointer. Then the entry for F is looked up in the symbol table and the pointer to its formal parameter vector is found. Assuming that the number of actual and formal parameters given in the two vectors agree, the information in the macro definition is copied, and the process of substitution

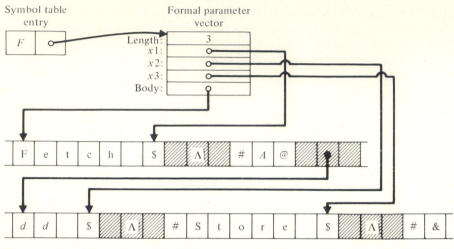

Symbol table entry   Formal parameter vector

FIGURE 7.19

of copies of actual parameters for formal parameters begins. To do this, the chain of occurrences of the ith formal parameter is followed, and copies of the ith actual parameter are inserted everywhere along this chain, for each i ($1 \leq i \leq 3$). This yields the expanded copy of the body shown in Fig. 7.21.

The expanded body is sometimes then processed further to detect and expand new occurrences of macro calls created as a result of the first expansion.

In many practical systems, the process of macroexpansion is considerably enriched with features allowing, for example, conditional expansion (based on assembly-time variables), iterated expansion of some body subject to some systematically varying condition, processing of actual parameter lists with a variable number of parameters, and so on (see McIlroy [1960], Strachey [1965], and Brown [1969]). This is clearly an application where efficient processing of variable-length strings is required. If space is at a premium, as on minicomputers with small core memories, Madnick's representation method 6, with pointer pairs used to specify

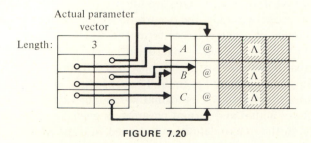

Actual parameter vector

Length:

FIGURE 7.20

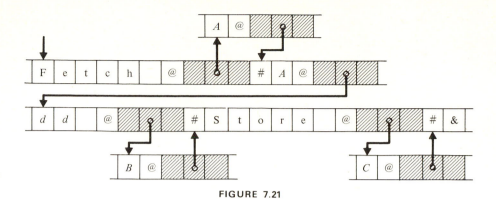

FIGURE 7.21

the beginning and ending of strings, may be the most economical of space. If time is at a premium, Madnick's representations 1 or 2 might be best, using again pointer pairs to specify the beginning and ending of strings.

7.5.2 Fast string-pattern matching

Suppose our task is to find whether some string S contains occurrences of another string P, called the pattern string. This arises in preprocessing macro definitions as discussed above, and in applications such as text editors and text-processing programs that search for and replace words, etc. Suppose, for example, that we are trying to determine the number of occurrences of the word "liberty" in the "Federalist Papers." It would be important to use the fastest recognition procedure possible. Two surprising developments have occurred recently in the area of string pattern matching. Knuth, Morris, and Pratt [1977] (see also Morris and Pratt [1970] and Knuth and Pratt [1971]) discovered a way to find whether S contains an instance of the pattern P using only one character comparison per character of string S. More recently, Boyer and Moore [1977] discovered how to do it without, on the average, having to look at all characters of S.

An elementary algorithm for string pattern matching is the following.

Algorithm 7.3 *Elementary pattern matching.*

Let $S = s_1 s_2 \cdots s_n$ be a string and let $P = p_1 p_2 \cdots p_m$ be a pattern where $m \le n$. If P is a leftmost substring of S starting at the ith character of S, the algorithm returns i. If P is not a substring of S, the algorithm returns 0.

1. [Initialize.] Set $i \leftarrow 1$ (i is the pointer to the leftmost character of a substring of S being tested against P). Set $j \leftarrow 1$ (j is a pointer to a current character of P being compared against a character of S).

2. [Failure?] If $i > n - m + 1$, then terminate the algorithm with the result 0

(since pattern P is either bigger than S initially, or has been slid off the right end of S).

3. [Test.] In the following cases, take the following actions:

Case	$\Rightarrow$	Action
a) $(p_j = s_{i+j-1})$ and $(j = m)$	$\Rightarrow$	terminate the algorithm with result i.
b) $(p_j = s_{i+j-1})$ and $(j < m)$	$\Rightarrow$	set $j \leftarrow j + 1$ and repeat this step.
c) $(p_j \neq s_{i+j-1})$	$\Rightarrow$	set $i \leftarrow i + 1$, set $j \leftarrow 1$, and go back to step 2.

In essence what this does is to superimpose P on top of each substring of S of length $|P|$ proceeding from left to right, and to check the characters of P, character by character, against the substring of S beneath it. As soon as a difference is detected, P is shifted to the right one character. If P matches the entire substring beneath it, a successful exit is taken. In the worst case (such as matching $P = aaab$ against $S = aa \cdots aaab$), Algorithm 7.3 takes time $O(n \times m)$. In the following sections, we will see how this result may be considerably bettered.

7.5.2.1 The Knuth–Morris–Pratt Algorithm

The idea behind the Knuth–Morris–Pratt pattern matching procedure is to construct a deterministic finite-state automaton M from P, which processes the characters of S one at a time in left-to-right order, reacting to each by making an appropriate state transition. If a subsequence of the characters of S matches the characters of P in order, M enters an accepting state. However, if, at any point, M detects a mismatch between a character of S and a character of P, it takes a "failure transition" back to the "best possible" state, from which pattern matching can continue.

Suppose $S = s_1 s_2 \cdots s_n$ and $P = p_1 p_2 \cdots p_m$ and that, after starting, M has found $p_1 p_2 \cdots p_i$ matches $s_1 s_2 \cdots s_i$. Suppose further that while the first i characters of S and P are identical, M finds that $s_{i+1} \neq p_{i+1}$. The best possible place to recover from this failure would be to slide P over to the right so that as many of its initial characters $p_1 p_2 \cdots p_j$ match as many of the final characters of $s_1 s_2 \cdots s_i$ as possible, provided we can continue matching s_{i+1} with p_{i+1} from this position. Thus, we want to find the longest *head* of P, $p_1, p_2 \cdots p_j$, that is equal to a *tail* of $s_1 s_2 \cdots s_i$, for which $s_{i+1} = p_{j+1}$. Then we want to enter a state M_{j+1} corresponding to the situation in which the first $j + 1$ symbols of P have been matched. M continues pattern matching from this state.

Knuth, Morris, and Pratt have shown how to construct M using only the information in the pattern P in an amount of time proportional to the number of characters in P. The machine M is then run using any string S as an input. The result is that it is possible to recognize whether P is a substring of S in time $O(|P| + |S|)$. (See Knuth, Morris, and Pratt [1977].)

We now show how to construct the automaton M. Supposing $P = p_1 p_2 \cdots p_m$, we first construct an initial part of M containing $m + 1$ states numbered $0, 1, \ldots, m$:

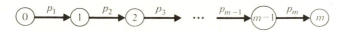

with "success" transitions p_i from each state $i - 1$ to state i. Each state j signifies a condition in which the first j characters of P match the last j characters of S scanned. In order to construct the "failure" transitions, we must first construct a table of "failure links," which are used in an intermediate stage of the construction of M and are later discarded.

Returning to the situation in which $p_1 p_2 \cdots p_j$ matches the last j characters of S scanned:

$$
\begin{array}{cccc}
p_1 & p_2 & \cdots & p_j \\
\updownarrow & \updownarrow & & \updownarrow \\
\cdots \quad s_{k-j+1} & s_{k-j+2} & \cdots & s_k
\end{array}
$$

we observe that finding the largest head of P identical to the longest tail of $s_{k-j+1} \cdots s_k$ (the last j characters of s scanned), is equivalent to finding the longest head of $p_1 p_2 \cdots p_j$ matching the longest tail of $p_1 p_2 \cdots p_j$, since $p_1 p_2 \cdots p_j$ is identical to the characters in S beneath it. Suppose we have a table of failure links $f\ell[j]$ with integer entries, where $0 \leq j \leq m$, there being one entry for each state j in the machine M. It is intended that $f\ell[j] = i$ should give the length i of the largest head of $p_1 p_2 \cdots p_j$ that is also a tail of $p_1 p_2 \cdots p_j$. The following algorithm computes the failure links.

Algorithm 7.4 *Compute failure links for pattern P.*

Let $P = p_1 p_2 \cdots p_m$ be a pattern.

1. [Initialize.] Set $f\ell[0] \leftarrow 0$ and set $f\ell[1] \leftarrow 0$.
2. [Compute links.] For $j \leftarrow 2, 3, \ldots, m$, first set fail $\leftarrow f\ell[j - 1]$ and then do step 3. (Step 3 is called as a subroutine for each value of j.)
3. [Cases.] In the following cases, take the following actions:

	Case	$\Rightarrow$	Action
a)	(fail = 0)	$\Rightarrow$ if $p_j = p_1$, then set $f\ell[j] \leftarrow 1$, otherwise, set $f\ell[j] \leftarrow 0$.
b)	(fail $\neq 0$) and $(p_j = p_{\text{fail}+1})$	$\Rightarrow$ set $f\ell[j] \leftarrow$ fail $+ 1$.
c)	(fail $\neq 0$) and $(p_j \neq p_{\text{fail}+1})$	$\Rightarrow$ set fail $\leftarrow f\ell[\text{fail}]$ and repeat step 3.

It is not at first obvious, but the fact is that Algorithm 7.4 runs in an amount of time at worst proportional to the length m of pattern P. Step 1 is executed once and has a constant cost. Step 2 has a cost proportional to $(m-1)$ since it sets and increments the variable j to $(m-1)$ distinct values and performs other operations of constant cost for each distinct value of j. The cost of executing step 3 is troublesome to contend with since not only is step 3 called by step 2 once for each value of j $(2 \le j \le m)$, but it is also possible that step 3 will call itself repeatedly when case 3(c) occurs. To get a handle on the number of times step 3 can call itself from within itself, we need to look at the way the variable fail gets incremented and decremented. The only way fail is incremented is when, in step 3(b), $f\ell[j] \leftarrow$ fail $+ 1$, after which control transfers back to step 2, where j is incremented by one and then fail $\leftarrow f\ell[j-1]$. This has the effect of incrementing fail by one. The only place fail can be decremented is in step 3(c); and in this case, performing the assignment fail $\leftarrow f\ell[\text{fail}]$ always decrements fail by one or more. But since fail $\leftarrow f\ell[\text{fail}]$ cannot decrement the value of fail more than the number of times fail is incremented elsewhere, and since fail is initialized to 0 and incremented at most $m-1$ times, we see that the number of times step 3 can be reentered from step 3(c) is at most $m-1$ times during the entire run of the algorithm. At worst, then, step 3 is entered $m-1$ times from itself, and $m-1$ times from step 2, so Algorithm 7.4 runs in a time bounded above by $2m-2$ times a constant of proportionality.

Our next step is to use the table of failure links $f\ell$ to complete the failure transitions of the machine M. Let $t(i, a) = k$ represent the state transition function for M wherein, if M is in state i and sees the letter a in the string S, it reacts by scanning past a and entering state k. We agreed earlier to construct success transitions such that $t(i, p_{i+1}) = i+1$ for each i $(0 \le i \le m-1)$. The failure transitions are computed as follows.

Algorithm 7.5 *Compute failure transitions for M from $f\ell$ and P.*

Let A be an alphabet of characters used in S and P.

1. [State 0.] For each $a \in A$, if $a \ne p_1$, then set $t(0, a) = 0$ (that is, if in state 0, return to state 0 for each letter in the alphabet A different from the first letter p_1 in the pattern P).

2. [Others.] *For* $i \leftarrow 1$ *step* 1 *until* m *do* for each letter $a \in A$ such that $a \ne p_{i+1}$, set $t(i, a) = t(f\ell[i], a)$, (that is, the reaction of M in state i to a letter a not equal to the $(i+1)$st letter of the pattern is the reaction of the state specified by the failure link $f\ell[i]$ to that same letter).

We now go through an example of the construction of M for a simple pattern. We use the binary alphabet $A = \{0, 1\}$. Let the pattern P be the string 1010110. We first compute the array $f\ell$ using Algorithm 7.4:

$$
\begin{array}{l|cccccccc}
i & 0 & 1 & 2 & 3 & 4 & 5 & 6 & 7 \\
p_i & & 1 & 0 & 1 & 0 & 1 & 1 & 0 \\
f\ell[i] & 0 & 0 & 0 & 1 & 2 & 3 & 1 & 2
\end{array}
$$

In Fig. 7.22, the failure links are indicated by dashed lines. Here, for example, $f\ell[4] = 2$, since 10 (the head of length 2) is the largest head of 1010 that is also a tail, while $f\ell[5] = 3$, since 101 is the largest head of 10101 that is also a tail.

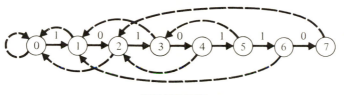

FIGURE 7.22

Now, using Algorithm 7.5 we can compute the state transitions for the machine M, as shown in Fig. 7.23. To find whether an arbitrary string S contains an instance of the pattern $P = 1010110$, one now starts machine M in state 0 with the first character of S under scan. Each character s_i of S causes a state transition along an arc labeled s_i in M to some new state of M. If the accepting state (state 7) is ever reached by this process, S contains an instance of P. If the last character s_n of S is scanned without state 7 ever having been entered, S contains no substring identical to P.

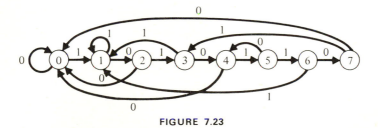

FIGURE 7.23

There is an interesting story behind the discovery of the Knuth–Morris–Pratt algorithm. Earlier, Cook had shown that any problem that could be solved using a two-way deterministic pushdown store automaton (2DPDA) could be solved in linear time on a random-access machine (see Cook [1971], Knuth and Pratt [1971], or Aho, Hopcroft, and Ullman [1974]). A 2DPDA has a read-only input tape whose symbols can be scanned left or right; it has an internal pushdown stack for temporary storage, onto which it can push symbols, from which it can pop symbols, and from which it can read the topmost symbol; and it has a finite-state control. In a given state s, with a character c under the read head on the input tape, and with the character p on top of its pushdown stack, it can determine a unique reaction $t(s, c, p)$ consisting in: (1) optionally moving left or right one symbol on its input tape, (2) optionally pushing or popping a symbol on its pushdown stack, and (3) entering some new successor state. Cook's theorem is rather remarkable, since even if the 2DPDA takes quadratic or even exponential time to solve a given problem, it can be shown that the same problem can be solved in linear time on a random-access computer.

It is fairly easy to program a 2DPDA to find out whether a string $S = s_1 s_2 \cdots s_n$ contains a pattern $P = p_1 p_2 \cdots p_m$.

Let the machine be called Q. The problem is given to Q on its input tape, say, in the following form:

$$\# s_1 s_2 \cdots s_n \$ p_1 p_2 \cdots p_m \mathcal{c},$$

where $\#$ is a left end marker, $\$$ is a middle marker, and $\mathcal{c}$ is a right end marker. Suppose, at the outset, that the left end marker $\#$ is under the read head of Q. Q scampers rightward along the tape pushing each symbol s_i of S onto its stack as it goes until it finds the middle marker $\$$. Now Q zips off toward the right in search of the right end marker $\mathcal{c}$, and when it finds it, it moves one symbol to the left so that the last character p_m of P is under its read head. (See Fig. 7.24.) Now it is ready to compare backwards the successive characters of the string $s_n s_{n-1} \cdots s_1$ on its pushdown stack with successive characters $p_m p_{m-1} \cdots p_1$ as it moves leftward along the input tape. Each time p_i matches s_i, Q pops s_i off the stack, moves left one symbol on the input tape, and proceeds to compare s_{i-1} on the stack with p_{i-1} on the input tape under the read head. If Q comes to the middle marker $\$$, it

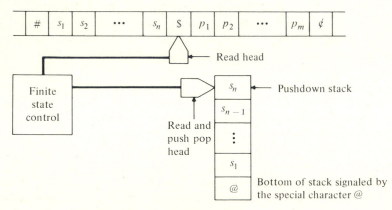

FIGURE 7.24

knows it has successfully matched all pattern characters against stored characters of S on its stack, so it enters an accepting state and halts. If, however, Q comes to the bottom of its stack (by hitting the special stack end marker @) before it comes to the middle marker $ on the input tape, it knows that S contains no instance of P and it enters a rejecting state and halts. If, at any point, a stack symbol s_i fails to match an input symbol p_i under the read head, Q knows it must abort the current attempt to match and it must find a way to try to match P against some other substring of S. It does this by reversing direction and scanning rightward along the input tape and pushing all the symbols of P onto its stack as it goes. This restores the characters of S (which were identical to those of P) back onto the pushdown stack. When Q hits the right end marker ¢, it pops one symbol of S off its pushdown stack, say s_k, and moves one symbol to the left on the input tape; now it starts again matching $s_{k-1} \cdots s_1$ @ on its stack against $p_m p_{m-1} \cdots p_1$ as it once again moves left on the tape. This time, a new substring of S one character to the left of the previous one tried is tested against P to see if it matches.

Since the 2DPDA can solve the pattern-matching problem (even though it takes quadratic time), Cook's theorem implies that there exists a program on a random-access machine that solves the same problem in linear time.

The story goes that when Knuth and Pratt found out about this, they knew there had to exist a linear string pattern-matching algorithm but they didn't know how to construct one. They laboriously went through Cook's linear simulation of the 2DPDA to find out how it could work and came up with a first version of their linear pattern-matching algorithm. It then turned out that Morris had a similar algorithm, but he had not been able to show that it could run in linear time. Putting all these results together, the Knuth–Morris–Pratt algorithm was born. Here is a case where a knowledge of theoretical computer science produced a surprising and important practical result.

7.5.2.2 The Boyer–Moore Algorithm. Recently, Boyer and Moore [1977] have come up with another surprising development—a string pattern-matching algorithm that can often find whether a pattern P is a substring of S *without, on the average, having to inspect all characters of S*! They call it a *sublinear* algorithm. They have experimental data that shows that it is very fast under appropriate circumstances.

The key idea is to superimpose the pattern $P = p_1 p_2 \cdots p_m$ on the string $S = s_1 s_2 \cdots s_n$,

$$p_1 \qquad p_2 \qquad \cdots \qquad p_m$$
$$\cdots \quad s_{k-m+1} \qquad s_{k-m+2} \qquad \cdots \qquad s_k \cdots$$

and to match characters of P against those of the underlying segment of S in *right-to-left* order while the pattern P is being moved to the right. If the rightmost character of P, namely p_m, does not match the underlying character s_k of S, it may also be the case that s_k doesn't occur in P at all. If so, the pattern P can be slid over to the right all the way past s_k, since no character of P superimposed above s_k will ever match s_k.

$$
\begin{array}{ccccc}
p_1 & p_2 & \cdots & p_m \\
\cdots \quad s_{k-1} \quad s_k & s_{k+1} & s_{k+2} & \cdots & s_{k+m} \cdots
\end{array}
$$

After the slide to the right, the match can be tried again starting with a comparison of p_m with s_{k+m}. Note that, since there was no need to compare any of the $s_{k-m+1} \cdots s_{k-1}$ with $p_1 \cdots p_{m-1}$, $m-1$ comparisons were omitted.

More generally, if the rightmost occurrence of s_k in P is r characters from the right end of P, then we can slide P right r characters without checking for matches since, if P were moved right any amount less than r, s_k would be aligned with a character p_j of P it couldn't possibly match, p_j being to the right of the rightmost occurrence of s_k in P.

Here r is a function of the characters in the string S. For characters $c \in S$ such that $c \notin P$, $r(c) = m$; and for characters $c \in S$ such that $c \in P$, $r(c) = m - j$, where j is the largest integer such that $c = p_j$.

Suppose now that we are checking the characters of P against those of S beneath in right-to-left order. If all characters of P match those of S beneath, we have found a substring of S to match P. If, however, a mismatch is detected, say at position p_j, after having matched the last $m - j$ characters of P, what can we do?

$$
\text{Last } m - j \text{ characters of } P
$$

$$
\begin{array}{cccc}
\cdots \quad p_j & \overbrace{p_{j+1}} & \cdots & p_m \\
\cdots \quad s_{k-m+j} & s_{k-m+j+1} & \cdots & s_k \quad \cdots \\
\uparrow \\
\text{Mismatch}
\end{array}
$$

There are two possibilities. First, if the second-to-last occurrence of the mismatching character s_{k-m+j} occurs in P to the left of p_j, we could slide P to the right by an amount $r(s_{k-m+j}) - (m-j)$ to align s_{k-m+j} and this next-to-last occurrence of s_{k-m+j} in P. The character pointer that points to the current character of S could then be incremented by $r(s_{k-m+j})$ to access the new character of S to match against the last character p_m of P.

Second, given that the last $m - j$ characters of P match the underlying characters of S, we could treat the last $m - j$ characters of P as a subpattern $P' = p_{j+1} \cdots p_m$; and we could find the next-to-last occurrence of P' in P, if it exists. We could then slide P to the right by some amount $R1$ so as to align the second-to-last occurrence of P' with $s_{k-m+j+1} \cdots s_k$. The character pointer to the character s_{k-m+j} can now be incremented by an amount $R1 + (m - j)$ so it will align with the last character p_m of P in P's new position, ready for the next character comparison.

So let $R(j)$ be the amount to increment the character pointer for S to the right, based on the second-to-last occurrence of P' in P. Then, if we have matched the final $m - j$ characters of P and we get a mismatch at p_j, we slide P to the right an appropriate amount, and increment the character pointer for S by the larger of the amounts $R(j)$ and $r(s_i)$, where $i = k - m + j$, to provide the maximum jump.

Before giving the precise definitions of the incrementing functions $r(c)$ and $R(j)$, it is convenient to define a slight extension of the concept of identical string matching called *unification*. Let θ be a character not in pattern P. Let us assume that pattern $P = p_1 p_2 \cdots p_m$ is extended as far to the left as we wish by defining $p_k = \theta$ for $k \leq 0$. Now we say that two sequences of characters $c_1 c_2 \cdots c_n$ and $d_1 d_2 \cdots d_n$ *unify* if $c_i = d_i$ or if either $c_i = \theta$ or $d_i = \theta$ for all i $(1 \leq i \leq n)$. As a special case, we agree that two empty sequences *unify*.

Letting m be the length of P, we state the formal definitions of the S-pointer incrementing functions $r(c)$ and $R(j)$ as follows:

For all characters $c \in S$, define

$$r(c) = \text{if } c \notin P \text{ then } m, \text{ else } m - j \text{ where } j \text{ is the largest integer such that } c = p_j.$$

For all integers j in the range $1 \leq j \leq m$, define

$$R(j) = m + 1 - (\text{the greatest } k \leq m \text{ such that } p_{j+1} \cdots p_m \text{ and } p_k \cdots p_{k+m-j-1} \text{ unify and either } k \leq 1 \text{ or } p_{k-1} \neq p_j).$$

The Boyer–Moore algorithm for finding whether P is a substring of S can now be given as follows:

Algorithm 7.6 *Boyer–Moore string pattern matching.*

Let $S = s_1 s_2 \cdots s_n$ be a string and let $P = p_1 p_2 \cdots p_m$ be a pattern. The algorithm terminates with result 0 if P is not a substring of S. Otherwise, it terminates with result i, where i is the position of the first character of the leftmost substring of S matching P.

1. [Initialize.] Set $i \leftarrow m$.
2. [Failure?] If $i > n$, terminate the algorithm with result 0. Otherwise, set $j \leftarrow m$.
3. [Success?] If $j = 0$, the algorithm terminates successfully with result $i + 1$.
4. [Compare.] If $s_i = p_j$ then set $j \leftarrow j - 1$, set $i \leftarrow i - 1$, and go to step 3.
5. [Advance i.] Set $i \leftarrow i + \max (R(j), r(s_i))$ and go back to step 2.

Boyer and Moore implemented their algorithm in machine code on a PDP-10 and compared its search speed with the search algorithm used in a PDP-10 text editor (TECO), which uses a tightly coded version of Algorithm 7.3 (quadratic search in worst-case, but not much above linear in practice). They wrote a test-data generator to select random substrings of a given length from some string S of given length. This program was used to select 50 strings randomly, each of length n for each n in the range $1 \leq n \leq 15$, and the speed of both search algorithms was compared. To get the speed of each algorithm in characters per second, for each n ($1 \leq n \leq 15$), the penetration depths into S for each match were summed up for each of the randomly chosen strings of length n; and this sum was divided by the cumulative total number of seconds to do all 50 searches. Figure 7.25 (from an earlier version of Boyer and Moore [1977]) plots the results as a function of the pattern length n. The figures for the Boyer–Moore algorithm include the time necessary for preprocessing the pattern.

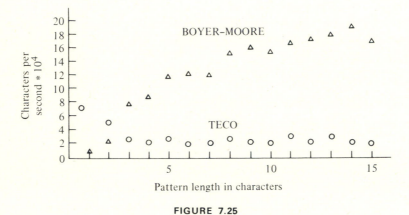

FIGURE 7.25

TECO is 12 times faster than Boyer–Moore on patterns of length 1, and 3.2 times faster on patterns of length 3, but on patterns of length 10 it is six times slower. Furthermore, as shown in Fig. 7.26, the Boyer–Moore algorithm skips more characters in S the larger the pattern P becomes. For example, if an average pattern of length 10 is found at location i in S, the Boyer–Moore algorithm looks

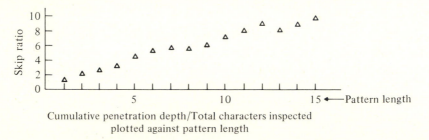

Cumulative penetration depth/Total characters inspected plotted against pattern length

FIGURE 7.26

at $i/7.2$ characters before finding it. By coding their algorithm tightly, Boyer and Moore were able to achieve the result that, on the average, the match is found at position i in S even though fewer than i machine instructions have been executed.

Knuth has proved that the Boyer–Moore algorithm has linear behavior in the worst case (see Knuth, Morris, and Pratt [1977], where it is shown that the linear worst case bound is due entirely to the R heuristic). One might hope for even stronger results in the form of a discovery of some string-matching algorithm whose worst case is provably sublinear; but Rivest [1977] has shown that this is impossible by proving that any algorithm for finding a pattern of length m in a string of length n must examine at least $n - m + 1$ of the characters in the string, in the worst case.

Boyer and Moore [1977] point out that the S-pointer incrementing functions $r(c)$ and $R(j)$ can be computed linearly during pattern preprocessing by the results of Knuth, Morris, and Pratt.

7.5.2.3 *Harrison's substring test using hash signatures.* Suppose we have a collection of strings S_i ($1 \le i \le N$) such as might be given as lines of a text. When there is a low probability of finding an instance of a pattern P in any average such string S_i, it may be useful to devise a cheap test $T(P, S_i)$ that is necessary but not sufficient for P to be a substring of S_i. That is, if $T(P, S_i) = false$, then P is known not to be a substring of S_i; but if $T(P, S_i) = true$, then P may or may not be a substring of S, and a more expensive test is required to determine the actual fact. An example of such a test is the comparison of the lengths of P and S_i,

$$T(P, S_i) \equiv (|P| \le |S_i|),$$

but this test is too weak to be of much value.

Harrison [1971] has given a cheap substring test using hashing techniques that is demonstrably strong under appropriate conditions and that relies on the ability of most computers to perform many Boolean operations in parallel.

We first define the *hashed k-signature* of a string S. Let $b_1 b_2 \cdots b_n$ be a bit vector with $b_i = 0$ ($1 \le i \le n$). For each substring s of S such that $|s| = k$, compute a hash function $i = \text{hash}(s)$ where the range of the hash function is $1 \le i \le n$; and set b_i to 1. This is called the hashed k-signature of S, and we denote it by $H^k(S)$.

If P is a substring of S, then $H^k(S)$ has ones in every position where $H^k(P)$ does, since any substring α of length k of P is also a substring of length k of S, implying that $b_{\text{hash}(\alpha)} = 1$ in both signatures. In other words, a necessary condition that P be a substring of S is that the hashed k-signature of S must "cover" that of P by having ones in every position where the hashed k-signature of P does.

By choosing the length of the bit vector $b_1 b_2 \cdots b_n$ equal to the length of a machine word, it is often possible to implement the signature test in two or three machine instructions. Letting Substring(P, S) denote a rigorous substring test that returns *true* or *false*, we can use the hashed k-signature test as a "filter", as shown in the following algorithm:

Algorithm 7.7 *Harrison's test for finding whether P is a substring of S.*

Let $H1$ and $H2$ be the respective hashed k-signatures of P and S.

1. [Test.] If $(H1 \wedge \sim H2) \neq 0$, then the algorithm terminates with the result *false*. Otherwise, the algorithm terminates with the result obtained by calling Substring(P, S).

Note that $H2$ covers $H1$ iff $(H1 \wedge (\sim H2)) = 0$, since the only way $H1 \wedge (\sim H2)$ can be nonzero is for at least one bit of $H1$ to be 1 when the corresponding bit of $H2$ is 0.

The two free parameters in this discussion are n and k. How should each be chosen? Suppose that n has been chosen as a multiple of the number of bits in a machine word (though this is not necessary). Given a random hash function, a value of k should be chosen so that the average number of ones in a hashed k-signature is neither too large nor too small. The larger k is, the smaller the number of bits in a signature; but if $k = 1$, no order information is being used in computing the signature. We must also choose n and k so that the probability of a false match is low enough to make the technique effective. For this purpose, we need to compute the probability of a false match; that is, the probability that the hashed k-signature of S will cover that of P, even though P is not a substring of S. To do this, we follow the argument given in Bookstein [1973].

Suppose that the hash function has been chosen to be random and that random strings P and S have been chosen. (This will not be exactly true in practice since there are dependencies in actual text.) Let there be ℓ_1 segments of size k in the pattern P (from which the length of P is seen to be $\ell_1 + k - 1$), and let there be ℓ_2 segments of size k in the string S (from which the length of S is seen to be $\ell_2 + k - 1$).

We want to estimate the probability that a bit hashed onto by a segment of P will already have been turned on by the hashing of some segment of S. The probability that a given k-segment of P will hash onto an arbitrarily chosen bit among the n possible bits in the signature is $1/n$. Hence, $(1 - 1/n)^{\ell_2}$ is the probability that all ℓ_2 segments of S will not hash onto the chosen bit, and $[1 - (1 - 1/n)^{\ell_2}]$ is the probability that a given segment of P hashes onto a bit already turned on in the signature of S. Therefore, the probability that each of the ℓ_1 segments of P will hash onto a bit already turned on in the signature of S is given by

$$p(\ell_1, \ell_2, n) = \left[1 - \left(1 - \frac{1}{n} \right)^{\ell_2} \right]^{\ell_1}. \tag{17}$$

Now since $(1 - 1/n)^n \approx 1/e$, we can replace $(1 - 1/n)^{\ell_2}$ with $e^{-\ell_2/n}$, getting

$$p(\ell_1, \ell_2, n) \approx (1 - e^{-\ell_2/n})^{\ell_1}.$$

For example, the probability of a 13-character string being falsely identified as a substring of a 52-character string, using 2-signatures with 32-bit words, is less than ten percent which means that at least ninety percent of nonsubstrings will be rejected by the signature test.

The signature test for locating substrings has been used in a conversational text editor in which one locates a line by specifying a substring contained in the line (see Harrison [1971]). If the hashed k-signature of each line of text is stored along with each line, rapid search is possible.

7.6 BIBLIOGRAPHIC NOTES

Karlgren's representation is studied in KARLGREN [1963]. Huffman codes are discussed in HUFFMAN [1952] and in KNUTH [1973a]. SCHWARTZ [1964] shows how to construct a Huffman tree that is "well balanced" in the sense that, among all possible Huffman trees with minimum weighted path length, Schwartz's procedure selects one with smallest depth.

A short readable introduction to some concepts in algebraic coding theory can be found in BERZTISS [1975]. The appearance of HAMMING [1950] stimulated much work in coding theory. Further treatment of Hamming codes can be found in PETERSON and WELDON [1961], BIRKHOFF and BARTEE [1970], and STONE [1973].

Interesting measurements of characteristics of FORTRAN programs are found in KNUTH [1971], and the technique of compressing blanks to produce "Squoze decks" is given in BOEHM and STEEL [1959]. Two studies of techniques for producing compressed representations of natural-language text are WOLFF [1978] and LOUIS-GAVET [1978]. Wolff's technique builds a dictionary of frequently occurring letter strings and replaces them by short codes, yielding compression of up to forty-nine percent.

Some early references on cryptography are VIGENÈRE [1586], KASISKI [1863], and KERCKHOFFS [1883]. In the nineteenth century, Kasiski and Kerckhoffs showed that polyalphabetic substitution is unsafe if used with a periodic key. The method named after the sixteenth-century Frenchman Vigenère consists of the use of a nonperiodic key in connection with a relatively simple polyalphabetic substitution, which is, if properly used, unbreakable (SHANNON [1949]).

Information on the Lucifer system is given in SMITH [1971], FEISTAL [1973], and FEISTAL, NOTZ, and SMITH [1975].

Public-key cryptosystems are discussed in HELLMAN [1978], DIFFIE and HELLMAN [1976b], RIVEST, SHAMIR, and ADLEMAN [1978], GARDNER [1977], MERKLE and HELLMAN [1978], and NEEDHAM and SCHROEDER [1978]. An interesting attack on the M.I.T. public-key cryptosystem, consisting of repeatedly applying the encrypting function in the forward direction until the original message appears, is examined in SIMMONS and NORRIS [1977], RIVEST [1978b], and HERLESTAM [1978]. In applying the Rivest, Shamir, and Adleman technique, it is especially important to observe precautions mentioned in the latter three articles and in the original paper (RIVEST, SHAMIR, and ADLEMAN [1978]) that were not covered in this book.

An interesting public controversy concerning the cryptographic strength of the National Bureau of Standards Data Encyption Standard (DES), and concerning other matters of public policy related to publication of research results on cryptography in the open literature, takes place in DIFFIE and HELLMAN [1976a, 1977], HELLMAN [1977], SHAPLEY and BARI KOLATA [1977], BARI KOLATA [1977ab, 1978], SHAPLEY [1977ab, 1978], MORRIS [1977, 1978], TUCHMAN [1977], BLAIR [1977], BRANSTAD [1975], and U.S. Senate Select Committee on Intelligence [1978].

Interesting history and background on cryptanalysis is found in KAHN [1967, 1975]. Elementary cryptanalytic techniques are given in GAINES [1956]. PURDY [1974] studies a secure log-in technique. BAYER and METZGER [1976] study encrypting in file systems.

Matula's test and a discussion of fixed-point number conversions and rounding are found in GOLDBERG [1967], MATULA [1968ab], METROPOLIS and ASHENHURST [1965], and KNUTH [1969].

Examples of representations of variable-length string representations are given in d'IMPERIO [1969], BERZTISS [1965], MADNICK [1967], and HARRISON [1973].

Macroexpansion is studied in McILROY [1960], STRACHEY [1965], and BROWN [1969]. FISCHER [1968] formalizes the concept of macroexpansion using the notion of a *macro grammar* and shows that "outside-in" expansion can generate more than "inside-out" expansion.

The Knuth–Morris–Pratt algorithm is discussed in MORRIS and PRATT [1970], KNUTH and PRATT [1971], KNUTH, MORRIS, and PRATT [1977], and AHO, HOPCROFT, and ULLMAN [1974]. Cook's theorem on linear simulation of 2DPDA's is given in COOK [1971], KNUTH and PRATT [1971], and AHO, HOPCROFT, and ULLMAN [1974].

The Boyer–Moore algorithm is studied in BOYER and MOORE [1977]. Harrison's hashed-signature test for substrings is presented in HARRISON [1971]; and an improved probability estimate for the success of the substring test is given in BOOKSTEIN [1973].

GIMPEL [1970] and HARRISON [1973] discuss algorithms for generalized pattern matching and extraction of substrings in the context of the SNOBOL programming language. AHO, HOPCROFT, and ULLMAN [1974] give a technique for recognizing strings that are instances of regular expressions in time proportional to the product of the length of the string and the length of the regular expression.

Matching strings containing "don't care" characters is discussed in FISCHER and PATTERSON [1974]. WEINER [1973] introduces "position trees" for solving problems such as finding the longest common substring of two strings in linear time. McCREIGHT [1976], and HIRSCHBERG [1973a, 1977, 1978] give further information on this problem. KARP, MILLER, and ROSENBERG [1972] give further techniques for fast identification of repeated structures in strings, arrays, and trees. The string-to-string correction process that finds the smallest number of deletions and insertions needed to transform one string into another is discussed in WAGNER and FISCHER [1974]. AHO and CORASICK [1975] discuss applications of fast string-pattern matching in bibliographic search problems.

EXERCISES

1. (Code size) Given an alphabet of 243 characters, how many bits are needed to represent each character if distinct codes of uniform length are assigned to each character?

2. (Self-correcting Huffman codes?) One night, Prof. Connie Lisst discovered by computer experiment that if a bit is spuriously changed in a Huffman-coded bit string, then even though decoding is "thrown off", it tends not to be thrown off for very long. That is, after processing the erroneous bit, the decoding tends to return to normal. Also, if the Huffman codes are of several different lengths, adding or dropping bits in the Huffman code throws the decoding off, but not for very long. Investigate these phenomenona under various conditions and characterize them.

3. (Code cracking) Suppose you know that the following string is an encrypted version of the initial part of the Gettysburg Address: "Fcnoodur-res--esaver-nso--uyareg-aofa-htbthr-eofruosgrttohhn-itosin-n-cennttei,   wo--nan,   -a-", where "-" represents a space. Can you crack the code?

4. (Cryptanalysis: Vernam ciphers) Mr. Alf Witt is proud of the encrypting scheme he has devised for protecting a user's personal calendar file stored in a popular operating system's files. The calendar file stores reminders, such as "April 15, 1980 10:00 a.m. Check Tax Returns Mailed". It stores them in chronological order, and deletes obsolete reminders (defined as those whose time is no longer in the future). Witt uses a Vernam cipher to encrypt calendar files by obtaining a secret key K from the user, transforming it into a seed for the public random-number generator (given by formula (8) of Section 7.3.1), and generating a sequence of random numbers k_i ($0 \leq i \leq n$), which are then exclusive-or'ed with the calendar file text to encrypt it. Mrs. Anna Leiser decides to prove Witt's method is vulnerable to a simple cryptanalytic attack. She enlists the support of two collaborators C. Ductive and D. Ceptive, to get Witt to plant an appointment for the first time the next morning into his calendar file "August 20, 1979 8:00 a.m. Meet with C. Ductive and D. Ceptive". Anna then obtains a copy of the encrypted version of Witt's file the next morning, which she knows has the planted record as its very first item. She then has a cryptogram–plaintext pair. Using this, how can she decrypt the rest of Witt's file without even knowing Witt's secret key K?

5. (Karlgren's representation) Given a matrix of the frequencies of digrams (i.e., two-letter pairs) for some sample text, give an algorithm for partitioning the alphabet A into two disjoint sets U and L of equal size, called "cases", so that the probability of a case shift between adjacent letters in the text is minimized.

6. (Code conversion: Robert Morris and K. E. Iverson) A programming language L accepts characters typed in at a terminal. Certain of the permissible characters in L must be typed by overstriking two or more characters of the character set used by the terminal. For example, the character " $\neq$ " can be generated by typing "=", then backspacing and typing "/". It is also permissible to type "/" first and then to backspace and type "=" second, in order to generate " $\neq$ ". The final visual appearance on the typed line determines what

overstruck characters are specified, not the order in which the keys are struck. This "what you see is what you get" philosophy is termed "visual fidelity" in the programming language manual for L. Write an algorithm to accept sequences of input characters in an alphabet A (including a backspace character) and to convert such sequences into characters in an extended alphabet A', where characters in A' are equivalent to nonempty subsets of no more than two characters of A overstruck in any order, and where A' contains no backspace character.

7. (Minimum-depth Huffman codes: Schwartz) In Algorithm 7.1, suppose we start with the frequencies in order $f_1 \leq f_2 \leq \cdots \leq f_n$, and suppose we keep them in order such that when f_1 and f_2 are removed, $f_1 + f_2$ is placed back into the sequence in the highest possible position (i.e., between f_j and f_{j+1} where $f_j \leq f_1 + f_2 < f_{j+1}$). Show that Algorithm 7.1 constructs then the Huffman tree with smallest depth among all trees with minimum weighted path length for the f_i $(1 \leq i \leq n)$. [Recall that the *depth* of a binary tree is the length in edges of the longest path from the root to a leaf.]

8. (Assessing the assessors) Profs. van Snipe and Lisst are making up an exam for their students. Lisst suggests using question 19 of the ACM Self-Assessment Procedure II. Van Snipe objects, saying no correct answer is given. What is your opinion? Question 19 (see Frederick [1977]) is as follows:

> "Assume a machine uses 36 bits to represent the unsigned fraction (mantissa) of floating-point numbers. To determine the maximum number of significant digits, d, that can be represented, which one of the following equations for d must be solved?
>
> a) $36 = 10d$ c) $36^2 = d^{10}$
> b) $36 \times 2 = 10 \times d$ d) $10^d = 2^{36}$"

The answer given is 19(d).

9. (Multiplicative inverses modulo n) To compute e where $e \times d \equiv 1 (\text{modulo } \phi(n))$ in the method of Rivest, Shamir, and Adleman for public-key cryptosystems, one can start with $x_0 = \phi(n)$ and $x_1 = d$, and using Euclid's algorithm, one can obtain successive remainders that form a series $x_0, x_1, \ldots, x_k$ until finally $x_k = 0$. Here, $x_{i+1} \equiv x_{i-1}(\text{modulo } x_i)$. In Euclid's algorithm, when $x_k = 0$, the gcd of x_0 and x_1 is known to be x_{k-1} (the last nonzero remainder in the sequence). Show how to combine the numbers x_i in some easy fashion that enables quick computation of the value e. (Rivest, Shamir, and Adleman [1978].)

10. (Knuth–Morris–Pratt) Construct the Knuth–Morris–Pratt pattern-matching machine M to recognize the pattern "abcababc" in strings over the alphabet $A = \{a, b, c\}$.

11. (Boyer–Moore) Given a pattern P over an alphabet A, write a linear-time algorithm for computing $r(c)$.

12. (Boyer–Moore) Given a pattern P over an alphabet A, give a linear algorithm for computing $R(j)$. [*Hint.* Use a Knuth–Morris–Pratt failure-link table computed in a certain fashion.]

13. (Longest common substrings) Write an algorithm for determining the longest common substring of two strings S and T (Weiner [1973]).

14. (String-to-string correction) Given two strings $S1$ and $S2$, write an algorithm to determine the smallest number of single character insertions and deletions to convert $S1$ to $S2$ (Wagner and Fischer [1972]).

15. (Repeated substrings) Given a string S, write an algorithm to determine the longest repeated substring of S. (Weiner [1973].)

16. (Implications of Cook's Theorem) Suppose that, for any context-free language L, a program could be written for a 2DPDA to accept strings in L and reject strings not in L. What would this imply about the time required to recognize context-free languages? (The best-known bound for general recognition of context-free languages, at the moment, is $N^{2.8}$.)

17. (R. Morris [1978]) Suppose one decides to use the NBS Data Encryption Standard (DES) technique having 56-bit keys. Show how one can get a longer effective key length by composing two DES chips in series, each with its own separate 56-bit key to get an equivalent key length of 112 bits. As Morris [1978] points out, we can view the DES essentially as a permutation operation on letters of a 2^{64}-character alphabet wherein the key selects one of 2^{56} possible substitution ciphers. Taking this point of view, and assuming that each of the 2^{56} possible keys selects a distinct permutation, how much would composing DES chips in series improve the security of the DES method against a brute-force exhaustion attack using fast, parallel-chip hardware?

ARRAYS

8.1 INTRODUCTION AND MOTIVATION

Arrays are systems of elements indexed by a system of integer coordinates. The system of indexes is used to access elements and to permit alteration of individual elements.

The primary memory of most contemporary computers is a linear array of words of uniform size addressed by a contiguous subset of the integers. Because of this, the linear array is an underlying representation that supports nearly every other kind of higher-level data structure. We have seen that techniques for allocating storage within linear arrays are of major importance in many places in this book.

Perhaps it is not surprising then, that nearly every programming language supports some form of array as a data structure. However, there is considerable variation in the flexibility of array use allowed. While some languages require allocation of arrays in advance of the running of programs, other languages, such as ALGOL 60, permit arrays to be allocated dynamically at block entry time—that is, the size of an array may be computed at block entry and remains fixed over the lifetime of the block. Languages such as APL use arrays as the basic composite data structure, and permit arrays to change size, shape, and dimension dynamically during program execution and even during the evaluation of expressions.

In some internal representations of arrays, traversal is made particularly efficient because elements in adjacent rows, columns, or planes are stored either at constant intervals or at intervals that are simple to compute.

There are a variety of choices for representations of arrays of higher dimensions in terms of linear storage allocation schemes. The properties of those representations naturally are susceptible to trade-offs.

In this chapter, for each of the array representations we shall study, we shall remark on four dimensions of "representation quality." These are: (1) simplicity of element access, (2) ease of traversal along various paths, (3) storage utilization efficiency, and (4) ease of growth. While these are not the only criteria we could use for comparison, their consistent use in this chapter helps establish a framework in which the characteristics of various underlying array representations can be portrayed, and it helps us understand which array-representation techniques to use in order to achieve efficiency in one or more of the desired aspects.

In fact, formal investigations suggest that the trade-off between several of these "representation qualities" is inviolable. For example, Rosenberg [1974] shows, under appropriate formal conditions, that simplicity of array extension precludes simplicity of certain traversals of elements; and deMillo, Eisenstat, and Lipton [1978] show that arrays cannot be stored as trees without unbounded loss in element proximity.

The primary purpose of this chapter is to come to grips with and to compare characteristics of underlying array representations. For this reason, we do not study applications of arrays as host representations for other data structures, nor do we apply arrays to the solution of other algorithmic problems.

8.2 BASIC CONCEPTS AND NOTATION

In order to discuss various underlying array-representation schemes, it is helpful to have a common representation-independent notion for arrays. Our starting point is the notion of a *bound pair* (a term taken from ALGOL 60).

Definition 8.1 Given two integers m and n, the *bound pair* $m:n$ is the set of integers from m to n,

$$m:n = \{i \mid (i \text{ is an integer) and } (m \leq i \leq n)\}.$$

A bounded rectangular set of n-tuples can be specified using a cartesian product of bound pairs. For example,

$$m_1:n_1 \times m_2:n_2 \times \cdots \times m_k:n_k$$

specifies the set of integer k-tuples $(i_1, i_2, \ldots, i_k)$ such that $m_j \leq i_j \leq n_j$ for all j in the range $1 \leq j \leq k$. The set of integer k-tuples $m_1:n_1 \times m_2:n_2 \times \cdots \times m_k:n_k$ can be visualized as the set of all lattice points in a "rectangular" region of k-space.

Let R be a set of array elements.

Definition 8.2 An *array* A is an association between integer k-tuples and elements of the set R such that, to each k-tuple in the set

$$m_1:n_1 \times m_2:n_2 \times \cdots \times m_k:n_k,$$

there corresponds an element of R.

An *element* of the array A is denoted $A[i_1, i_2, \ldots, i_k]$, where $(i_1, i_2, \ldots, i_k)$ is a k-tuple in $m_1:n_1 \times m_2:n_2 \times \cdots \times m_k:n_k$, and it consists of the element of R associated with $(i_1, i_2, \ldots, i_k)$. The k-tuples $(i_1, i_2, \ldots, i_k)$ are called array indices, and the individual components i_j $(1 \leq j \leq k)$ are called *subscripts*. Square brackets are used to denote array subscripts, while parentheses are used to denote other functional relations.

During most of our discussion of array representations, we will assume that the elements in R can each be stored in computer memory in a fixed amount of space, although in some representations this restriction can be relaxed.

Sometimes we will consider subarrays that are nonrectangular. We will normally specify these subarrays by relations on the subscripts of the general array element $A[i_1, i_2, \ldots, i_k]$. For example, a *lower triangular array* is a system of elements $A[i, j]$ for which $1 \le j \le i$. Here "$1 \le j \le i$" is the relation on subscripts i and j that describes the shape of the subarray under consideration.

Two special sorts of arrays that are defined in this fashion are *tetrahedral arrays* and *ragged arrays*.

Definition 8.3 A *tetrahedral array* A of dimension k and size n is a system of elements $A[i_1, i_2, \ldots, i_k]$ such that $1 \le i_k \le i_{k-1} \le \cdots \le i_1 \le n$.

Definition 8.4 A *ragged array* A is a system of elements $A[i_1, i_2, \ldots, i_k]$ with the property that, if $A[i_1, i_2, \ldots, i_k]$ is an element of A, then for each r in the range $1 \le r \le k$, so is $A[i_1, i_2, \ldots, i_{r-1}, j_r, i_{r+1}, \ldots, i_k]$, provided $1 \le j_r \le i_r$ and $i_s = 1$ if $s > r$.

Following the notation used in array declarations in ALGOL 60, we shall use the expression $A[m_1 : n_1, \ldots, m_k : n_k]$ to define A as an array having indices in the set $m_1 : n_1 \times \cdots \times m_k : n_k$; and we shall say that k is the *dimension* of A.

8.3 STORAGE ALLOCATION FUNCTIONS

Let $A[m_1 : n_1, m_2 : n_2, \ldots, m_k : n_k]$ be an array of dimension k. A storage allocation function $\text{Loc}(A[i_1, i_2, \ldots, i_k])$ is a mapping that assigns a distinct underlying machine address α to each distinct array index $(i_1, i_2, \ldots, i_k)$ of array A, where α is the address of a cell of suitable size for storing an element of A.

(Actually, the notation $\text{Loc}(A[i_1, i_2, \ldots, i_k])$ is somewhat of an abuse of normal mathematical notation. If the notation $\text{Loc}(A[i_1, i_2, \ldots, i_k])$ were interpreted in the usual mathematical fashion, it would signify that we should first obtain the value of the array element a denoted by $A[i_1, i_2, \ldots, i_k]$, and that we should then attempt to find the value $\text{Loc}(a)$. However, our usage follows that established by Knuth ([1973a], p. 231), in which Loc is a special notation with the property that $\text{Loc}(V)$ is defined to be the address of the cell holding the value that V names. For consistency with normal mathematical practice, we should have written $\text{Loc}(A, (i_1, i_2, \ldots, i_k))$ as a two-place function, to signify that the address α computed by Loc for index $(i_1, i_2, \ldots, i_k)$ of array A is a function of both the array name A and the index $(i_1, i_2, \ldots, i_k)$. Since the latter notation is clumsy, we shall use the former along with the special agreement about what it signifies.)

Since $\text{Loc}(A[i_1, i_2, \ldots, i_k])$ is defined to give distinct addresses α corresponding to distinct indices $(i_1, i_2, \ldots, i_k)$, it is a 1–1 function mapping indices into a region of memory $M : N$. If we require further that the mapping $\text{Loc}(A[i_1, i_2, \ldots, i_k])$ be an *onto* mapping of indices for $A[i_1, i_2, \ldots, i_k]$ onto $M : N$, we get the class of *sequential storage allocation* functions. These are deserving of attention because of their optimal storage utilization properties.

8.3.1 Lexicographic storage allocation

A *lexicographic ordering* of the integer k-tuples $(i_1, i_2, \ldots, i_k)$ in the set $m_1 : n_1 \times m_2 : n_2 \times \cdots \times m_k : n_k$ is defined as follows:

$$(a_1, a_2, \ldots, a_k) < (b_1, b_2, \ldots, b_k) \quad \text{iff there is some } j \text{ in the}$$
$$\text{range } 1 \leq j \leq k \text{ such that}$$
$$a_i = b_i \text{ for } 1 \leq i < j, \text{ and } a_j < b_j.$$

Thus, if $a_j < b_j$ and if a_j and b_j are the leftmost elements of $(a_1, a_2, \ldots, a_k)$ and $(b_1, b_2, \ldots, b_k)$ that differ, then

$$(a_1, a_2, \ldots, a_k) < (b_1, b_2, \ldots, b_k)$$

in lexicographic order. For example, the indices of the array $A[0:2, 0:3]$ in lexicographic order are:

$$(0, 0) < (0, 1) < (0, 2) < (0, 3) < (1, 0) < (1, 1)$$
$$< (1, 2) < (1, 3) < (2, 0) < (2, 1) < (2, 2) < (2, 3).$$

A *lexicographic storage allocation function* for the array A is a 1–1, *onto* function Loc such that, if $(a_1, a_2, \ldots, a_k) < (b_1, b_2, \ldots, b_k)$ according to lexicographic order, then $\text{Loc}(A[a_1, a_2, \ldots, a_k]) < \text{Loc}(A[b_1, b_2, \ldots, b_k])$ according to the normal integer ordering of the address space onto which Loc maps $A[i_1, i_2, \ldots, i_k]$. Figure 8.1 illustrates a lexicographic storage allocation for elements of the array $A[0:2, 0:3]$ on the address space $0:11$.

Location	Array element
0	$A[0, 0]$
1	$A[0, 1]$
2	$A[0, 2]$
3	$A[0, 3]$
4	$A[1, 0]$
5	$A[1, 1]$
6	$A[1, 2]$
7	$A[1, 3]$
8	$A[2, 0]$
9	$A[2, 1]$
10	$A[2, 2]$
11	$A[2, 3]$

FIGURE 8.1

The formula $\text{Loc}(A[i_1, i_2]) = 4 \times i_1 + i_2$ gives a lexicographic storage allocation function mapping array elements $A[i_1, i_2]$ onto locations $0:11$ matching those of Fig. 8.1. If we display the elements of $A[0:2, 0:3]$ as a rectangular array, as in Fig. 8.2, where we have three rows and four columns, we see that Fig. 8.1 provides

$$A[0,0] \quad A[0,1] \quad A[0,2] \quad A[0,3]$$
$$A[1,0] \quad A[1,1] \quad A[1,2] \quad A[1,3]$$
$$A[2,0] \quad A[2,1] \quad A[2,2] \quad A[2,3]$$

FIGURE 8.2

storage for the three rows of A in ascending order of memory addresses. First, row 0 of A is stored in locations $0:3$; then row 1 of A is stored in locations $4:7$; and finally row 2 of A is stored in locations $8:11$. Such a storage arrangement is said to be in *row-major* order.

If, instead, we store elements of A column by column, we get a storage arrangement for A said to be in *column-major* order, as illustrated in Fig. 8.3.

Location	Array element
0	$A[0,0]$
1	$A[1,0]$
2	$A[2,0]$
3	$A[0,1]$
4	$A[1,1]$
5	$A[2,1]$
6	$A[0,2]$
7	$A[1,2]$
8	$A[2,2]$
9	$A[0,3]$
10	$A[1,3]$
11	$A[2,3]$

FIGURE 8.3

Two-dimensional arrays are stored in column-major order in FORTRAN, using a storage allocation function such as $\text{Loc}(A[i_1, i_2]) = i_1 + 3 \times i_2$. However, column-major order is different from lexicographic order since, for instance, $A[2, 0]$ appears earlier in column-major order than $A[0, 1]$ even though $A[0, 1]$ comes before $A[2, 0]$ in lexicographic order.

To figure out how to construct lexicographic storage allocation functions for the general array $A[m_1 : n_1, \ldots, m_k : n_k]$, consider the two indices $(i_1, i_2, \ldots, i_k)$ and $(i_1 + 1, i_2, \ldots, i_k)$. Every array element with a first subscript i_1 and arbitrary values of the subscripts $i_2, \ldots, i_k$ comes before any element with a first subscript $i_1 + 1$ and arbitrary subscripts $i_2, \ldots, i_k$ according to lexicographic ordering. Therefore, we must arrange to map all elements $A[i_1, i_2, \ldots, i_k]$ with i_1 fixed and $i_2, \ldots, i_k$ varying onto a contiguous sequential set of locations that are immediately lower than those for the adjacent higher region onto which we map the elements $A[i_1 + 1, i_2, \ldots, i_k]$ with $i_1 + 1$ fixed and $i_2, \ldots, i_k$ varying. If $A[m_1 : n_1, \ldots, m_k : n_k]$ represents the entire set of array elements with indices in the set of k-tuples

$m_1 : n_1 \times \cdots \times m_k : n_k$, this means we must allocate $(n_1 - m_1 + 1)$† adjacent linear regions each of size S sufficient to contain subarrays determined by holding the first subscript fixed and varying the others. The size S of these linear regions therefore has to be

$$S = (n_2 - m_2 + 1)(n_3 - m_3 + 1) \cdots (n_k - m_k + 1).$$

Now, by the same reasoning, within the region assigned to $A[i_1, i_2, \ldots, i_k]$ where we hold i_1 fixed and vary $i_2, \ldots, i_k$, we must allocate storage in increasing linear adjacent blocks of size $(n_3 - m_3 + 1)(n_4 - m_4 + 1) \cdots (n_k - m_k + 1)$ corresponding to sub-subarrays of increasing lexicographic subsets where we hold i_1 and i_2 fixed and vary $i_3, \ldots, i_k$. Continuing in this fashion, we nest linear blocks of storage for subarrays of increasing lexicographic order until, finally, we allocate linear vectors of contiguous locations corresponding to variation on the final subscript i_k in direct increasing address order. This leads to the following general formula for lexicographic storage allocation functions for $A[m_1 : n_1, \ldots, m_k : n_k]$:

$$\mathrm{Loc}(A[i_1, i_2, \ldots, i_k]) = \mathrm{Loc}(A[m_1, m_2, \ldots, m_k])$$
$$+ \sum_{1 \leq j \leq k} \left(\prod_{j+1 \leq p \leq k} (n_p - m_p + 1) \right) (i_j - m_j). \quad (1)$$

When we multiply out the terms of this formula, treating $i_1, i_2, \ldots, i_k$ as variables, we discover that the storage allocation function assumes the following form:

$$\mathrm{Loc}(A[i_1, i_2, \ldots, i_k]) = \mathrm{Loc}(A[m_1, m_2, \ldots, m_k])$$
$$+ c_0 + c_1 i_1 + c_2 i_2 + \cdots + c_k i_k \quad (2)$$

for suitable constants c_i $(0 \leq i \leq k)$. This tells us that when we hold all subscripts fixed except for one, say i_j, and vary i_j in steps of 1, we find the corresponding locations in memory at constant intervals of size c_j apart from one another. In short, the array elements are stored in arithmetic progressions on single subscripts, with different step sizes for different subscripts.

Lexicographic allocation is therefore efficient in several respects. First, traversal of elements in a direction parallel to any arbitrary axis of the coordinate system is easy (and can usually be implemented using machine index registers). Second, the storage locations used are contiguous, so storage utilization is optimal. Third, access to an arbitrary element is convenient to compute in stages in compiled machine code by the following iterative process, using formula (2)

---

† In numerous places in this chapter, it is helpful to recall that the number of integers i in the range $a \leq i \leq b$ is $b - a + 1$.

above:

1. [Initialize.] Set $L \leftarrow \mathrm{Loc}(A[m_1, m_2, \ldots, m_k]) + c_0$.
2. [Sum up.] *For* $j \leftarrow 1, 2, \ldots, k$ *do*
   a) Execute the code for the jth subscript expression, getting a value i_j.
   b) Set $L \leftarrow L + c_j i_j$.
3. [Terminate.] L now holds the address of $A[i_1, i_2, \ldots, i_k]$.

Let us study this a bit further. Suppose we have a compiler that compiles code which, when executed at storage allocation time for array A, sets up a table $C[0]$, $C[1], \ldots, C[k]$ such that $C[0]$ contains $\mathrm{Loc}(A[m_1, m_2, \ldots, m_k]) + c_0$, and $C[j]$ contains c_j for $1 \leq i \leq k$, where the c_j are computed as in formula (2) above. Suppose further, that, corresponding to the array expression $A[e_1, e_2, \ldots, e_k]$, where the e_i ($1 \leq i \leq k$) are subscript expressions, the compiler produces code in the following order:

1. $L \leftarrow C[0]$.
2. $j \leftarrow 1$ (j is usually an index register).
3. Code to evaluate subscript expression e_1, leaving the value i_1 in accumulator ACC.
4. Code to call the subroutine NEXT.
5. Code to evaluate subscript expression e_2, leaving the value i_2 in accumulator ACC.
6. Code to call the subroutine NEXT.

$\vdots$ $\vdots$

$2k + 1$. Code to evaluate subscript expression e_k, leaving the value i_k in accumulator ACC.
$2k + 2$. Code to call the subroutine NEXT.

where the subroutine NEXT contains the following steps:

Subroutine NEXT

1. [Bounds check.] Optional bounds check on jth subscript of A using bounds information stored in tables.
2. [Multiply.] Set $\mathrm{ACC} \leftarrow \mathrm{ACC} \times C[j]$ (usually one indexed multiply instruction).
3. [Add.] Set $L \leftarrow L + \mathrm{ACC}$.
4. [Increment.] Set $j \leftarrow j + 1$.

This scheme has two advantages for compiler writers. First, the code for the array expression $A[e_1, e_2, \ldots, e_k]$ can be produced with ease in one left-to-right pass, since the instruction sequences for the subscript expressions $e_1, e_2, \ldots, e_k$ can be produced in order with only a call on NEXT inserted at the end of the evaluation of each subscript. Second, and more important, however, is the advantage for languages that permit array subscript expressions e_i to contain nested array expressions and procedure calls (as, for example, in the array expression

$$A[i + B[j, 3], k \times P(2, B[3, i])]$$

in ALGOL 60). In such cases, the current partially computed values of the subscript computation for A must be saved before computing nested array expressions or procedure calls that use the same accumulators and index registers. Later these values must be restored in order to resume the computation for A.

In the above case, all that need be saved are the values of L and j in order to facilitate proper restoration of the subscript computation after a nested evaluation requiring the same registers (ACC, L, and j). Code for saving the pair (L, j) is generated during processing of the expression e_i upon encountering nested subexpressions; and restorative code is inserted near the end of the compiled instruction sequence for e_i. Storage mapping functions not in the form $c_0 + \sum f_j(i_j)$, but instead in a form where some terms are multivariate in several of the $i_1, i_2, \ldots, i_k$ require more elaborate context-saving and restoration techniques with corresponding efficiency and programming complexity penalties.

Consider, now, the problem of enlarging an array A stored in lexicographic order. For instance, we may wish to add new rows or new columns to a rectangular array $A[0:2, 0:3]$, such as that shown in Fig. 8.2. In general, we may wish to add new bordering subarrays to $A[m_1 : n_1, \ldots, m_k : n_k]$. If A is stored lexicographically, it is easy to extend A only in the dimension of its first subscript i_1. In particular, it is possible to extend the storage area for $A[m_1 : n_1, \ldots, m_k : n_k]$ to a storage area for $A[m_1 : n_1 + 1, \ldots, m_k : n_k]$ merely by appending a sequential region for the subarray $A[n_1 + 1 : n_1 + 1, \ldots, m_k : n_k]$ directly after the storage area for the original array. No previously allocated elements need be moved. Such is not the case for adding subarrays in any other dimension but the first, all of which require previously allocated array elements to be moved. Thus, lexicographically allocated arrays grow "naturally" only in their first dimension. For this reason, Rosenberg [1974] has called them *prism arrays*. If the capacity for ease of growth along a dimension other than the first, or by subarrays of different shape, is of paramount importance, lexicographical storage functions are not ideal.

Clearly, we can arrange sequential storage allocation functions for prism arrays with ease of growth along some axis different from the first at the sacrifice of lexicographical ordering, without sacrificing ease of element access, or additive traversal of elements along directions parallel to the axes of the array index space (in arithmetic progressions), by devising analogous functions of the form of equation (2). Consideration of other growth patterns and of other emphases of ease of traversal along other paths leads to the study of additional sequential storage allocation techniques in the following subsections.

8.3.2 Triangular and tetrahedral storage allocation functions

Suppose we wish to store the elements of the lower-triangular array shown in Fig. 8.4 in lexicographic order in the region 1:10 of memory, in the fashion indicated in Fig. 8.5. In such an array, the second row has one more element than the first, the third row has one more element than the second, and, in general, the ith row has one more element than the $(i - 1)$st. Hence, the storage for the ith row can begin immediately after the storage of size $1 + 2 + \cdots + (i - 1)$ required for the first $(i - 1)$ rows. Since

$$1 + 2 + \cdots + (i - 1) = \sum_{1 \le j \le i-1} j = \frac{(i - 1)i}{2},$$

we see that we can provide a lexicographical storage allocation function for A by using the mapping:

$$\text{Loc}(A[i, j]) = \frac{i(i - 1)}{2} + j. \tag{3}$$

We note that, if we multiply out the first term of formula (3), we get a polynomial in i with an i^2 term. In addition, we note that column traversal involves accessing elements no longer spaced at constant intervals, but rather at intervals that grow in arithmetic progression.

$$
\begin{array}{llll}
A[1, 1] \\
A[2, 1] & A[2, 2] \\
A[3, 1] & A[3, 2] & A[3, 3] \\
A[4, 1] & A[4, 2] & A[4, 3] & A[4, 4]
\end{array}
$$

FIGURE 8.4

Location:	1	2	3	4	5	6	7	8	9	10
Element:	$A[1, 1]$	$A[2, 1]$	$A[2, 2]$	$A[3, 1]$	$A[3, 2]$	$A[3, 3]$	$A[4, 1]$	$A[4, 2]$	$A[4, 3]$	$A[4, 4]$

FIGURE 8.5

If we are fortunate enough to have two triangular arrays A and B of equal size, we can use the trick illustrated in Fig. 8.6 to store A and B in a common rectangular area. Here, the elements of A are stored in lexicographic order, and those of B in reverse lexicographic order by the two linear storage allocation functions:

$$\text{Loc}(A[i, j]) = (5i + j) - 5,$$
$$\text{Loc}(B[i, j]) = 26 - (5i + j).$$

$A[1,1]$	$B[4,4]$	$B[4,3]$	$B[4,2]$	$B[4,1]$
$A[2,1]$	$A[2,2]$	$B[3,3]$	$B[3,2]$	$B[3,1]$
$A[3,1]$	$A[3,2]$	$A[3,3]$	$B[2,2]$	$B[2,1]$
$A[4,1]$	$A[4,2]$	$A[4,3]$	$A[4,4]$	$B[1,1]$

FIGURE 8.6 *The* ◣ *trick.*

Let us now consider the more general case of tetrahedral arrays of k dimensions of size n. Figure 8.7 pictures a tetrahedral array of three dimensions and size four, defined by elements $A[i, j, k]$ such that $1 \le k \le j \le i \le 4$. By making observations about the three-dimensional array in Fig. 8.7, we aim to develop the general lexicographic allocation function for tetrahedral arrays of any size and dimension.

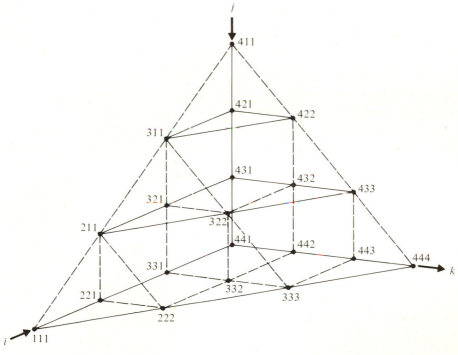

FIGURE 8.7

First, we need to make up a table that gives the number of elements in a tetrahedral array of k dimensions of size n. This is given as Table 8.1.

Examining Table 8.1 we see, for instance, that, in triangular arrays, which are tetrahedral arrays of dimension 2, each time we increase the size by one, we add a

TABLE 8.1
Number of Elements
in Tetrahedral Array of Dimension k and Size n.

Dimension	Size = maximum subscript n								
k	1	2	3	4	5	6	7	8	9
1	1	2	3	4	5	6	7	8	9
2	1	3	6	10	15	21	28	36	45
3	1	4	10	20	35	56	84	120	165
4	1	5	15	35	70	126	210	330	495

new row of length one greater than the longest row in the array of the previous size. Thus, the numbers in row 2 of Table 8.1 are just sums of the form $\sum_{1 \le j \le n} j$. Likewise, to extend a three-dimensional tetrahedron with n planes to have $(n + 1)$ planes, we must append a triangular array with $(n + 1)$ rows. Hence, we see that to get the number $T(k, n)$ in row k and column n of Table 8.1, we have to add the number $T(k, n - 1)$ to the number $T(k - 1, n)$. This gives the relation

$$T(k, n) = T(k, n - 1) + T(k - 1, n), \tag{4}$$

which is satisfied by the binomial coefficient

$$T(k, n) = \binom{n + k - 1}{k},$$

since (4) is exactly the relation used to generate Pascal's Triangle.

Thus, we see that to generate a lexicographical storage allocation function Loc($A[i, j, k]$), we need only add to Loc($A[1, 1, 1]$) the volume of a tetrahedron of size $(i - 1)$ plus a triangle of size $(j - 1)$ plus a linear displacement of size $(k - 1)$. This yields

$$\text{Loc}(A[i, j, k]) = \text{Loc}(A[1, 1, 1]) + \binom{i + 1}{3} + \binom{j}{2} + (k - 1)\dagger$$

or

$$\text{Loc}(A[i, j, k]) = \text{Loc}(A[1, 1, 1]) + \frac{i(i + 1)(i - 1)}{6} + \frac{j(j - 1)}{2} + (k - 1).$$

From the latter formula, we see that these lexicographical storage allocation functions are each of the form

$$\text{Loc}(A[1, \ldots, 1]) + \sum_{1 \le r \le k} f_r(i_r),$$

---

† Recall that $\binom{n}{k} = 0$ if $k > n$.

where each $f_r(i_r)$ is a polynomial of degree $k - r + 1$ in the variable i_r (or, alternatively, is a binomial coefficient of $k - r + 1$ factors).

The general formula for a lexicographic storage allocation function for the tetrahedral array of dimension k and size n is

$$\text{Loc}(A[i_1, i_2, \ldots, i_k]) = \text{Loc}(A[1, 1, \ldots, 1]) + \sum_{1 \leq r \leq k} \binom{k - r - 1 + i_r}{k - r + 1}. \quad (5)$$

Commenting now on our four characteristics of "representational quality" for these lexicographic functions for tetrahedral arrays, we find:

1. *Ease of access of arbitrary elements:* Computationally more expensive than for rectangular arrays, since polynomials, binomial coefficients, or their equivalents must be evaluated whose degrees are at most the dimension of the array (yet, for compiler writers, the storage allocation functions can still be incrementally computed from a sum of terms of the form $f_r(i_r)$);

2. *Ease of traversal along paths:* If the index i_r runs through the values $1, 2, \ldots, k$, the corresponding elements of A are stored at intervals computed by polynomials of degree $(r - 1)$ in the variable i_r, so traversal along paths parallel to one of the coordinate axes can be expensive in all but the last dimension i_k compared to traversal in lexicographically allocated rectangular arrays all of whose paths are allocated in arithmetic progressions;

3. *Efficiency of storage utilization:* Still 100% since storage is contiguous and sequential; and

4. *Ease of growth:* Tetrahedral arrays of dimension k and size n grow naturally by addition of new tetrahedral arrays of size $(n + 1)$ and dimension $(k - 1)$, without having to move elements in the original array.

8.3.3 Cubic and diagonal shell functions

In some algorithms, efficiency of traversal along certain paths in an array may take precedence over efficiency of access to arbitrary elements. Any sequence that enumerates all elements of an array exactly once can be used as the basis for a 1–1, *onto*, sequential storage allocation function. Indeed, recursive function theory is replete with examples of "tupling" functions with these properties. We shall only exemplify the idea in this section by considering the "shell" arrays of Rosenberg [1974].

Consider a 4×4 square array $A[1:4, 1:4]$, as depicted in Fig. 8.8. If we allocate storage to A in the order of locations given in Fig. 8.9, we have given an

$A[1,1]$	$A[1,2]$	$A[1,3]$	$A[1,4]$
$A[2,1]$	$A[2,2]$	$A[2,3]$	$A[2,4]$
$A[3,1]$	$A[3,2]$	$A[3,3]$	$A[3,4]$
$A[4,1]$	$A[4,2]$	$A[4,3]$	$A[4,4]$

FIGURE 8.8

1	4	9	16
2	3	8	15
5	6	7	14
10	11	12	13

FIGURE 8.9

enumeration in order of increasing "cubic" shells. A cubic-shell storage allocation function for A is given by

$$\text{Loc}(A[i, j]) = \text{Loc}(A[1, 1]) + (\max(i, j) - 1)^2 + \max(i, j) + (j - i) - 1.†$$

A can easily be extended by adding new cubic shells of elements without moving previously allocated elements or recomputing the storage allocation function. Hence, cubic shell functions provide ease of traversal on paths through the shells and ease of extension with bordering arrays. However, access to arbitrary elements involves multivariate functions containing quadratic polynomial terms. Storage utilization is still 100%.

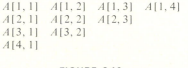

FIGURE 8.10   FIGURE 8.11

Figures 8.10 and 8.11 illustrate storage allocation of a triangular array by "diagonal" shells. The storage allocation function for A, in this case, is given by:

$$\text{Loc}(A[i, j]) = \text{Loc}(A[1, 1]) + \binom{i + j}{2} - i$$

$$= \text{Loc}(A[1, 1]) + \frac{i}{2}(i - 3) + ij + \frac{j}{2}(j - 1).$$

We see here that the storage allocation function contains both multivariate terms of the form $i \times j$ and terms that are quadratic polynomials. This means that the storage allocation function is not of the form

$$\text{Loc}(A[1, 1]) + c_0 + \sum_{1 \le r \le k} f_r(i_r),$$

but instead (to the dismay of compiler writers) involves terms of the form $f(i_1, i_2, \ldots, i_k)$.

If we generalize the above triangular array to tetrahedral shell arrays, we encounter the same multivariate terms in the storage allocation function. Such a tetrahedral shell array can be expressed as the set of $A[i_1, i_2, \ldots, i_k]$ such that

$$k \le i_1 + i_2 + \cdots + i_k \le (n + k - 1).$$

To find where to start to allocate the pth hyperplane (where $k \le p \le (n + k - 1)$),

---

† Another solution based on use of conditional expressions is:

$$\text{Loc}(A[i, j]) = \text{Loc}(A[1, 1]) + (\text{if } i > j \text{ then } (i - 1)^2 + j - 1 \text{ else } j^2 - i).$$

we have to sum up the number of elements in the hyperplanes above p in the tetrahedron. This is given by a binomial coefficient of the form

$$\binom{i_1 + i_2 + \cdots + i_k - 1}{k - 1}$$

whose expansion into polynomial form involves multivariate terms of the form $c \times i_1 \times i_2 \times \cdots \times i_k$. Thus, a compiler writer must produce code to evaluate and save all $i_1, i_2, \ldots, i_r$ in a table before computing the location of $A[i_1, i_2, \ldots, i_k]$. This requires more elaborate and costly mechanisms to save contexts across nested evaluations of array expressions and procedures used in the subscript expressions. For this reason, lexicographic allocation is preferable to allocation by tetrahedral shells, unless the efficiency of enumeration of elements by shells is of paramount importance.

In summary, evaluating shell functions with respect to our four dimensions of quality: (1) element access is complicated and costly, (2) traversal of shells is efficient, (3) storage utilization is 100%, and (4) natural growth takes place in tetrahedral shells of dimension one less and size one more.

8.3.4 Sacrificing storage utilization efficiency to gain extensibility

Each of the storage mapping functions we have considered thus far has been a 1–1, *onto*, sequential function. By virtue of being "onto," storage utilization was always 100%. And yet, each such storage function had an associated "natural" growth pattern, which allowed the addition of new bordering subarrays without the need for moving elements previously allocated. The shape of the subarray that could be naturally added was different for each different sequential storage function.

By arranging to use an "into" storage allocation function that leaves "gaps" between the storage locations assigned to various array elements, it is possible to provide for "natural" growth along several dimensions, or even along an infinite number of new dimensions added later. These techniques are more useful for demonstrating the existence of trade-offs between the various dimensions of quality than for practical use, since their poor storage utilization properties can be overcome through techniques using hash addressing and pointers (which we shall explore later). Indeed, consideration of a few examples motivates the need for the latter techniques.

We choose two examples from Rosenberg [1974]. Consider, first, $A[1:n, 1:m]$, where we use the allocation function:

$$\text{Loc}(A[i, j]) = \text{Loc}(A[1, 1]) + 2^{i-1} \times 3^{j-1} - 1.$$

Figures 8.12 and 8.13 give the correspondence between elements $A[i, j]$ and assigned locations, on the assumptions that $A[1, 1] = 1$ and $m = n = 4$.

$A[1, 1]$	$A[1, 2]$	$A[1, 3]$	$A[1, 4]$
$A[2, 1]$	$A[2, 2]$	$A[2, 3]$	$A[2, 4]$
$A[3, 1]$	$A[3, 2]$	$A[3, 3]$	$A[3, 4]$
$A[4, 1]$	$A[4, 2]$	$A[4, 3]$	$A[4, 4]$

1	3	9	27
2	6	18	54
4	12	36	108
8	24	72	216

FIGURE 8.12   **FIGURE 8.13**

Here, rows and columns are stored at locations that form geometric progressions and are easy to traverse since the locations differ by constant multiples of 2 or 3. New rows and columns can be added naturally without moving previously allocated elements. Access to arbitrary elements involves computing exponential functions of i and j, and storage utilization is intolerably poor. In the case of $A[1:4, 1:4]$ only 16 locations are occupied, but they are spread over 216 locations in memory because of gaps. Storage utilization in this case is a mere 7.41%. In general, storage utilization for $A[1:n, 1:m]$ is $mn/(2^{m-1}3^{n-1})$, and we can see that this rapidly approaches 0 as m and n increase. The capacity to add both rows and columns has exacted a high price for this type of storage allocation function.

Our second example uses the storage mapping function:

$$\text{Loc}(A[i, j]) = \text{Loc}(A[1, 1]) + 2^{j-1}(2i - 1) - 1.$$

This is a 1–1, *onto* mapping of the tuples (i, j) with $i, j \geq 1$ onto the integers $k \geq \text{Loc}(A[1, 1])$, since any positive integer can be expressed as the product of a power of 2 (special case $2^0 = 1$) times an odd integer (special case 1). Traversals are additive along columns, and multiplicative along rows. However, storage utilization degenerates very rapidly. Growth by addition of both new rows and columns is "natural," however, in that neither must previously allocated elements be moved, nor must we change the storage allocation function. Again, extensibility has been purchased at the expense of poor storage utilization, even though the blame, in this case, cannot be laid at the feet of "into" as opposed to "onto" mappings.

In fact, Rosenberg [1974] shows that no storage allocation function that enjoys additive traversal along rows and columns can admit "easy" extension of both rows and columns (wherein no previously allocated element need be moved) and, correspondingly, no easily extensible storage allocation function affords simple (i.e., additive) traversal along both rows and columns. Such trade-offs are inherent in the nature of storage allocation mappings.

8.4 LINKED ALLOCATION

Linked allocation of array elements can be useful under three conditions:

1. to provide fast access to arbitrary elements $A[i_1, i_2, \ldots, i_k]$ on machines with index registers at the price of reduced storage utilization,

2. to accommodate array growth in arbitrary directions at the expense of reduced storage utilization, and

3. to store elements of sparse or ragged arrays without allocating space for all array elements.

In this section we study schemes for linked allocation and develop a few quantitative facts about their behaviors along various dimensions of representation quality.

8.4.1 Techniques using vectors of pointers and linked lists

Consider allocating space for an array $A[1:n_1, 1:n_2, \ldots, 1:n_k]$. The elements of such an array can be placed at the leaves of an ordered tree such as that given in Fig. 8.14. This tree has uniform depth k, and each node at depth i ($0 \le i \le k-1$) has n_{i+1} direct descendants. The array element $A[i_1, i_2, \ldots, i_k]$ is stored in the leaf found at the end of the path from the root with edges labeled $i_1, i_2, \ldots, i_k$. The number of edges in this tree is given by:

$$n_1 + n_1 n_2 + n_1 n_2 n_3 + \cdots + n_1 n_2 \times \cdots \times n_k = \sum_{1 \le i \le k} \left(\prod_{1 \le r \le i} n_r \right). \qquad (6)$$

The internal nodes of the tree at all depths $< (k-1)$ can be represented by vectors of pointers. For example, the array $A[1:3, 1:4, 1:5]$ could be represented as shown in Fig. 8.15.

The internal nodes whose direct descendants are leaves are represented by vectors of array elements arranged in order of the last subscript i_k. The vectors of pointers and elements can be stored in physically noncontiguous regions of memory, permitting various array extensions provided there is an underlying storage management regime for handling vectors of arbitrary length.

The principal advantage of using such a scheme is that it permits extremely rapid access to arbitrary array elements using index registers. Suppose, for a moment, that the array under consideration is a "0-origin" array of the form $A[0:n_1, 0:n_2, \ldots, 0:n_k]$. Let α be the base address of the vector of pointers corresponding to the root of the tree, and suppose ACC is an accumulator and I is an index register. The idea is to initialize ACC to contain α and to compute and store the successive subscripts $i_1, i_2, \ldots, i_k$ in the index register I. Each time a new subscript i_r is stored in I, we replace the address in ACC with the address stored in location ACC + I, which is the i_rth element in the vector whose base address is in ACC. This is the base address of another vector if $r < k$, and it is an array element if $r = k$. Thus we step down a chain of pointers from the root to a leaf in order to access the array element stored at the leaf. On many machines, only a single instruction is required to perform the operation ACC ← Contents(ACC + I). This is faster than computing the location of rectangular array elements using lexico-

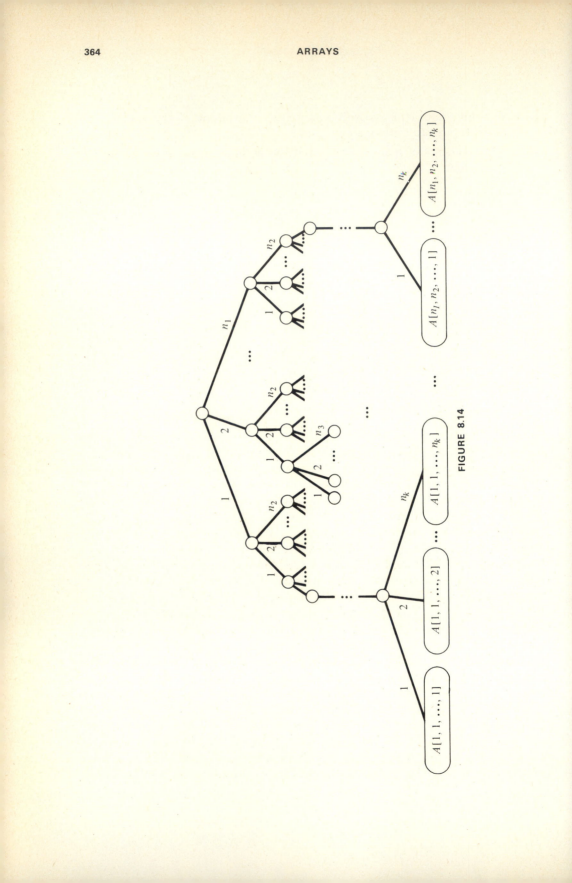

FIGURE 8.14

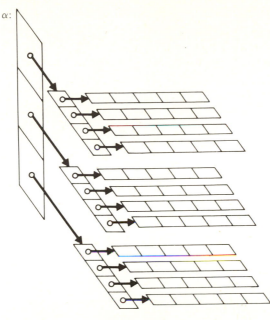

FIGURE 8.15

graphic storage mapping functions, since the latter method involves evaluating expressions of the form $L \leftarrow L + I \times C[I]$, where C is a table of multiplicative constants. Such operations can rarely be done as cheaply as following a chain of pointers using repeated indexing.

One important trick in connection with the use of vectors of pointers concerns the case where the array has a nonzero origin, as in $A[m_1:n_1, m_2:n_2, \ldots, m_k:n_k]$. Here the origin is at the point $(m_1, m_2, \ldots, m_k)$. In this case, instead of storing pointers that point directly to the base address of vectors at lower levels, one stores pointers that are offset by $-m_r$. This is illustrated in Fig. 8.16.

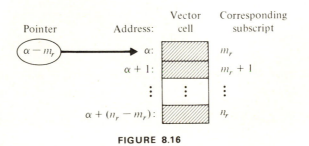

FIGURE 8.16

Since the subscript i_r lies in the range $m_r \leq i_r \leq n_r$, if we add i_r to a pointer whose value is $\alpha - m_r$, we get addresses in the range $\alpha : \alpha + (n_r - m_r)$. Hence, we can still use single indexing operations to follow pointer chains even if the origin is nonzero, provided we store offset pointers in our vectors instead of actual pointers.

The speed of access to arbitrary elements available through use of this technique exacts its price in reduced storage utilization. Here, storage utilization is defined as the ratio of storage used for array elements to the total space used for both array elements and pointers. The pointers are the "excess baggage" not devoted to storage of data. There are several minor observations we can make that help give a feeling for the kind of reduction in storage utilization implied by the use of pointers.

The number of pointers required to store an array of the form $A[1:n_1, 1:n_2, \ldots, 1:n_k]$ is almost the same as the number of edges in the tree of Fig. 8.14 (as given by formula (6)), since pointers correspond 1–1 to all edges in the tree except those touching the leaves (the leaves being represented directly in vectors of array elements). Hence, the formula for the number of pointers required to represent $A[1:n_1, 1:n_2, \ldots, 1:n_k]$ is

Number of pointers in $(A[1 : n_1, 1 : n_2, \ldots, 1 : n_k])$

$$= \sum_{1 \leq i \leq k-1} \left(\prod_{1 \leq r \leq i} n_r \right). \tag{7}$$

A crude but useful upper bound on the number of pointers can be obtained by observing that:

$$\left(\begin{array}{c} \text{Number of pointers in} \\ A[1 : n_1, 1 : n_2, \ldots, 1 : n_k] \end{array} \right) + \left(\begin{array}{c} \text{Number of array elements in} \\ A[1 : n_1, 1 : n_2, \ldots, 1 : n_k] \end{array} \right)$$

$$< \left(\begin{array}{c} \text{Number of array elements in} \\ A[1 : n_1 + 1, 1 : n_2 + 1, \ldots, 1 : n_k + 1] \end{array} \right). \tag{8}$$

That is, there are fewer pointers required to represent $A[1 : n_1, \ldots, 1 : n_k]$ than there are new elements to extend A by one element along every dimension. A slightly stronger observation is given in the following theorem.

Theorem 8.1 Let $A[1:n_1, 1:n_2, \ldots, 1:n_k]$ be an array in which each subscript can take on at least two values (that is, $n_i \geq 2$ for all i). Then the number of pointers required by the pointer vector representation of A is less than the number of elements of A.

Proof Since $n_k \geq 2$, we have $1 + \frac{1}{2} + \frac{1}{4} + \cdots + (\frac{1}{2})^{k-2} < n_k$ or, equivalently,

$$\sum_{1 \leq i \leq k-1} (\tfrac{1}{2})^{(k-1)-i} < n_k.$$

But, since all the n_r are at least 2, we can substitute any q of the n_r for q of the 2's in the denominators of the fractions of the form $1/2^q$. Hence, we get

$$\sum_{1 \le i \le k-1} \frac{1}{\prod_{i+1 \le r \le k-1} n_r} < n_k.$$

And now, multiplying both sides of the latter inequality by $\prod_{1 \le r \le k-1} n_r$ gives:

$$\sum_{1 \le i \le k-1} \left(\prod_{1 \le r \le i} n_r \right) < n_1 n_2 \times \cdots \times n_k. \qquad \blacksquare$$

　　　The condition of Theorem 8.1 nearly always holds in practice, since, in nearly every array A, the n_r have values 2 or greater. (Otherwise, if $n_r = 1$, the corresponding subscript i_r can have only one value, expresses no choice, and is therefore useless.)

　　　Now we look at the number of pointers required to represent k-dimensional, "cubic" arrays of the form $A[1:n, 1:n, \ldots, 1:n]$ each of which has n^k elements. Formula (7) shows that the number of pointers required is $n + n^2 + \cdots + n^{k-1}$, which is a geometric series with the sum:

$$T(n, k) = \frac{n^k - n}{n - 1}.$$

It is interesting to study the quantity $T(n, k)/n^k$, which is the ratio between the number of pointers and the number of elements for A. It turns out that:

$$\frac{1}{n - 1} - \frac{1}{(n-1)^k} < \frac{T(n, k)}{n^k} < \frac{1}{n - 1},$$

which implies, rather surprisingly, that $T(n, k)/n^k$ is almost independent of k, for respectable n and k. In particular, for any cubic array with $n > 100$, we find $1/(n - 1)$ approximates (and is an upper bound for) $T(n, k)/n^k$ within 1%. For example, a 20×20 square array, a $20 \times 20 \times 20$ cubic array, and a $20 \times 20 \times 20 \times 20$ hypercubic array would all have no more than approximately $\frac{1}{19}$ the number of pointers as they do elements. (In particular the upper-bound estimate gives $\frac{1}{19} = 0.0526$, and the true fractions are: 0.0500 for a 20×20 array, 0.0525 for a $20 \times 20 \times 20$ array, and 0.0526 for a $20 \times 20 \times 20 \times 20$ array.)

　　　Thus, for cubic arrays with n^k elements, the number of pointers required to support the pointer vectors is approximately $1/(n - 1)$ of the total number of elements as n increases, making the representation reasonably bearable in storage utilization efficiency for large n. For instance, on the (usually liberal) assumption that a pointer takes the same amount of space as an array element, the storage utilization efficiency is approximately equal to $(n - 1)/n$. This means that, almost independently of the dimension k, storage utilization efficiency approaches

$(n-1)/n$ as n increases, which is surprisingly close to 100% efficiency for larger arrays. This suggests that, for arrays that are approximately of cubic shape and are of reasonable size, it is worthwhile using pointers since the speed of element access is greatly increased at a very slight increase of space requirements; that is, we don't really pay very much space to gain a speed-up in access time.

We see, in general, that, under the very reasonable assumptions that all $n_i \geq 2$ and that pointers take no more space than array elements, the storage utilization for the pointer vector representation is never below 50%.

Examining the pointer vector representation on our four dimensions of representation quality we see that:

1. accessing arbitrary array elements can be made highly efficient;
2. easy additive traversals are possible only along paths $A[i_1, i_2, \ldots, i_k]$ for which i_k varies and the lesser subscripts are held fixed;
3. storage utilization is usually greater than 50% and can approach 100% for large arrays of approximately cubic shape; and
4. extensions require lengthening vectors (usually by allocating new vectors of longer length and copying in the old elements in the prefix).

Let us now consider representing an array $A[1:n_1, \ldots, 1:n_k]$ using linked lists. We agree that a list of arbitrary elements $(x_1, x_2, \ldots, x_n)$ is to be represented in the form:

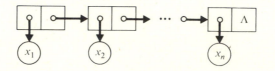

Thus, it takes $2n$ pointers to represent a list of n elements. The linked list representation of the array given in tree form in Fig. 8.14 can then be obtained by replacing each internal node of the tree of the form

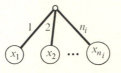

with the linked list representation of the list $(\bar{x}_1, \bar{x}_2, \ldots, \bar{x}_{n_i})$, where the $\bar{x}_i$ are the lists corresponding to the subtrees x_i. Formula (6) can be used to calculate the number of pointers required since there are two pointers in the linked list representation of A for every edge in the tree in Fig. 8.14. This gives:

Number of pointers in $(A[1:n_1, \ldots, 1:n_k])$

$$= 2 \sum_{1 \le i \le k} \left(\prod_{1 \le r \le i} n_r \right),$$

which is more than four times worse than the number of pointers required for the pointer vector technique (whenever all $n_i \ge 2$). To make matters worse, accessing the arbitrary array element $A[i_1, i_2, \ldots, i_k]$ requires us to traverse $i_1 + i_2 + \cdots + i_k$ links, so that accessing elements is inefficient. Traversals are efficient only along paths for which i_k increases in steps of 1 and other subscripts are held constant. About the only advantage to the linked list representation is that linked arrays can be extended nearly arbitrarily. It would not be unreasonable to use linked list array representations in a system where linked lists had already been implemented and the efficiency of array handling was not critical, especially if programming resources are the most critical factor.

Both the pointer vector and linked list representations save space for *ragged arrays* (as specified in Definition 8.4). For example, a piece of text might be conveniently represented as a ragged array by having a vector of pointers to "pages," each of which is a vector of pointers to "lines," each of which is a vector of "characters."

8.4.2 Techniques using orthogonal lists

Occasionally we have a sparse array for which it is important to be able to traverse both rows and columns and for which very few of the elements are nonzero. For example, consider an array $A[1:1000, 1:1000]$, having only the following 11 nonzero elements:

$A[2, 6]$	$A[2, 784]$	$A[2, 814]$
$A[64, 6]$	$A[64, 784]$	
$A[128, 153]$	$A[128, 784]$	$A[128, 814]$
$A[512, 6]$	$A[512, 153]$	$A[512, 814]$

On most contemporary computers it would be disastrous to attempt to allocate explicit space for all million of the elements of $A[1:1000, 1:1000]$, only 11 of which are nonzero, so we are urged to consider some representation in which the zero elements are not represented explicitly. Our desire for ease of row and column traversal leads to the idea of linking all the nonzero elements together in such a fashion that horizontal links link all nonzero elements in a given row, and vertical links link all elements in a given column. This leads to the following representation for A:

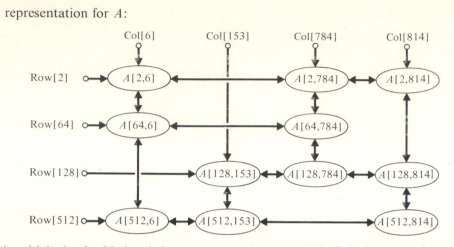

in which the double-headed arrows represent symmetric links between elements. As we have seen (in Section 5.3.2.5, Fig. 5.17), each element in such an orthogonal array can then be represented by a cell of the form:

Array element	
Left link	Right link
Up link	Down link

The elements in any given row (or column) can be linked into a symmetric ring by constructing links of the form leftmost ↔ rightmost (or topmost ↔ bottommost) or, alternatively, the null address can be used to signify the ends of rows and columns. Orthogonal arrays can also be constructed in higher dimensions.

Storage utilization is inversely proportional to the percentage of nonzero elements (the worst case occurring when a presumably sparse array turns out to have no nonzero elements). For example, taking the trial assumptions that a pointer requires half the space required for storing an array element, that we are given a k-dimensional orthogonal array, and that the sparse array is $X\%$ saturated (that is, contains $X/100$ of the total number of nonzero elements $Total$), we can write:

$$\text{Storage utilization} = \frac{Total \times 1}{(X/100) \times (k+1) \times Total} = \frac{100}{X(k+1)}.$$

Thus, for a two-dimensional orthogonal array ($k = 2$) that is, respectively, 10%,

50%, and 100% saturated, we get respective storage utilizations of 333%, 67%, and 33%. The orthogonal list representation is advantageous, therefore, whenever the saturation $X < 100/(k + 1)$ percent.

8.5 HASHED ALLOCATION TECHNIQUES

Let $A_j[i_1, i_2, \ldots, i_k]$ be a set of array elements using different array names A_j and having indices i_r that are arbitrary integers. Let $H(A_j, i_1, i_2, \ldots, i_k)$ be a hash function that operates on the array name A_j and on the k subscript values $i_1, i_2, \ldots, i_k$ to produce an address α in a hash space. When we perform the assignment $A_j[i_1, i_2, \ldots, i_k] \leftarrow X$, where X is a value for an array element, we first compute the address $\alpha = H(A_j, i_1, i_2, \ldots, i_k)$ and then, assuming that address α is unoccupied, we store the $(k + 2)$-tuple $(A_j, i_1, i_2, \ldots, i_k, X)$ at address α. (If address α is already occupied, we have a collision, and we must store the $(k + 2)$-tuple somewhere dictated by the collision-resolution policy associated with the hash allocation scheme). To retrieve the value of $A_j[i_1, i_2, \ldots, i_k]$, we again compute $H(A_j, i_1, i_2, \ldots, i_k)$, which yields α again, and we start searching at α for a $(k + 2)$-tuple whose first $(k + 1)$ elements match $(A_j, i_1, i_2, \ldots, i_k)$ and, upon finding it, we retrieve the value X stored in the last component.

The storage and retrieval times for arbitrary array elements are thus related to the efficiency of the underlying hashing technique. If array names and array subscripts take the same space as array elements, the storage utilization efficiency is at most $100/(k + 1)$ percent for storage of rectangular arrays, with advantages comparable to those for orthogonal arrays for storage of sparse arrays. There are no paths through any array for which hashed allocation provides especially efficient traversals (in contrast to all the other array representations studied in this chapter). However, array extensibility is uniform and easy for all dimensions and attains the optimum flexibility in hashed allocation techniques.

One of the most interesting applications of hashed array allocation is in languages that require neither array declarations nor execution of array space allocation expressions in advance of assigning particular array elements. Two different conventions can be used in this connection. First, one can consider that all possible arrays with all possible names A_j are predefined to have the value 0 for any possible set of subscripts. The value of $A_j[i_1, i_2, \ldots, i_k]$ is then either the value last assigned, or else is 0 if no value was ever assigned by explicit execution of the program. The second convention would treat the value of $A_j[i_1, i_2, \ldots, i_k]$ as undefined unless it had been previously assigned. Thus, assignment of values to array elements previously undefined causes incremental allocation of storage, with gaps of undefined elements permitted. The first scheme has the property that all possible array elements are always defined, and the second has the property that only previously assigned array elements are defined.

TABLE 8.2

Comparison of Array Representations.

Let $A[i_1, i_2, \ldots, i_k]$ be an arbitrary array element in an array of dimension k. The variable r lies in the range $1 \le r \le k$.

Representation technique	Ease of access of arbitrary elements	Easy path traversals	Storage-utilization efficiency	Natural extensions
Lexicographically allocated rectangular	*Fast:* Access function is of form $c_0 + \sum c_r * i_r$	Additive parallel to any axis i_r	100%	New subarrays along the i_1 axis of the form $A[n_1 + 1 : n_1 + 1, m_2 : n_2, \ldots, m_k : n_k]$
Lexicographically allocated tetrahedral	Access function of form $c_0 + \sum f_r(i_r)$ where $f_r(i_r)$ is polynomial of degree $k - r + 1$	Additive traversals only in last dimension i_k	100%	New tetrahedra of dimension $k - 1$ and size $n + 1$ can be added to tetrahedral arrays of size n and dimension k
Cubic-shell arrays	Access function is multi-variate polynomial of degree k in $i_1, i_2, \ldots, i_k$	Additive traversals of cubic shells	100%	New cubic shells
Diagonal-shell arrays	Access function is multi-variate polynomial of degree k in $i_1, i_2, \ldots, i_k$	Additive traversals of diagonal shells	100%	New diagonal shells (or, in general, new tetrahedra of size $n + 1$ and dimension $k - 1$)
Allocation using vectors of pointers	*Fast:* (Fastest if can use index regs. and indirect addressing on machine)	Additive traversals only in last dimension i_k	Usually 50% to 100%	Ragged growth in the last dimension i_k
Allocation using linked lists	*Slow:* Requires following $\sum i_r$ links	Successor link traversal only in i_k	Usually 12.5% to 50%	Insertion of arbitrary subarrays at any "slice"
Allocation using orthogonal lists	*Slow:* (Reasonable for very sparse arrays)	Link following parallel to any axis	Usually $> 1/(1 + 2k)$	Addition of new border arrays
Hash-allocated arrays	Dependent on speed of underlying hash scheme	No path favored	Normally $\approx 1/(k + 2)$	*Most flexible:* Can add arbitrary subarrays

For example, in such a language, executing a statement such as:

$$For \; i \leftarrow 1 \; to \; 10 \; do \; For \; j \leftarrow 1 \; to \; 10 \; do \; A[2^i, 3^j] \leftarrow i \times j$$

would define values for a sparse array with 100 nonzero values, one of which would be $A[1024, 59049]$ whose value is 100.

A further interesting generalization is to permit the use of names as subscripts. One can then write such expressions as $A[top, 3] \leftarrow 5$ or $A[4, 5, numerator] \leftarrow 9$. This feature is found in "associative" languages and it permits one to build up ragged tree structures as values.

8.6 COMPARISON OF REPRESENTATION TECHNIQUES

For each of the various array representations we have examined in this chapter, we have compared four dimensions of representation quality: (1) ease of access of arbitrary elements, (2) ease of traversal along various paths, (3) storage utilization efficiency, and (4) ease of extensions.

Table 8.2 summarizes the results for all the practical representations studied. Each representation excels in some quality that makes it advantageous to use under appropriate circumstances. Thus, the question of which representation to use must be settled in reference to the advantages and trade-offs exhibited amongst the various representations.

One can see from the table, for example, that the best representations are: (1) the pointer vector technique for speed of element access, (2) lexicographically allocated rectangular arrays for the greatest number of easy traversals, (3) any sequential storage mapping allocation technique for the best storage utilization efficiency, and (4) hash-allocated arrays for the best freedom for arbitrary natural extensions.

8.7 BIBLIOGRAPHIC NOTES

DeMillo, Eisenstat, and Lipton [1978] demonstrate that arrays cannot be stored as trees without unbounded loss of element proximity.

Pooch and Nieder [1973] survey techniques for indexing sparse matrices, and Mac-Veigh [1977] studies the cost of various operations on sparse matrices with respect to different representations including bit-map and address-map representations.

Hellerman [1962] studies addressing for multidimensional arrays. Rosenberg and Thatcher [1975] address the question: "What is a multilevel array?"

Extensive considerations of array theory have been given in a sequence of papers by Rosenberg ([1971], [1972], [1973], [1974], [1975], [1977abc], and [1978]).

Karp, Miller, and Rosenberg [1972] treat the problem of identifying patterns rapidly in arrays.

Iverson [1962], and Falkoff and Iverson [1973] discuss the array manipulation language APL.

HOFFMAN [1962] treats data structures that generalize rectangular arrays. Hashing schemes for extensible arrays are investigated in ROSENBERG and STOCKMEYER [1977a]. LEW and ROSENBERG [1978ab] study polynomial indexing of integer lattice-points. The storage of ragged arrays by hashing is studied in ROSENBERG [1977b]. WOOD [1978] introduces a "pyramid" tree encoding technique and shows it to be superior to binary tree encodings with regard to array access time, array storage, and average proximity.

EXERCISES

1. (Lexicographic storage function) Construct a lexicographic storage allocation function that maps the three-dimensional array $A[1:5, 2:4, 8:9]$ onto locations $100:129$ in memory such that $\text{Loc}(A[1, 2, 8]) = 100$ and $\text{Loc}(A[5, 4, 9]) = 129$.

2. (Multiword array elements) Suppose each element of the array A is stored in $p > 1$ machine words instead of one word. If $\text{Loc}(A[i_1, i_2, \ldots, i_k]) = \text{Loc}(A[m_1, m_2, \ldots, m_k]) + f(i_1, i_2, \ldots, i_k)$ is the sequential address-mapping function for an array A with one-word elements, what is the formula for an array A with p-word elements?

3. (Change of origin) Formula (5) for allocating storage lexicographically for tetrahedral array assumes that each tetrahedral array has an "origin" at the point $(1, 1, \ldots, 1)$. How should formula (5) be changed for tetrahedral arrays with origin $(n, n, \ldots, n)$ for any integer n? Formulate a substitution procedure for changing origins from $(1, 1, \ldots, 1)$ to $(n, n, \ldots, n)$ that works with any formula for sequential allocation of tetrahedral arrays.

4. (Another kind of tetrahedral array) Let $A[i_1, i_2, \ldots, i_k]$ be a system of quantities such that $1 \le i_1 \le i_2 \le \cdots \le i_k \le n$. Prove that the following formula defines a lexicographic storage allocation function for such an array.

$$\text{Loc}(A[i_1, i_2, \ldots, i_k]) = \text{Loc}(A[1, 1, \ldots, 1])$$
$$+ \sum_{1 \le r \le k} \left[\binom{(k - r + 1) + (n - i_{r-1})}{(k - r + 1)} - \binom{(k - r + 1) + (n - i_r)}{(k - r + 1)} \right],$$

where i_0 is a special symbol such that $i_0 = 1$.

5. (Nonlexicographic allocation of rectangular arrays) Change formula (1) so that it allocates storage sequentially for $A[m_1:n_1, \ldots, m_k:n_k]$ and allows for natural extensions by addition of subarrays of the form $A[m_1:n_1, \ldots, n_i + 1:n_i + 1, \ldots, m_k:n_k]$, where $i > 1$ (a natural extension being one that does not require previously allocated elements to be moved in storage).

6. (Allocating storage for prism arrays) Write a sequential storage allocation function for the prism array $A[i, j, k]$ such that $1 \leq i \leq j \leq n$ and $1 \leq k \leq m$.

A

7. (Allocating storage for cubic shell arrays) Write a sequential storage allocation function for cubic shell arrays of arbitrary dimension k. These are arrays of the form $A[1:n_1, \ldots, 1:n_k]$ such that $n_1 = n_2 = \cdots = n_k$ and for which the rth cubic shell is defined to be the set of elements $A[i_1, i_2, \ldots, i_k]$ such that max $(i_1, i_2, \ldots, i_k) = r$ for r in the range $1 \leq r \leq n_1$.

8. (Re-expressing cubic shell allocation functions without conditionals) Re-express the allocation function

$$\text{Loc}(A[i, j]) = \text{Loc}(A[1, 1]) + (\textit{if } i \geq j \textit{ then } (i - 1)^2 + j - 1 \textit{ else } j^2 - i)$$

without using conditional expressions (*if–then–else*), using only $|x|$ and the four arithmetic operations $+$, $-$, $\times$, and $/$.

9. (Tetrahedral shell allocation functions) Write a sequential storage allocation function for the tetrahedral shell array $A[i_1, i_2, \ldots, i_k]$ where $0 \leq i_1 + i_2 + \cdots + i_k \leq n$.

10. (Uniqueness of lexicographic mappings?) Let $A[0:n_1, 0:n_2, \ldots, 0:n_k]$ be a rectangular array and let $\text{Loc}(A[i_1, i_2, \ldots, i_k])$ be computed as specified in formula (1), which allocates storage lexicographically for A. Prof. van' Snipe conjectures that $\text{Loc}(A[i_1, i_2, \ldots, i_k])$ is unique in that there is no 1–1, *onto*, sequential storage mapping function F, distinct from Loc, such that if $(i_1, i_2, \ldots, i_k)$ is lexicographically less than $(j_1, j_2, \ldots, j_k)$, then $F(A[i_1, i_2, \ldots, i_k]) < F(A[j_1, j_2, \ldots, j_k])$, where F and Loc each map A onto the same region of memory $M:N$. Is van Snipe right? If so, prove it. If not, give a counterexample.

†11. (Selection sort) Let $A[1:n]$ be an array of n numbers. Devise a sorting algorithm to arrange the numbers in A into nondecreasing order according to the following general hint. [*Hint.* First locate the smallest number k in $A[1:n]$.

---

† The purpose of Exercises 11 and 12 is to complete the (modest) coverage of sorting in this book, since the algorithmic topic of sorting is not examined in any one place in detail, as is traditional for data structures books. We have already seen Quicksort in Chapter 2, and Heapsort in Chapter 3; and Exercise 3.39 covers tree-insertion sorting. Courses in analysis of algorithms usually cover sorting in more detail. The index to Knuth [1973b] lists names of thirty sorting methods, and Knuth [1973b] is an excellent reference for learning more about the topic of sorting.

Suppose k occurs in position j. Exchange $A[1] \leftrightarrow A[j]$. Now $A[1]$ contains the smallest number in A. Next, find the smallest number in $A[2:n]$ and suppose this occurs in position j. Exchange $A[2] \leftrightarrow A[j]$. Now $A[1]$ and $A[2]$ contain the two smallest numbers in A. Continuing in this fashion, work on smaller and smaller subproblems $A[i:n]$ for $i = 3, 4, \ldots, n - 1$. At each stage, locate the smallest number in $A[i:n]$ and exchange it with $A[i]$. When you have solved all the subproblems, A is sorted.] Analyze the running time of your algorithm.

†12. (Bubble sort) Let $A[1:n]$ be an array of n numbers. Devise a sorting algorithm to arrange the numbers in A into nondecreasing order according to the following hint. [*Hint*. Make repeated sweeps over the array $A[1:n]$ from left to right. Upon detecting any adjacent pair of numbers $A[i]$ and $A[i + 1]$ not in proper order, exchange them $A[i] \leftrightarrow A[i + 1]$. When a pass is completed with no exchanges having been made, the process terminates.]

---

† See footnote on page 375.

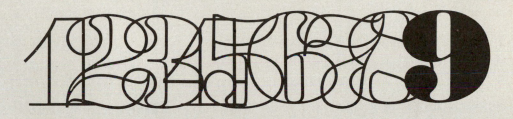

9.1 INTRODUCTION AND MOTIVATION

Files consist of large collections of individual records usually stored on external memory devices such as tapes, disks, or drums. Files are often too extensive to be brought into the main memory of a computer all at once, and therefore operations on them must be performed through a succession of piecewise accesses to groups of records of modest size.

For the purpose of this chapter, we will consider a slightly more general definition of the concept of a record than was given in the earlier chapter on tables. We start with two sets of undefined entities, a finite, nonempty set A of *attributes* and a set V of *values*. A *record* R is a subset of the cartesian product $A \times V$ in which no two distinct, ordered (attribute, value) pairs have identical attributes but different values; that is, each attribute in a record must have one and only one value. For example, consider a record R_1, where

$$R_1 = \left\{ \begin{pmatrix} \text{Constellation:} \\ \text{Ursa Major} \end{pmatrix}, \begin{pmatrix} \text{Abbrevia-} \\ \text{tion: UMa} \end{pmatrix}, \begin{pmatrix} \text{English name:} \\ \text{The Great Bear} \end{pmatrix}, \begin{pmatrix} \text{Area in square} \\ \text{degrees: 1279.7} \end{pmatrix}, \begin{pmatrix} \text{Map:} \\ 1 \end{pmatrix} \right\}.$$

A *file* is a finite set of records all of which possess values of a given set of attributes. Let the file F consist of records $R_1, R_2, \ldots, R_m$, and let each of the records R_j be of the form

$$\{(a_1 : v_1), (a_2 : v_2), \ldots, (a_n : v_n)\},$$

where the a_i $(1 \leq i \leq n)$ are distinct attributes, and where v_i is the value of attribute a_i $(1 \leq i \leq n)$. If there is some particular attribute a_k $(1 \leq k \leq n)$ such that each different record R_j in file F has a distinct value v_k of attribute a_k, we call the values v_k *keys*. In other words, distinct records have distinct keys. Therefore, given a *key* K, we can identify at most one record in F having $v_k = K$.

There are numerous ways we can choose to represent the individual records in a file, and numerous ways of storing and indexing collections of record representations on physical media such as tapes, disks, and drums. A *file-organization technique* is a method of representing, storing, and indexing the component records in a file on some species of physical storage medium in order to provide for the execution of categories of intended operations such as *retrieval, updating, inserting, deleting, report generation, querying,* and *maintenance.*

One purpose of this chapter is to introduce various file-organization techniques that have been found helpful for supporting various subsets of these operations on large files. We will also examine the properties of physical media in which large files are stored on contemporary computing systems.

Unfortunately, in dealing with a subject of such vast scope as this, on which dozens of books have been written, and on which hundreds of papers have appeared in the research literature, we find that exhaustive coverage is beyond the scope of a single chapter in a single volume such as this. We can only hope to give a few pointers to the literature and to examine a small subset of the topics that have been investigated.

An even more advanced topic is that of *data base systems*. A *data base* is a collection of files concerned with a particular organization or enterprise. A data base system consists of the data base itself, together with the set of machines, people, policies, and procedures that govern its use in the context of the enterprise. For instance, one major airline has a data base system that handles the following tasks:

1. maintenance of an on-line flight reservation system for passengers on flights in its schedule and those connecting to other airlines, accessible from 4,000 on-line terminals distributed over a 2,000-mile-long geographical area;

2. crew scheduling, including resolution of bids for route assignments by pilots and stewardesses;

3. delivery of up-to-date weather information including terminal, area, and winds-aloft data to pilots for preflight and en route navigation planning;

4. an aircraft-maintenance scheduling service that keeps track of the time in service of every part of every aircraft, together with its complete maintenance history, and which notifies the proper service personnel whenever an aircraft or one of its subsystems requires scheduled maintenance;

5. extensive management reporting capabilities on all phases of its operations; and

6. an on-line system for assigning passenger seating at airport gates and for printing boarding passes at over a hundred airports.

In a system such as this, issues of reliability and security are important. The system operates 24 hours a day, and each fifteen minutes it is out of service imposes a loss of $3 million on the airline. For example, to guard against failure of its external commercial power source, it is equipped with an "uninterruptible power source" consisting of batteries and generators. When the commercial line voltage fails, the batteries come on line to supply continuous power until the generators can be started up. Needless to say, the data structuring and file-maintenance capabilities in a system such as this must be designed to function reliably and efficiently over many years of continuous usage.

Unfortunately, the investigation of data base systems is beyond the scope of this volume. However, many of the file-organization techniques and management disciplines we shall examine are relevant to the implementation of data base systems.

An interesting aspect of the study of file-organization techniques is that many of the methods that work well for tables stored in internal memory do not work well for files stored on external memory; and variations have to be found that yield good performance.

For instance, in searching a table, balanced binary search trees provide a good solution if the intended operations include random accesses, insertions, deletions, and alphabetical listings. However, consider a file of a million records on which we wish to perform the same operations. (For example, perhaps the file is a file of credit-card records and we wish to query on-line the credit status of a particular cardholder randomly, to insert and delete records for new and discontinued cardholders, and occasionally to print a list of bad credit-card numbers for publication and distribution.) We know that AVL trees take at most $1.44 \lg n$ accesses to handle n records, so for a million records, we have $10^6 \approx 2^{20}$; thus we need at worst about $1.44 \times \lg 2^{20} \cong 29$ node comparisons in an AVL search tree with a million leaves, and on the average, we need perhaps $\lg n \approx 20$ node comparisons. If we naively place the nodes of the AVL tree one to a record in random locations on a disk, we will need 20 or more disk seeks to access a given record, using this technique. At perhaps 10^{-1} seconds per seek, it may take over two seconds to find the record (and the disk drive may be vibrating all over the floor from rapid motion of its read/write heads as they scamper back and forth switching access cylinders). Under the circumstances, it pays to use highly branching multiway trees, or to use a method we shall presently study, called an Indexed Sequential Access Method (or ISAM, for short). This enables us to cut the number of disk seeks down to four or less.

Suppose, now, that we drop the requirement for occasional alphabetic listings of the records. Under these new circumstances, we might think of using hash address techniques to access records, where we hash the record key K to obtain a disk address $h(K)$. If we try to use the techniques that work best for internal tables, however, such as chaining and open addressing with double hashing, to resolve collisions, we are likely to find ourselves hopping all over the disk attempting to follow chains or probe sequences. However, if we use linear open addressing or if we use large-size buckets to help resolve collisions, we tend to stay on the same local portion of a cylinder surface on the disk, and we can cut down substantially on the number of seeks required (particularly by reading in bunches of records from the bucket or linear probe sequence at a single gulp from tracks of the disk and conducting further search in internal memory).

Thus, we need a fresh point of view for considering the variations of tree-structured indexing and hashing policies that are to yield the best performance for large external files stored on relatively slow external storage media.

Additionally, the properties of media such as tape, lacking the random-access properties assumed for most of the storage media considered so far in this book, imply file structures and restrictions on applications that merit our attention.

A difficult and challenging area of exploration is that of *information retrieval*. Oftentimes, in information retrieval from large files, we ask difficult and complex questions, such as "How many married taxpayers who filed joint returns for the last three years had adjusted gross incomes between $15,000 and $17,500 in the last of these three years and, in the last of these three years, paid taxes that were less than 20 percent of their adjusted gross incomes?" and "What percentage were these of all taxpayers in the $15,000-to-$17,500 income bracket?" Sometimes queries such as this are called *multi-attribute retrievals* because they involve testing several of the attributes stored in a record for certain properties, as opposed to a simpler query such as the one considered earlier that involved finding a unique record containing a given unique search key K.

Generally, the queries in information retrieval are formulated in a *query language*, which may possess some subset of the following capabilities:

1. *Simple random access:* Find the record containing key K.
2. *Simple value queries:* Find all records R whose A-attribute has the value V.
3. *Range queries:* Find all records R whose A-attribute has a value V such that (a) $V < k$, (b) $V > k$, or (c) $k_1 \le V \le k_2$.
4. *Function queries:* Find f of the values of attribute A over all records in the file, where f is a function such as the average, minimum, maximum, sum, etc.
5. *Boolean queries:* Using the operators *and*, *or*, and *not*, find some Boolean combination of answers to queries 1 through 4. For example, find all records R such that $(\text{age}(R) \le 18)$ *and* $(\text{sex}(R) = \text{male})$ *or* $(not(45 \le \text{age}(R) \le 65)$ *and* (occupation $(R) = $ bricklayer)).
6. *Quantified queries:* For example, "Is it true of the airline schedule file that all flights that leave for Denver after 2 P.M. on Friday or Saturday from Boston stop either in Chicago, St. Louis, or Dallas?"
7. *Covering retrievals:* Find all records having at least some subset of attribute values; for example, find all documents with key-words "hashing," "scatter storage," and "file."
8. *Similarity retrievals:* For example, find all passengers in the airline reservation file with last names similar to "Schumacher" or "Shumaker."

Various indexing and organization techniques can be used to facilitate the processing of queries composed in query languages incorporating subsets of features drawn from the above list. These techniques include such methods as file inversion, multiple indexing, multilinking, and hybrids of the simpler organization techniques involving hashing, tree-indexing, and the like.

From this brief discussion, it is evident that the scope of inquiry for files is broad enough, and the known results large enough, to fill a number of chapters. Accordingly, we have restricted the scope of coverage to a few brief remarks and pointers to a selected portion of the literature.

9.2 PROPERTIES OF PHYSICAL STORAGE MEDIA

The types of file organizations appropriate to various external storage devices depend on device accessing time, storage, and cost properties. We first explore properties of tapes, and then properties of rotating storage devices such as disks and drums.

9.2.1 Tapes

A magnetic tape is a long strip of tough plastic coated with magnetic material capable of being magnetized in small local areas to hold bit encodings. For instance, tapes may be on the order of 800 to 1000 meters in length; and the bit encodings may occur along the tape at densities of from 300 to 700 bits per centimeter. Bit encodings are written across the width of the tape along, say, five to nine parallel tracks. One of the tracks is sometimes reserved for a parity bit. For example, on a nine-track tape, eight of the tracks can be reserved to hold an eight-bit byte and one of the tracks can hold a parity bit. (In turn, the eight-bit byte is sometimes used to encode a seven-bit ASCII character plus a parity bit.) Figure 9.1 illustrates a nine-track tape encoding.

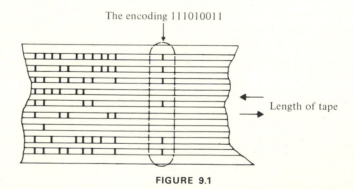

The encoding 111010011

Length of tape

FIGURE 9.1

Of course, technology changes rapidly and there is a spectrum of tape characteristics in use at the moment that fall outside the boundaries of the "typical" tapes we have been discussing. However, by studying a specific, imaginary, typical tape medium, we can gain an understanding that will help provide insights useful for dealing with other serial storage media of low cost and slow access time. Thus, we introduce the *TypiComp* tape (a hypothetical tape produced by TCC, the Typical Computer Corporation). TypiComp tapes have the characteristics listed in Table 9.1.

Let us compute the storage capacity of a single tape. The recording density allows us 500 eight-bit bytes per centimeter, and there are 1000 meters × 100

TABLE 9.1
TypiComp Tape Characteristics

Length	1000 meters
Number of tracks	9 tracks (holding 8 data bits and 1 parity bit)
Density	500 bits per centimeter
Read/write speed	300 centimeters/second
Cost/tape	$24.00

centimeters/meter × 500 bytes/centimeter = 50,000,000 bytes, or 400 megabits, on one tape. Thus, it costs only six cents per megabit to store data on a completely dense tape. A 300-page mystery novel requires on the order of four megabits to store so, theoretically, a TypiComp tape could store 100 such books at a cost of 24¢ each, if one could take advantage of completely dense encoding. However, because the TypiComp tape drives must accelerate and decelerate the tape before and after reading and writing, gaps of unwritten tape of length 1 cm may be created. These gaps may occur between adjacent records, or between adjacent blocks of records, depending on the policy used for grouping records on the tape; but the existence of interrecord and interblock gaps reduces the storage utilization factor for the tape to less than the theoretical maximum density of 400 megabits per tape.

Let us now compute the data-transfer rate of an active tape. If an active tape moves at 300 cm/sec, and holds 500 bytes/cm, it transfers 150,000 bytes/sec, or about 1 byte every $6\frac{2}{3}$ microseconds. To make a complete pass over the tape without stopping takes about $5\frac{1}{2}$ minutes.

Equipment manufacturers utilize a variety of policies for writing records on tapes. In one scheme, the tape is initially *calibrated* by writing sequentially ascending *block addresses* on it at regular intervals. It is then possible to search for particular block addresses and to read or write records in the associated block spaces. Such records can be grouped together into files by a combination of sequential and linked grouping; and a "directory," consisting of names of files, their starting block addresses, and their length in number of records, can be maintained at the beginning of the tape. This kind of policy is used for the small DecTapes (beloved by users of DEC equipment); and it is easy to see that the maintenance procedures can become elaborate.

Another policy is to write blocks of contiguous records on tape without first assigning an address space to the tape. Such blocks can be of variable length, and they are separated by interblock gaps. Sometimes the records in each block are separated by interrecord gaps. This situation is depicted in Fig. 9.2. In this case, the individual records may consist of sequences of fixed length.

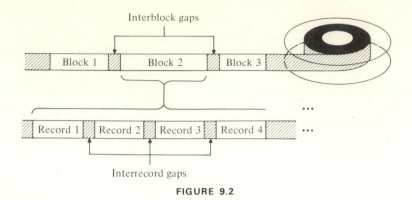

FIGURE 9.2

Blocks of records can be read and written from tape into contiguous "buffer" areas in the main memory of a computer. In some policies, the interrecord gap is set long enough to allow the tape unit to start and stop between each record. In other policies, only the interblock gaps are long enough to permit stop and start operations; so a whole block must be read or written as a unit.

9.2.2 Drums and disks

A *drum* is a cylinder coated with a magnetic material, which rotates under a set of read/write heads. In a *fixed-head* drum, the read/write heads stay in fixed positions and divide the cylindrical surface of the drum into a number of *tracks*, which are the portions of the drum surface that rotate beneath the respective heads. In a *movable-head* drum, the read/write heads can slide back and forth along the drum surface in a direction parallel to the axis of the drum. They must be moved to access tracks at distant points. Figure 9.3 illustrates these two kinds of drums.

Each *track* is divided into a number of *sectors*, and each sector contains a fixed number of bits. The sectors are individually addressable. Thus, to specify an

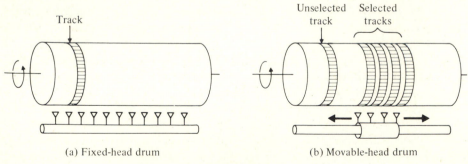

(a) Fixed-head drum   (b) Movable-head drum

FIGURE 9.3

addressable cell on a drum surface, we need the track number t and sector number s. In a fixed-head drum, the search for a cell (t, s) involves selecting the read/write head for track t electronically, and then waiting, if necessary, for the drum to rotate until the sector s is positioned under the read/write head. The transfer of data through the read/write head then occurs at a speed determined by the speed of rotation and the surface packing density. On the other hand, for a movable-head drum, an additional delay may be encountered if it is necessary first to move one of the movable read/write heads along the drum surface into position over track t. Thus, the time required to read a record from a drum consists of three components:

1. *Seek time:* The time to move a read/write head into place over the desired track (if applicable).

2. *Latency time:* The rotational delay until the proper sector moves under the read/write head.

3. *Transmission time:* The rotational delay while the portion of the track containing the record passes under the read/write head.

The advantage of fixed-head drums is that they eliminate the seek time. As examples, the Univac 1108 FH 432 fixed-head drum contains 128 tracks, each track contains 2048 sectors, and each sector contains six characters, for a total of 12,288 characters/track, and 1,572,864 characters/drum. The seek time is 0, the average latency is $4\frac{1}{4}$ ms, and the transmission rate is 1440 characters per millisecond. The Univac Fastrand II, by contrast, is a movable-head drum with a storage capacity of 132,120,756 characters. It has 6144 tracks, 64 sectors/track, and 168 characters per sector. The average latency is 35 ms, the average seek time is 58 ms, and the transmission rate is 153.8 characters/ms. Some drums such as the IBM 2301 have a variable number of characters per sector, and a variable number of sectors per track.

A *disk* is a rotating magnetic storage device constructed from a stack of circular plates coated with magnetic material. Disks have become more widely used than drums, principally because of lower cost for nearly as good performance. On the order of five to ten plates are involved in each stack. Read/write heads may be placed on each disk surface in fixed locations (giving a *fixed-head* disk), or a series of read/write heads may be arranged on a comblike access assembly, which permits them to be moved inward or outward atop the disk surfaces along a line from the rim toward the center of the stack (giving a *movable-head* disk). The surface of each disk is divided into a number of concentric rings called *tracks*; and each track is further divided into *sectors*, each containing a fixed number of bits. Figure 9.4 shows tracks and sectors on a disk surface. Figure 9.5 shows the movable heads of the comblike access assembly of a movable-head disk.

A set of tracks vertically above one another is called a *cylinder*. To locate a particular sector, one needs first to select a cylinder c, then a track t within that

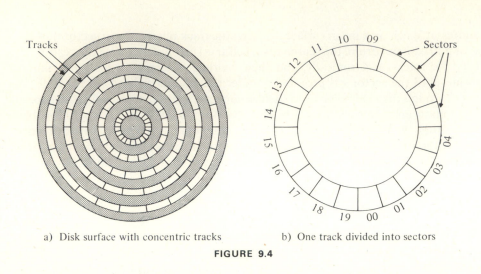

a) Disk surface with concentric tracks　　　　b) One track divided into sectors

FIGURE 9.4

cylinder, and then a sector s within that track. This leads to a three-component addressing system (c, t, s) for disks. The disk address space can then be thought of as a numbered sequence of cylinders, each of which contains a sequence of tracks, each track of which consists of a sequence of sectors.

The access time for a record stored on a disk has three components, similar to that for drums.

1. *Seek time:* The time to move the read/write heads to the proper cylinder.

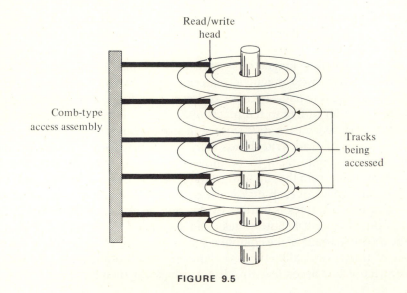

FIGURE 9.5

2. *Latency time:* The rotational delay until the proper sector moves beneath the read/write head on the appropriate track.

3. *Transmission time:* The rotational delay while the portion of the track containing the record passes under the read/write head.

Again, for fixed-head disks, the seek time is absent. Some movable-head disks permit the read/write heads to be retracted completely past the outer rim of the disk stack, and the stack of disks to be removed and exchanged. These are called *exchangeable-disk packs* (or sometimes *removable-disk packs*).

If the cylinders are numbered from 1 to N as the read/write heads move from the outer rim towards the center, the seek time for the heads to move from cylinder i to cylinder j in a movable-head disk can be given by a function such as $(25 + 0.5 \times |i - j|)$ milliseconds. The average seek time, under the assumption that i and j are chosen randomly on a 200-cylinder disk, is approximately 58.3 ms (since the average value of $|i - j|$ with i and j chosen randomly between 1 and 200 is

$$\frac{2 \times \binom{201}{3}}{200^2} \approx 66.7;$$

cf. Knuth [1973b], p. 362). If the disk rotates at 2400 rpm, each rotation takes 25 ms, so the average latency time is 12.5 ms.

Disks come in many sizes and speeds. For instance, CDC's 3300 model contains 100 cylinders of 10 tracks/cylinder, with 16 sectors/track and 256 characters per sector, for a total of

$$100 \times 10 \times 16 \times 256 = 4,096,000 \quad \text{characters per disk.}$$

The average seek time is 85 ms, the average latency is 12.5 ms, and the transmission rate is 288.3 characters/ms. IBM's 3330 disk contains over 100 million characters, while DEC's RS03 for the PDP-11 has under 300,000 characters.

For the purpose of further discussion, we will assume that TCC (the Typical Computer Corporation) manufactures the TypiComp Disk, a movable-head disk with exchangeable disk packs, having the characteristics listed in Table 9.2.

Devices such as drums and disks are sometimes called *direct access storage devices* (DASD's). In contrast to the fixed sector-size organization of the disks discussed above, several of the IBM disks have variable-size sectors formatted into blocks.

In using disks, it is important to minimize the number of seeks, since the seek times dominate the transaction times for most random accesses.

TABLE 9.2
TypiComp Disk Characteristics

Number of:	
cylinders	200
tracks/cylinder	20
sectors/track	64
characters/sector	64
Average seek time (ave. of $(25 + 0.75\|i - j\|)$ ms)	75 ms
Average latency time	12.5 ms
Number of characters/unit	16,384,000
Transmission rate	163.84 characters/ms

9.3 FILE ORGANIZATION TECHNIQUES

We begin our limited sampling of file organization techniques by studying *sequential files* and *direct-access files*.

Let $\alpha_1 < \alpha_2 < \cdots < \alpha_n$ be an ordered set of distinct addresses, belonging to an address space A. Sequential files are files whose records are stored on a sequential access medium, such as tape, with the equation $f(\alpha_1, \alpha_2) = k_1|\alpha_1 - \alpha_2| + k_2$ governing the time between consecutive accesses of locations α_1 and α_2, where $|\alpha_i - \alpha_j|$ is a distance function defined on $A \times A$, and where k_1 and k_2 are suitable constants.

9.3.1 Sequential files

9.3.1.1 *Sorting, merging, and reporting.* Certainly files stored on tape are not much good for rapid answering of on-line queries, such as interrogating the status of a credit-card user's revolving credit account, or determining whether an airline passenger has made a reservation on a certain flight on a certain day. What then are sequential files useful for?

To gain some insight into one answer to this question, we will study informally a telephone billing application. Let us assume that, when a person makes a chargeable phone call from a given phone number N_1 to another number N_2, some automatic equipment, whose nature need not concern us, creates a transaction record for the call of the following form:

Originating number	Destination number	Date today	Time	Charge
N_1	N_2	*MM/DD/YY*	*H:MM*	*DDD.cc*

For instance, a call from (714)–497–3064 to (617)–627–8923 on May 22, 1980 for two minutes at a cost of \$2.25 would generate the following transaction record:

Originating number	Destination number	Date today	Time	Charge
(714)–497–3064	(617)–627–8923	05/22/80	0:02	002.25

Let us suppose that these transactions are posted to an output tape where they are allowed to accumulate in the order in which they are generated for a period of a day. At the end of the day, the tape of transactions is sent to a computer center where it is sorted in order of increasing originating phone numbers. These sorted tapes of phone call transactions are allowed to accumulate each day until the monthly billing run is performed on the 23rd day of the month. Further suppose that during a given month, the phone company's main office is adding new customers whose phones have been installed recently, and deleting customers who have discontinued service.

The main office generates insertion and deletion transactions for these customers in the form of records having such information as the following in them:

Insertion transaction record:

$$\left\{ \left(\begin{array}{c} \text{Phone number} \\ N_1 \end{array} \right), \left(\begin{array}{c} \text{Name: 30} \\ \text{characters} \end{array} \right), \left(\begin{array}{c} \text{Billing address:} \\ \text{60 characters} \end{array} \right), \right.$$

$$\left. \left(\begin{array}{c} \text{Type of service: Special} \\ \text{two-character code} \end{array} \right), \left(\begin{array}{c} \text{Basic monthly charge:} \\ \text{\$DD.cc} \end{array} \right), \left(\begin{array}{c} \text{Balance of account:} \\ \text{\$0000.00} \end{array} \right) \right\}$$

Deletion transaction record:

$$\left\{ \left(\begin{array}{c} \text{Phone number:} \\ N_1 \end{array} \right) \right\}$$

Finally, the billing office, which receives payments from its customers, generates transactions to record payments received, using transaction records of the form:

Payment transaction record:

$$\left\{ \left(\begin{array}{c} \text{Phone number:} \\ N_1 \end{array} \right), \left(\begin{array}{c} \text{Date:} \\ \text{MM/DD/YY} \end{array} \right), \left(\begin{array}{c} \text{Amount received:} \\ \text{\$DDDD.cc} \end{array} \right) \right\}$$

All of these transactions are accumulated sequentially on tape and are forwarded to the computing center where they too are sorted in order of the phone numbers N_1 and stored in chronological order received.

The computing center keeps a *Master File* consisting of a master record for each phone number.

Master record for each phone number:

$$\left\{ \left(\begin{matrix} \text{Phone number:} \\ N_1 \end{matrix} \right), \left(\begin{matrix} \text{Name: 30} \\ \text{characters} \end{matrix} \right), \left(\begin{matrix} \text{Billing address:} \\ \text{60 characters} \end{matrix} \right), \right.$$

$$\left. \left(\begin{matrix} \text{Type of service: Special} \\ \text{two-character code} \end{matrix} \right), \left(\begin{matrix} \text{Basic monthly charge:} \\ \$DD.cc \end{matrix} \right), \left(\begin{matrix} \text{Balance of account:} \\ \$DDDD.cc \end{matrix} \right) \right\}$$

The master records, too, are stored on tape sorted in ascending order of their phone numbers.

When the 23rd of the month arrives it is time for the monthly billing run. The first operation is to take the Master file tape and the transaction tapes, all of which have been sorted in ascending order of their phone numbers N_1, and to merge them onto one big tape (or several tapes if required). These files are merged in the following order to create the *Merge tape(s)*:

1. Master file

2. Insertion and deletion transactions

3. Payment transactions

4. Phone call transactions (in chronological order)

The result of the *merge* operation is to group together all records for a given phone number N_1 in the order: (a) Master file for N_1 (if present), followed by (b) Insertion or deletion transaction for N_1 (if present), followed by (c) Payment transactions for N_1 in chronological order of receipt (if present), followed by (d) Phone call transactions for N_1 in chronological order (if present). The *Merge tape(s)* contain such groupings in order of ascending values of N_1. The Merge tape is now run through the billing and reporting process. Several output tapes are simultaneously created during the billing and reporting process:

a) the *Billing tape*, which contains bills to be printed and mailed to customers,

b) a new updated Master tape (containing updated master records for each phone number with new account balances), and

c) a *Management report tape* containing summary statistics for submission to the phone company managers (such as total local calls made, total long-distance calls made, total of accounts payable, total payments received, and various breakdowns of other data requested by the management).

Basically, the processing of the Merge tape proceeds by processing, one set at a time, the records grouped under a given phone number N_1. Without going into all contingencies, some of which are pathological (such as a group of records of phone call transactions not preceded by a master record or insertion transaction for the given number, which might trigger an investigation request on the management report), the following things take place:

1. If a master record for N_1 is received and it is followed by a deletion transaction for N_1, output a summary of the account closed to the management tape.

2. If no master record for N_1 occurs, but an insertion transaction for N_1 is encountered, a new master record for N_1 is created, using the information in the insertion transaction record. Further steps are taken at step 4.

3. If a master record for N_1 is received, and is not followed by an insertion or deletion transaction, further steps are taken at step 4.

4. The customer name and address (taken from the master record) are output to the Billing tape.

5. The payment transactions (if present) are read in from the Merge tape. Each payment is deducted from the amount in the account balance of the master record, and each payment and the new account balance are output as a line on the Billing tape.

6. The phone call transactions are read in from the Merge tape in chronological order. Each is processed by adding its cost to the account balance, and outputting a record of the call to the Billing tape.

7. At the end of the phone calls for N_1 (signaled by reading in a record for the next phone number N_2), the account balance is output as an amount due and payable to the Billing tape (supplemented by lines for taxes and surcharges, if applicable), and a new master record for N_1 is output to the new Master tape.

8. Finally, contributions from the master record for N_1 are combined with the summary statistics for the management report, the bill for N_1 is closed on the Billing tape, and the next group of records for N_2 is considered in sequence.

The Billing tape is now ready for printing and mailing, the Management report tape can be printed and sent to the management (perhaps after further analysis runs), and the new Master file can be shelved to await the next month's billing run.

While this is assuredly an oversimplified treatment of the myriad of details that must be considered, it gives the basic flavor of a sorting, merging, and reporting application with sequential files stored on tape. It is remarkable what can be done with inexpensive equipment and inexpensive tapes in this vein. Similar applications include billing systems for small corporations, monthly statement preparation for banks, and inventory control in a retail outlet. Basically, enough transactions must accumulate to make a pass through the Master file tape worthwhile, in these kinds of applications. The accumulation of transactions is called *batching*, and this method of file processing is called *batch processing*, for this reason.

9.3.2 Direct access files

Sometimes it is possible to use the address of a record stored on a direct-access storage device to gain access to the record. This is especially possible when the enterprise that controls access to a DASD can also control the issuing of keys for the records stored on it and can enforce use of the keys for access.

For example, suppose we consider an application in which we are to provide an on-line query service for certifying the credit of cardholders attempting to make a purchase. Let us suppose there are 10,240,000 credit-card holders in the system. Suppose the buyer holding the credit card wants to make a purchase from the seller for X. The seller makes a phone call (say, to an 800 number which connects him, toll-free) to the credit-certification agency, where he is put in touch with an operator at a keyboard. The seller gives the buyer's credit-card number and the intended purchase amount X to the operator, who types it on the keyboard. The computer responds with the name of the credit-card holder, his authorized credit limit, and the current amount of his unused revolving credit. Also, if the X dollar purchase falls within the bounds of the revolving-credit limit, the operator reports that the purchase is acceptable, and issues a transaction number to the seller to enter on the credit-card purchase slip. This transaction number is also posted to a transaction file together with the credit-card number and purchase amount X. Additionally, if the purchase is confirmed as made, the amount X is subtracted from the cardholder's revolving-credit limit. Credit-card payments by the cardholder are also periodically added to the revolving-credit limit stored on his account. If a cardholder is unable to make the purchase because the amount X exceeds his current revolving-credit limit, or because he holds an invalid card, the operator so informs the seller.

To see how a system of this sort could be implemented, suppose the credit-card company purchases 40 TypiComp disk pack units (with characteristics given in Table 9.2). Let the company issue credit cards to its customers of the following form:

$$PP\text{-}CCC\text{-}TT\text{-}SS$$

where **PP** is a disk pack number in the range $1 \le PP \le 40$, CCC is a cylinder number in the range $1 \le CCC \le 200$, TT is a track number in the range $1 \le TT \le 20$, and SS is a sector number in the range $1 \le SS \le 64$. Thus, the credit-card number identifies a unique sector on one of the 40 disk packs. This sector contains a 64-character record, enough capacity to hold a 30-character name for the credit-card holder, and two numbers giving the authorized credit limit and the current revolving-credit balance. Access to such a record on a given disk pack takes an average of

(75 ms seek time) + (12.5 ms latency time) + (0.4 ms transmission time)

for a total of 87.9 ms, or a little under a tenth of a second. Clearly an efficient on-line credit query system might be built on this basis. Further improvements might arise from batching the access requests for each disk pack, and arranging them in the optimal scheduling order of requests to minimize inter-cylinder switching time and rotational delay between sectors. (See Exercise 9.7.) However, here one must be careful that increasing the system throughput (i.e., number of queries handled per minute) is not purchased in the coinage of unacceptably increased variance in the waiting times for receiving answers to the queries.

9.3.3 The indexed sequential access method

In Sections 9.3.1 and 9.3.2 we have seen circumstances under which it was favorable to batch transactions, sort them, merge them, and process them, on the one hand, and, on the other hand, circumstances in which it was favorable to perform rapid, on-line queries to a large file of 10 million records. We also saw that the storage of ordered files on tape did not lend itself to good, rapid, on-line query operations. Conversely, the direct-access storage method does not lend itself to applications in which one needs, say, to process the records sequentially in the alphabetical order of the names they contain.

In some applications, however, we need the capacity for rapid random access, update, insertion, and deletion of records, as well as the capability for sequential processing of the records in an order furnished, say, by the alphabetical ordering on their *primary keys*.

We have already seen, in the introduction, that naive application of balanced search tree techniques, such as AVL trees or 2–3 trees, leads to on the order of 20 or so disk accesses for a file of a million records. If the nodes of such a search tree are placed randomly on the disk, we may incur unacceptable cumulative seek-time penalties. A popular method for organizing a file to permit both random access and sequential operations, incurring fewer than four disk accesses per random retrieval, on the average, is the ISAM or Indexed Sequential Access Method.

The idea behind the ISAM technique is to write records of a file sequentially on portions of each successive cylinder in a disk in order of increasing primary keys K, and then to prepare a *cylinder surface index*, which may be used to ascertain where the record containing a particular search key K resides. The cylinder surface index has a top-level index, which for key K tells on which cylinder the record for K resides. On each cylinder, a *track index* is stored, which, in turn, tells on which track the record containing K resides. The track index for each cylinder is stored on the lowest numbered track, say track 00. A few tracks of highest number, say M and $M - 1$, can be set aside for use as *overflow areas* to handle later insertions that don't fit on a given full track. Then the tracks used neither for holding the track index nor for holding overflow records, say tracks 1 to $M - 2$, are called the *primary area* and are used to hold the records initially written in sequential order.

This system of indexing is roughly analogous to a card catalogue in a library. Each tray of cards in the card catalogue can be thought of as analogous to a cylinder. The tray holds *tab cards* which divide its alphabetically arranged cards at intervals. These tab cards are analogous to the contents of the track index on track 00 of a cylinder (and are contained in the tray, just as the track index is contained in the cylinder). To locate an appropriate tray in which to search, an external tray index for the card catalogue is consulted. Usually, the range of alphabetical keys held by a tray is written on the outside of the tray, and the trays are arranged in increasing order of their alphabetical ranges. If such information were placed in an index that mapped the alphabetical ranges contained by trays into tray numbers, such an index would correspond to the cylinder index of an ISAM file. Perhaps such a card-catalogue tray index would require a booklet of several pages of alphabetical range listings corresponding to the trays. In the case, say, that there were 4096 trays, such a booklet might contain 32 pages, and each page might contain 128 individual tray listings. Then the table of contents for the booklet that tells which page to use to search further for the tray number containing a given listing, would be analogous to what is sometimes called a *master index* in some ISAM files. The master index enables one to locate a *cylinder index* containing key K. The cylinder index tells what cylinder K is located on, and the track index on that cylinder tells the track on which the record for K is located. The track must be searched in order to locate the record containing K. Thus, in the absence of overflows, an ISAM file with a master index requires at most four disk accesses if all three levels of indexes are stored on disk. In practice, however, the master index (or, more generally, the top-level index) is kept in main memory during file access, so that at most three accesses are required if no overflows occur.

In order to set a context for the discussion of overflow policies and to get a feeling for the specific details of how a particular instance of an ISAM technique can work, we examine an ISAM scheme for a TypiComp disk. Suppose we are operating an inventory-control system for a parts supply distributor, who has 200,000 parts in stock. The inventory-control system permits on-line query, update, insertion, and deletion for such things as purchase-order handling. Also, sequential processing is involved for reordering, price-list printing, and management reporting. Let us suppose, further, that the records in the system are each 64 characters in length, and that they are ordered on a primary key K consisting of a six-digit part number.

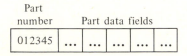

Space on a TypiComp disk is allocated as follows. Cylinder 000 is reserved for the *cylinder index* and various file maintenance statistics. Cylinders 001 through

184 are designated as *prime cylinders*, and cylinders 185 to 199 are designated as *general overflow cylinders*. On each of the prime cylinders, track 00 is reserved for the *track index*, tracks 01 through 17 are reserved as *prime tracks*, and tracks 18 and 19 are reserved as *overflow tracks*. Each of the prime tracks contains 64 records, stored one record to a sector.

For the initial loading of the file 200,192 parts records are stored in ascending order of their part-number keys on the prime tracks of the prime cylinders in ascending order of cylinders, and of tracks within cylinders. This exactly fills all the prime tracks on the prime cylinders (since $64 \times 17 \times 184 = 200,192$), leaving the overflow tracks on each prime cylinder and the general overflow cylinders empty (but poised for action). The track index on track 00 of each prime cylinder is a sequence of *index records* in which there is one index record for each of the 17 prime tracks. Each index record contains two pairs of the form (key, pointer). The first pair is the *maximum track entry*, and consists of the highest-numbered key stored on the track together with a pointer to the first record of the track. The second pair is the *overflow entry*, and consists of a part-number key and a pointer to an overflow record. When there are no overflows on a track, the overflow entry is identical to the maximum track entry. Figure 9.6 shows an example of a cylinder surface format after initial loading of the file in sequential order.

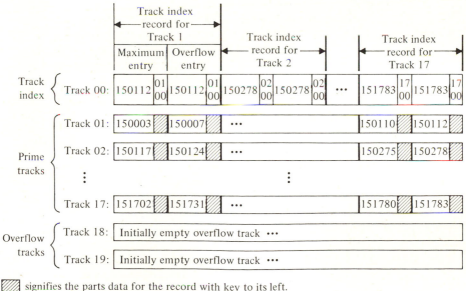

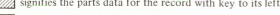 signifies the parts data for the record with key to its left.

$\boxed{\begin{smallmatrix}17\\00\end{smallmatrix}}$ is a pointer to record 00 of track 17.

FIGURE 9.6

If, for instance, it had been determined that the search key $K = 150124$ was located on the cylinder of Fig. 9.6, the track index would be read from track 00 and searched (perhaps by binary search in main memory) for the index record with the smallest key $K' \geq K$. Thus, the index record for track 02 would be selected because its associated maximum key entry $K' = 150278$ is the smallest key in the track index greater than or equal to the search key $K = 150124$. The track 02 is associated with K' by the pointer $\boxed{\substack{02\\00}}$ which points to record 00 of track 02. Track 2 is now read and searched for the record with key $K = 150124$. This record is found in the second sector position in sequence on track 2.

9.3.3.1 *Handling overflows.* How shall we handle overflow records when records are inserted randomly? In the specific scheme pictured in Fig. 9.6, all the prime tracks are full, so the next record to be inserted will cause an overflow into the overflow area on tracks 18 and 19. One method of handling this overflow is as follows. Suppose we wish to insert a new record $\boxed{150277 \hspace{0.5em} /\!/\!/}$ into the cylinder illustrated in Fig. 9.6. The record $\boxed{150278 \hspace{0.5em} /\!/\!/}$ must then be moved off the end of track 02 into overflow track 18, in order to preserve the sequential order of the records on track 02. Now, however, the maximum key on track 02 has changed, and must be adjusted in the index record for track 2 in the track index. Also, the overflow entry is changed in the index record for track 2 to hold the *largest* key value of any of the records that have overflowed track 2 while the associated pointer gives the address of the first record in an ordered linked list of overflow records for track 2, this list being ordered in increasing order of the keys of its elements. The last element of such an ordered linked overflow list points back to the beginning of the track whose overflows it stores. Figure 9.7 shows the status of the cylinder of Fig. 9.6 after the insertion of record $\boxed{150277 \hspace{0.5em} /\!/\!/}$, and Fig. 9.8 shows the status after the record $\boxed{150120 \hspace{0.5em} /\!/\!/}$ has been inserted into the configuration of Fig. 9.7.

Should the overflows exceed the capacity of overflow tracks 18 and 19, further overflows are placed on the reserved overflow cylinders (185 through 199). These records are linked into linked lists in ascending order of their chains. Thus, the general overflow cylinders are treated as an available space list for linked lists.

The cylinder index, stored on cylinder 000, is analogous to the track index for each cylinder. It contains an ordered sequence of index records, one for each of the prime cylinders in sequence. The highest key value stored on prime cylinder i is stored in the ith record of the cylinder index. Thus, to locate the cylinder containing search key K, the cylinder index on cylinder 000 is searched for the lowest key $K' \geq K$, and further search continues on its associated cylinder.

Clearly, other overflow policies are possible. For instance, Mullin [1972] examines a hashing technique for handling ISAM overflows.

9.3.3.2 *Deletions and file maintenance.* In some ISAM techniques, deletions of records are handled by marking the records as "deleted" but not removing the

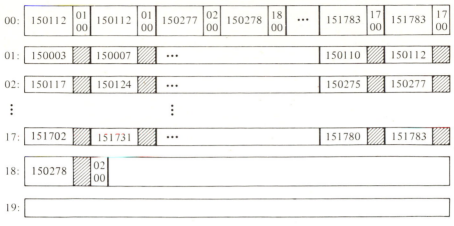

FIGURE 9.7

deleted record physically. As with the deletion problem in open addressing techniques for hashing, this method may lead to eventual clogging of the cylinders with physically present *deleted* records, and to overflow chains that are long and that perhaps incur extra seek-time penalties. Chapin ([1969b], p. 417) states that this overflow may amount to a third to a half more space than for the main file, but that typically the overflow can be held to a tenth or less additional space.

Periodically, such an ISAM file can be rewritten in order to eliminate the deleted records, to readjust the overflow areas, and to compute a new index. A question arises as to how often one should perform such file reorganizations. One might wish to choose an optimum time such that the cost of reorganization and the cost of degraded performance in the absence of reorganization are taken into

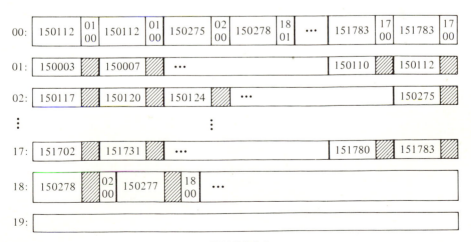

FIGURE 9.8

consideration. This question has been studied by Schneiderman [1973] and Tuel [1978].

9.3.3.3 *Random access by interpolation.* Ghosh and Senko [1969] have studied the question of whether or not it might be preferable to use linear interpolation techniques to guess where to look for a record in an ISAM file instead of using repeated levels of accessing in a hierarchical multiway tree index. Under certain favorable conditions, such as proper distribution properties for the keys, and record sizes in proper relationships to the device characteristics, Ghosh and Senko have shown that it is possible to reduce the typical two accesses to obtain the track index and track data down to a range of between 1.1 and 1.7 accesses per record.

9.3.4 Files indexed by multiway trees

In the ISAM files studied in the last section, we constructed a hierarchy of indexes to conform to the physical characteristics of a particular device. Thus, the ISAM index for a TypiComp disk could be viewed as a multiway search tree whose root node has one child for each prime cylinder, each of which has one child for each prime track, each of which has one child for each record. The branching factors of the nodes were thus 184, 17, and 64, respectively, at the three levels of nodes. Perhaps these device-oriented branching factors are not optimal, and perhaps we could do better with a completely balanced multiway tree with uniform branching factors m at each of its nodes.

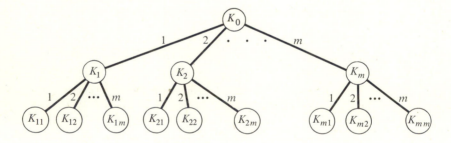

If the search key K does not match the key K_0 at the root, we could read the sequence $K_1, K_2, \ldots, K_m$ of the m children of the root from the disk into the main memory. Using binary search we could determine the smallest of these keys $K_i \geq K$ in time at most $(a + b \times \lg m)$ steps. If $K = K_i$, we are done, whereas if $K < K_i$, we must continue the search by reading in another sequence of m keys from the disk that are the children of node K_i, and so on. The question is, for what value of m do we minimize the total time to utilize the index and locate K?

Each time we read in the m children nodes of a given node from a TypiComp disk, we can assume it takes

(75 ms seek time) + (12.5 ms latency) + (0.049 × m ms transmission time),

on the average. (Here, we have assumed eight character units to hold each of the m (key, subtree disk address) pairs for a node, leading to a transmission time of 0.049 ms for each eight-character unit.) Hence, to access the children of a node takes

$$87.5 + 0.049 \times m \text{ milliseconds.}$$

Therefore, to descend one level in the multiway search tree takes

$$F(m) = (\text{Time to read } m \text{ nodes from disk})$$
$$+ (\text{Time to search } m \text{ nodes in main memory})$$
$$= (87.5 + 0.049 \times m)$$
$$+ (a + b \times \lg m) \text{ milliseconds.}$$

We can drop the term a since $a \ll 87.5$. The number of levels we must descend at cost $F(m)$ each for a file of N records is at most

$$\lceil \log_m (N) \rceil = \lceil \lg (N)/\lg (m) \rceil \text{ levels.}$$

Thus, if we take the derivative of $F(m)/\lg m$ and set it to zero, we find that a branching factor of $m \cong 371$ minimizes the function $F(m)$ for the given combination of parameters. If we had chosen 16-character components for each of the m components of a node record on a TypiComp disk, the optimal branching factor would have been $m \cong 207$. By examining the second derivative of $F(m)/\lg m$, we discover that the function is shallow in the region of the optimum (i.e., of low curvature). Since the region of the optimum is relatively flat, we can take branching factors in the range of 200 to 500 without ranging far from the optimum.

Actually, though, in most cases, multiway balanced tree indexes do not improve much over ISAM techniques, if they improve at all. For comparison, suppose we have $N = 16,777,216$ records, and circumstances under which the optimum branching factor in a multiway tree is $m = 256$. Then we need exactly $3 = \log_{256}(16777216)$ levels to the index, with 256-way nodes. Thus, it takes three disk seeks to determine the address of the record for a key K. With an ISAM technique on 69 TypiComp disks, assuming 64-character records, we would need one master index seek to determine one of 69 disk packs, one cylinder index seek on the selected pack to determine the cylinder, and one track index seek on the selected cylinder to determine the selected track. But then we are on the correct cylinder, and so can switch electronically and search the proper track without an additional seek. Each technique thus takes three seeks if the highest level of index is on disk, and two seeks if the highest level is already in main memory. If now we have $N = 33{,}554{,}432$ records, the ISAM technique still uses three seeks with double the master index and double the number of disk packs to select at the top level, but the multiway balanced tree uses up to

$$\lceil \lg N/\lg m \rceil = \lceil \lg 33{,}554{,}432/\lg 256 \rceil = \lceil 25/8 \rceil = 4 \text{ levels of access,}$$

in which the last level is sparsely occupied. Thus, four seeks are required, and the ISAM technique proves itself superior.

Another drawback of completely balanced multiway trees is the difficulty of maintenance of balanced tree shape under insertions and deletions. We have seen, however, in Chapter 3, that this problem can be overcome through the use of B-trees.

9.3.4.1 *B-tree indexes.* The use of B-trees as indexes combines the advantages of using large m for multiway branching at the nodes, yielding the corresponding shallow number of levels, together with low-cost easy maintenance of B-tree shape under insertions and deletions. In addition, sequential enumeration of records indexed by B-trees is possible using a generalized symmetric tree traversal of the index.

As we have seen in Chapter 3, the worst case number of nodes ℓ we have to search in a B-tree of order m that indexes N keys is constrained by the inequality $\ell \leq 1 + \log_{\lceil m/2 \rceil}((N + 1)/2)$, so that, for instance, ℓ is at most 3 if $N = 1{,}999{,}998$ and $m = 199$. Further, we have seen that, when splitting nodes during insertion, the average number of splits per insertion is $1/(\lceil m/2 \rceil - 1)$ at most, so maintenance costs for insertion are quite low.

Some important refinements and variations have been explored by McCreight and Knuth (see Knuth [1973b], pp. 476–479), which make use of the technique potentially attractive. See also Bayer and McCreight [1972] for maintenance algorithms and experimental results.

9.3.5 Random access with hashing methods

Suppose now that we drop the requirement for sequential processing, but retain the requirements for rapid random access for queries, updates, insertions, and deletions. However, suppose that, unlike the situation studied in Section 9.3.2, we do not have the luxury of using record addresses as keys, but instead must deal with some space of primary search keys K other than disk addresses. In these circumstances, the direct access techniques of Section 9.3.2 are inapplicable; but, using hashing methods (sometimes called *scatter storage* methods, when speaking of files), we should be able to do just about as well.

The only difference, in comparison to the hashing methods studied for accessing tables in Chapter 4, is that we must take care to avoid cascades of disk seeks that might be encountered if we naively apply collision-resolution techniques, such as chaining or open addressing with double hashing, that work so well for tables. For instance, if we use chaining, an attempt should be made to keep chains on the same cylinder, if possible.

In actual practice, the use of buckets containing b or less records for each of the M hash addresses that can be computed, and the use of open addressing with linear probing, have been found effective as hashing methods to use with external direct access storage devices.

For example, Table 9.3 presents a sample of the average number of accesses given by Knuth ([1973b], p. 535), when we use buckets of size b and when we assume that, when a bucket overflows, we plant a link to an overflow area and keep the overflowed records on separate chains (one for each overflowed bucket) in this overflow area. It is advantageous to put the overflow areas on the same cylinder as overflowed buckets, if possible. Here the load factor $\alpha = N/bM$, where N is the number of records.

Sometimes planting links on the end of records is inconvenient when the records are all of identical size. In this case, we might consider using the open-address method with linear probing. Here, however, instead of choosing a linear

TABLE 9.3
Knuth's Theoretical Data

Average accesses in an unsuccessful search by separate chaining

Bucket size, b	% Full = $100\alpha\%$						
	10%	50%	60%	70%	80%	90%	95%
1	1.0048	1.1065	1.1488	1.197	1.249	1.307	1.3
5	1.0000	1.0619	1.1346	1.249	1.410	1.620	1.7
10	1.0000	1.0222	1.0773	1.201	1.426	1.773	2.0
20	1.0000	1.0028	1.0234	1.113	1.367	1.898	2.3
50	1.0000	1.0000	1.0007	1.018	1.182	1.920	2.7

Average accesses in a successful search by separate chaining

Bucket size, b	% Full = $100\alpha\%$						
	10%	50%	60%	70%	80%	90%	95%
1	1.0500	1.2500	1.3000	1.350	1.400	1.450	1.5
5	1.0000	1.0358	1.0699	1.119	1.186	1.286	1.3
10	1.0000	1.0070	1.0226	1.056	1.115	1.206	1.3
20	1.0000	1.0005	1.0038	1.018	1.059	1.150	1.2
50	1.0000	1.0000	1.0000	1.001	1.015	1.083	1.2

TABLE 9.4
Knuth's Theoretical Data

Average accesses in a successful search by linear probing

Bucket size, b	% Full = $100\alpha\%$						
	10%	50%	60%	70%	80%	90%	95%
1	1.0556	1.5000	1.7500	2.167	3.000	5.500	10.5
5	1.0000	1.0307	1.0661	1.136	1.289	1.777	2.7
10	1.0000	1.0047	1.0154	1.042	1.110	1.345	1.8
20	1.0000	1.0003	1.0020	1.010	1.036	1.144	1.4
50	1.0000	1.0000	1.0000	1.001	1.005	1.040	1.1

probe increment of one-record size, we might instead choose an increment c that minimizes drum or disk latency delays due to rotation between consecutive addresses probed. Table 9.4 presents a portion of Knuth's data (Knuth [1973b], p. 536) for such an open-addressing scheme.

It is rather remarkable that at bucket size $b = 50$ and upwards of 80% saturation, the open-addressing method beats the separate chaining method for successful searches!

Table 9.5 presents a sample of empirical results obtained by Lum, Yuen, and Dodd [1971] for successful searches using the chaining and open-addressing methods on actual files. The division method of calculating hash addresses is used for both tables.

In these tables, the average number of accesses for linear probing is the average of $S + 1$, where S is the number of buckets away from the key's home bucket $h(K)$, whereas in separate chaining, each record located in the home bucket $h(K)$ is said to require one access, and the average number of accesses is the average of $T + 1$, where T is the position of K along the overflow chain.

The Lum, Yuen, and Dodd empirical data was calculated for eight different sets of keys used in actual practice. As they point out, a comparison of the empirical and theoretical data in Tables 9.3, 9.4, and 9.5 reveals that the division method of calculating hash addresses works out in practice slightly better than completely random hash functions for the larger bucket sizes when open addressing is used, and for almost all bucket sizes when chaining is used. More observations about the relative performance of various hashing functions on actual key sets can be gleaned by reading Lum, Yuen, and Dodd [1971].

9.3.6 Multi-attribute file techniques

So far, our discussion has centered on techniques for accessing records in files under the assumption that each record in a file is identified by a unique primary

TABLE 9.5
Lum, Yuen, and Dodd's Empirical Data

Average accesses for successful search by separate chaining

Bucket size, b	% Full = 100α%					
	50%	60%	70%	80%	90%	95%
1	1.19	1.25	1.28	1.34	1.38	1.41
5	1.02	1.05	1.09	1.13	1.24	1.25
10	1.00	1.01	1.03	1.08	1.16	1.20
20	1.00	1.01	1.01	1.04	1.09	1.17
50	1.00	1.00	1.00	1.01	1.03	1.08

Average accesses for successful search by linear probing

Bucket size, b	% Full = 100α%					
	50%	60%	70%	80%	90%	95%
1	4.52	5.04	4.73	10.10	22.42	25.79
5	1.02	1.05	1.10	1.31	1.94	4.47
10	1.00	1.01	1.02	1.08	1.32	2.32
20	1.00	1.00	1.01	1.03	1.08	1.25
50	1.00	1.00	1.00	1.00	1.01	1.03

key K. Sometimes, however, we want to find records in a file based on knowing values of some attributes other than the primary keys. Sometimes these values are called *secondary keys* but, since we are following the practice of using the word key to refer to values of attributes that uniquely identify records containing them, and since secondary keys often do not uniquely identify records, we prefer to use the term *secondary attributes* to refer to the quantities used as inputs to multi-attribute retrieval processes. For example, retrieval of documents containing certain key words is an instance of multi-attribute retrieval in which the key words are the attributes, and more than one record may be retrieved containing the given key words if the key words fail to identify some particular document uniquely. The queries listed in the introduction to this chapter are instances of multi-attribute queries.

9.3.6.1 *Inverted files. Inverted files* consist of files for which, in addition to listing the values of the attributes of each record, we list the records having attributes with given values. We can make sense out of this terminology by considering a file F as a function that maps a pair (α, a) consisting of an address of a record α and an attribute name a into the value v of attribute a of the record stored at α. Thus, $F(\alpha, a) = v$. The inverse function, $F^{-1}(v)$ is then the set of pairs (α, a) that F maps into v:

$$F^{-1}(v) = \{(\alpha, a) \mid F(\alpha, a) = v\}.$$

Thus, given a value v, $F^{-1}(v)$ locates all records having the value v as a value of some attribute. In this sense, an *inverted file* is a listing of the *inverse* of the file function F.

For example, consider each page of this book to be a record in a file, and consider the index to the book. The index contains, for each referenced word or name of interest, the list of pages on which this word or name is mentioned.

For a file F consisting of records of the form

$$\{(a_1 : v_1), (a_2 : v_2), \dots, (a_n : v_n)\},$$

suppose we choose the ith attribute a_i and prepare an *i-index* such that, for each value of v_j of a_i that appears in at least one record of the file, we list the addresses of all records having value v_j for a_i. The i-index looks like:

$$v_0 : (\alpha_{01}, \alpha_{02}, \dots, \alpha_{0k_0}), \qquad v_1 : (\alpha_{11}, \alpha_{12}, \dots, \alpha_{1k_1}), \qquad \dots, \qquad v_r : (\alpha_{r1}, \alpha_{r2}, \dots, \alpha_{rk_r}).$$

The file F together with each of its i-indexes for $(1 \le i \le n)$ is called a *fully inverted file*. If some of the i-indexes are missing, the file is called *partially inverted*.

We know of many techniques for representing lists, and so the lists in the i-indexes can be represented in many ways. For example, in a *multilist* file organization, we link together the records for value v_j of attribute a_i by linking (with links through the a_i field) all records having value v_j for attribute a_i. In terms of the analogy to the index in this book, this would be as if, for a word w in the index, we list only the last page p on which w is mentioned. Then on page p, next to w, we mention the next-to-last page on which w is mentioned, and so on. Searching for all occurrences of w by this technique involves following a linked list through many pages. Similarly, when multilist techniques are used on a disk, following such lists might lead to an excessive number of seeks if the links hop around across a number of cylinders. In the so-called *cellular-partition* methods, attempts are made to place the lists on the same cylinder or disk pack, in order to reduce the cost of list-following. The *cells* of the partition are arranged to conform to the characteristics of the physical device used. Another technique for controlling costs is the so-called *controlled list-length multilist organization*, in which an upper bound is placed on the length of the lists for an item in an i-index (but for which there may be more than one item in an i-index with the same indexed value v_j). (See Tremblay and Sorensen [1976], Chapter 7, for more details and explanation.)

Sometimes instead of storing record addresses α_{i_j} in an i-index, we use primary keys K instead. This way, if the file is reorganized, and some records moved, the keys do not have to be readjusted. For example, Bible references are usually given in the form (book, chapter, verse). To give Bible references by page would be sheer folly since so many printings of the Bible are in existence. A concordance for a Bible is an inverted file. For example, under the heading for the Angel Gabriel, we might find entries such as Daniel 8:16, Daniel 9:21, Luke 1:19, and Luke 1:26.

One way of organizing a (partially) inverted file is to toss all of the i-indexes onto the same disk in variable-length records with keys v_j and associated lists of records. The practice of putting author, subject, and title cards in the same alphabetical file in a card catalogue is an instance of this. Suppose, for example, that we want to organize an on-line query service for a telephone company permitting records of the form

$$\left\{ \begin{pmatrix} \text{Phone number:} \\ N \end{pmatrix}, \begin{pmatrix} \text{Name:} \\ 30 \text{ characters} \end{pmatrix}, \begin{pmatrix} \text{Address:} \\ 60 \text{ characters} \end{pmatrix} \right\}$$

to be retrieved using either a name, a phone number, or an address. Since people and organizations tend to have only a few phone numbers, and since, for each phone number, there are only a few people or organizations using it, we could expect the i-indexes for phone numbers, names, and addresses to be reasonably short. One way of organizing the file would therefore be to hash on names, phone numbers, and addresses, and to represent each record three times for each of its three keys. Alternatively, the phone number could be used as the primary key for a record, and the name and address could hash to records giving the phone number.

9.4 BIBLIOGRAPHIC NOTES

General references on file organization techniques are DZUBAK and WARBURTON [1965], BECKER and HAYES [1963], HSIAO and HARARY [1970], SEVERANCE [1975], FLORES [1970], LEFKOWITZ [1969], GILDERSLEEVE [1971], TREMBLAY and SORENSEN [1976], HOROWITZ and SAHNI [1976], KNUTH [1973b], and JODEIT [1968]. CLIMENSON's work on file organization ([1966]) contains 97 references. CHAPIN [1968] gives a graph-theoretic approach to file organization, while CHILDS [1968ab] gives a set-theoretic approach, and SALTON [1968] and YU, SALTON, and SIU [1978] treat the subject in the context of information retrieval problems.

MOHAN [1978] gives an overview of database research and lists 415 references. General references on database systems are DATE [1977], DODD [1969], ENGLES [1972], FRY and SIBLEY [1976], LEFKOWITZ [1969], LOWE [1968], MARTIN [1976], McGEE [1968], SUNDGREN [1975], and MINKER and SABLE [1967]. Database security is studied in KAM and ULLMAN [1977], CHIN [1978] and REISS [1979]. VERHOFSTAD [1978] studies database recovery techniques.

File compression techniques are studied in LYNCH [1973], LESK [1970], MARRON and DEMAINE [1967], FILES and HUSKEY [1969], MYERS, TOWNSEND, and TOWNSEND [1966], FRASER [1967], HAHN [1974], and RUTH and KREUTZER [1972].

Multi-attribute files are studied in LUM [1970], WEXELBLAT and FREEDMAN [1967], PRYWES [1966], and GOWER [1962]. An especially enlightened discussion is presented in

KNUTH [1973b], including the topic of multi-attribute retrieval on files of binary attributes. For a study of the problem of partial-match retrievals, see BURKHARD [1976ab].

The topic of files on multilevel stores is examined in ROSE and GOTTERER [1973]. MUNTZ and UZGALIS [1970] study how to allocate a binary tree to pages in a two-level memory.

The topic of overflow in files is treated in MULLIN [1972] and OLSON [1969].

Tree structured indexes are a topic with many variations of relevance to file techniques. BAYER and MCCREIGHT [1972] study the use of *B*-trees for file indexes. BRUNO and COFFMAN [1971] study techniques for obtaining nearly optimal binary search trees with a heuristic. TRIE indexes are studied in FREDKIN [1960], SUSSENGUTH [1963], and CLAMPETT [1964], as well as in KNUTH [1973b]. CASEY [1973] studies optimal search trees based on a bit-vector technique. SCIDMORE and WEINBERG [1963] treat the problem of searching for variable-length keys in a tree structured index.

BACHMAN [1965] reports on GE's IDS system, which uses rings to implement file organization. CHAPIN ([1969a], p. 277, and [1969b], p. 419) comments on this system.

GHOSH [1972] studies the consecutive-retrieval property in files. A file has the C-R property if the records answering every query in a query set *Q* can be stored in consecutive locations without redundant storage of any record. GUPTA [1979] generalizes the C-R organization to permit redundant storage of records and explicit pointers.

An interesting technique for multidimensional searching problems is given in DOBKIN and LIPTON [1976].

VAN DER POOL [1972] studies the question of selecting storage bucket size when files are loaded onto a DASD assuming no subsequent additions and deletions and a uniform distribution of hash addresses. VAN DER POOL [1973ab] extends the analysis to files in a steady state of insertions and deletions, and formulates the cost of retrieval as a function of storage space and accesses.

SCHNEIDERMAN [1973] and TUEL [1978] study optimal reorganization points for files and databases.

SISKIND and ROSENHEAD [1976] characterize the number of cylinders separating consecutive cylinders accessed on a movable-head disk using the theory of order statistics and they analyze performance under some scanning policies. MCKELLER and WONG [1978] study minimization of disk seek time.

GAIROLA and RAJARAMAN [1976] introduce a modified ISAM technique (MISAM) which has good response times when block sizes are small.

EXERCISES

1. (Storage utilization efficiency) Using the characteristics of the TypiComp tapes, assume a one-cm interblock gap and blocks written from groups of *N* contiguous bytes (characters). Discover a function relating bytes/tape stored to bytes/block. What should *N* be to achieve at least 80-percent storage utilization?

2. (Tape transfer time) How long would it take to read a four-megabit mystery novel from tape if it is stored in blocks of 1000 characters (8 bits per character)

with one-cm interblock gaps? (See specifications for TypiComp tape, Table 9.1.)

3. (Drum transfer time) Using the specifications for the Univac 1108 FH32 and the Univac Fastrand II, given in the text, calculate the average elapsed time to read an 840-character record into main memory for each of the two pieces of equipment.

4. (Average disk seek time) Prove that the average value of $|i - j|$, when i and j are track numbers chosen randomly between 1 and 200, is

$$\frac{2\binom{201}{3}}{200^2} = 66.7.$$

(See Knuth [1973b], p. 362.)

5. (Disk transfer time) How long on the average does it take to locate and transmit a record of 64 characters from a TypiComp disk? (See specifications, Table 9.2.)

6. (Phone system billing) Study your phone bill and develop a hypothesis as to how it could have been prepared in a batch-process file system with sequential files stored on tape.

7. (Disk schedule optimization) Let (C_i, T_i, S_i) be a sequence of direct-access queries for $1 \le i \le n$, where C_i is a cylinder number, T_i is a track number, and S_i is a sector number. These queries are for 64-character credit-card records on a TypiComp disk. How can the order of the queries be arranged to minimize the total throughput time for processing the schedule of requests?

8. (Sequential processing of an ISAM file) Given the overflow and deletion policies for ISAM files described in Section 9.3.3, show how to enumerate the records sequentially in ascending order of their keys.

ABRAHAM, C. T., GHOSH, S. P. and RAY-CHAUDHURI, D. K. [1968]. File Organization Schemes Based on Finite Geometries, *Inform. & Control* **12**, 143–163.

ABRAMOWICH, J. [1967]. Storage Allocation in a Certain Iterative Process, *CACM* **10**:**6** (June), 368–370.

ACKERMAN, A. F. [1974]. Quadratic Search for Hash Tables of Size p^n, *CACM* **17**:**3** (March), 164.

ADEL'SON-VEL'SKII, G. M. and LANDIS, E. M. [1962]. An Algorithm for the Organization of Information, *Dokl. Acad. Nauk SSSR Math.* **146**:**2**, 263–266. English translation in *Sov. Math. Dokl.* **3**, 1259–1262.

AHO, A. V. and CORASICK, M. J. [1975]. Efficient String Matching: An Aid to Bibliographic Search, *CACM* **18**: **6** (June), 333–340.

AHO, A. V., HOPCROFT, J. E. and ULLMAN, J. D. [1974]. *The Design and Analysis of Computer Algorithms*, Addison-Wesley, Reading, Massachusetts, 470 pp.

AHO, A. V. and ULLMAN, J. D. [1972]. *The Theory of Parsing, Translation, and Compiling, Vol. 1*, Prentice-Hall, Englewood Cliffs, New Jersey.

AHO, A. V. and ULLMAN, J. D. [1973]. *The Theory of Parsing, Translation, and Compiling, Vol. 2*, Prentice-Hall, Englewood Cliffs, New Jersey.

AJTAI, M., KOMLÓS, J. and SZEMERÉDI, E. [1978]. There is No Fast Single Hashing Algorithm, *Info. Proc. Letters* **7**:**6** (October), 270–273.

ALLEN, B. and MUNRO, I. [1978]. Self-Organizing Search Trees, *JACM* **25**:**4** (October), 526–535.

AMBLE, O. and KNUTH, D. E. [1974]. Ordered Hash Tables, *Computer Journal* **17**:**2** (May), 135–142.

ANDERSON, M. R. and ANDERSON, M. G. [1979]. Comments on Perfect Hashing Functions: A Single Probe Retrieving Method for Static Sets, *CACM* **22**:**2** (February), 104.

ARORA, S. R. and DENT, W. T. [1969]. Randomized Binary Search Technique, *CACM* **12**:**2** (February), 77–80.

BACHMAN, C. W. [1965]. Integrated Data Store, *DPMA Quarterly* **1**:**2** (January), 10–13.

BAECKER, H. D. [1970]. Implementing the ALGOL 68 Heap, *BIT* **10**, 405–414.

BAECKER, H. D. [1972]. Garbage Collection for Virtual-Memory Computer Systems, *CACM* **15**:**11** (November), 981–986.

BAER, J.-L. and SCHWAB, B. [1977]. A Comparison of Tree-Balancing Algorithms, *CACM* **20**:5 (May), 322–330.

BAILEY, M. J., BARNETT, M. P. and BURLESON, P. B. [1964]. Symbol Manipulation in FORTRAN—SASP I Subroutines, *CACM* **7**:6 (January), 339–346.

BAKER, H. G. [1977]. List Processing in Real Time on a Serial Computer, AI Working Paper 139, MIT AI Lab. (March).

BANDYOPADHYAY, S. K. [1977]. Comment on Weighted Increment Linear Search for Scatter Tables, *CACM* **20**:4 (April), 262–263.

BANERJI, R. B. [1962]. The Description List of Concepts. *CACM* **5**:8 (August), 426–432.

BARI KOLATA, G. [1977a]. Computer Encryption and the National Security Agency Connection, *Science* **197** (July 29), 438–440.

BARI KOLATA, G. [1977b]. Cryptography: On the Brink of a Revolution, *Science* **197** (August 19), 747–748.

BARI KOLATA, G. [1978]. Cryptology: A Secret Meeting at IDA?, *Science* **200** (April 14), 184.

BARNARD, T. J. [1969]. A New Mask Rule Technique for Interpreting Decision Tables, *Computer Bulletin* **13**:5 (May), 153–154.

BARRETT, J. A. [1960]. Abbreviating Words Systematically, *CACM* **3**:5 (May), 323–324.

BARTH, J. M. [1977]. Shifting Garbage Collection Overhead to Compile Time, *CACM* **20**:7 (July), 513–518.

BATAGELI, V. [1975]. The Quadratic Hash Method When the Table Size is Not a Prime Number, *CACM* **18**:4 (April), 216–217.

BATSON, A. P. and BRUNDAGE, R. E. [1977]. Segment Sizes and Lifetimes in ALGOL 60 Programs, *CACM* **20**:1 (January), 36–44.

BATSON, A. P., JU, S. M. and WOOD, D. C. [1970]. Measurements of Segment Size, *CACM* **13**:3 (March), 155–159.

BAYER, R. [1972a]. Symmetric Binary B-Trees: Data Structure and Maintenance Algorithms, *Acta Informatica* **1**:4, 290–306.

BAYER, R. [1972b]. Oriented Balanced Trees and Equivalence Relations, *Info. Proc. Letters* **1**, 226–228.

BAYER, R. and MCCREIGHT, E. [1972]. Organization and Maintenance of Large Ordered Indexes, *Acta Informatica* **1**, 290–306.

BAYER, R. and METZGER, J. K. [1976]. On the Encipherment of Search Trees and Random-Access Files, *TODS* **1**:1 (March), 37–52.

BAYES, A. J. [1973]. A Dynamic Programming Algorithm to Optimise Decision Table Code, *Australian Computer J.* **5**:2 (May), 77–79.

BAYS, C. [1973a]. The Reallocation of Hash-Coded Tables, *CACM* **16**:1 (January), 11–14.

BAYS, C. [1973b]. Some Techniques for Structuring Chained Hash Tables, *Computer Journal* **16**:2 (May), 126–131.

BAYS, C. [1973c]. A Note on When to Chain Overflow Items Within a Direct-Access Table, *CACM* **16**:**1** (January), 46–47.

BAYS, C. [1977]. A Comparison of Next-Fit, First-Fit, and Best-Fit, *CACM* **20**:**3** (March), 191–192.

BECKER, J. and HAYS, R. M. [1963]. Theories of File Organization, Chapter 14 in *Information Storage and Retrieval*, Wiley, New York, 359–397.

BELADY, L. A. and KUEHNER, C. J. [1969]. Dynamic Space-Sharing in Computer Systems, *CACM* **12**:**5** (May), 282–288.

BELL, C. G. and NEWELL, A. [1971]. *Computer Structures: Readings and Examples*, McGraw-Hill, New York.

BELL, J. R. [1970]. The Quadratic Quotient Method: A Hash Code Eliminating Secondary Clustering, *CACM* **13**:**2** (February), 107–109.

BELL, J. R. and KAMAN, C. H. [1970]. The Linear Quotient Hash Code, *CACM* **13**:**11** (November), 675–677.

BENTLEY, J. L. [1975]. Multi-Dimensional Binary Search Trees Used for Associative Searching, *CACM* **18**:**9** (September), 509–517.

BERGE, C. [1968]. *The Theory of Graphs and Its Applications*, Wiley, New York.

BERMAN, G. and COLIJN, A. W. [1974]. A Modified List Technique Allowing Binary Search, *JACM* **21**:**2** (April), 227–232.

BERZTISS, A. T. [1965]. A Note on Storage of Strings, *CACM* **8**:**8** (August), 512–513.

BERZTISS, A. T. [1975]. *Data Structures: Theory and Practice*, Academic Press, New York (Second edition 1975, 586 pp.).

BETTERIDGE, T. [1973]. An Analytical Storage Allocation Model, *Acta Informatica* **3**, 101–122.

BIRKHOFF, G. and BARTEE, T. C. [1970]. *Modern Applied Algebra*, McGraw-Hill, New York, 431 pp.

BLAAUW, G. A. [1959]. Indexing and Control Word Techniques, *IBM J. R. & D.* **3** (July), 288–301.

BLAIR, C. [1977]. Cryptology and National Security, *Science* **198** (November 4), 408.

BLUM, M., FLOYD, R. W., PRATT, V. R., RIVEST, R. L. and TARJAN, R. E. [1972]. Time Bounds for Selection, *JCSS* **7**:**4**, 448–461.

BOBROW, D. [1975]. A Note on Hash Linking, *CACM* **18**:**7** (July), 413–415.

BOBROW, D. G. and MURPHY, D. L. [1967]. Structure of a LISP System Using Two-Level Storage, *CACM* **10**:**3** (March), 155–159.

BOBROW, D. G. and MURPHY, D. L. [1968]. A Note on the Efficiency of a LISP Computation in a Paged Machine, *CACM* **11**:**8** (August), 558, 560.

BOBROW, D. G. and RAPHAEL, B. [1964]. A Comparison of List Processing Languages, *CACM* **7**:**4** (April), 231–240.

BOEHM, E. M. and STEEL, T. B., JR. [1959]. The Share 709 System: Machine Implementation of Symbolic Programming, *JACM* **6**:**2** (April), 134–140.

BOOKSTEIN, A. [1973]. On Harrison's Substring-Testing Technique, *CACM* **16**:**3** (March), 180–181.

BOOTH, A. D. and COLIN, A. J. T. [1960]. On the Efficiency of a New Method of Dictionary Construction, *Information & Control* **3**, 327–334.

BOSE, R. C. and KOCH, G. C. [1969]. The Design of Combinatorial Information-Retrieval Systems for Files with Multiple-Valued Attributes, *SIAM J. Appl. Math.* **17**:**6** (November), 1203–1214.

BOYER, R. S. and MOORE, J. S. [1977]. A Fast String Searching Algorithm, *CACM* **20**:**10** (October), 762–772.

BRANSTAD, D. K. [1975]. Encryption Protection in Computer Data Communications, *Proc. Fourth Data Communications Symposium* (ACM–SIGCOMM & IEEE Computer Society co-sponsors), ACM, New York (October) 8.1–8.7.

BRENT, R. P. [1973]. Reducing the Retrieval Time of Scatter-Storage Techniques, *CACM* **16**:**2** (February), 105–109.

BRILLINGER, P. C. and COHEN, D. J. [1972]. *Introduction to Data Structures and Non-Numeric Computation*, Prentice-Hall, Englewood Cliffs, New Jersey.

BROOKER, R. A., MORRIS, D. and ROHL, J. S. [1962]. Trees and Routines, *Computer Journal* **5**:**1** (April), 33–47.

BROWN, M. R. [1978]. A Storage Scheme for Height-Balanced Trees, *Info. Proc. Letters* **7**:**5** (August), 231–232.

BROWN, P. J. [1969]. A Survey of Macro Processors, *Ann. Rev. of Automatic Programming* **6**, Pergamon Press, Oxford, 37–88.

BRUNO, J. and COFFMAN, E. G. [1971]. Nearly Optimal Binary Search Trees, *Proc. IFIP Congress* 1971, North-Holland, Amsterdam, 99–103.

BUCHHOLZ, W. [1963]. File Organization and Addressing, *IBM Syst. J.* **2** (June), 86–111.

BURKE, J. M. and RICKMAN, J. T. [1973]. Bitmaps and Filters for Attribute-Oriented Searches, *Int. J. of Comp. & Info. Sci.* **2**:**3**, 187–200.

BURKHARD, W. A. [1975a]. Full Table Quadratic Quotient Searching, *Computer Journal* **18**:**2** (May), 161–163.

BURKHARD, W. A. [1975b]. Nonrecursive Traversals of Trees, *Computer Journal* **18**:**3** (August), 227–230.

BURKHARD, W. A. [1976a]. Partial Match Retrieval, *BIT* **16**, 13–31.

BURKHARD, W. A. [1976b]. Hashing and Trie Algorithms for Partial Match Retrieval, *TODS* **1**:**2** (June), 175–187.

BURTON, W. [1976]. A Buddy System Variation for Disk Storage Allocation, *CACM* **19**:**7** (July), 416–417.

CAMPBELL, J. A. [1971]. A Note on an Optimal-Fit Method for Dynamic Allocation of Storage, *Computer Journal* **14**:**1** (February), 7–9.

CAMPBELL, J. A. [1974]. Optimal Use of Storage in a Simple Model of Garbage Collection, *Info. Proc. Letters* **3**, 37–38.

CARDENAS, A. F. [1973]. Evaluation and Selection of File Organization—A Model and a System, *CACM* **16**:9 (September), 540–548.

CARDENAS, A. F. [1975]. Analysis and Performance of Inverted Database Structures, *CACM* **18**:5 (May), 253–263.

CARR, J. W., III [1959]. Recursive Subscripting Compilers and List-Type Memories, *CACM* **2**:2 (February), 4–6.

CASEY, R. G. [1973]. Design of Tree Structures for Efficient Querying, *CACM* **16**:9 (September), 549–556.

CAVOURAS, J. C. [1974]. On the Conversion of Programs to Decision Tables: Method and Objectives, *CACM* **17**:8 (August), 456–462.

CHAPIN, N. [1968]. A Deeper Look at Data, *Proc. 1968 ACM Nat. Conf.*, Brandon Systems Press, Princeton, New Jersey, 631–638.

CHAPIN, N. [1969a]. A Comparison of File-Organization Techniques, *Proc. 24th ACM Nat. Conf.*, 273–283.

CHAPIN, N. [1969b]. Common File-Organization Techniques Compared, *Proc. AFIPS FJCC 1969*, **35**, 413–422.

CHEN, T. C. and HO, I. T. [1975]. Storage-Efficient Representation of Decimal Data, *CACM* **18**:1 (January), 49–52.

CHENEY, C. J. [1970]. A Nonrecursive List-Compacting Algorithm, *CACM* **13**:11 (November), 677–678.

CHILDS, D. L. [1968a]. Descriptions of a Set-Theoretic Data Structure, *Proc. AFIPS 1968 FJCC*, **33**, Thompson Book Co., Washington, D.C., 557–564.

CHILDS, D. L. [1968b]. Feasibility of a Set-Theoretic Data Structure—a General Structure Based upon a Reconstituted Definition of Relation, *IFIP Congress 1968, Part B*, The Hague.

CHIN, F. Y. [1978]. Security in Statistical Databases for Queries with Small Counts, *TODS* **3**:1 (March), 92–104.

CHOW, D. K. [1969]. New Balanced File-Organization Schemes, *Information & Control* **15**, 377–396.

CHVALOVSKY, V. [1976]. Problems with Decision Tables, *CACM* **19**:12 (December), 705–706.

CLAMPETT, H. A., JR. [1964]. Randomized Binary Searching with Tree Structures, *CACM* **7**:3 (March), 163–165.

CLAPSON, P. [1977]. Improving the Access Time for Random-Access Files, *CACM* **20**:3 (March), 127–135.

CLARK, D. W. [1975a]. A Fast Algorithm for Copying Binary Trees, *Info. Proc. Letters*, **4**:3 (December), 62–63.

CLARK, D. W. [1975b]. Copying List Structures Without Auxiliary Storage, TR, Carnegie-Mellon University, Pittsburgh, Pa. See also *CACM* **21**:5 (May), 351–357.

CLARK, D. W. [1976]. An Efficient List-Moving Algorithm Using Constant Workspace, *CACM* **19**:6 (June), 352–354.

CLARK, D. W. [1979]. Measurements of Dynamic List Structure Use in LISP, *IEEE TSE* **SE-5**:1 (January), 51–59.

CLARK, D. W. and GREEN, C. C. [1977]. An Empirical Study of List Structure in LISP, *CACM* **20**:2 (February), 78–87.

CLARK, D. W. and GREEN, C. C. [1978]. A Note on Shared List Structure in LISP, *Info. Proc. Letters* **7**:6 (October), 312–314.

CLIMENSON, W. D. [1966]. File Organization and Search Techniques, *Ann. Rev. of Info. Sci. & Tech.* **1**, 107–135.

CODD, E. F. [1970]. A Relational Model of Data for Large Shared Data Banks, *CACM* **13**:6 (June), 377–387.

COFFMAN, E. G. and BRUNO, J. [1970]. On File Structuring for Nonuniform Access Frequencies, *BIT* **10**, 443–457.

COFFMAN, E. G. and EVE, J. [1970]. File Structures Using Hashing Functions, *CACM* **13**:7 (July), 427–432.

COHEN, D. J. and GOTLIEB, C. C. [1970]. A List Structure Form of Grammars for Syntactic Analysis, *C. Surveys* **2**:1 (March), 65–82.

COHEN, J. [1967]. A Use of Fast and Slow Memories in List Processing Languages, *CACM* **10**:2 (February), 82–86.

COHEN, J. and TRILLING, L. [1967]. Remarks on Garbage Collection Using a Two-Level Storage, *BIT* **7**, 22–30.

COLLINS, G. E. [1960]. A Method for Overlapping and Erasure of Lists, *CACM* **3**:12 (December), 655–657.

COLLINS, G. O. [1961]. Experience in Automatic Storage Allocation, *CACM* **4**:10 (October), 436–440.

COMER, D. and SETHI, R. [1977]. The Complexity of Trie Index Construction, *JACM* **24**:3 (July), 428–440.

COMFORT, W. T. [1964]. Multiword List Items, *CACM* **7**:6 (June), 357–362.

COOK, S. A. [1971]. Linear-Time Simulation of Deterministic Two-Way Pushdown Automata, *Proc. IFIP Cong. 1971*, TA-2, North-Holland, Amsterdam, 172–179.

CRANE, C. A. [1972]. Linear Lists and Priority Queues as Balanced Binary Trees, Ph.D. Dissertation, Stanford University (March).

CRANSTON, B. and THOMAS, R. [1975]. A Simplified Recombination Scheme for the Fibonacci Buddy System, *CACM* **18**:6 (June), 331–332.

DATE, C. J. [1977]. *An Introduction to Database Systems*, Addison-Wesley, Reading, Massachusetts, (First edition 1975).

DAY, A. C. [1970]. Full Table Quadratic Searching for Scatter Storage, *CACM* **13**:8 (August), 481–482.

DE BALBINE, G. [1968]. Doctoral dissertation, California Institute of Technology, Pasadena, California.

DE MILLO, R. A., EISENSTAT, S. C. and LIPTON, R. J. [1978]. Preserving Average Proximity in Arrays, *CACM* **21**:3 (March), 228–231.

DEUEL, P. [1966]. On a Storage Mapping Function for Data Structures, *CACM* **9**:**5** (May), 344–347.

DEUTSCH, L. P. [1973]. A LISP Machine with Very Compact Programs, *IJCAI3*, Stanford, California, 697–703.

DEUTSCH, L. P. and BOBROW, D. G. [1976]. An Efficient Incremental Automatic Garbage Collector, *CACM* **19**:**9** (September), 522–526.

DEWAR, R. B. K. [1973]. A Stable Minimum-Storage Sorting Algorithm, *Info. Proc. Letters* **2**, 162–164.

DIFFIE, W. and HELLMAN, M. E. [1976a]. A Critique of the Proposed Data-Encryption Standard, *CACM* **19**:**3** (March), 164–165.

DIFFIE, W. and HELLMAN, M. E. [1976b]. New Directions in Cryptography, *IEEE Trans. Info. Theory* **IT-226** (November), 644–654.

DIFFIE, W. and HELLMAN, M. E. [1977]. Exhaustive Cryptanalysis of the NBS Data-Encryption Standard, *Computer* **10** (June), 74–84.

DIJKSTRA, E. W., LAMPORT, L., MARTIN, A. J., SCHOLTEN, C. S. and STEFFENS, E. F. M. [1977]. On the Fly Garbage Collection: An Exercise in Cooperation, *CACM* **21**:**11** (November), 966–975.

D'IMPERIO, M. E. [1969]. Data Structures and Their Representation in Storage, *Ann. Rev. of Automatic Programming* **5**, Pergamon Press, Oxford, 1–75.

DOBKIN, D. and LIPTON, R. J. [1976]. Multi-Dimensional Searching Problems, *SIAM J. Comp.* **5**:**2** (June), 181–186.

DODD, G. G. [1969]. Elements of Data Management Systems, *C. Surveys* **1**:**2** (June), 117–133.

DUMEY, A. I. [1956]. Indexing for Rapid Random Access Memory Systems, *Computers & Automation* **5**:**12** (December), 6–9.

DZUBAK, B. J. and WARBURTON, C. R. [1965]. The Organization of Structured Files, *CACM* **8**:**7** (July), 446–452.

ECKER, A. [1974]. The Period of Search for the Quadratic and Related Hash Methods, *Computer Journal* **17**:**4** (November), 340–343.

EHRSAM, W. F., MATYAS, S. M., MEYER, C. H. and TUCHMAN, W. L. [1978]. A Cryptographic Key Management Scheme for Implementing the Data-Encryption Standard, *IBM Syst. J.* **17**:**2**, 106–125.

EISNER, M. G. and SEVERANCE, D. G. [1976]. Mathematical Techniques for Efficient Record Segmentation in Large Shared Data Bases, *JACM* **23**:**4** (October), 619–635.

ELGOT, C. C. and SNYDER, L. [1977]. On the Many Facets of Lists, Tech. Rept. RC-6449, IBM Watson Research Center, Yorktown Heights, N.Y., 50 pp.

ELIAS, P. [1974]. Efficient Storage and Retrieval by Content and Address of Static Files, *JACM* **21**:**2** (April), 246–260.

ELSON, M. [1975]. *Data Structures*, Science Research Associates, Chicago, Illinois, 307 pp.

ENGELFRIET, J. [1972]. A Note on Infinite Trees, *Info. Proc. Letters* **1**, 229–232.

ENGELS, R. W. [1972]. A Tutorial on Data Base Organization, *Ann. Rev. of Automatic Programming* **7**:**1**, 1–65.

EVEN, S. [1973]. *Algorithmic Combinatorics*, Macmillan, New York, 260 pp.

FABRIZIO, L. [1972]. Weighted-Increment Linear Search for Scatter Tables, *CACM* **15**:**12** (December), 1045–1047.

FAGIN, R., NIEVERGELT, J., PIPPENGER, N. and STRONG, R. H. [1978]. Extendible Hashing— A Fast Access Method for Dynamic Files, *Research Rept. RJ2305*, IBM Research Division, Yorktown Heights, N.Y.

FALKOFF, A. D. and IVERSON, K. E. [1973]. The Design of APL, *IBM J. of R. & D.* **17**, 324–334.

FARBER, D. J., GRISWOLD, R. E. and POLONSKY, I. P. [1964]. SNOBOL, A String Manipulation Language, *JACM* **11**:**1** (January), 21–30.

FEDERAL REGISTER [1975]. Computer Data Protection, *Federal Register* **40**:**52** (March 17), 12067–12250. (See also Vol. **40**, no. **149**, August 1, 1975).

FEISTAL, H. [1973]. Cryptography and Computer Privacy, *Sci. Amer.* **228** (May), 15–23.

FEISTAL, H., NOTZ, W. and SMITH, J. L. [1975]. Some Cryptographic Techniques for Machine-to-Machine Data Communications, *Proc. IEEE* **63** (November), 1545–1554.

FELDMAN, J. A. [1965]. Aspects of Associative Processing, *Tech. Rept. ESD-TDR-65-65*, MIT Lincoln Laboratory, Lexington, Massachusetts (April), 45 pp.

FELDMAN, J. A. and ROVNER, P. R. [1969]. An ALGOL-Based Associative Language, *CACM* **12**:**8** (August), 439–449.

FELLER, W. [1957]. *An Introduction to Probability Theory and its Applications* (Second ed.), Wiley, New York.

FENICHEL, R. R. [1971]. Comment on Cheney's List-Compaction Algorithm, *CACM* **14**:**9** (September), 603–604.

FENICHEL, R. R. and YOCHELSON, J. C. [1969]. A LISP Garbage Collector for Virtual-Memory Computer Systems, *CACM* **12**:**11** (November), 611–612.

FERGUSON, D. E. [1960]. Fibonaccian Searching, *CACM* **3**:**12** (December), 648.

FILES, J. R. and HUSKEY, H. D. [1969]. An Information Retrieval System Based on Superimposed Coding, *Proc. AFIPS 1969 FJCC* **35**, 423–432.

FINKEL, R. A. and BENTLEY, J. L. [1974]. Quad Trees: A Data Structure for Retrieval on Composite Keys, *Acta Informatica* **4**:**1**, 1–10.

FISCHER, M. J. [1968]. Grammars with Macro-Like Productions, Doctoral dissertation, Harvard University, Cambridge, Massachusetts.

FISCHER, M. J. and PATERSON, M. S. [1974]. String Matching and Other Products, Proj. MAC Tech. Memo. 41, MIT, Cambridge, Massachusetts.

FISHER, D. A. [1974]. Bounded Workspace Garbage Collection in an Address Order-Preserving List Processing Environment, *Info. Proc. Letters* **3**, 29–32.

FISHER, D. A. [1975]. Copying Cyclic List Structures in Linear Time Using Bounded Workspace, *CACM* **18**:**5** (May), 251–252.

FISHER, D. L. [1966]. Data Documentation and Decision Tables, *CACM* **9**:1 (January), 26–31.

FITCH, J. P. and NORMAN, A. C. [1978]. A Note on Compacting Garbage Collection, *Computer Journal* **21**:1 (February), 31–34.

FLECK, A. C. [1971]. Towards a Theory of Data Structures, *JCSS* **5**, 475–488.

FLECK, A. C. [1978]. Recent Developments in the Theory of Data Structures, *Computer Languages* **3**:1, 37–52.

FLORENTIN, J. J. [1976]. Information Reference Coding, *CACM* **19**:1 (January), 29–33.

FLORES, I. [1970]. *Data Structure and Management*, Prentice-Hall, Englewood Cliffs, New Jersey, 390 pp.

FLOYD, R. W. [1962]. Algorithm 97: Shortest Path, *CACM* **5**:6 (June), 345.

FLOYD, R. W. [1964]. Algorithm 245: Treesort 3, *CACM* **7**:12 (December), 701.

FLOYD, R. W. [1967]. Nondeterministic Algorithms, *JACM* **14**:4 (October), 636–644.

FOSTER, C. C. [1965]. Information Storage and Retrieval Using AVL Trees, *Proc. ACM 20th Nat. Conf.*, Spartan Books, Washington, D.C., 192–205.

FOSTER, C. C. [1973]. A Generalization of AVL Trees. *CACM* **16**:8 (August), 513–517.

FOSTER, J. M. [1967]. *List Processing*. MacDonald, London.

FRANTA, W. R. and MALY, K. [1977]. An Efficient Data Structure for the Simulation Event Set, *CACM* **20**:8 (August), 596–602.

FRANTA, W. R. and MALY, K. [1978]. A Comparison of Heaps and the TL Structure for the Simulation Event Set, *CACM* **21**:10 (October), 873–875.

FRASER, A. G. [1967]. Data Compression and Automatic Programming, *Computer Journal* **10**, 165–167.

FREDERICK, T. J. *et al.* [1977]. Self-Assessment Procedure: II. *CACM* **20**:5 (May), 297–300.

FREDKIN, E. H. [1960]. Trie Memory, *CACM* **3**:9 (September), 490–500.

FRY, J. P. and SIBLEY, E. H. [1976]. Evolution of Database Management Systems, *C. Surveys* **8**:1 (March), 7–42.

GAINES, H. F. [1956]. *Cryptanalysis*, Dover, New York.

GAIROLA, B. K. and RAJARAMAN, U. [1976]. A Distributed Index Sequential Access Method, *Info. Proc. Letters* **5**:1 (May), 1–5.

GANPATHY, S. and RAJARAMAN, V. [1973]. Information Theory Applied to the Conversion of Decision Tables to Computer Programs, *CACM* **16**:9 (September), 532–539.

GARDNER, M. [1977]. Mathematical Games, *Sci. Amer.* **237**:2 (August), 120–124.

GAREY, M. R., GRAHAM, R. L. and ULLMAN, J. D. [1972]. Worst-Case Analysis of Memory Allocation Algorithms, *Proc. 4th Ann. ACM Symp. on the Theory of Computing*.

GARWICK, J. V. [1964]. Data Storage in Compilers, *BIT* **4**, 137–140.

GELENBE, E. [1971]. The Two-Thirds Rule for Dynamic Storage Allocation Under Equilibrium, *Info. Proc. Letters* **1**, 59–60.

GELENBE, E., BOCKHORST, J. C. A. and KESSELS, J. L. W. [1973]. Minimizing Wasted Space in Partitioned Segmentation, *CACM* **16**:6 (June), 343–349.

GELERNTER, H., HANSEN, J. R. and GERBERICH, C. L. [1960]. A FORTRAN-compiled List Processing Language, *JACM* **7**:2 (April), 87–101.

GHOSH, S. P. [1972]. File Organization: The Consecutive Retrieval Property, *CACM* **15**:9 (September), 802–808.

GHOSH, S. P. [1974]. File Organization: Consecutive Storage of Relevant Records on Drum-Type Storage, *Information & Control* **25**, 145–165.

GHOSH, S. P. and SENKO, M. E. [1969]. File Organization: On the Selection of Random-Access Index Points for Sequential Files, *JACM* **16**:4 (October), 569–579.

GILBERT, E. N. and MOORE, E. F. [1959]. Variable-Length Binary Encodings, *Bell Syst. Tech. J.*, **38**, 933–968.

GILDERSLEEVE, T. R. [1971]. *Design of Sequential File Systems*, Wiley, New York, 49 pp.

GIMPEL, J. [1973]. A Theory of Discrete Patterns and Their Implementation in SNOBOL 4, *CACM* **16**:2 (February), 91–100.

GOLD, D. E. and KUCK, D. J. [1974]. A Model for Masking Rotational Latency by Dynamic Disk Allocation, *CACM* **17**:5 (May), 278–288.

GOLDBERG, I. B. [1967]. 27 Bits are Not Enough for 8-Digit Accuracy, *CACM* **10**:2 (February), 105–106.

GOLOMB, S. W. and BAUMERT, L. D. [1965]. Backtrack Programming, *JACM* **12**:4 (October), 516–524.

GONNET, G. H. [1976]. Heaps Applied to Event-Driven Mechanisms, *CACM* **19**:7 (July), 417–418.

GONNET, G. H. and MUNRO, I. [1977]. The Analysis of an Improved Hashing Technique, *Proc. 9th Ann. ACM Symposium on the Theory of Computing* (May), 113–121.

GOTLIEB, C. C. and TOMPA, F. W. [1974]. Choosing a Storage Schema, *Acta Informatica* **3**, 297–320.

GOWER, J. C. [1962]. The Handling of Multiway Tables in Computers, *Computer Journal* **4**:4 (January), 280–286.

GRAY, J. C. [1967]. Compound Data Structures for Computer-Aided Design: A Survey, *Proc. ACM 22nd Nat. Conf.*, 355–365.

GRIES, D. [1971]. *Compiler Construction for Digital Computers*. Wiley, New York, 493 pp.

GRIES, D. [1977a]. On Believing Programs to be Correct, letter to ACM Forum, *CACM* **20**:1 (January), 49–50.

GRIES, D. [1977b]. An Exercise in Proving Parallel Programs Correct, *CACM* **20**:12 (December), 921–930 (Corrigendum: *CACM* **21**:12 (December), 1048).

GRISWOLD, R. E., PONGE, J. F., and POLONSKY, I. P. [1968]. *The SNOBOL 4 Programming Language*, Prentice-Hall, Englewood Cliffs, New Jersey (Second edition 1971).

GUIBAS, L. J. [1978]. The Analysis of Hashing Techniques that Exhibit k-ary Clustering, *JACM* **25**:4 (October), 544–555.

GUIBAS, L. and SZEMERÉDI, E. [1976]. The Analysis of Double Hashing, *Proc. 8th Ann. Symp. on Theory of Computing*, ACM-SIGACT (May), 187–191.

GUPTA, U. [1979]. Bounds on Storage for Consecutive Retrieval, *JACM* **26**:1 (January), 28–36.

HADDON, B. K. and WAITE, W. M. [1967]. A Compaction Procedure for Variable-Length Storage Elements, *Computer Journal* **10**, 162–165.

HAHN, B. [1974]. A New Technique for Compression and Storage of Data, *CACM* **17**:8 (August), 434–436.

HALATSIS, C. and PHILOKYPROU, G. [1978]. Pseudochaining in Hash Tables, *CACM* **21**:7 (July), 554–557.

HALL, P. A. V. [1975]. *Computational Structures: an Introduction to Non-Numerical Computing.* Macdonald and Jane's, London.

HAMMING, R. W. [1950]. Error-Detecting and Error-Correcting Codes, *Bell System Tech. J.* **29**, 147–160.

HANSEN, W. J. [1969]. Compact List Representation: Definition, Garbage Collection, and System Implementation, *CACM* **12**:9 (September), 499–507.

HANSEN, W. J. [1978]. A Predecessor Algorithm for Ordered Lists, *Info. Proc. Letters* **7**:3 (April), 137–138.

HARARY, F. [1969]. *Graph Theory*, Addison-Wesley, Reading, Massachusetts.

HARRISON, M. C. [1971]. Implementation of the Substring Test by Hashing, *CACM* **14**:12 (December), 777–779.

HARRISON, M. C. [1973]. *Data Structures and Programming.* Scott Foresman and Co., Glenview, Illinois, 322 pp.

HELLERMAN, H. [1962]. Addressing Multidimensional Arrays, *CACM* **5**:4 (April), 205–207.

HELLMAN, M. E. [1977]. Computer Encryption: Key Size. *Science* **198** (October 7), 8.

HELLMAN, M. E. [1978]. An Overview of Public Cryptography, *IEEE Comm. Soc. Magazine* **16**:6 (November), 24–32.

HERLESTAM, T. [1978]. Critical Remarks on Some Public-Key Cryptosystems, *BIT* **18**:4, 493–496.

HIBBARD, T. [1962]. Some Combinatorial Properties of Certain Trees With Applications to Searching and Sorting, *JACM* **9**:1 (January), 13–28.

HINDS, J. A. [1975]. An Algorithm for Locating Adjacent Storage Blocks in the Buddy System, *CACM* **18**:4 (April), 221–222.

HIRSCHBERG, D. S. [1973a]. A Linear Space Algorithm for Computing Maximal Common Subsequences, TR-138, E.E. Dept., Princeton University, Princeton, New Jersey. (See also *CACM* **18**:6 (June 1975), 341–343.)

HIRSCHBERG, D. S. [1973b]. A Class of Dynamic Memory Allocation Algorithms, *CACM* **16**:10 (October), 615–618.

HIRSCHBERG, D. S. [1976]. An Insertion Technique for One-Sided Height-Balanced Trees, *CACM* **19**:8 (August), 471–473.

HIRSCHBERG, D. S. [1977]. Algorithms for the Largest Common Subsequence Problem, *JACM* **24**:3 (October), 664–675.

HIRSCHBERG, D. S. [1978]. An Information-Theoretic Lower Bound for the Longest Common Subsequence Problem, *Info. Proc. Letters* **7**:1 (January), 40–41.

HOARE, C. A. R. [1961]. Algorithm 63: Partition, and Algorithm 64: Quicksort. *CACM* **4**:7 (July), 321.

HOARE, C. A. R. [1962]. Quicksort, *Computer Journal* **5**:1, 10–15.

HOARE, C. A. R. [1974a]. Optimization of Store Size for Garbage Collection, *Info. Proc. Letters* **2**, 165–166.

HOARE, C. A. R. [1974b]. Monitors: An Operating System Structuring Concept, *CACM* **17**:10 (October), 549–557.

HOFFMAN, S. A. [1962]. Data Structures that Generalize Rectangular Arrays. *Proc. JCC AFIPS*, 325–333.

HOLT, A. W. [1963]. A Mathematical and Applied Investigation of Tree Structures, Doctoral dissertation, Univ. of Pennsylvania, Philadelphia, Pennsylvania.

HONIG, W. L. and CARLSON, C. R. [1978]. Toward an Understanding of (actual) Data Structures, *Computer Journal* **21**:2 (May), 98–104.

HOPCROFT, J. E. and ULLMAN, J. D. [1969]. *Formal Languages and Their Relation to Automata*. Addison-Wesley, Reading, Massachusetts.

HOPGOOD, F. R. A. [1968]. A Solution to the Overflow Problem for Hash Tables, *Computer Bulletin* **11**:4 (March), 297–300.

HOPGOOD, F. R. A. and DAVENPORT, J. [1972]. The Quadratic Hash Method when the Table Size is a Power of 2, *Computer Journal* **15**:4, 314–315.

HOROWITZ, E. and SAHNI, S. [1976]. *Fundamentals of Data Structures*, Computer Science Press, Woodland Hills, California, 564 pp.

HSIAO, D. and HARARY, F. [1970]. A Formal System for Information Retrieval from Files, *CACM* **13**:2 (February), 67–73.

HU, T. C. and TUCKER, A. C. [1971]. Optimal Computer Search Trees and Variable-Length Alphabetic Codes, *SIAM J. Appl. Math.* **21**:4 (December), 514–532.

HUFFMAN, D. A. [1952]. A Method for the Construction of Minimum-Redundancy Codes, *Proc. IRE* **40**, 1098–1101.

HYAFIL, L. and RIVEST, R. L. [1976]. Constructing Optimal Binary Decision Trees is NP-Complete, *Info. Proc. Letters* **5**:1 (May), 15–17.

IBRAMSHA, M. and RAJARAMAN, V. [1978]. Detection of Logical Errors in Decision Table Programs, *CACM* **21**:12 (December), 1016–1025.

ILLIFE, J. K. and JODEIT, J. G. [1962]. A Dynamic Storage Allocation Scheme, *Computer Journal* **5**:3 (October), 200–209.

INGERMAN, P. Z. [1961]. Thunks, *CACM* **4**:1 (January), 55–58.

ISODA, S., GOTO, E. and KIMURA, I. [1971]. An Efficient Bit Table Technique for Dynamic Storage Allocation of 2^n-Word Blocks, *CACM* **14**:9 (September), 589–592.

IVERSON, K. E. [1962]. *A Programming Language*. Wiley, New York.

JODEIT, A. [1968]. Storage Organization in Programming Systems, *CACM* **11**:**11** (November), 741–746.

JOHNSON, D. S. [1974]. Fast Algorithms for Bin Packing, *JCSS* **8**, 272–314.

JOHNSON, D. S., DEMERS, A., ULLMAN, J. D., GAREY, M. R. and GRAHAM, R. L. [1974]. Worst-Case Performance Bounds for Simple One-Dimensional Packing Algorithms, *SIAM J. Computing* **3**:**4** (December), 299–325.

JOHNSON, W. L., PORTER, J. H., ACKLEY, S. I. and ROSS, D. T. [1968]. Automatic Generation of Efficient Lexical Processors Using Finite-State Techniques (A Tutorial), *CACM* **11**:**12** (December), 805–813.

JONES, B. [1970]. A Variation on Sorting by Address Calculation, *CACM* **13**:**2** (February), 105–107.

KAHN, D. [1967]. *The Codebreakers*. Macmillan Co., New York.

KAHN, D. [1975]. The Code Battle, *Playboy* **22**:**12** (December), 132 ff.

KAIN, R. Y. [1969]. Block Structures, Indirect Addressing and Garbage Collection, *CACM* **12**:**7** (July), 395–398.

KAM, J. B. and DAVIDA, G. I. [1978]. A Structured Design of Substitution-Permutation Encryption Network, *TR-CS-78-1*, Dept. EE-CS, University of Wisconsin, Milwaukee.

KAM, J. B. and ULLMAN, J. D. [1977]. A Model of Statistical Databases and Their Security, *TODS* **2**:**1** (March), 1–10.

KARLGREN, H. [1963]. Representation of Text Strings in Binary Computers. *BIT* **3**, 52–59.

KARLTON, P. L., FULLER, S. H., SCRUGGS, R. E. and KAEHLER, E. B. [1976]. Performance of Height-Balanced Trees, *CACM* **19**:**1** (January), 23–28.

KARP, R. M., MILLER, R. E. and ROSENBERG, A. L. [1972]. Rapid Identification of Repeated Patterns in Strings, Trees, and Arrays, *Proc. 4th Ann. ACM Symp. on Theory of Computing*, 125–136.

KASISKI, F. W. [1863]. *Die Geheimschriften und die Dechiffrir–Kunst*, Mittler und Sohn, Berlin.

KERCKHOFFS, A. [1883]. *La Cryptographie Militaire*, Baudoin et Cie, Paris.

KING, P. J. H. [1966]. Conversion of Decision Tables to Computer Programs by Rule Mask Techniques, *CACM* **9**:**11** (November), 796–801.

KING, P. J. H. [1967]. Decision Tables, *Computer Journal* **10**:**2** (August), 135–142.

KING, P. J. H. [1968]. Ambiguity in Limited-Entry Decision Tables, *CACM* **11**:**10** (October), 680–684.

KING, P. J. H. [1969]. The Interpretation of Limited-Entry Decision Table Format and Relationships Among Conditions, *Computer Journal* **12**:**4** (November), 320–326.

KING, P. J. H. and JOHNSON, R. G. [1973]. Some Comments on the Use of Ambiguous Decision Tables and Their Conversion to Computer Programs, *CACM* **16**:**5** (May), 287–290.

KING, P. J. H. and JOHNSON, R. G. [1974]. Comments on the Algorithms of Verhelst for the

Conversion of Limited-Entry Decision Tables to Flowcharts, *CACM* **17**:1 (January), 43–45.

KIRK, G. W. [1965]. Use of Decision Tables in Computer Programming, *CACM* **8**:1 (January), 41–43.

KNOTT, G. D. [1975]. Hashing Functions, *Computer Journal* **18**:3 (August), 265–278.

KNOTT, G. D. [1977]. A Numbering System for Binary Trees, *CACM* **20**:2 (February), 113–115.

KNOWLTON, K. C. [1965]. A Fast Storage Allocator, *CACM* **8**:11 (October), 623–625.

KNUTH, D. E. [1961]. Minimizing Drum Latency Time. *JACM* **5**:2 (April), 119–150.

KNUTH, D. E. [1969]. *The Art of Computer Programming; Vol. 2: Semi-Numerical Algorithms*, Addison-Wesley, Reading, Massachusetts, 624 pp.

KNUTH, D. E. [1971a]. An Empirical Study of FORTRAN Programs, *Softw.-Practice and Experience* **1**, 105–133.

KNUTH, D. E. [1971b]. Optimum Binary Search Trees, *Acta Informatica* **1**:1, 14–25.

KNUTH, D. E. [1973a]. *The Art of Computer Programming; Vol. 1: Fundamental Algorithms*, Addison-Wesley, Reading, Massachusetts, 634 pp. (First edition 1968).

KNUTH, D. E. [1973b]. *The Art of Computer Programming; Vol. 3: Searching and Sorting*, Addison-Welsey, Reading, Massachusetts, 722 pp.

KNUTH, D. E. [1977]. Algorithms, *Sci. Amer.* **236**:4 (April), 63–80.

KNUTH, D. E. and PRATT, V. R. [1971]. Automata Theory Can be Useful, *TR*, Stanford University, Stanford, California.

KNUTH, D. E., MORRIS, J. H. and PRATT, V. R. [1977]. Fast Pattern Matching in Strings, *SIAM J. Comp.* **6**:2 (June), 323–350.

KNUTH, D. E. and STEVENSON, F. R. [1973]. Optimum Measurement Points for Program Frequency Counts, *BIT*, **13**, 313–322.

KOSARAJU, S. R. [1978]. Insertions and Deletions in One-Sided Height-Balanced Trees, *CACM* **21**:3 (March), 226–227.

KRÁL, J. [1971]. Some Properties of the Scatter-Storage Technique with Linear Probing, *Computer Journal* **14**:2 (May), 145–149.

KRIEGEL, H. P., VAISHNAVI, V. K. and WOOD, D. [1978]. 2-3 Brother Trees, *BIT* **18**:4, 425–435.

KROGDAHL, S. [1973]. A Dynamic Storage Allocation Problem, *Info. Proc. Letters* **2**, 96–99.

KRUSKAL, J. B. [1956]. On the Shortest Spanning Subtree of a Graph and the Traveling Salesman Problem, *Proc. Amer. Math. Soc.* **7**:1, 48–50.

KUNG, H. T. and SONG, S. W. [1977]. An Efficient Parallel Garbage Collection System and Its Correctness Proof, *TR*, Computer Science Dept., Carnegie-Mellon University, Pittsburgh, Pa.

LAMPORT, L. [1970]. Comment on Bell's Quadratic Quotient Method for Hash Code Searching, *CACM* **13**:9 (September), 573–575.

LAMPORT, L. [1975]. Multiple Byte Processing with Full-Word Instructions, *CACM* **18**:**8** (August), 471–475.

LANG, C. A. and GRAY, J. C. [1968a]. ASP—A Ring-Implemented Associative Structure Package, *Proc. ACM 23rd Nat. Conf.*, Brandon Systems Press, Princeton, N.J.

LANG, C. A. and GRAY, J. C. [1968b]. ASP—A Ring-Implemented Associative Structure Package, *CACM* **11**:**8** (August), 550–555.

LARSON, P. [1978]. Dynamic Hashing, *BIT* **18**:**2**, 184–201.

LEFKOWITZ, D. [1969]. *File Structures for On-Line Systems*, Hayden Book Company, Rochelle Park, N.J.

LESK, M. E. [1970]. Compressed Text Storage, Bell Labs. Tech. Rept. 3, November, 34 pp.

LEW, A. [1978]. Optimal Conversion of Extended-Entry Decision Tables with General Cost Criteria, *CACM* **21**:**4** (April), 269–279.

LEW, J. S. and ROSENBERG, A. L. [1978a]. Polynomial Indexing of Integer Lattice-Points, I. General Concepts and Quadratic Polynomials, *J. Number Theory* **10**:**2** (May), 192–214.

LEW, J. S. and ROSENBERG, A. L. [1978b]. Polynomial Indexing of Integer Lattice-Points, II. Nonexistence Results for Higher-Degree Polynomials, *J. Number Theory* **10**:**2** (May), 215–243.

LINDSTROM, G. [1973]. Scanning List Structures Without Stacks or Tag Bits, *Info. Proc. Letters* **2**, 47–51.

LINDSTROM, G. [1974]. Copying List Structures Using Bounded Workspace, *CACM* **17**:**4** (April), 198–202.

LOMBARDI, L. [1960]. Theory of Files, *Proc. 1960 EJCC*, IRE, New York, 137–141.

LONDON, K. [1972]. *Decision Tables: A Practical Approach for Data Processing*, Auerbach, Princeton, N.J.

LORIN, H. [1971]. A Guided Bibliography to Sorting, *IBM Syst. J.* **10**, 244–254.

LOUIS-GAVET, G. [1978]. Diverses Applications Issues d'une Fonction de Compactage Basée sur une Étude Mathématique du Langage Naturel, *R.A.I.R.O. Informatique* **12**:**1**, 47–71.

LOWE, T. C. [1968]. The Influence of Database Characteristics and Usage on Direct-Access File Organization, *JACM* **15**:**4** (October), 535–548.

LOWE, T. C. [1969]. Analysis of Boolean Program Models for Time-Shared, Paged Environments, *CACM* **12**:**4** (April), 199–205.

LUCCIO, F. [1967]. A Comment on Index Register Allocation, *CACM* **10**:**9** (September), 572–574.

LUCCIO, F. and PAGLI, L. [1978]. Power Trees, *CACM* **21**:**11** (November), 941–947.

LUM, V. Y. [1970]. Multi-Attribute Retrieval with Combined Indexes, *CACM* **13**:**11** (November), 660–665.

LUM, V. Y. [1973]. General Performance Analysis of Key-to-Address Transformation Methods Using an Abstract File Concept, *CACM* **16**:**10** (October), 603–612.

LUM, V. Y. and YUEN, P. S. T. [1972]. Additional Results on Key-to-Address Transform

Techniques: A Fundamental Performance Study on Large Existing Formatted Files, *CACM* **15**:**11** (November), 996–997.

LUM, V. Y., YUEN, P. S. T. and DODD, M. [1971]. Key-to-Address Transform Techniques: A Fundamental Performance Study on Large Existing Formatted Files, *CACM* **14**:**4** (April), 228–239.

LURIÉ, D. and VANDONI, C. [1973]. Statistics for FORTRAN Identifiers and Scatter-Storage Techniques, *Softw. Prac. & Exp.* **3**, 171–177.

LYNCH, M. F. [1973]. Compression of Bibliographic Files Using an Adoption of Running-Length Coding, *Info. Storage Retrieval* **9**, 207–214.

LYON, G. [1978]. Packed Scatter Tables, *CACM* **21**:**10** (October), 857–865.

LYON, G. [1979]. Batch Scheduling from Short Lists, *Info. Proc. Letters* **8**:**2** (February), 57–59.

MACVEIGH, D. T. [1977]. Effect of Data Representation on Cost of Sparse Matrix Operations, *Acta Informatica* **7**:**4**, 361–394.

MADNICK, S. E. [1967]. String Processing Techniques, *CACM* **10**:**7** (July), 420–424.

MAES, R. [1978]. On the Representation of Program Structures by Decision Tables: A Critical Assessment, *Computer Journal* **21**:**4** (November), 290–295.

MALY, K. [1976]. Compressed Tries, *CACM* **19**:**7** (July), 409–415.

MARRON, B. A. and DE MAINE, P. A. D. [1967]. Automatic Data Compression, *CACM* **10**:**11** (November), 711–715.

MARTIN, J. [1976]. *Principles of Data-Base Management*, Prentice-Hall, Englewood Cliffs, New Jersey.

MARTIN, W. A. [1971]. Sorting, *C. Surveys* **3**:**4** (December), 147–174.

MARTIN, W. A. and NESS, D. N. [1972]. Optimizing Binary Trees Grown with a Sorting Algorithm, *CACM* **15**:**2** (February), 88–93.

MARUYAMA, K. and SMITH, S. E. [1976]. Optimal Reorganizations of Distributed Space Disk Files, *CACM* **19**:**11** (November), 634–642.

MATULA, D. W. [1968a]. In-and-Out Conversions, *CACM* **11**:**1** (January), 47–50.

MATULA, D. W. [1968b]. The Base-Conversion Theorem, *Proc. Amer. Math. Soc.* **19**, 716–723.

MATYAS, S. M. and MEYER, C. H. [1978]. Generation, Distribution, and Installation of Cryptographic Keys, *IBM Syst. J.* **17**:**2**, 126–137.

MAURER, W. D. [1968]. An Improved Hash Code for Scatter Storage, *CACM* **11**:**1** (January), 35–38.

MAURER, W. D. and LEWIS, T. G. [1975]. Hash Table Methods, *C. Surveys* **7** (March), 5–20.

MAYOH, B. H. [1972]. Recursion and Stacks, *Info. Proc. Letters* **1**, 115–116.

MCBETH, J. H. [1963]. On the Reference Counter Method, *CACM* **6**:**9** (September), 575.

MCCARTHY, J. [1960]. Recursive Functions of Symbolic Expressions and Their Computation by Machine: Part I, *CACM* **3**:**4** (April), 184–195.

McCarthy, J. [1975]. Proposed Criterion for a Cipher to be Probable-Word-Proof, *CACM* **18**:2 (February), 131–132.

McCarthy, J., Abrahams, P. W., Edwards, D. J., Hart, T. P. and Levin, M. I. [1962]. *Lisp 1. 5 Programmer's Manual*, MIT Press, Cambridge, Massachusetts.

McCreight, E. W. [1976]. A Space-Economical Suffix Tree Construction Algorithm, *JACM* **23**:2 (April), 262–272.

McCreight, E. M. [1977]. Pagination of B*-Trees with Variable Length Records, *CACM* **20**:9 (September), 670–674.

McGee, W. C. [1968]. File Structures for Generalized Data Management, *IFIP Cong. 1968, Part F*, The Hague, 68–73.

McIlroy, M. D. [1960]. Macro Instruction Extensions of Compiler Languages, *CACM* **3**:4 (March), 214–220.

McKellar, A. C. and Wong, C. K. [1978]. Dynamic Placement of Records in Linear Storage, *JACM* **25**:3 (July), 421–434.

Mealy, G. H. [1967]. Another Look at Data, *Proc. FJCC 1967*, AFIPS, **31**, 525–534.

Merkle, R. C. and Hellman, M. E. [1978]. Hiding Information and Signatures in Trap-Door Knapsacks, *IEEE Trans. Inform. Theory*, **IT-24** (September), 525–530.

Metropolis, N. and Ashenhurst, R. L. [1965]. Radix Conversion in an Unnormalized Arithmetic System, *Math. Comp.* **19**, 435–441.

Metzner, J. R. and Barnes, B. H. [1977]. *Decision Table Languages and Systems*, Academic Press, New York.

Miller, R. E., Pippenger, N., Rosenberg, A. L. and Snyder, L. [1977]. Optimal 2, 3-Trees, *Tech. Rept. RC-6505*, IBM Watson Research Center, Yorktown Heights, N.Y. (April), 31 pp.

Minker, J. and Sable, J. [1967]. File Organization and Data Management, *Ann. Rev. of Info. Sci. & Tech.* **2**, 123–160.

Minsky, M. [1963]. A Lisp Garbage Collector Algorithm Using Serial Secondary Storage, *A.I. Memo 58*, Proj. MAC, MIT, Cambridge, Mass. (December).

Minsky, N. [1972]. Rotating Storage Devices as Partially Associative Memories, *Proc. FJCC*, 587–595.

Minsky, N. [1973]. Representation of Binary Trees on Associative Memories, *Info. Proc. Letters* **2**, 1–5.

Mohan, C. [1978]. An Overview of Recent Data Base Research, *Data Base* (ACM SIGBDP Quarterly Newsletter) **10**:2 (Fall 1978), 3–24.

Montalbano, M. [1974]. *Decision Tables*, Science Research Associates, Palo Alto.

Morgan, H. L. [1974]. Optimal Space Allocation on Disk Storage Devices, *CACM* **17**:3 (March), 139–142.

Morris, F. L. [1978]. A Time- and Space-Efficient Garbage Compaction Algorithm, *CACM* **21**:8 (August), 662–665.

Morris, J. H. and Pratt, V. R. [1970]. A Linear Pattern Matching Algorithm, *TR-40*, Computing Center, Univ. of California, Berkeley.

MORRIS, R. [1968]. Scatter-Storage Techniques, *CACM* **11**:**1** (January), 38–44.

MORRIS, R. [1977]. Computer Security and the Bell System, *Science* **197** (August 19), 716.

MORRIS, R. [1978]. The Data Encryption Standard—Retrospective and Prospects, *IEEE Comm. Soc. Magazine* **16**:**6** (November), 11–14.

MULLIN, J. K. [1972]. An Improved Index Sequential Access Method Using Hashed Overflow, *CACM* **15**:**5** (May), 301–307.

MUNTZ, R. and UZGALIS, R. [1970]. Dynamic Storage Allocation for Binary Search Trees in a Two-Level Memory, *Proc. 4th Princeton Conf.*, Princeton, New Jersey.

MUTHUKRISHNAN, C. R. [1971]. Reply to Comment by Pollack, *CACM* **14**:**1** (January), 52.

MUTHUKRISHNAN, C. R. and RAJARAMAN, V. [1970]. On the Conversion of Decision Tables to Computer Programs, *CACM* **13**:**6** (June), 347–351.

MYERS, W., TOWNSEND, M. and TOWNSEND, T. [1966]. Data Compression by Hardware or Software, *Datamation* (April), 35–43.

NEEDHAM, R. M. and SCHROEDER, M. D. [1978]. Using Encryption for Authentication in Large Networks of Computers, *CACM* **21**:**12** (December), 993–999.

NEWELL, A. [1964]. *Information Processing Language-V Manual*, Prentice-Hall, Englewood Cliffs, New Jersey.

NEWELL, A. and SHAW, J. C. [1957]. Programming the Logic Theory Machine, *Proc. Western JCC*, 230–240.

NEWELL, A., SHAW, J. C. and SIMON, H. A. [1956]. The Logic Theory Machine, *IRE Trans. on Info. Theory*, **IT-2** (September), 61–70.

NEWELL, A. and TONGE, F. M. [1960]. An Introduction to Information Processing Language V, *CACM* **3**:**4** (April), 205–211.

NIELSEN, N. R. [1977]. Dynamic Memory Allocation in Computer Simulation, *CACM* **20**:**11** (November), 864–873.

NIEVERGELT, J. [1974]. Binary Search Trees and File Organization, *C. Surveys*, **6**:**3** (September), 195–207.

NIEVERGELT, J., PRADELS, J., WONG, C. K. and YUE, P. C. [1972]. Bounds on the Weighted Path Length of Binary Trees, *Info. Proc. Letters* **1**, 220–225.

NIEVERGELT, J. and REINGOLD, E. M. [1973]. Binary Search Trees of Bounded Balance, *SIAM J. Computing* **2**:**1** (March), 33–43.

NIEVERGELT, J. and WONG, C. K. [1973]. Upper Bounds for the Total Path Length of Binary Trees, *JACM* **20**:**1** (January), 1–6.

NILSSON, N. J. [1971]. *Problem-Solving Methods in Artificial Intelligence*, McGraw-Hill, New York.

OLSON, C. A. [1969]. Random Access File Organization for Indirectly Accessed Records, *Proc. ACM Nat. Conf.* **24**, 539–549.

OTTMANN, TH. and WOOD, D. [1978]. Deletion in One-Sided Height-Balanced Search Trees, *Int. J. Computer Math.* **6**:**4**, 265–271.

OTTMANN, TH., SIX, H. W. and WOOD, D. [1978]. Right Brother Trees, *CACM* **21**:9 (September), 769–776.

OVERHOLT, K. J. [1973]. Efficiency of the Fibonacci Search Method, *BIT* **3**, 92–96.

PALMER, E. M., RAHIMI, M. A. and ROBINSON, R. W. [1974]. Efficiency of a Binary Comparison Storage Technique, *JACM* **21**:3 (July), 376–384.

PATT, Y. N. [1969]. Variable-Length Tree Structures Having Minimum Average Search Time, *CACM* **12**:2 (February), 72–76.

PERL, Y., ITAI, A. and AVNI, H. [1978]. Interpolation Search—A log log *N* Search, *CACM* **21**:7 (July), 550–553.

PERL, Y. and REINGOLD, E. M. [1977]. Understanding the Complexity of Interpolation Search, *Info. Proc. Letters* **6**:6 (December), 219–222.

PERLIS, A. J. [1972]. *Introduction to Computer Science*, Harper & Row, New York.

PERLIS, A. J. and THORNTON, C. [1960]. Symbol Manipulation by Threaded Lists, *CACM* **3**:4 (April), 195–204.

PETERSON, J. L. and NORMAN, T. A. [1977]. Buddy Systems, *CACM* **20**:6 (June), 431–431.

PETERSON, W. W. [1957]. Addressing for Random-Access Storage, *IBM J. of R. & D.* **1**:2, 130–146.

PETERSON, W. W. and WELDON, E. J. [1961]. *Error-Correcting Codes*, MIT Press, Cambridge (Second ed. 1972), 560 pp.

POHL, I. [1971]. Bi-Directional Search, *Machine Intelligence* **6**, 127–140.

POLLOCK, S. L. [1965]. Conversion of Limited-Entry Decision Tables to Computer Programs, *CACM* **8**:11 (November), 677–682.

POLLOCK, S. L. [1971]. Comment on the Conversion of Decision Tables to Computer Programs, *CACM* **14**:1 (January), 52.

POLLOCK, S. L., HICKS, H. T. and HARRISON, W. J. [1971]. *Decision Tables: Theory and Practice*, Wiley, New York, 179 pp.

POOCH, U. W. [1974]. Translation of Decision Tables, *C. Surveys* **6**:2 (June), 125–151.

POOCH, U. W. and NIEDER, A. [1973]. A Survey of Indexing Techniques for Sparse Matrices, *C. Surveys* **5**:2 (June), 109–133.

POONAN, G. [1976]. Optimal Placement of Entries in Hash Tables, *ACM Computer Sci. Conf.* (abstract only), **25**. (Also *DEC Internal Tech. Rept. LRD-1*, Digital Equipment Corp., Maynard, Mass.)

PRESS, L. J. [1965]. Conversion of Decision Tables to Computer Programs, *CACM* **8**:6 (June), 385–390.

PRICE, C. E. [1973]. Table Look-Up Techniques, *C. Surveys* **3**:2 (June), 49–66.

PRYWES, N. S. [1966]. Man-Computer Problem Solving with Multilist, *Proc. IEEE* **54**:12 (December), 1788–1801.

PURDOM, P. W. and STIGLER, S. M. [1970]. Statistical Properties of the Buddy System, *JACM* **17**:4 (October), 683–697.

PURDOM, P. W., STIGLER, S. M. and CHEAM, S. O. [1971]. Statistical Investigation of Three Storage Allocation Algorithms, *BIT* **11**, 187–195.

PURDY, G. B. [1974]. A High Security Log-In Procedure, *CACM* **17**:**8** (August), 442–445.

QUINE, W. V. [1952]. The Problem of Simplifying Truth Functions, *Amer. Math. Monthly* **59**, 521–531.

RADKE, C. E. [1970]. The Use of the Quadratic Residue Search, *CACM* **13**:**2** (February), 103–105.

RANDELL, B. [1969]. A Note on Storage Fragmentation and Program Segmentation, *CACM* **12**:**7** (July), 365–372.

RANDELL, B. and KUEHNER, C. J. [1968]. Dynamic Storage Allocation Systems, *CACM* **11**:**5** (May), 297–306.

RANDELL, B. and RUSSELL, L. J. [1964]. ALGOL-*60 Implementation*, Academic Press, New York.

REINGOLD, E. M. [1972]. On the Optimality of Some Set Algorithms, *JACM* **19**:**4**, 649–659.

REINGOLD, E. M. [1973]. A Nonrecursive List-Moving Algorithm, *CACM* **16**:**5** (May), 305–307.

REINWALD, L. T. and SOLAND, R. M. [1966]. Conversion of Limited-Entry Decision Tables to Optimal Computer Programs I: Minimum Average Processing Time, *JACM* **13**:**3** (July), 339–358.

REISS, S. P. [1979]. Security in Databases: A Combinatorial Study, *JACM* **26**:**1** (January), 45–47.

RISSANEN, J. [1973]. Bounds for Weight-Balanced Trees, *IBM J. R. & D.* **17**:**2** (March), 101–105.

RIVEST, R. [1976]. On Self-Organizing Sequential Search Heuristics, *CACM* **19**:**2** (February), 63–67.

RIVEST, R. L. [1977]. On the Worst-Case Behavior of String Searching Algorithms, *SIAM J. Comp* **6**:**4** (December), 669–674.

RIVEST, R. L. [1978a]. Optimal Arrangement of Keys in a Hash Table, *JACM* **25**:**2** (April), 200–209.

RIVEST, R. L. [1978b]. Remarks on a Proposed Cryptanalytic Attack on the M.I.T. Public-Key Cryptosystem, *Cryptologia* (January), 62–65.

RIVEST, R. L. and KNUTH, D. E. [1972]. Bibliography 26: Computing Sorting, *Computing Reviews* **13**:**6** (June), 283–289.

RIVEST, R. L., SHAMIR, A. and ADLEMAN, L. [1978]. A Method for Obtaining Digital Signatures and Public-Key Cryptosystems, *CACM* **21**:**2** (February), 120–126.

ROBERTS, D. C. [1972]. File-Organization Techniques, *Advances in Computing* **12**, 115–174.

ROBERTS, L. G. [1965]. Graphical Communication and Control Languages, *Proc. 2nd Congress on Information System Sciences*, Spartan Books, N.Y., 211–217.

ROBSON, J. M. [1971]. An Estimate of the Store Size Necessary for Dynamic Storage Allocation, *JACM* **18**:**3** (July), 416–423.

ROBSON, J. M. [1973]. An Improved Algorithm for Traversing Binary Trees Without Auxiliary Stack, *Info. Proc. Letters* **2**, 12–14.

ROBSON, J. [1974]. Bounds for Some Functions Concerning Dynamic Storage Allocation, *JACM* **21**:**3** (July), 491–499.

ROBSON, J. M. [1977]. A Bounded Storage Algorithm for Copying Cyclic Structures, *CACM* **20**:**6** (June), 431–433.

ROCHFELD, A. [1971]. New LISP Techniques for a Paging Environment, *CACM* **14**:**12** (December), 791–795.

ROHL, J. S. and CORDINGLY, G. [1970]. List Processing Facilities in Atlas Autocode, *Computer Journal* **13**:**1** (February), 20–24.

ROSE, L. and GOTTERER, M. H. [1973]. A Theory of Dynamic File Management in a Multilevel Store, *Int. J. of Comp. & Inf. Sci.* **2**, 249–256.

ROSENBERG, A. L. [1971]. Data Graphs and Addressing Schemes, *JCSS* **5**, 193–238.

ROSENBERG, A. L. [1972]. Addressable Data Graphs, *JACM* **19**:**2** (April), 309–340.

ROSENBERG, A. L. [1973]. Suffixes of Addressable Data Graphs, *Information & Control* **23**, 107–127.

ROSENBERG, A. L. [1974]. Allocating Storage for Extendible Arrays, *JACM* **21**:**4** (October), 652–670.

ROSENBERG, A. L. [1975]. Preserving Proximity in Arrays, *SIAM J. Comp.* **4**:**4** (December), 443–460.

ROSENBERG, A. L. [1977a]. On Storing Concatenable Arrays, *JCSS* **14**:**2** (April), 157–174.

ROSENBERG, A. L. [1977b]. On Storing Ragged Arrays by Hashing, *MST* **10**, 193–210.

ROSENBERG, A. L. [1977c]. Direct-Access Storage of Data Structures, *Rivista di Informatica* **8**:**1**, 127–151.

ROSENBERG, A. L. [1978]. Data Encodings and Their Costs, *Acta Informatica* **9**:**3**, 273–292.

ROSENBERG, A. L. and SNYDER, L. [1978]. Minimal-Comparison 2-3 Trees, *SIAM J. Comp.* **7**:**4** (November), 465–480.

ROSENBERG, A. L. and STOCKMEYER, L. J. [1977a]. Hashing Schemes for Extendible Arrays, *JACM* **24**:**2** (April), 199–221.

ROSENBERG, A. L. and STOCKMEYER, L. J. [1977b]. Storage Schemes for Boundedly Extendible Arrays, *Acta Informatica* **7**:**3**, 289–303.

ROSENBERG, A. L. and THATCHER, J. W. [1975]. What is a Multilevel Array?, *IBM J. of R. & D.* **19**:**2** (March), 163–169.

ROSS, D. T. [1961]. A Generalized Technique for Symbol Manipulation and Numerical Computation, *CACM* **4**:**3** (March), 147–150.

ROSS, D. T. [1967]. The AED Free Storage Package, *CACM* **10**:**8** (August), 481–492.

ROTEM, D. and VARAL, Y. L. [1978]. Generation of Binary Trees from Ballot Sequences, *JACM* **25**:**3** (July), 396–404.

ROTHNIE, J. B. and LOZANO, T. [1974]. Attribute-Based File Organization in a Paged Memory Environment, *CACM* **17**:**2** (February), 63–69.

RUBIN, F. [1976]. Experiments in Text File Compression, *CACM* **19**:**11** (November), 617–623.

RUSKEY, F. [1978]. Generating *t*-ary Trees Lexicographically, *SIAM J. Comp.* **7**:**4** (November), 424–439.

RUSSELL, D. L. [1977]. Internal Fragmentation in a Class of Buddy Systems, *SIAM J. Comp.* **6**:**4** (December), 607–621.

RUTH, S. S. and KREUTZER, P. J. [1972]. Data Compression for Large Business Files, *Datamation* **18**:**9**, 62–66.

SALTON, G. [1962]. Manipulation of Trees in Information Retrieval, *CACM* **5**:**2** (February), 103–114.

SALTON, G. [1968]. *Automatic Information Organization and Retrieval*, McGraw-Hill, New York.

SALTON, G. and SUSSENGUTH, E. H. [1964]. Some Flexible Information Retrieval Systems Using Structure-Matching Procedures, *Proc. SJCC 1964*, AFIPS, 587–597.

SCHNEIDERMAN, B. [1973]. Optimum Database Reorganization Points, *CACM* **16**:**6** (June), 362–365.

SCHNEIDERMAN, B. [1974]. A Model for Optimizing Indexed File Structures, *Int. J. of Comp. and Info. Sci.* **3**, 93–103.

SCHNEIDERMAN, B. [1978]. Jump Searching: A Fast Sequential Search Technique, *CACM* **21**:**10** (October), 831–834.

SCHORR, H. and WAITE, W. M. [1967]. An Efficient Machine-Independent Procedure for Garbage Collection in Various List Structures, *CACM* **10**:**8** (August), 501–506.

SCHUMACHER, H. and SEVCIK, K. C. [1976]. The Synthetic Approach to Decision Table Conversion, *CACM* **19**:**6** (June), 343–351.

SCHWARTZ, E. S. [1963]. A Dictionary for Minimum-Redundancy Encoding, *JACM* **10**:**4** (October), 413–439.

SCHWARTZ, E. S. [1964]. An Optimum Encoding with Minimum Longest Code and Total Number of Digits, *Information & Control* **7**, 37–44.

SCHWAYDER, K. [1974]. Extending the Information-Theory Approach to Converting Limited-Entry Decision Tables to Computer Programs, *CACM* **17**:**9** (September), 532–537.

SCHWAYDER, K. [1975]. Combining Decision Rules in a Decision Table, *CACM* **18**:**8** (August), 476–480.

SCIDMORE, A. K. and WEINBERG, B. L. [1963]. Storage and Search Properties of a Tree-Organized Memory System, *CACM* **4**:**1** (January), 28–31.

SEDGEWICK, R. [1977]. The Analysis of Quicksort Programs, *Acta Informatica* **7**:**4**, 327–355.

SEDGEWICK, R. [1978]. Implementing Quicksort Programs, *CACM* **21**:**10** (October), 847–857.

SETHI, R. [1973]. A Note on Implementing Parallel Assignment Instructions, *Info. Proc. Letters* **2**, 91–95.

Severance, D. G. [1974]. Identifier Search Mechanisms, *C. Surveys* **6**:3 (September), 175–194.

Severance, D. [1975]. A Parametric Model of Alternative File Structures, *Inf. Syst.* **1**:2 (April), 51–55.

Severance, D. and Duhne, R. [1976]. A Practitioner's Guide to Addressing Algorithms, *CACM* **19**:6 (June), 314–326.

Shannon, C. E. [1949]. Communication Theory of Secrecy Systems, *Bell Syst. Tech. J.* **28**:4 (October), 656–715.

Shapley, D. [1977a]. Telecommunications Eavesdropping by NSA on Private Messages Alleged, *Science* **197** (September 9), 1061–1064.

Shapley, D. [1977b]. Cryptography Meeting Goes Smoothly, *Science* **198** (November 4), 476.

Shapley, D. [1978]. Security Agency's Role in DES Confirmed, *Science* **200** (April 28), 412–413.

Shapley, D. and Bari Kolata, G. [1977]. Cryptology: Scientists Puzzle Over Threat to Open Research, Publication, *Science* **197** (September 30), 1345–1349.

Sheil, B. A. [1978]. Median Split Trees, *CACM* **21**:11 (November), 947–958.

Shen, K. K. and Peterson, J. L. [1974]. A Weighted Buddy Method for Dynamic Storage Allocation, *CACM* **17**:10 (October), 558–562.

Shore, J. E. [1975]. On the External Storage Fragmentation Produced by First-Fit and Best-Fit Allocation Strategies, *CACM* **18**:8 (August), 433–440.

Shore, J. E. [1977]. Anomalous Behavior of the Fifty-Percent Rule in Dynamic Memory Allocation, *CACM* **20**:11 (November), 812–820.

Sibley, E. H. and Taylor, R. W. [1973]. A Data Definition and Mapping Language, *CACM* **16**:12 (December), 750–759.

Siklóssy, L. [1972]. Fast and Read-Only Algorithms for Traversing Trees without an Auxiliary Stack, *Inf. Proc. Letters* **1**, 149–152.

Simmons, G. J. and Norris, M. J. [1977]. Preliminary Comments on the M.I.T. Public–Key Cryptosystem, *Cryptologia* (October), 406–414.

Siskind, V. and Rosenhead, J. [1976]. Seek Times for Disc File Processing: Some Results from Probability Theory, *Computer Journal* **19**:4 (November), 301–305.

Smith, J. L. [1971]. The Design of Lucifer, A Cryptographic Device for Data Communications, *Research Rept. RC*-3326, I.B.M.

Smyth, W. F. and Rădăceanu, E. [1974]. A Storage Scheme for Hierarchic Structures, *Computer Journal* **17**:2 (May), 152–156.

Solntseff, N. [1974]. On a Notational Device for the Description of Pointer Free Operations on Structured Data, *Inf. Proc. Letters* **2**, 158–159.

Sprugnoli, R. [1977]. Perfect Hashing Functions: A Single Probe Retrieving Method for Static Sets, *CACM* **20**:11 (November), 841–850.

Standish, T. A. [1978]. Data Structures—An Axiomatic Approach, in *Current Trends in*

Programming Methodology, Vol. IV: Data Structuring (R. Yeh, ed.), Prentice-Hall, Englewood Cliffs, N.J., 30–59.

STANFEL, L. E. [1970]. Tree Structures for Optimal Searching, *JACM* **17**:**3** (July), 508–517.

STANFEL, L. E. [1972]. Practical Aspects of Doubly Chained Trees for Retrieval, *JACM* **19**:**3** (July), 425–436.

STEELE, G. L. [1975]. Multiprocessing Compactifying Garbage Collection, *CACM* **18**:**9** (September), 495–508 (Corrigendum: *CACM* **19**:**6** (June 1976), 354.)

STONE, H. S. [1972]. *Introduction to Computer Organization and Data Structures*, McGraw-Hill, New York, 321 pp.

STONE, H. S. [1973]. *Discrete Mathematical Structures and Their Applications*, SRA, Palo Alto, California.

STONE, H. S. and SIEWIOREK, D. P. [1975]. *Introduction to Computer Organization and Data Structures: PDP-11 Edition*, McGraw-Hill, New York, 368 pp.

STRACHEY, C. [1965]. A General-Purpose Macrogenerator, *Computer Journal* **8**:**3** (October), 225–241.

SUNDGREN, B. [1975]. *Theory of Data Bases*, Mason/Charter, London.

SUSSENGUTH, E. H., JR. [1963]. Use of Tree Structures for Processing Files, *CACM* **6**:**5** (May), 272–279.

SZWARCFITER, J. L. and WILSON, L. B. [1978]. Some Properties of Ternary Trees, *Computer Journal* **21**:**1** (February), 66–72.

TADMAN, M. [1978]. Fast-Fit: A New Hierarchical Dynamic Storage Allocation Technique, U.C. Irvine, Computer Science Dept., M.S. Thesis.

TENNENBAUM, A. [1978]. Simulations of Dynamic Sequential Search Algorithms, *CACM* **21**:**9** (September), 790–791.

THORELLI, L.-E. [1972]. Marking Algorithms, *BIT* **12**, 555–569.

TREMBLAY, J. P. and SORENSON, P. G. [1976]. *An Introduction to Data Structures with Applications*, McGraw-Hill, New York.

TROJANOWSKI, A. E. [1978]. Ranking and Listing Algorithms for *k*-ary Trees, *SIAM J. Comp.* **7**:**4** (November), 492–509.

TUCHMAN, W. L. [1977]. Computer Security and IBM, *Science* **197** (September 2), 938.

TUEL, W. G. [1978]. Optimal Reorganization Points for Linearly Growing Files, *TODS* **3**:**1** (March), 32–40.

ULLMAN, J. D. [1972]. A Note on the Efficiency of Hashing Functions, *JACM* **19**:**3** (July), 569–575.

U.S. SENATE SELECT COMMITTEE ON INTELLIGENCE [1978]. Unclassified Summary: Involvement of NSA in the Development of the Data Encryption Standard, *IEEE Comm. Soc. Magazine* **16**:**6** (November), 53–55.

VAN DER POOL, J. A. [1972]. Optimum Storage Allocation for Initial Loading of a File, *IBM J. of R. & D.* **16**, 579–586.

VAN DER POOL, J. A. [1973a]. Optimum Storage Allocation for a File in Steady State, *IBM J. of R. & D.* **17**, 27–38.

VAN DER POOL, J. A. [1973b]. Optimum Storage Allocation for a File with Open Addressing, *IBM J. of R. & D.* **17**, 106–114.

VARNEY, R. C. [1972]. Priority Processes Used for Scheduling Within a Tree Structured Operating System, *Inf. Proc. Letters* **1**, 187–190.

VERHOFSTAD, J. S. M. [1978]. Recovery Techniques for Database Systems, *C. Surveys* **10**:2 (June), 167–195.

VIGENÈRE, B. [1586]. *Traicté des Chiffres.*

VUILLEMIN, J. [1978]. A Data Structure for Manipulating Priority Queues, *CACM* **21**:4 (April), 309–315.

WADLER, P. L. [1976]. Analysis of an Algorithm for Real-Time Garbage Collection, *CACM* **19**:9 (September), 491–500. (See GRIES [1977] and also Wadler's reply *CACM* **20**:2 (February 1977), 120.)

WAITE, W. M. [1973]. *Implementing Software for Non-Numeric Applications*, Prentice-Hall, Englewood Cliffs, New Jersey, 510 pp.

WAITE, W. M. and SCHORR, H. [1964]. A Note on the Formation of Free List, *CACM* **7**:8 (August), 478.

WAGNER, R. A. and FISCHER, M. J. [1974]. The String-to-String Correction Problem, *JACM* **21**:1 (January), 168–173.

WEGBREIT, B. [1972a]. A Generalised Compacting Garbage Collector, *Computer Journal* **15**:3 (August), 204–208.

WEGBREIT, B. [1972b]. A Space-Efficient List Structure Tracing Algorithm, *IEEE Trans. Comp. C-21* **9** (September), 1009–1010.

WEINER, P. [1973]. Linear Pattern Matching Algorithms, *Conf. Record IEEE 14th Ann. Symp. on Switching and Automata Theory*, 1–11.

WEINSTOCK, C. B. [1976]. Dynamic Storage Allocation Techniques, Doctoral dissertation Carnegie-Mellon Univ., Pittsburgh, Pennsylvania.

WEIZENBAUM, J. [1962]. Knotted List Structures, *CACM* **5**:3 (March), 161–165.

WEIZENBAUM, J. [1963]. Symmetric List Processor, *CACM* **6**:9 (September), 524–544.

WEIZENBAUM, J. [1969]. Recovery of Reentrant List Structures in SLIP. *CACM* **12**:7 (July), 370–372.

WEXELBLAT, R. L. and FREEDMAN, H. A. [1967]. The Multilang On-Line Programming System, *Proc. AFIPS 1967 SJCC* **30**, 559–569.

WHITT, J. D. and SULLENBERGER, A. G. [1975]. The Algorithm Sequential Access Method: An Alternative to Index Sequential, *CACM* **18**:3 (March), 174–176.

WILKES, M. V. [1965]. Lists and Why They are Useful, *Computer Journal* **7**:4 (January), 278–281.

WILKES, M. V. [1972]. Associative Tabular Data Structures, *Int. J. of Comp. & Info. Sci.* **1**:3 (September), 225–233.

WILLIAMS, F. A. [1959]. Handling Identifiers as Internal Symbols in Language Processors, *CACM* **2**:**6** (June), 21–24.

WILLIAMS, J. W. J. [1964]. Algorithm 232: Heapsort, *CACM* **7**:**6** (June), 347–348.

WILLIAMS, R. [1973]. A Survey of Data Structures for Computer Graphic Systems, *C. Surveys*, **3**:**1** (March), 1–23.

WIRTH, N. [1971]. The Design of a Pascal Compiler, *Softw. Prac. & Exp.* **1**, 309–333.

WODON, P. L. [1969]. Data Structure and Storage Allocation, *BIT* **9**, 270–282.

WOLFF, J. G. [1978]. Recording of Natural Language for Economy of Transmission or Storage, *Computer Journal* **21**:**1** (February), 142–144.

WONG, E. and CHIANG, T. C. [1971]. Canonical Structure in Attribute-Based File Organization, *CACM* **14**:**9** (September), 593–597.

WOOD, D. [1978]. A Comparison of Two Methods of Encoding Arrays, *BIT* **18**:**2**, 219–229.

YAMAMOTO, S., TERAMOTO, T. and FUTAGAMI, K. [1972]. Design of a Balanced Multiple-Valued Filing Scheme of Order Two, Based on Cyclically Generated Spread in Finite Projective Geometry, *Information & Control* **21**, 72–91.

YAO, A. C. [1978]. On Random 2-3 Trees, *Acta Informatica* **9**, 159–170.

YAO, S. B. [1977]. Approximating Block Accesses in Database Organizations, *CACM* **20**:**4** (April), 260–261.

YAO, A. C. and YAO, F. F. [1976]. The Complexity of Searching an Ordered Random Table, *Proc. 17th Ann. Symp. on Foundations of Computer Sci.*, IEEE Computer Society (October), 173–177.

YNGVE, V. [1963]. COMIT, *CACM* **6**:**3** (March), 83–84.

YU, C. T., SALTON, G. and SIU, M. K. [1978]. Effective Automatic Indexing Using Term Addition and Deletion, *JACM* **25**:**2** (April), 210–225.

ZIPF, G. K. [1949]. *Human Behavior and the Principle of Least Effort: An Introduction to Human Ecology*, Addison-Wesley, Reading, Massachusetts.

ZOBRIST, A. L. and CARLSON, F. R. [1977]. Detection of Combined Occurrences, *CACM* **20**:**1** (January), 31–35.

ZWEBEN, S. H. and McDONALD, M. A. [1978]. An Optimal Method for Deletions in One-Sided Height-Balanced Trees, *CACM* **21**:**6** (June), 441–445.

INDEX